KANSAS

ITS POWER AND ITS GLORY

Edited by PEG VINES

Published by John R. Peach, Topeka, Kansas

FOREWORD

How do you say thank you to one who has been a kind and protective mother and a generous and understanding father for over 60 years yet who has not ears to hear your thanks, nor eyes to see your face light up in appreciation of her beauty and grandeur? To cast a medal for her bosom would not suffice, for Kansas — the object of my affection — stretches 200 miles north and south and 400 miles east and west.

For over 100 years millions have proudly called it home. Others, though they deserted her to seek greener pastures, sought the companionship of their fellow wanderers and banded together to relive pleasant memories in groups they called "Kansas Societies."

Kansas — whatever the name means in Indian lore — means many things to her sons and daughters who have reaped the fruits of the rich earth from which one seed sprouts and produces hundreds of kernels. Strata thousands of feet down shoot up oil and gas worth billions of dollars. Coal and other minerals add to her bounty. Creative sons dot the Kansas plains with factories making thousands of items.

I think I have loved Kansas from the day I was born. I've heard that I kicked the covers off my buggy in delight when my mother wheeled me out in the warm sunshine and I saw and heard the birds singing overhead, watched the boughs of the stately elms on Union Street moving in the gentle breeze, and smelled the fragrant flowers from plants, shrubs and trees.

I swam in her creeks and rivers, fed from springs gushing from limestone formations that filtered and sweetened the cool, refreshing waters. I traveled over her thousands of miles of roads which bring into view an ever-changing panorama to delight the eye. I came to know well her cities, large and small, where her spirited people built their homes, churches and schools and championed enterprise and industry. I watched in wonder the rising sun in all its beauty announcing the coming of another day, and relished this setting ball of fire creating, in the clouds, a beautiful doxology. Here in Kansas I enjoyed the life and love given me by my parents, found my wife, raised our children, found work, opportunity and reward equal to my labors, I met my neighbors and made friends with people of many races and creeds.

Yet, with all of these treasures, enough of the trials and burdens came, also, to keep me mindful of the Kansas motto, "To the stars through difficulties."

So now, after all of these blessings, I want you to share with me a book in dedication to Kansas. Share it with me and my fellows who have helped to give a picture and to recite our pride in words, "Kansas — Its Power and Its Glory."

Credit is given those contributing from their areas of interest. Many others have supplied facts and pictures, but we especially want to acknowledge the help of the Kansas Historical Society, Mr. Nyle Miller and his fellows; the Kansas Department of Economic Development, Mr. Jack Lacy and his associates; Mrs. Peg Vines for her editorial talents; Mr. W. J. van Wormer for his help in make-up and composition details; and to my valued friend from boyhood, Mr. William L. White, who said, "John, it sounds like a good idea."

John R. Peach

PHOTO CREDITS

Acknowledgement for photographs is extended to the chambers of commerce of many cities across the state of Kansas and to newspapers and industries which helped the local chambers in this endeavor. Also, special thanks to the following:

Division of Institutional Management
Kansas Bankers Association
Kansas Board of Agriculture
Kansas Department of Economic Development
Kansas Power & Light Company
Kansas Savings and Loan League
Kansas State Chamber of Commerce
Kansas State Department of Education
Kansas State Highway Commission
Kansas Water Resources Board
The Kansas State Historical Society

PREFACE

Come, Kansas! — come, my lovely — look now into this mirror which John Peach, your old friend and mine, holds up before your eyes, and be startled by your own beauty of which, busy with the daily chores of earning a living, you have taken small account.

And how — in this book which is that mirror — the new beauty blends with the old! There is Old Chief Smoky, that giant fist of alluvial rock thrust from the plains south of Oakley up into the sky — a fist shaken at the fat thunderheads as lazily they drift into Kansas from the Colorado Rockies, a fist which was there before ever the first Indians crossed the Bering Straits into our New World.

There is the stark white beauty of the Buick Assembly Plant in Kansas City, as simple and sheer a surface as any that Courbusier ever built in France — lines as pure and as new as tomorrow morning.

There are, back across the state at Victoria, the twin spires and gothic buttresses of St. Fidelis's church, built back in the last century, with each parishioner contributing 6 loads of native limestone and 45 preinflation dollars.

There is, in Wichita, the floating disc of the proposed auditorium complex, a beautiful flying saucer seemingly supported only by the brimming confidence of those people in their over-grown cow town.

There is the magnificent loosely-knotted ascot and satin-trimmed frock coat of John J. Ingalls, probably the most exquisitely literate Kansan ever to sit in the United States Senate.

There is the sparkle of dancing water on the huge reservoir at Tuttle Creek and countless other lakes. In covered wagon days, horses leaned against their collars, their hanging tongues grey with dust, pulling these wagons across what then was known as the Great American Desert. But today, old Doc Brinkley's promise of the 1930's of "a lake in every county" has been gloriously overfulfilled; if our statesmen continue at this rate, by 2000 A.D. they will have turned Kansas into the nation's sixth Great Lake, its surface laced with outboards, and its depths a tangle of catfish lines.

There are the slender Victorian-Gothic wood pillars holding up the porch of the

William L. White of Emporia, nationally known author, editor and publisher.

Officers Quarters at Old Fort Larned, so charmingly whittled by a craftsman in the last century, and also the limestone walls of the building, stone exactly like the yellow travertine of which Republican Rome was built, that noble native Kansas building material which gives Kansas State at Manhattan the most beautiful campus of all our schools.

So beautiful you are, O my Kansas and, stranger still, as you grow older — instead of shriveling into wrinkles — with each decade you become fresher and more youthful — with the stark beauty of new industrial parks and shopping centers, which at night bejewel our prairies with a necklace of glowing neon jewels.

What a miracle you are, O Kansas, to grow ever younger with the drifting years.

W. L. White

CONTENTS

Governor Avery

KANSAS STATE GOVERNMENT IN MODERN AMERICA

by Wm. H. Avery

Governor of Kansas

Contrary to much current opinion, state governments in America still have a significant role to play in determining the broad paths followed by our society. Much that lies within the province of state governmental authority can determine the manner in which a particular region responds to the changes inherent in contemporary America. In these comments, I should like to explore briefly some of the major areas in which Kansas state government has sought to meet and anticipate the needs of her citizens as a part of the development of the modern American culture and economy.

One does not have to be in Kansas long to realize that the Sunflower State puts a unique stamp on what it does, even in those cases where it may be borrowing from others' experience.

9

In this regard, Dr. Emory Lindquist, President of Wichita State University, has made a significant observation:

> Kansas in the dimension of time, like every populated geographic area, has a history which casts long shadows into the future — some good, some evil — a history not always fully understood nor interpreted in accordance with the facts, but creating, nevertheless, that indefinable quality called a "tradition," to inspire or to console, as circumstances called for inspiration or consolation.*

Today, in the manner in which Kansas state government is meeting its challenges, I believe our history is providing more cause for inspiration than for consolation.

When elected officials turn to reflecting upon the course of the institutions within their area of responsibility, they often lapse into a recitation of specific acts of legislation or administration of current interest to them. There have been many such items in recent Kansas history which have impressed me as being of vital significance. But to see their impact, I have found it useful to look at the way in which specific actions, policies, or events fit into the general movement of modern society. This does not lead to a minimization of the significance of specific occurrences. Rather, it enhances their significance by seeing them as a part of a larger pattern.

Today, more than ever before, if one looks at the public statements and the policies advocated by the governors of the various states, it is readily apparent that the economic development of their particular areas is of prime importance to them. Yet, as the states have turned their attention increasingly to recognizing and attempting to solve their own economic problems, we have also seen American society moving to the stage where less and less of each citizen's time and talents are expended on strictly economic pursuits. The state that has the whole interest of its citizens in mind will show an awareness of these shifts in our patterns of life. I want to show, therefore, how Kansas state government has responded to both the economic developments of contemporary America and also to some of the challenges in developing human resources not directly related to economic matters.

Economic Development Activities in Kansas

Nearly everything done by state or local government today has an impact on the state's economy. And nearly everything that is done for economic development also has an impact upon what I am calling the "human resources" of the state. Highway improvements, for example, clearly aid the movement of people to their jobs and the distribution of their products to market. Yet good highways are also an essential part of modern recreational activities. With this over-lapping in mind, I would like to look at a few aspects of Kansas' economic development activities in recent years.

Two-thirds of the way through the twentieth century, Kansas is still one of the major agricultural states of the nation. Kansas leads the nation in production of wheat, sorghum silage, and certain other crops. It is among the top five states in production of nearly a score of other commodities. Agriculture and industries related to agriculture continue to be the major sources of employment of the Kansas work force.

Due to its position as a leading agricultural state, Kansas has led most other states in experimenting with and developing new agricultural methods. Many improved seeds, new methods of cultivation, advancements in mechanization, and marketing innovations have had their beginning in Kansas.

But Kansas is a state of many contrasts. The tremendous agricultural resources of the state form an interesting backdrop for ultra-modern industrial plants. An example of this is the

---

*"Kansas: A Centennial Portrait," *Kansas Historical Quarterly*, Spring 1961.

extensive array of aircraft manufacturing facilities that operate in Kansas. Kansas leads the nation in the production of private aircraft and is rapidly establishing itself as the producer of many space-age products.

A more extensive discussion of the history of industrial development and efforts to promote the Kansas economy is contained in the Industrial Section of this book. But I want to discuss here a few other factors which are intimately related to economic development.

The American economy generally is undergoing rapid changes. We have grown from a nation predominantly devoted to the production of food and fibre for subsistence to a nation of complex technology and industrial production. It has been said by noted economists that we are now moving from the stage of a "production" economy to a "consumption" economy. This is evident in the rapid growth of "service trades" and related professions. Just as employment in manufacturing surpassed employment in agriculture some years ago on a national basis, so now the rate of increase in services is far greater than in manufacturing. And by services, I am including everything from a hamburger stand to an opera company.

This growing significance of the service occupations goes back to the point I made earlier: namely, less and less of the time of the average American's life is devoted exclusively to making a living. More on this and its relation to Kansas government later. There is a further economic consideration of these changes which should be explored at this point.

As manufacturing grows to a certain point, it becomes profitable to decentralize operations. For example, each year there is a lower percentage of the nation's automobile workers employed in the Detroit metropolitan area. Furthermore, the growing service professions do not require and cannot justify the kind of geographic centralization that characterized heavy industry in its earlier stages.

This decentralization of industry and the growth of services creates a demand for state governmental action in a number of areas. One of these, obviously, is transportation. Kansas, of all states, can appreciate the relationship between economic growth and an efficient transportation network. Much of Kansas' history parallels the growth of the railroads and is closely linked with it. What once held true for the railroads is equally true today for our highways.

Located as it is in the heart of the nation, Kansas is a vital link in national highway transportation. Kansans are aware of this position. While it is a matter for constant scrutiny and planning, Kansas has responded to its role admirably in many areas. The state made rapid progress in fulfilling its part in the creation of the Interstate Highway system. Interstate #70, connecting Kansas City with the Colorado line is a key link in a modern, transcontinental artery. The 10,000 miles of state highway and the Kansas Turnpike compare well to facilities in other states.

Certainly Kansas is not going to stand still with its present transportation network. As this is being written, investigation is under way to assess the present situation and to propose plans for meeting the future highway needs of those traveling in Kansas. Many alternatives are being considered, and hard, practical reasoning is being given to methods for achieving the goals decided upon.

But increased transportation demands are not the only results of the sophistication of the American economy. As the productive mechanisms of the nation decentralize, they also specialize. As they specialize, the requirements in training and insight of the men and women who operate them are heightened. Kansas has a firmly established position of leadership in providing its citizens with the skills and knowledge necessary for success in the contemporary economy.

Given the kind of pressures faced by American education after World War II, it is a mark of considerable accomplishment to have moved as far as has Kansas. The birth rate in the late

(Continued on page 268)

11

Kansas' own Deborah Bryant — "Miss America of 1966."

A royal Kansas welcome is Debbie's upon her return "back home."

REIGNING 'MISS AMERICA'

Loyal Kansans exclaim and proclaim that much natural beauty exists in their state.

One such natural beauty is Miss Debbie Bryant of Overland Park, winner of the coveted title, "Miss America of 1966."

Recognition of her beauty, talent, poise and personality brings added recognition to Kansas. Now, for the first time, this state has an ambassadress of good will that is as vibrant as the new Kansas she represents.

Her naturalness appears to have been a big factor in her success at the Miss America Pageant. According to Debbie, girls from the Midwest have more opportunity than ever before to be chosen Miss America. Judges are favoring the natural look. Girls here have it!

Deborah Irene Bryant, daughter of Mr. and Mrs. Hurley D. Bryant of Overland Park, was 19 when she won the crown in Atlantic City. In the talent competition, she gave a dramatic reading. Miss America's father is a civil engineer for the U. S. Air Force. He was stationed in Viet Nam at the time of the pageant. Debbie has a background of travel, having lived in Germany three years with her family. She understands several foreign languages.

Miss America is 5 feet 7 inches tall, weighs 115 pounds, has brown hair and radiant blue-grey eyes. The Kansas City, Kansas Junior Chamber of Commerce was her local pageant sponsor. The Miss Kansas Pageant was directed by the Pratt Jaycees. Debbie received a $1,000 scholarship at her state pageant and a $10,000 scholarship as Miss America. It was the first time in the 37-year history of the event that a Kansas girl won the top honor.

She is a 1963 graduate of Shawnee Mission East High School and 1965 graduate of Christian College (2 years) where she was a member of scholastic, science and language honorary sororities. She took drama and speech training in high school; public speaking, piano and dancing lessons in college.

Miss America plans to use her scholarship money to complete her college education. She will enter Kansas University as a junior after her reign. Following graduation, she hopes to attend medical school and specialize in pediatrics. She stated that by following a career in the medical profession she hoped to contribute something to our society instead of always taking from it. She desires to specialize in pediatrics because of her love for children and the desire to see every child have the opportunity to grow to full adulthood.

Debbie's year as reigning Miss America is filled with public appearances from coast to coast, most of them covered by the press. As flashbulbs illuminate her smile and eager reporters toss questions at her, the name "Kansas" comes into the limelight, into the news and magazine stories, and into the conversation of her admirers everywhere. She's selling Kansas every inch of the way . . . and Kansans are proud of their new No. 1 salesgirl!

MAGNIFICENT PEACE
of KANSAS

by Bob Linder

A barefoot boy with a cane fishing pole over his shoulder flexes his toes in the dust of a cow trail. His tracks in the warm powder lead toward a den of torpid bullheads.

He pauses to watch a ribbon of red ants cross the path. The twisting whistle of a meadowlark breaks the absolute quiet. The bitter scent of sunflowers joins the sweetness of clover, invading his awareness as he waits for the tiny parade to pass.

This is the magnificent peace of Kansas.

No sights to stagger the imagination here, no mile deep canyons or towering peaks. The beauty of Kansas is in its simplicity. The unshorn Flint Hills in the east, boundless and beautiful, fail to assail the senses with sheer size. Their beauty is in their closeness to man, in the gentle sloping roundness of their curves, that, like a woman, belies their strength.

In the spring, the hills are damp with dew and bright with the greens, reds and pinks of new life. There is freshness in the air. The white lace tablecloth of winter has lifted, and the banquet of spring spreads its tantalizing aroma over a nation.

Spring melts into summer, and life in the hills is as peaceful as a nap after Sunday dinner. Angus and Hereford cattle stroll lazily through knee-deep blue stem grass and an occasional cowboy can be seen riding slowly around the slopes.

Then comes the autumn season, and the hills blush red in anticipation of the nakedness of winter.

This is the magnificent peace of Kansas.

A great change occurs when one leaves the eastern part of Kansas and journeys into the plains regions. The sky seems larger here and a huge white thunderhead gains in stature. Under this giant of skies, the land seems more bountiful. Here is the beauty of productivity. Endless miles of wheat rippled by a completely uninhibited breeze create a natural, peaceful ballet across the land. This is Kansas, the meat and bread of a nation.

But a kind creator also provided parks for the people of Kansas, such as the white spires of the Monument Rocks in Gove County and the red wilderness of the Gyp Hills.

Rising thirty feet or more above the prairie, Monument Rock and the chalk pyramids of Gove County must have provided a thrilling sight to early travelers on the dozens of trails that criss-crossed the heart of the nation.

The wilderness of the Gyp Hills in Barber and Comanche Counties in southwestern Kansas creates a completely different aspect of the state. Sparkling lakes, cedar groves and grassy slopes mark this part of the Wheat State providing a park-like atmosphere for travelers on U. S. Highway 160.

The atmosphere of Kansas is conducive to happiness. Kansans show this spirit in a variety of ways. Almost every community in the state has a time to celebrate. From full scale productions such as Newollah at Independence and Arkallalah at Arkansas City, each attended by about 50,000 people, to the annual Medora Picnic seen by less than 200 people, the variety and color of festivals in the Sunflower State are almost endless.

Goblins of orange and witches of black at the Newollah and Arkallalah Halloween festivals are local children dressed not to scare, but to reap prizes for the best costume. Originally, the celebrations were started as a means to keep the youngsters out of trouble on Halloween, but the citizens soon discovered they were having a lot of fun. Now parades are of top-notch quality sometimes stretching for more than two miles. Queens are crowned at a Grand Ball on the last day, and the entire programs are saturated with games, contests and a general carnival atmosphere for three days. While these two events have a rather spontaneous look, due to their present size, they are well-planned and completely coordinated, "Right down to the last scoop full of litter on the morning after," as one local citizen commented at Arkansas City this year.

It would seem, at a glance at the list of Kansas festivals, that almost any theme is an excuse for a grand celebration. The people of Baldwin City in the eastern half of the state, for instance, invite guests to their Maple Leaf Festival each year in October just to share the beauty of their 400 maple trees.

Under the flaming umbrella of red maple leaves, the town turns out for parades, a beauty contest, and a steak barbeque in the middle of main street. Several busses are always on hand to haul visitors through the wooded hills that surround the city with regular stops at the local historic sites. These bus tours are usually quite lengthy because almost every spot around Baldwin has some historic attachment, including the site of the pre-Civil War battle at Black-jack and the oldest library in Kansas at Vinland. But most enjoyable is a stroll through the beauty of the brilliant fall colors.

Long before the Spanish explorers trekked north from the Gulf of Mexico, the Indians were holding annual festivals. The Pottawatomie, Kickapoo, and Iowa tribes, each with a reservation in Kansas, continue to gather each year at Mayetta, Horton, and White Cloud for a pow wow. While visitors are quite welcome to observe the proceedings, the Indians are there basically for a reunion. They pitch their teepees and make their campfires just as their ancestors did, and dancing in full feathered regalia is the order of the day while trading of arts and crafts and other business is taken care of.

A completely different sort of dancing is seen every other year at Lindsborg, former home of Birger Sandzen, world famous artist. Swedish folk dancing in native costume is the main attraction at the Svensk Hyllnings Fest, a reminder of the heritage of the early settlers of this valley.

A few years ago, farmers from Bird City in a nostalgic mood, decided to put all their antique farming equipment in working condition for an after-harvest get-together. The idea spread like a prairie fire and there are now 150 members of the Antique Threshers Association with over 30 antique steam threshers and scores of other antique farm implements. Every fall, the group meets amid the belching steam and smoke of the old threshers for pulling contests, threshing meets and picnics.

Late summer and early fall is Fair time in Kansas. Kansans have always been proud of the product of their fertile land and have long used their state and county fairs as a means to display the fruit of their toil.

The fair means bright lights and cotton candy. It means carnival rides and salt taffy. It means panda bears, dart games, and it means a chance to look at the best livestock and crops in the

Neewollah parade in Independence.

Queen Neewollah receives her crown.

A delightful scare at the fair!

16

world. The fair means quarter horse racing and trotting races, motorcycle and auto racing and competition of all kinds for everyone from horseshoe pitching to sack racing. There is color and excitement at the fair, and the ultimate in Fairs is the Kansas State Fair at Hutchinson, and the Mid America Fair in Topeka.

At the Hutchinson State Fair, the winners of all the judging competitions from the County Fairs gather for the grand competition. Dozens of varieties of fruit, vegetables, corn, and grains are on display in the huge exhibition halls along with jams, jellies, canned fruit, colorful quilts, fancy beadwork, and a huge panorama of other crafts.

Spectator sports from the National Coursing Races at Abilene each year to the dozens of rodeos throughout the state are another way in which Kansas citizens enjoy the good life. The coursing races at Abilene are used as a show ground for the sleek greyhounds that are matched against live rabbits in their early years. The races are held twice a year and are attended by several thousand spectators.

Bucking horses and calf-roping along with the dozens of other exciting events of a rodeo can be seen almost all summer some place in Kansas, ranging from the world famous Flint Hills Rodeo at Strong City to Dodge City Days where the entire city takes on the look of the past for the duration of the celebration.

This love of competition in Kansas has produced some great athletes. Kansas milers have almost dominated the field for a number of years with such great runners as Wes Santee, Glen Cunningham, Archie San Romani, Archie San Romani, Jr., and the new sensation of this generation, Jim Ryun of Wichita.

A full round of championship basketball and football are provided by Kansas State University, the University of Kansas and Wichita State University in addition to some 17 smaller independent universities and a full athletic program on the high school level.

Interest in the various aspects of Kansas and midwestern history runs high in Kansas. There are 156 zoos and museums in the Wheat State, ranging from the Post Rock Museum at LaCrosse and the Santa Fe Museum at Ashland to the huge Kansas Historical Museum at Topeka and the Museum of Natural History at Kansas University at Lawrence. In Wichita, the Art Association recently opened a new art gallery and school to complement the existing Wichita Art Museum.

In the major metropolitan areas, concerts and theater are on a par with any in the nation.

This is the magnificent Peace of Kansas. A peace that allows the people time to relax, time to enjoy the result of their work and a grand atmosphere in which to enjoy the good life.

Kansas has grown. Growing pains have left their marks on Kansas and a number of these mark the westward movement of the United States in graphic detail. Old Fort Larned was one of several early forts strung across Kansas. After it was no longer needed, it was used as a ranch headquarters for a half century in almost the same condition it was in when Custer, Sheridan, and others walked through the officer's mess. In the last few years, the old fort has been changed into a museum and is now a National Historical Monument.

Reminders of the past are scattered across Kansas in an almost continuous string, from the replicas of the early day west at Dodge City, Wichita and Abilene to the John Brown Memorial in Osawatomie. The tradition is carried on in the Eisenhower Memorial and Museum in Abilene and the Agricultural Hall of Fame in Bonner Springs.

The history of Kansas has filled several volumes, and the future will probably fill many more. The aircraft industry, for instance, is making history every day and modern agricultural methods born in Kansas offer a ray of hopefulness to generations in the future.

This is the land of enjoyment, where people live, work and enjoy their efforts.

This is the magnificent peace of Kansas.

PLANNING
for WATER *the management of*

Kansas water

Kansas Water Resources Board, June, 1965

Tuttle Creek Reservoir

Stanton County

A windmill turning briskly in the western Kansas wind, pulling up cool fresh water — A small farm pond satisfying the thirst of cattle and inviting a young fisherman — Tuttle Creek, 16,000 acres of water ready to help satisfy an entire river valley's thirst, store a flood, or transport a water skier —

All across the state, Kansans are using their considerable water resources and curbing the problems which these same resources occasionally pose. This chapter is intended to provide a quick look at water in Kansas, with its problems and promises.

A Restless Resource

Kansas is a 200 by 400 mile rectangle located in the center of the 48 contiguous states. This size and location result in wide ranges in precipitation and abrupt changes in temperature. The primary source of water in Kansas is precipitation which falls on the land. To this is added the streamflow into Kansas from adjacent states and the slow movement of a very small amount of water in some ground-water reservoirs that extend across the state boundary. Almost 99 per cent of the gross amount of water available to Kansas comes from precipitation which falls within the state. Of this total, 85-90 per cent is consumed by evaporation or by transpiration from plants. Most of the remainder runs off and forms the streams of the state. A small portion moves downward through the soil and becomes ground water.

An understanding of Kansas water resources must start with a knowledge of some basic climatic and geologic conditions. Because of higher precipitation, eastern Kansas has much more water in streams than does the west while geologic deposits allow much more water to be stored underground in western and southcentral Kansas than in eastern Kansas.

Variability is the keynote of the Kansas climate. Kansas receives an average of 27 inches of precipitation each year, but the distribution varies with location and time. For example, the average annual precipitation ranges from 16 inches in the extreme west to 42 inches in the southeast. This variation produces an even greater variation in runoff. The amount of water which finds its way into streams ranges from less than 0.1 inch yearly in the west to over 10 inches in the southeast. This 100-fold variation in runoff means that *eastern Kansas has more and bigger streams* than does western Kansas. Water flowing out of the state totals about 12 million acre-feet per year, or enough to fill a freight train which would extend around the world 89 times. An acre-foot is an amount of water which would cover one acre to a depth of one foot, or 326,000 gallons.

The total amount of water stored underground in Kansas has been estimated to be about 500,000,000 acre-feet, enough to cover the entire state to a depth of almost 10 feet. This is more water than all of the streams carry out of the state in 40 years of average flow. Geology accounts for the ground-water paradox in Kansas: in humid eastern Kansas the underground geologic formations, mostly limestone and shale, store very little water, while *in drier western and southcentral Kansas underground deposits of sands and gravels yield large amounts of water.*

These variations in average water conditions across the state set the pattern of long-term development. If average conditions always existed there would be few water problems. Unfortunately, large seasonal and annual fluctuations are typical. Water planning and development are aimed at minimizing the effects of these fluctuations.

Recent Kansas history has recorded wide variations in precipitation. The 15 years from 1949 through 1963 offer excellent examples of the extremes of Kansas climate. (See graph) During this period, average precipitation for the state was 27 inches per year, which equals the long-term average. However, "normal" years were the exception rather than the rule. This 15-year period included both the wettest year and the driest year in Kansas since records began in

Republican River near Alida

1887. It also included 5 of the 15 driest years of record, and 5 of the 15 wettest years of record. These examples demonstrate that average precipitation values in Kansas are useful only as an indication of the long-term water supply which is available for development and management.

Runoff varies much more than does precipitation. In 1951 Kansas streams carried about 42 million acre-feet of water out of the state. In dry years the total outflow from the state has been less than 2 million acre-feet. Thus, the maximum annual runoff has been more than 20

I-70 roadside park near Paxico

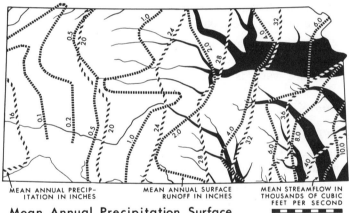

MEAN ANNUAL PRECIP-
ITATION IN INCHES

MEAN ANNUAL SURFACE
RUNOFF IN INCHES

MEAN STREAMFLOW IN
THOUSANDS OF CUBIC
FEET PER SECOND

0   18

Mean Annual Precipitation, Surface Runoff, And Streamflow In Kansas

YIELDS OF MORE THAN
500 GALLONS PER
MINUTE POSSIBLE

YIELDS OF 50 TO 500
GALLONS PER MIN-
UTE POSSIBLE

YIELDS OF 0 TO
50 GALLONS PER
MINUTE POSSI-
BLE IN WHITE
AREAS

DATA PROVIDED BY THE U.S. WEATHER BUREAU
AND THE U.S. AND STATE GEOLOGICAL SURVEYS.

KANSAS WATER RESOURCES BOARD. JUNE, 1964.
A.C.M.

Generalized Ground Water Regions In Kansas

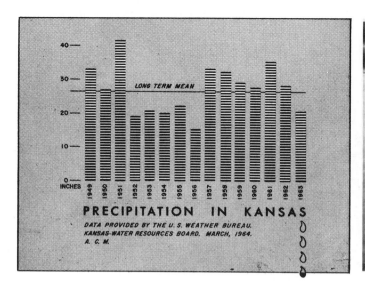

PRECIPITATION IN KANSAS
DATA PROVIDED BY THE U. S. WEATHER BUREAU.
KANSAS-WATER RESOURCES BOARD. MARCH, 1964.
A. G. M.

times greater than the minimum, while the maximum annual precipitation has not reached 3 times the minimum.

Because of the wide variation in the amount of surface runoff, it is necessary to provide storage in reservoirs. For this reason, Kansas is rapidly becoming a land of man-made lakes. Completed lakes, ranging in size from small farm ponds to the huge Tuttle Creek Reservoir, have a total conservation storage capacity of more than two million acre-feet and a total normal surface area of over 200,000 acres, almost twice the size of Wyandotte County.

Water quality is as important as quantity to many water users. Except for a few small areas where natural deposits of chloride or sulfate salts contaminate the runoff the natural quality of surface water is good. Ground water is of generally good quality.

How Kansans Use Water

Evapo-transpiration

The largest use of water in the state is by evapo-transpiration. This includes every natural and artificial means of returning water to the atmosphere whether it be through evaporation from land or water surface, or plant transpiration. In an average year evapo-transpiration consumes enough water to cover the entire state to a depth of nearly two feet, and ranges from about 98 per cent of the average precipitation in western Kansas down to 75 per cent in the east. *Over one-third of this total is used by crops and pastures, helping Kansas rank among the top six states of the nation in agricultural production.* Virtually all of the remainder **evaporates** directly from land and water surfaces or is transpired by trees and weeds.

Near Topeka

22

Kansas Gas and Electric, Parsons plant.

Withdrawal Uses of Water

Water is withdrawn from the state's streams or ground water for municipal and industrial purposes, rural domestic uses, and irrigation. These uses support much of Kansas commerce, industry, and agriculture. The average annual use is estimated at 2,644,000 acre-feet, about two per cent of the average annual precipitation. Only about 40 per cent of the water withdrawn is consumed; the remaining 60 per cent is returned to the streams or ground-water reservoirs, and is available for re-use. By 1975 these uses will require an estimated 5,937,000 acre-feet, of which 50 per cent will be returned.

Municipal Water Use. Water uses in homes are increasing at a rate of two per cent per year. When Kansas was being settled, five gallons would meet the average daily needs per person mostly for washing and drinking. Today automatic clothes washers, dishwashers, lawn sprinklers, garbage grinders, and sanitary facilities all add greatly to water use in homes — add up in fact, to an average daily use of 70 gallons per person. Meanwhile, such public uses as swimming pools, street washing, and fire fighting, plus water sold by cities to industries add to the total municipal water use. Municipal water use in Kansas totals about 220,000 acre-feet per year, an average of 125 gallons per person per day. This use is increasing and by 1975 will likely total 385,000 acre-feet. About two-thirds of the water diverted for municipal use is returned to the streams or ground water.

Industrial Water Use. Water and steam have played a vital part in determining the type and extent of industrial development in Kansas. Since the early days, Kansas industries have located near water supplies. In 1875, for example, most of the industries in Kansas were saw mills, grist mills, or flour mills located along the streams and powered by water wheels or steam. Today Kansas industries produce a wide variety of items ranging from airplanes to fly swatters, and while in most cases their dependence on water is not as direct as in the case

23

Smoky Hill River, Lindsborg

of the early mills, they must have water. Industries use water for everything from drinking water to washing products, but about 75 per cent is used for cooling. Although most industries obtain water from cities, many large industries have their own private source of supply.

Average annual industrial water use in Kansas totals about 970,000 acre-feet. Almost 96 per cent of this water is returned to the streams or ground water and is available for re-use. *Industrial water use is accelerating with the location of new industries and the expansion of existing industries.* Industrial water use is expected to reach 1,560,000 acre-feet per year by 1975.

Rural Domestic Use. Water use for domestic purposes on Kansas farms, a small but vital part of the total water used in the state, includes water for household purposes, lawns and gardens, and livestock. The total amount of water used for these purposes is currently estimated at 94,000 acre-feet per year, and it will probably increase to about 102,000 acre-feet per year by 1975. About 30 per cent of this water is returned. Most rural domestic water is obtained from individual wells or ponds developed by the farmers. However, in some areas where it is difficult for an individual to develop a dependable supply, rural water districts have been organized to distribute water to farms.

Irrigation. *Irrigation is the largest withdrawal use of water in Kansas.* Irrigation not only results in increased crop production; it also permits growing of a wider variety of crops including vegetables. Currently, more than a million acres are under irrigation, receiving an estimated 1,360,000 acre-feet of water each year. Most of this water comes from ground-water reservoirs via an estimated 9,000 wells. By 1975, the irrigated acreage may double, requiring an estimated annual water use of 3,890,000 acre-feet. About one-third of the water diverted for irrigation purposes is returned to the streams or ground water.

Low Flow Supplementation

The treatment of wastes has been required of cities and industries in the past and will continue to be needed in the future. However, even with a high degree of treatment, a certain amount of water is needed to dilute those wastes which cannot be removed by conventional treatment methods. This is one of the largest uses which will be made of the conservation storage in the federal reservoirs in the state.

Recreation

The most spectacular increase in water use by Kansans in recent years has been for recreation. The state has for many years provided state lakes and wildlife management areas for hunting, fishing, and wildlife refuges. Currently 36 state lakes and seven wildlife and waterfowl areas provide 21,000 acres of water surface. The many city, county, and township lakes and private ponds are also an important part of the recreation potential. Sixty-two municipal lakes over 10 acres in surface area and 25 county and township lakes add almost 10,000 acres of water to the Kansas recreation picture. In addition there are 70,000 small private ponds in Kansas, mostly on farms.

The big federal reservoirs built during the past few years have added a new element to recreation in Kansas. The 14 federal reservoirs now in operation provide a normal water surface area of almost 80,000 acres and a combined shoreline of more than 700 miles. Additional reservoirs which will be completed by 1975 will double the present surface area. One of the most pleasing aspects of this new recreation bonanza is that the recreation generally takes place on water which is provided for other purposes and requires no additional water. Kansans are participating in the nationwide increase in outdoor activity and in the growth of interest in water centered recreation. In 1950, attendance at the two federal reservoirs in Kansas was 700,000 visitor days; the 1963 visitation at eight Kansas reservoirs was over 3.5 million visitor days. In 1960, 15,700 motorboats were registered under the new state boat registration law; two years later the number had nearly doubled to 27,100. Sales of fishing and hunting licenses in Kansas were almost two and one-half times greater in 1960 than in 1940. Camping, hiking, and sightseeing around lakes also have been growing in popularity.

Missouri River Uses

In addition to the uses described above of water within the state, Kansas also uses the water which the Missouri River carries along the northeastern border for 127 miles. The large flow of the Missouri, averaging nine times that of the Kansas River, plus the regulation provided by six mainstem dams in South Dakota, North Dakota, and Montana, make this river a great boon to Kansas. The river and the ground-water in the valley alluvium provide virtually unlimited water for municipal, agricultural, or industrial use. Here too are the Kansas outlets to the vast U. S. inland waterway network for grain and other products loaded on barges at Atchison, Leavenworth and Kansas City.

Water Problems

Water problems in Kansas stem from the yo-yo tendency of the precipitation.

Floods

Average annual flood losses in Kansas have been estimated to exceed $35 million. Flood damage intensifies from west to east across the state, because of the more frequent occurrence of flood-producing storms and because the valleys are more intensely occupied.

The words "flood" and "1951" are synonymous in much of Kansas. That year Kansas suffered an estimated $650 million in flood damages. Especially hard hit was the Kansas River basin, which experienced $600 million of damages. Kansas has experienced other major floods and

Urban flood problems.

more are sure to follow. The damages caused by the floods of the past have resulted in demands for remedial action; great progress has been made toward reducing flood losses along the major streams in Kansas through the construction of major reservoirs and local protection works.

Floods along small streams occur more frequently and have caused much damage over the years. They also pose problems which are now receiving attention, particularly through the watershed program.

Drought

Droughts are less spectacular than floods, but they hurt more people in more ways. Almost everyone feels the sting of a drought to some degree, ranging from a little lower crop yield to total crop failure for the farmer, and from a little higher water bill to water rationing for the city dweller. Average annual losses due to water deficiency in past years are thought to have approached $75 million in Kansas. Indirect losses have added an unknown amount to the cost of drought.

The drought of 1952-1956 was one of the most severe in Kansas history. In 1956 the value of crops grown in Kansas barely exceeded $500 million (still among the best in the nation) compared with a record high of well over $900 million and an average of more than $800 million for the years 1959-1962. Kansas farmers spent an estimated $10 million in both 1954 and 1956 hauling water for household and livestock use. In 1954, 153 cities and towns experienced water shortages, and 72 of these spent over $4 million to provide emergency supplies. The lessons of this drought stimulated water resource planning, and as a result Kansans are much better prepared for drought now than in the 1950's.

Solving the Problems

The First Step

Adequate basic data is the foundation of a sound water planning, development, and management program. Measurements of precipitation, streamflow, ground-water levels, quality of water, sediment loads in streams — all are needed. In Kansas, a team of state and federal agencies is cooperating to fill this need.

Solutions to Water Problems

Overshadowing all physical solutions to water problems is the need for water conservation. Conservation, to be effective, must have widespread application, from the farmer who builds terraces and irrigates efficiently, to the industry which recirculates cooling water, to the city that carefully treats its wastes. While much water could be saved by presently known conservation practices, research is needed in other areas. This is particularly true of finding ways to reduce evapo-transpiration, which consumes 85-90 per cent of our precipitation.

Physical solutions to water needs and problems include wells and ponds to meet the domestic and irrigation needs on farms, well fields or reservoirs to provide a water supply for cities, levees for local flood protection, and large reservoirs for flood reduction and water supply storage. Often a combination of these methods is used. For example, Wichita has a large well field and also cooperated with the Bureau of Reclamation in the construction of Cheney Reservoir for additional municipal water.

Wells tapping ground water are the key to meeting water needs over much of western and southcentral Kansas.

Flood control works which provide strictly local benefits include levees, channel changes and bank clearing. Such works are used to protect a high-damage center, often supplementing protection provided by reservoirs upstream.

Since the basic water problems over a large portion of Kansas stem from the variation in runoff, *a key solution is the construction of reservoirs and ponds to reduce the fluctuations by storing water during high flows for use later.* Storage structures built in Kansas range from small farm ponds, used mostly to provide water for livestock, to multi-purpose reservoirs covering thousands of acres. Multi-purpose reservoirs may provide temporary storage for flood control and holdover storage for municipal, industrial, and agricultural uses and for maintaining minimum desirable stream flows. Recreation is usually a side benefit resulting from the availability of the water stored for the other purposes although it is now receiving more emphasis in reservoir planning. The trend is toward multi-purpose reservoirs as a means of making more efficient use of water.

Cooperation

Sound development and use of the water resources in Kansas depends upon teamwork between local, state and federal entities.

The Local Role. The local people are closest to both the problems and the potential posed by water, and much of the task of water planning and conservation lies with individuals and local communities. Many projects are accomplished through local efforts, including the municipal water supply systems and sewage treatment works. Larger projects require the assistance of the state and/or federal government. However, in these large projects local interests still play a vital role. It is largely from expressions of local concern that water projects receive their initial impetus. As the project progresses from conception to completion, local interests can play a major role in shaping its uses. The specific responsibilities of local citizens vary widely from project to project. In the case of local protection works or water supply storage in federal reservoirs, local interests may be required to make a major financial contribution to the project. Watershed projects are considered local projects and the local interests assume primary responsibility for their completion, with the technical and financial assistance of the state and federal governments.

The State Role. The primary responsibilities of the state are in long-range planning, administration of laws concerning quality and quantity of water, basic data collection, research, and providing financial assistance for water projects.

Work is underway on a unique state plan designed to make the best possible use of Kansas water resources. An example of the benefits of state planning is the conservation storage which has been added to several federal reservoirs in Kansas at the request of the state. Recognition of the need for this storage came from the state planning studies. By 1966, this storage will amount to about one-third of the total conservation storage in Kansas reservoirs, a significant addition to our water resources.

Laws which insure the right to use water and which protect against pollution are necessary for the best use of water. The Water Appropriation Act dedicates all water within the state to the use of the people, subject to control and regulation by the state. It provides for a system of water rights based on the principle of "first in time is first in right." The law has been the basis for administering water rights since 1945, and it has withstood the tests of time and courts. Since 1907, Kansas industries and cities have been required to obtain a permit to discharge wastes into streams. Adequate waste treatment is a condition for receiving a permit. The state constructs recreational lakes and recreational facilities around lakes and reservoirs. The role of the state in construction of larger water projects is that of coordinating the programs of the federal construction agencies and representing the interests of the state and the local people. The state may also guarantee the repayment to the federal government of the cost of water supply features of a federal reservoir or provide financial assistance to public corporations such as watershed districts.

The Role of State Agencies in Water Activities

State Department of Health — Environmental Health Services. Water quality investigations and analysis of data. Water pollution control by review of plans and operational supervision of municipal and industrial waste treatment facilities. Supervision of public water supplies by review of plans, appraisal of water systems, and analysis of water supplies. Provide assistance in the development of adequate water supplies and waste treatment facilities in rural areas.

State Geological Survey. Geological studies, descriptive (county) reports, problem oriented investigations, topographic mapping. Collection and analysis of basic data, research on occurrence and movements of ground water.

Kansas State University. Research on rural water supplies, irrigation, drainage, soil moisture conservation and use, crop production and weed control. Soil surveys and economic studies of agriculture, rural area development.

University of Kansas. Legal, economic, biologic, hydrologic, and engineering studies of water resource development programs.

State Board of Agriculture — Division of Water Resources. Administration of water rights, water law, inter-state compacts, irrigation districts, and watershed districts. Permits for construction of dams, levees, and channel improvements.

Soil Conservation Committee. Soil conservation districts programs in each county and related activities such as watersheds.

Webster Dam

Status of Federal Water Projects in Kansas
Kansas Water Resources Board

The U. S. Army Corps of Engineers constructs reservoirs and local protection works such as levees and channel improvements. The first reservoirs were constructed primarily for flood control but the newer reservoirs provide storage for low-flow supplementation and for municipal, industrial, or agricultural uses. Local interests pay for water supply storage in the reservoirs and part of the costs of local protection works.

The Bureau of Reclamation of the U. S. Department of Interior constructs reservoirs and irrigation facilities. The primary purpose of the reservoirs is to provide water for local irrigation districts except for Cheney which is being built in cooperation with Wichita for municipal water supply. These reservoirs also provide flood protection. The irrigation districts pay part of the cost of the irrigation water and local interests pay for any other water supply storage.

The Soil Conservation Service of the U. S. Department of Agriculture, cooperates with local watershed districts in the construction of watershed projects which include land treatment measures and center around small dams which provide temporary flood storage. A few watershed structures in Kansas include storage for water supply or recreation. Local interests pay for conservation storage and part of the flood control costs.

29

Park and Resources Authority. Development and operation of state park system and related recreation facilities.

Forestry, Fish and Game Commission. Fish and wildlife development. State lakes, construction and management. Boat registration and safety. Game management area development for ducks, fur bearers and game habitat.

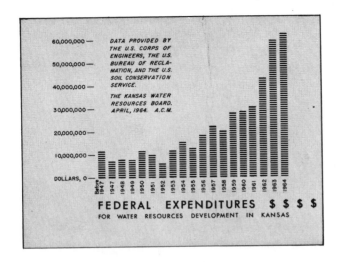

Water Resources Board. Preparation of state plan of water resources development. Collection and analysis of basic data. Studies and reports on state and federal water legislation. Coordination of state water activities. Review of state water activities. Review of state and federal projects and reports. Recommendations for state purchase of storage.

The Federal Role. The primary water activities of the federal government are basic data collection and the construction of various water projects. The U. S. Geological Survey spearheads the data collection activities and interpretation of the data, in cooperation with several state and federal agencies. The construction programs of the Corps of Engineers, Bureau of Reclamation, and watershed districts (working with the Soil Conservation Service) are outlined on page 29. The federal construction programs in Kansas were initially keyed to one major purpose: flood control in the case of the Corps of Engineers and the Soil Conservation Service, and the storage of irrigation waters in the case of the Bureau of Reclamation. The evolution of water development has seen increasing emphasis placed on multi-purpose development, which will permit better use of water for a wide variety of purposes. The importance of federal participation can be illustrated by the fact that federal expenditures for water resources development in Kansas will total over $530 million by July 1966. A total federal investment in Kansas water development approaching a billion dollars is conceivable in the remainder of this century.

Inter-State and Inter-Agency Coordination. *Rivers which cross state lines demand inter-state cooperation* if they are to be used effectively. In several instances Kansas has negotiated inter-state compacts, legal documents which set out the rights of the states to use the water involved. Kansas currently has compacts in effect with Colorado for the Arkansas River and with Colorado and Nebraska for the Republican River. Compacts are being negotiated with Oklahoma for the Arkansas River basin and with Nebraska for the Big Blue River.

Another means of coordinating water development and use is the inter-agency committee, which consists of representatives of states and federal agencies involved in water development.

Kansas participates in two: the Arkansas, White, and Red and the Missouri basin inter-agency committees.

Progress Through Planning

Kansas is now reaping some of the initial benefits of planned water development — benefits with roots in the efforts of many individuals, groups, and agencies — hastened to reality by the dramatic revelation of the hazards of unregulated water during the floods and drought of 1951-1956.

Flood Control Progress

Since 1953, 11 reservoirs and 12 local protection works have been completed in Kansas. Six more reservoirs and five local protection projects are under construction. One hundred fifty-eight floodwater retarding structures have been completed and 46 are under construction in the growing watershed program. The protection provided by these projects ranges from protection against only the smaller floods in some areas to protection against all known floods in other areas.

An adequate flow way which can be used for parks

Water Supply Progress

From 1954 through 1963, 132 cities containing almost 600,000 people have improved their water supplies to prevent the recurrence of shortages which they experienced in 1954. Since 1953, 90 rural water districts serving over 24,000 persons have been placed in operation with an additional 60 in planning stages. During this same period conservation storage in federal

Missouri River, looking north from White Cloud, Kansas.

reservoirs has increased from 260,000 acre-feet to 1,800,000 acre-feet. The six federal reservoirs now under construction will boost the total conservation storage to 3,100,000 acre-feet. Land irrigated from ground-water sources increased from about 400,000 acres in 1954 to over a million acres in 1963. In addition, the Bureau of Reclamation has constructed irrigation facilities and provided storage reservoirs for irrigation districts containing more than 60,000 acres.

Pollution Abatement

Kansas has an outstanding pollution abatement program. From 1954 through 1963, 106 cities and towns in Kansas have constructed sewage treatment plants. Good progress also has been made in abatement of pollution from industrial wastes. For example, more than 99 per cent of all oil field brine is now properly disposed of in Kansas, whereas, in 1953, an estimated 10,000 tons of brine were being improperly disposed of each day, much of which eventually reached the streams or ground water. Streams which could not be used 10 years ago are supporting game fish today.

Planning for the Future

The ultimate goal of water resources planning goes beyond the solving of current problems to the anticipation and avoidance of future difficulties. This involves not only careful planning but even more importantly an informed public — for it is largely the private decisions of individual cities, industries, and citizens which determine or deter future water problems. Some possible future problems could spring from changes in flood plain development, increases in irrigation water use, and changing pollution hazards.

Flood Plain Development

Great progress has been made in the construction of flood protection works in recent years and many Kansas cities and farms now enjoy a high degree of flood protection. However, preliminary studies indicate that *urban development along streams is creating future flood problems* in many areas. For example, in one Kansas city a housing area and a shopping center have been constructed on the flood plain of a small stream which is certain to overflow in the future — covering some living room floors. This is typical of many situations over the state. How should flood plains be used? The first step in answering this question is to understand how much flood risk exists. Flood risk estimates based on old legends and the optimistic hope that floods won't occur again have given way to modern engineering analysis which can provide a sound basis for local decisions as to the best flood plain usage. Kansas is cooperating with the Corps of Engineers in flood risk studies of the major streams in the state. Several Kansas cities also have expressed an interest in such studies.

Two methods of avoiding flood problems in areas undergoing urbanization are: (1) provide *an adequate flow way which can be used for parks,* golf courses, parking lots, and other purposes which would not be subject to high damages and would not seriously obstruct flood flows; and (2) in cases where building on a flood plain is essential, prevent loss by developing flood-resistant structures or building protective measures before development occurs. Flood protection is then recognized as a necessary part of the cost of development. Regardless of the method used, the potential problems must be clearly defined by flood risk studies before a proper solution can be agreed upon.

Increased Irrigation Use

While western Kansas has extensive ground-water reserves, the recharge, the amount of precipitation which filters down into the ground-water reservoir, is generally quite small. In several areas the current use, mostly for irrigation, is many times the amount of annual recharge and water levels are declining. In some local areas the decline has been great enough to require the lowering of pumps. Although the problem is not generally critical at present, it will intensify as irrigation increases.

Fishing, Boating and Hunting are year around pleasures found at the many lakes and reservoirs which serve every section of Kansas.

Any possible solution to this problem rests first on learning more about the storage, recharge, and other characteristics of the ground-water reservoirs. This information is difficult to obtain. However, work now in progress will provide a better understanding of the changing conditions and how they affect the individual users. Future studies may include research on possible means of increasing the recharge by artificial means.

One obvious need is to use the water more efficiently. Forty to sixty per cent of the water made available for irrigation to Kansas farms is lost before it can be used by crops. Some of these losses are inevitable, but a large portion can be prevented by more efficient operation. How much can be saved? Enough to increase the irrigated acreage in Kansas by 250,000-400,000 acres with no increase in water use, according to irrigation experts. In areas of declining water levels these savings could be used to reduce the amount of pumping to irrigate the present acreage. This could prolong the life of the ground-water reservoirs. Many western Kansas farmers are already increasing their irrigation efficiency as indicated by the fact that about 2,500,000 feet of underground irrigation pipe has been installed recently.

Changing Pollution Hazards

A vigorous program of pollution abatement is being carried out in Kansas with the result that our streams are now generally in good condition. New problems keep arising as the state continues to intensify agriculture and industry. The new hazards will be associated largely with the new chemical environment in which we live. The growing use of insecticides, new products from the petro-chemical industry, and the wastes of livestock feedlots will cause problems which require changed methods of waste handling and treatment.

Lake Shawnee

34

The Challenge

Kansas has enough water to support great economic growth — but not enough to be careless about it. Years of progress in solving water problems make the Kansas water picture brighter than ever before. But old problems are not completely solved and new ones threaten.

Kansas water problems and needs can be met. However, widespread understanding of the problems and what can be done about them is essential. It is hoped that these pages have answered many questions and stirred up others — for the future of Kansas water depends upon public understanding of water problems and upon the public support of measures to correct the water problems and prevent new ones from developing.

Selected Reading List

Governor's Economic Development Committee; *Economic Development for Kansas — Mineral and Water Resources;* Center for Research in Business, University of Kansas; 1962.

Grimes, Marcene; *Government and Natural Resources in Kansas: Water;* Governmental Research Center, University of Kansas; 1957.

Hutchins, Wells A.; *The Kansas Law of Water Rights;* Kansas Board of Agriculture and Kansas Water Resources Board; 1957.

Kansas Water Resources Board, *Kansas Water News,* a Bimonthly Newsletter.

Kansas Water Resources Board; *State Water Plan Studies, Part A, Preliminary Appraisal of Kansas Water Problems, Sections 1-12;* 1958-1962.

Kansas Water Resources Fact-Finding and Research Committee, *Water in Kansas,* Kansas State Finance Council, 1955.

Leopold, L. B. and Langbein, W. B.; *A Primer on Water,* U. S. Geological Survey, 1960.

The Kansas Geological Survey publishes geology and ground water reports for individual counties and special study areas. The Kansas Department of Health publishes reports on quality of water in Kansas.

These publications can be found in most Kansas libraries.

For additional information write: The Kansas Water Resources Board, Room 1134-S, State Office Building, Topeka, Kansas 66612.

Acknowledgements

Much of the information contained herein is based on reports and data from the various state and federal agencies involved in water resources. The cooperation extended by these agencies is greatly appreciated.

Members: FRED N. SIX, *Chairman,* Lawrence, Kansas; EDWARD GORDON, *Vice Chairman,* Highland, Kansas; CHRIS C. GREEN, Courtland, Kansas; DONALD CHRISTY, Scott City, Kansas; C. Y. THOMAS, Shawnee Mission, Kansas; WM. C. SALOME, Wichita, Kansas; WADE WILLCOXEN, Arkansas City, Kansas; DWIGHT F. METZLER, *Executive Secretary.*

PUBLIC EDUCATION IN KANSAS

by Adel F. Throckmorton
state superintendent of public instruction

Article 6 of the Kansas constitution provides that the legislature "shall encourage the promotion of intellectual, moral, scientific, and agricultural improvement by establishing a uniform system of common schools and schools of higher grade." The constitution also created the offices of state superintendent of public instruction and county superintendent of public instruction.

One of the first steps taken by the Legislature to reach these objectives was to authorize the county superintendent to divide each county into a convenient number of school districts. The early day system was uniform but, with convenience as the only other state criterion to guide this county official, an excessive number of districts were formed and the general pattern of a district with a governing board for each school was established.

By 1896, 35 years after Kansas became a state, 9,284 such districts had been organized. These schools met the needs of a pioneer society by providing instruction in reading, writing, spelling, arithmetic, history and other tool subjects. They also became centers around which community activities centered. Under these conditions there developed a sentimental attachment to the one-room school with its spelling bees, ciphering matches, box suppers, community sings, and other social activities that at a much later date made difficult the establishment of school district organizational patterns within which educational programs appropriate for the space age could develop. As recently as the 1940's rural education was thought of in terms of one-room schools.

With the increased number of automobiles and tractors after World War I, there followed a sharp decrease in the number of farms. By the close of World War II the resulting population shift from rural to urban areas accounted for a substantial reduction in the number of operating school districts. The movement of population from rural to urban areas had reached such proportions by 1945 that 2,200 organized rural elementary districts were unable to maintain school. The few pupils remaining in these districts were sent to neighboring schools.

It was during this period that a new kind of rural school began to develop. The need for instruction in fundamentals to supplement those that were adequate for a pioneer era became evident. These included courses designed to advance vocational and technical skills, more study about other peoples and cultures, and studies to prepare an increasing number of young people to enter college. In many sections of the state it was found difficult to meet the new challenges because of an outmoded district system that limited educational opportunity. However, the mid-forties did mark the beginning of new concepts of rural education and the expansion of educational offerings in all schools.

Typical of the modern school facilities over Kansas is this high school complex at Manhattan.

Modernizing the District System

The 1945 legislature sensed these needs and sought to meet them by enacting a school district reorganization law. Although this measure was strongly resisted in many parts of the state, county committees, working under provisions of the act, reduced the 8,438 existing school districts by 2,671 before the law was declared unconstitutional in 1947. The need for new organizational patterns was highlighted by the fact that more than 25,000 school board members were required to govern the 8,438 districts. This was about one and one-half times the total number of teachers in the state.

Impact of the reorganization act and subsequent legislation reduced the total number of school districts in Kansas to 3,517 during the period 1945-1955. Although results of the 1945 reorganization act were spotted, it set in motion educational reforms later climaxed by 1963 and 1965 legislative action.

By 1950, no semblance remained of the uniform system of school districts prescribed by the constitution. There had developed no less than 16 kinds of school districts as to organization or function, with an ever increasing number of special laws needed to enable such a variety of organizations to operate. More than one-half of the high schools were under the jurisdiction of districts that had no responsibility for elementary instruction. This double deck system of school districts compounded the difficulties as the state finally took steps to modernize the organizational patterns within which educational programs are conducted.

In order to obtain a clear picture of the state's school needs, the 1957 legislature appropriated funds with which to conduct a statewide comprehensive survey of education. The survey report, following completion of the project, was published in 1960. The data assembled, school conditions revealed by the survey, and recommendations of the survey team set the stage for unprecedented educational improvements in the state.

In 1963 a law was enacted which again provided for the establishment of a uniform system of school districts throughout the state. In order to qualify, each district must enroll a minimum of 400 pupils, provide instruction in grades one through 12, and teach 30 unit courses

Modern school library and instructional materials center. School libraries in all areas of the state are making unprecedented growth.

in each high school. An exception to the 400 pupil requirement was made for sparsely populated areas.

County planning boards were named by representatives of existing school districts in the county. It was the duty of each board to make a comprehensive study of the educational needs of the county and develop a redistricting proposal for submission to the voters. The governing bodies of qualified districts in counties that failed to adopt the planning board's proposal could petition the state superintendent who was authorized by the unification act to declare such districts to be unified. By means of county-wide elections and the petitions a total of 294 unified districts were established by Oct. 1, 1965. It is estimated that by July 1, 1966, at least 305 unified districts will have been formed which will include more than 97% of the territory of the state. When the unification program has been completed the 1,799 school districts that existed in 1963 will have been reduced to approximately 315, which will provide Kansas with a sound system of district organization that is basic to the operation of efficient elementary and secondary schools.

The unified school districts can offer opportunities and services formerly denied many Kansas boys and girls. These include a wider choice of elective courses consistent with the abilities and interests of each student. Typical of such courses are a great number of vocational and technical subjects, modern foreign languages, music, art, and advanced work in science and other fields that require modern laboratories and other costly equipment.

Complete guidance, counseling and testing programs under the direction of qualified personnel can be established, provision made for specialized instruction for gifted and handicapped children, health and physical education activities expanded, adequate libraries developed, and many other advantages given students who heretofore have not had the benefit of such services.

School Finance

The 1965 legislative session made another major improvement in elementary and secondary education by the adoption of a foundation finance measure. This act increases to $80,760,000 state revenues for direct school support which, added to the $7,359,000 residue returned to school districts for property tax reduction, provides more than $88,000,000 for elementary and high schools from non-ad valorem tax sources. This does not include state money used to reimburse schools for driver training courses and special education programs.

As recently as 1937, the financial support for Kansas schools was derived almost exclusively from local and county ad valorem taxes. Revenues from other sources totaled less than 5 per cent of the amount spent for public schools. The first state elementary aid law was passed by the 1937 legislature but because of the nature of the formula and the inadequacy of funds, by 1944 the amount distributed was less than one and one-quarter million dollars. A high school support measure enacted in 1905 and known as the Barnes Law provided some revenue from a county property tax for the 40 participating counties. This statute was replaced by another in 1945 which substantially increased the amount of property tax revenue for the high schools of all counties. In 1947, a two-mill county wide levy became mandatory for the support of elementary schools. Under the 1965 foundation program these sources of revenue have been replaced by a uniform system for financing elementary and secondary education.

School Government and Administration

In addition to a sound system of school district organization and provision for the financial support of schools, there remains one other element in the framework within which elementary and secondary education operates; namely, provision for the government, administration, and supervision of schools.

For the most part the control of education in Kansas has been delegated by the Legislature to boards of education elected by voters of the school districts. It is the duty of these boards to adopt budgets, administer the financial affairs of the district, employ teachers, approve instructional courses over and beyond minimums required by the state, and adopt policies for the guidance of the board in discharging these responsibilities.

The Legislature has assigned to a number of state agencies the responsibility to coordinate programs and policies of local boards of education, establish educational standards, prescribe courses of study, collect statistical data, distribute state funds to local districts under formulas established by law, provide consultative services in many fields, and provide general supervision of the educational interests of the state.

This is one of more than 175 laboratories in Kansas schools provided with electronic equipment to improve instruction in modern foreign languages.

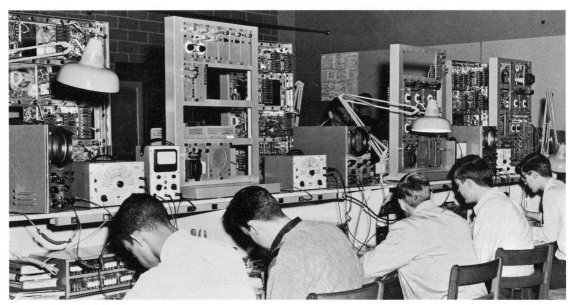

Electronic equipment in a Kansas Area Vocational-Technical School. These schools are designed to make quality vocational-technical education available in all sections of the state.

The agency charged with general responsibility for elementary and secondary education is the state department of public instruction, which by law is defined as consisting of the state superintendent of public instruction and a state board of education composed of seven members appointed by the governor.

This department is charged with developing standards and policies under which teachers are certified, schools accredited, instructional programs developed, and special services provided. The department also collects statistical data from the schools, distributes state funds to school districts and junior colleges, conducts educational conferences for school boards, school administrators and teachers, administers a state scholarship program and other activities, assists in school district organization matters, works with the colleges in coordinating teacher education programs, and cooperates with numerous official and private agencies and organizations.

The chief educational officer in each county is the county superintendent of public instruction. Prior to school district unification it was his duty to supervise education in the county, assist school boards in carrying out their responsibilities, collect information from the schools and keep official school records in his office, organize and disorganize school districts, change school district boundaries when such change was warranted in the educational interests of the county, establish in-service programs for the improvement of instruction, prepare county school budgets, distribute funds to school districts and in general provide educational leadership for the county.

With district unification and the reduction in number of school districts the role of the county superintendent will change. It is too early to predict the future of this office although there now appears to be considerable support for replacing the office with bigger intermediate units to perform over a wider geographic area many of the duties now carried out in each county. In the meantime the work of these officials will be unusually heavy during the period of transition from the present school district system to full operation under the unified districts.

A second state agency is the state board of education which serves as the board for vocational education. This board administers vocational programs in high schools and junior colleges and has major responsibility in the establishment and operation of the area vocational technical schools. The board is also in charge of the state rehabilitation program. Other agencies with some school responsibility include the state department of health, the state fire marshal's office, the highway department, the Kansas state high school activities association, and the state teacher retirement board.

A movement is under way to modernize the state administration of education by placing responsibilities now distributed among a number of state agencies in the hands of one state board of education. A study committee appointed by the legislative council recently filed its report recommending that such a board be established.

Within this general framework, Kansas elementary schools with a 1964-65 enrollment of 365,727, including kindergarten, give basic instruction in the traditional elementary subjects and in other fundamental courses as required by law. High schools of the state which last year enrolled 141,476 students, make available an ever expanding list of courses as required by developments in social, economic, technological, vocational, and citizenship fields. The total public school enrollment of 507,203 in September, 1964, shows an increase of 111,986 over the 395,217 enrollment in 1954.

Dramatic educational changes within the past 10 years are indicated by what has happened in the field of modern foreign language instruction. In 1955, Kansas ranked near the bottom among the states in the number of students enrolled in modern foreign language courses. In 1953-54, only 196 high schools or 28% of the secondary schools then operating, taught any modern foreign language. There were only 265 teachers of modern foreign language in all the schools of the state at that time. By 1964-65, 523 schools or 76.6% of the operating schools, gave instruction in one or more foreign languages. Prior to 1958, there were no language laboratories in Kansas secondary schools. Today, there are 177 such laboratories supplied with electronic equipment to speed up foreign language study. In 1958, only 6,496 secondary school students were enrolled in the study of Spanish. By 1964, the number of such students had increased to 21,350.

Comparable, or even greater expansion, has occurred in the fields of science, at both the elementary and secondary levels, and in vocational education. Organized physical education programs have likewise expanded in both elementary and secondary schools. The schools not only offer instruction in these basic courses but, in addition, render such specialized services as counseling, guidance and testing, special education for gifted and handicapped children, school lunch programs, and health services. A specialized service of the state is the teacher retirement system.

Vocational Education

Vocational education had its beginning in Kansas with the passage of the Smith-Hughes Act in 1917. The Smith-Hughes Act was specifically designed to train young people for the labor market in trade and industrial education, home economics, distributive education and agriculture. The Smith-Hughes Act resulted from the World War I emergency when there was a drastic shortage of skilled workers available for industrial production and defense purposes. Vocational education has moved forward with high points and low points for the past 40 years. The agriculture education program was the largest division of vocational education from 1917 to approximately 1955. Thousands of successful farmers of this state can trace their prosperous farming operations to vocational agriculture programs in the schools. Trade and industrial education has served a great need in industrial centers, such as the aircraft industry in Wichita. Because of the expensive nature of trade and industrial vocational education, it has not yet been made available in all parts of the state. Home economics education, designed for the training of homemakers, has covered the entire state with very successful and productive programs. Distributive education has made its mark in the business community of this state over a long period of years.

41

Since issuance of the Kansas economic development committee report in 1962, vocational education has taken a great step forward. One of the recommendations of this committee was the establishment of a state system of area vocational-technical schools. This proposed state system makes available the kinds of quality vocational education that are needed by both students and the labor market throughout Kansas. It was also the express purpose of this legislation to equalize the educational opportunities for all students in the state and to make quality vocational education available within commuting distance of all students who want, need, and can benefit from such training. Authorized by the 1963 Legislature, the state system of area vocational-technical schools gives local communities the opportunity to band themselves together and pool their resources with those of the state and the nation to provide vocational education to all Kansas citizens.

The state board for vocational education is now developing the state system of area vocational-technical schools as authorized by the legislature. Schools have been established and are serving students in the communities of north central Kansas at Beloit, southeast Kansas at Coffeyville and Columbus, southwest Kansas at Dodge City, northwest Kansas at Goodland, central Kansas at a combination center at Hutchinson-Newton-McPherson, northeast Kansas at Topeka, and in the areas of Emporia, Salina, Manhattan, and Wichita. The area vocational-technical school centers are vocational education centers and not industrial education centers only. Programs are offered for any segment of the labor market in which there is an actual or anticipated need locally or statewide or where there are known national shortages of skilled workers and technicians. Programs are offered in agriculture and agriculture-related occupations, home and community service, health occupations, distributive occupations, office occupations, trade and industrial occupations, and for the highly skilled technician.

Two area vocational-technical schools are now operating in all-new facilities, a third is on the drawing board, and three additional schools have funds available for construction as soon as plans can be finalized.

Practices and policies developed by the state board for vocational education provide for not more than 20 area vocational-technical schools. The state has also authorized the establishment of a technical institute designed to provide occupational education of less-than-professional level at the deactivated Schilling Air Force Base in Salina. This vocational education facility will fill an obvious void in vocational and technical training in the state.

As the state economy moves forward, it is anticipated there will develop a total vocational and technical education program that will provide for occupational orientation in junior high school programs, exploratory skill development training programs at the secondary school level, and then, real, occupational-oriented vocational education at the posthigh school level, in the area vocational-technical school system, the community junior college system, or the Schilling Technical Institute.

Special Education

Special education in Kansas is rapidly expanding. In 1949, private organizations interested in the educational welfare of handicapped and gifted children obtained legislation, a small appropriation, and authorization for the establishment of a division of special education in the state department of public instruction. In 1951, the Legislature gave further impetus to the movement by making an appropriation of $80,000 to reimburse local school systems that initiated special education programs.

Today, special education reimbursement to local public schools approaches $2,000,000. Even so it is estimated that only a little more than one-fourth of the educational needs of handicapped and gifted children are being met. One of the most positive features for advancing special education has been the formation of unified school districts. However, some small schools have conducted special education programs successfully on a cooperative basis with other districts.

Historically there has been a shortage of teachers adequately prepared in special education, a lack of money to finance these expensive programs, ranging from two to seven times the cost of regular instruction, and inadequate facilities to house special classes.

An important breakthrough to alleviate the teacher shortage has been provided in Public Law 88-164, the scholarship and fellowship program in special education. Last year Kansas awarded a total of 35 summer traineeships in various areas of exceptionality, and three year-long fellowships, similar awards will be made for the 1966-67 school year. Also, there are special training institutes for teachers.

Special education programs making the most significant gain in Kansas are in the fields of the educable mentally retarded and speech correction. It is anticipated there will be 300 programs for the educable mentally retarded for the 1966-67 school year. The statewide planning study in mental retardation recommends there should be more than 800 such programs in the state. Programs for the trainable retarded are being given additional consideration, although they have been slow to move in public school settings. There is also increasing concern for the border-line mentally retarded — slow learning group. Local school districts have been planning itinerant-resource programs for the visually impaired, as well as for the physically limited. Programs for hard of hearing children are beginning to develop in public schools. It is thought there are at least 1,500 hard of hearing children in the public schools who do not yet have appropriate types of special education. Supportive services for exceptional children are on the increase by the establishment of more school psychological and social

Geometry for the gifted fifth-grader. Well prepared teachers and modern school facilities provide unlimited opportunities for Kansas elementary pupils.

work services. Specialized itinerant-resource programs for intellectually gifted children, usually those above 130 IQ level, should expand as a result of the district unification movement.

It is fortunate that Kansas legislation is sufficiently broad to give latitude for experimental programs such as those for slow learners and learning disability areas. In many states it is necessary to introduce special legislation in order to initiate new programs, but such is not the case in Kansas. Kansas has been given nationwide recognition by other states and national organizations for the flexible legislative authorization under which provision has been made for the education of exceptional children. The 1965 legislative session issued a mandate for the reporting of visually and hearing impaired children. Psychological evaluation and team planning are also required for better educational placement.

The following table indicates the scope of special education services during the school year 1964-65:

Name of Program	Teachers	Children Served
Educable Mentally Retarded	201	2,587
Trainable Mentally Retarded	17	162
Speech and Hearing	121	11,950
School Psychological Services and School Social Work	51	7,650
Directors of Special Education	7	10,500
Gifted	18	280
Visually Impaired	6	120
Emotionally Disturbed and Neurologically Impaired	17	190
Orthopedically Handicapped	12	
Homebound and Hospitalized	14 full-time 225 part-time	616
Deaf-Blind (and combinations of other severe handicaps)		6
	690	24,061

School Health Services

Among the state agencies that play an important role in Kansas education, is the Kansas state department of health.

The school health program of the department is centered in the division of maternal and child health and is concerned not only with health services to children but with the school environment and health education. Basic public health functions include investigation of the causes of death and disease, survey making, analysis of vital statistics, standard setting, and promotion of preventive health services for school children. The department furnishes schools with a large variety of health and dental records and forms, pamphlets on health problems and normal growth and development of children, and guides on various phases of school health. The film library, widely used by schools throughout the state, has an excellent selection of health education films for school children of all ages. As accidents are a number one health problem, the department issues a biennial student accident report based upon information provided by schools. Consultation is provided by the school nurse consultant to school nurses employed by school districts, and to county public health nurses who provide school nursing services. Physician consultation is also available to communities in evaluating their school health programs. Epidemiological services may be provided whenever an unusual outbreak of disease occurs among school children. Immunizing biologicals are furnished to local health departments and physicians for school immunization programs.

The department furnishes guides and forms for the annual inspection of schools made by local health officers, as required by law, and gives consultation to local health departments

This blind girl was president of the student council in her local public school. Special education programs in Kansas schools make such achievement possible.

This is one of 1,400 Kansas school lunchrooms. Well qualified cooks and balanced meals contribute to the health of participating students.

who work with school boards and communities to make improvements in the school environment which affects the health of children.

It encourages preschool and periodic health examinations and special athletic examinations, and provides forms for this program. Except for the dental inspection law, most school health legislation has been enacted in the past six years. These include the vision screening requirement every two years, the certification of immunization for school entrance, and certification of health of school personnel at the time of employment and at three year intervals. The department of health prints the forms used in these programs and guides relating to these health concerns. A special mobile hearing unit travels throughout the state for the purpose of demonstrating the value of audiometric screening to schools not presently staffed and equipped for this hearing screening procedure.

An interdepartmental committee on school health, composed of representatives of the state departments of health and public instruction, meets regularly to develop and coordinate the school health program. They jointly sponsor the annual school health education workshops held at Wichita and Washburn Universities, attended by school administrators, teachers, school nurses, public health nurses and physicians.

The state department of health, in cooperation with the state department of public instruction, has recently published a School Health Handbook for the guidance of boards of education, school administrators and teachers.

Counseling and Guidance

Counseling, guidance, and testing programs in Kansas high schools have expanded rapidly since enactment of the National Defense Education Act of 1958. The number of qualified counselors has increased to keep pace with the expansion of these programs. Today, 789 qualified counselors serve in some 600 Kansas high schools and junior high schools. Complexities of the space age and technological developments have placed added responsibilities upon schools to employ qualified persons to assist students in choosing the courses they are best fitted to study and to guide them in selecting the vocation for which they are best fitted. The state department of public instruction through the state testing center at Emporia administers approximately 30,000 tests to ninth grade students and 20,000 tests to tenth grade students each year as one means of evaluating the abilities, aptitudes and interests of students.

School Lunch Programs

The United States Congress enacted the National School Lunch Act in 1946 in order to assist school lunch programs both through grants-in-aid and food distributions. The United States department of agriculture, which administers the national school lunch program, and the state department of public instruction maintain an agreement under which the former grants funds to the state for reimbursing approved local schools, and the latter agrees to adopt certain national standards and procedures in the state program.

The state superintendent of public instruction first appointed a school lunch director in 1946. As the administrative officer, the director exercises general supervision of the lunch program. He and his staff also train the supervisors and cooks in the schools of Kansas since the majority of the women in this area are not professionally prepared.

The school lunch program has expanded rapidly. Today, more than 230,000 Kansas school children in some 1,400 schools participate in the Type A lunch program, which represents a 6% increase over the previous year. Almost $14,000,000 was spent during the 1964-65 school year to operate the Kansas school lunch program. About $11,500,000 of this amount was paid by the children themselves. The federal cash subsidy is only 4c for each meal served, with a minimum of about 8c provided from commodities, much of which is from federal surplus. The average cost to the pupil for each meal is 28c.

The school lunch section of the state superintendent's office conducts a field visit program during which attention is devoted to such matters as menu planning, serving recipes, record keeping and food storage. The supervisors and the director visit about 90 per cent of the participating schools annually.

Teacher Retirement

Kansas has provided retirement benefits for teachers and other school personnel through a state teacher retirement system and authorization for teachers to participate in the federal social security program. Currently, there are 29,402 school employees contributing to the state retirement system as required by law. Some 5,960 inactive persons are carried on the rolls of the system and under its provisions will receive benefits upon reaching retirement age. As of June 30, 1965, 3,480 persons were receiving retirement benefits under the system. Only 4% of the first $3,000 of a school employee's salary was withheld for retirement purposes until 1965 when the Legislature required that 4% of the first $5,000 be withheld. The system, established in 1941, now has invested $38,850,000 in government securities.

Community Junior Colleges

The first public junior colleges established in Kansas were founded at Fort Scott, Garden City, Holton and Marysville in 1919. During the period from 1919 to 1963, 14 junior colleges were established and operated in Kansas.

The early growth in enrollment of Kansas public junior colleges was very slow during the period of 1919 to 1925, with only eight such colleges and an enrollment of 705 students. How-

A Blind Child in a Regular Classroom: The braille writer and the typewriter are tools which the blind child uses in preparation of assignments to hand in to the teacher.

Home-to-school telephone brings the classroom to a physically handicapped child. The child recites when called upon by the teacher, becoming a contributing member of the class in the two-way telephone hook-up.

ever, the next 15 years were characterized by very rapid growth in enrollment, with six additional institutions established, and a total of 5,103 students enrolled.

The growth in enrollment has continued steadily upward, with a total enrollment of 6,100 in the school year 1963-4 and 7,400 in October 1964. The 1965 fall enrollment will approximate 9,500 students. Since 1964, three new junior colleges have been established making a total of 17 such institutions in Kansas. The Kansas junior colleges have, since their establishment, offered quality education comparable to the four-year colleges and universities.

During the regular session of the 1965 Kansas Legislature, an act was passed establishing a state system of community junior colleges. This is the first major change in legislation for such colleges since 1917. The act provides for the expansion of community junior college taxing districts, increases state aid for operational purposes, establishes out-of-district tuition to be paid by counties sending students to community junior colleges, and increases local levy limits for operation and capital outlay. The law further provides that a state plan of community junior colleges be developed by the state superintendent which will basically outline criteria for the establishment of new community junior colleges in Kansas.

The law also authorized the establishment of an advisory council for community junior colleges responsible to the state superintendent of public instruction who is designated as the state authority for these institutions. The council is composed of representatives from the state board of education, the community junior colleges, the state board of regents, private colleges, state colleges, secondary schools, labor, business, industry and agriculture. The major purpose of the advisory council is to articulate, coordinate between all levels of Kansas education, and advise the state superintendent on matters pertaining to the state system of community junior colleges.

Kansas in accepting the community junior college title and philosophy assumes the responsi-

Equipment in the machine shop of our Area Vocational-Technical School. Ten Area Vocational-Technical schools have been established in Kansas with 10 additional such schools tentatively planned.

bilities associated with it. Such colleges must make available educational opportunities beyond high school to the youth and adults of Kansas.

Programs must be available for:

1. The high school graduate who plans, after two years of study at the community college, to transfer to a four-year institution for the purpose of attaining a baccalaureate degree.

2. The high school graduate who desires training as a highly trained technician, skilled craftsman or other semi-professional specialty who will enter the world of work following training.

3. The individual who desires special training, upgrading, or retraining vocationally.

4. The individuals who desire to continue their educational opportunities for personal, vocational, or avocational reasons.

The future mission of Kansas community junior colleges, therefore, will be to meet those educational needs not now being met by other institutions of higher education.

These educational developments in Kansas during the past decade may appropriately be designated as an educational revolution. The movement has also been marked by the building of new school facilities, improved qualifications of elementary and secondary teachers, the establishment of a program under which 400 Kansas students each year are awarded state scholarships financed by legislative appropriations, the extension of modern foreign language study to elementary schools, the development of a statewide interest in economic education and numerous other indications that Kansans believe in education.

49

A look at one unified school . . . seven years later

How is rural high school consolidation working out in Kansas? For the boys and girls who gave up their hometown schools? For the teachers? For the citizens who pay the costs of education and want the very best for their money?

Here, in a close-up view of one of the first rural high school consolidated districts to build and occupy a central school, the consensus seven years later is that the youths get more educational opportunities at less cost. And everyone seems to approve!

Formed by the towns of Allen, Miller, Admire and Bushong, all in Lyon County, the school district now covers an area of 308 square miles. The consolidation was approved first, then the questions of bonds for a new building and site for it were solved by elections. Two sites were proposed, both of which were apart from the four towns involved. The winning location was one mile east of Allen. The patrons voted $375,000 in bonds. The building cost $370,000, or about $10.50 per square foot which is considered an economical figure. Operating costs are running cheaper than costs of the four old schools.

How was the school named? By the students. Their choice was Northern Heights. Official address is Allen, Kansas.

New opportunities for students included classes in shorthand, welding, auto mechanics, shop, advanced algebra, solid geometry, advanced math, physics, chemistry and biology — many of which had not been offered in the former schools. A broad music program was offered. School paper and annual were published by the journalism class. The Business students could affiliate with the Future Business Leaders of America. The consolidated school now takes part in football, basketball, track and baseball competition and the four surrounding communities provide enthusiastic spectators. Football posed a dilemma at first, as none of the boys had come from a school big enough to field a team. They caught on quickly, however, and squads have done well. Basketball is probably the favored sport at Northern Heights. The school's gymnasium-auditorium easily seats 800.

Northern Heights is doing a good job of educating young people and serving the community. Glen Atherly, principal, expressed the feelings of many in the area. "Though each town gave up something dear in its school," he said, "it is practically impossible to walk down the short main streets of any of the towns and find a person who would want to go back to the old system."

Looking west from Government Hill near Junction City. This photo looks down on I-70. The route cuts through the south edge of Fort Riley and across the Smoky Hill River valley, bypassing the city on the south.

KANSAS HIGHWAYS: *800 miles of*
multi-lane interstate routes under construction

One measure of the development of Kansas is the evolution of its modern highway system. The Santa Fe, Overland and Oregon trails were in use a century ago. Today 800 miles of multi-lane interstate routes are under construction and there are dreams of an additional 1,400 miles of freeways that one day will span the state and serve its major traffic arteries.

Now, Kansas has 133,400 miles of public roads, streets and highways, a total that is exceeded by only two states. Residents of Kansas in the early years needed adequate land service roads, and to insure that these would be available, the Legislature dedicated practically every section line to be a public road.

From this basic grid system has evolved nearly 10,000 miles of rural state highways; 22,000 miles of county secondary roads; 9,000 miles of city streets; and 92,000 miles of county and township roads.

Kansas has an investment of about $650,000,000 in its state highway system. All resulting from the great love affair of America and the automobile.

This is truly a nation on wheels — wheels that increase in numbers each year and roll faster and faster.

In 1914, Kansas had a motor vehicle registration of 39,900 vehicles, and to demonstrate the possibilities of motor vehicle transportation, Governor Hodges headed a "Good Roads Caravan" that drove from Hutchinson to Kansas City in a single day — from dawn to dark — a feat unparalleled at that time. Today, there are 1,335,000 registered vehicles and a similar trip takes about 3½ hours.

Kansas began a partnership with the federal government in 1917, to provide a system of highways using federal grants-in-aid and state matching revenues. From a very meager beginning, this joint effort has produced a system that compares quite favorably with surrounding states.

Between 1917 and 1929, the State Highway Commission served only as an advisory body for the counties, since the Kansas Constitution did not permit the state to engage in works of internal improvement. A vote of the people amended this section of the Constitution and the Legislature then set up the agency to plan, design, construct and maintain an interconnected highway system.

Hard surfaced state highways now connect every county seat town and every major city. Rural state highways are only a part of the Commission's responsibility. Building the 600 miles of connecting highway links through towns and cities has been a part of the job. In many towns, these comprise their major arterial streets.

In 1934, using state and federal matching funds, the first roadside park was built in Kansas near Baldwin along US 56. We now have more than 160 of these rest areas. These have brought more favorable comments from the traveling public than any other single feature of the state highway system.

In 1964, an estimated 3,500,000 persons stopped at the parks. With the increased federal

Through the heart of Topeka, the I-70 expressway is only two blocks from the central business district. This picture looks east from the Adams Street interchange.

Winding its way through the beautiful hills of north central Kansas, this section of I-70 between Salina and Dorrance is fitted to the landscape to provide an outstanding safe, scenic highway. This picture shows the K-14 interchange north of Ellsworth.

interest in highway beautification, Kansas has a head start on a great many states. Future plans call for development of scenic overlooks; improvements at some of the established parks and development of new areas.

One of the keys to the success of the roadside parks and the highway system as a whole, is a first-rate maintenance organization equipped with machines to do the work and experienced men with the knowledge of what needs to be done and the best method of accomplishing it.

Through the years, the progressive engineering departments of the State Highway Commission have been quick to adapt new engineering concepts to highway work and have pioneered in several new developments now in use by other highway departments throughout the country.

These include continuous reinforced concrete girder design for bridges, use of geologists for bridge foundation studies, correction of subsurface water problems, and more precise classification of excavation. Another development is test work in materials to adapt many local aggregate deposits for concrete mixer by adding crushed limestone "sweetners."

In 1953, the Kansas Legislature enacted the first access control law at the request of the State Highway Commission. This is the basis for the concept of freeways by controlling the right of ingress and egress to the traveled lanes.

That same legislature provided for a feasibility study for a proposed Kansas Turnpike that would connect Kansas City, Topeka and Wichita. Using private capital, the Turnpike was built, and opened to traffic in October, 1956. This toll road relieved the Highway Commission of the responsibility of building a freeway through the same traffic corridor.

The interstate and national defense system of highways had been in the planning stage since 1944, but until President Eisenhower asked for a further study in 1954, the early plans did not result in legislation. In 1956, the Congress passed the bill that set up the 41,000 interstate system. In Kansas, 800 miles were designated that included 187 miles of the Turnpike.

The toll road gave the Highway Commission a head start on building the interstate routes. Kansas also was allocated a route connecting Wichita and Salina that will do a great deal for economic growth of Central Kansas.

West of Topeka in late summer, 1956, the Kansas Highway Commission completed the first interstate contract in the nation, using 90 per cent federal and 10 per cent state-collected road user tax collections.

While the interstate construction program is perhaps the most spectacular portion of the work for the last 10 years, the Highway Commission has continued improvement of the primary, secondary and urban highway systems in every section of Kansas.

Beginning with the long range highway improvement program made possible by the Kansas Legislature in 1949, the Highway Commission made rapid advances on the backlog of road needs. However, in recent years, increased population which has increased motor vehicle registration, additional travel by all vehicles, higher construction standards, and inflation all have tended to slow the rate at which road deficiencies are being overcome.

The Kansas Legislature has given the Highway Commission the responsibility for construction of interior park roads at the many state parks being developed by the Park and Resources Authority. These roads will do a great deal to increase the use of the parks, and this will assist in raising the level of the outdoor recreation facilities available.

Good roads and highways, good schools, plenty of recreational facilities, adequate labor supply, and ample raw materials all go together to provide the climate needed for a robust economic growth of Kansas.

A future freeway system of four-lane highways is one of the keys that will open the door to the future of Kansas.

Our highways are good now, but they need to be better to save lives, save time, and save money.

Today's covered wagons are the house trailers and station wagons used by thousands of motorists for vacations every year. These two vehicles are stopped at the roadside park near Solomon along I-70.

Concrete shelters shade picnic tables at roadside park along I-70 near Paxico. Kansas has 160 roadside parks along nearly 10,000 miles of rural state highways.

The 18th Street Expressway in Kansas City, Kansas, running left to right in photo, intersects the Kansas Turnpike and spans the Rock Island and Union Pacific Freight Yards.

Aerial photo shows the roadside park along I-70 near Paxico. The sheltered picnic tables, clean restrooms, wide drives where motorists can pull off the main traveled way for a cool drink of water all help to make these rest areas popular.

HISTORY OF KANSAS MENTAL HEALTH PROGRAM 1863-1965

by Dick Mann, Public Information Director
Division of Institutional Management
State Department of Social Welfare

Kansans can look back with pride on more than 100 years of concern for the state's mentally ill. From its inception in 1863, when the Kansas Legislature passed an act for the purchase of land for the first State Insane Asylum, the Osawatomie State Hospital (so re-named in 1901) was conceived as a hospital for the reception of patients, not as an institution for the detention of inmates.

By the 1870's the need for beds for the state's mentally ill had outgrown the single institution at Osawatomie. In 1879, a second hospital, The Topeka Insane Asylum (later re-named The Topeka State Hospital) was established.

One goal of the Board of Trustees of State Charities and Corrections in the early 1900's was to provide enough hospital beds that all insane indigents could be removed from county jails and local asylums. In 1904, the Board proudly announced that for the first time since the state was organized no indigent insane were being kept in county or private asylums.

This achievement was made possible by expanding the Osawatomie and Topeka institutions and by opening a new State Hospital for Epileptics at Parsons in 1904. Fifty epileptic insane male patients were transferred to Parsons from Topeka and 60 from Osawatomie. Officials noted at the time that separating the epileptics from the non-epileptic hospital residents was beneficial to both types of patients.

When modern drug treatment for epilepsy made the epileptic hospital obsolete the state changed this institution in 1953 to The Parsons State Training School for the care, treatment and training of ambulatory mentally retarded children from six to 21 years of age who required special services for physical, mental, emotional and social growth. Because of crowded conditions at the Winfield institution for retarded, some mentally retarded patients had been committed to mental hospitals prior to 1953. Redesignation of the Parsons State Training School in 1953, then, was another forward step in the program of providing better treatment for both mentally ill and the mentally retarded. The Parsons institution was renamed the Parsons State Hospital and Training Center in 1957.

The 1881 Kansas Legislature had established the Kansas State Asylum for Idiotic and Imbecile Youth at Lawrence. The institution was moved to Winfield in 1884. The name of the institution was changed several times over the years due to changes in function and became the Winfield State Hospital and Training Center in 1957. Opening of the Parsons State Training School in 1953 changed the pattern of admissions to the Winfield State Hospital, limiting it to the adult retarded, the multihandicapped retarded of all ages and retarded children under six years of age.

Outside view of a team unit of two wards of the new Woodsview Section at Topeka State Hospital. The one-story buildings and large windows keep the patient in close contact with the outside.

However, the existing state mental hospitals soon were again unable to keep up with the demand for beds and, in 1911, the Kansas Legislature appropriated funds for a third state mental hospital to be located in the western part of the state. Larned was selected in 1912 as the site and the first Larned State Hospital building was completed in 1914. The hospital's first patients were transfers from the overcrowded Topeka and Osawatomie institutions.

In 1919 the Kansas Legislature provided for voluntary admission of mentally ill persons to the state's mental hospitals.

Another forward step in the care of the state's mentally ill was made in 1937 when the Kansas Legislature authorized funds to establish the State Hospital for the Dangerous Insane on the Larned State Hospital campus. This hospital provides treatment for mentally ill male patients transferred from Kansas penal and correctional institutions. In addition, district courts may commit patients directly to the security unit for evaluation, diagnosis, and/or treatment, and other institutions of the Division of Institutional Management may make administrative transfers to the Larned unit for security purposes. The 1963 Legislature changed the name of this hospital section to The State Security Hospital.

Dramatic progress in the Kansas mental hospital program occurred during a 10-year period from 1948 to 1958. A series of newspaper articles aroused public concern with the desperate needs of the overcrowded and understaffed state mental hospitals. Governor Andrew Schoeppel started some preliminary investigation to see what the problems were and what could be done about them. Governor Frank Carlson and the Kansas Legislature followed with a program for widespread improvement.

It was decided that rather than embark upon a crash building program for approximately 3,800 additional needed beds, the state would build a program of improved personnel and train its own people to provide an active treatment program that would enable patients to return to their families and useful community living instead of spending years (sometimes a lifetime) in the mental hospital under custodial care.

Topeka State Hospital was selected as the "pilot training institution" and became affiliated with the Menninger School of Psychiatry. Topeka State Hospital was given special funds for training purposes by the 1949 Legislature. As this program proved its worth, the 1953 Legislature appropriated funds for a "Mental Hospital Training Fund," to be allocated by the State Board of Social Welfare to all institutions having approved training programs.

Physicians taking their residency training in psychiatry at Topeka State Hospital were allowed to participate in a "package plan," which was put into effect July 1952. Under this plan, a resident physician takes three years of training at Topeka State Hospital then is assigned to another state hospital in Kansas for a period of two years. Thus all Kansas mental hospitals benefit from the training program and the resident will have completed all of his hospital requirements before taking the examination to be certified as a specialist in psychiatry. Today the Menninger School of Psychiatry attracts physicians from all over the world. Many of these go through the residency program just described.

At the 1952 general election, Kansans approved a constitutional amendment authorizing the legislature to levy a special tax for a permanent building fund for the mental institutions. This levy was set at one-half mill by the 1953 Legislature and first fruits from it were gathered in the form of new buildings commenced early in 1954.

Under this impetus of training and modernization of facilities our Kansas mental hospitals quickly jumped to the forefront and became recognized as among the best in the nation. The 1953 Legislature reorganized the State Department of Social Welfare to create the Division of Institutional Management, which was given responsibility for the mental health program. It was to carry out the improved care and treatment of patients and better management practices begun in 1949. The Advisory Commission on Institutional Management, which advised on the operations of the institutional programs, was enlarged from five to eight members in 1953 and construction of a treatment center for children was authorized.

The years 1953 and 1954 saw expansion of the employe training programs at all institutions and, as staff became available, patients were given more individual attention. In addition to the physician's psychiatric residency program at Topeka State Hospital, other training programs were established at the mental hospitals for senior medical students, affiliate nurses, psychology interns and psychiatric social workers. The largest inservice training program was developed for psychiatric aides, who are most closely working with mental patients.

To help in screening and giving treatment to those who did not require hospitalization, an adult outpatient clinic and a children's outpatient clinic were established at Topeka State Hospital and separate inpatient facilities for treatment of teenage children were opened at Topeka State Hospital.

By 1958, the increase in the number of adolescent children needing psychiatric treatment was illustrated by enlargement of the Topeka State Hospital Children's Unit from an original 34 beds to 60 beds, and use of the Treatment Center for Children's 30 beds for those aged six to 12. By 1963, a traveling psychiatric team had been authorized for the Kansas Treatment Center for Children. This team now works anywhere in Kansas with parents of emotionally disturbed children waiting for admittance to the Treatment Center to help them handle their problems during the waiting period.

With the cooperation of the hospital social service departments and with county welfare departments doing pre-admission social histories, arrangement for return to the patient's home or to boarding or nursing home and followup supervision, it was possible to increase mental hospital patient releases and shorten the stay of patients.

Reorganization and improvement of administrative practices within the institutions began in 1953 and 1954 and included inauguration of a complete and permanent running inventory of non-expendable equipment and a uniform cost accounting system. Many printed forms were standardized, increased efficiency was gained in the purchase and use of utilities, fuel, food, etc. Sewing rooms for making patients' clothing were eliminated when it was found many clothing and linen items could be purchased more cheaply; dairy operations were discontinued as it was shown to be more economical to purchase dairy products than to maintain a herd and pasteurizing equipment. Kitchens and dining rooms were consolidated to curtail waste and improve food service; cafeteria food service was expanded. As a result institutional administrators were able to budget more intelligently, eliminate duplication and waste, and provide up-to-date comparative cost figures on every phase of operation. Unnecessary paper work was eliminated.

In 1955 there was increasing use of the new tranquilizing drugs for the mentally ill. Experience proved that the drugs themselves were not the complete answer to successful treatment, but that they did make it possible for the patient to benefit more readily from other forms of psychiatric treatment.

Early in the 1950's, the Division of Institutional Management took the initiative in moving many elderly patients no longer needing active treatment out into nursing homes to make room for new patients. Along with this move, the hospitals provided training of nursing home personnel in meeting the special needs of elderly ex-mental patients.

All these improvements, by 1956, allowed the three hospitals for the mentally ill to admit more than twice as many patients as they did in 1950 and to increase discharges by more than four times. While more patients were being admitted, treated, and discharged, the total average hospital resident population dropped from 5,000 in 1950 to 4,400 in 1956. It has been going down ever since and in 1965 was below 3,000.

In 1964, an employe at the Larned State Hospital pointed out, "Although there are only half as many patients living at the hospital today as there were 15 years ago, more than three times as many people are receiving some form of psychiatric care at the institution and another 400 outside the hospital are still receiving hospital attention."

Early in the 1950's the Osawatomie, Topeka and Larned state hospitals for the mentally ill developed the treatment philosophy of milieu therapy, which means treatment by regulating the environment of the patient. Both individual and group psychotherapy were established as part of the overall treatment program.

Later in the 1950's and continuing into the 1960's, these same three hospitals have reorganized under what is called the "Kansas Plan," which has attracted national recognition. Each of these Kansas mental hospitals serves a geographic district of the state with each hospital district having a comparable state population. Under the "Kansas Plan," each hospital is further divided into three or four sections, with each section serving as a complete mental hospital for a smaller geographic area within the total hospital district. This means that incoming patients are always placed with other patients from their own or nearby counties and remain within the same section during their entire hospitalization. This plan of having several small hospitals within one large hospital allows for a much closer relationship among patients, between patient and staff, and between the staff and relatives and officials in the county where the patient lives.

Since the last week of May, 1964, the Larned State Hospital has been operating a specialized 15-bed department called "walk-in." This specialized treatment function was started to fill a gap in service that existed between inpatient and outpatient treatment functions. This "walk-in" department offers help to anyone seeking it day or night any day of the week. On an average, 30 persons are admitted to the walk-in unit for treatment each month and the average length of stay is about 10 days. Only one in five patients coming to the walk-in unit shows need for more prolonged treatment. These are transferred to the regular inpatient service. Another 15 persons per month come just to see if they do need help and are moved directly to outpatient treatment if needed.

All three hospitals for the mentally ill operate outpatient clinics. In addition Osawatomie State Hospital has developed a Day Hospital and Treatment Center for 40 adolescent inpatients. These adolescents live on the adult wards but spend their days in intensive treatment at the Day Hospital and Treatment Center, where they can benefit from a program designed especially for them. Purpose of the adolescent center is to help these young people through establishment of satisfying learning experiences, both academic and inter-personal.

During 1965 Topeka State Hospital opened a complete Day Hospital on the campus to fill the gap between inpatient and outpatient services. This Day Hospital serves persons in the community who live off the grounds but need to come to the hospital during the day. The range of treatment activities includes group therapy, work in creative arts, woodworking, home management, music and recreation therapy.

A traveling psychiatric team was added to services of the Osawatomie State Hospital during 1965. This team works on a consultation request basis with groups and agencies in the hospital district to help them with all problems concerning prospective or former mental hospital patients.

Some patients are unable to make a direct return from the mental hospital wards to the community. For these patients Osawatomie and Topeka State Hospitals have resocialization housing and programs on campus, where small groups of patients can live under a family type situation until they feel enough confidence to face the outside world. In some cases, these patients live in the resocialization area at night and on week ends while working off campus during week days. Larned State Hospital has a 13-week resocialization course for women patients who need this help.

Over the years, Kansans have learned that just turning the mentally ill over to a hospital staff and then forgetting them is not enough. Hundreds of Kansans now work as volunteers, many directly with patients in the hospitals. Osawatomie State Hospital even has a volunteer grandfather for its teenage patients. His sympathetic understanding and advice have helped many young patients over the rough spots of hospitalization. At the other end of the age bracket, teenage volunteers are doing marvelous service with older mental patients in all three hospitals for the mentally ill. Volunteers of all ages are helping hospitalized mental patients toward quicker recovery through many types of supervised services and activities.

As more patients returned home each year, communities began looking to the mental hospital staffs for help with local problems. Consultation was and is provided by hospital staff to community agencies as staff time is available. The community-wide mental health program also was served by using the institutions for training personnel such as nursing home operators, holding seminars for ministers and other professional people; special meetings at the hospitals for probate judges, physicians and others helped extend the knowledge and philosophy of mental health to the community.

Several research programs are being carried on at the Topeka, Osawatomie and Larned state hospitals. These cover such things as experiments with drugs, to studies of staffing patterns, etc. One project at Topeka State Hospital is a study of the effect of architectural design of mental hospital buildings on the behavior of mental patients. The Osawatomie State Hospital has a Hospital Design and Demonstration project which proposes to achieve a comprehensive patient-centered program of psychiatric care. Purposes of the project are to design an efficient therapeutic system or therapeutic milieu which will exploit the institution's social environment to its maximal advantage and facilitate development of an integrated community-oriented

A ward building in the new Eastman Section of Topeka State Hospital. The ground-level ward buildings provide a homelike atmosphere and convey to patients that there is a stable order of things moving on all the time they struggle with what appear to them to be earth-shaking inner conflicts.

service. The hospital will implement this program through extensive reorganization of the system's properties and intensive educational and training efforts. It is hoped to demonstrate that these comprehensively designed changes will result in an increase in the quality and level of direct patient care, a corresponding rise in the social-personal competence of patients, and facilitation of the hospital's role as a regional mental health center.

Benefits of Kansas psychiatric training programs have not been limited to the three hospitals for the mentally ill. Other Kansas social welfare institutions also have been included in the upgrading process.

The Parsons and Winfield institutions' functions were changed in 1953 to State Training Schools and are now (since 1957) called the Parsons State Hospital and Training Center and the Winfield State Hospital and Training Center. These institutions are charged with the responsibility of examining, treating, educating, training, and rehabilitating the mentally deficient. Intensive treatment and training programs in these institutions proved that many mentally retarded patients can be rehabilitated to return to productive community life rather than remain under institutional care for life.

The Parsons State Hospital and Training Center has developed into a nationally-recognized center of research and research training. A joint research program between the hospital and the Bureau of Child Research at the University of Kansas began in 1958 with a grant to the K. U. Bureau from the National Institute of Mental Health for a study of the language and communication problems of the hospital population. Research training was added in 1961 with financial support from the National Institute of Neurological Diseases and Blindness. In 1963, after a two-year study and on-site inspection by various advisory groups, the Public Health Service endorsed an additional plan to expand the research program under the newly-created National Institute of Child Health and Human Development.

New projects underway at the hospital include comparative studies of normal and retarded children in the areas of learning and retention processes, language development, and social

A modern Rehabilitation Center which was constructed at the Osawatomie State Hospital was completed in July, 1963. The Center includes twin gymnasiums, exercise rooms, swimming pool and auditorium. The auditorium is used for church services, entertainments and meetings. Because of the ramp construction, wheelchair patients now are able to attend worship services and special entertainment.

Many of the patient activity programs at the Larned State Hospital are held in this auditorium on the campus. The auditorium also is used for many other purposes, including presentation of information on hospital treatment programs for visiting groups.

interaction; a study of the social behavior of retarded children in natural, uncontrolled situations in cottage and play areas; and application of research findings to the development of improved treatment and training techniques for the retarded. Because an estimated 70 percent of retarded patients have language and communication defects, the program will also include continuing investigation of the approaches to this problem.

Research training is now operating at both the pre- and post-doctoral levels with new grants from the National Institute of Mental Health and extension grants from the National Institute of Neurological Diseases and Blindness.

The K. U. Bureau of Child Research also collaborates in presenting workshops, short courses and similar advanced training programs at the Parsons hospital. They are held primarily for speech pathology and audiology training. Parsons State Hospital and Training Center was one of the first institutions for the retarded to have complete facilities and staff for a speech and hearing clinic.

Twenty-eight students and professional workers were training in seven clinical areas of the hospital program at the close of the 1964-65 biennium. New programs include one for graduate students in the school of social work at the University of Missouri to take a year of field training at the hospital. A grant made to the University of Kansas by the National Institute of Mental Health supports a joint program of the hospital and the K. U. department of music education and music therapy to provide 10 traineeships each year for graduate students in music therapy.

A grant through the Menninger Foundation for inservice training is designed to bring hospital nursing service personnel the most recent research findings applicable to direct care, treatment and training of the mentally retarded. Another grant through the Menninger Foundation will assist retarded young adults in the transition from institutional to community work placement. The project also will train personnel to staff sheltered workshops, with supporting funds from the Hospital Improvement Project Section of the National Institute of Mental Health.

A Speech and Hearing clinic has officially begun operation at the Winfield State Hospital and Training Center, with a wide range of speech and hearing services provided to patients through a program supported by a hospital improvement grant from the U. S. Public Health Service. Needs of patients in the area of speech and hearing will be determined and necessary therapy provided to help them reach their maximum ability in developing speech and hearing skills. An expanding research program is underway also at the Winfield institution.

A research program now underway by the dietary department is designed to teach some mentally retarded, physically handicapped children how to suck, chew and swallow so they can learn to eat normally rather than being fed by tubes or intravenously. This is being done by using the department's past experience with motivation and adding the use of the techniques used by speech pathologists to stimulate sucking and swallowing. Another new research project is for an intensive training and rehabilitation program for the mentally retarded, multi-handicapped patients, with emphasis on development of new methods and procedures in treatment. Handicaps most prevalent are cerebral palsy and hearing and sight deficiencies.

Ultimate goal is to help multi-handicapped patients become self-sufficient enough to return to community facilities, such as boarding homes, nursing homes, half-way houses or sheltered workshops.

The Winfield State Hospital and Training Center also has a successful workshop project on the campus, where patients are doing contract work for manufacturers. Some Winfield patients who are able to hold down jobs in the community but are unable to cope with community social problems are allowed to live on the campus in as near an independent situation as possible. They are given counseling and other services by staff if needed. Some of these are eventually able to go out on their own. Both Parsons and Winfield provide outpatient services. Increased applications for admission to the Parsons and Winfield institutions (far beyond their capacity) resulted in the acquisition in 1959 of the old Winter Veterans Hospital in Topeka and its renovation to care for mentally retarded patients. It was named the Kansas Neurological Institute. By 1961 the State Vocational Rehabilitation Services had established a special unit on the Kansas Neurological Institute campus to provide job placement training for mentally retarded who are able to benefit from vocational training. They take some patients from all three institutions for the retarded plus some from other sources of referrals. During the first four and one-half years of its operation, the Rehabilitation Unit admitted more than 500 male and female retardates and more than 270 of these completed the course and went out on job placements.

A special Child Study Unit at the Kansas Neurological Institute has two psychiatric teams doing diagnostic and evaluation services to determine the needs of retarded children referred to it and to recommend the proper treatment or care for them.

Further expansion in the state hospital program for the retarded began when the 1963 Kansas Legislature provided for the transfer of approximately 120 ambulatory mentally retarded patients from the Parsons and Winfield institutions to buildings at the State Sanitorium for Tuberculosis, at Norton. Three buildings were unused due to a drop in the number of TB patients.

Psychiatric evaluation and treatment programs are available at the Girls Industrial School, Beloit, and the Boys Industrial School, Topeka. Psychiatric evaluation with recommendations is provided at the Childrens Receiving Home, Atchison.

A sweeping revision of mental hospital admission laws was made by the 1965 Kansas Legislature which, in effect, means that the mentally ill will be treated more like other sick people in our society. One new law, House Bill 902, Chapter 348, of the 1965 laws of Kansas, became effective January 1, 1966.

This law provides for several different methods by which mentally ill persons can obtain hospital treatment without delay, or by which (if disturbed or potentially dangerous) they can temporarily be placed in general hospitals or mental health facilities for their own and others' protection rather than be put in jail as has often occurred in the past. The new law also allows a mentally ill person to be sent under court order to a mental hospital without being adjudged "insane" or determined to be "incapacitated," thus losing his civil rights until discharged as "restored." This should greatly reduce the stigma of hospitalization and the fear which some mental patients have about losing their civil rights. Another law, HB 905, does provide, however, that a separate court hearing can be held, if necessary, to determine whether the patient is incapacitated. Previously, all patients committed to the mental hospital automatically lost their civil rights. Briefly, the new law makes appropriate treatment easily available to each person, when and where it is needed, without necessarily sacrificing his rights as a citizen or subjecting him to undue legal delays or emotional stress in obtaining treatment.

Although the history of community mental health services in Kansas is short, it is replete with rapid and sound growth. Thousands of Kansans have given their time and efforts to carry out their vision of making high quality community mental health services available to every community and easily accessible to every citizen.

The Kansas community mental health movement officially began in 1948, when the State Board of Health was appointed the state mental health authority and became eligible to receive federal financial assistance in developing community mental health services.

When this program started there were just two community mental health facilities in Kansas — child guidance clinics in Atchison and Wichita. Under the guidance and support of the State Board of Health Mental Hygiene Division, mental health centers were established in Douglas, Finney, Franklin, Lyon, Riley, Saline, Shawnee and Wyandotte counties.

All of these centers, with the exception of the one in Shawnee county, were organized under state legislation which provided for the establishment of centers under administration of a local joint board of health, and which allowed county commissioners to levy a one-quarter mill tax to support local mental health services. The center in Shawnee county was supported with United Fund monies.

In 1961, the Kansas Legislature transferred the state mental health authority to the State Board of Social Welfare, the agency already responsible for administering the institutional mental health program. The Board then delegated responsibility for community services to the Division of Institutional Management and a new section — Community Mental Health Services — was then established within the Division.

The 1961 Kansas Legislature also enacted new legislation (KSA 19-4001-4009) which allowed Kansans much more latitude in establishing community mental health centers. This legislation enlarged the permissive scope of services which community mental health centers could provide. It enabled county commissioners to appoint a citizen governing board representative of community agencies and helping professionals. It raised the allowable tax levy for services to one-half mill. It allowed centers to be organized as nonprofit corporations or as units of county government. And it enabled several counties to join together in the establishment and support of one center to serve a district of counties.

This latter provision is particularly helpful in Kansas, where many single counties cannot raise enough tax money through the allowable levy to support a mental health center and a full range of services to the community.

Following the 1961 legislative changes, the centers in Atchison, Finney, Franklin, Lyon, Riley and Saline counties were reorganized under provisions of the new legislation. Between 1961 and 1965 they were joined by adjacent counties in the support of multiple county centers.

New centers also were established at an increased rate. Butler and Crawford counties organized centers in 1962. By January, 1963, new centers were established in Harvey, Johnson, and Allen-Neosho counties. A second center was organized in Wichita to serve Sedgwick County. By January, 1964, multiple-county centers were established in Hays and Independence. Single county centers were established in Bourbon, Brown and Seward counties.

By January, 1965, there were 21 operating community mental health centers in Kansas. They are tax supported by a total of 46 counties, and serve about 70 per cent of the state's population. Still other Kansas counties are actively working toward provision of local mental health services.

In the spring of 1963, a proposal for Comprehensive Planning for Mental Health in Kansas was approved by the National Institute for Mental Health and a two-year planning project under federal grant was initiated in July, 1963, and was carried out by the Division of Institutional Management and Community Mental Health Services.

More than 2,000 Kansans participated in this two-year planning activity which involved 27 statewide planning committees, six regional planning meetings, 11 separate publications and 335 specific recommendations. Purpose of the project was to make long range plans for the next 10 years.

The first Kansas Congress on Mental Illness and Health was held in Topeka October 24, 1963. Sponsored by the Kansas Medical Society in cooperation with the Kansas Psychiatric Society, the Kansas Chapter of the American Academy of General Practice, the Kansas Association for Mental Health and the Division of Institutional Management, the Congress obtained participation of more than 500 individuals. The needs and problems associated with mental retardation received the attention of a topical committee of the Congress.

In February, 1964, the Governor appointed a 19-member Advisory Council on Mental Retardation Planning. Members of this Council are heads of state or private agencies and organizations. In July, 1964, an 18-month planning project to combat mental retardation was initiated by the Division of Institutional Management with the aid of federal funds made available under Public Law 88-156.

Following completion of this mental retardation planning period additional federal funds may be available to the Division for a continuation of planning and for implementation.

Community mental health centers in Kansas which provide *comprehensive* services (inpatient and outpatient treatment, emergency care, partial hospitalization, and consultation to other community agencies) are eligible to receive federal financial assistance in construction of facilities. The 89th Congress also passed a law that provides for short-term financial assistance in staffing community mental health centers.

The 1965 Kansas Legislature passed laws which enable county commissioners to levy a one-quarter mill tax for construction of mental health facilities. Other laws permit some counties to levy a three-quarters mill tax to support the services of local mental health centers.

Backed by the intensive planning studies and a firm foundation of laws, Kansas now looks forward to eventually having adequate mental health services of high quality within possibly a one-hour drive of any citizen's home. If past performance can be taken as a guide to the future, Kansas will reach that goal within the next few years.

PROSPECTS UNLIMITED FOR KANSAS WHEAT

by President James A. McCain
Kansas State University

Kansas agriculture faces an incredibly attractive future and of no segment of our agriculture is this more the case than wheat. Unfortunately, this happy prospect is obscured by three false but pervasive assumptions that assign the farmer an increasingly minor role in our economy. These are:

First, in seeking economic growth, it is high time Kansas turned its back on agriculture and sought industrial development instead.

Secondly, the steady decline in the farm population and numbers of farms is undermining the future of agriculture.

Third, in view of mounting farm surpluses, agricultural research, especially as it relates to wheat, is no longer necessary or desirable.

The general public must be disabused of these fallacies if agriculture here in Kansas and in the nation is to enjoy the favorable atmosphere for the continued progress so essential to not only the economic well-being of the farmer but to the health and prosperity of people generally. Kansans should be the last people in the nation to underestimate the economic importance of agriculture. Our annual net income for farming is now averaging a billion dollars a year, money that finds its way from farmer to merchant to fuel prosperity throughout the business and professional communities of our towns and cities.

But, this is less than half the story. Farmers provide both the raw materials and the markets for Kansas agri-businesses with a total annual income from sales now approaching four billion dollars.

In a state such as ours, it is the height of futility to try to draw a line between agriculture and industry. Two experts on economic growth recently brought to Kansas to fill key positions of leadership, Jack Lacy, director of the Department of Economic Development, and Dr. Christopher Barthel, director of the Research Foundation, have both significantly stressed the central role of agriculture and the agri-business to the achievement of their goals.

The declining farm population reflects not stagnation but increased efficiency in food production through substituting capital for labor in achieving mechanization, better use of fertilizers and improved cropping practices. Furthermore, the drop in numbers of farm workers is paralleled by an increase in jobs in the agri-businesses, now exceeding 16 million.

It is not by accident that enrollment in agriculture at K-State rose 23 per cent this fall, more than any other college. Actually, men with college training in agricultural curriculums are in growing short supply.

The third fallacy poses the most serious threat to the future of Kansas agriculture and especially our notable wheat industry. For without continued support and stimulation from scientific investigations, agriculture faces a bleak future, indeed.

To insure a role for research, however, requires a reorientation in the attitudes of consumers, the business community, and even, I suspect, many farmers themselves.

Four such attitudes are:

1. Agricultural research is not concerned exclusively with increasing production as many people mistakenly insist, but serves such goals as improving efficiency, reducing costs, expanding markets and in general helping solve all major problems plaguing the farmer.

2. Furthermore, research designed to increase production is not necessarily incompatible with surplus production.

3. The ultimate beneficiary of agricultural efficiency is the consumer.

4. And finally, the supply-and-demand status of American agriculture should increasingly be evaluated on a world-wide instead of a national basis.

In assessing the present and future role of agricultural research, I would stress two facts.

First, K-State is far better equipped to serve Kansas farmers than ever before in our 102-year history. Completion of our new dairy-poultry building alongside the animal industries building constructed seven years ago gives us laboratory and teaching facilities in poultry and livestock second to none in the nation.

The addition of bakery management to the program in flour milling and feed manufacturing round out the most comprehensive faculty and laboratories anywhere in the world in cereal grain processing.

The national water resources research program established by the last Congress will provide Kansas State, in cooperation with Kansas University, with expanded scientific resources in this important field so vital to our farmers and ranchers.

My second fact, several agricultural research programs already under way or in prospect hold unusual promise for the future of the Kansas wheat grower. These involve hybrid wheat, water conservation, marketing studies, and a proposed new utilization laboratory.

The development of a hybrid wheat as a result of research initiated at the Fort Hays Branch Experiment Station could well become a major break-through in the history of Kansas and American agriculture.

Dr. Ron Livers, plant geneticist on the Station staff, deserves major credit for his contributions to this significant development.

The prospects for hybrid wheat document many of the points I have emphasized relative to the contemporary role of agricultural research.

The hybrid under study would, by a conservative estimate, increase yields 25%. Too often I've heard this figure greeted with protests that we need more wheat about like we need a hole in the head.

But let's look at the *positive* facts!

First, a 25% increase in yields is actually a reduction in production costs of almost the same proportion. Thus, the farmer's cost versus benefit ratio is improved almost one fourth.

Secondly, the ultimate beneficiary of improved farming efficiency, the consumer, will profit. The American family spends 19% of its income, or around $1,000 a year, on food. By a rough estimate, a quarter of this bill is for wheat foods. Such a reduction in the cost of producing wheat passed on to the consumer would represent a savings of from $50 to $60, or enough for a down payment on an electric refrigerator or a color TV set.

Third, it is estimated that the release of hybrid wheat would create *50 new seed processing plants* in the state *with 5,000 new jobs,* a formidable increment to Kansas' industrial economy.

Fourth, increased wheat yields would free thousands of acres of marginal crop land for soil conserving crops and other uses.

Water resources is another area in which we are on the threshold of major research achievements.

Water is the lifeblood of Kansas agriculture as agriculture is the lifeblood of the Kansas economy. This relationship is graphically demonstrated by charts which show that almost every significant drop in our state's annual per capita income in recent times coincides with subnormal rainfall.

The K-State Agricultural Experiment Station can cite notable past accomplishments from research involving water resources. Irrigated land in our state has risen from 80,000 acres 15 years ago to one and a quarter million today. Thanks to better soil management practices, the drought of the 1950's caused far less havoc than that of the 1930's although the latter was less severe.

The new Water Resources Research Institute will increase funds for investigations and involve close cooperation between our Experiment Station, the K. U. geological survey, and many scientists and engineers in other fields on our two faculties.

Of the most immediate possible benefit to agriculture is research seeking methods of reducing evaporation which is the greatest source of moisture waste in the Great Plains area.

About 65% of the precipitation in the Great Plains is lost by evaporation. A reduction of this loss by 5% would save more than one inch of water where the average precipitation is 20 inches.

Projected over the cultivated acreage of Western Kansas, 15 million acres, this would be 1,250,000 acre-feet of water or about three times the total water stored in Kansas' five major reservoirs in the western half of Kansas. That 5% reduction would produce 62 million dollars in crops for Kansas. And, of course, water thus saved is vital to industrial and urban as well as agricultural use.

Research already conducted by the Experiment Station has shown that such a 5% reduction in evaporation is within reach. At the Garden City Branch Station a paper mulch has been used to decrease evaporation from the soil between sorghum rows. The water saved increased sorghum production per acre from 2,000 to 4,290 pounds and yields for an acre from 15.9 bushels on the unmulched plots to 54.5 bushels.

Similar results have come from similar experiments in the Manhattan area on the eastern edge of the Great Plains where polyethylene plastic cloth between sorghum rows increased the storage of soil under the mulch by 1½ inches.

The expanded resources for water research will insure substantial further progress in this important area.

A third research area holding great promise for agriculture is in the development of industrial uses for the raw materials produced by our farms and ranches. It was gratifying to note that candidates for governor in the current election have advocated such investigations as a principal means of stimulating the state's economy.

The Board of Regents has authorized Kansas State University to request a $75,000 appropriation from the 1965 legislature to establish an agricultural utilization laboratory. It is our intention to bring to the University one of the outstanding scientists in the nation in this field to direct the laboratory and to augment our already excellent laboratory facilities in flour, feed milling and baking. If space permitted, I could list for you nine promising projects we would undertake immediately in this institute. These include in the wheat and sorghum area:

(1) Determination of the properties of wheat and processing changes required to make flour best suited to the continuous baking procedure now in use by commercial bakeries.

(2) Use of milled cereal grains or of milled fractions of cereal grains in road construction.

(3) Development of waxy and non-waxy varieties of grain sorghums, with good agronomic characteristics, as raw materials for starch production.

(4) Development of new chemicals from cereal grains by fermentation processes.

Finally, several important investigations are under way and others are needed in the area of agricultural marketing.

The proposed federal grain marketing research laboratory has the endorsement of all the directors of the Agricultural Experiment Stations of the Great Plains states and many other experts as well and is coming to the campus of Kansas State University where it will have access to the most complete and modern laboratories and the strongest research staff in grain and related fields.

Marketing research is broader and more varied than most people realize. It includes the highly complex problem of transportation rates, the condition of stored grain, the nutritional and milling qualities of grain, the palatability of processed grain products to consumers both here and abroad and a maze of relationships in the field of international trade and diplomacy. In Dr. Leonard Schruben and his associates, Kansas State has a staff second to none in the transportation field.

By no means are we ignoring the remarkable increase of vending machines in the dispensing of food, both hot and cold. For example, vending machines alone representing only a fraction of this market are dispensing daily the production of 150,000 cows.

Kansas State is developing a research project involving experimental psychologists, environmental engineers, and nutritional experts in home economics for improving the taste and quality of hot foods dispensed by vending machines with emphasis on breads and meats.

Studies designed to increase the nutritional value of wheat and wheat flour, principally through increasing its protein content, show promise of expanding foreign markets. The Indian minister of agriculture, for example, declared recently at Kansas State University that the Indian people had ample food. What he failed to say was that they suffered grievously from malnutrition and widespread disease, the direct result of improper diet! Thus, nutritional quality takes on surpassing importance to efforts to expand markets in developing countries.

So, for that matter does palatability. Great Plains Wheat, for example, employed a Kansas State consumer economist to survey the consumer acceptability of bulgur in two African countries as a substitute for rice foods. It should be noted parenthetically that the consumer reaction was very favorable. I applaud the "Salute Kansas Wheat Commission," an exciting report on the expanding sales of bulgur.

However, transcending all these other opportunities by a wide margin is the world-wide imbalance involving agricultural production and population growth.

When viewed from a global perspective, there are no food surpluses; rather the human race may be facing the stark prospect of starvation. The United Nations Food and Agricultural Organization recently reported that whereas last year the world's population increased another 2% — 3.218 billion — farm production increased only 1%.

If this trend continues, India, for example, will fall short of her food needs by 28 million tons a year by 1966.   And, some forecasts anticipate widespread famine throughout three continents during the decade of the 1970's.

The total food producing capacity of the American farmer is the strongest single safeguard against such a catastrophe. But how to mobilize this incomparable resource will tax our ingenuity.

I propose the organization immediately of a world-wide conference of official representatives of the nations involved — those facing eminent food shortage crises and those capable of major food exports.

This should not be — heaven forbid! — just another forum for economic reports. Rather a systematic and precise plan should be developed and agreed upon for anticipating needs and increasing food production to meet them, with specific quotas assigned the "overproducing" nations for five, ten and twenty-year periods subject to modification by five-year intervals. This conference should be served by a permanent secretariat charged with administration and evaluation.

Assuming that grains are the key to the solution of these problems and, further, the preeminence of Kansas is grain production and processing, why not Kansas as the site for such a conference? Certainly we would provide fewer obstacles and diversions to effective functioning than the bureaucracy of national capitals and complex international organizations.

The stereotyped and often sterile mechanisms of diplomacy should be subordinated in such a conference to expert agricultural knowledge coupled with humanitarian assessment of the basic food requirements of people wherever they are.

Bankers and their families tour data processing center.

BANKING: *automation permits*
wider scope of services

Kansas banks continue to expand and each year establish new record highs in total assets, total deposits, and in total loans to finance the activities of business, agriculture and industry.

For the year ending December 31, 1965, the 598 commercial banks, state and national, in Kansas reported total assets of nearly $4 billion — $3,745,344,255. Total deposits were $3,368,321,789, and loans totaled $1,750,359,641.

Reflecting increased lending activities by the banks, the ratio of loans to deposits has been climbing steadily in recent years, which means more money has been put to work financing commercial enterprise, agricultural operations, and for increasing purchasing power of individual consumers.

Kansas banks have made notable progress, the record shows, advancing the "full service" concept of the financing enterprise — providing all the normal and many special services of money and credit. These include savings accounts, checking accounts, safe deposit boxes, all types of loans, trust services and management record counseling.

Particularly noteworthy are the advances Kansas banks have been making in recent years in the areas of consumer lending and in electronic data processing. Automation, entered into by many banks, has enabled them to broaden their types of services and to serve more people.

In consumer lending, for example, banks have seen a rapid rise in the demand from students to meet the increased costs of higher education. Most Kansas banks are participating in the United Student Aid Fund program of providing low-cost, long-terms loans to thousands of students needing help in financing their college education.

Kansas banking activity generally has a high rating compared with banking in surrounding states, and with banks nationally.

A comprehensive study of performance of banks of the state since 1953 conducted by two members of the faculty at the University of Kansas and completed in 1964, showed that Kansas banks have increased total assets, and have hiked their lending activity generally at a faster rate than have banks of surrounding states.

The evaluation reported that Kansas banks gained faster than did banks of surrounding states and banks of the United States in the categories of agricultural loans, consumer loans, and in their investment in U. S. Government bonds.

They gained at a faster rate also in real estate loans than banks of neighboring states.

The study observed that "whether or not the credit-creating potential of the Kansas banks expands over a period of time largely depends on what happens to the level of economic activity within the state.

"If current efforts to attract industry and research are successful, Kansas probably will experience a relative gain in income and employment. Correspondingly, this will tend to set into motion forces which will enhance not only the credit-creating potential but also the credit-expansion opportunities of the Kansas banks."

This report and others pointing to the need of expanding the state's economy have encouraged Kansas banks to join in a united effort to provide more expansion capital. A tool to provide extra stimulus in business and industrial growth is the new Kansas Development Credit Corporation.

Its purpose is to create more jobs, by providing so-called "grey area" expansion capital through a lending pool arrangement supported by banks of the state in cases where normal bank loans are not readily available. The plan calls for several millions of dollars made available to the corporation's loan pool. Such development credit corporations have been successful in the New England states, and in others.

Large corporations and utilities operating in the state purchase stock for the Kansas Development Credit Corporation, and most of the banks of the state are providing the loan pool of several million dollars.

Elected first president of the corporation was R. C. Clevenger, president of First National Bank of Topeka. Other first officers elected were: vice presidents, R. A. Acker, Southwestern Bell Telephone Co., Topeka; Mark Robeson, Yellow Transit Co., Prairie Village; W. E. Lehmberg,

Banker Soil Conservation Award Meeting in Montgomery County. Here, and at similar gatherings, outstanding practices in agricultural conservation are recognized and landowners given awards.

Officers of the first statewide Kansas Development Credit Corporation organized in Kansas for the purpose of making more long-term expansion capital available to industry are: seated, left to right; Carl A. Bowman, Kansas Bankers Association, assistant secretary; Harrison Johnson, Union Gas Co., treasurer; R. C. Clevenger, First National Bank, Topeka, president; Robert Harkins, Panhandle Eastern Pipe Line Co., Liberal, secretary. Standing, left to right, Paul Woods, First National Bank, Wichita, and W. E. Lehmberg, McPherson & Citizens State Bank, McPherson, vice presidents; Maurice Fager, First National Bank, Topeka, assistant treasurer; and R. A. Acker, Southwestern Bell Telephone Co. and Mark Robeson, Yellow Transit Co., vice presidents.

McPherson & Citizens State Bank, McPherson; Paul Woods, First National Bank, Wichita; secretary, Robert Harkins, Panhandle Eastern Pipe Line Co., Liberal; assistant secretary, Carl A. Bowman, Kansas Bankers Association, Topeka; treasurer, Harrison Johnson, Union Gas Co., Independence; assistant treasurer, Maurice Fager, First National Bank, Topeka; members of the executive committee: Clevenger, Acker, Robeson, Lehmberg, Woods; Tom Griffith, Union National Bank, Manhattan; Art Collins, Hutchinson National Bank, Hutchinson; and A. K. Sewell, Citizens National Bank, Independence.

The 36 directors of the KDCC are:

R. A. Acker, Southwestern Bell Telephone Co., Topeka; D. E. Ackers, Kansas Power & Light Co., Topeka; Gordon Evans, Kansas Gas & Electric Co., Wichita; Harrison Johnson, Union Gas Systems, Inc., Independence; John P. Harris, Harris Publications, Inc., Hutchinson; Robert Harkins, Panhandle Eastern Pipe Line Co., Liberal; Kirby Crenshaw, Cities Service Gas Co., Oklahoma City; R. M. Powers, Gas Service Co., Kansas City; Gordon Angwin, McNally-Pittsburg Mfg. Co., Pittsburg; Mark Robeson, Yellow Transit Co., Prairie Village;

Russell C. Harris, Phillips Petroleum Co., Shawnee Mission; H. M. Sampson, Northern Natural Gas Co., Omaha, Neb.; Henry Blanchard, Commercial National Bank, Kansas City; John W. Breidenthal, Security National Bank, Kansas City; Robert M. Bunten, Merchants National Bank, Topeka; R. Charles Clevenger, First National Bank, Topeka; W. C. Hartley, Miami County National Bank, Paola; Riley Burcham, Lawrence National Bank, Lawrence; J. J. Flynn, The State Bank of Parsons; A. K. Sewell, Citizens National Bank, Independence; C. W. Hunt, First National Bank, Coffeyville; Ernest A. Morse, The Citizens Bank, Abilene; T. J. Griffith, Union National Bank, Manhattan; John Peck, Cloud County Bank, Concordia; E. J. Rolfs, Central National Bank, Junction City; Glenn Mason, First National Bank & Trust Co., Salina; A. Dwight Button, Fourth National Bank & Trust Co., Wichita; Clarence Coleman, Union National Bank, Wichita;

A. J. Collins, Hutchinson National Bank & Trust Co., Hutchinson; W. E. Lehmberg, McPherson & Citizens State Bank, McPherson; Philip Hamm, El Dorado National Bank, El Dorado; Paul H. Woods, First National Bank in Wichita, Wichita; C. M. Miller, Farmers & Merchants State Bank, Colby; Willis E. Stout, First National Bank, Goodland; John R. Burnside, Fidelity State Bank, Garden City; and Lester M. Bauer, Burdett State Bank, Burdett.

Such promotional efforts of the banks of the state are organized through the Kansas Bankers Association, one of the oldest and most active of such associations among the states.

The Kansas Bankers Association, organized in 1887 also is one of the oldest trade associations in Kansas. It was the third state bankers association to be formed. All the banks in Kansas are members of the association, and this is one of the first states to gain the distinction of 100% membership of banks in their state association.

Kansas banks, working through their association, have an enviable record of other "first" and near firsts in its broad activity program of working for the best interests of banking and for the development and progress of the state.

Among them are these other achievements:

One of the first to establish the Banker Agricultural School, conducted every two years in cooperation with Kansas State University, for "country bankers" and agricultural representatives of larger banks.

Kansas banks pioneered in establishing organized encouragement of soil and water conservation. Since the KBA Conservation Awards program was established 20 years ago, nearly 9,000 banker certificates have been awarded to farmers and land owners in furthering conservation practices. All Kansas counties have participated. This recognition program, along with 4-H Club work and other agricultural activities sponsored by Kansas banks, has won for Kansas for many years running the American Bankers Association's annual Achievement Award, the highest recognition for work in agriculture.

Kansas was one of the first to establish a Bank Management Commission and annual school for bank management to study problems and procedures of management. In this connection, the KBA established 28 years ago the Annual Bank Management Report, giving comprehensive data on operation of Kansas banks for study and improvement.

Kansas was credited with being the first state to establish, four years ago, a Statewide Advertising and Public Information program designed to better inform the public of bank services, developments, and of the bank's place in the community.

In recent years, Kansas has taken a leading role in encouraging more economic education in our schools. Banks are providing economics study materials for schools of their respective communities, and are providing scholarships for teachers to attend summer workshops on economics instruction.

When the Kansas Council on Economic Education — sponsored by business leaders, educators and private foundations — pointed to a "great need for economics education in our schools" — Kansas bankers were among those who picked up the challenge. The economic workshops in our various colleges were among the results.

In the words of Dr. Maynard Peck, dean of the Department of Business and Commerce at Sterling College, in charge of the workshop there: "We think we are accomplishing a lot of our review of how every-day economics is working, and our teachers like it. We hope the workshops will continue."

Progressive Kansas bankers, business leaders and educators also want the workshops, and other such teaching encouragements, continued.

LIFE INSURANCE INDUSTRY IN KANSAS

The idea of life insurance began as early as the idea of mutual existence. A hunter returning without game might be supplied food by other tribe members, with the understanding that he, in turn, may contribute his share to help the next luckless hunter.

As civilization reached early men, and as they moved from rural communities to cities, they faced hazards which required dependency upon something more certain than the good will of their neighbors. Also, as trade and commerce expanded and grew more complicated, men pooled their resources in order to make a cooperative stand against dangers.

When little was yet understood of nature, when science was yet unborn and the course of human destiny was thought to be controlled by dark and unfathomable forces, there was little justification for life insurance. In the 20th century the prevalent idea is that death, disaster and other calamities occur because of natural, explicable causes. This is the fundamental assumption underlying insurance.

Life insurance came to America on the Mayflower and grew with the colonies. Ben Franklin, statesman, author and inventor, found time in his career to help found a fire insurance firm and to print the first book in this country dealing with insurance. He furnished useful data to the country's first life insurance company, the Presbyterian Ministers Fund.

A common hazard faced by life insurance firms in the early 1800's was dueling. So common, in fact, that companies had to state their policies would be voided if the insured was in a single combat. In 1860, just a few months before being elected President of the United States, Abraham Lincoln applied for life insurance. General Custer rode into combat well insured and his wife received a check for $4,750 from an insurance firm following his death.

During the first half of this century, medical advances brought sharp reductions in mortality from diseases of pregnancy, childbirth, infancy and childhood, and such diseases as respiratory infections, tuberculosis and diabetes. Control of these diseases greatly diminished deaths at the younger ages but increased the percentage of deaths due to diseases of old age.

Most persons who apply for life insurance are able to purchase it. According to a recent survey, life insurance companies accept over 97 per cent of the applications submitted. Of the remaining, about three-fifths are rejected for serious health impairments; the rest for extremely hazardous occupations or other reasons.

Here in Kansas, life insurance protection for families has continued to grow at a faster rate than family income the past 20 years. More than $8,225,000,000 in life insurance was in force in Kansas at the end of 1965. The average of $12,000 of life insurance for each Kansas family equaled about 22 months of family income.

Most Kansas families are protected by life insurance. The amount and kind of coverage varies, depending upon the family's status. Social and economic situations, ages and the number of family members are factors determining the amount of coverage.

As to types of life insurance issued, a recent survey indicates that individual insurance is by far the most frequently owned. Among men, 65 per cent owned individual policies for an average amount of $6,290. Of women surveyed, 54 per cent owned an average coverage of $1,760. Fifty-one per cent of the children polled owned policies averaging $1,310.

Group insurance was the second most frequently held type of coverage in Kansas. Group policies protected 39 per cent of the men, 11 per cent of the women and 2 per cent of those under 18 years old.

At the end of 1965 there were 21 life insurance companies with home offices in Kansas. Three hundred other companies were licensed to do business in the Sunflower State. These companies receive their income from two main sources. These are premiums from policyowners and earnings on investments held to meet future obligations.

Companies licensed in Kansas received more than $3 billion in income. Of that amount, 74 per cent was from premiums and annuity considerations. Twenty per cent was from investment earnings. Six per cent came from various other sources, principally policy proceeds left with the companies under supplementary contracts.

The life insurance industry is one of the state's largest taxpayers. It paid over $3 million in taxes, licenses and fees to federal, state and local governments in 1965. Federal income taxes, based partly on investment earnings, account for more than one-half of the total.

One out of 11 of the working population in Kansas is employed full or parttime in the life insurance business. More than 100,000 are employed in the insurance business. Sales personnel account for 35 per cent of that number. About 75 per cent of non-sales personnel are women.

Four of five deaths of ordinary life insurance policy owners in Kansas during 1964 were caused by heart and circulatory diseases, cancer and accidents. A significant trend in recent years has been the increasing percentage of deaths due to motor vehicle accidents.

Money at work through the assets of the life insurance industry in Kansas reached over $15 billion at the end of 1965. One of the main responsibilities of the life companies is to see that funds accumulated in premiums and from other sources are put to work as promptly, profitably and safely as possible. A life company has two divisions with responsibility for placement of these funds — the investment department and the mortgage loan department. The first deals with bonds, stocks and other securities. The latter makes mortgages on commercial and residential property and buys real estate for investment purposes. Before actual receipt of funds the investment and mortgage loan departments often commit funds for investment.

Policyowners' money forms a substantial flow of capital funds seeking investment. This money helps bring gas, water and electricity into every Kansas home. It helps produce the Kansan's car, the tires it rolls on, the gasoline for the tank, glass in the windshield, upholstery and instruments on the dash panel.

Life insurance dollars help construct super markets and department stores and produce the goods that Kansans purchase there. Through federal, state and municipal taxes, Kansas life insurance companies help provide adequate schools, safer highways and contributions to the national defense program.

KANSAS SAVINGS & LOAN ASSOCIATION: *near 100 years of service*

Everything has a beginning, and the savings and loan business is no exception. As they did many other things, early settlers brought the savings and loan idea or theory with them from England, and the first association was established in Pennsylvania in 1831.

The basic theory of the business is mutual or collective finance; English building societies were the immediate ancestors of the American "building and loan associations." In the early history of our country, the development of a wage-earning class was compelled to depend largely on collective effort for any real economic advance. Thrown on their own resources, these early settlers combined their efforts to accomplish for each other greater achievements than they could each attain on their own.

In the middle of the 19th century a notable scholar wrote: "The form of financial enterprise that has attained far greater results in the United States than all others combined, is that of the well-known and almost invariably successful building and loan association. It is immensely important in the period of a city's early and most rapid development that the proportions of tax-paying, property-holding citizens should be as large as possible. Of all the various plans in vogue for acquiring property by small periodic payments from current wages, the building and loan associations provide the best."

The *building and loan* movement grew up with the country, and spread with the opening of the West. With its growth, conditions changed, including the name, and in some respects the *savings and loan* associations changed also. It adopted several slightly different forms to aid in carrying out its functions in the community. But whatever its variation in form, it continues to encourage thrift through safeguarding savings, and homeownership by its exclusive investment in mortgage loans on real property.

The function of savings and loans is quite simple. The combined savings of investors are loaned to those persons desiring to own their own homes, and the loans are paid off over a period of time by way of a regular, systematic payment schedule. The interest paid by borrowers provides the income for payment of dividends to savers.

The first savings and loan association to be established in Kansas was in Topeka on April 16, 1869; another in Atchison followed four days later. Neither of these early charters are active now. Three associations chartered in the spring of 1884 are still serving the public; the oldest is the Citizens Mutual Building and Loan Association of Leavenworth, dating from March 4, 1884. The Erie Savings and Loan Association followed on March 5, 1884, and the Home Savings and Loan Association of Girard on April 4, 1884.

The great depression of the early 1930's left its effect on the financial world. Through a series of consolidations and mergers, the process of segregation of assets, and the creation of the Federal Home Loan Bank System, the savings and loan industry in Kansas survived, rallied and began to flourish again. The dual chartering system (both state and federal charters)

Kansas Savings and Loan League officers gather. Left to right, Robert G. Lake, 1st vice president, Pratt; George B. Dicus, 2nd vice president, Hutchinson; Kenneth P. Brasted, president, Wichita; and Joe J. Morris, Treasurer, Emporia.

came into being along with insurance of savings accounts by the Federal Savings and Loan Insurance Corporation.

The first Kansas statute regulating savings and loan associations was enacted in 1899. On two occasions since then, 1927 and 1943, a complete revision of the statute was made, and there have been numerous subsequent amendments in an effort to provide associations with the necessary tools to accommodate the demands of business. The "code" of 1927 established a state agency, the Kansas Savings and Loan Department; the agency director is the State Commissioner, also referred to as the Supervisor. The Commissioner and his staff are responsible for the annual examination of all state savings and loan association books and records. The responsibility for the examination of federal savings and loan association books and records rests with the Examining Division of the Federal Home Loan Bank Board, and there is an area office in Topeka. The dual-chartering system requires separate examining agencies. Also, federal insurance of savings accounts for state-chartered associations results in a dual-examination; both the state and federal agencies examiners perform the task concurrently.

The Federal Home Loan Bank System is a "credit bank" for the savings and loan industry. Twelve area banks serve as a back-stop; a source of counsel and money to assist in any situation, be it routine or an emergency. The Federal Home Loan Bank of Topeka serves the states of Kansas, Colorado, Nebraska and Oklahoma. Savings and loan associations in Kansas and in the nation are the largest single source of mortgage money. As a "specialty shop," savings and loan associations loan exclusively on real estate, principally on home loans; home loans are defined as one to four family dwellings. On a limited basis (a percentage of assets), associations make some business and farm loans.

The associations in Kansas have enjoyed considerable growth since World War II, and our state boasts having one of the largest associations in the country. In 1962, Kansas' 102 savings and loan associations reached the billion dollar mark in total assets, and on Dec. 31, 1964, the total assets were $1.4 billion. This is a billion dollar increase over 10 years ago when total assets were $400,000,000.

The industry's trade organization, the Kansas Savings and Loan League, has served its member associations for 70 years; the League was founded in 1895. The League enjoys 97% membership; maintains an office in Topeka, and has had full-time management since 1928. This record is rather unique in that even today there are a few less than 40 states that have full-time trade organization executives. The function of the League is to provide business guidance through the distribution of essential information and statistics, to develop the business through a broad program of publicity and public relations, and to maintain an alertness on state and federal legislative matters.

Along with their success in our state, savings and loan association managers are cognizant of the obligation involved; an obligation to give service to their customers and adequately provide the two-phased facility of *savings and loan.*

Kansas Savings and Loan League, 612 Capitol Federal Building,
700 Kansas Avenue, Topeka, Kansas 66603

Executive Committee: President, Kenneth P. Brasted, Wichita; First Vice President, Robert G. Lake, Pratt; Second Vice President, George B. Dicus, Hutchinson; Treasurer, Joe J. Morris, Emporia; Immediate Past President, Lawrence Reed, Ellis; Kansas Director, United States League, John C. Dicus, Topeka; Kansas Governor, National League, Damon A. Willbern, Coffeyville; Chairman, Northeast District, Chester C. Pennock, Osawatomie; Chairman, Southeast District, Robert N. Allen, Chanute; Chairman, South Central District, Drew W. Noble, Wichita; Chairman, Southwest District, Jack Greenwood, Medicine Lodge; Chairman, Northwest District, Richard H. Reynolds, Russell; Executive Vice President, Thomas L. Wilson, Topeka; Office Secretary, Mrs. Frances M. Elder, Topeka; Office Assistant, Stephen K. Brownell, Topeka.

THE KANSAS STORY IN BRIEF CHAPTERS

SYMBOLS — Kansas is an Indian word meaning "People of the South Wind." The sunflower is the official state flower; the buffalo, the state animal; meadowlark, state bird; cottonwood, state tree.

"Home on the Range" is the state song. It was adopted by the Legislature in 1947. Originally entitled "My Western Home," the words were written by Dr. Brewster Higley in his cabin on Beaver Creek near Smith Center in 1871 or 1872. Dan Kelly composed the music. The song has six verses but the first and fourth are most often used. They are:

> Oh, give me a home where the buffalo roam,
> Where the deer and the antelope play,
>
> Where seldom is heard a discouraging word
> And the sky is not cloudy all day.

(Chorus)

> Home, Home on the range
> Where the deer and the antelope play,
>
> Where seldom is heard a discouraging word
> And the sky is not cloudy all day.
>
> How often at night, when the heavens are bright
> With the light of the glittering stars,
>
> Have I stood here amazed and asked as I gazed
> If their glory exceeds this of ours.

The Great Seal of Kansas was adopted in May, 1861, by the Legislature. The design embraces a prairie landscape, with a buffalo pursued by Indian hunters, a settler's cabin, a river with a steamboat, a cluster of 34 stars surrounding the motto, "Ad Astra per Aspera," the whole encircled by the words, "Great Seal of the State of Kansas, 1861." The official state flag of Kansas has this seal, in colors, with a sunflower above, the word KANSAS below on a field of blue.

Kansas was admitted as the 34th state in the Union on January 29, 1861.

AREA — 82,276 square miles. Kansas is 411 miles from east to west; 208 miles north to south. The state is rectangular in shape except for the northeastern corner which is cut off by the Missouri River.

POPULATION — 2,197,815 as of January 1, 1965.

CLIMATE — Kansas has an average annual temperature of 55 degrees. Rainfall varies greatly from western, with less than 20 inches a year, to eastern Kansas, with 40 inches or more.

TOPOGRAPHY — Western section is largely tableland with few trees. Eastern Kansas is varied — near the Missouri River hilly with timbered areas. Southeastern Kansas is rough and hilly. Central is a combination of the eastern and western sections.

TIME BELTS — Kansas is located in the Central Standard Time Belt except a small portion of the western part of the state which is in Mountain Standard Time Belt.

RIVERS — Eleven principal rivers and many smaller streams make up the Kansas river drainage. Most of the northern half of the state is drained by the Kansas River. The Arkansas River system drains the southern part of Kansas except the southwestern edge where the Cimarron River cuts across, and the Verdigris and Neosho Rivers drain most of the southeastern district.

PRINCIPAL RIVERS —

1. Kansas
2. Blue
3. Republican
4. Solomon — N. Fork, S. Fork
5. Saline
6. Smoky Hill
7. Arkansas
8. Cimarron
9. Verdigris
10. Neosho
11. Marais des Cygnes

RESERVOIRS, FEDERAL (County and Location) —

1. Kanopolis — Ellsworth — S. of Kanopolis.
2. Fall River — Greenwood — K-96 N. of Fall River.
3. Lovewell — Jewell — US-36 NE. Mankato.
4. John Redmond — US-75 NW. Burlington.
5. Kirwin — Phillips — K-9 S. Kirwin.
6. Pomona — 15 W. Ottawa.
7. Tuttle Creek — K-13 N. Manhattan.
8. Webster — Rooks — US-24 W. Stockton.
9. Cedar Bluff — Trego — S. WaKeeney.
10. Toronto — Woodson — S. Toronto.
11. Cheney — W. Wichita.
12. Council Grove — Morris — N. Council Grove.
13. Milford — Geary — NW. Junction City.
14. Wilson — Russell — E. Russell.
15. Norton — Norton — W. Norton.
16. Perry — Jefferson — NE. Topeka.
17. Glen Elder — Mitchell — W. Beloit.
18. Elk City — Montgomery — W. Independence.

LAKES, STATE —

1. Allen-Bourbon
2. Atchison
3. Barber
4. Brown
5. Butler
6. Chase
7. Clark
8. Cowley
9. Crawford No. 1
10. Crawford No. 2
11. Decatur
12. Douglas
13. Finney
14. Geary
15. Hamilton
16. Hodgeman
17. Jewell
18. Kingman
19. Leavenworth
20. Logan
21. Lyon
22. McPherson
23. Meade
24. Montgomery
25. Nemaha
26. Neosho
27. Osage
28. Ottawa
29. Pottawatomie No. 1
30. Pottawatomie No. 2
31. Rooks
32. Scott
33. Shawnee
34. Sheridan
35. Washington
36. Wilson
37. Woodson

WILDLIFE AND WATERFOWL MANAGEMENT AREAS —

1. Cheyenne Bottoms
2. Marais des Cygnes
3. Miami
4. Morton
5. Neosho
6. Republic
7. Sheridan

STATE SCHOOLS AND INSTITUTIONS —

Boys' Industrial School . . . . Topeka
Girls' Industrial School . . . . Beloit
Kansas Technical Institute . . . . Topeka
Kansas State Industrial Reformatory . . . Hutchinson
Kansas State Penitentiary . . . . Lansing
Larned State Hospital . . . . Larned
Osawatomie State Hospital . . . . Osawatomie

School for the Blind . . . . Kansas City
School for the Deaf . . . . Olathe
State Hospital for Epileptics . . . . Parsons
State Industrial Farm for Women . . . . Lansing
State Orphans' Home . . . . Atchison
State Sanatorium for Tuberculosis . . . . Norton
State Training School . . . . Winfield
Topeka State Hospital . . . . Topeka

RAILROADS — Kansas ranks fifth in the nation in its amount of railroad mileage. Leading railroads in Kansas:

Atchison, Topeka and Santa Fe
Union Pacific Railroad Co.
Missouri Pacific
Missouri, Kansas, Texas

Chicago, Rock Island & Pacific Railroad Co.
Frisco
Chicago, Burlington & Quincy Railroad Co.

GOVERNMENT — The Kansas government has three separate branches.

EXECUTIVE — The governor is the chief officer of the executive branch of Kansas government. The laws of the state are administered and enforced and the policies and programs carried out through the executive departments, agencies, boards and commissions. Eight other elected officers serve with the governor in the executive branch of the government.

These are the lieutenant governor, secretary of state, auditor, state treasurer, attorney general, superintendent of public instruction, commissioner of insurance and state printer. All elected officers in the executive branch are elected for two-year terms.

LEGISLATIVE — This power is vested in a house of representatives and a senate, with the number of members in each regulated by law. Maximum number of representatives is 125, senators 40. (Reapportionment of legislative membership is underway during the 1966 special session.) Senators are elected for four-year terms and members of the house are elected every two years.

JUDICIAL — The Kansas judiciary is made up of the Supreme Court and 38 district courts. The Supreme Court has a chief justice and six justices, all of whom are initially appointed to the court by the governor, after being nominated by the Supreme Court nominating committee which is made up of lawyers and other individuals from all parts of the state. The justices may be returned to their positions every six years if the voters approve such action. The 57 Kansas district court judges run for office to fill four-year terms.

Road grading before the days of paved highways. In 1910, Kansans were becoming aware of the need for better roads. Equipment like this grader in Hill City became a familiar sight.

GROWING UP

The story of industrial growth in Kansas is the story of brainpower and manpower at work to harness mineral assets and other natural resources.

Photographs on the following pages show the contrasts between early day efforts and modern methods of oil and natural gas production, rural electrification, the building of aircraft and other manufacturing enterprises.

An early industry — putting up ice. Scene on Pipe Creek, Ottawa County, in the 1890's. Each winter, when the ice grew thick, it was cut and stored for summer use.

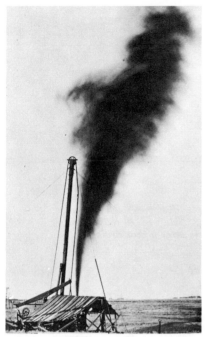

Drilling for gas, Iola, about 1902.

Aurora oil well No. 9, near Chanute, 1904.

Standard Oil Refinery at Neodesha about 1900. Considered the first commercially successful refinery in Kansas, it is still in operation.

Stapleton No. 1, discovery well of the El Dorado oil field, as it looked in 1920, five years after it was drilled.

A mobile car loader hundreds of feet underground in the Carey Salt Mine near Hutchinson. Kansas ranks high in salt production.

Pan American natural gas plant at Ulysses in southwestern Kansas.

Monarch Cement Company's Humboldt plant.

The one millionth Buick produced in Kansas City, Kansas, rolls off the assembly line of the General Motors Corporation in mid-1965.

Foundry of the L.F.M. division, Rockwell Manufacturing Company, Atchison, specializing in oil field and railroad equipment.

The first airplane built and flown by A. K. Longren at Topeka, 1911. Longren, with his brother and another partner, established the first successful aircraft manufacturing firm in Kansas.

Walter Beech, Kansas aviation pioneer (left), and Brice Goldsborough with the Beech Travel Air in which they demonstrated the practicability of blind flying, 1926.

Production of military aircraft was on a round-the-clock schedule at Boeing's Wichita plant during World War II. Photograph shows part of a B-29 assembly line.

Modern aircraft production, mid-1960's, in two Wichita plants.

University of Kansas 900-acre campus at Lawrence. KU also has 25-acre medical center at Kansas City. Centennial is 1966.

UNIVERSITY OF KANSAS:

substantial claims to excellence

The year of 1966 is centennial year for the University of Kansas, located on a hilly, 900-acre campus at Lawrence, and a 25-acre Medical Center campus at Kansas City.

The university is representative of the nation's 97 state universities and land-grant colleges which enroll more than 25 per cent of the nation's college students. KU is in the 15,000-student range, modest sized for a state university, yet continually a national leader in many avenues of education.

The school is ranked among the top six to 12 institutions in the nation in such graduate fellowship competitions as Rhodes (five in the past seven years) and Woodrow Wilson (88 in the past five years). It is one of the first five recipients of the Institute of International Education-Reader's Digest Foundation Award for distinguished service in international education and cultural relations. It is also a national leader in post-graduate medical education, music therapy, invertebrate paleontology and numerical taxonomy.

Each year 50,000 volumes are added to its 1,150,000-volume library which includes special collections in at least 14 subjects. The language arts education available at KU has been cited by the National Council of Teachers of English as "a beacon for guidance." The school also has a gifted student program. It provides a music and drama program with such features as the annual Symposium of Contemporary American Music, the annual Midwestern Music and Art Camp, a permanent acting company with guest professionals, and the premier of Douglas Moore's new opera, "Portrait of Carry."

KU is the site of the Hall Laboratory for Mammalian Genetics, the Burt Environmental Health Laboratory, and the Center for Research in Engineering Science. (Other University of Kansas data on page 171, Lawrence listing.)

CITY INDEX GUIDE to Kansas

SOURCES:

1964 County Assessor Population Report, Kansas State Board of Agriculture; Kansas Corporation Commission; League of Kansas Municipalities; Planning Division, State Highway Department; Official Guide of the Railways; Superintendent of Public Instruction.

CODE KEY:

1 Electricity	3 Water	5 Highways	7 Educational Institutions
2 Gas	4 Railroads	6 Airlines	

Banks are listed with total deposits for each city. All newspapers — weekly and daily.

MOTOR CARRIERS

Truck facilities are available throughout the state and provide excellent trucking services to every Kansas community. Because the number of motor carriers serving the state is large, it is not possible to identify them individually.

ABBREVIATIONS

RAILROADS

Atchison, Topeka and Santa Fe Ry...AT&SF
Chicago, Burlington & Quincy R. R...CB&Q
Chicago Great Western Ry...........CGW
Chicago, Rock Island and Pacific R. R. CRIP
Garden City Western Ry............GCW
Hutchinson and Northern Ry.........H&N
Joplin-Pittsburg R. R. ....J-P
Kansas City, Kaw Valley R. R., Inc...KCKV
Kansas City Southern Ry............KCS
Kansas, Oklahoma and Gulf Ry.....KO&G
Midland Valley R. R.................MV
Missouri-Kansas-Texas R. R........MKT
Missouri Pacific R. R................MP
Northeast Oklahoma R. R...........NEO
St. Louis-San Francisco Ry.........SLSF
Union Pacific R. R. ....UP

UTILITIES

American Gas Co....................AG
Caney Electric Co...................CEC
Central Kansas Power Company......CKP
Central West Utility Co.............CWU
Cities Service Gas Company.........CSG
Commercial Gas Pipeline Co........CGPC
Consolidated Gas Utilities Corp.....CGUC
Drillers Gas Co.....................DrG
Eastern Kansas Gas Co..............EKG

Empire District Electric Co..........EDE
Gas Service Company...............GSC
Kansas City Power and Light Co.....KCPL
Kansas City Suburban Water Co.....KCSW
Kansas Gas and Electric Co.........KGE
Kansas-Nebraska
    Natural Gas Co., Inc............K-NG
Kansas Power and Light Co.........KPL
Municipal Utility...................Mun.
Northern Natural Gas Co............NNG
Plateau Natural Gas, Inc............PNG
Southeastern Kansas Gas Co., Inc...SEKGC
Southwestern Public Service Co.......SPS
Tri-City Gas Company.............T-CG
Union Gas System, Inc..............UGS
United Gas Service Co..............UGSv
Western Light and Telephone, Inc....WLT

AIRLINES

Braniff International Airways........BNF
Central Air Lines...................CEN
Continental Air Lines...............CAL
Delta Air Lines....................DAL
Frontier Airlines...................FAL
Ozark Air Lines....................OZA
Trans World Airlines...............TWA
United Air Lines...................UAL

(Occasionally in editorial matter, a city's population figure differs slightly from City Index Guide listing. The former is usually a more recent unofficial figure, while City Index Guide shows official year-end statistics.)

Prairie skyscrapers store the millions of bushels of wheat produced annually. This elevator at Hutchinson is one of the largest and longest in the world.

CITY INDEX

Indicates County Seat

ABBYVILLE, Reno (E-7) pop. 119; 1 KPL; 2 Mun.; 4 AT&SF.

*ABILENE, Dickinson (C-9) pop. 7,327; 1 KPL; 2 KPL; 3 Mun.; 4 AT&SF, CRIP, UP; 5 I-70, US 40, K-15; Abilene National Bank, Citizens Bank, Farmers National Bank, United Trust $19,400,000; newspaper — Abilene Reflector-Chronicle. The Eisenhower Memorial Museum and the Boyhood Home of President Dwight D. Eisenhower are among the nation's leading tourist attractions. Also here are the new Eisenhower Presidential Library and replica of Old Abilene Town as it was in frontier days. Mamie Eisenhower Doll Collection is in the City Library. The Dickinson County Historical Museum is in the basement of the new courthouse. A boulder on the post office lawn marks the end of the famous extended Chisholm Trail, over which hundreds of thousands of cattle were driven from Texas to the railroad here in the late 1860's and early 1870's. In Abilene Cemetery is a boulder marking the grave of Marshal Tom Smith, noted frontier peace officer.

Dickinson County — Earnings per cap. $1,845; sales tax collections $663,396; employed in industry 2,579; number of farms 1,712; crop value $1,687,130; livestock value $9,088,880; mineral production $785,639. Limestone was quarried and crushed for concrete aggregate, roadstone, riprap and agstone. Crude petroleum production amounted to 48,000 barrels. Recovery of natural gas was 10 million cubic feet.

ADMIRE, Lyon (D-11) pop. 131; 1 KPL; 4 MP; 5 K-99; Admire State Bank $800,000.

AGENDA, Republic (A-9) pop. 131; 1 WLT; 2 Kansas Gas & Pipeline; 3 Mun.; 4 CRIP; 5 K-148.

AGRA, Phillips (A-6) pop. 330; 1 WLT; 2 K-NG; 3 Mun.; 4 CRIP; 5 US 36; Farmers National Bank $2,100,000.

ALBERT, Barton (D-6) pop. 202; 1 Central Kansas Electric Co-op.; 2 Mun.; 4 AT&SF; 5 K-96; Farmers State Bank $2,300,000.

ALDEN, Rice (E-7) pop. 263; 1 KPL; 4 AT&SF; Alden State Bank $800,000.

ALEXANDER, Rush (D-5) pop. 152; 1 WLT; 2 WLT; 4 AT&SF; 5 K-96; Alexander State Bank $1,200,000.

ALLEN, Lyon (D-11) pop. 223; 1 KPL; 3 Mun.; 4 MP; 5 US 56.

*ALMA, Wabaunsee (C-11) pop. 843; 1 Mun.; 2 Mun.; 3 Mun.; 4 AT&SF, CRIP; 5 K-99; First National Bank $3,300,000; newspaper — Signal-Enterprise. Mill Creek Museum is a short distance from Alma. Museum features pioneer farm items. Baby farm animals are an attraction for children.

Wabaunsee County — Earnings per cap. $1,522 sales tax collections $106,365; employed in industry 146; number of farms 972; crop value $4,228,270; livestock value $7,496,100; mineral production $852,621. Crude petroleum production 250,000 barrels. Quarried and crushed limestone for concrete aggregate and roadstone.

ALMENA, Norton (A-5) pop. 620; 1 WLT; 2 K-NG; 3 Mun.; 4 CB&Q, CRIP; 5 US 383, K-60; First State Bank $1,000,000; newspaper — Almena Plaindealer.

ALTAMONT, Labette (G-12) pop. 690; 1 Mun.; 2 Mun.; 3 Mun.; 4 SLSF; 5 K-96; Labette County State Bank $1,600,000; newspaper — George Publications.

ALTA VISTA, Wabaunsee (C-10) pop. 452; 1 KPL; 3 Mun.; 4 CRIP; 5 K-180; Alta Vista State Bank $900,000; newspaper — Alta Vista Journal.

ALTON, Osborne (B-6) pop. 261; 1 Mun.; 3 Mun.; 4 MP; 5 US 24.

ALTOONA, Wilson (F-12) pop. 584; 1 KGE; 2 UGS; 3 Mun.; 4 MP; 5 US 75, K-47; newspaper — Altoona Tribune.

AMERICUS, Lyon (D-11) pop. 270; 1 KPL; Americus State Bank $960,000.

ANDALE, Sedgwick (F-8) pop. 484; 1 KGE; 2 Arkansas & Louisiana Gas; 4 MP; 5 K-96.

ANDOVER, Butler (F-9) pop. 169; 1 KGE; 4 SLSF; Andover State Bank $2,400,000.

°ANTHONY, Harper (G-8) pop. 2,791; 1 Mun.; 2 WLT; 3 Mun.; 4 AT&SF, MP; 5 K-14, K-44, K-179; Citizens National Bank, First National Bank $10,110,000; newspaper — Anthony Republican.

Harper County — Earnings per cap. $2,032; sales tax collections $273,493; employed in industry 784; number of farms 1,062; crop value $8,993,650; livestock value $5,074,870; mineral production $4,087,430. Crude petroleum output totaled 1.1 million barrels, 17 per cent more than in previous year. Marketed production of natural gas was 5.8 billion cubic feet, an increase of 5 per cent. Building and paving sand and gravel are produced.

ARCADIA, Crawford (F-13) pop. 484; 1 Mun.; 3 Mun.; 4 SLSF; Home State Bank $1,300,000.

ARGONIA, Sumner (G-8) pop. 544; 1 WLT; 2 Argonia Gas; 3 Mun.; 4 AT&SF, MP; 5 K-210; Farmers & Merchants State Bank $2,900,000; newspaper — Argonia Argosy. Argonia is the home of the first woman mayor in the United States and probably the world. Elected in 1887, Mrs. Susanna Madora Salter lived in a house still standing in Argonia. A museum in Township Hall contains Mrs. Salter's mementoes and other historical items. Plaque commemorating her election is in front of the hall and another in Salter Park outlining details of the election.

ARKANSAS CITY, Cowley (G-9) pop. 14,607; 1 KGE; 2 GSC; 3 Mun.; 4 AT&SF; SLSF, MV, MP; 5 US 116, US 77; 7 Arkansas City Junior College; Home National Bank, Union State Bank $16,-200,000; newspaper — Arkansas City Daily Traveler. A natural bridge at the base of a bluff on the east edge of the city is formed by two large rocks that arch over a spring. The bluff was a camping place for Buffalo Bill Cody in 1869-70 and his initials are carved on a boulder here. A granite marker south of town on US 77 at the Oklahoma line marks area from which 20,000 early homesteaders started at noon on Sept. 16, 1893, in the run for the opening of the Cherokee Strip.

ARLINGTON, Reno (E-7) pop. 443; 1 KPL; 2 GSC; 3 Mun.; 4 CRIP; 5 K-14, K-66; Citizens State Bank $740,000.

ARMA, Crawford (F-13) pop. 1,374; 1 Mun.; 3 Mun.; 4 MP; 5 US 69; First State Bank $1,700,000; newspaper — Arma Record.

°ASHLAND, Clark (G-4) pop. 1,418; 1 Mun.; 2 KPL; 3 Mun.; 4 AT&SF; 5 US 160; Citizens State Bank, Stockgrowers State Bank $6,000,000; newspaper — Clark County Clipper. Thirteen miles west of Ashland on US 160 are Big Basin and Little Basin, geological sinkholes. The larger is a mile-wide depression, 100 feet deep, formed by underground water dissolving supporting rock strata and forming caverns which eventually collapsed.

Clark County — Earnings per cap. $1,790; sales tax collections $88,476; employed in industry 322; number of farms 406; crop value $2,438,360; livestock value $5,143,060; mineral production $2,122,000. Natural gas recovery totaled nearly 12.5 billion cubic feet, an increase of 22 per cent. Over 189,000 barrels of crude petroleum was recovered, an increase of 18 per cent. Gravel available for paving and road maintenance.

1 2 3 4 5 6

A

Cheyenne
St. Francis
Bird City

Rawlins
Herndon
McDonald
Atwood

Decatur
Oberlin
Norcatur
Clayton
Jennings
Dresden
Selden

Norton
Almena
Norton
Lenora Edmond

Phillips
Long Island
Prairie View
Phillipsburg Agra
Logan Speed Glade Kirwin

Smith
Athol Lebanon
Kensington Smith Center
Cedar Gaylord

B

Sherman
Kanorado
Goodland

Thomas
Brewster Colby

Sheridan
Rexford
Gem
Menlo
Hoxie

Graham
Morland Hill City Bogue

Rooks
Woodston
Stockton
Damar
Palco Zurich Plainville

Osborne
Portis
Alton
Osborne
Natoma
Down

C

Wallace
Wallace
Sharon Springs

Logan
Winona
Russell Springs

Oakley
Grinnell Park
Gove Grainfield Quinter
Gove City

Trego
Collyer
WaKeeney

Ellis
Ellis
Hays Victoria

Paradise Waldo Luray
Russell
Russell
Gorham Bunker Hill Luca
Dorrance

D

Greeley
Horace Tribune

Wichita
Leoti

Scott
Scott City

Lane
Dighton

Ness
Utica
Ransom Brownell
Ness City Bazine

Rush
Schoenchen
Liebenthal
McCracken
La Crosse Bison Otis
Alexander Rush Center Timken
Albert
Pawnee

Barton
Galatia Susank
Olmitz
Hoisington Claf
Ellinwood
Great Bend

E

Hamilton
Coolidge
Syracuse

Kearny
Deerfield
Lakin

Finney
Holcomb
Garden City

Hodgeman
Jetmore
Gray

Burdett Rozel
Radium Seward
Hanston
Stafford
Hudson
Edwards Garfield
Kinsley Lewis Belpre Macksville St. John
Offerle
Larned
Pawnee Rock
Stafford

F

Stanton
Johnson
Manter

Grant
Ulysses

Haskell
Montezuma
Copeland
Sublette
Satanta

Ford
Ingalls Cimarron
Ensign
Spearville
Dodge City
Ford
Bucklin

Kiowa
Mullinville Greensburg
Haviland Cullison
Wellsford

Pratt
Byers
Iuka Presto
Pratt
Coats Sawyer
Barber
Isabel

G

Morton
Richfield
Rolla
Elkhart

Stevens
Moscow
Hugoton

Seward
West Plains
Kismet
Liberal

Meade
Fowler
Meade

Clark
Minneola
Ashland
Englewood

Comanche
Wilmore
Coldwater
Protection
Sun City

Medicine L
Hardtner K

1 2 3 4 5 6

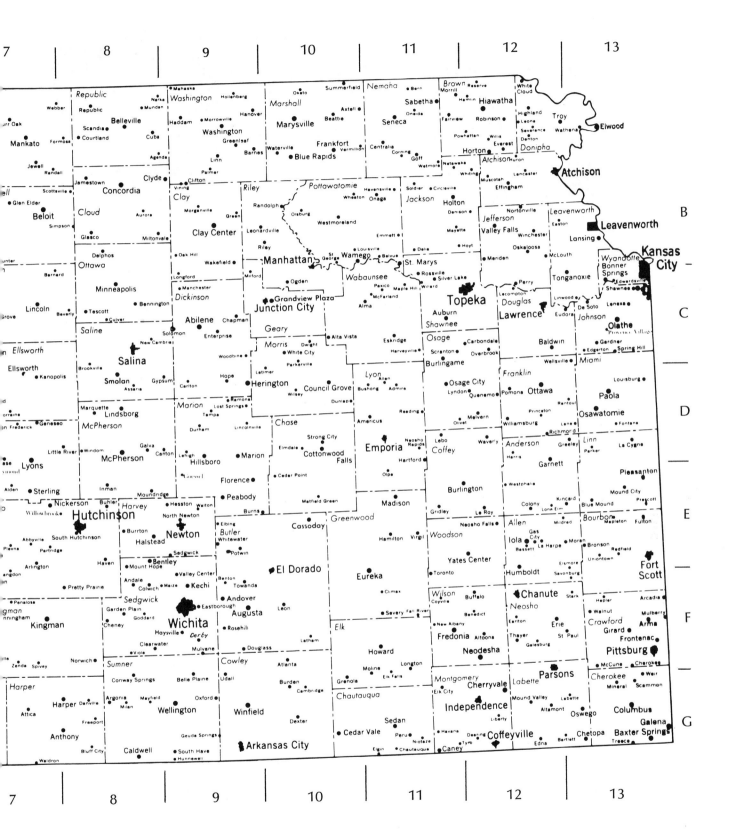

Visitors flock to "Old Abilene Town."

ABILENE: *city of opportunity*
in the heart of the nation

Greyhounds, manufacturing and tourist attractions steadily are bolstering the economy of the seat of Dickinson County.

Abilene claims today to be the foremost tourist center in Kansas. Tourists and residents enjoy Kansas hospitality, re-live the Old West and still live as modern as tomorrow.

Once the wildest boom town on the frontier and end of the famous Chisholm cattle trail from Texas, Abilene today is known as the boyhood home of former President Dwight D. Eisenhower. Over 300,000 visitors a year tour the Eisenhower Center — museum, library and home. Meditation Chapel will be completed by spring, 1966. It will be located west of the library and will complete the physical structures of the Center.

Old Abilene Town, an authentically recreated portion of Texas Street, continues to draw tourists. Can-can dancers entertain at some of the old saloons along this street where two-gun marshals Tom Smith and Wild Bill Hickok once shot it out with gunslingers and rampaging Texas cowhands.

Other tourist attractions are the Greyhound Hall of Fame, antique car museum, Mamie Eisenhower's doll collection and numerous historical markers. Close proximity to new Milford and Tuttle Creek Reservoirs, fine highways, unusual scenery, good camping, boating and fishing facilities are helping the community to become Mid-America's newest vacationland. The largest free fair in Kansas is held in Abilene each August, along with the Wild Bill Hickok Rodeo. Two weeks of greyhound racing in April and October add to entertainment. Offices of the National Coursing Association and Greyhound Hall of Fame are located here. Records of more than 550,000 registered greyhounds in the United States, Mexico and Cuba are kept here. National coursing meets are held here each spring and fall. In this community are 24 greyhound kennels and stud farms and three training tracks. The National Coursing Park is one mile west of the city.

The economy is based primarily on agriculture. However, Dickinson County is fast becoming one of the top counties in livestock production. Two large commercial feed lots with capacity of 5,000 cattle are located just west of the city. Two livestock companies hold weekly auctions. The county is the first in Kansas in production of turkeys and third in sheep. Wheat is the main crop. But alfalfa, oats, rye, corn, clover, watermelons, cantaloupes and sweet potatoes are raised here.

Flour and feed milling are the largest Abilene industries. Others include a steel products

Eisenhower Library, newest facility in the Center.

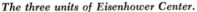

The three units of Eisenhower Center.   *New Memorial Hospital provides modern health facilities.*

manufacturing firm, concrete mixing plant, concrete building panel manufacturer, cooking utensil assembly plant and soft drink bottlers. The Ehrsam Manufacturing Company, manufacturers of heavy industrial equipment shipped around the world, is located just six miles from here at Enterprise. Main offices of Ehrsam's, with staff of 90 people, are moving to Abilene. Armour & Co. will locate a commercial fertilizer plant at the west edge of Abilene.

General offices of the A. L. Duckwall Stores Company are located here on the site of the original Chisholm Trail stockyards. The company operates a chain of 90 variety stores in midwest states.

Kansas Power and Light Company serves Abilene and adjacent areas with power and natural gas. Municipally-owned water supply is plentiful and water quality excellent. A new sewer disposal plant is capable of handling waste for a city of 10,000. The city's airport has all-weather runways and ramps and around-the-clock service to accommodate the largest twin-motor aircraft. Abilene is a hub for traffic along highways Interstate-70, US 40 and K-15 and from at least eight other main highways within a 50-mile radius.

A new Dickinson County courthouse is located adjacent to the business district. Also new are Abilene high school, three elementary schools and 70-bed hospital. Numerous businesses have remodeled or added new store fronts. Abilene is the trade center for 50,000 persons. The city has three banks and a trust company with total resources over $22 million. It was the smallest city in the United States with four banks, all of which reopened and stayed open after the "bank holiday" in 1933.

The colorful history of Abilene dates from pioneer cattle days when great herds of longhorns were driven overland from Texas to the western terminus of the first railroad through Kansas. Many legends and traditions of cowbody days had their origin here three-quarters of a century ago. Abilene was founded in 1858 when Timothy F. Hersey and his family chose a spot on the present site of the city for their log cabin. It was named by Mrs. Hersey. She allowed her Bible to fall open at random. In the first verse, third chapter of Luke was the name Abilene, meaning City of the Plains.

A livestock dealer from Illinois, Joseph G. McCoy, saw opportunities presented by the new railroad for transporting Texas cattle to eastern markets. He built a stockyards and hotel for the purpose. From 1867 to 1871, over three million head of cattle were shipped from Abilene. Stores, saloons and gambling houses sprang up to compete for cowboy patronage. It required the fast-gun reputation of Wild Bill Hickok to relieve townspeople of terror over prospects of anarchy and chaos.

Abilene grew rapidly as a rail terminal. Once the city was laid out for a population of 50,000. But, after the initial boom, settlers discouraged over-development and stressed, instead, making it an ideal home town.

95

St. Jacob's Well, in Clark County. This photograph was taken in the 1890's.

ASHLAND: *noted for city housekeeping*

This Clark County seat prairie town of 1,400 people is noted for its good housekeeping. Streets are clean and adequately lighted. Well-painted and well-roofed houses add to the brightness. There are 130 city blocks of paved streets.

All public buildings, including a million-dollar junior-senior high school (1963), were constructed within the past 15 years. Bonded indebtedness has been paid on most public buildings. Clark County courthouse was built in 1950. City Hall was a 1962 project. Electrical power and water supply systems, airport and swimming pool are municipally owned. Voters approved fluoridation of city water in 1965.

Not more than a half-dozen Kansas towns in the 1,000-1,500 class have lower taxes than Ashland.

Recently constructed was Ashland District Hospital with a 22-bed capacity. Cost was $280,000. The hospital is free of indebtedness. Most churches here have been newly constructed or remodeled during the past five years.

Located in the heart of wheat and cattle ranch country, Ashland has experienced a cultural boom in recent years. Ashland Art Association was created in 1960 to sponsor art exhibits and instruction for young and old. Nationally-known instructors conduct classes in painting, modeling and sculpture. As many as 100 children receive art instruction each year. Capacity audiences attend school concerts. Local businessmen have purchased murals and paintings done especially for their establishments.

Ashland schools have rated high every year in Kansas state scholarship tests. Each October, citizens here open their homes to foreign students studying at nearby colleges. Forty foreign students were entertained here in the 1965 United Nations Weekend event. They came from a half-dozen colleges in Oklahoma and Kansas.

Concern for the economic future of the town led the Chamber of Commerce to organize an industrial development corporation in 1964. Purpose was to offer long-term credit to finance new plants and equipment for industries. Aid also is available for expansion of existing businesses.

The Chamber of Commerce this year is promoting Saint Jacob's Well as a tourist attraction. The centuries old well is 13 miles west of town near highway US 160. Depth of the well never has been determined. It never went dry in the memory of Ashland's oldest residents. The well is believed to have been created by an earth spasm deep underground. A move was initiated in 1964 to have the well and surrounding area designated a state park. It would require legislative approval. Big Basin and Little Basin sinkholes are located in this area. Big Basin measures a mile across.

Augusta Library, built in 1962, now has 15,000 volumes.

Mobil Oil Company refinery averages 330 employees. It recently completed major expansion of facilities.

AUGUSTA: prospered first with discovery of oil; now agriculture, manufacturing aid economy

In March, 1914, Butler County's first commercial oil well was brought in just southwest of Augusta. From that discovery came the foundation of a growing and thriving city of nearly 7,000 people.

Oil still is important to this city located near the center of Kansas' largest oil fields. But Augusta also may rely now on agriculture and manufacturing for its continued economic stability.

Oil production and refining, oil field service and supply provide the first vital spoke in the city's wheel of progress.

Augusta is the home of more than two dozen businesses engaged in these activities.

Agriculture is the second important segment of the city's economy. Livestock and 21 field crops grown in the county have contributed an average $18 million to the county economy the past 10 years.

Oil brought $21 million a year during the same period.

Manufacturing other than the oil industry provides one job per dozen residents here. Augusta has a major Mobil Oil Company refinery; Spencer-Safford Loadcraft, manufacturer of commercial trailers; Augusta Unit Step, producer of pre-formed concrete products; Minuteman Nylon Products, and Pioneer Optical, Inc., both of which manufacture nylon eyeglass frames; Augusta Boat Company, maker of paddleboats; Criss Concrete Company, a ready-mix facility; and two printing firms — Gazette Publishing Company and Lytton's, Inc.

The Chamber of Commerce has formed an industrial development corporation to secure and develop industrial sites.

More than 300,000 people live within 20 miles of Augusta. This provides a sizeable work force from which local industries may draw.

For leisure time and recreation, Augustans enjoy a 200-acre city park. The park offers three lighted baseball diamonds, lighted tennis courts, picnic areas and fishing in a large lake.

The city-owned Santa Fe Lake five miles northwest of Augusta provides picnicking, boating and fishing.

Augusta Country Club has a nine-hole, grassed-green golf course open to the public. The city operates a municipal swimming pool and Moyle Field — a lighted baseball field and park.

Other attractions are a bowling alley, indoor and outdoor theaters, Augusta Historical Museum and a summer baseball program for youngsters.

Scheduled for completion in 1966 are a new municipal airport, with paved runways, and a 30-bed memorial hospital.

Augusta has 16 churches, six schools and a modern public library.

Colorful Kansas

Colorful Kansas . . .
CLIMATE

The stimulation and beauty of changing seasons gives a superior, natural advantage to a Kansas location for industry. Pure air, sunshine, and invigorating temperatures combine to produce high working efficiency and production. Kansas has an abundance of sunshine. Annually, more than 66 per cent of the days have sunshine. No other part of the country with as much rain has as many clear days and little fog.

Such weather conditions have proved to be excellent for raising families, and enjoying the retirement years. The state has one of the highest life expectancy rates in the nation, and only one other state has a smaller percentage of men rejected for military service for health reasons during World War II.

Temperatures are moderate, with only short durations of extremes. Average annual temperatures as recorded by the U. S. Weather Bureau in Kansas City and Wichita are 56° and 57°, respectively. The normal monthly average temperature at these two stations ranges from 30° in January to 80° in July.

AVERAGE MONTHLY TEMPERATURES
(degrees Fahrenheit)

	Wichita	Kansas City
January	32	30
February	37	34
March	45	43
April	56	55
May	64	65
June	75	75
July	80	80
August	79	79
September	71	70
October	60	59
November	45	44
December	35	33
Annual	**57**	**56**

Kansas slopes gently toward the east to the Missouri border. Elevation at the junction of the Kansas and Missouri rivers is 755 feet. Lowest spot is in southeastern corner (south of Coffeyville) where it drops to 686 feet above sea level. Highest point is a hill near the Colorado border which measures 4,135 feet above sea level.

Rainfall is moderate, providing excellent conditions for crop raising, and sufficient moisture for luxuriant, well kept lawns, gardens, and parks. The average annual precipitation ranges from 40 inches in the southeast, to 25 inches in the central region, and decreases to 20 inches in western Kansas.

ASSARIA, Saline (D-8) pop. 351; 1 KPL; 2 KPL; 3 Mun.; 4 UP; 5 US 81, K-4; Assaria State Bank $1,500,000.

°ATCHISON, Atchison (B-12) pop. 11,835; 1 KPL; 2 KPL; 3 Atchison Water Works; 4 AT&SF, CB&Q, CRIP, MP; 5 US 73, K-4, K-7, K-9, K-48; 7 Mt. St. Scholastica, St. Benedict's College; City National Bank, Exchange National Bank $26,600,000; newspaper — Atchison Daily Globe. Plaque in the courthouse square marks spot where Lincoln in 1859 first delivered his Cooper Union speech. Lewis and Clark camped near Atchison on July 4, 1804. A monument in front of Memorial Hall commemorates the organization of the Santa Fe Railway in 1860. Amelia Earhart's birthplace overlooks the Missouri River from one of Atchison's bluffs.

Atchison County — Earnings per cap. $1,833; sales tax collections $500,613; employed in industry 3,302; number of farms 1,142; crop value $5,394,320; livestock value $4,630,930; mineral production $307,211. Limestone is quarried and crushed for concrete aggregate, roadstone, riprap, and agstone.

ATHOL, Smith (A-6) pop. 162; 1 WLT; 4 CRIP; 5 US 36.

ATLANTA, Cowley (F-10) pop. 268; 1 KGE; 2 GSC; 3 Mun.; 4 SLSF; Citizens State Bank $1,200,000.

ATTICA, Harper (G-7) pop. 782; 1 Mun.; 2 Mun.; 3 Mun.; 4 AT&SF; 5 US 160; First National Bank $1,400,000; newspaper — Attica Independent.

°ATWOOD, Rawlins (A-2) pop. 1,819; 1 CKP; 2 K-NG; 3 CKP; 4 CB&Q; 5 US 36, K-25; Farmers National Bank, State Bank of Atwood $8,900,000; newspaper — Citizen Patriot.

Rawlins County — Earnings per cap. $1,863; sales tax collections $118,216; employed in industry 256; number of farms 750; crop value $5,554,300; livestock value $4,574,510; mineral production $2,220,608. Crude petroleum output totaling 766,000 barrels. Atwood Sand & Rock Co. Produced are crushed opal (miscellaneous stone) for concrete aggregate, roadstone, and roofing granules, and sand for building and paving.

AUBURN, Shawnee (C-11) pop. 241; 1 Kaw Valley; 3 Rural Water Supply Dist. 2, Shawnee Co.; Security State Bank $1,200,000.

AUGUSTA, Butler (F-9) pop. 6,307; 1 Mun.; 2 CSG; 3 Mun.; 4 AT&SF, SLSF; 5 US 77, US 54, K-96; Augusta State Bank, Prairie State Bank $9,200,000; newspaper — Augusta Daily Gazette. The first building in Augusta, a log structure built in 1868, is still preserved as a landmark and now houses a historical museum owned by the Augusta Historical Society, operated by the Chamber of Commerce. The museum displays hundreds of authentic pioneer items preserved from early Augusta life. East of Augusta 6½ miles on highway 54 is the Glenn Cunningham Wild Animal Farm.

AURORA, Cloud (B-8) pop. 152; 1 WLT; 3 Mun.; 4 AT&SF.

AXTELL, Marshall (A-11) pop. 502; 1 Mun.; 2 KPL; 3 Mun.; 4 UP; 5 K-110; State Bank of Axtell $1,100,000; newspaper — Axtell Standard.

BALDWIN, Douglas (C-12) pop. 1,494; 1 Mun.; 2 GSC; 3 Mun.; 4 AT&SF; 5 US 56; 7 Baker University; Baldwin State Bank $3,200,000; newspaper — Baldwin Ledger. Black Jack Park, an attractive spot for tourists and picnickers, is located on US 56 about three miles east of Baldwin. The park is near the marker describing the Battle of Black Jack (1856), which has been termed "one of the first battles of the Civil War." Also near the park can be seen ruts of the old Santa Fe Trail. Baker University (Methodist) is oldest four-year college (1858) in Kansas. The Bishop Quayle Collection of Bibles and manuscripts in campus library contains two copies of the first edition of the King James version of the Bible and earlier Bibles handprinted by early monks. Library features an entire antique drawing room of the King James (Jacobean) Period which was originally in Urishay Castle in Herefordshire, England. There is also a museum containing thousands of specimens including North Polar artifacts and Chinese coins. Another building houses Santa Fe Trail relics, Masonic records and other items of historical interest.

BARNARD, Lincoln (B-7) pop. 244; 1 KPL; 2 GSC; 3 Mun.; 4 AT&SF; First National Bank $1,200,000.

BARNES, Washington (A-9) pop. 251; 1 WLT; 2 KPL; 3 Mun.; 4 MP; 5 K-9, K-15E; State Exchange Bank $800,000; newspaper — Barnes Chief.

BARTLETT, Labette (G-13) pop. 137; 1 KPL; 2 T-CG; 4 MP; 5 K-134.

BASSETT, Allen (E-12) pop. 64; 1 City of Iola; 2 City of Iola; 3 City of Iola; 5 US 169, US 59, K-57.

BAXTER SPRINGS, Cherokee (G-13) pop. 4,561; 1 EDE; 2 Baxter Springs Gas; 3 Mun.; 4 SLSF, KCS, KO&G; 5 US 166, US 66; American National Bank, Baxter State Bank $12,500,000; newspaper — Baxter Springs Citizen. Once a wild cattle town established in 1858, was the site of the Baxter Springs Massacre by Quantrill's Guerrillas in October, 1863. Monument in National Cemetery commemorates victims. Military Avenue, the main street (US 66), is named for the old military road which linked Fort Leavenworth and the Indian Territory to the south. Great chat piles are evidence of the lead and zinc mining in the vicinity.

BAZINE, Ness (D-5) pop. 479; 1 WLT; 2 WLT; 3 Mun.; 4 AT&SF; 5 K-96; Bazine State Bank $2,200,000.

BEATTIE, Marshall (A-10) pop. 355; 1 KPL; 2 KPL; 3 Mun.; 4 UP; 5 K-99; First National Bank $700,000.

BELLE PLAINE, Sumner (F-9) pop. 1,607; 1 KGE; 2 GSC; 3 Mun.; 4 AT&SF, MV, MP; 5 K-55; Valley State Bank $2,100,000; newspaper — Belle Plaine News. Bartlett Arboretum, a 25-acre formal garden, is nationally famous for its collection of flowers, shrubs, trees and grasses. Paradise Valley Ranch, membership recreation area, is being developed.

*BELLEVILLE, Republic (A-8) pop. 3,035; 1 Mun.; 2 KPL; 3 Mun.; 4 CRIP; 5 US 81, US 36; First National Bank, Peoples National Bank $8,400,000; newspaper — Belleville Telescope. Thirteen miles southeast of Belleville on US 81 is the Seapo Salt Marsh, a 4,000-acre pool of brine where early settlers obtained salt by evaporating the water. Pike-Pawnee Monument, a Kansas State Park, marks the reported site of the first raising of the United States flag west of the Mississippi by Zebulon Pike. It is located 12 miles west and 6 miles north of Belleville. Authentic replica of a Conestoga wagon weighing 1½ tons and capable of hauling 3 to 4 tons of freight has been constructed and is on display in Belleville.

Republic County — Earnings per cap. $1,422; sales tax collections $218,499; number of farms 1,483; crop value $9,647,860; livestock value $7,246,800. Minerals produced are sand and quarried and crushed limestone for concrete aggregate and road maintenance.

*BELOIT, Mitchell (B-7) pop. 4,089; 1 Mun.; 2 GSC; 3 Mun.; 4 MP; UP; 5 US 24, K-9, K-14, K-124, K-129; First National Bank, Guaranty State Bank $8,800,000; newspapers — Beloit Daily Call, Beloit Weekly Call, Gazette. State Industrial School for Girls is in Beloit. City is in the heart of the post-rock area where early settlers made posts of rock because of the scarcity of wood.

Mitchell County — Earnings per cap. $1,594; sales tax collections $345,100; employed in industry 788; number of farms 954; crop value $7,851,350; livestock value $4,195,350; mineral production $25,000. Sand and gravel for building, paving and fill are produced.

BELPRE, Edwards (E-6) pop. 199; 1 KPL; 2 KPL; 3 Mun.; 4 AT&SF; 5 US 50, K-19.

BELVUE, Pottawatomie (B-11) pop. 191; 1 KPL; 2 KPL; 4 UP; 5 US 24.

BENEDICT, Wilson (F-12) pop. 116; 1 KPL; 2 UGS; 4 AT&SF, MP; 5 K-39.

BENNINGTON, Ottawa (C-8) pop. 588; 1 KPL; 3 Mun.; 4 UP; 5 K-18; Bennington State Bank $3,005,000.

BENTLEY, Sedgwick (E-8) pop. 203; 1 KGE; 2 GSC; 4 SLSF; State Bank of Bentley $670,000.

BENTON, Butler (F-9) pop. 456; 1 KGE; 2 GSC; 3 Mun.; 4 MP; Benton State Bank $1,000,000.

BERN, Nemaha (A-11) pop. 202; 1 KPL; 3 Mun.; 4 CRIP; 5 K-71; State Bank of Bern $1,200,000.

BEVERLY, Lincoln (C-8) pop. 235; 1 KPL; 2 KPL; 4 UP; 5 K-18; Beverly State Bank $1,100,000.

BIRD CITY, Cheyenne (A-2) pop. 691; 1 CKP; 2 K-NG; 3 Mun.; 4 CB&Q; 5 US 36, K-161; Security State Bank $2,600,000; newspaper — Bird City Times.

BISON, Rush (D-6) pop. 333; 1 WLT; 2 KPL; 3 Mun.; 4 MP; Bison State Bank $1,020,000.

BLUE MOUND, Linn (E-13) pop. 358; 1 Mun.; 2 Blue Mound Gas & Supply Co.; 3 Mun.; 5 K-31, K-52; Farmers State Bank $911,000.

BLUE RAPIDS, Marshall (A-10) pop. 1,320; 1 KPL; 2 KPL; 3 Mun.; 4 MP, UP; 5 US 77, K-9;

TRANSPORTATION

Kansas business has the unique advantage of operating from the geographic center of the United States. Because of extensive railway, highway, air, pipeline and water systems of the state, manufacturers find no problem in moving their products to local, regional, national and international markets.

Inland Waterways — Due to channel improvements on the Missouri and the expanding dock facilities at Atchison, Leavenworth and Kansas City, commercial tonnage through these port cities increased over 550 per cent in five years, reaching approximately 1.4 million tons in 1963.

Trucking — Steady growth has been the pattern for trucking operations. Kansas has approximately 2,550 interstate routes operated by 2,250 companies. The number of truck and bus licenses issued annually in the state is more than 300,000.

Railroads — Sixteen railroads blanket the state with 8,159 miles of track, ranking fifth among the 50 states. They carry over 15 billion ton miles of freight annually and operating revenues exceed $260 million a year. An innovation to cut time and cost of rail shipment is the trailer train (piggy back) service in which fully loaded trailers are carried by rail to all parts of the country.

Air Transportation — Scheduled commercial service to 12 industrial areas in the state is provided by two international, one continental and one regional airlines. Kansans also have access to four additional airlines which serve Kansas City, Mo. Kansas has 219 airports of which 102 are municipal and more than 178 available for public use.

Highways — By 1972, 800 miles of Interstate highway will be located in Kansas and the state will rank third nationally in total public highway mileage. The 224 state-maintained routes extend for 10,000 miles and join with the 8,800 miles of city streets to form a network over Kansas.

Colorful Kansas . . .
UTILITIES

The impressive growth of Kansas utilities reflects the steadily expanding industrial and domestic demands for heat, power, light, and water. Serving the state are private utilities, municipal plants and rural electric cooperatives.

ELECTRIC

Kansas electric utilities can provide low-cost power to industry as well as commercial, rural and residential customers. Gas reserves located in the state. Because of the proximity to these fields, generating plants are able to obtain fuel at prices far below the national average. Since fuel costs represent 75 to 80 per cent of the production cost, Kansas utilities are in a favored position to offer low power rates.

Seven investor-owned companies, 124 municipal systems, and 36 rural electric cooperatives serve Kansas industrial areas. Generating capacity of electric power companies has grown remarkably in recent years and major expansions are scheduled for the immediate future. Kansas is laced together with a vast network of high voltage transmission lines and more than one-thousand additional miles of high voltage lines are scheduled for installation during the next five years. This expansion will include a 345,000 volt line connecting Wichita, Topeka and Kansas City, Missouri by 1967.

GAS

The natural gas utility industry is booming. Kansas ranks fifth nationally in the marketed production of natural gas, and the pipeline system stretching across the state assures an adequate low-cost gas supply to industry. The cost of natural gas for Kansas users across the board is about 50 per cent lower than the national average. Over 38,000 miles of pipeline criss-cross Kansas, and both residential and industrial users have easy access to this plentiful supply of energy.

WATER

Large quantities of surface and ground water are available for industrial use. There is nearly 200 million acre-feet available in ground water storage and approximately 12 million acre-feet flow from the state. The bulk of this water leaving Kansas is unused.

It is estimated that 2,700 million gallons per day (2 million acre-feet annually) is withdrawn from the net supply. Nearly half of the withdrawals are for industrial use and are supplied from privately developed surface and ground water sources. However, over 96 per cent of this water used for industrial purposes is returned to net supply.

BELOIT: *where the growing is showing*

Industry in the Great Plains relies upon Beloit to train personnel for specific jobs. Located here is a new heavy equipment operator and diesel mechanics school — one of four such public schools in the United States and the only one in the Great Plains states. This is part of the North Central Kansas Area Vocational-Technical School which serves 10 counties. Courses include auto mechanics, electricity and electronics, welding, building trades, agri-business and business training. Day and night class enrollment totals 376 at present, 16 of these in heavy equipment training.

Bond issue votes in Beloit show the trend is to stronger backing of improved school facilities on all levels. In 1953, the school district voted 60 per cent in favor of a bond to build a new elementary school.

Beloit, county seat of Mitchell County, is in north central Kansas in the rich Solomon River valley. Cash grains are principally wheat and grain sorghum on dry land and irrigated corn.

Livestock programs consist of beef cow herds, wintering steer calves and heifers, some creep feeding and some full feeding. Mitchell County is one of the top quality ewe and spring lamb marketing areas of the state. Swine production is becoming more and more important.

The territory within a 50-mile radius of Beloit is one of the most advanced water resource development areas of Kansas. In addition to the $76 million Glen Elder and Waconda Lake project 12 miles upstream from Beloit, the city itself will be the nucleus of a 22,000-acre irrigation district. Primarily it will serve livestock farms and furnish some specialty crop and cash grain production. The district will have half its acreage in Mitchell County with the balance in Cloud and Ottawa counties. Beloit's water supply is currently from the Solomon River and fed out of the Webster Reservoir. After 1968, and upon completion of the Glen Elder Dam, it will be supplied from the Waconda Lake in amounts adequate for industrial and business expansion.

Beloit, long referred to as the "Queen City of the Solomon Valley," has a new motto — "Our Growing Is Showing!" This is no pipe dream. It symbolizes the positive attitude of the community toward balancing the economy formerly weighted heavily to basic agricultural production but now fast gaining in industry. Among the 154 building permits (valued at $1.5 million) issued in the past 29 months are these: a government office building for Agriculture Stabilization and Conservation Service and Soil Conservation Service, a supermarket expansion, two fertilizer bulk distributing plants, service station, two shop buildings for the area V-T school, machine shop building, auto body shop, automatic car wash, bank concrete land-scaped parking lot, roofing and paint company office, drive-in Burger-Bar, city water tower and educational wing for a church. Balance of the permits were 90 per cent new homes construction.

A major industry, the Sunflower Manufacturing Company, employs 38 people in the manu-facturing of various types of farm equipment and attachments. Another industry for Beloit is the Professional Photographers Color Corporation which develops color film. Its employ-ment will jump from 25 to 100-150 when a planned new plant becomes reality. Other businesses in town include an electrical wholesale firm, farm chemical, fertilizer and supply center, a large feed mill and a livestock auction. There are four major manufacturing com-panies within a 30-mile radius of Beloit.

Transportation facilities include two railroads, three truck lines and a municipal airport with runways of 2200, 2500 and 3000 feet.

The town has two banks, two savings and loan associations and a credit unit with combined financial resources of $33.5 million. There is a 54-bed Community Hospital, staffed by 12 doctors, which serves Mitchell and neighboring counties. During the summer of 1966 work is slated to start on construction of a million dollar county hospital and connected extended care or skilled nursing facility.

Beloit is more than a place for industrious people to earn a living . . . it is a good place to enjoy the living! The public library contains 12,000 volumes. There are 44 civic, fraternal and social organizations. There are 13 churches, embracing many faiths.

The Municipal Building, with seating capacity of 1200, hosts many area and state conventions as well as musical and cultural events. Other avenues of creative life in Beloit are clubs for art, music and gardening and Dale Carnegie Classes sponsored by Rotary.

For recreation there are the City Park and several smaller parks, two lighted and 12 un-lighted baseball diamonds, two lighted football fields, two quarter-mile cinder and dirt tracks, a modern county fairgrounds and buildings, three indoor basketball courts, three tennis courts, a city-owned swimming pool 75 x 150 feet, a country club and golf course, a movie theater and one drive-in theater, gun club and volley ball courts.

Auto and horse races are held on the half-mile 60-foot track located at the Mitchell County Fair Grounds. Plans are underway to construct a 440-yard straightaway approach to the half-mile track so that nationally recognized quarter horse and harness racing can be added in the near future.

The Beloit Industrial Development Corporation, started in 1958 as a non-profit corporation to encourage and lend financial aid to industrial development, has directly benefited the V-T School and the color film company. Original industrial site was about 20 acres, now fully developed. The corporation plans to acquire another site at least that large for accelerated development. The word "accelerated" describes Beloit and its business atmosphere. Its growing is definitely showing!

Municipal swimming pool and park
— popular on hot days.

Students handle heavy equipment
at Vocational-Technical School.

One of five schools in Beloit.

Colorful Kansas...
AGRIBUSINESS

Kansas is among the 10 leading states in total agricultural production.

U. S. Department of Agriculture reporters have predicted a $1.5 billion farm income in 1966, a 10 per cent increase over 1965.

Hog prices of $28.25 a hundred at the close of 1965 were about double of the price 18 months earlier. The U. S. Crop and Livestock Reporting Service estimated the 1965 pig crop at 2,096,000 head. A survey indicated farmers were planning a 7 per cent increase in pig production in 1966.

Beef marketings during 1965 were up 2 per cent over 1964. Lamb and mutton sales were down 7 per cent. Marketing of chickens through federally-inspected plants was up 7 per cent from 1964. Turkey sales were up 5 per cent. Ready availability of feed throughout most of 1965 was the reason given for high production of livestock. Substantial rains provided ideal wheat pasturing generally over the state.

Crops in 1965 were valued at nearly $100 million higher than the previous year, according to Kansas Crop and Livestock Reporting Service. It was the fourth best harvest of record. Value of all crops was estimated at $753,729,000. Yields in field crops were from acreages substantially lower than record production years of 1958, 1960 and 1961. Sorghum grains and corn brought record yields. Near record highs were production of hay, forage, small grains and wheat.

Wheat production in 1965 amounted to 243,-624,000 bushels, highest in the nation. It was 13 per cent above the 1964 yield and seventh largest crop of record. Yield average was 24 bushels per acre. Sorghum grain in 1965 totaled 136,710,000 bushels. It was a 39 per cent increase from 1964.

Corn had a record yield of 59 bushels per acre. It was eight bushels more than the 1952

106

record and 15 bushels per acre better than 1964. Soybean harvest was up 51 per cent from 1964 at 18,240,000 bushels. This was despite drouth which brought abandonment of 18,000 acres. Excessive winter kill hurt the barley crop. Many acres were abandoned. Oats production was up three bushels per acre from 1964 but the number of acres planted was considerably below average.

Sugar beets totaled 312,000 tons in 1965. It was the second largest crop on record. Planted acreage was down 17 per cent from 1964.

In other production, Irish potatoes produced were 190,000 hundredweights, up 6 per cent; sweet potatoes, 135,000 hundredweights, up 13 per cent; popcorn, 10,500,000 pounds, sharp increase; dry edible beans, 110,000 bags, up 43 per cent; apples 280,000 bushels, down 3 per cent; peaches, 160,000 bushels, down 9 per cent.

While income from farming during this period was at record highs, nearly a billion dollars a year was also being spent by farmers for such production items as farm machinery and equipment, petroleum, tires, fertilizers, chemicals, prepared feeds, fencing materials, seeds and other items. As each dollar of this farm income is spent, an additional three dollars worth of activity is generated in the Kansas economy, with the result that the entire agricultural industry of Kansas, fourth ranking state in the nation in acres devoted to farming, produces more than four billion dollars in income to Kansas each year.

Many projects of the research organizations in the state are agriculture-related studies, proving beneficial to business and industry.

This substantial, growing agriculture-industry complex relating to the marketing and processing of farm commodities as well as servicing the producers' basic requirements is referred to as agribusiness.

Years of research, much of it still being carried on through Kansas' scientific-research facilities, has led to discovery of new uses for agricultural products which can be manufactured right in the area. Other research projects have effected entirely new marketing channels for Kansas' agricultural production.

These developments, evidencing the technological advances made in the state in recent years, have added new vitality to the area's agricultural economy, both through investment in capital expenditures for new industries as well as creation of new employment.

Typical Kansas agribusiness enterprises are large automated livestock feeding operations; Lawrence's farm chemical manufacturing plant; and some of the world's largest grain elevators, this one located at Hutchinson.

107

First completed building of Agricultural Hall of Fame and National Center.

AGRICULTURAL HALL OF FAME

A $6 million tribute to agriculture is now taking shape 12 miles west of Kansas City. Here, on a rolling 275-acre tract surrounded by an additional 350-acres of beautiful park ground is the first' of several buildings which will comprise the Agricultural Hall of Fame and National Center. It is located at the Bonner Springs interchange of the Kansas Turnpike and just off highways US 24 and 40.

In the spring of 1965, the First Hall with its numerous exhibits and displays was opened to the public. During the four-month tourist season thousands of American and foreign visitors have passed through its doors.

The role of this huge Center will be to provide a year-round exhibit depicting the past, present and future of agriculture and agribusiness. Another aim of the Center is to develop a greater understanding between rural and urban groups, the producer and consumer of food. It is designed to become an education display and to give state, national and international visitors an opportunity to learn of the competition involved in the operation of a private enterprise system.

The Agricultural Hall of Fame and National Center is a nationwide project. Oliver Wilhem, president of Oklahoma State University, is president; Harry Bryson is executive secretary. A Board of Governors comprised of 149 agriculture and business leaders are responsible for establishing policies of this National Center. Fund raising campaigns are being conducted now or planned for the future with quotas for each state.

First Hall is a general purpose building housing administrative headquarters and a large Exhibition Hall with exhibits showing the development of farm machinery and other automated devices that have made changes in farming methods and family living. Future buildings will include: a Hall of States, a Hall of Industry, a Livestock Building, an Agronomy Hall, an Association Display Hall, an Auditorium, and other buildings as the need arises. Other areas will show restoration and replicas of historical buildings, a country village, a children's farm and plots to display new varieties in horticulture, agronomy and forestry as they are developed. An outdoor amphitheater and area of demonstration of farm machinery and equipment will be included in the completed center.

Boy Scout marker along Santa Fe Trail.

Federated Church unites three major denominations.

BURLINGAME: *where the rail meets the trail*

This pleasant community midway between Topeka and Emporia keeps pace with today's progress, yet keeps its pioneer history alive, too. Burlingame strives to provide all the facilities for modern living while pointing with pride to its beginning, in 1854, as an early settlement along the famed Old Santa Fe Trail. Once it furnished many of the state's leading political figures and also was one of the principal suppliers of coal for Topeka and the Santa Fe Railway.

Since the passing of that industry, it has become the center of a diversified farming area.

The city now has a municipal electric power plant, a water and disposal system, natural gas and fire-fighting equipment serving both the town and surrounding rural area.

Recreational facilities include the new Pomona Reservoir about 15 miles distant; the Osage County Lake, 15 miles away; and Lake Wabaunsee, 25 miles. Two nearby streams are available for fishing. Quail hunting is excellent in the area. In addition, plans are being developed by a local watershed district for construction of a large flood control dam and reservoir two miles from town. This would provide an almost unlimited supply of water for both city and community.

Burlingame is located on U. S. highway 56 and is 75 miles southwest of Kansas City. It has a mayor-council form of government. There is a fully accredited grade and high school, the latter housed in a modern building constructed in 1960. Five colleges and universities are located within 45 miles.

Burlingame is the only place in Kansas where the Santa Fe Railway crosses the Old Santa Fe Trail. A small museum at the railway station contains relics of pioneer days, ranging from early railroad records and equipment to medical instruments. To preserve the town's link with its early history, the local Boy Scout organization has marked a 50-mile route along county, state and federal highways. It runs as close as possible to the original Old Trail between Burlingame and Council Grove. The route has been designated by the national Scout organization as an official hike route. A campsite has been provided near where the railroad and Trail cross, offering overnight camping facilities for Boy Scouts who come here to hike the Trail.

Colorful Kansas . . .
MINERALS

Kansas' mineral industry for many years has maintained a high and relatively stable production level. The state has ranked among the 10 leading mineral producing states for more than three decades. The 1965 production estimate was $552,430,000, according to the Kansas Geological Survey. Less than one per cent under the 1964 value of $557,931,000 — an all-time high for the state — the 1965 value completes a decade of annual mineral production values exceeding one-half billion dollars.

Manufacturers depending on minerals as a raw material source, or those engaged in the primary metals industry, will find opportunities in Kansas. Of the state's 105 counties, 103 are engaged in mineral extraction. Fifty-eight counties each produce minerals valued at $1 million or more. The four principal counties — Ellis, Barton, Russell and Butler — produce minerals valued at $20 million or more.

Possibilities are good for expanding the array of minerals being produced. Within the state, 22 minerals are produced commercially, five others are available but currently not exploited, and at least six more are known to occur, but have not been studied sufficiently to determine their commercial possibilities.

The backbone of Kansas' mineral wealth is petroleum products, chiefly crude oil and natural gas. Along with natural gas liquids and helium, the petroleum industry's contribution is about 81 per cent of the total 1965 value.

Principal products and most merchandise are gasoline and jet fuel. Together they comprise approximately 60 per cent of Kansas plant products. They add up to three billion gallons a year, or 71-plus million barrels. Kansas motorists burn a billion gallons of it. Distillate and kerosene account for 25 per cent of the products. Residual fuel, asphalt and coke account for seven per cent. Balance of the output is spread among a wide variety of products including lube oils, grease, butane, propane, naphtha and various chemical intermediates.

The Kansas refiners are: Phillips Petroleum Co., Kansas City, 70,000 barrels per day; Skelly Oil Co., El Dorado, 48,000 barrels daily; Mobil Oil Co., Augusta, 45,000 barrels; National Cooperative Refinery Assn., McPherson, 37,000 barrels; American Oil Co., division of Standard, Ind., in Neodesha, 30,600; Derby Refining Co., division of Colorado Oil & Gas Corp., Wichita, 21,000 barrels; American Petrofina, El Dorado, 20,000 barrels; APCO Oil Corp., Arkansas City, 19,500; Century Refining Co., Shallow Water, subsidiary of Panhandle Eastern Pipe Line Co., 6,000 barrels; Mid-America Refining Co., Inc., Chanute, 3,000 barrels. Vickers Refining Co., Wichita and Potwin, has shifted to manufacture of petro-chemicals, 3,000 barrels of feedstock daily.

Helium, only a few years ago a minor part of the total mineral industry, has gained increased prominence partially resulting from its use in the nation's space program. Three multi-million dollar helium extraction plants were constructed in 1963.

The world's largest salt deposits cover a wide area of Kansas, with several of the nation's most productive salt mines located in the Hutchinson-Lyons area. The state is the seventh largest producer of salt in the United States. Salt production has been on the increase since 1940, with 980,000 tons — valued at $12.4 million — produced in 1963. This was 65 per cent rock salt and 35 per cent evaporated salt. Brine, important in the manufacturing of industrial inorganic chemicals, is also produced. Meat packers, livestock raisers and leather tanners were the largest consumers of salt.

Significant sidelight to the operation of the salt mines is their development for storage of government and business records. The extensive underground reaches provide unusual safekeeping conditions as there is a total absence of water seepage, vermin and inflammable substances. A natural atmospheric condition maintains a temperature of 65-70 degrees and a humidity range from 35-50 per cent year-round in the mines, ideal conditions for the preservation of paper, film and magnetic tape. A Wichita firm, Underground Vaults & Storage, Inc., has leased 128 acres (more than 3½ times the acreage of the Pentagon at Washington) at the Carey Salt Company mines in Hutchinson for use as a records storage center.

Other mineral development involves production of coal, cement, clay and stone products. Although coal production generally has been declining since the discovery of oil and natural gas in the state, coal mined in Kansas annually has an estimated worth of $5 million-plus. Kansas has large deposits of sand and gravel. Over 80 per cent of the production is used for building and highway construction; however, sand for blasting, grinding and polishing, engines, filtration, fill, hydra-fraction, ballast, glass and other uses is produced. Sand and gravel production is near 12 million tons; 84 per cent for commercial purposes.

State Bank of Blue Rapids $1,700,000; newspaper — Blue Rapids Times. Camping, picnicking facilities and children's playground at Alcove Springs on historic grounds where travelers on the Oregon Trail camped as early as 1827. Site was named by ill-fated Donner Party and a member of the Donner Party carved the words, still visible, "Alcove Spring" on a stone. Also visible are trail ruts left by thousands of early trail travelers. Alcove Spring is at the bottom of Naomi Pike falls. Another spring has been piped for drinking water supply. Site is near fine fishing area of Blue River at north end of Tuttle Creek Reservoir. Purest gypsum in United States is mined at Blue Rapids and a wallboard plant is located at the mine site.

BLUFF CITY, Harper (G-8) pop. 159; 1 WLT; 4 AT&SF.

BOGUE, Graham (B-5) pop. 243; 1 Norton-Decatur Co-op. Electric Co., Inc.; 2 K-NG; 3 Mun.; 4 UP; 5 K-18; Farmers State Bank $1,500,000.

BONNER SPRINGS, Wyandotte (C-13) 3,568; 1 KPL; 2 Greeley Gas Co.; 3 Mun.; 4 AT&SF, KCKV, UP; 5 K-32, K-7; Commercial State Bank $4,000,000; newspaper — Chieftain Publishers.

BREWSTER, Thomas (B-2) pop. 325; 1 Great Plains Electric Co-op., Inc.; 2 K-NG; 3 Mun.; 4 CRIP; 5 US 24, K-184.

BRONSON, Bourbon (E-13) pop. 432; 1 Mun.; 2 SEKGC; 3 Mun.; 4 MP; 5 US 54, K-3; Bank of Bronson $1,700,000.

BROOKVILLE, Saline (C-8) pop. 282; 1 KPL; 3 Mun.; 4 UP; 5 US 40. The Brookville Hotel is nationally famous for its fried chicken, hot biscuits, and old-fashioned atmosphere. Built in 1870, it is probably the oldest hotel in Kansas still operating as a hotel in its original location.

BROWNELL, Ness (D-15) pop. 116; 1 WLT; 3 Mun.; 4 MP; 5 K-4.

BUCKLIN, Ford (F-5) pop. 833; 1 WLT; 2 GSC; 3 Mun.; 4 CRIP; 5 US 54, K-34; Bucklin State Bank $1,700,000; newspaper — Bucklin Banner.

BUFFALO, Wilson (F-12) pop. 412; 1 B&M Electric Service; 2 UGS; 4 MP; 5 US 75.

BUHLER, Reno (E-8) pop. 960; 1 KGE; 2 KPL; 3 Mun.; 4 SLSF; Buhler State Bank.

BUNKER HILL, Russell (C-6) pop. 219; 1 WLT; 3 Mun.; 4 UP.

BURDEN, Cowley (G-10) pop. 560; 1 City of Winfield; 2 GSC; 3 Mun.; 4 AT&SF; 5 US 160; State Bank of Burden $920,000; newspaper — Burden Times.

BURDETT, Pawnee (E-5) pop. 332; 1 KPL; 2 Individual, Bill Wiley; 3 Mun.; 4 AT&SF; 5 US 156; Burdett State Bank $1,800,000.

BURLINGAME, Osage (C-11) pop. 1,086; 1 Mun.; 2 Mun.; 3 Mun.; 4 AT&SF; 5 US 56, K-31; First State Bank $2,400,000; newspaper — Enterprise Chronicle.

*BURLINGTON, Coffey (E-10) pop. 2,233; 1 Mun.; 2 UGS; 3 Mun.; 4 AT&SF; 5 US 75; Peoples National Bank $5,400,000; newspaper — Daily Republican.
Coffey County — Earnings per cap. $1,579; sales tax collections $177,562; employed in industry 543; number of farms 1,233; crop value $6,209,560; livestock value $6,820,780; mineral production $558,000. Limestone is quarried and crushed for concrete aggregate, roadstone, riprap and agstone. Coal is strip mined near Lebo. Crude petroleum output totaled 99,000 barrels, a 2 per cent increase. Natural gas recovery doubled the previous year, totaling 200,000 cubic feet. U. S. Army Corps of Engineers completed construction of John Redmond dam and spillway and it is filled to conservation level.

BURNS, Marion (E-10) pop. 325; 1 KGE; 2 GSC; 3 Mun.; 5 US 77; Burns State Bank; newspaper — Burns News.

BURR OAK, Jewell (A-7) pop. 442; 1 WLT; 2 GSC; 3 Mun.; 4 MP; 5 K-28; Burr Oak State Bank; newspaper — Burr Oak Herald.

BURRTON, Harvey (E-8) pop. 784; 1 KGE; 2 Mun.; 3 Mun.; 4 AT&SF, SLSF; 5 US 50; State Bank of Burrton $695,000; newspaper — Burrton Graphic.

BUSHONG, Lyon (D-11) pop. 60; 1 KPL; 4 MP.

BUSHTON, Rice (D-7) pop. 442; 1 KPL; 2 KPL; 3 Mun.; 4 MP; 5 K-171; Bushton State Bank; newspaper — Bushton News.

BYERS, Pratt (F-6) pop. 60; 1 WLT.

A favorite spot below the dam.

BURLINGTON: *catfish capital*
located on international highway

Fishing is fine here in the Neosho River and in more than 2,000 nearby farm ponds which are stocked for anglers. Most farm ponds are open to the public for fishing.

The $32 million John Redmond Reservoir was completed recently just above Burlington on the Neosho. Built for flood control and water conservation, the reservoir also brings to the community excellent facilities for fishing, duck hunting, boating and other water sports.

Burlington is known as the "Catfish Capitol of the World." One of the city's major businesses deals in live and prepared bait and fishing supplies.

Other business firms here manufacture fire trucks, agricultural lime, sand, gravel and other building materials. The city has an industrial fund tax levy to aid new and existing industries. Downtown stores have completed extensive remodeling projects. Fifty homes and three churches were constructed the past five years. Also finished recently was an elementary school with cafeteria. There is a 22-bed county hospital. A National Guard armory, built in 1955, is the center for civic and community functions.

Burlington is outspoken about the congeniality of its citizens. Residents meet on downtown streets, golf course, municipal swimming pool and at beautiful Kelley Park for football and baseball games. Always there's that good fellowship atmosphere that makes folks welcome. There's no such thing as a stranger in Burlington.

The city has an unusually large business district and a municipally-owned electrical utility plant. Burlington is the home of the Coffey County Fair, oldest continuous annual fair in the state. The city is located on Highway U. S. 75, the nation's only truly international highway. U. S. 75 extends from Galveston, Tex., to Winnipeg, Ontario, Canada.

Colorful Kansas ...

RESEARCH

Kansas business and industry rely heavily on the state's 18 colleges and universities for valuable technical assistance and a ready source of highly trained personnel. At the University of Kansas in Lawrence are the Center for Research in Business, Center for Engineering Research, and Nuclear Reactor Center. Kansas State University in Manhattan maintains continuing research projects in its world renowned milling industry complex; its engineering, veterinary medicine, home economics and agriculture schools; its Institute for Environmental Research; and nuclear engineering department, including a Triga Mark II Reactor.

Several prominent research organizations in the area direct major scientific projects. Midwest Research Institute has undertaken studies to explore new and expanded uses for the state's raw materials as well as more extensive industrial use of agricultural products.

Menninger Foundation in Topeka, long recognized as the world's leading mental health center, has developed clinical research and other experimental projects which have established new concepts in the prevention and treatment of mental illness. Pioneering studies in industrial mental health also are in progress at Menninger's. Its executive seminars have gained widespread distinction among the nation's leading corporations.

The State Geological Survey at KU encourages the manufacture of mineral products resulting from its discovery and research. Significant research is being conducted at KU's Medical Center and its Communicable Disease Center. Agri Research in Manhattan is involved in studies of uses of agricultural materials while Morris Research Laboratory, Topeka, specializes in animal nutrition and disease research projects.

115

Pleasant residential area.

CLAY CENTER: *adds industry to*
agricultural economy

Primarily a farm marketing center on the Republican River, Clay Center has made significant strides in manufacturing the past 10 years.

The Chamber of Commerce organized an industrial development corporation. One of the corporation's first successes was financial aid which lured a young Gilmore-Tatge Manufacturing Company here from Osborne, Kans. Extensive remodeling of an old slaughterhouse provided a home for the manufacturer of grain dryers and other lines of agricultural machinery. Today, the company makes 16 items of agricultural machinery. Products are sold over the United States and Canada.

Gilmore-Tatge employs about 90 persons. Annual payroll is just under $500,000. Three years ago employment was 35. Business growth necessitated a move to a new plant. Continued success brought construction of two additional buildings in 1965. The original plant was sold to Simlo Corporation, grain elevator equipment manufacturer, which employed 56 at the close of 1965.

Hutchinson Manufacturing Company moved to Clay Center in 1957 and now employs 90 people to make all types of grain conveying equipment. The present factory covers 26,000 square feet with an addition of 25,000 square feet under construction. The firm sells its product in 48 states, Canada and foreign countries.

In 1964, the industrial development corporation financed construction of the Key Milling Company's first poultry house. Its business was egg production. A second poultry house was built early in 1965. The company has 20,000 laying hens. Key Milling currently is considering supplying canned eggs under a military contract.

Kansas State Highway Department has a division office here. Sixty-four employes maintain state highways in a multi-county area.

Clay Center's approach to gaining new industry has been to "get what you can when you can." New industries in November, 1965, were a honey processing plant and a golf cart manufacturing company. New buildings were under construction for both.

Community support enabled all new industries here to begin small and experience "phenomenal growth."

Nearly $500,000 in new building permits were issued here in 1965. Thirty-two new homes were built. Thirteen more were moved here from the Wakefield area.

Clay Center, population just under 5,000, is government seat of Clay County. The city has mayor-council form of government. A new $1.5 million community high school, with accommodations for 750 students, was completed in 1963.

Extensive improvements have been made in recent years by businesses in the 13 block downtown area. Seventeen buildings were remodeled or had new store fronts added in a two-year period.

Annual sale of crops and livestock exceed $13 million in the county. Principal crops are corn, wheat, milo and legumes.

Clay Center is 30 miles from Tuttle Creek Reservoir with its abundance of recreational attractions. Milford Reservoir, which will be completed in 1966, has between 300 and 400 miles of shoreline in Clay County.

The city has municipally-owned power, water and sewage plant utilities and a swimming pool. There are 30.5 acres of parks in the immediate area.

Research institutions and an engineering school are 38 miles from Clay Center at Kansas State University, Manhattan.

Gilmore-Tatge Manufacturing Company, lured to city by industrial development corporation.

Owners of Key Milling Company, John McKee and son Jack, talk over egg production at their farm southeast of the city. Some of their 20,000 laying hens can be seen in the background.

Hutchinson Manufacturing Company makes grain conveying equipment.

Colorful Kansas . . .
RECREATION AND CULTURE

Something for every taste, indoors or out, the year around! This is the goal in planning for cultural, artistic and recreational opportunities in Kansas. At present, many thousands find cultural fulfillment in art galleries, orchestral groups such as Topeka's Civic Symphony, choral, music and theater groups, libraries, museums and such historical collections as Abilene's Eisenhower Center and Presidential Library.

The centers for cultural activity are usually the state's colleges and universities. The University of Kansas, for example, has an outstanding museum of art and museum of natural history which annually attract more visitors than its football games. The state's progressive urban centers also support organizations, events and institutions fostering greater appreciation of the fine arts and performing arts.

An important new development on the Kansas scene was the creation, early in 1966, of the state's Cultural Arts Commission. Kansas is one of the early states to have an arts council to encourage, develop and coordinate the cultural arts. Gov. William Avery, indicating it will become a positive force in Kansas' future, appointed 12 people from different parts of the state to this commission. Martin Umansky of Wichita is president; Mrs. Jerry Moxley of Council Grove, vice president; and Mrs. Paul Ward of Hays, secretary-treasurer.

"First business of our group," according to Umansky, "is to inventory the state's cultural assets, which are *many* and *varied*." He said the commission then will evaluate its findings and seek means of better communication among local groups fostering the arts. As projects and needs develop, the group will be available for advice and guidance. Many facets of culture are represented on the commission — music, drama, painting, photography,

118

radio and television, sculpture, architecture, literature, dance, allied arts and patrons of the arts.

Far reaching results of an active water conservation and reclamation program are becoming apparent in Kansas. Major dams — some completed and others under construction or in various stages of planning — have created new reservoirs of water for industrial and recreational uses. They also have created a rising interest in water sports, boating, fishing and camping activities while providing new impetus to a growing tourist industry.

In a report to the 1965 Legislature, the Governor's Advisory Council on Outdoor Recreation stressed that demands for this type of recreation are increasing at a fast pace. It estimated that attendance at recreational facilities in Kansas will more than double by 1975, from over eight million annually at present to over 17 million. This will be the result of growth in population, mobility of the population, increased income, and an increase in leisure time. Existing public and private recreation resources in 1965 approached 289,-000 acres. This area was developed approximately one-third by the federal government, one-third by state and local governments, and one-third private individuals. There are 35 state lakes, 11 federal reservoirs, 14 state parks and many city parks. One of the major pheasant hunting areas in the United States is in central and western Kansas, and is visited by thousands of hunters during the autumn shooting season. Quail and dove are usually abundant. Ducks and wild geese also frequent Kansas' many rivers, lakes and streams. Several major waterfowl migration routes cross the area and one of the nation's outstanding migratory waterfowl refuges is located here.

Golf's widespread, year-round popularity is due partly to the generally mild climate in

Kansas. One of the many outstanding golf courses here is located at Hutchinson and was the site of the 1964 U. S. Women's Amateur Golf Championship.

Contrary to popular misconception, the state has many picturesque and scenic drives. The surface features range from gently rolling to irregular countryside, dominated by the expansive plains. There are unlimited opportunities to study the state's colorful history at more than 350 historic sites and museums.

Officers' quarters at old Fort Larned.

CALDWELL, Sumner (G-8) pop. 1,738; 1 WLT; 2 WLT; 3 WLT; 4 AT&SF, CRIP; 5 US 81, K-49; Caldwell State Bank, Stock Exchange Bank $7,300,000; newspaper — Caldwell Messenger. On the Chisholm Trail, Caldwell was wild and wooly in the 1880's, when it was receiving thousands of Texas cattle for shipment by rail. A historical marker on US 81, one mile south of town, marks the place where the Chisholm Trail entered Kansas. The Border Queen Museum is located here.

CAMBRIDGE, Cowley (G-10) pop. 148; 1 KGE; 2 GSC; 4 AT&SF; 5 US 160.

CANEY, Montgomery (G-11) pop. 2,711; 1 Caney Electric Co.; 2 UGS; 3 Mun.; 4 AT&SF, MP; 5 US 166, US 75; Caney Valley National Bank $3,300,000; newspaper — Chronicle.

CANTON, McPherson (D-9) pop. 850; 1 KPL; 2 KPL; 3 Mun.; 4 AT&SF, CRIP; 5 K-86; Farmers State Bank, State Bank of Canton $3,000,000; newspaper — Canton Pilot. Six miles north of Canton is the Maxwell State Game Preserve with buffalo, elk, deer, beaver and other native animals and birds. A lookout tower is available and also at the site is a 47-acre State Lake with concession and campsites. The preserve has one of the state's largest herds of buffalo. With a sense of humor its two water towers are designated "Hot" and "Cold."

CARBONDALE, Osage (C-12) pop. 925; 1 KPL; 3 Mun.; 4 AT&SF; 5 US 75.

CARLTON, Dickinson (D-9) pop. 66; 1 KPL; 4 MP; 5 K-4.

CASSODAY, Butler (E-10) pop. 126; 1 KPL; 4 AT&SF; 5 KTA, I-35, K-13.

CAWKER CITY, Mitchell (B-7) pop. 743; 1 KPL; 2 Mun.; 4 MP; 5 US 24, K-9; Farmers & Merchants State Bank $1,500,000; newspaper — Cawker City Ledger. It is on the banks of the Glen Elder Reservoir.

CEDAR, Smith (A-6) pop. 63; 1 WLT; 4 MP; 5 K-9.

CEDAR POINT, Chase (E-10) pop. 97; 1 KPL; 4 AT&SF; 5 US 50; Cedar Point State Bank $885,000.

CEDAR VALE, Chautauqua (G-10) pop. 758; 1 Caney Valley Electric Co-op. Assn.; 2 UGS; 3 Mun.; 4 MP; 5 US 166; Cedar Vale National Bank $2,700,000; newspaper — Cedar Vale Messenger. City has a miniature village which contains 54 buildings, all replicas of early day and present buildings in the city. This "Quail Heaven" of the Flint Hills region is located on picturesque Big Caney River, a fine fishing stream. On Main Street is a handcrafted steam engine about 50 years old.

CENTRALIA, Nemaha (A-11) pop. 544; 1 Mun.; 2 KPL; 3 Mun.; 4 MP; 5 K-187, K-9; First

National Bank of Centralia $2,000,000; newspaper — Nemaha County Journal-Leader & Sun Press.

CHANUTE, Neosho (F-12) pop. 10,532; 1 Mun.; 2 Mun.; 3 Mun.; 4 AT&SF, MKT; 5 US 169, K-57, K-39; 7 Chanute Junior College; Bank of Commerce, First National Bank $20,500,000; newspapers — Chanute Publishing Co., Chanute Tribune. The late Osa Johnson, a native of Chanute, and her husband, Martin Johnson, noted explorers, are buried here. The Safari Museum contains trophies and souvenirs of their African trips. There is a herd of buffalo 12 miles west of Chanute.

CHAPMAN, Dickinson (C-9) pop. 1,079; 1 Mun.; 2 KPL; 3 Mun.; 4 UP; 5 K-206; Chapman State Bank $2,100,000; newspaper — Chapman Advertiser.

CHASE, Rice (D-7) pop. 858; 1 KPL; 2 GSC; 3 Mun.; 4 AT&SF; 5 US 56, K-96; Chase State Bank $701,000; newspaper — Chase Index.

CHAUTAUQUA, Chautauqua (G-11) pop. 139; 1 Caney Valley Electric Co-op. Assn.; 2 UGS; 5 K-99.

CHENEY, Sedgwick (F-8) pop. 1,131; 1 KGE; 2 Tri-County Gas, Inc.; 3 Mun.; 4 AT&SF; Citizens State Bank $4,100,000; newspaper — Cheney Sentinel.

CHEROKEE, Crawford (F-13) pop. 862; 1 KGE; 2 AG; 3 Mun.; 4 SLSF, MP; 5 US 160, K-7.

CHERRYVALE, Montgomery (G-12) pop. 2,864; 1 KGE; 2 GSC; 3 Mun.; 4 AT&SF, SLSF; 5 US 169, US 160; Peoples State Bank $4,000,000; newspaper — Cherryvale Republican. The Bender Museum here is a replica of the home of the infamous Bender family which killed and robbed numerous travelers about 1871-73, vanished and were never brought to trial. Mannequins reenact one of the crimes in the Bender Museum.

CHETOPA, Labette (G-13) pop. 1,556; 1 Mun.; 2 T-CG; 3 Mun.; 4 MKT, MP; 5 US 166, US 59; Chetopa State Bank, $2,200,000; newspaper — Chetopa Advance.

*CIMARRON, Gray (F-4) pop. 1,239; 1 Mun.; 2 NNG; 3 Mun.; 4 AT&SF; 5 US 50, K-23; First National Bank $3,000,000; newspaper — The Jacksonian. Cimarron Crossing Park, on the Arkansas River, marks a noted crossing and a short cut on the old Santa Fe Trail; also favorite crossing of Indians. A pioneer museum is housed in the city hall. North of US 50 may be seen remnants of the Soule Irrigation Ditch built in the 1880's by a New York patent medicine millionaire. Stretching from Ingalls for about 75 miles east, it was intended to transform the prairie into a Garden of Eden.

Gray County — Earnings per cap. $1,499; sales tax collections $120,629; employed in industry 309; number of farms 617; crop value $6,126,870; livestock value $3,779,950; mineral production $55,700.

CIRCLEVILLE, Jackson (B-11) pop. 156; 1 KPL; 5 K-79; Farmers State Bank $1,300,000.

CLAFLIN, Barton (D-7) pop. 1,012; 1 KPL; 2 KPL; 3 Mun.; 4 MP; 5 K-45, K-4; Farmers & Merchants State Bank $5,000,000; newspaper — Claflin Clarion.

*CLAY CENTER, Clay (B-9) pop. 4,938; 1 Mun.; 2 KPL; 3 Mun.; 4 CRIP, UP; 5 US 24, K-15; The Peoples National Bank, Union State Bank $12,500,000; newspapers — Clay Center Times, Clay Center Dispatch.

Clay County — Earnings per cap. $1,814; sales tax collections $356,460; employed in industry 1,164; number of farms 1,207; crop value $6,683,930; livestock value $6,449,340; mineral production $92,366. Sand and gravel for building, paving and fill purposes are produced. Slightly over 6,000 barrels of crude petroleum is produced.

CLAYTON, Norton-Decatur (A-4) pop. 154; 1 Norton-Decatur Co-op. Electric Co., Inc.; 3 Mun.; 4 CRIP; 5 US 383.

CLEARWATER, Sedgwick (F-8) pop. 1,240; 1 KGE; 2 UGSv; 3 Mun.; 4 MP; Home State Bank $3,000,000.

CLIFTON, Wasington-Clay (B-9) pop. 831; 1 WLT; 2 KPL; 3 Mun.; 4 CRIP, MP; 5 K-9; First National Bank $1,100,000; newspaper — Clifton News.

CLIMAX, Greenwood (F-11) pop. 66; 1 KPL; 4 AT&SF; 5 K-99.

CLYDE, Cloud (B-9) pop. 999; 1 WLT; 2 KPL; 3 Mun.; 4 CRIP, MP; 5 K-9; Elk State Bank, Exchange National Bank $3,600,000; newspaper — Clyde Republican.

Colorful Kansas...
MANPOWER

The selection of a location for a new facility, whether it be a petrochemical plant or an insurance company's regional office building, is greatly influenced by the local labor market. In Kansas, an adequate labor supply, a good wage level, and constructive union activities combine to provide favorable conditions.

The constantly declining need for farm workers, the steady arrival of young people in the labor group for the first time, plus a consistently expanding population (50% in each of the last two decades) combine with reduced demands in defense manufacturing to produce this sizable labor force.

The distribution of nonagricultural workers has changed in the last decade. The numbers of workers in manufacturing, government, service, trade, construction, finance, insurance and real estate activities have increased substantially. These categories will continue to demand the greatest share of the labor supply in the future. Evidence of productive efficiency is underscored by the record of growth established by Kansas manufacturers which compete on a national level. Top executives in many of these firms express the opinion that Kansas is suited to industrial development because its people have a high aptitude for understanding and operating complicated precision equipment. The companies "get a full measure of sincere work effort from the personnel," as one administrator said.

Kansans also have one of the nation's highest literacy rates; a low drop-out rate in high school; and a high proportion of college age students in college. The resulting high intelligence level has helped them adapt to the area's rapid technological changes and given them the means to improve their technical skills.

Colorful Kansas...
SCHOOLS

Kansas has the second highest percentage in the nation of school-age population enrolled in full-time public elementary and secondary schools with 94 per cent. There are 47 institutions of higher learning, including 26 four-year colleges and universities, and 21 junior colleges.

COLLEGES AND UNIVERSITIES

State

University of Kansas	Lawrence
Kansas State University	Manhattan
Kansas State Teachers College	Emporia
Kansas State College of Pittsburg	Pittsburg
Fort Hays Kansas State College	Hays
Wichita State University	Wichita

Municipal

Washburn University	Topeka

Private

Baker University	Baldwin
Bethany College	Lindsborg
Bethel College	North Newton
Central Baptist Theological Seminary	Kansas City
College of Emporia	Emporia
Friends College	Wichita
Kansas Wesleyan University	Salina
Manhattan Bible College	Manhattan
Marymount College	Salina
McPherson College	McPherson
Mt. St. Scholastica College	Atchison
Ottawa University	Ottawa
Sacred Heart College	Wichita
St. Benedict's College	Atchison
St. Mary College	Xavier
St. Mary of the Plains	Dodge City
Southwestern College	Winfield
Sterling College	Sterling
Tabor College	Hillsboro

PUBLIC COMMUNITY JUNIOR COLLEGES

Allen County CJC	Iola
Arkansas City CJC	Arkansas City
*Barton County CJC	Great Bend
Butler County CJC	El Dorado
Cloud County CJC	Concordia
Coffeyville CJC	Coffeyville
Colby CJC	Colby
Dodge City CJC	Dodge City
Fort Scott CJC	Fort Scott
Garden City CJC	Garden City
Highland CJC	Highland
Hutchinson CJC	Hutchinson
Independence CJC	Independence
Kansas City, Kansas, CJC	Kansas City
Labette CJC	Parsons
Neosho County CJC	Chanute
Pratt CJC	Pratt

*Scheduled to open September, 1967

PRIVATE TWO-YEAR COLLEGES

Central College	McPherson
Donnelly College	Kansas City
Hesston College	Hesston
Miltonvale Wesleyan College	Miltonvale
St. Johns College	Winfield

AREA VOCATIONAL SCHOOLS

Beloit • Coffeyville • Newton (Hutchinson, Newton, McPherson region) • Emporia • Topeka Goodland • Salina • Dodge City

Aerial view of Acme Foundry & Machine Company.

ACME OF COFFEYVILLE: *foundry,*
machine company serves Kansas over 50 years

Officers and employees of a Coffeyville foundry can look back with pride on more than 50 years of service to Kansas. However, they choose to look ahead to continued progress in the future.

The Acme Foundry & Machine Company manufactures a diversified line of castings for all types of manufacturers. These include producers of transmission equipment, valves, machine tools, pumps, road machinery, laundry machinery, oil field and refinery equipment.

Acme castings are shipped to all points of the United States, and some ultimately find their way overseas as parts of customers' finished products.

Incorporated in October, 1914, Acme purchased the old Coffeyville Foundry Company, then consisting of one foundry building 50' x 100' and one machine shop building, about 40' x 80'. There were 40 employees at that time.

Since then, Acme has expanded to a total of 28 buildings housing a gray iron foundry, machine shop, pattern shop, oil field and industrial supply division, welding shop and warehouses. Total employment is now 190 employees.

Iron being poured into molds from one of the ladles.

Spo molding machines in operation.

Molten iron being tapped from cupola.

COATS, Pratt (F-6) pop. 168; 1 Mun.; 4 AT&SF; Coats State Bank $1,650,000.

COFFEYVILLE, Montgomery (G-12) pop. 16,738; 1 Mun.; 2 UGS; 3 Mun.; 4 AT&SF, MKT, MP; 5 US 169, US 166; 6 CEN 7 Coffeyville College (Jr.); Condon National Bank, First National Bank $22,600,000; newspapers — Coffeyville Daily Journal, Coffeyville Press. The Dalton family of desperadoes made their bloody raid on the city Oct. 5, 1892, in an attempt to rob two banks at the same time. Still to be seen is Death Alley down which the gang raced to their horses through a withering crossfire from aroused citizens. Three members of the gang, Bob and Grat Dalton and Bill Powers, are buried in Elmwood Cemetery. Dalton Museum is open daily; mementoes of gun battles and replica of frontier street included in displays. Mementoes of Walter Johnson, famous baseball pitcher, are also in the museum and a memorial to Johnson is in Memorial Park.

°COLBY, Thomas (B-2) pop. 4,248; 1 Mun.; 2 K-NG; 3 Mun.; 4 CRIP, UP; 5 US 24, K-25; 7 Colby Jr. College; Farmers & Merchants State Bank, Thomas County National Bank $16,800,000; newspapers — Prairie Printer, Inc., Colby Free Press Tribune. Tourist attraction is Sod Town two miles east of Colby on US 24, headquarters for the organization "Sons and Daughters of the Soddie." Anyone who has lived or attended church or Sunday School in a sod house is eligible for membership.

Thomas County — Earnings per cap. $2,259; sales tax collections $291,402; employed in industry 878; number of farms 672; crop value $6,323,020; livestock value $4,334,680; mineral production $75,970. Produced is sand and gravel for building, paving, fill and road maintenance.

°COLDWATER, Comanche (G-5) pop. 1,061; 1 WLT; 2 KPL; 3 WLT; 4 AT&SF; 5 US 183, US 160; Coldwater National Bank, Peoples State Bank $4,000,000; newspapers — Western, Star. Rich Rose Ranch, 5½ miles southwest of Coldwater, attracts thousands of visitors annually showing hundreds of varieties of newest championship roses. Display rosarian shows over 1,200 roses in spring. Open May 15 to October 15. Coldwater is home of historical "Comanche Pool" which once had 84,000 acres of pasture inside one fence.

Comanche County — Earnings per cap. $1,661; sales tax collections $81,932; employed in industry 189; number of farms 333; crop value $1,781,240; livestock value $4,646,380; mineral production $1,161,448. Marketed production of natural gas was 7.5 billion cubic feet, an increase of 26 per cent. Exploratory drilling resulted in discovery of Tuttle East gas field. Output of crude petroleum increased to 73,000 barrels. Gravel for paving was produced by various operators.

°COLUMBUS, Cherokee (G-13) pop. 3,374; 1 EDE; 2 AG; 3 Mun.; 4 SLSF, MKT, NEO; 5 US 69, K-96, K-7; Columbus State Bank, First National Bank $9,500,000; newspapers — Modern Light, Columbus Daily Advocate. Columbus is a coal, lead and zinc center. It is the site of some of the finest strip pit fishing in the world. Within the area are underground mine tours. One of the largest electric shovels in the U. S. is in operation nearby.

Cherokee County — Earnings per cap. $1,579; sales tax collections $403,622; employed in industry 2,974; number of farms 1,347; crop value $7,782,150; livestock value $3,054,640; mineral production $4,668,310. County ranked first in coal production. Coal was strip mined by Pittsburg & Midway Coal Co., Wilkinson Coal Co., and Black Diamond Coal Co. Pittsburg & Midway Coal Co. completed construction of a 90-cubic-yard shovel at its strip mine near Hallowell. The entire production of lead and zinc in Kansas was mined in Cherokee County. Miscellaneous stone (chats) was produced by The Eagle-Picher Co. and Southwest Rock & Chat Co. for railroad ballast, concrete aggregate and roadstone. Acme Brick Co. (formerly United Brick & Tile Co.) mined miscellaneous clay for manufacturing building brick near Weir.

COLWICH, Sedgwick (F-8) pop. 785; 1 KGE; 2 Arkansas-Louisiana Gas; 4 MP; 5 K-96.

COLONY, Anderson (E-12) pop. 418; 1 KGE; 2 GSC; 3 Mun.; 4 AT&SF; 5 US 169, US 59.

°CONCORDIA, Cloud (B-8) pop. 7,391; 1 WLT; 2 KPL; 3 Mun.; 4 AT&SF, CB&Q, MP, UP; 5 US 81, K-28, K-9; Cloud County Bank, Fidelity State Bank, First National Bank $11,000,000; newspapers — The Kansan, The Blade Empire. Concordia is the home of the Nazareth Motherhouse and Novitiate for Sisters of St. Joseph. A plaque marks the Kansas homestead of Boston Corbett, the man who shot John Wilkes Booth, assassin of President Abraham Lincoln. The Cloud County Junior College was established in 1964.

Colorful Kansas . . .

BUSINESS, INDUSTRY

Kansas' traditional agricultural economy is being reshaped by industrial development. Manufacturing payrolls now constitute the largest single source of annual personal income.

Hundreds of new industries began operations in Kansas since 1960. Growing population and rising per capita consumption assures unlimited growth to a company which meets its consumer's demands.

Manufacturers in Kansas produce chemicals, batteries, cellophane, plastics, cement, minerals, flour, petroleum products, meat, clothing, heavy metal castings, machinery, railroad and automotive equipment and aircraft.

Kansas government has provided a favorable climate of operations for industry. New state programs assist in the expansion of existing business and industry, as well as new enterprises.

Kansas Research Foundation has been inventorying public and private research efforts to coordinate and urge research among all facets of business and industry. The Office of Economic Analysis reports on the Kansas economy. The State Department of Economic Development directs a broad program for making industrial climate more favorable in Kansas.

Kansas has ranked among the top 10 mineral producing states for more than 30 years. Production exceeded the $500 million mark for nine consecutive years. Most of this production has been crude oil and natural gas, primarily from western and south central Kansas. Production of helium added to the industry in 1963 with the construction of three extracting plants.

Cloud County — Earnings per cap. $1,745; sales tax collections $454,284; employed in industry 1,634; number of farms 1,112; crop value $9,052,500; livestock value $4,434,520; mineral production $582,220. County ranked first in value of clay production. Cloud Ceramics mined fire clay for manufacturing building brick. Quarried and crushed limestone produced for concrete aggregate and roadstone as well as dimension limestone. Also produces sand and gravel for building, paving and fill uses.

CONWAY SPRINGS, Sumner (F-8) pop. 1,145; 1 WLT; 2 UGSv; 3 Mun.; 4 MP; 5 K-49; First National Bank, State Bank of Conway Springs $2,500,000; newspaper — The Star.

COOLIDGE, Hamilton (E-1) pop. 133; 1 Wheatland Electric Co-op., Inc.; 2 Thornburgh Gas; 3 Mun.; 4 AT&SF; 5 US 50. Twelve miles south of town is the Hamilton Sink, a depression about 100 feet in diameter and about 50 feet deep. In the vicinity of Coolidge are several artesian wells.

COPELAND, Gray (F-3) pop. 261; 1 WLT; 2 NNG; 3 Mun.; 4 AT&SF; 5 US 56.

CORNING, Nemaha (A-11) pop. 203; 1 KPL; 4 MP; 5 K-63, K-9; Farmers State Bank $640,000.

°COTTONWOOD FALLS, Chase (D-10) pop. 958; 1 KPL; 2 Cottonwood Falls Gas; 3 Mun.; 4 AT&SF; 5 K-13; Exchange National Bank $2,805,000; newspaper — Chase County Leader-News. The Chase County courthouse built in 1870's is admired for its Monsard roof architecture. Knute Rockne monument is 13 miles southeast of here near K-13. The Roniger Memorial Museum contains Indian artifacts, stuffed native animals and local historical mementoes. Beautiful Chase County State Lake is 3 miles west.

Chase County — Earnings per cap. $1,417; sales tax collections $84,946; employed in industry 184; number of farms 432; crop value $3,028,650; livestock value $7,965,720; mineral production $360,923. Petroleum production totaled 72,500 barrels, a decrease of 16 per cent. Secondary recovery operations accounted for most of the production. Natural gas recovery totaled 77 million cubic feet, an increase of 127 per cent. Limestone is mined and crushed for concrete aggregate, roadstone, riprap and agstone. Dimension limestone was prepared by J. T. Lardner Cut Stone Co., Bayer Stone Co., and H. J. Born Stone Co.

°COUNCIL GROVE, Morris (D-10) pop. 2,654; 1 KPL; 2 Home Gas Co.; 3 Mun.; 4 MP; 5 US 56, K-57, K-13; Council Grove National Bank, Farmers & Drovers Bank $7,500,000; newspaper — Council Grove Republican. Council Grove is the most historic town on the old Santa Fe Trail. For many years it was the last outfitting post between the Missouri River and Santa Fe. Two trees on Main Street are Post Office Oak, where letters were left for passing caravans, and the remaining stump of Council Oak, near which a treaty with the Indians was signed in 1825, giving the government the right of way for the Santa Fe Trail. Kaw Mission, a school for Indians, and one of the first in Kansas for white children, is now a state-owned museum. Council Grove Lake is 3 miles northwest of the city. Council Grove Dam and Reservoir on the Neosho was completed in 1965.

Morris County — Earnings per cap. $1,438; sales tax collections $159,953; employed in industry 608; number of farms 935; crop value $5,830,330; livestock value $7,093,940; mineral production $1,550,032. Crude petroleum production totaled 404,000 barrels, a decrease of 7 per cent. Output of natural gas decreased 17 per cent to 296 million cubic feet. Limestone was quarried and crushed for concrete aggregate, roadstone, riprap and aglime and gravel for paving and road maintenance.

COUNTRYSIDE, Johnson (C-13) pop. 421; 1 KCPL; 2 GSC; 3 Kansas City Suburban Water Co.; 5 US 69, US 56, US 50.

COURTLAND, Republic (A-8) pop. 426; 1 WLT; 2 KPL; 3 Mun.; 4 AT&SF, CRIP; 5 K-179; Swedish-American State Bank $1,400,000; newspaper — Courtland Journal; is the center of an irrigated area served by the Lovewell Reservoir.

COYVILLE, Wilson (F-11) pop. 118; 1 KPL.

CUBA, Republic (A-8) pop. 321; 1 WLT; 2 KPL; 3 Mun.; 4 CB&Q, CRIP; 5 K-139.

CULLISON, Pratt (F-6) pop. 145; 1 WLT; 2 KPL; 3 Mun.; 4 CRIP; 5 US 54.

CULVER, Ottawa (C-8) pop. 232; 1 KPL; 4 UP.

CUNNINGHAM, Kingman (F-7) pop. 570; 1 WLT; 2 KPL; 3 Mun.; 4 AT&SF; 5 US 54; First National Bank $1,300,000; newspaper — Cunningham Clipper.

Crowd gathers for 1965 Tractor Show.

COLBY: *agricultural-educational center*

Located in the heart of the Great Plains wheat country of northwest Kansas is Colby, seat of Thomas County. The city is known as "The Golden Buckle on the Wheat Belt," and serves as the trade, industrial and activity center of a nine-county area.

The Colby Experiment Station, a branch of Kansas State University, has conducted agricultural research here for 50 years. In new crops the station developed Colby milo and assisted in development of Pawnee, Comanche and Wichita wheat varieties. The station is open daily to visitors.

The city also is the home of the Colby Community College, a two-year junior college. The school is the result of long planning and intensive work of many local educators and civic leaders. Organized effort began in 1957. Progress was slow until publication of the controversial Eurich Report in 1962 which brought general public awareness to the problem of increasing college enrollments.

Promoters of a college for northwest Kansas formed a committee. Legislators from this part of Kansas introduced a bill in 1963, seeking legislative authorization for establishment of a full state-supported college here. It passed the House of Representatives but was tabled in the Senate. The Senate education committee held up consideration of the bill to await results of a study of two-year colleges in Kansas. Community support for a college continued to grow. Citizens donated $20,000 to finance preliminary work. The development committee decided to establish the college without delay.

A special election was held July 14, 1964, on the question of a five-mill tax levy to open the college that fall. The vote was 1,201 to 167 in favor of the school. An administrative officer and faculty were hired. Classes were held temporarily in the new junior high school building in 1964. Temporary classes have been established in the Colby Community Building for the 1965-66 season. Enrollment in September of 1965 was over 200. A bond election was held on Sept. 7, 1965, for construction of buildings and campus on a site obtained south of Colby near the new Interstate-70. The bond issue ($1,000,000) passed by a 90 per cent margin.

According to the Colby Board of Education: "We believe that the community college offers the best opportunity to serve the needs of the youth who wish to continue on to four or more years of advanced education, to the group who might wish to terminate their formal education at the end of two years, and to the adult population of the community who wish to add to their knowledge in their present line of work, take further work for enrichment or to enter into a new field of work."

Colby is noted for its community social events. There is an annual Gun and Coin Show in March, Chamber of Commerce banquet in April, the Northwest Home and Implement Show and the Colby Appaloosa and Quarter Horse Show both occurring in May, Thomas County Free Fair in August and Town and Country Get Together in November.

Pioneer Memorial Library was constructed recently — not by a bond issue, but by public subscription of $100,000. City taxes and gifts support the library program. The library board of directors announced plans to spend the major portion of its book budget for reference materials related to Colby Community College courses. Several branches of Colby library have been established in smaller towns nearby. A bookmobile was provided to travel throughout the community, offering books to those without access to a library.

Kansas Library Association thought so highly of the community spirit and forward-looking policies of the library staff, it nominated Pioneer Memorial Library as the only entry for its annual award in 1963.

Dedicated in 1955, Colby Community Building makes it possible for the city to host numerous state and district conventions. The building's seating capacity is 3,625. Cost of the community building was $350,000. An additional $20,000 went for equipment. A day seldom passes that the building is not in use. It is the meeting center for northwest Kansas. The Colby Community College uses some of the rooms for classes and office for temporary quarters.

Years of effort by a group of Colby men resulted in the opening of St. Thomas Hospital in 1941. Under the direction of Sisters of St. Agnes, the hospital has grown from 32 to 73 beds. It serves patients from Decatur, Gove, Logan, Rawlins, Sheridan and Sherman counties.

Colby, with a population of nearly 4,500, has a council-manager-mayor government. The police department has four officers trained in law enforcement. They operate two patrol cars. The fire department has three fulltime and 15 volunteer firemen. Reduction in fire insurance rates here in recent years is equal to many times the fire department payroll and operation cost.

The city has completed a $200,000 expansion of its sewage disposal plant and sewer systems.

The city provides a summer recreation program with organized baseball, swimming instructions, tumbling, handicrafts and other activities. Recently established was a teenage club. Boys and girls developed it into a "tropical paradise" and named it Colby Cabana.

New buildings include Radio Station KXXX, an affiliate of Columbia Broadcasting System; Thomas County Home for the Aged; Great Plains Electric Co.; Kansas State Highway Department office and shops, which also houses a branch of the Kansas Highway Patrol, and a parochial elementary school.

Many purebred cattle breeders are within a short distance of Colby. They own some of the finest bloodlines in Angus, Hereford and Shorthorn. Colby Sale Barn handles about 50,000 head of cattle a year, in addition to large numbers of sheep and hogs.

Radio station occupies new building.

*Junior High School also serves as
temporary college campus.*

DAMAR, Rooks (B-5) pop. 364; 1 WLT; 2 K-NG; 3 Mun.; 4 UP; 5 K-18.

DANVILLE, Harper (G-8) pop. 93; 1 WLT; 4 AT&SF; 5 US 160.

DEARING, Montgomery (G-12) pop. 329; 1 CEC; 2 UGS; 4 MP.

DEERFIELD, Kearny (E-2) pop. 473; 1 Wheatland Co-op.; 2 K-NG; 3 Mun.; 4 AT&SF; 5 US 50.

DELIA, Jackson (B-11) pop. 176; 1 KPL; 3 Mun.; 4 UP.

DELPHOS, Ottawa (B-8) pop. 646; 1 KPL; 2 KPL; 3 Mun.; 4 UP; 5 K-41; State Bank of Delphos $1,800,000; newspaper — Delphos Republican. Delphos was the home of Mrs. Grace Bedell Billings, the "little girl" who wrote to Abraham Lincoln suggesting that he grow a beard. The original of Lincoln's reply is at the Delphos State Bank.

DENISON, Jackson (B-12) pop. 205; 1 KPL; 3 Mun.; 5 K-16.

DENTON, Doniphan (A-12) pop. 180; 1 KPL; 4 CRIP; 5 K-20; Bank of Denton $1,300,000.

DERBY, Sedgwick (F-9) pop. 6,675; 1 KGE; 2 GSC; 3 El Paso Water Co.; 4 AT&SF; 5 K-15; Farmers & Merchants State Bank $7,500,000; newspapers — Star-Herald, Daily Reporter.

DE SOTO, Johnson (C-13) pop. 1,400; 1 Mun.; 2 Greeley Gas Co.; 3 Mun.; 4 AT&SF; 5 K-10; De Soto State Bank $2,400,000; newspaper — De Soto News.

DEXTER, Cowley (G-10) pop. 278; 1 Mun.; 2 GSC; 3 Mun.; 4 MP; 5 K-15; Farmers & Merchants State Bank $551,000.

°DIGHTON, Lane (D-3) pop. 1,741; 1 Mun.; 2 K-NG; 3 Mun.; 4 AT&SF; 5 K-96, K-23; First National Bank $5,300,000; newspaper — Herald. Dighton has a sod house on highway K-23.

Lane County — Earnings per cap. $1,668; sales tax collections $101,788; employed in industry 211; number of farms 362; crop value $4,052,580; livestock value $4,192,280; mineral production $223,357.

°DODGE CITY, Ford (F-4) pop. 13,661; 1 WLT; 2 NNG; 3 Mun.; 4 AT&SF, CRIP; 5 US 283, US 56, US 50, US 154, US 50 Alt.; 6 CEN; 7 Dodge City College (Jr.), St. Mary of the Plains College; Fidelity State Bank, First National Bank $25,000,000; newspapers — Dodge City Daily Globe, High Plains Publishers, Inc. Established in 1872, Dodge City became known as the "Queen of the Cow Towns." During the following 13 years, millions of Texas Longhorns were driven up the cattle trails from Texas, herded by hundreds of cowboys, and Dodge City became famous as "the wickedest little city in America." The cowboy statue that stands in front of the City Hall marks the site of world famous Boot Hill. Near this site is a memorial cemetery with its Hangman's Tree and museum where at least 28 unfortunate cowboys were buried "with their boots on." Inside the museum is an "open grave" and one of the finest gun collections in the country. A replica of Old Front Street allows visitors to absorb the colorful history as they stroll down the Board Walk and tour the old stores, the Beeson Museum and the Long Branch Saloon (only soft drinks are served). Five miles east of town on US 154 is old Fort Dodge, established in 1864. The first westbound pack train on the Santa Fe Trail was snow-bound four miles west of what is now Dodge City in 1823. Losing their animals, the pioneer traders cached their merchandise on the slope of a hill north of present US 50 and the depressions left by the later removal of their goods are known as The Caches.

Ford County — Earnings per cap. $1,911; sales tax collections $958,939; number of farms 1,102; crop value $6,918,380; livestock value $9,693,200; mineral production $463,373. Bucklin gas field was an important discovery. Skelly Oil Co. recovers natural gas liquids at its Minneola plant. Sand and gravel is produced mainly for building and paving.

DORRANCE, Russell (C-7) pop. 340; 1 WLT; 3 Mun.; 4 MP; 5 US 40, K-231.

DOUGLASS, Butler (F-9) pop. 1,074; 1 KGE; 2 GSC; 3 Mun.; 4 AT&SF; 5 US 77; Exchange State Bank $1,830,000; newspaper — Douglass Tribune.

DOWNS, Osborne (B-7) pop. 1,348; 1 WLT; 2 GSC; 3 Mun.; 4 MP; 5 US 24, K-181, K-9; Downs National Bank, State Bank of Downs $5,566,000; newspaper — Downs News.

DRESDEN, Decatur (A-3) pop. 129; 1 CKP; 4 CRIP; 5 US 383, K-123.

DUNLAP, Morris (D-10) pop. 138; 1 KPL.

DURHAM, Marion (D-9) pop. 158; 1 KPL; 4 CRIP; 5 K-15; Durham State Bank $723,000.

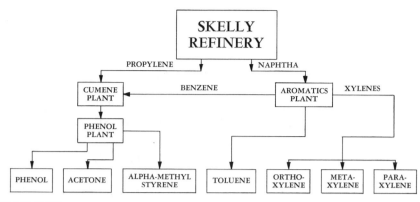

```
                    ┌──────────────┐
                    │    SKELLY    │
                    │   REFINERY   │
                    └──────────────┘
        PROPYLENE        │        NAPHTHA
    ┌──────────┐    BENZENE    ┌──────────────┐   XYLENES
    │  CUMENE  │──────────────▶│  AROMATICS   │
    │  PLANT   │               │    PLANT     │
    └──────────┘               └──────────────┘
    ┌──────────┐
    │  PHENOL  │
    │  PLANT   │
    └──────────┘
```

| PHENOL | ACETONE | ALPHA-METHYL STYRENE | TOLUENE | ORTHO-XYLENE | META-XYLENE | PARA-XYLENE |

UTILIZING ANY OF THE ABOVE CHEMICALLY-PURE PRODUCTS, YOUR PLANT IN THE CENTER OF THE UNITED STATES AT EL DORADO, KANSAS WILL ALSO BENEFIT FROM————

PLENTIFUL, LOW COST-ELECTRIC POWER —
NON-INTERRUPTIBLE NATURAL GAS

Butler County Community Junior College.

EL DORADO: *oil and college*

Raw products and finished products are the story of El Dorado, seat of Butler County.

Skelly Oil Company utilizes raw products to make a vast variety of finished commodities for commercial sale.

New Butler County Junior College (1965) turns out finished products to contribute to the usefulness and welfare of mankind.

Skelly, through operation of its highly-modern petro-chemical complex, breaks down molecules of crude petroleum, drawn from beneath the county's broad acres, into a huge number of chemically-pure products. These products form the backbone for a great array of manufacturing plants over much of the nation.

At the same time, the new community college takes Butler County's boys and girls from town and farm homes and perfects them in the art of useful occupations through first-class vocational training. It sends them into the world fully equipped for gainful jobs.

In this manner Butler County is helping to build Kansas' power and glory. The community's material resources are massive. But its human resources are just as huge and far more valuable. Its boys and girls now have opportunity to become highly skilled members of the American society through the medium of a home institution.

The county's resources go hand in hand. Their possibilities are limitless.

Flanked by oil fields, El Dorado is seat of the largest county in Kansas. Late in 1915, a wildcat oil well at the northwest edge of El Dorado converted a small town into a prosperous, progressive city. Butler County ranks among the top three or four in Kansas in petroleum production.

DWIGHT, Morris (C-10) pop. 334; 1 KPL; 4 CRIP; 5 K-57, K-4; Farmers State Bank $851,000.

EARLTON, Neosho (F-12) pop. 122; 1 City of Chanute; 2 Gamble, Anderson & Crumbley Gas Co.; 4 AT&SF; 5 US 169.

EASTBOROUGH, Sedgwick (F-9) pop. 849; 1 KGE; 2 GSC; 3 Wichita Water Co.; 5 I-35, US 54, K-96.

EASTON, Leavenworth (B-12) pop. 386; 1 KPL; 3 Mun.; 5 K-192; Easton State Bank $1,700,000.

EDGERTON, Johnson (C-13) pop. 392; 1 KCPL; 2 Mun.; 4 AT&SF; 5 US 56.

EDMOND, Norton (B-4) pop. 94; 1 CKP; 4 MP; 5 K-9.

EDNA, Labette (G-12) pop. 455; 1 KPL; 2 T-CG; 3 Mun.; 4 MP; 5 K-101; First State Bank $1,296,000; newspaper — Edna Sun.

EDWARDSVILLE, Wyandotte (C-13) pop. 498; 1 KPL; 2 UGS; 3 Wyandotte Twp. Water Works; 4 KCKV, UP; 5 K-107, K-32; Edwardsville State Bank $600,000.

EFFINGHAM, Atchison (B-12) pop. 560; 1 KPL; 3 Mun.; 4 MP; 5 US 159, K-9; Farmers & Merchants State Bank $1,412,000.

ELBING, Butler (E-9) pop. 76; 1 KGE; 2 GSC; 4 CRIP.

*EL DORADO, Butler (E-10) pop. 12,627; 1 KGE; 2 GSC; 3 Mun.; 4 AT&SF, MP; 5 US 77, US 54, K-196 Alt., K-13; 7 El Dorado Junior College; Citizens State Bank, El Dorado National Bank, Walnut Valley State Bank $21,976,000; newspapers — El Dorado Times, Butler County News, Times Publishing Co.

Butler County — Earnings per cap. $1,931; sales tax collections $1,145,008; employed in industry 5,893; number of farms 1,772; crop value $10,158,240; livestock value $12,848,020; mineral production $19,408,806. The county ranked fourth in petroleum production and sixth in total mineral production value. Petroleum output totals 6.5 million barrels. Secondary recovery operations supplied over half the crude output. Exploratory drilling resulted in discovery of three important oil fields — Benfer, Harlan and Wehrman. Mobil Oil Co. operates its refinery at Augusta. Mobil Chemical Co. produced carbon black oils and sodium cresylate solutions, using petroleum fractions as feedstock. Skelly Oil Co. operated its refinery at El Dorado and completed construction of its aromatics complex. Using naphtha fractions as feedstock, the plant produced phenol and other naphtha compounds. Vickers Refining Co., division of Vickers Petroleum Co., Inc., operated its refinery at Potwin. Vickers Petroleum Co., Inc., produced benzene, toluene, xylenes and other chemicals at its Potwin petro-chemical plant using catalytic reformate as feedstock. American Petrofina Co. of Texas operated its refinery at El Dorado. Over 121 million cubic feet of natural gas was recovered in the county. Limestone was quarried and crushed for concrete aggregate, roadstone, agstone and riprap.

ELGIN, Chautauqua (G-11) pop. 154; 1 Caney Valley Electric Co-op. Assn.; 2 UGS; 3 Mun.

ELK CITY, Montgomery (G-11) pop. 489; 1 KGE; 2 UGS; 3 Mun.; 4 AT&SF; 5 US 160, K-39; First National Bank $1,018,000; newspaper — Elk City Sun.

ELK FALLS, Elk (F-11) pop. 165; 1 KGE; 2 UGS; 4 AT&SF; 5 US 160.

*ELKHART, Morton (G-1) pop. 2,247; 1 Southwestern Public Service Co.; 2 NNG; 3 Western Gas Service Co.; 4 AT&SF; 5 US 56, K-27; First State Bank $5,718,000; newspaper — Elkhart Tri-State News. Each year in the latter part of October, cattle are rounded up by their owners in one of the last real general roundups to be witnessed in the United States. Here, working cowmen can be seen in chaps, hats and boots, skillfully herding, cutting and roping as a necessary part of their work. The area is open to the public for hunting, fishing and sightseeing.

Morton County — Earnings per cap. $2,213; sales tax collections $118,672; employed in industry 432; number of farms 288; crop value $2,191,660; livestock value $1,140,250; mineral production $16,601,741. Morton County ranked third in natural gas production with 82.5 million cubic feet. Crude petroleum output increased to more than 2.1 million barrels. Anadarko Production Co. recovered natural gas liquids at its Interstate plant near Elkhart.

ELLINWOOD, Barton (D-7) pop. 2,667; 1 Mun.; 2 KPL; 3 Mun.; 4 AT&SF; 5 US 56, K-96; The Peoples State Bank $7,620,000; newspaper — Ellinwood Leader. Three miles north of Ellinwood is the Frank W. Robl Game Refuge and Banding Station where migratory birds are banded so

Aerial view of Ehrsam plant in Enterprise.

EHRSAM'S: *worldwide market*

As a manufacturer of conveying equipment, The J. B. Ehrsam and Sons Manufacturing Company recently expanded its markets into the mining, fertilizer and aggregate industries. Further expansion is under way in general industrial conveying and vertical transportation equipment (elevators).

Near the end of 1965, the company moved its general office headquarters from Enterprise to Abilene to provide additional office space and consolidate office personnel of the firm and its three subsidiaries. Ehrsam's big plant at Enterprise will continue to manufacture conveyors, mixers, lifts, car pullers, power shovels and accessory items for all phases of the grain industry. The office move allows space for an eventual plant expansion. Ehrsam also is the leading supplier of machinery for automated gypsum wallboard plants. It designed, manufactured and installed all of the equipment for Republic Gypsum Corporation's new multimillion dollar plant at Duke, Okla., in 1964.

"Our markets are forecasting another good year for Ehrsam in 1966," said William J. Ehrsam, Jr., president - general manager. The firm grossed $10 million in 1965. Ehrsam employs nearly 600 people. Subsidiaries of the firm are Simlo, Inc., Clay Center; Ehrsam Wichita Foundry, Inc., Wichita; and Ehrsam, Inc., Elevator Division, Abilene. Simlo, which manufactures grain handling equipment, also is building a small plant at Concordia. The elevator division manufactures passenger and freight elevators. The foundry makes iron castings.

The company at Enterprise began when Jacob Ehrsam, a Swiss immigrant, built a dam and milling equipment for the Hoffman mill, owned by the town's founder, Christian Hoffman. The mill was established in 1869. Ehrsam built machinery for handling wheat and processing flour. Also in the 1890's, the firm began manufacturing iron kettles needed by many small plaster mills for cooking plaster.

Many of the company's work force are second and third generation employes. About 60 per cent live at Enterprise; the rest commute from nearby towns. The firm is establishing a national network of distributors of Ehrsam products. It has sales forces at the home plant and 15 cities over the nation.

In 1964, the firm received a $2 million contract to supply conveyors to the Post Office Department for handling mail. Recently, conveying equipment to handle fertilizer was shipped by Ehrsam to Bataan in the Philippine Islands.

Desk of automobile industrialist.

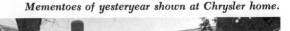

Mementoes of yesteryear shown at Chrysler home.

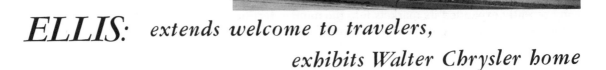

ELLIS: extends welcome to travelers, exhibits Walter Chrysler home

Civic leaders of Ellis are promoting development of their community to accommodate travelers on Interstate-70 and US 40 highways. Ellis is located midway between Kansas City and Denver.

Latest development here is an up-to-date park program. A well-planned seven-acre city park and lake area is equipped with modern restrooms, swimming pool, baseball facilities and overnight trailer park. There is a nine-hole sand green golf course. Two miles of US 40 west of the city are lined with cottonwood trees. Cedar Bluff Reservoir and Irrigation District, with 6,600 acres of water, is 18 miles southwest.

Ellis is the boyhood home of Walter P. Chrysler, automobile industrialist. The home of the man who founded Chrysler Corporation is a museum, located on US 40. An estimated 3,200 tourists visit the museum annually.

Grain, cattle, oil and Union Pacific Railroad Company shops are the principal industries here. Union Pacific employs 76. The city has 23.2 acres available for an industrial park. Ellis Industries, Inc., was opened here in October, 1965. The company manufactures metal cattle gates, stock racks and cattle chutes.

A new water tower was built in 1965 to improve water service.

Ellis YMCA is the center of activity for boys' clubs, American Legion, home demonstration units, election boards, irrigation and recreation committees, dance classes, Co-op Credit union, 4-H, wedding showers and anniversaries, railroad employee organizations, Boy and Girl Scouts, youth and old-timer parties, civic and industrial events, bowling and other sports. Daily attendance averages more than 100 throughout the year in these activities.

Nearly 1,000 boys and girls attend schools here. Washington Elementary School was built in 1962. Fort Hays State College is a 15-minute drive from Ellis.

The community of Ellis provides a senior citizens home.

Last unaltered Pony Express Station at Hanover houses a museum.

their movement across the country can be studied. Over 22,000 birds have been banded and they have been recovered in the entire North American continent, as far north as Alaska and a few as far south as South America. Hundreds of geese winter here from November to March.

ELLIS, Ellis (C-5) pop. 2,348; 1 Mun.; 2 CKP; 3 Mun.; 4 UP; 5 US 40; Ellis State Bank $2,906,000; newspaper — Ellis Review. The Walter Chrysler boyhood home is a popular tourist attraction. "Cottonwood Lane," US 40 for two miles west of Ellis is lined with cottonwood trees. Eighteen miles southwest of town is Cedar Bluff Dam and Reservoir.

°ELLSWORTH, Ellsworth (D-7) pop. 2,635; 1 WLT; 2 GSC; 3 Mun.; 4 SLSF, UP; 5 US 40, K-45, K-14; Citizens State Bank $7,329,000; newspapers — Messenger, Reporter. Ellsworth succeeded Abilene as the Northern Terminus of the Texas cattle trail in 1872. A historical museum displays pioneer artifacts. Mushroom Rocks and Red Rock Canyon are located near Carneiro, 12 miles east of Ellsworth. South on K-14 at Ash Creek, buffalo tracks still can be seen in the creek's steep sandstone banks. Kanopolis Dam and Reservoir are 18 miles southeast of Ellsworth.

Ellsworth County — Earnings per cap. $1,635; sales tax collections $189,484; employed in industry 785; number of farms 772; crop value $4,368,840; livestock value $4,388,300; mineral production $16,454,407. County ranked first in production of natural gas liquids and rock salt, and seventh in total mineral production value. Northern Gas Products Co., subsidiary of Northern Natural Gas Co., began operating its natural gas liquids extraction plant at Bushton. The company had a 2-million-barrel natural gas liquids storage facility in a salt formation in the county. Northern Helex Co., another subsidiary of Northern Natural Gas Co., operated its helium extraction plant adjacent to the natural gas liquids plant. Crude petroleum output totaled 1.6 million barrels. Gregory and Oxhide oil fields were important discoveries. Natural gas production totaled 64 million cubic feet. Independence Salt Co. mined salt near Kanopolis. Sand and gravel for building, paving and fill uses are produced. Fire clay for building brick is mined by Acme Brick Co.

ELMDALE, Chase (D-10) pop. 128; 1 KPL; 2 Kline-Roniger-Thurston Gas Co.; 3 Mun.; 4 AT&SF; 5 US 50; Peoples Exchange Bank $954,000. Nearby is Camp Wood, a YMCA boys camp.

ELSMORE, Allen (E-13) pop. 129; 2 UGS; 4 MKT; 5 K-203.

ELWOOD, Doniphan (A-13) pop. 1,296; 1 Mun., 2 GSC; 3 Mun.; 4 CRIP, UP; 5 US 36.

EMMETT, Pottawatomie (B-11) pop. 166; 1 KPL; 3 Mun.; 4 UP; 5 K-63.

Bust of
William Allen White
in Peter Pan Park.

Kansas State Teachers College, looking northeast.

EMPORIA: *rich in cultural heritage,*
city adds industrial growth

Bluestem grass and flint hills are predominant physical features of much of East Central Kansas. They provide a setting of lush, quiet beauty where thousands of cattle graze.

Within this environment is Emporia. The city appreciates the importance of its agricultural community. But it is equally proud of its own cultural, educational and industrial development. Made famous by the late William Allen White, editor of The Emporia Gazette, Emporia basically remains a college town with tree-lined streets, which the editor loved so well. The two colleges, Kansas State Teachers College and College of Emporia, more than tripled combined enrollment the past 10 years. Enrollment exceeds 7,000. College of Emporia is a Presbyterian liberal arts school. Opened here the summer of 1965 was Flint Hills Area Vocational-Technical School. Costing in excess of $600,000, it was designed to train young people in industrial and technical skills. Adults may enroll in night classes. Enrollments are from a 5½-county area.

In 1956, local businessmen financed a 160-acre industrial park at the city's west edge. Three major new industries have located in the park.

Didde-Glaser, Inc., manufactures graphic arts equipment. Forty per cent of its sales are outside of the United States — all over the world. Employment is 200. A new addition in the fall of 1965 provided new offices and nearly tripled manufacturing space. The plant located here in 1956.

Two years later came Crawford Manufacturing Company. It employs up to 280 in its peak season for manufacturing auto seat covers, marine fabric items, hassocks and decorator pillows. Products are marketed throughout the Midwest.

New in 1965 was Interstate Bakeries Corporation. The city issued $3.5 million in industrial revenue bonds to finance the major part of the plant cost. About 200 employees produce cakes for distribution in 12 to 15 states.

Sauder Tank Company, established in 1954, manufactures tanks of all kinds and oil field equipment. Missile fuel storage tanks are made here. Twice expanded, the company is planning further enlargement. Aeroglide Corporation produces large commercial grain driers in Emporia. Future plans are for considerable expansion. Hopkins Manufacturing Company produces a wide range of high quality automotive accessories and related items.

Armour and Company established a beef abattoir here in 1964. Prime Flint Hills beef fattened in this area reaches a nationwide market. More than four hundred carcasses are shipped daily by Armour.

Soybeans shipped here from Eastern Kansas and Western Missouri are processed at Kansas Soya Products Company. Storage capacity is 1,550,000 bushels. Wheat, corn and milo also are processed here. Second largest soybean processing mill in Kansas, the firm has branch elevators at Hartford and Sharp, Kansas.

In recent years, Emporia has experienced a quiet but solid boom in educational and industrial growth. All indications are the city will continue to flourish. Founded in 1857, Emporia was not long in becoming a center of higher education. A legislative act of 1863 established a state normal school here. It opened in 1865 with 18 students. Further educational and cultural progress was made in 1882 when the Presbyterian Synod voted to establish College of Emporia. Santa Fe Railroad reached here in 1870 with the aid of two Lyon County bond issues totaling $400,000 to help finance construction.

William Allen White purchased The Emporia Gazette in 1895. Three years later, he and Emporia became famous because of White's editorial "What's the Matter With Kansas?" His was one of the most influential and widely quoted small newspapers in the nation. White wrote that Kansas does not take advantage of its resources in people and capital. We import much we should make here. Well-educated people and big dollars leave our state for greener pastures. We have everything here if we know how to marshal our abilities and take advantage of our potential.

The combined influence of White and the two colleges gave Emporia a cultural heritage which present leaders strive to maintain. Concerts, lectures and dramatic productions are frequent attractions at the schools and civic auditorium.

The face of Emporia is drastically changing from the sleepy, cultural typical little midwest college town to a bustling, growing city. Its industry is processing more natural resources, taking advantage of its strategic geographic location and rail and highway network, but solidly spurred by the tremendous growth of its best salable commodity — education. Teachers, scientists, American and foreign exchange students trained at the two colleges leave their mark in all parts of the world.

New Interstate Bakeries plant — south view.

Southwest corner of Emporia Industrial Park looking north-northeast.

°EMPORIA, Lyon (D-11) pop. 17,735; 1 KPL; 2 KPL; 3 Mun.; 4 AT&SF; 5 I-35, US 50, K-99, K-57; 7 Kansas State Teachers College, College of Emporia; Citizens National Bank, Emporia State Bank, Lyon County State Bank $25,090,000; newspapers — Gazette, Times. Here are the late William Allen White's Emporia Gazette, now published by his son, W. L. White; the William Allen White home, "Red Rocks"; and Peter Pan Park donated by Mr. and Mrs. White as a memorial to their daughter. In the park is the William Allen White Memorial by sculptor Jo Davidson and dedicated in 1950 by former President Herbert Hoover. On the campus of Kansas State Teachers College are many of the famous editor's mementoes including the original of his widely published editorial "Mary White." The Museum of the Lyon County Historical Society is in Civic Auditorium. Reading State Lake is 11 miles northeast and Lake Kahola 20 miles northwest.

Lyon County — Earnings per cap. $1,903; sales tax collections $953,080; employed in industry 4,226; number of farms 1,501; crop value $5,906,730; livestock value $10,269,980; mineral production $537,474. Crude petroleum output totaled 93,000 barrels. Sand and gravel for building, paving and road maintenance are produced. Limestone is quarried and crushed for concrete aggregate, roadstone, riprap and agstone.

ENGLEWOOD, Clark (G-4) pop. 241; 1 WLT; 2 KPL; 3 Mun.; 4 AT&SF; 5 US 283.

ENSIGN, Gray (F-4) pop. 243; 1 WLT; 2 NNG; 3 Mun.; 4 AT&SF; 5 US 56.

ENTERPRISE, Dickinson (C-9) pop. 955; 1 Mun.; 2 KPL; 3 Mun.; 4 AT&SF, CRIP, UP; 5 K-43; Dickinson County Bank $1,278,000; newspaper — Enterprise Journal.

°ERIE, Neosho (F-12) pop. 1,371; 1 Mun.; 2 GSC; 3 Mun.; 4 AT&SF, MKT; 5 US 59, K-108, K-57; The Home State Bank $2,125,000; newspaper — Erie Record.

Neosho County — Earnings per cap. $1,681; sales tax collections $569,276; employed in industry 2,575; number of farms 1,380; crop value $6,037,580; livestock value $5,140,340; mineral production $8,009,066. Neosho County ranked second in portland and masonry cement production and sixth in value of stone production. Ash Grove Lime & Portland Cement Co. quarried limestone, sandstone and shale for manufacture of cement. Limestone was quarried and crushed for concrete aggregate, roadstone and agstone. Also produced are sand and gravel. A major part of crude petroleum production was recovered by water-flooding methods. Mid-America Refining Co., Inc., operated its petroleum refinery at Chanute.

ESBON, Jewell (A-7) pop. 231; 1 WLT; 2 GSC; 3 Mun.; 4 CRIP; 5 K-112; State Bank of Esbon $824,000.

ESKRIDGE, Wabaunsee (C-11) pop. 542; 1 KPL; 3 Mun.; 4 AT&SF; 5 K-99, K-4; Eskridge State Bank $1,337,000; newspaper — Eskridge Independent. Lake Wabaunsee, four miles west of Eskridge on K-4 and K-99, is owned and operated by the city. A commercial resort, it has a 14-room lodge, rental cabins and restaurant. Eskridge stages an annual rodeo on Labor Day.

EUDORA, Douglas (C-13) pop. 1,626; 1 Mun.; 2 Greeley Gas Co.; 3 Mun.; 4 AT&SF; 5 K-10; Kaw Valley State Bank $2,092,000.

°EUREKA, Greenwood (E-11) pop. 4,330; 1 KPL; 2 WLT; 3 Mun.; 4 AT&SF, MP; 5 US 54; 7 Midwest Institute of Business Administration; Citizens National Bank, Home National Bank $10,866,000; newspaper — Eureka Herald. On Eureka's south Main Street is Spring Park, complete with old schoolhouse, windmill, livery stable, antique farm implements, etc. An outdoor museum contains items of historical interest.

Greenwood County — Earnings per cap. $1,911; sales tax collections $279,056; employed in industry 959; number of farms 1,053; crop value $3,523,490; livestock value $8,562,830; mineral production $9,586,750. Secondary recovery operations yielded most of the 3.3 million barrels of crude petroleum; production decreased 10 per cent. Natural gas production totaled over 65 million cubic feet, considerably greater than previous year. Limestone is quarried and crushed for concrete aggregate and roadstone.

EVEREST, Brown (A-12) pop. 375; 1 KPL; 2 GSC; 3 Mun.; 4 MP; 5 K-114; Union State Bank $1,029,000.

FAIRVIEW, Brown (A-11) pop. 351; 1 KPL; 2 GSC; 4 CRIP; 5 US 75, US 36; Farmers State Bank $1,121,000; newspaper — Fairview Enterprise.

Harness racing at fairgrounds track.

EUREKA: *"Capital of the Magic Circle"*

Eureka means "I have found it!" To many pioneer families it also means "I have found it pleasant." For, through the years, they have remained loyal to Eureka. Many of today's residents are direct descendants of hardy folk who first settled the village in August 1857.

Eureka covers 1100 acres and serves as the seat of Greenwood County in southeastern Kansas. It is situated on Fall River on the eastern slope of the Flint Hills where thousands of cattle graze each year on the famous blue stem grass.

In 1946, Roger W. Babson, economist, selected a six-state region within a 400-mile radius of Eureka as the "Magic Circle." He believed the material resources of these six states exceeded those of any equal area in any part of the world and would support 400 people per square mile. It then had only 40 persons per square mile. Eureka — in the exact center — is "The Capital of the Magic Circle." Here Babson established the Midwest Institute of Business Administration, a junior college. The 54 students enrolled this year hail from Bermuda, Canada, Haiti, France, Hawaii, Mexico, Panama and the United States.

Eureka has 300 stores or business firms representing 76 different services. Among the businesses are two mills which manufacture commercial livestock feed, an alfalfa mill, and Cook's Aluma-Fab Manufacturing Company which makes storm windows, doors, screens and other aluminum products. The town has an industrial levy which will aid in business expansion.

There are $2 million worth of educational facilities — three public elementary, a junior and senior high school and a Catholic elementary school. Students have an organized summer recreation program. Another attraction is Christian Hills Camp, accommodating more than 1000 Christian Church youths each summer.

Besides a 40-bed hospital there are three nursing homes in operation and a 48-bed rest home under construction. Air travelers use the FAA-approved airport two miles north of town. The 2600-foot runway is suitable for twin-motored planes.

Eureka is six miles from the upper reaches of Fall River Reservoir; 18 miles from the dam. Toronto Reservoir is also 18 miles away.

The Fall River Watershed project northwest of Eureka comprises 201,000 acres and affects 918 landowners in the area. When completed in 1967 it will have 29 lakes, averaging 8 to 68 acres each. Fourteen of the structures are completed and four are now under construction.

Eureka is the site of the Greenwood County Fair, now in its 64th year. Harness racing has been a major attraction at the fair since 1956 and racing horses are trained here the year 'round. The fairgrounds grandstand erected in 1964 is set at an agle to allow unobstructed view of the entire track at all times. The town also has the first state-approved quarter horse race track. With both harness and running races featured, Eureka is known as the "Horse Racing Capital of Kansas."

FAIRWAY, Johnson (C-13) pop. 5,396; 1 KCPL; 2 GSC; 3 J. C. Nichols & Water Dist. No. 1, Johnson Co.; 5 US 69, US 56, US 50. The old Shawnee Methodist Mission, established in 1830 and moved to this site in 1839, was a manual training school for the Indians and twice the territorial capitol of Kansas. It is located in Fairway. Here three buildings more than a century old still are standing. The East Building contains a state-owned pioneer museum, and the North Building has been restored and furnished to look as it did when it was used for living quarters and classrooms.

FALL RIVER, Greenwood (F-11) pop. 234; 1 KPL; 2 UGS; 3 Mun.; 4 SLSF; 5 K-96; Fall River State Bank $407,000; newspaper — Fall River Star. Fall River Dam and Reservoir is slightly north of K-96 west of Fall River.

FALUN, Saline (C-8) pop. 125; Falun State Bank $717,000.

FLORENCE, Marion (E-9) pop. 853; 1 KPL; 2 Citizens Gas Co.; 3 Mun.; 4 AT&SF; 5 US 77, US 50; Florence State Bank $923,000; newspaper — Florence Bulletin.

FONTANA, Miami (D-13) pop. 157; 1 KCPL; 4 SLSF.

FORD, Ford (F-5) pop. 213; 1 WLT; 4 CRIP; 5 US 154.

FORMOSA, Jewell (A-8) pop. 220; 1 WLT; 2 GSC; 3 Mun.; 4 CRIP; First National Bank $773,000.

°FORT SCOTT, Bourbon (E-13) pop. 9,549; 1 KGE; 2 GSC; 3 Mun.; 4 SLSF, MKT, MP; 5 US 69, US 54, K-7; 7 Fort Scott Junior College; Citizens National Bank, City State Bank, Security State Bank $15,619,000; newspapers — Fort Scott Tribune, Fort Scott Weekly Tribune. Fort Scott, the outgrowth of a frontier military outpost established in 1842, is rich with tourist attractions — Fort Blair, renovated Civil War blockhouse; Carroll Plaza, the parade ground of the original Fort; the well preserved 100-year-old Officers' Quarters which house a historical museum; National Cemetery, first officially designated cemetery in the nation to be used for burial of soldiers. Historical marker in memory of Eugene Ware, "Ironquill," American poet of international fame who called Fort Scott his hometown, is in the National Cemetery. Lake Fort Scott, southwest of town, has a surface area of 352 acres.

Bourbon County — Earnings per cap. $1,625; sales tax collections $461,395; employed in industry 2,534; number of farms 1,378; crop value $5,554,720; livestock value $6,782,430; mineral production $792,530. Petroleum production totaled 72,000 barrels. Coal was strip mined by Palmer Coal Co. and Garrett Coal Co. Fort Scott Hydraulic Cement Co., Inc., manufactured natural and masonry cement near Fort Scott. Bandera Stone Quarry mined and prepared dimension sandstone near Redfield. Limestone is quarried and crushed for concrete aggregate, roadstone, agstone and coal mine dust.

FOWLER, Meade (F-4) pop. 743; 1 WLT; 2 NNG; 3 Mun.; 4 CRIP; 5 US 54, K-98; Fowler State Bank $2,438,000; newspaper — Fowler News.

FRANKFORT, Marshall (A-10) pop. 1,192; 1 KPL; 2 KPL; 3 Mun.; 4 MP, UP; 5 K-99, K-9; First National Bank $2,158,000; newspaper — Frankfort Index.

FREDERICK, Rice (D-7) pop. 36; 1 KPL; 2 GSC; 4 SLSF, MP; 5 K-4.

°FREDONIA, Wilson (F-11) pop. 3,846; 1 Mun.; 2 UGS; 3 Mun.; 4 AT&SF, SLSF, MP; 5 K-96, K-47, K-39; First National Bank, State Bank of Fredonia $10,503,000; newspapers — Fredonia Daily Herald, Wilson County Citizen. Twenty miles northwest of Fredonia is the Fall River Dam and Reservoir. On a clear day, five or more counties can be seen from Skyline Drive where the lighted Star and Cross also may be seen.

Wilson County — Earnings per cap. $1,730; sales tax collections $304,932; employed in industry 1,588; number of farms 1,080; crop value $5,566,000; livestock value $4,227,550; mineral production $5,715,236. Wilson County ranked fourth in production of portland cement. Victor Portland Cement Division, General Portland Cement Co., mined shale and limestone for manufacture of portland and masonry cements. Excelsior Brick Co. and Acme Brick Co. mined shale for building brick. Limestone is quarried and crushed for concrete aggregate, roadstone, aglime and riprap. Crude petroleum output near previous year's; secondary recovery projects accounted for most of output. Production of natural gas increased to 497 million cubic feet, compared with 134 million cubic feet in previous year. American Oil Co. operated its petroleum refinery at Neodesha.

Water tower — spring water.

New motel.

Modern school.

First Harvey House
in Kansas
outside of Topeka.

FLORENCE: *proud of schools and*
new flood-control dike

Located at the west edge of the beautiful Flint Hills, Florence is the trading center for a rich Cottonwood River farming area. Population in 1964 was 853.

A dike was constructed around the city to prevent flooding. The structure was completed in the fall of 1964.

One of the major industries is a rock quarry. The quarry currently is operating under contracts to furnish rock for Marion Reservoir, now under construction; Atchison, Topeka and Santa Fe Railroad Company to build and repair tracks and limestone for agricultural fertilizer.

Many stripper oil wells add to the community's economy.

A high school annex with gymnasium, band room and Future Farmers of America work shops was completed in 1956.

Florence's municipal water supply system could accommodate a 5,000 population.

Cottonwood River at the east edge of town is one of the better fishing streams in Kansas. Six miles northwest is the 152-acre Marion County Lake. It is a popular resort for swimming, boating, skiing and fishing.

Founded in 1872, the town was named after Florence Crawford. She was the daughter of Samuel J. Crawford, former governor of Kansas and president of the town company which founded this town. Miss Crawford married Arthur Capper who also was governor of Kansas and later United States senator for many years.

A landmark here is the first Harvey House built outside of Topeka. All Santa Fe trains stopped in Florence so their passengers could dine here. The rooming-boarding house was built in 1876. Currently, it is the home of Mrs. Lillian Jackson, town librarian.

141

FREEPORT, Harper (G-8) pop. 27; 1 WLT; 4 MP; Freeport State Bank $623,000.

FRONTENAC, Crawford (F-13) pop. 1,832; 1 KGE; 2 GSC; 3 Mun.; 4 AT&SF; 5 US 160; Miners State Bank $2,403,000.

FULTON, Bourbon (E-13) pop. 229; 1 KCPL; 2 CGPC; 4 SLSF; 5 US 69, K-31.

GALATIA, Barton (D-6) pop. 75; 1 WLT; 4 AT&SF; Galatia State Bank $553,000.

GALENA, Cherokee (G-13) pop. 4,024; 1 EDE; 2 AG; 3 Mun.; 4 SLSF, MKT; 5 US 66, K-26; Citizens State Bank of Galena $1,421,000; newspaper — Sentinel-Times.

GALESBURG, Neosho (F-12) pop. 118; 1 KPL; 2 UGS; 3 Mun.; 4 MKT.

GALVA, McPherson (D-8) pop. 463; 1 Mun.; 2 KPL; 3 Mun.; 4 AT&SF, CRIP; 5 US 56; Farmers State Bank $698,000.

°GARDEN CITY, Finney (E-3) pop. 13,407; 1 Mun.; 2 NNG; 3 Mun.; 4 AT&SF, GCW; 5 US 156, US 50; 6 CEN; 7 Garden City Junior College; Fidelity State Bank, Garden National Bank $25,137,000; newspaper — Garden City Telegram. Garden City is the center of the state's irrigation industry. A state branch experimental farm station is located here. Garden City is the home of famous Finnup Park which includes the world's largest free concrete municipal swimming pool and a large zoo. The Windsor Hotel, "Waldorf of the Prairies," in the downtown area was built in 1886 with a lobby court three stories high. Lillian Russell, Eddie Foy, Buffalo Bill Cody, Jay Gould and General Dodge stayed here. The lobby is open for tourists to see the ornate decor of the time. Located a short distance south of town on US 83 is a 3,600-acre State Game Preserve, home of the largest buffalo herd in the state. Oakarah Herb Gardens are an attraction for gardeners.

Finney County — Earnings per cap. $1,984; sales tax collections $846,224; employed in industry 2,562; number of farms 682; crop value $11,619,340; livestock value $7,081,920; mineral production $12,970,218. The county ranked fifth in natural gas production; 52.9 billion cubic feet were recovered, an 11 per cent decrease. Output of crude petroleum increased 16 per cent to over 2 million barrels. Northern Natural Gas Co. recovered natural gas liquids at its plant near Holcomb. Sand and gravel is produced, mainly for building and paving.

GARDEN PLAIN, Sedgwick (F-8) pop. 634; 1 KGE; 4 AT&SF; 5 US 54.

GARDNER, Johnson (C-13) pop. 1,763; 1 Mun.; 2 GSC; 3 Mun.; 4 AT&SF; 5 US 56; Farmers Bank $4,003,000; newspapers — Gardner News, New Era Printing Co.

GARFIELD, Pawnee (E-5) pop. 314; 1 KPL; 2 KPL; 4 AT&SF; 5 US 56.

°GARNETT, Anderson (D-12) pop. 3,127; 1 Mun.; 2 Mun.; 4 AT&SF, MP; 5 US 169 Alt., US 59, K-31; Garnett State Savings Bank, Kansas State Bank $6,895,000; newspapers — Garnett Review, Anderson Countian. Garnett is the birthplace of the late U. S. Sen. Arthur Capper, noted newspaper publisher and first native Kansan to be elected governor. The Walker Collection of Art and Letters, housed at the public library, includes works of John Steuart Curry, Henry Varnum Poor and other noted artists. The Lake Garnett National Grand Prix Sports Car Races are held here. The unusual race course winds around Lake Garnett.

Anderson County — Earnings per cap. $1,607; sales tax collections $218,826; employed in industry 728; number of farms 1,131; crop value $7,035,570; livestock value $6,257,950; mineral production $1,175,055. Petroleum output was about equal previous year; secondary recovery projects accounted for most of the production. Over 65 million cubic feet of natural gas was recovered. Limestone is quarried and crushed for concrete aggregate, roadstone and railroad ballast.

GAS CITY, Allen (E-12) pop. 395; 1 City of Iola; 2 GSC; 3 Mun.; 5 US 54.

GAYLORD, Smith (A-6) pop. 236; 1 WLT; 3 Mun.; 4 MP; 5 K-9; First National Bank $695,000.

GEM, Thomas (B-3) pop. 125; 1 CKP; 2 K-NG; 4 CRIP.

GENESEO, Rice (D-7) pop. 574; 1 KPL; 2 GSC; 3 Mun.; 4 AT&SF, MP; 5 K-4; Citizens State Bank $524,000.

GEUDA SPRINGS, Sumner-Cowley (G-9) pop. 196; 1 KGE; 2 Arkansas-Louisiana Gas; 3 Mun.; 4 AT&SF, MV.

°GIRARD, Crawford (F-13) pop. 2,410; 1 Mun.; 2 GSC; 3 Mun.; 4 AT&SF, SLSF, J-P; 5 K-57, K-7; First National Bank, Girard National Bank $7,089,000; newspaper — Girard Press. One of the largest soybean processing mills in the state is located at Girard.

Home of Trailcraft Canoes.   *Crowd gathers for beef cattle auction.*

GLASCO: *busiest little city in*
North Central Kansas

Glasco is the home of Trailcraft, Inc., manufacturer of canoe kits and fiberglass boats. Distribution is nationwide.

It is headquarters for Polly-Dell Stencils, with nationwide distribution of textile stencils for women's handicrafts. Also here are LESCO, Plush Mills and Glasco Livestock Exchange. LESCO stands for Livestock Equipment and Supply Company. It is distributor of livestock handling equipment produced by Casewell Manufacturing Company, Des Moines, Iowa; W. W. Manufacturing Company, Dodge City, Kansas; Pride of the Farm, Waterloo, Iowa. Products are scales, hog feeders and waterers, stock racks, loading chutes and many more. Plush Mills mixes proportioned feeds for all livestock.

Glasco Livestock Auction draws beef cattle from a 100-mile radius. It is one of the largest cattle auctions in the area. Also it is the location of an annual show and sale of North Central Kansas Hereford Association.

Spencer Chemical Division of Gulf Oil Corporation recently constructed one of Kansas' largest bulk fertilizer mixing plants in an industrial area just west of here. Capacity is 800 tons of nitrogen and super phosphate.

Newly installed this summer by Spencer Chemical Company is an anhydrous ammonia storage tank with 18,000 gallons capacity. Natural Gas Pipeline Company of America has one of its largest gas pressure boosting stations at Glasco.

Kansas-Nebraska Pipeline Company has a bulk station 10 miles east of here for delivery of refined petroleum products. The largest processor of alfalfa seed in this area is here.

Glasco residents have time for recreation, too. Lovewell Reservoir is 40 miles northwest, Milford Reservoir 45 miles east, Tuttle Creek Reservoir 62 miles east, Kanopolis Reservoir 70 miles south, Wilson Dam 75 miles southwest and Kirwin Dam 82 miles west. Thirty miles west, Glen Elder Dam (Waconda Lake) now is under construction. Glasco Country Club has a nine-hole, sand green golf course east on highway U. S. 24.

Glasco is the home of the Cloud County Fair. Dairy breeders of the North Central Kansas Brown Swiss Canton meet here each summer.

Glasco High School ranked first in the state scholastically among Class B schools in 1962, 1963 and 1965. It ranked second in 1964.

Crawford County — Earnings per cap. $1,861; sales tax collections $1,117,306; employed in industry 4,844; number of farms, 1,498; crop value $6,552,590; livestock value $4,170,690. Crawford County ranked second in coal production. Two strip mines were operated by Clemens Coal Co. and one strip mine each by Cliff Carr Coal Co. and Joe E. Gobl Coal Co. Fire clay and miscellaneous clay were used to manufacture sewer pipe and stoneware by W. S. Dickey Clay Mfg. Co. and Pittsburg Pottery Co., Inc. Petroleum output increased 55 per cent to 63,000 barrels. Farlington oilfield was an important discovery. Recovery of natural gas increased 161 per cent to 65 million cubic feet.

GLADE, Phillips (A-5) pop. 176; 1 WLT; 2 K-NG; 4 MP; 5 US 183, K-9.

GLASCO, Cloud (B-8) pop. 796; 1 Mun.; 2 Ruth Fuel Co.; 3 Mun.; 4 UP; 5 US 24; First National Bank $1,720,000; newspaper — Glasco Sun.

GLEN ELDER, Mitchell (B-7) pop. 447; 1 Mun.; 2 GSC; 3 Mun.; 4 MP; 5 US 24, K-9; Traders State Bank $1,599,000.

GODDARD, Sedgwick (F-8) pop. 537; 1 KGE; 3 Mun.; 4 AT&SF; 5 US 54.

GOESSEL, Marion (E-9) pop. 318; 1 KGE; 5 K-215.

GOFF, Nemaha (A-11) pop. 261; 1 Mun.; 3 Mun.; 4 MP; 5 K-9; First National Bank $708,000.

*GOODLAND, Sherman (B-1) pop. 4,814; 1 Mun.; 2 PNG; 3 Mun.; 4 CRIP; 5 US 24, K-27; 6 CEN; First National Bank, Goodland State Bank $10,861,000; newspapers — Goodland Daily News, Sherman County Herald. Goodland has a Pioneer Museum housing frontier artifacts, Indian items and a collection of musical instruments. The Northwest Kansas Area Vocational-Technical School is located here.

Sherman County — Earnings per cap. $2,158; sales tax collections $314,711; employed in industry 668; number of farms 557; crop value $7,436,030; livestock value $3,602,180; mineral production $177,470. Output of crude petroleum totaled 44,000 barrels. Produces building and paving sand and gravel.

GORHAM, Russell (C-6) pop. 422; 1 CKP; 2 KPL; 3 Mun.; 4 UP; 5 US 40; Gorham State Bank $2,252,000.

*GOVE, Gove (C-3) pop. 214; 1 CKP; 3 Mun.; 5 K-23; newspaper — Gove County Republican Gazette.

Gove County — Earnings per cap. $1,604; sales tax collections $108,272; employed in industry 282; number of farms 579; crop value $4,385,750; livestock value $5,422,130; mineral production $266,143. Crude petroleum output totaled 83,000 barrels, an increase of 21 per cent. Garvey Ranch oil field was an important discovery. Building and paving sand and gravel are produced.

GRAINFIELD, Gove (C-3) pop. 437; 1 CKP; 2 K-NG; 3 Mun.; 4 UP; 5 I-70, US 40, K-23 Alt.; Citizens State Bank $1,040,000; newspaper — Grainfield Cap Sheaf.

GRANDVIEW PLAZA, Geary (C-10) pop. 450; 1 Flint Hills Rural Elec. Co-op. Assn.; 2 KPL; 3 Plaza Water Co., Inc.; 5 I-70, US 77.

GREELEY, Anderson (D-13) pop. 403; 1 KCPL; 2 GSC; 3 Mun.; 4 MP; 5 US 169; Bank of Greeley $1,100,000.

GREEN, Clay (B-9) pop. 224; 1 Mun.; 3 Mun.

GREENLEAF, Washington (A-9) pop. 568; 1 WLT; 2 KPL; 3 Mun.; 4 MP; 5 K-119; Citizens National Bank $2,614,000; newspaper — Greenleaf Sentinel.

*GREENSBURG, Kiowa (F-5) pop. 2,132; 1 Mun.; 2 KPL; 3 Mun.; 4 CRIP; 5 US 54; Greensburg State Bank $3,149,000; newspaper — Kiowa County Signal. Greensburg claims the world's largest hand-dug well, measuring 32 feet in diameter and 109 feet deep, with steps leading to the water level. Adjacent to the well is the Celestial Museum containing the largest Pallasite Meteorite ever found and many other articles. Burketown Museum has collection of antique vehicles, classic automobiles and other pioneer equipment on display. Front of museum depicts a frontier town.

Kiowa County — Earnings per cap. $2,037; sales tax collections $142,469; employed in industry 538; number of farms 445; crop value $2,992,490; livestock value $3,321,420; mineral production $3,037,010. Crude petroleum output totaled 476,000 barrels. Production of natural gas increased 22 per cent to 12.9 billion cubic feet. Ursula Northeast gas field was an important discovery.

144

For Great Bend and Barton County listings see page 312.

Produces sand and gravel for building, paving and road maintenance.

GRENOLA, Elk (G-10) pop. 366; 1 KGE; 2 GSC; 3 Mun.; 4 AT&SF; 5 US 160.

GRIDLEY, Coffey (E-11) pop. 346; 1 KGE; 4 AT&SF; 5 K-57; Citizens State Bank $1,400,000; newspaper — Gridley Light.

GRINNELL, Gove (C-3) pop. 484; 1 CKP; 2 K-NG; 3 Mun.; 4 UP; 5 US 40, K-216; Peoples State Bank $1,170,000; newspaper — Grinnell Record-Leader.

GYPSUM, Saline (D-9) pop. 489; 1 KPL; 2 KPL; 3 Mun.; 4 MP; 5 K-4; Gypsum Valley National Bank $1,544,000; newspaper — Gypsum Advocate.

HADDAM, Washington (A-9) pop. 298; 1 WLT; 2 KPL; 3 Mun.; 4 CB&Q; 5 K-22; Citizens State Bank $742,000.

HALSTEAD, Harvey (E-8) pop. 1,609; 1 KGE; 2 Mun.; 3 Mun.; 4 AT&SF; 5 K-89; Halstead Bank $2,569,000; newspaper — Independent. Halstead is the home of Halstead Hospital built by Arthur E. Hertzler whose autobiography, Horse and Buggy Doctor, attracted nationwide attention. A Kansas Health Museum is located here.

HAMILTON, Greenwood (E-11) pop. 383; 1 KPL; 3 Mun.; 4 AT&SF; 5 K-99; First National Bank $865,000.

HAMLIN, Brown (A-12) pop. 114; 1 KPL; 2 GSC; 4 UP.

HANOVER, Washington (A-9) pop. 828; 1 KPL; 2 KPL; 3 Mun.; 4 CB&Q, UP; 5 K-15E; Community State Bank $1,550,000; newspaper — Hanover News. The Hollenberg Station, only original unaltered Pony Express station left standing today in its original location, is two miles northeast of Hanover. It is now owned by the state and contains a small pioneer museum. Also in Hanover is the Neugebauer Rock Garden. "Days of '49," an annual celebration, is held at Hanover in July.

HANSTON, Hodgeman (E-5) pop. 308; 1 Central Kansas Electric Co-op., Inc.; 5 US 156; Hanston State Bank $1,360,000.

HARDTNER, Barber (G-6) pop. 356; 1 WLT; 2 Zenith Gas System; 3 Mun.; 4 MP; 5 US 281, K-14; Farmers State Bank $2,176,000; newspaper — Hardtner Press.

HARPER, Harper (G-8) pop. 1,819; 1 WLT; 2 UGSv; 3 Mun.; 4 AT&SF; 5 US 160, K-14, K-2; First National Bank $4,162,000; newspaper — Harper Advocate. Harper has old Runnymede Church which once stood in an English settlement, Runnymede, established about 10 miles northeast of Harper. The church was dedicated in 1889, and moved to town in 1893 by the Episcopalians of Harper. Interior furnishings such as stone baptismal font and bronze memorial plaque imported from England; pews, kneeling benches, organ, choir seats, etc., are original in the old church. The church is open to tourists. A tape recording tells the story of Runnymede, established by an Irish promoter who mustered wealthy English and Irish scions to the English-patterned village to study farming methods. The British playboys took better to polo, steeplechase and horse racing and the community passed into oblivion after five hectic English years on the prairie.

HARRIS, Anderson (D-12) pop. 51; 1 KCPL; 5 K-31.

HARTFORD, Lyon (D-11) pop. 391; 1 KPL; 2 AG; 3 Mun.; 5 K-130; Hartford State Bank $787,000; newspaper — Hartford Times.

HARVEYVILLE, Wabaunsee (C-11) pop. 238; 1 KPL; 4 AT&SF; 5 K-195; First National Bank $458,000; newspaper — Harveyville Monitor.

HAVANA, Montgomery (G-11) pop. 147; 1 Caney Valley Electric Co-op. Assn.; 2 UGS; 4 AT&SF.

HAVEN, Reno (E-8) pop. 1,068; 1 Mun.; 2 GSC; 3 Mun.; 4 MP; 5 K-96; Haven State Bank $2,193,000; newspaper — Haven Journal.

HAVENSVILLE, Pottawatomie (B-11) pop. 156; 1 KPL; 3 Mun.; 5 K-63; Havensville State Bank $473,000.

HAVILAND, Kiowa (F-6) pop. 602; 1 WLT; 2 KPL; 3 Mun.; 4 CRIP; 5 US 54; Haviland State Bank $1,596,000; newspaper — Haviland Journal.

*HAYS, Ellis (C-5) pop. 12,989; 1 CKP; 2 CKP; 3 Mun.; 4 UP; 5 US 183, US 40, US 40 Alt.; 6 CEN; 5 Fort Hays Kansas State College; Farmers State Bank, First National Bank, Hays National Bank $22,210,000; newspapers — Ellis County Farmer, Hays Daily News. City was named for Fort Hays, one of the famous military posts on the old frontier. The stone blockhouse, guard-

145

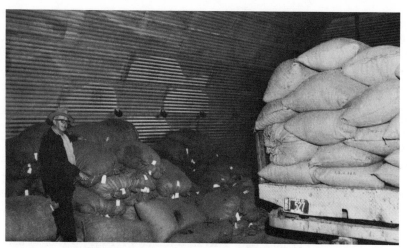

Loading brome grass seed at Harveyville Seed Company.

Banking services available locally.

HARVEYVILLE: *commuters*

Located on Dragoon Creek 30 miles south of Topeka, Harveyville is primarily an agricultural business center in Wabaunsee County. Population is 243.

Many of the younger people of this prosperous agricultural community prefer to remain on farms. They are, however, taking advantage of rapid industrialization of the state capital. About half of the farm population commutes daily to industrial jobs at Topeka for additional income.

Harveyville civic leaders took action in 1963 to keep the community's economy from stagnation and meet demands in this era of competition for industrial development. The community invested $90,000 to construct a dam and 40-acre lake for a new municipal water supply.

Another $90,000 was appropriated in 1965 for a sanitary sewer system. Completed early in 1966 was a $100,000 natural gas utility. Dial telephone service was installed recently. Harveyville City Council and the local Businessmen's Association promoted the capital improvements. Deposits in the First National Bank of Harveyville passed the $1 million mark in 1965.

With a strong tradition for good education, the town has modern elementary and high schools with total enrollments of about 250. Other organizations working to better the community are Lions Club, Masonic Lodge, Eastern Star, American Legion and Auxiliary, Oddfellows, Grange, Rebekah Lodge, 4-H clubs and Boy Scouts.

The community is noted for excellent quail and prairie chicken hunting and pond and stream fishing.

Harveyville is located on State Highway 31 and a branch line of the Santa Fe Railroad.

Kansas grasslands feed thousands of cattle. Here, a group of Hereford graze in the Flint Hills.

house and parade grounds may still be seen in Frontier Historical Park. Old Fort Hays museum in the Fort blockhouse contains articles from the frontier and military days. At Fort Hays Kansas State College, in Forsyth Library, are geological, paleontological, natural history and historical museums. They include a fossil fish 13 feet long, a flying reptile skeleton with a wing expanse of 22 feet and other collections. Also on the campus is the Kansas car of the Merci Train, France's "thank you" to Americans for the Friendship Train in 1947. There is a Buffalo Bill Cody Memorial Statue and a stone hitching post used by Cody for target practice on the courthouse square at Hays. Ellis County — Earnings per cap. $1,781; sales tax collections $875,778; employed in industry 2,675; number of farms 977; crop value $4,409,680; livestock value $4,573,550; mineral production $27,445,146. Ellis County ranked first in petroleum production and total value of mineral production. Crude petroleum production totaled 9.5 million barrels. Minerals are sand and gravel for building and paving and crushed limestone for concrete aggregate, roadstone and dimension limestone.

HAYSVILLE, Sedgwick (F-9) pop. 4,905; 1 KGE; 2 GSC; 3 Mun.; 4 CRIP; Haysville State Bank $7,931,000.

HAZELTON, Barber (G-7) pop. 271; 1 WLT; 3 Mun.; 4 AT&SF, MP; 5 K-14; Farmers State Bank $462,000.

HEALY, Lane, pop. 219; First State Bank $1,784,000.

HEPLER, Crawford (F-13) pop. 192; 1 KGE; 4 MKT; 5 K-3; Hepler State Bank $1,062,000.

HERINGTON, Dickinson (D-9) pop. 3,576; 1 Mun.; 2 Greeley Gas Co.; 3 Mun.; 4 CRIP, MP; 5 US 77, US 56, K-218; Bank of Herington, First National Bank $6,333,000; newspaper — Herington Advertiser Times. In the city park of Herington is a tall granite shaft erected as a monument to Father Padilla, the soldier-priest who accompanied Coronado and later (1542) was killed near here by the Indians, making him the first Christian martyr on what is now United States soil.

HERNDON, Rawlins (A-3) pop. 314; 1 Mun.; 2 K-NG; 3 Mun.; 4 CB&Q; 5 K-117; State Bank of Herndon $2,099,000.

HESSTON, Harvey (E-9) pop. 1,264; 1 KGE; 2 Mun.; 3 Mun.; 4 MP; 5 US 81; 7 Hesston College; Hesston State Bank $2,342,000; newspaper — Hesston Record. Hesston College, high school and junior college (Mennonite) are located here. Schowalter Villa, Old Peoples Home (Mennonite) is here.

147

Hesston Manufacturing Company, view toward the northwest.

HESSTON MANUFACTURING COMPANY *of Hesston: specialized farm equipment firm thrives in agricultural environment*

Kansas is a spawning ground for "agri-business" — one of the newest concepts in industrial development.

Involved is research, commerce and industry directly related to the state's basic economy, agriculture. Scores of thriving industrial ventures have breathed life into the theory that a predominantly agricultural state can make an effective economic transition to an agri-business state.

A prime example of such an industrial venture is Hesston Manufacturing Company of Hesston. Here is an industrial complex where specialized farm machinery is produced for sale in all parts of the U. S., Canada and at least 20 foreign countries. Here, in a little farming community of some 600 population, an industry was launched in 1947. It was started on an idea for a useful farm product. It grew over the years on more ideas for more useful farm products.

The modern plant, spread on 125 acres of company-owned land on the north edge of town, represents more than $3,000,000 worth of facilities, with plant expansion a continuing process. Peak employment near the 950-mark involves persons from many central counties. Some live over 40 miles away.

Company founders were raised on farms. Most of the workmen are farm-bred, raised around tools and machinery. Farm-oriented men with skills in sales, accounting, engineering and a variety of other required fields are easy to find for positions at Hesston. Products which truly fill a need are better conceived and built by men who are close to the ultimate user — in Hesston's case, the farmer.

The business thrives in its agricultural environment. Hesston's first product was an unloading auger to attach to combines, a device which permitted harvesting combines to unload "on the run." This saved substantial harvesting time in the field. It has since become standard equipment on all makes of combines.

Hesston's first major product, introduced in 1955, was the self-propelled windrower. It still is the company's best seller, and has carried the Hesston name to six continents. The windrower is a machine which replaces three — the mower, conditioner and rake.

The company's windrower line now includes four models, the broadest offered in the industry. Largest of these, the Model 500, is famous for its all-metal auger header introduced in 1963. The big, fast machine is particularly effective with big acreage growers and custom cutters.

Hesston still makes the 280 draper model, refined from the first basic design produced. Popular with small acreage farmers are the compact Model 110 and the pull-type PT-10 which cut and condition hay crops as efficiently as the larger machines.

Hesston has set the pace in the windrower field, not only in design, but also in selling to American farmers the concept of windrowing — that is, using the one machine only while getting better quality hay at much less cost in labor and equipment.

Hesston's windrower line is strongly supported by its line of cotton and beet harvesters and two useful combine attachments, straw choppers and row harvesters. The SP-50 and V-22 Cotton Harvesters introduced to cotton country an efficient new method of removing cotton from the plant mechanically: "brush action" harvesting. The Hesston Beet Harvester line was acquired in 1965 from the Gemco Company, a leader in this specialized field. The complete production facilities, patents and assets of the Utah firm were purchased and transferred to Kansas.

Hesston places heavy emphasis on engineering and market research in its quest for new specialized equipment which might be useful to the farmer. It employs 46 persons in its engineering-research division, 14 of whom are engineers. New plant structures completed in 1965 include two engineering buildings.

Gross sales exceeded $16 million in 1965. But, the remarkable story of the company's growth is revealed in sales figures of broader scope. Over the past five years Hesston Manufacturing has steadily experienced annual sales increases of around 20 per cent of gross income. And, this pace is predicted to continue through 1966 — a truly phenomenal rate of growth for any industry, anywhere!

Hesston '500' Windrower.

Hesston-Gemco Beet Harvester.

Hesston SP-50 Cotton Harvester.

New school completed in 1965.

HERINGTON: *rail terminal eyes industry*

Long known as a railroad town, Herington also has gained notice as an agricultural trade center and as the home of the Tri-County 4-H Free Fair. In addition, it has taken positive action for city improvement and for growth in business and industry.

Railroading began when the town was in its infancy. Through the efforts of Monroe D. Herington, town founder and first mayor, the Rock Island and Missouri Pacific Railroads came through in 1888. Now Herington is a terminal for the Chicago, Rock Island and Pacific Railroad, and is on the Missouri Pacific main line from St. Louis to Pueblo. The Rock Island Depot here has become a Kansas landmark. It was erected in part in 1887; the south third of the building added in 1906. The McSweens, stonemasons of this territory, helped with its construction. The clean white limestone they fashioned and laid in place now is stained by smoke of many locomotives and weather beaten by storms of many winters.

Herington is located in the southeast corner of Dickinson County and serves a tri-county trade area including Dickinson, Marion and Morris counties. More than 400 youths from these three counties exhibited at the 1965 4-H Free Fair, with $2,350 premium money paid. The Fair is held annually in August. The fairgrounds and 12 buildings are rated among the best in the state. Largest, the T-Building, accommodates 2,000 people. Rodeo arena and ball parks are under floodlights.

The city has set aside part of the former Herington Army Airfield as an Industrial Park, with more than 500 acres available. The park has adequate water supply, electricity, sewage plant, fire protection and a 6,300-foot concrete landing strip with an attendant on duty at all hours. Industries located here are Welch Mfg. Co., Mid Continent Wholesale Warehouse and Herington Cattle Co.

Industrial sites are available in Herington proper, also. The city has Tatge Chemical Co.; Paragon Products, infants and girls fashions; Herington Packing Company; Pearl's Ceramic & Gift Studio and Anderson-Oxandale Rock Co.

The Herington Industrial Development Corporation makes loans at special rates for business expansion and new industries. It has 70 stockholders. A new $300,000 Lutheran United Home for the Aged was financed through the corporation. This 50-bed nursing home also has physical therapy facilities. The 39-bed Herington Municipal Hospital is served by a staff of 46.

School facilities are a source of pride to Herington citizens. The town has a new elementary building, junior high and Catholic grade school and a high school completed in August, 1965. The modern, functional design of the high school includes four circular complexes. The double gymnasium, which seats 1,800 spectators, has a barrel vault roof.

Herington has 13 churches, a public library, city park, swimming pool, bowling alley, theaters, Teen Club supervised by parents, and many civic, fraternal and social clubs. It also has an active Chamber of Commerce and this slogan — "You'll Be Hearing More About Herington."

°HIAWATHA, Brown (A-12) pop. 3,741; 1 KPL; 2 GSC; 3 Mun.; 4 MP, UP; 5 US 159, US 73, US 36; Citizens State Bank, The Morrill & Janes Bank $10,554,000; newspaper — Hiawatha Daily World. The John M. Davis Memorial in Mount Hope Cemetery is an unusual monument with a vault, pavilion and 11 life-sized portrait statues, all but one carved in Italy, of Mr. and Mrs. Davis at various stages in their lives. Brown County State Lake is 7½ miles east. Hiawatha Lake Park is ¾ mile south.

Brown County — Earnings per cap. $1,549; sales tax collections $353,830; employed in industry 1,395; number of farms 1,410; crop value $10,319,060; livestock value $8,184,420; mineral production $6,395.

HIGHLAND, Doniphan (A-12) pop. 709; 1 KPL; 3 Mun.; 5 US 36, K-120; 7 Highland Junior College; Farmers State Bank $1,220,000; newspaper — Highland Vidette. Two miles east of Highland is the old Iowa, Sac and Fox Indian Mission (1837). A portion of the building erected in 1846 is now a state museum.

°HILL CITY, Graham (B-4) pop. 2,227; 1 Mun.; 2 K-NG; 3 Mun.; 4 UP; 5 US 283, US 24; Consolidated State Bank, Farmer & Merchants Bank $7,650,000; newspaper — Hill City Times. Hill City is located in the artesian well district. The Rovenstine Gardens contain every flower and shrub known to the area; and hand-carved figures, depicting pioneer modes of transportation, are made and displayed by a local resident. An Oil Museum and derrick are open to the public. Buck's Pony & Buffalo Farm is a children's favorite. An FAA weather station is at the Municipal Airport.

Graham County — Earnings per cap. $1,999; sales tax collections $151,797; employed in industry 453; number of farms 659; crop value $4,114,850; livestock value $3,438,750; mineral production $15,419,962. Graham County ranked eighth in petroleum production; totaled 5.2 million barrels. Kohart oil field was an important discovery. Anderson-Oxandale quarried and crushed minerals are limestone for concrete aggregate and roadstone.

HILLSBORO, Marion (D-9) pop. 2,471; 1 Mun.; 2 Greeley Gas Co.; 3 Mun.; 4 AT&SF; 5 US 56; 7 Tabor College; First National Bank $4,602,000; newspaper — Hillsboro Star-Journal. Tabor College (Mennonite) has in its library a collection of books on Mennonite history. Mennonite Brethren Headquarters of North America are here. A pioneer adobe house in City Park is reconstructed and furnished as a replica of a type of home built by Mennonite settlers of the 1870's. The attached barn contains over 10,000 museum pieces depicting the pioneer and agricultural practices of this area. Hillsboro claims the largest creamery in the state and one of the few honey factories in Kansas.

HOISINGTON, Barton (D-6) pop. 4,556; 1 Mun.; 2 KPL; 3 Mun.; 4 MP; 5 US 281, K-45, K-4; First National Bank in Hoisington, Hoisington National Bank $8,643,000; newspaper — Hoisington Dispatch. The city is located at the northwest corner of Cheyenne Bottoms, one of the nation's outstanding migratory water fowl refuges, public shooting grounds and recreational areas. It is a state-federal project composed of a deep, central lake surrounded by four shallow lakes. Total water area is 13,000 acres.

HOLCOMB, Finney (E-2) pop. 279; 1 Wheatland Elec. Co-op., Inc.; 2 K-NG; 3 Mun.; 4 AT&SF; 5 US 50.

HOLLENBERG, Washington (A-9) pop. 64; 1 Nemaha-Marshall Elec. Co-op. Assn. Inc.; 4 UP.

°HOLTON, Jackson (B-11) pop. 2,890; 1 Mun.; 2 GSC; 3 Mun.; 4 CRIP; 5 US 75, K-116, K-16; Denison State Bank, The Kansas State Bank in Holton $9,374,000; newspapers — Holton Recorder, Jackson County Clipper.

Jackson County — Earnings per cap. $1,622; sales tax collections $228,197; employed in industry 983; number of farms 1,476; crop value $5,808,690; livestock value $6,214,440; mineral production $89,809. Crude petroleum output totaled slightly more than 2,400 barrels.

HOLYROOD, Ellsworth (D-7) pop. 645; 1 Mun.; 2 KPL; 3 Mun.; 4 AT&SF; 5 K-45; The Bank of Holyrood $2,157,000; newspaper — Holyrood Gazette.

HOPE, Dickinson (D-9) pop. 480; 1 KPL; 3 Mun.; 4 AT&SF, MP; 5 K-43, K-4; First National Bank $1,938,000; newspaper — Hope Dispatch.

HORACE, Greeley (D-1) pop. 210; 1 Wheatland Elec. Co-op., Inc.; 2 K-NG; 3 Mun.; 4 MP.

Oil Museum is tourist attraction.   *Central Kansas Power Plant, valued at $7 million.*

HILL CITY: *honors oil industry in museum*

Extending hospitality to travelers is becoming a tradition in Hill City. The town is situated along the north-south highway US 283 and on US 24 — "the scenic, hospitality route" from Detroit to Los Angeles. This location gives residents here the opportunities to provide lodging and accommodations and, at the same time, show off their city.

Comfortable motels, good food and car servicing are only the beginning of Hill City's hospitality to travelers. A roadside park has facilities for overnight camping. Under construction north of town is Trexler Lake where modern trailer parking sites will permit stays of longer duration. Tenting is encouraged, too! Boating, fishing and horseback riding will tempt the tourist to linger in Hill City. A municipal pool and nine-hole grass green golf course are summer features; hunting for pheasants, ducks, quail and deer are cool weather sports.

Hill City Chamber of Commerce invites travelers to be guests at the Oil Museum, located at the west edge of the city. During the summer of 1965, 1,200 people visited the attraction. Oil companies have provided the exhibits which show the history and modern methods of the oil industry. The museum was started in 1958, 20 years after the first commercial oil well was completed. Since then, several other pools have been developed in Graham County which regularly ranks among the top petroleum producers in the state. The county had 1,093 wells in 1963 and 1,107 the following year when it produced in excess of 4.1 million barrels of petroleum with a value of $14,744,350. Major oil companies with offices in Hill City are Cities Service, Texaco, Magnolia and Peel-Hardman. Several other oil firms have men assigned here. Another thriving business is the Hill City Sales Barn which realizes about $4 million yearly in sales, attracting buyers from four states. Grain storage is also important in Hill City; elevators hold from 250,000 to 500,000 bushels of grain. The Central Kansas Power Plant is located here, employing 19 people. With an output of 35,000 kilowatts of electricity, it serves a territory from Russell to Bird City. Through help from Graham County Development Association and the Small Business Administration, a new firm — the Kansas Food Products, Inc. — will be in operation by May, 1966. The company will employ about 15 people to process rabbits, poultry and other animals.

Hill City school facilities include elementary, junior, and senior high buildings. The city has over 320 days of sunshine every year and an average high of 70 degrees, a low of 40. Fishermen find these temperatures perfect for their favorite sport and have the convenience of three lakes to choose from — Webster, Cedar Bluff and Norton Lakes — all within 40 minutes driving time!

HORTON, Brown (A-12) pop. 2,830; 1 Mun.; 2 GSC; 3 Mun.; 4 CRIP; 5 US 159, US 73, K-20; Bank of Horton $2,515,000; newspaper — Horton Headlight. Five miles west of Horton is the 6,500-acre Kickapoo Indian Reservation. An annual Indian Pow-Wow is usually held in July.

°HOWARD, Elk (F-11) pop. 971; 1 KGE; 2 Mun.; 3 Mun.; 4 AT&SF; 5 K-99; First National Bank, Howard National Bank $3,613,000; newspaper — Howard Courant-Citizen.

Elk County — Earnings per cap. $1,634; sales tax collections $87,064; employed in industry 188; number of farms 732; crop value $2,016,480; livestock value $5,350,980; mineral production $1,148,584. Limestone is quarried for concrete aggregate, roadstone, railroad ballast and agstone. Crude petroleum production totaled 153,000 barrels. Recovery of natural gas increased 272 per cent to 464 million cubic feet.

°HOXIE, Sheridan (B-3) pop. 1,294; 1 CKP; 2 K-NG; 3 Mun.; 4 UP; 5 US 24, K-23; First National Bank, Hoxie State Bank $10,385,000; newspaper — Hoxie Sentinel.

Sheridan County — Earnings per cap. $1,417; sales tax collections $87,975; employed in industry 148; number of farms 557; crop value $7,436,030; livestock value $3,602,180; mineral production $1,064,579.

HOYT, Jackson (B-11) pop. 343; 1 KPL; 3 Mun.; 4 CRIP; 5 US 75.

HUDSON, Stafford (E-6) pop. 222; 1 KPL; 4 MP; Hudson State Bank $913,000.

°HUGOTON, Stevens (G-2) pop. 3,044; 1 Mun.; 2 NNG; 3 Mun.; 4 AT&SF; 5 US 270, US 56, K-51, K-25; Citizens State Bank $7,293,000; newspaper — Hugoton Hermes. In Hugoton is the Stevens County Gas and Historical Museum with rig at the well-site of what is the first municipally owned gas well and the only one of its kind in the world.

Stevens County — Earnings per cap. $2,190; sales tax collections $158,953; employed in industry 562; number of farms 390; crop value $222,460; livestock value $1,416,480; mineral production $20,504,181. Stevens County ranked second in output of natural gas; production down 2 per cent to 153.7 billion cubic feet. Production of crude petroleum totaled 432,000 barrels, an increase of 8 per cent. Gooch gas field was an important discovery.

HUMBOLDT, Allen (E-12) pop. 2,484; 1 KGE; 2 Mun.; 3 Mun.; 4 AT&SF, MKT; 5 US 169, US 59, K-57; Humboldt National Bank $4,332,000; newspaper — Humboldt Union. At Humboldt is the Monarch Cement Company plant, one of the most modern cement plants in the world. Annual Biblesta Parade in fall features floats depicting biblical scenes.

HUNNEWELL, Sumner (G-9) pop. 91; 1 WLT; 2 WLT; 4 AT&SF; 5 US 177.

HUNTER, Mitchell (B-7) pop. 172; 1 WLT; 3 Mun.; 4 AT&SF; 5 K-181; Farmers State Bank $500,000.

HURON, Atchison (A-12) pop. 122; 1 KPL; 2 GSC; 4 MP; 5 K-73.

°HUTCHINSON, Reno (E-8) pop. 37,914; 1 KPL; 2 GSC & Arkansas-Louisiana Gas (not residential); 3 Mun.; 4 H&N, AT&SF, CRIP, MP; 5 US 50, K-96, K-61, K-17; 6 CEN; 7 Hutchinson Junior College; Central State Bank, First National Bank of Hutchinson, Hutchinson National Bank & Trust Co. $69,356,000; newspapers — Hutchinson News, Hutchinson Record. The city is atop the greatest salt deposits in the world. It is a major salt production center with three of the largest salt evaporation plants and one of the most modern salt mines. Hutchinson is the largest primary hard wheat market in the country. The Kansas State Fair is held each September; the National Junior College basketball tournament each March. The State Industrial Reformatory is here. At the entrance of Carey Municipal Park is the Emerson Carey Memorial Fountain with its beautiful, ever changing, colored lights and water sprays.

Reno County — Earnings per cap. $2,071; sales tax collections $2,356,724; employed in industry 13,009; number of farms 2,289; crop value $16,668,840; livestock value $9,695,620; mineral production $13,976,745. Reno County ranked first in salt production. Evaporated salt from brine wells was produced by the Carey Salt Co., Morton Salt Co. and the Barton Salt Co. Rock salt was mined by the Carey Salt Co. Sand and gravel is produced mainly for building and paving. Cities Service Oil Co. has began recovering natural gas liquids at its new fractionation plant in Hutchinson. A new 180-mile pipeline from Ulysses delivers a de-ethanized feedstock for the 650,000-gallon-per-day plant. Crude petroleum output, 975,000 barrels, was near previous year's. Natural gas production up 15 per cent to 3.3 billion cubic feet.

Large lawn, huge trees provide picturesque setting for Sheridan County Courthouse.

Sheridan County Hospital in Hoxie.

HOXIE: *bustling community in the irrigation country*

An agricultural center, Hoxie is located in the heart of an important wheat area and is the seat of Sheridan County. Situated at the junction of highways US 24 and K-23, it is the trade center for the territory 50 miles south, 20 miles north, 20 miles east and 30 miles west.

While wheat is the major crop, silage, corn, feed grains and cattle also are substantial products of this area. Unlimited underground water charges approximately 200 irrigation wells in the county.

Manufacturing plants here are The Apache Oil Filter Cleaner Company and Triflex Farm Machinery Company.

Hoxie has a municipal swimming pool, three parks, bowling alley, junior and adult baseball

A. M. Shatzell, banker and civic leader.

programs, golf (with summer instruction for juniors), tennis, and lakes and federal reservoirs nearby for fishing and boating. Sheridan County Lake is 10 miles from here. Webster, Cedar Bluff and Norton Reservoirs are less than a one-hour drive.

The city has a public library with more than 10,000 volumes of books and a bookmobile carrying 6,000 volumes to four other communities in the county. One-third of Sheridan County residents hold library cards.

Recently constructed elementary and high schools enroll 750 boys and girls. Sheridan County Hospital opened in 1952 with a 14-bed capacity and was expanded to 20-bed capacity in 1963. A new 24-bed long-term nursing care home also was added to the hospital that year at a cost of $250,000. The hospital has intensive care facilities. Three doctors have offices at Hoxie.

In recent years, the main street of Hoxie has taken on a new look. Several merchants constructed new buildings. Others redecorated existing store fronts.

At an altitude of 3,400 feet, Hoxie is noted for sunshiny days, cool nights and low humidity. The roadside park in town attracts thousands of tourists each summer to eat, rest and relax.

First National Bank and Hoxie State Bank total more than $10 million in deposits.

Typical of Kansas bankers is A. M. Shatzell, president of the Hoxie State Bank. For years he has been active in the civic affairs of his city and state. He has taken a personal interest in young people, promoting scholarships for students seeking higher education, and serving as a national adviser to Boy and Girl Scouts. He is a director of the Kansas State Chamber of Commerce, National Institute of Logopedics, People to People Program, Western Kansas Development Association, and is a past president of Rotary Club. He established an irrigation district which now serves more than 200 wells in Sheridan County. Also typical of Kansas bankers is his progress in his chosen field. He started as a bookkeeper in the bank in 1920, advanced to cashier in 1926 and became president in 1941.

Hoxie has Rotary, Lions Club, American Legion, Chamber of Commerce, Junior Chamber of Commerce, two federated women's clubs, Girl and Boy Scouts, home demonstration units and numerous church organizations.

Carey Salt Company's Hutchinson office.

Blasted rock salt is loaded.

CAREY SALT COMPANY: *mines at four locations*

Common table salt and salt byproducts used in 28 states and Puerto Rico are mined by Carey Salt Company at Hutchinson.

The salt deposit underlying Hutchinson is one of the largest in the world. It covers several thousand square miles and reaches a thickness of 400 feet in some places. It is the remains of an old salt sea. The deposit contains enough salt to supply the United States for the next 250,000 years! The company uses two methods to obtain the salt — mining in much the same way as coal, and pumping by use of wells. The Carey Salt Mine is 648 feet below the surface of the earth. More than 120 rooms have been cut from the solid rock salt vein. The salt is blasted from the walls, loaded into "dinkies" which operate over a network of tracks, then hoisted by elevator to the breaker house.

The evaporation process entails the boring of the well through 1) 100 feet of topsoil, 2) a layer of red rock a few feet in thickness, 3) the thick strata that is the Arkansas River underflow and quicksand, and 4) several hundred feet of blue shale. Then the boring pierces the salt. Fresh water is pumped into the hole and allowed to stand long enough to dissolve the salt. Brine that is made is then pumped to the surface and put into open settling tanks to clarify.

Back in 1896, Emerson Carey went into the ice manufacturing business with a rented plant. He built a 10-ton plant of his own the following year. In 1901, he started the Carey Salt Company, now known from coast to coast. Using exhaust steam from the ice plant, his salt plant's capacity at first was only 250 barrels daily. In the two years from 1910 to 1912, the East plant was built. It increased the capacity for production of evaporated salt to 700 tons daily.

On June 23, 1923, the Carey Rock Salt Mine was dedicated by Gov. Jonathan David. Capacity now is 1,000 tons of rock salt daily.

The Carey Salt Company has established a mine at Winnfield, La., and purchased the Diamond Crystal Salt mine and plant at Lyons, Kansas. Salt was first taken from the Winnfield mine in 1931. Recently, a new mine was opened by the Carey Salt Company on Cote Blanche Bay, La. Location of the new mine permits barge transportation to many points.

Within the company there are three selling divisions — Grocery, Agricultural and Industrial. The company has five district offices — Atlanta, Denver, Houston, Kansas City and Omaha. The home office is in Hutchinson, with plant offices at Hutchinson, Winnfield and Cote Blanche. Company employment is approximately 375.

°INDEPENDENCE, Montgomery (G-12) pop. 11,366; 1 KGE; 2 UGS; 3 Mun.; 4 AT&SF, MP; 5 US 160, US 75, K-96; 6 CEN; 7 Independence Community College (Jr.); Citizens National Bank, Independence State Bank $17,468,000; newspapers — Daily Reporter, News. In 1870, Drum Creek Treaty, near here, moved the Osage Indians to Oklahoma where, ironically, they struck oil and became among the wealthiest people on earth. Riverside Park includes a vari-colored illuminated fountain, monkey island and zoo. Montgomery County state lake and park are 4 miles south of town.

Montgomery County — Earnings per cap. $1,858; sales tax collections $1,315,721; employed in industry 8,189; number of farms 1,571; crop value $5,804,380; livestock value $5,628,320; mineral production $5,320,696. Mined shale and limestone for use in making portland and masonry cements. Limestone was quarried and crushed for concrete aggregate, roadstone, agstone and riprap. Experimental project began on production of metal oxide for industrial use. Output of crude petroleum was down 9 per cent; secondary recovery projects accounted for about half total oil production. Natural gas production was 816 million cubic feet, up 133 per cent. Petroleum refinery operated at Coffeyville.

INGALLS, Gray (E-3) pop. 213; 1 WLT; 4 AT&SF; 5 US 50; Farmers State Bank $1,120,000.

INMAN, McPherson (E-8) pop. 809; 1 KPL; 2 KPL; 3 Mun.; 4 CRIP; 5 K-61; Bank of Inman $1,541,000; newspaper — Inman Review.

°IOLA, Allen (E-12) pop. 7,369; 1 Mun.; 2 Mun.; 3 Mun.; 4 AT&SF, MKT, MP; 5 US 169, US 59, US 54, K-57; 7 Iola Junior College; Allen County State Bank, Iola State Bank $16,555,000; newspaper — Iola Register. Boyhood home of Gen. Frederick Funston, hero of the Philippine campaign, is 4½ miles north. It is a museum containing historical mementoes. Iola claims largest courthouse square in the U. S., and oldest jail in continuous use.

Allen County — Earnings per cap. $1,722; sales tax collections $468,724; employed in industry 2,331; number of farms 1,283; crop value $5,624,280; livestock value $4,901,590; mineral production $11,789,250. Allen County first in cement production, second in value of clay output, and third in value of stone production. Portland and masonry cements were produced at Iola and Humboldt. Limestone and clay for cement were obtained near the plant sites. Miscellaneous clay for heavy clay products mined. Limestone quarried and crushed for concrete aggregate and roadstone. Yield of crude petroleum, mainly by secondary recovery operations, totaled 858,000 barrels, down 9 per cent. Natural gas production up 264 per cent to 656 million cubic feet.

ISABEL, Barber (F-7) pop. 175; 1 Mun.; 3 Mun.; 4 AT&SF; 5 K-42; Isabel State Bank $830,000.

IUKA, Pratt (F-6) pop. 222; 1 Mun.; 2 GSC; 3 Mun.; 4 MP; 5 US 281; Iuka State Bank $536,000.

JAMESTOWN, Cloud (B-8) pop. 463; 1 Mun.; 3 Mun.; 4 MP; 5 K-28; Jamestown State Bank $1,409,000; newspaper — Kansas Optimist.

JENNINGS, Decatur (A-4) pop. 268; 1 CKP; 3 Mun.; 4 CRIP; 5 US 383; First State Bank $1,293,000; newspaper — Jennings Journal.

°JETMORE, Hodgeman (E-4) pop. 1,074; 1 Mun.; 2 NNG; 3 Mun.; 4 AT&SF; 5 US 283, US 156; Farmers State Bank $2,578,000; newspaper — Jetmore Republican.

Hodgeman County — Earnings per cap. $1,441; sales tax collections $56,165; employed in industry 281; number of farms 568; crop value $3,507,500; livestock value $5,965,400; mineral production $5,715,714. Almost 2 million barrels of crude petroleum was produced, up 116 per cent. Exploratory drilling resulted in 5 important oil field discoveries — Eakin Northwest, Goebel East, Lippoldt, Mellecker and Saw Log Creek Southeast. Sand for paving and road maintenance was produced.

JEWELL, Jewell (A-7) pop. 587; 1 WLT; 2 GSC; 3 Mun.; 4 MP; 5 K-28, K-14; Citizens State Bank $1,568,000; newspaper — Jewell County Republican.

°JOHNSON, Stanton (F-1) pop. 1,020; 1 Mun.; 2 PNG; 3 Mun.; 4 AT&SF; 5 US 270, US 160, K-27; Johnson State Bank $3,375,000; newspaper — Johnson Pioneer.

Stanton County — Earnings per cap. $2,220; sales tax collections $75,287; employed in industry 97; number of farms 245; crop value $5,710,440; livestock value $1,895,750; mineral production $2,806,506. The county ranked 10th in natural gas output; marketed production up 2 per cent to 22 billion cubic feet. Crude petroleum production 17,000 barrels, up 1,000 barrels.

°JUNCTION CITY, Geary (C-10) pop. 19,896; 1 KPL; 2 KPL; 3 Mun.; 4 UP; 5 I-70, US 77, US 77 Alt., US 40, US 40 Alt., K-207, K-207 spur, K-18; 6 CEN; Central National Bank, First National Bank $21,911,000; newspapers — Daily Union, Republic. Rock Springs Ranch, a 348-acre 4-H Club camp, is 13 miles south. Scenic tours of Junction City, nearby Fort Riley, and the area south of the city have been mapped and marked with signs.

Geary County — Earnings per cap. $1,636; sales tax collections $756,132; employed in industry 2,810; number of farms 455; crop value $3,168,450; livestock value $3,056,690; mineral production $692,749. Limestone quarried and crushed for concrete aggregate, roadstone, riprap and agstone. Dimension limestone prepared. Building and paving sand and gravel produced. Crude petroleum production totaled 1,000 barrels.

KANOPOLIS, Ellsworth (D-7) pop. 789; 1 Mun.; 2 GSC; 3 Mun.; 4 MP, UP; 5 K-111; Kanopolis State Bank $940,000. City is the site of old Fort Herker, a starting point for stage lines to Santa Fe and a freighting and supply depot for southern and western forts. Old guardhouse has been converted into a museum containing documents, files, guns and war equipment of the 1870's plus a rock collection and Indian relics. Salt mines are visible south of US 40 near here. Kanopolis Reservoir is 12 miles southeast.

KANORADO, Sherman (B-1) pop. 186; 1 Great Plains Electric Co-op., Inc.; 3 Mun.; 4 CRIP; 5 US 24.

°KANSAS CITY, Wyandotte (C-13) pop. 126,431; 1 Mun.; 2 GSC; 3 Mun.; 4 AT&SF, CGW, CRIP, Kan. & Mo. RY. & TERM, KCS, MP, KCKV, UP; 5 I-70, I-35, US 169, US 73, US 69, US 40, US 24, K-32, K-10, K-5; 6 CAL, BNF, TWA, Frontier, DAL, UAL, CEN, OZA; 7 Kansas City Junior College, Donnelly College (Catholic); Brotherhood State Bank, Commercial National Bank, Douglass State Bank, Exchange State Bank, Fidelity State Bank, First State Bank, Guaranty State Bank, Home State Bank, Industrial State Bank, Kaw Valley State Bank, Quindaro State Bank, Rosedale State Bank, Security National Bank, Twin City State Bank, Victory State Bank, Westgate State Bank, Wyandotte County State Bank $269,118,000; newspapers — The Press, Kansas City Kansan, Wyandotte County Record. In the heart of Kansas City's business district is Huron Cemetery, tribal burial ground of the Wyandotte Indians, with an estimated 400 burials from 1844-55. Other historic points include Kaw Point, upon which Lewis and Clark camped in their exploratory expedition up the Missouri River; Old Grinter House and frontier military road ferry site on the Kaw. Tours of large industries in Kansas City, Kansas, are held twice daily for groups only if advance arrangements are made.

Wyandotte County — Earnings per cap. $1,934; sales tax collections $5,275,947; employed in industry 46,030; number of farms 556; crop value $1,222,390; livestock value $543,350; mineral production $8,183,798. County ranked first in stone, sand and gravel output, third in portland cement production, and fifth in value of clay production. Limestone and shale obtained for manufacturing portland and masonry cements at Bonner Springs. Limestone quarried and crushed for concrete aggregate, roadstone, riprap, and flux. Sand and gravel produced mainly for building and paving. Crude perlite, mined in Western States, was expanded at Kansas City plant for use as building material. Phillips Petroleum Co., operated its petroleum refinery at Kansas City; producing rubber extender and process oils, using petroleum fractions as feedstock. Reichold Chemicals, Inc., produced phenol-formaldehyde resins, polyvinyl acetate emulsions, and formaldehyde at its chemical plant in Kansas City.

KECHI, Sedgwick (F-9) pop. 230; 1 KGE; 2 Mun.; 4 CRIP; 5 K-254.

KENSINGTON, Smith (A-6) pop. 638; 1 WLT; 2 K-NG; 3 Mun.; 4 CRIP; 5 US 36; First National Bank $1,965,000; newspaper — Kensington Mirror.

KINCAID, Anderson (E-13) pop. 242; 1 KGE; 2 Yant Enterprise Gas; 3 Mun.; 4 MKT; 5 K-52, K-31; Bank of Kincaid $1,263,000..

°KINGMAN, Kingman (F-7) pop. 3,881; 1 Mun.; 2 KPL; 3 Mun.; 4 AT&SF, MP; 5 US 54, K-17, K-14; First National Bank, State Bank of Kingman $7,951,000; newspapers — Kingman Journal, Inc., Leader-Courier. The Kingman Rodeo is held annually in late May. Kingman County State Lake is 8 miles west on US 54. The park contains a game refuge, quail farm and buffalo herd.

Kingman County — Earnings per cap. $1,819; sales tax collections $233,260; employed in industry

Major highways branch out to all parts of mid-America from the Inter-City Viaduct spanning the Missouri-Kansas Rivers confluence. Straight ahead one block is the heart of downtown Kansas City, Kansas.

KANSAS CITY: *no doubt about it,*
this is Kansas!

People of Kansas City, Kansas, are blunt and outspoken in holding on to their identity and traditions as a Kansas community.

Circumstances, not affectation, cause them to do this. To the unaware, particularly the out-of-towner, the two Kansas Citys — one in Kansas and the other in Missouri — appear to merge into one. Even the waters of the Kansas (KAW) and Missouri rivers flowing between them fail to mark them as separate communities.

Yet, though both closely edge opposite banks of the two rivers, each is an entity in itself, politically, historically and particularly so in terms of state and civic loyalties. Ties of statehood stretch west from Kansas City, Kansas, across rolling wheat and cattle lands, past humming factories and tops of the earth's resources — gas, oil and coal — to the Kansas-Colorado line.

Residents of Kansas City, Kansas, are quick to assert that their city is no less Kansas, even though it stands at the eastern edge of the state, only a stone's throw from another city of the same name in another state. Just as quickly, they will tell you that their city is the oldest and second largest in Kansas.

To assure its present position as the second largest city in the state, Kansas City, Kansas, extended its boundaries in 1965 to embrace a population of 186,000. History, however, clinches its position as the state's oldest city. The year 1965 marked its 108th birthday.

It was founded as the city of Wyandotte by some 700 members of the Wyandotte Indian tribe. This was a near-white tribe, resulting from the tribe's deliberate intermarriage and mingling of white blood with their own. When forced to sell their land on the Upper Sandusky River in northwestern Ohio, the Wyandottes came here to the junction of the KAW and

Missouri rivers and purchased from the Delaware Indians 36 sections of land running from the rivers west to the middle of what is now Wyandotte County.

Building homes and a community, they welcomed new settlers of all national descents. Many Wyandottes were educated. Some were of the professions — doctors, lawyers, Christian clergy. Others were canny, astute tradesmen. Several were community leaders of early Kansas City, Kansas.

Famed University of Kansas Medical Center.

KANSAS CITY: *community of schools, parks, churches, homemakers*

One of the outstanding medical institutions in the Midwest — the University of Kansas Medical Center — is located here. It is the only school of medicine and the only university referral hospital in the state.

Also in Kansas City are Central Baptist Theological Seminary, Donnelly College, St. Augustine Seminary, Kansas City Kansas Junior College, Our Savior of the World Catholic Seminary, State School for the Blind and 17 senior and junior high schools.

Forty-one parks within the city provide 342 acres for recreation. Boating, fishing, hiking, camping, bridle paths and ice skating in winter are available at five county parks nearby. Largest of these is Wyandotte County Lake and Park on 1,500 acres just northwest of the city on Highway K-5. The lake covers 300 acres.

There are 280 churches in Kansas City, ranging the full spectrum of denominations.

It is also a community of homemakers. Sixty-seven per cent of homes in Kansas City are owned by the occupants.

Kansas University Medical Center had a 1965-66 enrollment of 1,115 medical students. The center offers medical treatment in every area of human illness to people from every county in Kansas, 49 other states and even foreign countries in such fields as open-heart surgery and eye diseases. Primarily a medical educational institution in all the basic fields of medicine, it also does research in all basic medical sciences.

Fifty-one students were enrolled for the 1965-1966 term at Central Baptist Theological Seminary in college-level training for the clergy. Enrollment at Our Savior of the World Catholic Seminary was 92 students at the high school level. Kansas City Junior College had 1,338 students in day or night classes.

Employees depart lobby entrance of 43-acre GM Assembly Division, General Motors Corp. Plant which turned out its millionth Buick during 1965.

KANSAS CITY: *pioneers industrial park*
concept

Kansas City, Kansas, has pioneered the industrial park concept in its planning for industry along the western banks of the Missouri River and astride the Kansas River.

This has been the "green-grass" approach to siteing industrial plants, avoiding willy-nilly location of industry and not permitting them to become community eyesores.

Industry is located at ample sources of water and power supply, as well as inlets and outlets to rail, highway, water and air transport. Industrial planning also provides city zoning, tax-leveling and industrial revenue bond ordinances which permit the city's industries to flourish.

Long-range projection of such planning now makes available large tracts of industrial land which invite new industrial tenants to the city.

The industrial park concept is the setting aside of land for industrial use, setting forth restrictions in the conveyances of property for protection of owners, and includes controlled architecture among restrictions. Normally, as has been the experience in Kansas City, Kansas, land is acquired for development of an industrial district by private enterprise. But now, in cooperation with civic authority, land within the tract is offered to companies for industrial use. Civic authority gets into the act, not only from the standpoint of drawing industry to the city, but also from the standpoint of promoting industrial revenue bonds if the potential tenants desire to purchase sites within the development by this method.

New industries here in 1965 include All-Metal Products Company, manufacturer of fumigating equipment; Koch Brothers Bag Company, burlap mats for curing concrete; Rock Island Railroad Company, general offices; Grandview Steel, Inc., fabricator of industrial and structural steel; Drive-In Theater Manufacturing Company, equipment for drive-in theaters; K. C. Industries, Inc., commercial and residential plastic draperies; Sealy Mattress Company, mattresses; King Koil Sleep Products Company, mattresses, box springs and beds; Irving Subway Grating Company, Inc., metal gratings for oil refineries, power, chemical and sewage disposal plants; Killians Company, fabrication of water softeners; Missouri Native Stone, finishers and distributors of domestic and imported stone products; Goldblatt Tool Company, subsidiary of Bliss & Laughlin Industries, manufacturers of "tools for the trowel trade"; Acme Plating Company, electro-plating operations; H. D. Lee Company, manufacturers of western and sports wear; and Motive Parts Warehousing, distributor of automobile replacement parts.

Industrial parks permit avoidance of unsightly developments often accompanying location of industry in the absence of any planning whatsoever. It is then but a small step for the development entrepreneur, either on his own volition or in response to civic pressure, to include underground power and communication transmission lines, and planting of trees and grass in his plans.

Kansas City's industrial park program started in 1923 when Union Pacific Railroad Company purchased 2,000 acres and developed them in intervening years. This was the first — or pioneer — planned industrial effort of this kind in the United States. More than 150 firms now are located in Fairfax.

Then came development of Armourdale, Santa Fe and Wolcott industrial parks. The 60-acre Armourdale site is occupied by a dozen firms engaged in light and heavy industry. Plans are under way to annex 80 additional acres to the project. Santa Fe has 500 acres and six tenant industries. The park has 360 acres available to new tenants. Still under development is Wolcott with 600 acres of Missouri River front.

Union Pacific announced that it would develop 260 acres of KAW river valley farm land eight miles west of here into an industrial district early in 1966. The park will be bounded on the north by Union Pacific tracks and on the south by Highway K-32.

Colgate-Palmolive Co. employs 750.

A million dollars a day changes hands in trading at the Kansas City stockyards.

Fairbanks-Morse Pump Division of Colt Industries employs 1,100.

Low-cost barge transportation is advantage.

KANSAS CITY: *transportation center*

Kansas City, Kansas, is easy to ship to and from by rail, highway, air and waterway. Near the center of the United States, Kansas City is the hub of transportation facilities reaching out over the length and breadth of the nation.

A dozen trunkline railroads make 78 freight and 142 scheduled passenger departures daily. Over two million freight cars of raw materials and finished products roll in and out of the city annually.

Three million tons aboard vehicles of 147 trucking firms, several of which are transcontinental carriers, enter and exit the city annually.

Overnight airline service to either sea coast and to major cities in between makes Kansas City, Kansas, a mainline air hub. Annually, eight airlines carry 8.5 million pounds of freight into terminals serving Kansas City, Kansas. They also carry 1,229,000 passengers and over four million pounds of mail.

Eight barge lines provide low-cost transport plus modern loading and unloading facilities to other inland ports and to all parts of the world. Revenue from barge transport for 1963 was $2.6 million. Most of the volume consisted of grain and grain products, iron and steel and pipe products, liquid chemicals such as soap ingredients, and salt and fertilizer products.

In the past, low-cost barge transportation has experienced substantial increases in tonnage each year. Linking of Kansas City, Kansas, with other large industrial centers by the Missouri River waterway is one more advantage to local industries.

Kansas City, Kansas, products that go to foreign markets are quartz crystals and cooling towers. Typical products that go or come by trucks are foods, insulation materials, plywood products and autos.

Rail shipments carry grain and food products, steel, iron and automobiles. Products that come and go by air are component units of manufactured items and other critical products on short order.

In 1965 Rock Island Railroad Company made Kansas City, Kansas, its operating heart for a 9,000-mile rail system in 14 states. Rock Island consolidated its two operation division offices in Des Moines, Iowa, and El Reno, Okla., into a single operations office in Kansas City.

KANSAS CITY: *hospitable, accessible*

Since the time it accorded a wide-open, lustful welcome to pioneers setting out to trek west on the Santa Fe and Oregon trails, Kansas City, Kansas, has clung to its traditions as a hospitable community.

As the hub of modern transport reaching out to the breadth and length of the nation, Kansas City today is the halfway point to everywhere American, via airline, railroad, car or bus.

Community cooperation adds the practical touch to Kansas City hospitality, particularly for conventioneers. The Chamber of Commerce lends a hand to help get conventions rolling. City government and civic groups promote their city as the best place in the nation for conventions. Free parking is accorded convention visitors in all street and municipally-owned parking facilities. Convention parking stickers are provided by the chief of police.

Among the larger convention facilities available are Memorial Hall auditorium downtown, Battenfeld Auditorium at Kansas University Medical Center student union building and National Guard Armory.

Memorial Hall seats 3,400 in the auditorium, 600 in the ballroom and smaller numbers in other meeting rooms. Hotels, motels, YMCA and YWCA accommodate many smaller conventions.

National Guard Armory, seven minutes from downtown, has auditorium seating 3,000.

On the fringe of Kansas City is Wyandotte Lake and Park.

1,071; number of farms 1,134; crop value $8,642,040; livestock value $6,605,870; mineral production $16,459,535. Almost 4 million barrels of crude petroleum was produced, a decrease of 10 per cent. Production of natural gas up 7 per cent to 28.5 billion cubic feet. Nashville gas field was an important discovery. Natural gas liquids were recovered at the Mobil Oil Co. Spivey plant and at the Kansas Hydrocarbons Co. Cheney plant. Sand and gravel produced mainly for building and paving.

*KINSLEY, Edwards (E-5) pop. 2,455; 1 KPL; 2 KPL; 3 Mun.; 4 AT&SF; 5 US 183, US 56, US 50; The Kinsley Bank $4,711,000; newspaper — Kinsley Mercury. A pioneer sod house replica has been erected at Kinsley.

Edwards County — Earnings per cap. $1,790; sales tax collections $144,690; employed in industry 417; number of farms 586; crop value $4,612,390; livestock value $2,934,960; mineral production $1,677,006. Crude petroleum production decreased for third consecutive year; total output 415,000 barrels. Natural gas output totaled 3 billion cubic feet. Bordewick, Britton, and McClanahan East gas fields were important discoveries. Sand and gravel for building, paving and fill uses.

KIOWA, Barber (G-7) pop. 1,551; 1 WLT; 2 UGSv; 3 WLT; 4 AT&SF, MP; 5 K-14, K-8; Bank of Kiowa, First State Bank $6,631,000; newspaper — Kiowa News. Building where Carry Nation smashed her first saloon is located on Main Street. One mile south of Kiowa is location of one of the starting places for Cherokee Strip Run of 1893.

KIRWIN, Phillips (A-6) pop. 335; 1 WLT; 3 Mun.; 4 MP; 5 K-9. Kirwin Dam and Reservoir southwest of town.

KISMET, Seward (G-3) pop. 282; 1 WLT; 2 GSC; 3 Mun.; 4 CRIP; 5 US 54.

LABETTE, Labette (G-13) pop. 97; 1 KPL; 4 MKT.

*LA CROSSE, Rush (D-5) pop. 1,798; 1 Mun.; 2 KPL; 3 Mun.; 4 MP; 5 US 183, K-4; Farmers & Merchants State Bank, Home State Bank $5,402,000; newspaper — Rush County News.

Rush County — Earnings per cap. $2,072; sales tax collections $177,144; employed in industry 392; number of farms 871; crop value $5,276,840; livestock value $3,416,540; mineral production $2,882,795. Volume of shipments of helium with a purity of 99.995 per cent or greater from the Bureau of Mines plant at Otis increased 9 per cent. Crude petroleum production totaled 358,000 barrels, down 5 per cent. Output of natural gas up 8 per cent to nearly 1.8 billion cubic feet. Sand produced for paving and road maintenance.

LA CYGNE, Linn (D-13) pop. 911; 1 KCPL; 2 LaCygne Gas Co.; 3 KCPL; 4 SLSF; 5 K-135; Linn County Bank $1,466,000; newspaper — LaCygne Journal.

LA HARPE, Allen (E-12) pop. 596; 1 Mun.; 2 GSC; 3 Iola Water; 4 MKT, MP; 5 US 54.

*LAKIN, Kearny (E-2) pop. 1,581; 1 Mun.; 2 K-NG; 3 Mun.; 4 AT&SF; 5 US 50, K-25; Kearny County Bank $4,652,000; newspaper — Lakin Independent. Two miles east of Lakin is Lake McKinney, a 3,000-acre area. One mile west of Lakin is Sod House Museum.

Kearny County — Earnings per cap. $1,990; sales tax collections $71,879; employed in industry 331; number of farms 310; crop value $4,506,430; livestock value $2,207,590; mineral production $10,291,667. County ranked fourth in natural gas production; over 77 billion cubic feet produced. Natural gas liquids were recovered at Colorado Interstate Gas Co. Lakin plant and at Kansas-Nebraska Natural Gas Co. Deerfield plant. Output of crude petroleum near previous year's. Sand and gravel for building, paving and fill produced.

LANCASTER, Atchison (B-12) pop. 202; 1 KPL; 4 MP; 5 US 73, K-9; State Bank of Lancaster $742,000.

LANE, Franklin (D-13) pop. 306; 1 KCPL; 2 GSC; 3 Mun.; 4 MP.

LANGDON, Reno (E-7) pop. 88; 1 KPL; 2 GSC; 4 CRIP; 5 K-61.

LANSING, Leavenworth (B-13) pop. 2,014; 1 KPL; 2 KPL; 4 AT&SF, UP; 5 US 73.

*LARNED, Pawnee (E-6) pop. 5,257; 1 Mun.; 2 KPL; 3 Mun.; 4 AT&SF, MP; 5 US 156, US 56, K-19 spur; First National Bank, First State Bank $15,457,000; newspaper — Tiller and Toiler. Fort Larned, established in late 1850's, about six miles west, was the most important Kansas military post on the Santa Fe Trail. The fort was a quadrangle with parade grounds in the center.

This complex limestone handling system does the following: raises limestone from ground level to top of building where it automatically feeds hoppers located inside the building. These distribute the rock to various points in the water purification system.

MID-WEST CONVEYOR COMPANY: *keeps industries 'on the move'*

A Kansas industry is responsible for keeping many other industries "on the move" in 24 states and in foreign countries!

All types of conveyor systems and mechanical handling equipment are designed, manufactured and erected by Mid-West Conveyor Company, Inc., of Kansas City, Kansas.

Mid-West Conveyor and its subsidiary company, Mid-West Metal Products, Inc., and other industrial operations are on the southeastern edge of the Fairfax Airport. This complex of large buildings which house the two firms is located on a 42-acre plot with nine acres under roof. Employment averages nearly 400.

Specialized engineering and custom equipment are required for most conveyors. This is necessary because of the variety of problems encountered in many industrial plants.

In addition to the manufacture of all types of conveyor systems, the company manufactures storage and handling racks for heavy duty service. This includes platform trucks, adjustable pallet racks, portable steel containers, bins and objects of rolled sheet steel. Also, the company is equipped to install heavy machinery and equipment in industrial plants. Among the many services offered to customers are engineering, product development, machine design, machine shop production, steel erection, welding (gas, arc, spot, heliarc), metal fabrication, phosphatizing, painting and assembly.

The design staff is headed by capable and experienced engineers. The manufacturing personnel produce intricate close-tolerance parts and assemblies of all kinds. The erection department is comprised of experienced supervisors and qualified craftsmen, many of whom have been with the company since it was organized in December, 1946.

Mid-West Conveyor occupies 252,900 square feet of manufacturing space including 25,000 square feet warehouse storage and 17,000 square feet for engineering and administrative departments. The company and its customers benefit from the location in the Fairfax Industrial District. Airport runways extend to the company buildings, major truck lines have easy access to the plant, rail spurs enter the buildings, and Missouri River loading docks are but a few blocks from the plant.

The firm has conducted business in the East — New York, Delaware, New Jersey, Massachusetts, Pennsylvania and Maryland; in the South — Alabama, Arkansas, Georgia and Louisiana; in the Midwest — Ohio, Illinois, Indiana, Iowa, Michigan, Wisconsin, Missouri, Nebraska, Kansas and Oklahoma; and in the Southwest — Texas, New Mexico, Arizona and California. The company has fabricated and shipped conveyor parts for erection in foreign countries. In August, of 1955, a subsidiary company was formed to supply a need for precision light metal fabrication. This company, Mid-West Metal Products, Inc., manufactures precision metal cabinets for sophisticated electronics equipment. It specializes in the design and manufacture of consoles, control boxes, racks, instruments and other devices which require a high degree of stability and quality finished appearance. Such equipment is seen in teletype and communication operations at airports, aboard naval vessels, submarines, airplanes and at communication centers. This company is fully equipped to supply specialized parts and assemblies. Mid-West Metal Products, Inc., has participated in Government contracts both on a prime and sub-contract basis. Products have been supplied for the U. S. Navy, Western Electric Company, Inc., The Strategic Air Command, American Telephone and Telegraph Company and many others.

The officers and board of directors of Mid-West Conveyor Company, Inc., hold the same positions with Mid-West Metal Products, Inc. Both companies are Equal Employment Opportunity firms. Both employ handicapped people although the number is limited because of the normal hazards of production equipment.

Both firms maintain a policy of on-the-job training. Supervised training is provided in the design, manufacturing and erection departments of Mid-West Conveyor. Also, training is provided new personnel in the manufacture of cabinetry, consoles, communication and electronic equipment and other specialized manufacture of Mid-West Metal Products. This policy enables inexperienced personnel to become qualified and capable in a particular trade.

Since the market for products of both companies is expanding annually, the future for both Mid-West companies holds exciting promise. Excellent opportunities exist within the companies for new people — as apprentice engineers, draftsmen, welders, machinists, tool and die makers and painters.

Kansas City Star's conveyor system moves paper rolls from three levels in one building, across the street through tunnel and through pressroom.

167

THE DARBY CORPORATION: *Kansas City, Kansas,*
pioneer manufacturer of iron and steel products

The Lewis and Clark Expedition of 1804 chose the junction of the Kaw and Missouri Rivers as their main campsite prior to exploration of the great Northwest Pacific areas. Today, some 160 years later, this same site is the principal location of another pioneer . . . a growing industrial firm.

The Darby Corporation of Kansas City, Kansas, fabricator and erector of steel and alloy plate and structural steel, has been in business for over 50 years. It is extremely diversified. Its plant facilities are equipped to perform all types of fabrication. These include shearing, stamping, rolling, forming, upsetting, welding, stress relieving, X-raying, sandblasting and painting. Darby manufactures its products from the various carbon steels including the new extra high tensile alloys, as well as stainless, Monel, Inconel, nickel and aluminum in both the solid and clad forms. For many years the company has been authorized to apply the ASME Code symbol to fired and unfired pressure vessels produced in its plants.

At present, Darby manufactures tanks, pressure vessels, large off-the-road trailers, smoke stacks, elevated water tanks, radio relay towers, bunkers and bins. It also makes process equipment for refineries, chemical plants and soap plants. Darby diversifies into such fields as contract manufacturing of farm implements, truck mounted hydraulic cranes, welded steel girders for bridges, etc.

The company makes automobile racks for installation on flatbed railroad cars and patented tie-down equipment for securing automobiles to the automobile racks. Darby also manufactures large penstocks. In 1947, it completed penstocks for the Department of Interior, 96″ and 108″ in diameter for Estes Park and Marys Lake, Colorado. These penstocks are part of a system to carry water from the western side of the Continental Divide to the eastern side for irrigation and power purposes.

In addition to its plant operations, The Darby Corporation erects large numbers of storage tanks, elevated water tanks, stacks and breechings. It currently performs services in the area of "Maintenance by Contract" for refineries and chemical and food processing plants.

During World War II, the facilities of the plant were converted primarily to Government defense contract work. The company earned five Army and Navy "E" awards for outstanding performance on Government contracts. These were for producing LCT and LCM landing craft for the Navy, 1,000-pound semi-armor piercing bombs and 4,000-pound block buster bombs for the Army and Air Force, locomotive boilers for the lend-lease program and submarine mine cases for harbor and coastal protection of the country. It also conducted research and development programs for floatation devices for tracked vehicles and mine exploders.

After the war, Darby Corporation, along with its normal custom fabrication work, engaged in high production manufacturing of cultivators for a nationally known implement manufacturer.

In 1962, the company was given an award of merit by the American Institute of Steel Construction for its part in furnishing the steel for the prize winning Randolph Bridge over the Tuttle Creek Reservoir in central Kansas. This is the longest highway bridge in the state. Darby's Middle West location — at the crossroads of the nation — facilitates delivery to a national market by truck, rail or barge.

112-cubic yard coal hauling trailer designed and built by Darby.

Steel penstocks for Continental Divide.

Refinery tower, 145' long, being moved from plant.

Aluminum process tanks made by Darby.

40,000 barrel solid stainless steel ammonium nitrate storage tank.

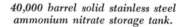

Solid stainless steel special process vessel 14'-6" x 45' long.

New auto rack, designed and built by Darby Corp., and mounted on flat car.

Old Fort Larned is National Historic Site.

LARNED: *industrial frontier today*

Larned is named for an old military post that is now a national tourist attraction. It serves as psychiatric center for 47 western counties and industrial, agricultural and governmental center for Pawnee County.

Old Fort Larned, six miles west of town, stands today as the first National Historic Site in Kansas! The National Park Service controls 700 acres including the 20-acre site on which the original buildings stand. Visitors to this outstanding historic and educational attraction on U. S. 56 will see what life on the frontier was like a century ago. They will see a museum with Indian artifacts, hundreds of military and pioneer items, the "guns that won the West," Officers Quarters carefully refurnished and an old escape tunnel now open to the public.

In the 1860's, Fort Larned stood as the most valued military post on the Santa Fe Trail. It was headquarters for more than 100 skirmishes with Indians. Over 500 troopers, plainsmen and Indians were killed or wounded within 30 miles of the fort. It was established as a base for troops to guard the mails and travelers.

The Larned State Hospital, three miles west of the city, provides diagnosis, care and treatment for one-third of the state's patients with psychiatric and neurologic disorders. It has the first walk-in clinic in Kansas. The hospital employs 700 people and has an annual payroll in excess of $2 million. In addition to the hospital proper, the State Security Hospital is located on the grounds. This unit serves the entire state.

Larned's trade territory has two abundant water supplies, the Arkansas and Pawnee rivers. Now under irrigation are 25,000 acres from streams and 125 wells. Still untapped is underground water and stream water that could expand irrigation to 100,000 acres to produce alfalfa, sorghum, corn, vegetables and specialty crops.

One of the larger industries in Larned is Doerr Metal Products Co. It manufactures a variety of articles — metal boats, stock tanks, grain beds, bulk feeders and irrigation pipe. Newacheck Supply Co. makes combine, binder and swather canvases, irrigation dams, tarpaulins and boat covers. Twin Feed Blower Co. manufactures hydraulic power equipment for farm machinery — power mowers, etc. The three firms ship nationwide and overseas. Schultz Home Modernizing Co. manufactures storm doors, windows and many other items from extruded aluminum. Other industries make hydraulic lifts, power steering for tractors and combines. Phinney's is a local manufacturer and applicator of liquid fertilizers. Three dehydrating plants in the county process alfalfa into pellets and meal for livestock feeders.

Five large feed yards, within a radius of 10 miles, are equipped to handle 30,000 head of cattle in their yards at one time and all are still growing.

Larned is a city which appreciates its role in frontier history and enjoys sharing this heritage with others. It is, however, giving attention to today's and tomorrow's living. Civic leaders recently acquired an industrial park through the Community Development Corporation. The citizens backed up this action at a special election by favoring an industrial levy to aid business growth and promote industrial frontiers.

Every building still stands to be viewed by the public as a National Historic Site, the first one for Kansas. Larned State Hospital (mental) is 3½ miles west of the city. A historical museum is in Larned Library.

Pawnee County — Earnings per cap. $1,973; sales tax collections $316,387; employed in industry 821; crop value $6,263,480; livestock value $4,019,480; mineral production $3,307,501. Output of crude petroleum slightly more than 1 million barrels, down 4 per cent. Production of natural gas down 15 per cent to 2 billion cubic feet. Eddy gas field was important discovery. Sand and gravel produced mainly for building and paving.

LATHAM, Butler (F-10) pop. 207; 1 KGE; 4 SLSF. Butler County state lake (Lake Clymer) is 3 miles northwest of here.

LATIMER, Morris (C-10) pop. 41; 1 KPL; 4 CRIP; 5 K-4.

°LAWRENCE, Douglas (C-12) pop. 27,024; 1 KPL; 2 Kansas Public Service Gas; 3 Mun.; 4 AT&SF, CRIP, UP; 5 I-70, US 59, US 40, US 24, K-10; 7 University of Kansas; Douglas County State Bank, First National Bank of Lawrence, Lawrence National Bank $36,081,000; newspapers — Lawrence Daily Journal-World, World Co., Lawrence Outlook. Lawrence, established in 1854 as a Free-State stronghold, was sacked and burned twice by proslavery forces. There is a monument in Oak Hill Cemetery to the 150 victims of the Quantrill raid. Points of interest on the University of Kansas campus are the 120-foot Campanile dedicated as World War II Memorial; Dyche Museum with one of the largest collections of fossil remains and mounted animals displayed in natural habitats; Spooner Thayer Art Museum with collections of Indian craftwork, glassware, silverware and Oriental paintings; Wilcox Museum with Greek sculpture, Greek and Roman antiquities; and Snow Entomological Museum, one of the most complete in the nation, with two million specimens.

Douglas County — earnings per cap. $2,072; sales tax collections $1,459,784; employed in industry 6,236; number of farms 1,331; crop value $6,607,200; livestock value $5,731,790; mineral production $245,847. Quarried and crushed limestone for concrete aggregate, roadstone, and agstone. Sand and gravel for building, paving and fill was produced. Crude petroleum output dropped 32 per cent; secondary recovery operations supplied most of production. Natural gas production 24 million cubic feet. Cooperative Farm Chemicals Assn., producers of ammonia, nitric acid and fertilizers, completed expansion of petrochemical complex at Lawrence.

°LEAVENWORTH, Leavenworth (B-13) pop. 23,837; 1 KPL; 2 KPL; 3 Mun.; 4 AT&SF, CB&Q, CGW, MP, UP; 5 US 73, K-92, K-7; First National Bank, Leavenworth National Bank, Manufacturers State Bank $24,517,000; newspapers — Chronicle, Times. This oldest city in Kansas has played host to such famous personages as Lincoln, John Wilkes Booth, Sara Bernhardt and Generals Grant, Sherman, Sheridan and Lee. General Custer's ill-fated command was stationed at Ft. Leavenworth and Carry Nation brought her famous hatchet to the city's bar rooms. Leavenworth has steel and iron plants, and a shipyard builds landing craft, commercial river boats and barges and house boats for river, lake and ocean use. The Federal Penitentiary adjoins the city to the northwest. The Veterans Administration Center with its hospital and the former old soldiers' home is on the southeast edge of town. St. Mary College and the Mother House of the Sisters of Charity adjoin the city on the south; Fort Leavenworth on the north.

Leavenworth County — Earnings per cap. $1,923; sales tax collections $904,225; employed in industry 6,690; number of farms 1,467; crop value $5,300,700; livestock value $5,044,140; mineral production $148,845. Quarried and crushed limestone produced for concrete aggregate, roadstone and agstone; sand for fill and other uses. Production of natural gas was 294 million cubic feet, a 135 per cent increase. Crude petroleum production 9,300 barrels.

LEAWOOD, Johnson (C-13) pop. 9,424; 1 KCPL; 2 GSC; 3 Water Dist. No. 1, Johnson Co.

LEBANON, Smith (A-7) pop. 620; 1 WLT; 2 GSC; 3 Mun.; 4 CRIP; 5 US 281; First National Bank $1,239,000; newspaper — Lebanon Times. The historical geographical center of the United States (exclusive of Alaska and Hawaii) is located two miles northwest.

LEBO, Coffey (D-11) pop. 493; 1 KPL; 2 Lebo Gas Co.; 4 AT&SF; 5 US 50, K-131; State Bank of Lebo $2,514,000; newspaper — Lebo Enterprise.

LECOMPTON, Douglas (C-12) pop. 355; 1 KPL; 2 GSC; 3 Mun.; 4 AT&SF. Here is Constitution

PANHANDLE
EASTERN: natural gas pioneer

Thirty-six years ago Panhandle Eastern Pipe Line Company ushered in a new and exciting phase of Kansas history. It completed an 800-mile pipeline from Liberal to Dana, Ind. The project marked the beginning of large scale natural gas deliveries from the vast Hugoton field of Kansas to the industrial urban centers of the East.

Today, Panhandle Eastern spans the industrial heartland of America from the Texas Panhandle to the Great Lakes, and with its subsidiary, Trunkline Gas Company of Houston, Tex., operates a network of more than 11,000 miles of high-pressure pipeline.

Starting with an initial capacity of 85 million cubic feet daily, the Panhandle transmission system has grown to a daily sales capacity of more than 2.5 billion cubic feet. It serves a market area of 22 million people in Kansas, Texas, Missouri, Illinois, Indiana, Ohio, Michigan, Kentucky, Tennessee, Arkansas, Mississippi, Louisiana and Ontario, Canada.

The Panhandle-Trunkline system draws from the nation's two most prolific areas for its gas supply. Fountainhead of the Panhandle main line is the Anadarko Basin, comprising the Hugoton field of Kansas, Oklahoma, and Texas, and the Panhandle field of Texas. Trunkline draws upon the Louisiana and Texas Gulf Coast areas and offshore Gulf of Mexico for its supplies.

While its primary business is the transmission and sale of natural gas, Panhandle during the last 15 years has diversified into allied fields. Anadarko Production Company, a subsidiary gas and oil producing company with division offices at Liberal, was organized in 1959. Through Anadarko's acquisition of Ambassador Oil Co. in 1965, the company acquired vast oil and gas reserves in 19 states in this country and Canada, plus exploration permits in several foreign countries. Panhandle is half owner of the world's largest helium extraction plant near Liberal. Helium contained in natural gas from the Hugoton field is extracted at the plant and utilized by the Federal government in the nation's defense and scientific needs.

Another Panhandle subsidiary, Century Refining Company, operates the only refinery between Wichita and Denver, providing a market for oil produced by Anadarko and by various other independent Kansas and Oklahoma producers.

The steady, orderly growth of Panhandle Eastern over the past 36 years provides a sound basis for the company's future; its position in the industry supports confidence in its progress. Kansas, the birthplace of the company and the focal point of its operations for nearly two score years, will share in that progress.

172

Hall where the Proslavery constitution was drafted in 1857. The building which housed old Lane University is also still to be seen. Here, in the middle 1880's, Dwight Eisenhower's parents met for the first time.

LEHIGH, Marion (D-9) pop. 205; 1 KPL; 2 KPL; 4 AT&SF; 5 US 56.

LENEXA, Johnson (C-13) pop. 3,067; 1 KCPL; 2 GSC; 3 Mun.; 4 SLSF; 5 I-35, US 169, US 50, US 56, K-58; Lenexa State Bank $1,843,000.

LENORA, Norton (A-4) pop. 536; 1 CKP; 3 Mun.; 4 MP; 5 K-9; Exchange Bank $3,319,000; newspaper — Lenora News.

LEON, Butler (F-10) pop. 555; 1 KGE; 3 Mun.; 4 SLSF; 5 K-96; State Bank of Leon $875,000; newspaper — Leon News.

LEONA, Doniphan (A-12) pop. 112; 1 Leona Power & Light Co.; 4 UP; Farmers Bank of Leona $1,120,000.

LEONARDVILLE, Riley (B-10) pop. 376; 1 KPL; 3 Mun.; 4 US 24; Leonardville State Bank $1,263,000; newspaper — Riley Countian.

*LEOTI, Wichita (D-2) pop. 1,599; 1 Wheatland Elec. Co-op., Inc.; 2 K-NG; 3 Mun.; 4 MP; 5 K-96, K-25; First State Bank $4,730,000; newspaper — Leoti Standard. Leoti has a 490,000-bushel elevator, one of the largest all-gravity feed elevators ever built. Another one, similar to it, is located at Selkirk, 9 miles west of Leoti. The town is also the center of a 50,000-acre irrigated area.

Wichita County — Earnings per cap. $1,923; sales tax collections $102,261; employed in industry 322; number of farms 392; crop value $6,653,180; livestock value $2,278,040; mineral production $36,893. Crude petroleum production slightly over 1,000 barrels, down 22 per cent. Gravel for paving was produced; sand obtained for paving and road maintenance.

LE ROY, Coffey (E-12) pop. 608; 1 KGE; 2 UGS; 3 Mun.; 4 MP; 5 K-57; First National Bank $679,000; newspaper — Le Roy Reporter.

LEWIS, Edwards (E-5) pop. 505; 1 KPL; 2 KPL; 3 Mun.; 4 AT&SF; 5 US 50; Home State Bank $2,593,000; newspaper — Lewis Press.

*LIBERAL, Seward (G-2) pop. 15,077; 1 WLT; 2 Liberal Gas Co.; 3 Mun.; 4 CRIP; 5 US 270, US 83, US 54; 6 CEN; Citizens State Bank, First National Bank, Peoples National Bank $21,-257,000; newspaper — Southwest Daily Times. Liberal is the home of the International Pancake Race where housewives compete with housewives of Olney, England, on Shrove Tuesday. Liberal is key city of Hugoton-Oklahoma-Texas Panhandle natural gas field. Seward County Coronado Museum is on east edge of city.

Seward County — Earnings per cap. $2,082; sales tax collections $780,710; employed in industry 4,159; number of farms 314; crop value $3,684,730; livestock value $2,263,530; mineral production $9,329,137. County ranked third in natural gas liquids output. National Helium Corp. began operating its helium extraction plant near Liberal. Natural gas liquids recovered by three firms. Production of crude petroleum down 4 per cent to 1.2 million barrels. Natural gas production 27.4 billion cubic feet, down 34 per cent. Arkalon West and March gas fields were important discoveries. Sand and gravel produced mainly for building and paving.

LIBERTY, Montgomery (G-12) pop. 229; 1 KGE; 2 UGS; 4 AT&SF; 6 CEN.

LIEBENTHAL, Rush (D-5) pop. 199; 1 WLT; 3 Mun.; 5 US 183.

*LINCOLN, Lincoln (C-7) pop. 2,009; 1 Mun.; 2 GSC; 3 Mun.; 5 K-18, K-14; Farmers National Bank, Saline Valley Bank $5,444,000; newspaper — Sentinel-Republican. Quartzite quarries still are used one mile southeast of Lincoln. Indians used the quartzite along with flint for their arrow and spear points. Evergreen Museum has pioneer artifacts, photos, and demonstrations of process used in making stone fence posts.

Lincoln County — Earnings per cap. $1,318; sales tax collections $156,770; employed in industry 526; number of farms 873; crop value $5,170,800; livestock value $5,377,560; mineral production $941,494. Sandstone quarried and crushed for concrete aggregate, roadstone, riprap, railroad ballast and filter use. Crushed limestone for riprap, paving sand and gravel produced. Small quantity of volcanic ash produced.

Pancake Race at Liberal — an international event.

LINCOLNVILLE, Marion (D-9) pop. 268; 1 KPL; 2 Greeley Gas Co.; 4 CRIP; 5 US 77, US 56; Pilsen State Bank $1,158,000.

LINDSBORG, McPherson (D-8) pop. 2,312; 1 Mun.; 2 KPL; 3 Mun.; 4 MP, UP; 5 US 81, K-14; 7 Bethany College (Lutheran); Farmers State Bank $3,746,000; newspaper — News Record. Three miles northwest is Coronado Heights where Coronado is believed to have camped in his search for mythical kingdom of Quivira. Bethany College is world-famous for its Messiah Festival held annually during Holy Week since 1882. Birger Sandzen Memorial Gallery honors the internationally recognized Swedish-American painter and teacher of art. Many of Sandzen's paintings and graphic works are on display, as well as works of other artists. Swedish Pavilion on Bethany campus was gift of Swedish Government. Popular are tours of practicing artists' studios. Swedish Hyllnings Fest is held on the odd years in October. Smoky Hill Flour Mill, water powered, is historical attraction.

LINN, Washington (A-9) pop. 528; 1 WLT; 2 KPL; 3 Mun.; 5 K-15, K-9; Linn State Bank $868,000; newspaper — Linn-Palmer Record.

LINWOOD, Leavenworth (C-13) pop. 320; 1 KPL; 2 T.A. Goff Gas.; 3 Mun.; 4 UP; 5 K-32.

LITTLE RIVER, Rice (D-8) pop. 555; 1 KPL; 2 Mun.; 3 Mun.; 4 AT&SF; 5 K-46; Home State Bank $1,389,000; newspaper — Rice County Monitor-Journal.

LOGAN, Phillips (A-5) pop. 935; 1 WLT; 2 K-NG; 3 Mun.; 4 MP; 5 K-9; First National Bank $3,061,000; newspaper — Logan Republican.

LONE ELM, Anderson (E-12) pop. 64; 1 KGE; 5 K-31.

LONGFORD, Clay (C-9) pop. 124; 1 KPL; 2 Longford Mill Products Gas; 3 Mun.; 4 AT&SF.

LONG ISLAND, Phillips (A-5) pop. 256; 1 WLT; 3 Mun.; 4 CB&Q; 5 US 383; Commercial State Bank $1,064,000.

LONGTON, Elk (F-11) pop. 368; 1 KGE; 2 Longton Gas Co.; 3 Mun.; 4 AT&SF; 5 US 160; Home State Bank $861,000; newspaper — Longton News.

Swimmers flock to modern pool in its first season.

Golfer slams down the No. 1 fairway.

Louisburg's Main Street.

LOUISBURG: small Kansas town
envisions rapid growth

Louisburg businessmen are frank to admit they exist largely from the purchasing power of farmers in eastern Miami County. Consequently, all planning of capital improvements is designed to serve both urban and rural people.

The Louisburg Area Chamber of Commerce was formed in the fall of 1964. Its purpose is to improve the entire community.

Biggest attraction of the Louisburg year is the Labor Day Picnic, sponsored by the American Legion Post. There are parades, pulling contests, a carnival company, and just plain renewing old acquaintanceships.

Lions Club sponsors a farmers' night banquet to bring farmers and townsmen together. Louisburg community hall is used extensively by 4-H clubs and home demonstration units. A community library was designed to bind urban and rural people closer together.

At a time when many small towns are deeply concerned about dwindling populations, Louisburg is growing. Population was 700 in 1947, grew to 875 in 1960 and now stands at 1,050. It is predicted that planned development of highway U. S. 69 into a four-lane highway down the eastern side of Kansas will bring further growth. U. S. 69 and K-68 form a junction here. Both are being improved this year. Louisburg streets were resurfaced recently.

About 10 per cent of the residents commute 35 miles north to jobs in Kansas City. In turn, Kansas City residents continually inquire about moving to Louisburg.

At the south edge of town, Panhandle Eastern Pipe Line Company employs more than 50 men at its compressor station. It is one of the town's major assets.

The surrounding area is a prosperous farm and dairy community. There are several large cattle ranches.

Fishing and camping sites are plentiful. New Pomona Reservoir is 50 miles west. Lake of the Ozarks lies to the east. There is an abundance of smaller lakes and streams nearby.

Within easy driving distance are metropolitan department stores, shopping centers, professional sports and cultural facilities at Kansas City.

The Louisburg Herald weekly newspaper is in its 90th year of continuous publication.

LORRAINE, Ellsworth (D-7) pop. 167; 1 WLT; 2 KPL; 3 Mun.; 4 AT&SF, SLSF; Lorraine State Bank $806,000.

LOST SPRINGS, Marion (D-9) pop. 130; 1 KPL; 2 Greeley Gas Co.; 4 AT&SF, CRIP.

LOUISBURG, Miami (D-13) pop. 956; 1 KCPL; 2 Louisburg Gas Co.; 3 Mun.; 5 US 69, K-68; Bank of Louisburg, First National Bank $3,545,000; newspaper — Herald.

LOUISVILLE, Pottawatomie (B-10) pop. 209; 1 KPL; 2 KPL; 5 K-99.

LUCAS, Russell (C-7) pop. 652; 1 Mun.; 2 GSC; 3 Mun.; 4 UP; 5 K-176, K-18; Farmers State Bank $2,510,000; newspaper — Lucas Independent. In Lucas is a man-made "Garden of Eden" consisting of three-dimensional cartoons in concrete of Adam and Eve, other biblical and social characterizations created by S. P. Dinsmoor. Miller's Rock Gardens is located at west edge of town.

LURAY, Russell (C-6) pop. 361; 1 Mun.; 2 GSC; 3 Mun.; 4 UP; 5 US 281, K-18; Peoples State Bank $3,895,000.

*LYNDON, Osage (D-12) pop. 1,005; 1 KCPL; 2 UGSv; 3 KCPL; 4 MP; 5 US 75, K-31; Lyndon State Bank $2,526,000; newspaper — Peoples Herald.

Osage County — Earnings per cap. $1,532; sales tax collections $265,184; employed in industry 569; number of farms 1,482; crop value $6,753,000; livestock value $6,332,270; mineral production $7,936. County ranked fourth in coal production. Coal mined underground and strip mined. Limestone quarried and crushed.

*LYONS, Rice (D-7) pop. 4,787; 1 KPL; 2 Mun. & Ark.-La. (residential); 3 Mun.; 4 AT&SF, SLSF, MP; 5 US 56, K-96, K-14; Chandler National Bank, Lyons State Bank $7,339,000; newspaper — Lyons Daily News. Four miles west is historical marker describing Quivira and next to it a 30-foot granite cross commemorating Father Juan de Padilla who accompanied Coronado to Kansas in 1541. In courthouse is museum with outstanding collection of pioneer and Indian relics. Near Lyons is a salt mine, and a new and modern salt processing plant.

Rice County — Earnings per cap. $1,790; sales tax collections $366,898; employed in industry 1,968; number of farms 982; crop value $7,535,980; livestock value $5,311,510; mineral production $18,076,224. County ranked second in value of salt production and sixth in petroleum output. American Salt Co. produced evaporated salt from brine wells and mined rock salt near Lyons. Crude petroleum production up 20 per cent. Output of natural gas increased 59 per cent to 500 million cubic feet. Lyons West oil field was important discovery. Quarried and crushed limestone produced for concrete aggregate, roadstone, aglime and riprap. Sand and gravel, mainly for building and paving, was produced.

MACKSVILLE, Stafford (E-6) pop. 522; 1 KPL; 2 KPL; 3 Mun.; 4 AT&SF; 5 US 50; Farmers & Merchants State Bank, Macksville State Bank $2,848,000; newspaper — Enterprise.

MADISON, Greenwood (D-11) pop. 1,123; 1 KPL; 2 GSC; 3 Mun.; 4 AT&SF; 5 K-99, K-57; First National Bank, The Madison Bank $3,398,000; newspaper — Madison News.

MAHASKA, Washington (A-9) pop. 165; 1 Mun.; 2 KPL; 3 Mun.; 4 CRIP.

MAIZE, Sedgwick (F-9) pop. 684; 1 KGE; 2 Ark.-La. Gas; 4 MP; 5 K-96.

MANCHESTER, Dickinson (C-9) pop. 129; 1 KPL; 3 Mun.; 4 AT&SF.

*MANHATTAN, Riley (B-10) pop. 21,126; 1 KPL; 2 KPL; 3 Mun.; 4 CRIP, UP; 5 US 24, K-18, K-13; 6 CEN; 7 Kansas State University of Agriculture and Applied Science; Citizens State Bank, First National Bank, Union National Bank $33,837,000; newspaper — Manhattan Mecury. The 175-acre main campus of Kansas State University with its native white stone buildings is one of the most attractive in the nation. Anderson Hall, on campus, is a historical landmark. Five miles north of Manhattan is Tuttle Creek Dam and Lake. A bridge across the 16,000-acre lake is one of the longest in the Midwest. A number of public area parks around the perimeter help make Tuttle Creek Lake a major recreational attraction. The Riley County Historical Museum is in City Memorial Building. Damon Runyon birthplace is marked. Pottawatomie County State Lake No. 2 is located northeast of the city.

Riley County — Earnings per cap. $1,857; sales tax collections $1,182,413; employed in industry 4,227; number of farms 829; crop value $4,695,740; livestock value $5,815,280; mineral production $743,922. Limestone quarried and crushed for concrete aggregate and roadstone. Dimension

Education at Kansas State University and recreation at Tuttle Creek Reservoir (top of photo) are income producers for Manhattan business and industry.

MANHATTAN: *education, research, industry*

Manhattan is the capital and natural market for a rich north-central Kansas farm empire. Two of the nation's most productive river valleys — the Kansas (Kaw) and the Blue — join three miles east of here.

Immediately to the south rise the famous Flint Hills blue stem pasture lands where grasses rank among the world's best for fattening cattle. Other thousands of acres are under intensive cultivation by farmers who long have owned and operated their farms. The large number of farm products from here are field crops, livestock, dairy and poultry. Truck farming abounds in the river valleys, adding an important source of revenue.

The stabilized economy of Manhattan is based primarily upon Kansas State University, agriculture, Fort Riley eight miles southwest of here, tourists, conventions, research, industry, insurance companies, governmental agencies and contracting services.

Manhattan is headquarters for several state and federal agencies. These are Kansas Agriculture Stabilization and Conservation Service, Agricultural Extension Service by Kansas State University, Production Credit Association, Soil Conservation Service, Bureau of Entomology and Kansas State Employment Service.

177

Manhattan has city commission (5) - city manager form of government.

One of the assets of the city is health facilities. Memorial Hospital (100 beds) was completed in 1955. St. Mary Hospital, of equal size, was opened in 1961. Kansas State University Hospital, built in 1959, has 40 beds. Irwin Army Hospital at Fort Riley, with 250 beds, was built in 1957. Several medical clinics and homes for the aged are operated here. North Central Guidance Center serves Riley, Geary, Marshall and Clay counties.

Recently, Manhattan has looked toward industrial development and research. City, county and university officials are cooperating in the venture. Voters approved a tax levy to provide revenue for attracting and locating new industries. The university provides qualified professional personnel in many industrial fields, plus a reactor for nuclear research and computing centers.

The Chamber of Commerce has options on a 45-acre research park and several industrial sites. Local corporations were formed to assist in construction of industrial and research installations. Plants can be developed through revenue bonds or private capital.

Manhattan is recognized as having one of the finest city park and recreation programs in the United States. In summer, 1,500 participate in a swimming program and almost an equal number of boys, girls and adults play regularly scheduled ball games at eight parks.

Under development is the 100-acre Ci-Co (City-County) recreation park, jointly developed by the city, county and public schools. Facilities will include a fair grounds, football stadium, baseball diamonds, swimming pool and picnic grounds. Parking will be available for 5,000 cars.

Tuttle Creek Dam, seventh largest earthen dam in the world, is five miles north of here. It provides a 16,000-acre lake with facilities for all types of recreation. The lake is bordered by several planned recreational parks and marinas, all easily accessible over good roads.

Also in this area are two other federal reservoirs, three state lakes, one private lake, streams and rivers, all accessible for fishing and boating.

A national scenic drive (north-south on K-177) is being developed through this area for tourists to view the great North American prairie, home of the Indian, bluestem grass, bison and wolf.

Riley County Historical Society Museum in the basement of Memorial Auditorium depicts much of the history of the pioneer and this section of the nation.

K-State's $2 million flour and feed milling facility, unmatched anywhere in the world.

MANHATTAN: *Kansas State University*

This is the home of Kansas State University with over a century of distinguished service to Kansas, the nation and the world. Now 104 years old, it is one of the leading examples of the highly-successful system of land-grant colleges and universities developed only in the United States. Kansas State University was the first land-grant institution in America.

With eight distinct colleges of professional stature and the graduate school, instruction offered to students has advanced dramatically from primarily agricultural toward a more diversified and industrial society, according to James A. McCain, KSU president.

The Master's degree is offered in 73 departments and the Doctor of Philosophy in 30 fields. More than 2,000 degrees are conferred annually. K-State has a faculty of national and international reputation. Nearly half the teaching and research staff has the doctorate. In 1965, full-time equivalent enrollment was 10,519. Projection of enrollment indicates 14,200 students by 1970 and approximately 18,750 by 1975. This increase will be accompanied by additional faculty and research personnel, buildings for student housing, academic needs and research.

Adjacent to the 153-acre campus here are 3,853 acres of university land for agricultural research. Five branch agricultural stations are at Hays, Colby, Garden City, Mound Valley and Tribune. These comprise an additional 4,529 acres of university land.

Agricultural agents in each of the 105 counties disseminate research results throughout the state through continuing programs of adult education, including extension services in agriculture, engineering, home economics, 4-H club work, veterinary medicine, and community and public affairs. The K-State extension service strives to make a "campus" of the entire state by taking the university to all the people of Kansas.

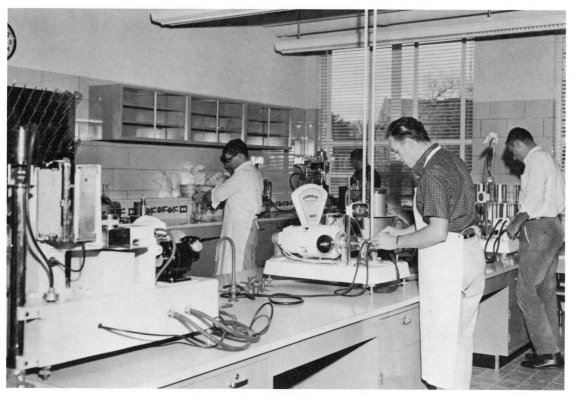

Students working in dough-testing laboratory.

MANHATTAN: *flour and feed milling study*

Kansas State University offers the world's only complete flour, feed milling and bakery management curriculum as an outstanding program in the College of Agriculture. Young people of all nationalities migrate annually to the KSU campus to take advantage of this new facility.

Interest in this field was generated before the turn of the century. It had become obvious there was a difference in milling qualities of wheat varieties grown at the time.

By 1910, a KSU milling department was established and equipment was moved into the classroom to process wheat into quality flour. And, as the formulation of feeds for livestock became more of a technical science, funds were raised within the formula feed industry to establish in 1951 the first pilot feed mill ever to become a part of an educational institution.

A continual modernization plan keeps both flour and feed milling facilities up to date with latest equipment. Kansas State University's Department of Flour and Feed Milling Industries has been providing a complete professional four-year curriculum and, more recently, the curriculum in bakery management. Incoming wheat is tested for protein content, gluten type and milling quality. Then it goes to a model bakery department where baking quality is tested in a multitude of baked products. Laboratories operate continually to study biological and physical properties of wheat and other grains to determine desirability for use in flour and feed. X-ray is used to investigate the sanitary properties of grain.

Cereal and feed grains will continue to play such an important part in providing feed for man and animals. The demand for students trained in this field is expanding rapidly.

A student adjusts automatic proportioning system for the batch mixer in K-State's new pilot feed mill. Scale to the right indicates weight of each ingredient as it is added to the hopper above the batch mixer.

Two feeders in the foreground are gravometric feeders which measure by weight, automatically adjusting to deliver a pre-set amount of dry ingredients. Other feeders are of the volumetric type, which deliver fixed volumes of feed.

limestone, building sand and paving sand available. Crude petroleum production down 4 per cent to 211,000 barrels.

*MANKATO, Jewell (A-7) pop. 1,353; 1 Mun.; 2 GSC; 3 Mun.; 4 CRIP, MP; 5 US 36, K-28; First National Bank, State Exchange Bank $2,714,000; newspaper — Jewell County Record. First clinic built under nationally famous Kansas Rural Health Plan at Mankato. Here also is Jewell County Historical Museum. Lovewell Dam and Reservoir 15 miles northeast; Jewell County State Lake six miles south and four miles west.

Jewell County — Earnings per cap. $1,567; sales tax collections $112,033; employed in industry 272; number of farms 1,243; crop value $9,814,530; livestock value $7,489,400. County ranked fifth in value of stone produced. Limestone was quarried and used for cement.

MANTER, Stanton (F-1) pop. 197; 1 Pioneer Co-op. Assn., Inc.; 2 PNG; 3 Mun.; 4 AT&SF; 5 US 160.

MAPLE HILL, Wabaunsee (C-11) pop. 257; 1 KPL; 3 Mun.; 4 CRIP; 5 K-30; Stockgrowers State Bank $743,000.

MAPLETON, Bourbon (E-13) pop. 146; 1 KCPL; 2 CGPC; 5 K-65, K-31.

*MARION, Marion (D-9) pop. 2,250; 1 Mun.; 2 Greeley Gas Co.; 3 Mun.; 4 AT&SF, CRIP; 5 US 56; Farmers & Drovers National Bank, Marion National Bank $6,152,000; newspaper — Marion County Record. The Marion County 152-acre lake is four miles southeast of town.

Marion County — Earnings per cap. $1,943; sales tax collections $407,495; employed in industry 976; number of farms 1,758; crop value $12,940,420; livestock value $10,587,790; mineral production $7,530,652. Crude petroleum production 1.8 million barrels. Natural gas production 7.3 billion cubic feet. Limestone quarried and crushed for concrete aggregate, roadstone, agstone and riprap.

MARQUETTE, McPherson (D-8) pop. 613; 1 KPL; 2 KPL; 3 Mun.; 4 MP; 5 K-175; Farmers State Bank, Marquette State Bank $1,704,000; newspaper — Tribune. Kanopolis Dam and Reservoir 10 miles northwest.

*MARYSVILLE, Marshall (A-10) pop. 4,171; 1 KPL; 2 KPL; 3 Mun.; 4 UP; 5 US 77, US 36; Citizens State Bank, Exchange Bank of Schmidt & Koester $10,563,000; newspapers — Marshall County News, Marshall Advocate. Marysville was the first home station out of St. Joseph, Mo., on the Pony Express route and one of the buildings used to stable horses is still standing in remodeled form. Swim's Pony Express Museum has more than 3,000 items and mementoes. Tuttle Creek Dam is 30 miles south of Marysville; Nemaha Lake 30 miles east; Washington Lake 25 miles west. Marshall County — Earnings per cap. $1,679; sales tax collections $391,694; employed in industry 1,238; number of farms 1,852; crop value $10,504,080; livestock value $9,112,950; mineral production $1,049,180. Gypsum mined and plaster and plaster products produced. Sand and gravel produced mainly for building and paving. Limestone quarried and crushed for concrete aggregate, roadstone and aglime.

MATFIELD GREEN, Chase (E-10) pop. 102; 1 Flint Hills Rural Elec. Co-op. Assn., Inc.; 3 Mun.; 4 AT&SF; 5 K-13.

MAYFIELD, Sumner (G-8) pop. 113; 1 WLT; 3 Wellington Water Co.; 4 AT&SF; Mayfield State Bank $570,000.

MAYETTA, Jackson (B-11) pop. 257; 1 KPL; 4 CRIP; 5 US 75. Pottawatomie Indian Reservation, largest in Kansas, is located west of Mayetta.

McCRACKEN, Rush (D-5) pop. 435; 1 WLT; 2 WLT; 3 WLT; 4 MP; 5 K-4; Citizens State Bank $2,471,000.

McCUNE, Crawford (F-13) pop. 432; 1 KGE; 2 UGS; 3 Mun.; 4 SLSF; 5 K-126; McCune State Bank $976,000; newspaper — McCune Herald.

McDONALD, Rawlins (A-2) pop. 325; 1 CKP; 2 K-NG; 3 Mun.; 4 CB&Q; 5 US 36; Peoples State Bank $1,780,000.

McFARLAND, Wabaunsee (C-11) pop. 216; 1 KPL; 2 Mun.; 4 CRIP; 5 K-185.

McLOUTH, Jefferson (B-12) pop. 535; 1 KPL; 2 Mun.; 3 Mun.; 5 K-92, K-16; Bank of McLouth $1,219,000; newspaper — Times.

MANKATO: *county seat town on the move*

Vigorous economic development the past two years is the mark of this governmental center of Jewell County.

Mankato gained nearly 100 in population. No business establishments or homes have been vacant.

More than $4 million in loans and local investment capital is being poured into business and industrial expansion and community improvements.

Mankato was not always this aggressive. In 1962, it had a population of 1,288. Many homes and business buildings were vacant.

Business leaders went into action. At their request, the Kansas State Chamber of Commerce Research Department in 1963 prepared an economic status report on Mankato and Jewell County. Among other things, the report showed that Mankato had lost 17.4 per cent of its population in the 1952-1962 period. Citizens were alarmed at the serious loss of income and property values due to a declining population. After a period of study, they launched a vigorous effort to stimulate community development.

Community improvements the past year include a $125,000 addition to the elementary school, city park on highway U. S. 36, National Guard Armory, two motels, whiteway, additional and widened streets, sewage system, swimming pool, bowling center and golf course clubhouse.

Mankato Commercial Development Association was incorporated to finance new businesses and industries. In September, 1965, Mr. and Mrs. Joe C. LeBow of Mankato purchased a city block from the association and donated it to Jewell County for a new 40-bed county convalescent hospital.

A contract was let for a 20-unit senior citizens home. The site has been cleared. Cost will be $191,000.

Several business firms have invested in extensive remodeling. New houses have been built. Mankato Endowment Association was organized to accept gifts for charitable and educational purposes.

Progressive city officials arranged for one million gallons of additional water storage for any new industry desiring to relocate here. Water supply is from White Rock and Lovewell Reservoir areas.

Small Business Administration processed a $255,000 loan for a new shopping center. Another SBA loan will help finance a new $60,000 steak house. Due to expansion of the business community, the City Council annexed 65 acres into the city Sept. 9, 1965.

Mankato is located on highway U. S. 36 at the gateway to Lovewell Reservoir. Lovewell has 44 miles of shoreline. The reservoir is a favorite hunting, fishing and recreation area for residents of several midwestern states.

Agriculture is the community's main industry. Jewell ranks 12th among Kansas counties in total agricultural income. It ranks second in counties west of highway U. S. 81. Agriculture is diversified. Primary crops are corn, wheat, milo and alfalfa seed. Much of the grain is used to feed hogs and cattle. Jewell is the third leading county in Kansas in hog production. The first soil conservation project in the state was in Jewell County. The county boasts of having the most conservation development contracts among Kansas counties.

Headquarters of the Jewell-Mitchell Cooperative Electric Co., Inc., is located at Mankato. It serves four counties and parts of others. Another business for Mankato is the State Highway Department's district maintenance shop.

The main portion of the elementary school building was constructed in 1957. The swimming pool is municipally owned. A private group, Mankato Golf Club, operates the nine-hole, sand green golf course.

Money received from the LeBow family for the county hospital site will be used by the development corporation to develop other sites for residential and commercial use.

Mankato citizens agreed to provide funds for utilities for the new county hospital.

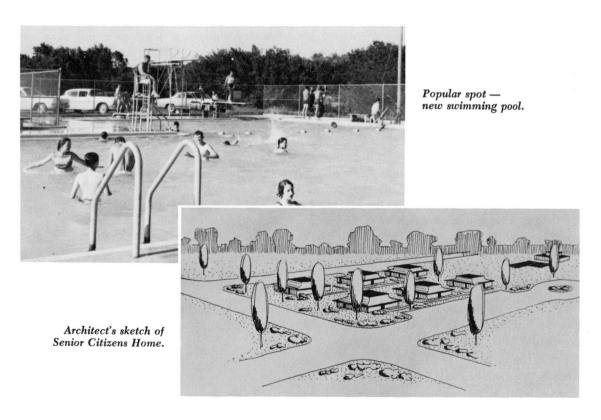

Popular spot —
new swimming pool.

Architect's sketch of
Senior Citizens Home.

Looking west from the courthouse down Marysville's main street.

MARYSVILLE: *positive thinking*

For nearly a century, this North Central Kansas town enjoyed slow, steady growth with little concern over economic pressures. Situated in the Big Blue River valley, it became the marketing center for Marshall County farmers. The community was populated by immigrants from Northern Europe. Prairie grass along the valleys and gentle slopes of Marshall County were transformed by immigrants into fertile acres of corn, milo, wheat, alfalfa and soybeans.

Descendants of the first Hereford cattle brought into the county from England still are bred here, along with large herds of Angus and dairy cattle.

The Oregon and Mormon Trails converged at a river crossing just south of town. Marysville became the first major station out of St. Joseph, Mo., on the Pony Express route. It was an important stopover point on the Overland Stage Lines and the military route from Fort Leavenworth to Fort Kearny.

Later, it became a railroad town on Union Pacific Railroad's main freight line between Kansas City, Kan., to Hastings, Neb. At least 25 mile-long freight trains pass through here daily. The railroad provides a $1 million annual payroll here for about 100 employees.

However, recent years brought a cutback in railroad employment here as it did in many communities of the nation. For the first time, businessmen were forced to seek new directions to fill an economic gap. Months of study brought a firm decision of businessmen to establish an industrial corporation to promote industry.

"Negative thinking on the part of many citizens has turned to positive," one businessman said with pride. Voters approved an annual levy to finance industrial promotion. Also approved was a recreation levy and funds for a new junior high school building. Cost of the school was just under $1 million.

Bestwall Gypsum Company financed a new plant and equipment. Cost was near $4 million. The firm mines gypsum and manufactures wallboard used in construction of homes and office buildings over the nation. Local financial assistance enabled Richard and Clark Manufacturing Company to get into production in October, 1965. Campers and trailers produced here are delivered as far distant as cities in Missouri, New Mexico and Texas.

Marysville is the "gateway to Tuttle Creek Reservoir" for visitors from Omaha, Lincoln and other Nebraska cities. Tuttle Creek Dam is 40 miles south of here. Recreation is nearby Washington Lake, 25 miles west, and Tuttle Creek Reservoir.

Marysville has the largest covered railroad stockyards in the world at the Union Pacific yards. Carloads of cattle, sheep and hogs from western ranches are unloaded here to await shipment to Kansas City and St. Joseph stockyards.

One of the buildings used to stable Pony Express horses was renovated for its historical value. Nearby is Swim's Pony Express Museum in the old Wells Fargo carriage barn. More than 3,000 historical mementoes are kept on exhibit.

*McPHERSON, McPherson (D-8) pop. 10,035; 1 Mun.; 2 KPL; 3 Mun.; 4 AT&SF, CRIP, MP, UP; 5 US 81, US 81 Alt., US 56; 7 McPherson College, Central College; Home State Bank, McPherson & Citizens State Bank, Peoples State Bank $21,517,000; newspapers — McPherson County News, McPherson Sentinel. McPherson College has world's first man-made diamond on display. Statue of General McPherson, Civil War leader for whom the city is named, is in Central Park. Five miles southeast is a monument on Dry Turkey Creek where United States commissioners made a treaty with the Kansas Indians in 1825 for the right of way on the Santa Fe Trail through central Kansas.

McPherson County — Earnings per cap. $1,887; sales tax collections $814,718; employed in industry 3,814; number of farms 1,977; crop value $12,330,730; livestock value $9,635,980; mineral production $7,812,510. Crude petroleum production 2.7 million barrels, down 17 per cent. Natural gas production up 40 per cent to 315 million cubic feet. Shale mined and expanded-shale lightweight aggregate produced. Gravel for paving and road maintenance.

*MEADE, Meade (G-3) pop. 2,133; 1 Mun.; 2 NNG; 3 Mun.; 4 CRIP; 5 US 160, US 54, K-98, K-23; First National Bank $4,529,000; newspaper — Meade Globe-Press. Meade is the home of the Dalton Gang Hideout and Museum on US 54. Visitors go through the secret escape tunnel from the house to the barn which houses a Western museum, including one of the nation's finest gun collections. The world's largest volcanic ash mine is located near the city. Meade County State Lake, 13 miles southwest, has pheasant farm and fish hatchery maintained by State Forestry, Fish and Game Commission. A half section of game preserve in the park contains buffalo and elk, while deer have the run of the entire 1,240 acres of wildlife management area. There is museum on Highways US 160 and US 54.

Meade County — Earnings per cap. $1,630; sales tax collections $155,444; employed in industry 486; number of farms 571; crop value $4,897,050; livestock value $4,912,880; mineral production $4,058,699. Crude petroleum output 712,000 barrels. Natural gas production slightly less than 16 billion cubic feet. Crooked Creek and Meyers gas fields important discoveries.

*MEDICINE LODGE, Barber (G-7) pop. 2,931; 1 WLT; 2 KPL; 3 Mun.; 4 AT&SF; 5 US 281, US 160; First National Bank $5,850,000; newspaper — Barber County Index. Medicine Lodge is the site of peace treaties negotiated by United States government and five hostile Plains Indian tribes in 1867. Once every five years a cast of 1,500 presents Peace Treaty Pageant at Memorial Peace Park, natural amphitheater seating 25,000 persons. Medicine Lodge was home of Carry A. Nation, stormy anti-liquor crusader. Her home is now a W.C.T.U. shrine and museum. A bank president and cashier were shot and killed during a robbery in 1884. The bandits' leader was the marshal of Caldwell. Pursued by a posse, the four thieves were boxed in and captured at Jackass Canyon southwest of town. Later, citizens stormed the jail, shot the leader and hanged the others from Hangman's Tree, symbolized by the macabre rope and tree in the city park. The National Gypsum Company here operates the most modern wallboard plant in America. South of Medicine Lodge are the Gypsum Hills. Deep canyons and hills, carved by erosion into towering mesas and buttes, give tourists another type of Kansas scenery. The red shale of the mesas is capped with white gypsum. The Gyp Hills Trails are well-marked with more than 200 markers. A 42-mile stretch along US 160 between this city and Coldwater is called Cedar Tree Lane, with thousands of trees planted there. Replica of a frontier stockade surrounds a museum building housing pioneer artifacts. North of the city is the 77-acre Barber County State Lake.

Barber County — Earnings per cap. $1,917; sales tax collections $249,629; employed in industry 963; number of farms 683; crop value $5,141,270; livestock value $6,505,790; mineral production $8,830,117. County ranked first in gypsum production and seventh in natural gas production. National Gypsum Co. mined and processed gypsum at Medicine Lodge. Natural gas production totaled 41 billion cubic feet. Crude petroleum output 995,000 barrels. Exploratory drilling resulted in two important gas fields, DeGeer Southwest and Groendycke. Skelly Oil Co. recovered natural gas liquids at Medicine Lodge plant. Sand and gravel produced for building and paving.

MELVERN, Osage (D-12) pop. 430; 1 KCPL; 2 UGSv; 4 AT&SF; 5 K-174.

MENLO, Thomas (B-3) pop. 65; 1 CKP; 2 K-NG; 5 K-186.

MERIDEN, Jefferson (B-12) pop. 366; 1 KPL; 2 GSC; 3 Meriden-Grantville Co-op. Water Corp.; 4 AT&SF; 5 K-4; State Bank of Meriden $1,471,000.

Three different models of El Dorado campers.

HONORBUILT: *Minneapolis firm builds popular El Dorado camper*

A Kansas firm is contributing to the popularity of camping, an outdoor recreation growing at fast pace across the entire nation. This plant in Minneapolis, Kansas — known as the Honorbuilt Division of Ward Manufacturing, Inc., of Hamilton, Ohio — makes the El Dorado pickup coach. Fourteen different models are manufactured here and distributed nationally.

This popular camper has made many network television appearances on such series as "Flipper" and "The Fred MacMurray Show." The company also has a factory at Lakeview, Calif.

As camping has grown, so also have the Minneapolis facilities of Honorbuilt Trailer Mfg. Co. In recent years, the company purchased an additional 5.5 acres of ground adjoining the original plant and constructed a 140x80-foot addition to the building. The extra ground also allowed for more parking of finished coaches.

The firm attributes its successful enterprise in Kansas to a combination of engineering know-how, manufacturing techniques, keen sense of the recreation-travel industry, and the technical skills of Kansans who build for them a quality product. Robert Stewart is manager and executive vice president of the Kansas plant.

MERRIAM, Johnson (C-13) pop. 7,138; 1 KCPL; 2 GSC; 3 Water Dist. No. 1, Johnson Co.; 4 SLSF; 5 I-35, US 169, US 56, US 50, K-10.

MILAN, Sumner (G-8) pop. 177; 1 WLT; 4 AT&SF; 5 K-205.

MILDRED, Allen (E-12) pop. 58; 1 KGE; 2 Kansas Gas & Fuel; 4 MKT; 5 K-52.

MILFORD, Geary (C-9) pop. 249; 1 KPL; 3 Mun.; 4 UP.

MILTONVALE, Cloud (B-9) pop. 680; 1 KPL; 3 Mun.; 4 AT&SF, UP; 5 K-189; 7 Miltonvale Wesleyan College; Citizens State Bank $1,696,000; newspaper — Record.

MINERAL (West Mineral), Cherokee (G-13) pop. 263; 1 EDE; 3 Mun.; 4 MKT; 5 K-102.

°MINNEAPOLIS, Ottawa (C-8) pop. 3,142; 1 Mun.; 2 GSC; 3 Mun.; 4 AT&SF, UP; 5 K-106; Citizens National Bank, The Ottawa County Bank $5,316,000; newspaper — Messenger. Two and one-half miles southwest is Rock City, noted for its 200 or more unusually well-formed large sandstone concretions. Some are almost perfect spheres with diameters exceeding 12 feet. Others, with diameters ranging from 8 to 27 feet, vary from rounded to elliptical forms. Ottawa County State Lake is east of Minneapolis on Highway 93.

Ottawa County — Earnings per cap. $1,534; sales tax collections $141,632; employed in industry 394; number of farms 883; crop value $6,586,820; livestock value $4,225,100; mineral production $30,230.

MINNEOLA, Clark (F-4) pop. 705; 1 WLT; 2 GSC; 3 Mun.; 5 US 283, US 54; Peoples State Bank $1,616,000; newspaper — Minneola Record.

MISSION, Johnson (C-13) pop. 8,227; 1 KCPL; 2 GSC; 3 Water Dist. No. 1, Johnson Co.; 5 US 69, US 56, US 50, K-158; Centennial State Bank, Mission State Bank $30,452,000.

MISSION WOODS, Johnson (C-13) pop. 268; 1 KCPL; 2 GSC; 3 J. C. Nichols Co. & KC Suburban Water; 5 US 69, US 56, US 50.

MOLINE, Elk (F-11) pop. 707; 1 KGE; 2 UGS; 3 Mun.; 4 AT&SF; 5 US 160, K-99; Exchange State Bank $1,026,000; newspaper — Moline Advance. Some of the state's largest rock quarries are two miles east of Moline.

MONTEZUMA, Gray (F-3) pop. 631; 1 Mun.; 2 NNG; 3 Mun.; 4 AT&SF; 5 US 56, K-96; Montezuma State Bank $2,434,000; newspaper — Montezuma Press.

MORAN, Allen (E-13) pop. 581; 1 Mun.; 2 SEKGC; 3 Mun.; 4 MKT, MP; 5 US 54, K-52, K-6; newspaper — Moran Sentinel.

MORGANVILLE, Clay (B-9) pop. 256; 1 KPL; 2 KPL; 3 Mun.; 4 CRIP; 5 K-80; newspaper — Tribune.

MORLAND, Graham (B-4) pop. 361; 1 CKP; 3 Mun.; 4 UP; 5 K-85; Citizens State Bank $1,620,000.

MORRILL, Brown (A-11) pop. 331; 1 Mun.; 2 GSC; 3 Mun.; 4 UP; Morrill State Bank $1,106,000; newspaper — Northwest Brown Countian.

MORROWVILLE, Washington (A-9) pop. 204; 1 WLT; 2 KPL; 3 Mun.; 4 CB&Q; 5 K-15W.

MOSCOW, Stevens (G-2) pop. 247; 1 Pioneer Co-op. Assn., Inc.; 2 NNG; 3 Mun.; 4 AT&SF; 5 US 56.

°MOUND CITY, Linn (E-13) pop. 685; 1 KCPL; 2 Mound City Gas; 3 Mun.; 5 K-52, K-7; Farmers & Merchants Bank $2,358,000; newspaper — Mound City Republic.

Linn County — Earnings per cap. $1,609; sales tax collections $167,217; employed in industry 525; number of farms 1,252; crop value $6,302,490; livestock value $5,964,380; mineral production $296,602. Crude petroleum production 52,000 barrels, a 4 per cent increase, with waterflood projects accounting for large part. Natural gas production up 161 per cent to 130.5 million cubic feet. Limestone quarried and crushed for concrete aggregate, roadstone and aglime. Gravel produced for paving and road maintenance.

MOUNDRIDGE, McPherson (E-8) pop. 1,260; 1 Mun.; 2 Mun.; 3 Mun.; 4 UP; 5 US 81; Citizens State Bank $2,693,000; newspaper — Moundridge Journal.

MOUND VALLEY, Labette (G-12) pop. 438; 1 KPL; 2 UGS; 3 Mun.; 4 SLSF, MKT; 5 K-96; newspaper — Times-Journal.

MOUNT HOPE, Sedgwick (E-8) pop. 590; 1 Mun.; 2 GSC; 3 Mun.; 4 MP; 5 K-96; First National

Strawn, on the hill upper right, overlooks dam.

Tainter Gates, Redmond Reservoir.

NEW STRAWN: *brand-new little city*

Strawn, a small town in Coffey County upstream from Burlington, just picked up and moved to make way for the John Redmond Reservoir. It also has made way for a bright new future! Today, a four-lane highway is under construction on U.S. 75 through the townsite, new businesses are opening and 1,000-yard landing strip has been staked and soon will be ready for aircraft!

The John Redmond Dam on the Grand (Neosho) River is in a fertile valley controlling runoff from 3,000 square miles of rolling Kansas prairies. Heavy runoffs for many years made farming hazardous. The valley was flooded 57 times in 34 years, the worst in 1951.

Dam construction started in 1959. The town of Strawn was relocated six miles eastward on higher ground. The old townsite now is completely under water. Nothing is left to show that a town was even there!

The move to the new site in 1962 was a gradual process. The government purchased the old homes; families arranged for building new. Two homes, moved into the town from the previous location, were remodeled. All the others, and the stores, were built new, making the town's name appropriate in two aspects — new location and new facilities. A few businesses were lost due to the move, but others were gained. The dam was dedicated in June, 1965. The Redmond Reservoir impounds more water and covers more acres of land than any other lake in Kansas except Tuttle Creek.

New Strawn is situated on the north rim of the reservoir. It is adjacent to the recreation and public use area on U.S. 75, four miles north of Burlington. The town is supplied with water by the Coffey County Rural Water District No. 1 and has complete municipal sewer system. Electric power is by Coffey County REA. Union Gas soon will have natural gas in the area. New Strawn has grown from nothing to a village of 55 new homes and 10 business buildings housing 23 firms. A new elementary grade school has been in use for two years and is completely free of debt. It will accommodate 100 children. High school youths are serviced at their doors by a Burlington rural high school bus.

The town expects tourists by the thousands now that it is located in a water sports area. Plans are complete for construction of a 20-unit motel. Both bait-and-tackle and boat storage shops are looking forward to business growth. A new attraction, the Ryan Antique Auto Museum, will be open in 1966 for its first visitors.

In mid-1965, an editorial in the Iola Register predicted fast growth for the Redmond Dam vicinity. "Its value as a pleasure facility to residents of the state — if there were any way to measure it — would be at least equal to its value as a device for flood control and water conservation. Make a special trip to Redmond Dam real soon to take a look . . . then watch it grow. I'll wager that 10 years from now, you will never recognize the place."

Bank $2,086,000; newspaper — Clarion.

MULBERRY, Crawford (F-13) pop. 655; 1 Mun.; 3 Mun.; 4 SLSF, KCS; newspaper — News Journal.

MULLINVILLE, Kiowa (F-5) pop. 429; 1 WLT; 2 GSC; 3 Mun.; 4 CRIP; 5 US 154, US 54; First State Bank $1,939,000.

MULVANE, Sedgwick and Sumner (F-9) pop. 3,042; 1 Mun.; 2 GSC; 3 Mun.; 4 AT&SF; 5 K-53, K-15; Mulvane State Bank $2,891,000; newspaper — Mulvane News.

MUNDEN, Republic (A-8) pop. 173; 1 WLT; 2 KPL; 3 Mun.; 4 CRIP; Munden State Bank $828,000.

MUSCOTAH, Atchison (B-12) pop. 240; 1 Mun.; 3 Mun.; 4 MP; 5 US 159, K-9.

NARKA, Republic (A-9) pop. 162; 1 WLT; 2 KPL; 3 Mun.; 4 CRIP.

NASHVILLE, Kingman (F-7) pop. 136; 1 WLT; 4 AT&SF; 5 K-42.

NATOMA, Osborne (B-6) pop. 740; 1 WLT; 2 K-NG; 3 Mun.; 4 UP; 5 K-18; First National Bank $3,340,000; newspaper — Natoma-Luray Independent.

NEODESHA, Wilson (F-12) pop. 4,105; 1 Mun.; 2 Mun. and UGS; 3 Mun.; 4 SLSF, MP; 5 US 75; First National Bank $5,823,000; newspapers — Neodesha Daily Sun, Neodesha Register. City is the site of the Norman No. 1, first successful commercial oil well west of the Mississippi River. A replica of the original rig has been built over the old well and a park area developed.

NEOSHO FALLS, Woodson (E-12) pop. 221; 1 KGE.

NEOSHO RAPIDS, Lyon (D-11) pop. 190; 1 KPL; 4 AT&SF; 5 K-130.

*NESS CITY, Ness (D-4) pop. 2,055; 1 WLT; 2 WLT; 3 Mun.; 4 AT&SF; 5 US 283, K-96; The First State Bank $3,847,000; newspaper — Ness County News.

Ness County — Earnings per cap. $1,753; sales tax collections $160,149; employed in industry 320; number of farms 834; crop value $4,937,050; livestock value $5,196,990; mineral production $3,044,180. Crude petroleum production up 43 per cent to 1.1 million barrels. Buda, McDonald, Sunshine and Wunder oil fields were important discoveries. Sand for paving and road maintenance produced.

NETAWAKA, Jackson (B-11) pop. 164; 1 Mun.; 4 MP; 5 US 75, K-9.

NEW ALBANY, Wilson (F-11) pop. 87; 1 KGE; 4 SLSF.

NEW CAMBRIA, Saline (C-8) pop. 155; 1 KPL; 4 UP; 5 K-220.

*NEWTON, Harvey (E-9) pop. 14,860; 1 KGE; 2 GSC; 3 Mun.; 4 AT&SF, MP; 5 I-35W, US 81, US 81 Alt., US 50, K-15; First National Bank, The Kansas State Bank, Midland National Bank $21,260,000; newspaper — Newton Kansan. Area in and around Newton is home of the largest Mennonite settlement in the United States. In Athletic Park is a tall limestone shaft, memorial to Mennonites who brought Red Turkey hard winter wheat to this country from Russia in 1874 and thus helped Kansas to march toward fame as the "Breadbasket of the World." The city has flour mills and mobile home manufacturing companies. Central Kansas Area Vocational-Technical School is located here.

Harvey County — Earnings per cap. $1,880; sales tax collections $788,972; employed in industry 3,745; number of farms 1,221; crop value $10,259,690; livestock value $6,837,970; mineral production $2,078,646. Crude petroleum output up 13 per cent to 662,000 barrels. Natural gas production slightly more than 1 billion cubic feet. Sand and gravel produced, mainly for building and paving.

NICKERSON, Reno (E-7) pop. 1,161; 1 KPL; 2 Ark.-La. Gas Co.; 3 Mun.; 4 AT&SF, MP; 5 K-96; Nickerson State Bank $1,526,000; newspaper — Nickerson Argosy.

NIOTAZE, Chautauqua (G-11) pop. 109; 1 Caney Valley Elec. Co-op. Assn., Inc.; 2 UGS; 4 MP; 5 US 166.

NORCATUR, Decatur (A-4) pop. 334; 1 Norton-Decatur Co-op. Elec. Co., Inc.; 2 K-NG; 3 Mun.; 5 US 36; Citizens State Bank $1,551,000.

NORTH NEWTON, Harvey (E-9) pop. 575; 1 KGE; 2 GSC; 3 Newton Water; 5 US 81, K-15; 7 Bethel College.

*NORTON, Norton (A-4) pop. 4,062; 1 Mun.; 2 K-NG; 3 Mun.; 4 CB&Q, CRIP; 5 US 383, US 283,

Newton — seat of Harvey County.

NEWTON: *manufactured goods, farm products help to supply worldwide market*

Mobile homes are causing excitement in the industrial field at Newton.

The city is on the move to put the nation on the move! Three major manufacturers of mobile homes and six manufacturers of mobile home equipment are here. A majority of these plants are located in an industrial park southwest of the city.

Guerdon Industries, American Coach Co. and Namco Industries are the three mobile homes plants operating in Newton, in the order of their locating here. Their combined employment is about 450, with a daily production of about 20 homes. Suppliers of the industry include manufacturers of frames and axles, furniture and aluminum windows. Additional suppliers include warehouse distributors of plywood paneling, hardware and fixtures.

Other industrial sites have been developed northwest of town, where one plant is in operation, and southeast adjoining proposed route of Highway I-35. All areas are platted, public roads provided and utilities available. Land is privately owned. In addition, there is industrial acreage adjoining Newton's Municipal Airport, three miles east of town. The airport has a 7,000-foot lighted concrete runway. At present, this city owned property has one aircraft service firm located at the site.

Newton is a major division point for Santa Fe Railroad, serving both areas to the east and west and to the south. By combining operations of transportation, train, yard, maintenance, mechanical and store departments, there are almost 1,000 employees of Santa Fe living in Newton. The city also is served by Missouri Pacific and is a north-south and east-west federal highway junction.

Industrial promotion is a continuing function of the Chamber of Commerce and its financial arm — the Newton Industrial Foundation. In the past 10 years, more than a dozen new firms have located in Newton. Each of these has received information and assistance from the community. About half a dozen are currently using funds provided by the industrial

190

foundation to finance a part of their operations.

Other industries at Newton include two food processing plants, a modern flour mill, two wood products plants and a pre-stressed concrete plant.

Newton, governmental seat of Harvey County, is in the 15,000-population range. It is located 24 miles north of Wichita in the heart of a rich agricultural area. Farm products of Harvey County, especially wheat, are feeding the hungry in many parts of the world. Soybeans are used to make meal for Kansas feedlots and for export abroad. Sorghum grown in the area goes to local cattle feeders, to the West Coast or to Egypt. Pork is sent across the nation and beef goes to markets in Wichita, Kansas City, Chicago and Omaha for shipment anywhere in the country. Both sheep and wool find nationwide markets. Alfalfa and dairy products help supply regional needs.

Newton has three banks and two savings and loan associations. Located here are home offices of the Railroad Building, Loan and Savings Association; the Midland Mutual Fire Insurance Company, and the First Kansas Life Insurance Company.

Newton's educational facilities cover the range from kindergarten through the arts and science degree. Within the city are eight grade schools, two junior high schools, a parochial school accommodating eight grades, and a Class AA high school. The school system also includes an area vocational school to train skilled workmen for industry in Harvey, Reno and Mc-Pherson counties; an adult education department, and a cooperative industrial and office practices department.

Adjacent in North Newton is Bethel College, a fully accredited, four-year liberal arts school. Founded in 1887, it is the oldest Mennonite college in America. Each year some 500 students from more than 20 states and 10 foreign countries choose Bethel because of its high academic rating. They represent about 20 church denominations.

Cultural activities center around the college. The Bethel lecture and music series brings internationally recognized speakers and music groups to the community. The nearly completed Fine Arts Building will provide excellent facilities for the drama and music departments. Kauffman Museum, on campus, attracts many visitors each year. In its Alumni Hall is the historical collection telling the story of the Mennonites and other pioneers who settled here in the last quarter of the 19th century. The Museum Annex contains a natural history collection, ethnological and anthropological displays. The Balcony contains natural history displays including stuffed small animals, birds, fish and reptiles.

Serving the health needs of a large area are two general hospitals, both with new wings under construction. Axtell Christian Hospital has 42 beds and eight bassinets. The new wing will add 25 beds. Bethel Deaconess Hospital has more than 74 beds and 12 bassinets, and an accredited school of nursing. There are seven homes for the aged in Newton.

Prairie View Hospital is a modern psychiatric treatment center. It serves the surrounding communities with its outpatient facilities and accommodates more than 40 inpatients.

Spiritual needs of the community are served by 31 churches of many denominations. The daily newspaper and radio station provide news coverage and entertainment. Three major TV networks are viewed in the area. Rural and urban dwellers exhibit at the Harvey County Town and Country Fair each August in Newton. The event is sponsored by the Harvey County Fair Assn.

Five parks in the city cater to those hunting fun and relaxation. Athletic Park has a municipally owned swimming pool, tennis courts and playground equipment. Newton also has both 9- and 18-hole golf courses and two bowling establishments. Yentruoc Lakes is a resort area eight miles southeast of town with cabins, tennis and volleyball courts, fishing and swimming areas.

US 36; First National Bank, First State Bank $7,852,000; newspaper — Daily Telegram. One of the largest volcanic ash mines in the state is seven miles east of Norton. A State Sanatorium for Tuberculosis is four miles east.

Norton County — Earnings per cap. $1,826; sales tax collections $275,910; employed in industry 832; number of farms 879; crop value $4,867,910; livestock value $5,032,590; mineral production $2,007,805. Crude petroleum output 692,000 barrels. Sandstone quarried and crushed for concrete aggregate, roadstone and riprap. Crushed limestone produced for concrete aggregate and roadstone. Gravel produced for paving and road maintenance; volcanic ash mined and prepared.

NORTONVILLE, Jefferson (B-12) pop. 631; 1 KPL; 3 Mun.; 4 AT&SF; 5 US 159, US 59, K-4; First National Bank $1,776,000; newspaper — Nortonville News.

NORWICH, Kingman (F-8) pop. 451; 1 WLT; 2 Mun.; 3 Mun.; 4 AT&SF, MP; 5 K-42; Farmers State Bank $1,159,000.

OAK HILL, Clay (B-9) pop. 55; 1 KPL; 4 AT&SF.

*OAKLEY, Logan (C-3) pop. 2,495; 1 Mun.; 2 K-NG; 3 Mun.; 4 UP; 5 US 83, US 40, I-70; Farmers State Bank $6,040,000; newspaper — Oakley Graphic. The largest cretaceous fossil beds in the United States are found in chalk deposits along the Smoky Hill River south of Oakley. Large fossil collection in Oakley High School. Monument Rocks 27 miles southeast.

Logan County — Earnings per cap. $2,060; sales tax collections $182,947; employed in industry 382; number of farms 378; crop value $2,965,250; livestock value $2,854,610; mineral production $34,700. Paving sand produced; gravel obtained for paving and road maintenance.

*OBERLIN, Decatur (A-3) pop. 2,624; 1 Mun.; 2 K-NG; 3 Mun.; 4 CB&Q; 5 US 83, US 36; Decatur County National Bank, Farmers National Bank $8,443,000; newspaper — Herald. Here are the Decatur County Historical Museum and reconstructed sod house. Monument in Oberlin Cemetery erected to settlers killed in the last Indian raid in Kansas, made by renegade Cheyennes Sept. 30, 1878. Seventeen of the victims have marked graves. Five survivors met at the museum for a reunion dinner in 1961. A community festival is held on September 30 each year. Decatur County-Sappa Creek State Lake is east of Oberlin.

Decatur County — Earnings per cap. $1,644; sales tax collections $147,626; employed in industry 369; number of farms 796; crop value $4,634,590; livestock value $5,476,130; mineral production $1,533,261. Crude petroleum production 517,000 barrels, up 3 per cent. Building sand, fill sand and paving gravel produced.

OFFERLE, Edwards (E-5) pop. 216; 1 KPL; 4 AT&SF; 5 US 56, US 50; Farmers State Bank $1,047,000.

OGDEN, Riley (C-10) pop. 1,429; 1 KPL; 2 KPL; 3 Mun.; 5 K-18.

OKETO, Marshall (A-10) pop. 154; 1 KPL; 3 Mun.; 4 UP; Oketo State Bank $1,059,000.

*OLATHE, Johnson (C-13) pop. 12,121; 1 KPL; 2 UGS; 3 Mun.; 4 AT&SF, SLSF; 5 I-35, US 169, US 56, US 50, K-150, K-7; First National Bank, Patrons Co-operative Bank $23,297,000; newspapers — Olathe Mirror, The Daily News. Olathe, called the "Cowboy Boot Capital" for its nationally known boot factories, is the location of the State School for Education of the Deaf. A U. S. Naval Air Station is five miles southwest of the city. The Federal Aviation Agency Air Route Traffic Control Center is located here. Olathe is the hometown of five governors — John P. St. John, Kansas 1878-1882; George H. Hodges, Kansas 1910-1912; James H. Brady, Idaho 1908-1910; Herbert S. Hadley, Missouri 1908-1912; John Anderson, Jr., Kansas 1960-1964.

Johnson County — Earnings per cap. $3,216; sales tax collections $5,152,881; employed in industry 15,182; number of farms 1,257; crop value $5,594,170; livestock value $4,296,080; mineral production $1,103,777. Johnson County ranked fourth in value of stone production. Limestone quarried and crushed for concrete aggregate, roadstone and agstone. Building and paving sand, fill sand, filtration sand and building gravel produced. Crude petroleum production totaled 30,000 barrels. Marketed production of natural gas up 173 per cent to 273 million cubic feet.

OLIVET, Osage (D-11) pop. 101; 1 KPL; 4 AT&SF.

OLMITZ, Barton (D-6) pop. 174; 1 WLT; 2 KPL; 3 Mun.; 4 MP.

OLPE, Lyon (E-11) pop. 412; 1 KPL; 2 GSC; 4 AT&SF; 5 K-99, K-57; Olpe State Bank $1,433,000.

OLSBURG, Pottawatomie (B-10) pop. 145; 1 KPL; 3 Mun.; 5 K-16; Union State Bank $1,048,000.

ONAGA, Pottawatomie (B-11) pop. 867; 1 KPL; 2 KPL; 3 Mun.; 4 UP; 5 K-16; First National Bank $2,187,000; newspaper — Onaga Herald.

ONEIDA, Nemaha (A-11) pop. 92; 1 KPL; 4 UP.

OSAGE CITY, Osage (D-11) pop. 2,444; 1 Mun.; 2 Mun.; 3 Mun.; 4 AT&SF, MP; 5 K-170, K-31; Citizens State Bank $3,405,000; newspaper — Journal-Free Press.

OSAWATOMIE, Miami (D-13) pop. 4,500; 1 Mun.; 2 GSC; 3 Mun.; 4 MP; 5 US 169, K-7; American State Bank, First National Bank $5,400,000; newspaper — Graphic News. Town was headquarters for John Brown in turbulent days preceding the Civil War. The John Brown Memorial State Park contains museum in the cabin where Brown stayed for a time. An old Land Office in town houses a travel information center and Chamber of Commerce office. Osawatomie State Hospital (mental) is northeast of town.

*OSBORNE, Osborne (B-6) pop. 2,139; 1 Mun.; 2 GSC; 3 Mun.; 4 AT&SF, MP; 5 US 281, US 24; Farmers National Bank, First State Bank $5,600,000; newspaper — Osborne County Farmer. On a ranch about 18 miles southeast of Osborne a bronze plate marks the geodetic center of North America. Southwest of Osborne is the Buffalo Hunter Museum dedicated to Jeff Durfey.

Osborne County — Earnings per cap. $1,577; sales tax collections $186,971; employed in industry 640; number of farms 940; crop value $5,395,300; livestock value $5,765,700; mineral production $161,572; newspaper — Osborne County Farmer. Crude petroleum production down 21 per cent to 46,000 barrels. Gravel and crushed limestone produced for paving and road maintenance; gravel for paving. Work on Glen Elder project of Bureau of Reclamation continues; expected completion date near 1969.

*OSKALOOSA, Jefferson (B-12) pop. 802; 1 KPL; 2 GSC; 3 Mun.; 5 US 59, K-92, K-16; State Bank of Oskaloosa $2,500,000; newspaper — Oskaloosa Independent.

Jefferson County — Earnings per cap. $1,665; sales tax collections $190,255; employed in industry 483; number of farms 1,355; crop value $6,976,460; livestock value $6,330,240. Jefferson County ranked second in value of stone production. Limestone quarried and crushed for concrete aggregate, roadstone, riprap and aglime. Work continues on Perry Dam and Reservoir.

*OSWEGO, Labette (G-13) pop. 2,150; 1 Mun.; 2 AG; 3 Mun.; 4 SLSF, MKT; 5 US 59, K-96; American State Bank, First National Bank $6,100,000; newspapers — Oswego Democrat & Carpenter Press, Oswego Independent. The corner of 4th and Union streets is the site of an old town well and a trading post established in the 1840's. Riverside Park is on a high bluff overlooking the broad Neosho River Valley. Below the park is scenic dam, favorite fishing place of southeastern Kansas and northeastern Oklahoma.

Labette County — Earnings per cap. $1,694; sales tax collections $671,867; employed in industry 3,092; number of farms 1,661; crop value $6,908,940; livestock value $6,271,420; mineral production $343,073. Crude petroleum production 85,000 barrels, down 16 per cent. Output of natural gas double previous year and totaled 130.5 million cubic feet. Limestone was quarried and crushed for concrete aggregate, roadstone and riprap.

OTIS, Rush (D-6) pop. 382; 1 WLT; 2 KPL; 3 Mun.; 4 MP; 5 K-4; Otis State Bank $1,100,000.

*OTTAWA, Franklin (D-12) pop. 11,195; 1 Mun.; 2 GSC; 3 Mun.; 4 AT&SF, MP; 5 I-35, US 59, US 50 spur, K-68; 7 Ottawa University; First National Bank, Kansas State Bank, Peoples National Bank $15,400,000; newspapers — Ottawa Herald, Ottawa Times. On campus of Ottawa University (Baptist) is Crevecoeur Entomological Collection of 21,000 specimens. Four miles northeast of Ottawa is the Tauy Jones Home, once an underground railroad station and stopping place for John Brown. Also northeast of the city is the Ottawa Indian Burial Ground, containing the marked grave of Rev. Jotham Meeker, missionary and printer who established the Ottawa Mission and earlier printed the first periodical in Kansas at the Shawnee Baptist Mission. Pomona Reservoir is west of Ottawa.

Franklin County — Earnings per cap. $1,743; sales tax collections $633,968; employed in industry 2,190; number of farms 1,501; crop value $7,708,220; livestock value $6,927,950; mineral production $874,160. County ranked fourth in value of clay production. Expanded shale lightweight aggregate produced; crude shale mined. Limestone was quarried and crushed for concrete aggre-

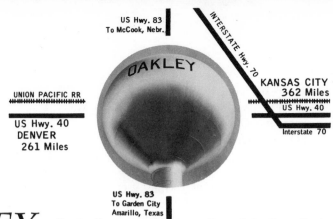

US Hwy. 83
To McCook, Nebr.

OAKLEY

UNION PACIFIC RR

US Hwy. 40
DENVER
261 Miles

INTERSTATE Hwy. 70

KANSAS CITY
362 Miles

US Hwy. 40

Interstate 70

US Hwy. 83
To Garden City
Amarillo, Texas

OAKLEY: *bright spot on the high plains*

Dedication of the new courthouse on October 2, 1965, culminated the transition of the county seat of Logan County from Russell Springs with population 93 to Oakley, population 2,647 and growing. Oakley's population has increased 1,000 in the past 10 years.

Other major new facilities were built during this period. Another new engine was installed at the municipal power plant boosting the plant's power generation to a firm 3,400 kilowatts and a peak of 4,900 kilowatts, assuring adequate power for manufacturing firms.

A new sewage disposal plant was constructed with capacity for double the current population. The water supply is also municipally owned, with unlimited capacity. Water is from Smoky Hill River deep underground storage.

Another new facility is Parkside Manor Rest Home for the aged. Capacity is 45 residents; cost more than $300,000. Logan County Hospital, a modern facility of 26-bed capacity, is also located in Oakley, and is fully equipped for all major surgery.

Although the community is presently an agricultural market, it has all the prerequisites for industrial manufacturing. It is situated on the main line of the Union Pacific Railroad, and Interstate Highway 70, with US 40 and 83 junctioning at this point, providing through travel from coast to coast and border to border.

Income basically is from cattle, wheat and sorghum. Farms are large, averaging a section or more. Oakley Livestock Commission Company is annually one of the top five leaders in Kansas in cattle sales. Pioneer Feed Yards near here fattens 30,000 head of cattle a year. Counties in this area are among top producers of choice milling wheat, which is in demand. A 24 hour municipal airport serves private aircraft.

The $1 million high school and grade school system serves a 300-square-mile district. There is a $200,000 Catholic grade school.

A mayor-council city government plans for future expansion and development under a Home Rule system.

Tourists add to the economy here, with many attractions within a few miles of the city. The largest cretaceous fossil beds in the United States are in deposits near the Smoky Hill River south of here. As early as 1870, expeditions from Yale University collected specimens from the beds. There is a large fossil collection at the Oakley High School. A page out of history is re-created by "Wagons Ho Inc." offering 2, 3 and 4-day trips over the Butterfield Overland Dispatch Trail, in covered wagons, stage coaches and horseback. Starting at Quinter — 40 miles east of Oakley — and culminating just south of here, the wagon train takes tourists from the space age to the days of Indian raids, cavalry attacks, campfire meals and outdoor sleeping. "Wagons Ho" has gained international acclaim.

Horsemanship is popular in this western country. Oakley Range Riders won Kansas saddle club riding skills contests 10 of the past 11 years. The community is steeped in history, with names of such notables as General George Custer, Buffalo Bill Cody, Billy Comstock, Chief Dull Knife and Chief Grey Wolf.

Pheasant hunters find success.

Modern "swimmin' hole."

Pioneer Feed Yards.

Old Chief Smoky, south of Oakley.

195

John Brown Memorial Park.

Adair Center for treatment of mentally ill.

OSAWATOMIE: center for mental treatment

Two slogans tell of Osawatomie's unusual role in Kansas.

"Cradle of Freedom Movement" refers to the first open warfare between pro- and anti-slavery forces at Osawatomie. "One Hundred Years of Concern for the Mentally Ill" refers to Osawatomie State Hospital with some of the finest facilities for treatment of mental illness.

Both the John Brown legend and hospital activities figure prominently in the city. Site of the famous battle over whether Kansas would be free or slave is now the John Brown Memorial State Park. Here, in 1856, some 400 men from Missouri and other slave states clashed with a group of 40 free-staters under the leadership of John Brown. Later, Brown operated the "underground railroad," aiding slaves in escaping to free territory. The 23-acre park has a bronze statue of the abolitionist created by George Fite Waters; the original Samuel Adair log cabin used as Brown's headquarters; and other relics of early days. Historic spots in the area have been preserved by organizations for tourist attractions. The original land office has been restored and is now used as an information center and Chamber of Commerce office.

Adair, Congregational minister who aided Brown, was a key figure in the history of the hospital. He served the mentally ill from 1866 to 1891, living to see a building named for him in 1895. In 1962, Dr. Karl Menninger dedicated the $2,500,000 seven-building patient treatment unit — Adair Center. The only thing the new center retains from the old building is the name. In 1963, a modern Rehabilitation Center was completed. In 1964, an unused industrial building was converted into the Adolescent Day Hospital and Treatment Center to meet the needs of the increasing number of 16-to-19-year-olds being admitted.

There are 701 people employed at the State Hospital; more than 300 psychiatric aides. In 1964, the hospital admitted 997 patients and discharged 1054. It serves mentally ill people 16 years of age and older from 22 counties in southeast Kansas.

Along with feeding, housing, diagnosing and treating patients, one of the goals of the hospital staff is to work with the community toward the patient's total rehabilitation as a productive citizen. A hospital bus enables patients to make trips to parks, museums, art galleries — and also to attend the theater, concerts, county fairs, etc., as guests of community organizations.

Osawatomie is about 45 miles south of Kansas City on U.S. 169. Three major railroads are within easy reach of this community. Located in the city is the Central District Office of the Missouri Pacific Railroad.

The Behm Company, a metal fabrication firm, transports its products to a worldwide market. Mode O'Day employs 50 women to make blouses for shipment to their stores.

Agriculture plays an important part in the economy of the area along with dairy herds and the feeder cattle industry. Farming is diversified. Oil production adds to the economy of the area, much of it from shallow wells and secondary recovery.

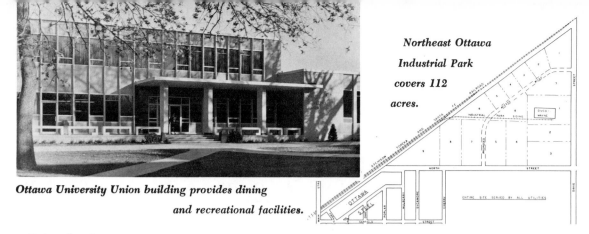

Ottawa University Union building provides dining and recreational facilities.

Northeast Ottawa Industrial Park covers 112 acres.

OTTAWA: *century-old town with century-old university*

Ottawa's civic leaders, who are working to bring in new industries, are the same persons who worked for many years to bring flood control to the beautiful Marais des Cygnes River Valley and improve highways in the area.

Today, Ottawa has much to offer new industries and their employees.

It has its own Ottawa (Baptist) University — a four-year school with degrees in 17 departments. Enrollment in 1965 was 900. Students came from 43 states and seven foreign countries.

Baptists of 100 years ago joined with Ottawa Indians and founded the town. Ottawa is the seat of Franklin County.

Ottawa Industrial Development, Inc., offers new industrial sites on a 112-acre industrial park northeast of the city. The park has been platted with 17 sites, serviced by utilities and railroad sidings.

The industrial park is six blocks from highways U. S. 50 and U. S. 59 and less than a mile from Interstate-35 to Kansas City and Wichita. The industrial corporation is a non-profit development, owned by citizens of Ottawa. It is a committee of the Ottawa Chamber of Commerce. The organization is authorized to buy, sell and lease land, and to construct and sell buildings for industrial development.

Already occupying a site is Divco-Wayne Industries. Divco-Wayne employs 120 persons to manufacture mobile homes.

A major segment of Ottawa's economy continues to be centered around agriculture. Franklin County is the largest milk producing county in Kansas. Bennett Creamery Company in Ottawa has 115 employees. Major crops in the community are corn, milo, beans and wheat.

H. D. Lee Company manufactures men's jackets. Mode O'Day Corporation produces women's dresses. Lee is the city's largest industry with 300 employees. Mode O'Day hires 130. Parmelee Products Company manufactures optical frames and components. It employs 90 people.

Ottawa Steel manufactures steel equipment, employs 85. Baldwin-Ward Manufacturing Company, world's largest manufacturer of "Sky Hooks" for hanging signs and other overhead uses, employs approximately 50 men.

Close-in Forest Park has fine recreational facilities. Pomona Reservoir is 18 miles west. The 4,000-acre lake is open for fishing, boating, water-skiing and other water sports.

The flood control plan for the Marais des Cygnes River Valley embraces five reservoirs and flood protection works at Ottawa and Osawatomie. Pomona, upstream from Ottawa, is completed, as well as local flood protection. Planning is completed for Melvern Reservoir, also upstream.

Ottawa's new high school, to cost $1,200,000, is scheduled for completion in July, 1966.

gate, roadstone and aglime. Gravel produced for paving and road maintenance. Crude petroleum production 262,000 barrels; natural gas output 65 million cubic feet.

OVERBROOK, Osage (C-12) pop. 581; 1 KPL; 3 Mun.; 4 MP; 5 US 56; First National Bank, Kansas State Bank $3,400,000; newspaper — Overbrook Citizen.

OVERLAND PARK, Johnson (C-13) pop. 51,292; 1 KCPL; 2 GSC; 5 I-35, US 50, US 56, US 169, US 69, K-58, K-150; Metcalf State Bank, Overland Park State Bank $19,800,000.

OXFORD, Sumner (G-9) pop. 1,064; 1 Mun.; 2 GSC; 3 Mun.; 4 AT&SF, MV; 5 US 160; The Oxford Bank $1,700,000; newspaper — Oxford Register. An old mill built in 1874 still stands in Oxford.

PALCO, Rooks (B-5) pop. 514; 1 WLT; 2 K-NG; 3 Mun.; 4 UP; 5 K-18; First National Bank $1,800,000.

PALMER, Washington (B-9) pop. 164; 1 WLT; 3 Mun.; 4 MP; 5 K-115; Bank of Palmer $800,000.

°PAOLA, Miami (D-13) pop. 4,801; 1 KCPL; 2 GSC; 3 Mun.; 4 SLSF, MKT, MP; 5 US 169, K-7; Citizens State Bank, Miami County National Bank $14,300,000; newspapers — Miami Republican, Western Spirit. The Miami County Fair and Horse Show is held annually, usually in mid-August, in Paola. Miola Lake has overnight camping areas.

Miami County — Earnings per cap. $1,845; sales tax collections $425,848; employed in industry 1,677; number of farms 1,661; crop value $7,265,720; livestock value $6,994,120; mineral production $760,154. Crude petroleum production 241,000 barrels; waterflood production accounting for most. Natural gas output 65 million cubic feet, compared with 20 million cubic feet previous year. Limestone was quarried and crushed for concrete aggregate, roadstone and agstone.

PARADISE, Russell (C-6) pop. 153; 1 WLT; 3 Mun.; 4 UP; 5 K-18.

PARK, Gove (C-4) pop. 222; 1 CKP; 2 K-NG; 5 K-211.

PARKER, Linn (D-13) pop. 176; 1 KCPL; 4 MKT.

PARKERVILLE, Morris (C-10) pop. 45; 1 KPL.

PARSONS, Labette (F-12) pop. 12,927; 1 KPL; 2 GSC; 3 Mun.; 4 SLSF, MKT; 5 US 160, US 59; 6 CEN; 7 Parsons Junior College; First National Bank, Parsons Commercial Bank, The State Bank of Parsons $15,000,000; Newspapers — Parsons News, Parsons Sun. The Parsons State Hospital and Training Center is here. Neosho County State Lake (Lake McKinley) is 6 miles east on US 160 and 2 miles north. Lake Parsons, 1,000-acre lake built as a water supply and recreation spot, is 5 miles northwest. The St. Paul Wildlife Refuge is northeast of town. About 12 miles west are the Bender Mounds named for the Bender Family.

PARTRIDGE, Reno (E-7) pop. 263; 1 KPL; 2 Mun.; 4 AT&SF, CRIP; 5 K-61.

PAWNEE ROCK, Barton (E-6) pop. 426; 1 KPL; 4 AT&SF; 5 US 56. One-quarter mile north of town and visible from US 56 is Pawnee Rock, a famous landmark on the Santa Fe Trail. As a lookout and ambush point for hostile Indians, the rock was one of the most dangerous spots on the Central Plains. Kit Carson, on sentry duty, shot his own mule in the mistaken belief it was a hostile Indian. The site is now a state park. A shelter house and monument are on the summit.

PAXICO, Wabaunsee (C-11) pop. 260; 1 KPL; 4 CRIP; 5 K-138.

PEABODY, Marion (E-9) pop. 1,387; 1 KPL; 2 Greeley Gas Co.; 3 Mun.; 4 AT&SF, CRIP; 5 US 50; Peabody State Bank $2,500,000; newspaper — Gazette-Herald. Four miles east of Peabody is Indian Guide Hill, an early-day guidepoint now topped by a concrete pylon. Peabody claims the oldest Masonic building still standing in Kansas. It is a stone structure 9 miles south of here.

PENALOSA, Kingman (F-7) pop. 63; 1 WLT; 4 MP.

PERRY, Jefferson (C-12) pop. 532; 1 KPL; 2 GSC; 3 Mun.; 4 UP; 5 US 24; Bank of Perry $1,800,000; newspaper — Jefferson County Mirror-Times.

PERU, Chautauqua (G-11) pop. 319; 1 Caney Valley Elec. Co-op. Assn.; 2 UGS; 3 Mun.; 4 MP; 5 US 166; Peru State Bank $408,000.

°PHILLIPSBURG, Phillips (A-5) pop. 3,916; 1 WLT; 2 K-NG; 3 Mun.; 4 CRIP; 5 US 183, US 36; First National Bank $7,000,000; newspaper — Phillips County Review. City is the site of the state's largest rodeo, held annually, beginning in late July. At Phillipsburg is the Jess Boyce Rock Garden and Museum, consisting of miniature castles and towers made from tiny rock and pebbles,

Downtown Park Square —
touch of serenity
in a bustling city.

PAOLA: *new breed among Kansas communities*

Centered in Kansas' eastern tier of counties is Paola — one of the best examples of this state's "New Breed" of communities. It is a blend of earliest Kansas history and one of the most progressive modern small cities.

This bustling city of 4,850 is Miami County seat. It is the marketing center for a prosperous community of 20,000 people. On three major highways and three mainline railroads, Paola is headquarters for a number of industrial operations and branch plants. One major truck line and eight contracting firms headquarter here.

Manufacturers produce fine women's clothing, forged iron items, metal and ceramic drainage pipe, electrical hoists, food products, and agricultural feeds, seeds and chemicals.

Power, water and fuel supplies virtually are unlimited. Soft water can be pumped at the rate of three million gallons per day. Nineteen pipelines cross the immediate area. Natural gas access is unlimited. Rates are competitive and attractive.

The city is situated among some of the state's most beautiful terrain. Miola Lake, a municipal recreation facility, and other surface waters are nearby. Hunting and fishing are excellent.

Two hunting preserves are nearby. There is boating, water skiing and swimming. The country club has a challenging grass green course and swim pool.

Paola's Park Square is a scenic hub for the city's downtown commercial center. A National Guard armory is headquarters for a howitzer battery. Located here are nine nursing care homes and the new Miami County hospital. The state mental treatment center is five miles southwest at Osawatomie. Kansas School for the Deaf is 21 miles away at Olathe.

Major highways are U.S. 169, main route between Kansas City and Tulsa; K-68, newly-improved Central Kansas' link with the Mississippi Valley states; and K-7, direct route to Eastern Kansas playground areas. This route also has a direct interchange on Kansas Turnpike. The name Paola is believed to have derived from a mispronunciation of the name of Baptiste Peoria, chief of the allied tribes of Miami, Wea, Piankeshaw, Peoria, Ottawa, Kaskaskia and Pottawatomie Indians. Chief Peoria owned the land which became the townsite of Paola.

Forested rolling hills in this community were chosen by Indian tribes as an ideal hunting ground. Whites later settled here as "a place of extraordinary beauty."

Ursuline Academy for Catholic women was established here beginning in 1894.

Oil was discovered near here in 1854 and was produced commercially in 1885. Natural gas and oil came to the surface in springs of water. In 1860, three oil wells began producing here. It was the first serious oil production attempted west of Pennsylvania.

and a large collection of pioneer relics. Kirwin Dam and Reservoir are nearby. A gun collection is in reconstructed Fort Bissell at the city park. Phillipsburg has the state's only gas-lighted airport.

Phillips County — Earnings per cap. $1,594; sales tax collections $248,230; employed in industry 915; number of farms 1,011; crop value $5,098,750; livestock value $6,350,680; mineral production $6,213,228. Crude petroleum output remained steady. Cooperative Refinery Assn. operated its petroleum refinery at Phillipsburg. Limestone for concrete aggregate and roadstone was quarried and crushed; sand obtained for paving and road maintenance.

PITTSBURG, Crawford (F-13) pop. 19,539; 1 KGE; 2 GSC; 3 Mun.; 4 AT&SF, SLSF, KCS, MP; 5 US 160, US 69 Alt., K-126, K-57; 7 Kansas State College of Pittsburg; First State Bank of Pittsburg, The National Bank of Pittsburg $29,000,000; newspapers — Pittsburg Headlight, Pittsburg Publishing Co., Pittsburg Sun.

PLAINS, Meade (G-3) pop. 827; 1 WLT; 2 NNG; 3 Mun.; 4 CRIP; 5 US 160, US 160 spur, US 54; Plains State Bank $2,600,000; newspaper — Plains Journal. One item developed here has been especially outstanding in its contribution to Kansas agriculture. The Angell One-Way Disc-Plow, invented, perfected, manufactured and named by Charlie Angell. He manufactured 430 of these plows on his farm near Plains from 1924 to 1926, then selling his rights to the Ohio Cultivator Co. of Bellevue, O. It was the Angell One-Way which started the revolution in tillage practices that occurred on the Great Plains during the 1920's. Two original Angell plows have been accepted by the Kansas Historical Society and the Agricultural Hall of Fame for permanent display.

PLAINVILLE, Rooks (B-5) pop. 2,797; 1 WLT; 2 K-NG; 3 Mun.; 4 UP; 5 US 183, K-18; Plainville State Bank $3,500,000; newspaper — Plainville Times.

PLEASANTON, Linn (E-13) pop. 1,158; 1 KCPL; 2 Pleasanton Gas Co.; 3 Mun.; 4 SLSF; 5 US 69, K-52; Bank of Pleasanton, First State Bank $6,300,000; newspaper — Pleasanton Observer-Enterprise. Two miles south is the site of the Battle of Mine Creek between 25,000 Union and Confederate forces in October, 1864. The Union victory ended the threat of a Confederate invasion of Kansas. The 6,000-acre Marais des Cygnes Wildlife Refuge is north of Pleasanton and west of US 69.

Fall River Dam and Reservoir form 2600-acre lake in Greenwood County.

Kansas State College of Pittsburg.

PITTSBURG: *"I like it here"*

For the past five years Pittsburg has progressed steadily and is continuing to do so. Coal, lead, zinc, oil, gas, clay and an unlimited supply of underground water are among the natural resources readily available in Pittsburg.

A 300-acre industrial park was established in the southeast quadrant of the city. Currently occupying about one-third of the park are Cook Paint and Varnish Company, Foodtown Super Markets, Inc., Delletters, Southwest Milk Producers and Midwest Tank and Reservoir Company. Delletters produces embroidered emblems.

New industry came to Pittsburg. Established firms underwent expansion to provide additional jobs. A boost to the economy came with expansion of Kansas State College. Enrollment grew from 636 to 5,280 in 20 years. This required additional faculty and staff.

Another boost came from the Federal Government. For lack of space in Washington, D.C., the Bureau of the Census moved its Personal Census Service branch here in 1958. The agency employs nearly 200 people to process more than 200,000 requests annually from persons over the United States needing legal proof of their age, place of birth, citizenship and kinship. New operations established here were an aircraft corporation, an aluminum foundry, a garment company, department stores, a nursing school, steel, tool, machine and plastic plants. New construction included a $1.5 million shopping center, city hall, rest homes, three schools, several churches and a number of housing developments.

Also located here is one of the nation's largest ammonium nitrate plants, the nation's largest plant devoted largely to production of coal preparation equipment, the main repair shops of Kansas City Southern Railroad Company, and one of the largest clay sewer pipe plants. The Pittsburg and Midway Coal Company installed the second largest electric shovel in the world. Pittsburg has master plans for projected growth for the next 20 years. Plans include zoning, water, sewers and street development, annexation and schools. If the college continues to grow at its present rate, enrollment will be 12,000 by 1970.

PLEVNA, Reno (E-7) pop. 119; 1 KPL; 2 Mun.; 4 AT&SF; State Bank of Plevna $648,000.

POMONA, Franklin (D-12) pop. 546; 1 Mun.; 2 UGSv; 3 Mun.; 4 AT&SF, MP; 5 K-68; Citizens State Bank $2,000,000. Pomona Reservoir has three major recreation areas.

PORTIS, Osborne (B-6) pop. 228; 1 WLT; 3 Mun.; 4 MP; 5 US 281, K-9; First State Bank $500,000.

POTWIN, Butler (E-9) pop. 584; 1 KGE; 3 Mun.; 4 MP; 5 K-196; Potwin State Bank $1,000,000; newspaper — Potwin Ledger.

POWHATTAN, Brown (A-12) pop. 161; 1 KPL; 4 CRIP.

PRAIRIE VIEW, Phillips (A-5) pop. 205; 1 WLT; 3 Mun.; 4 CRIP; 5 K-122.

PRAIRIE VILLAGE, Johnson (C-13) pop. 28,762; 1 KCPL; 2 GSC; 3 J. C. Nichols Water and Water Dist. No. 1, Johnson Co.; Johnson County National Bank & Trust Co., Kansas State Bank, Southgate State Bank $47,400,000. City awarded first place by the National Association of Home Builders in 1950 as the "Best Complete Community Development in the U. S."

*PRATT, Pratt (F-6) pop. 8,068; 1 Mun.; 2 KPL; 3 Mun.; 4 AT&SF, CRIP; 5 US 281, US 54, K-64, K-61; 7 Pratt Junior College; First National Bank in Pratt, The Peoples Bank $18,000,000; newspaper — Pratt Daily Tribune. Headquarters for the Kansas Forestry, Fish and Game Commission are southeast of Pratt on the grounds of the state fish hatchery. One of the world's largest freshwater hatcheries and the first channel catfish hatchery, it covers 187 acres and has 105 brood ponds as well as a museum, aquarium, zoo and the Commission's headquarters. Thousands of visitors annually visit the hatchery.

Pratt County — Earnings per cap. $1,967; sales tax collections $459,835; employed in industry 1,758; number of farms 757; crop value $6,219,050; livestock value $3,790,030; mineral production $4,464,091; crude petroleum production 1.4 million barrels, down 11 per cent. Natural gas output 2.9 billion cubic feet. Gereke West and Pratt Airport gas fields were important discoveries. Sand produced for building and paving.

PRESCOTT, Linn (E-13) pop. 286; 1 Mun.; 2 CGPC; 4 SLSF; 5 US 69; Prescott State Bank $445,000.

PRESTON, Pratt (F-7) pop. 306; 1 KPL; 2 GSC; 3 Mun.; 4 CRIP, MP; 5 US 61.

PRETTY PRAIRIE, Reno (F-8) pop. 581; 1 KGE; 2 KPL; 3 Mun.; 4 AT&SF; The State Bank $2,400,000; newspaper — Pretty Prairie Times. Town is the site of Kansas' largest night rodeo usually held in July or August.

PRINCETON, Franklin (D-12) pop. 166; 1 KCPL; 2 GSC; 4 AT&SF; 5 US 59.

PROTECTION, Comanche (G-5) pop. 739; 1 Mun.; 2 KPL; 3 Mun.; 4 AT&SF; 5 US 160, US 183, K-34; Farmers State Bank $1,500,000; newspaper — Protection Post.

QUENEMO, Osage (D-12) pop. 422; 1 KCPL; 2 UGSv; 3 Mun.; 4 AT&SF; 5 K-68.

QUINTER, Gove (C-4) pop. 847; 1 CKP; 2 K-NG; 3 Mun.; 4 UP; 5 K-212; First National Bank $3,500,000; newspaper — Gove County Advocate. Castle Rock rises from the plains 22 miles southeast of here.

RADIUM, Stafford (E-6) pop. 78; 1 Mun.; 4 MP.

RAMONA, Marion (D-9) pop. 127; 1 KPL; 2 Greeley Gas Co.; 4 CRIP; Ramona State Bank $300,000.

RANDALL, Jewell (B-7) pop. 235; 1 WLT; 3 Mun.; 4 MP; 5 K-28; Randall National Bank $1,000,000.

RANDOLPH, Riley (B-10) pop. 58; 1 KPL; 5 K-77, K-213.

RANSOM, Ness (D-4) pop. 470; 1 WLT; 3 Mun.; 4 MP; 5 K-4; Farmers State Bank, First State Bank $2,500,000.

RANTOUL, Franklin (D-13) pop. 153; 1 KCPL; 2 GSC; 4 MP.

RAYMOND, Rice (D-7) pop. 149; 1 KPL; 3 Mun.; 4 AT&SF; Raymond State Bank $540,000.

READING, Lyon (D-11) pop. 260; 1 KPL; 3 Mun.; 4 AT&SF; 5 K-170; Reading State Bank $688,000.

REDFIELD, Bourbon (E-13) pop. 152; 1 KGE; 2 Bourbon County Gas; 4 MP.

REPUBLIC, Republic (A-8) pop. 299; 1 WLT; 3 Mun.; 4 MP.

RESERVE, Brown (A-12) pop. 142; 1 Mun.; 2 GSC; 3 Mun.; 4 MP; 5 US 73.

REXFORD, Thomas (B-3) pop. 240; 1 CKP; 3 Mun.; 4 CRIP; 5 US 383, US 83; Rexford State Bank $460,000.

RICHFIELD, Morton (G-1) pop. 125; 5 K-51, K-27.

RICHMOND, Franklin (D-12) pop. 386; 1 KCPL; 2 GSC; 3 Mun.; 4 AT&SF; 5 US 59; Peoples State Bank $1,600,000.

RILEY, Riley (B-10) pop. 587; 1 KPL; 3 Mun.; 4 CRIP; 5 US 77, US 24; The State Bank of Riley $1,800,000.

ROBINSON, Brown (A-12) pop. 372; 1 Mun.; 3 Mun.; 4 UP; The Bank of Robinson $1,300,000.

ROELAND PARK, Johnson (C-13) pop. 10,519; 1 KCPL; 2 GSC; 3 Water Dist. No. 1, Johnson Co.; 5 US 56, US 50, K-158, K-58; Roeland Park State Bank $10,500,000.

ROLLA, Morton (G-1) pop. 448; 1 Pioneer Co-op. Assn., Inc.; 2 NNG; 3 Mun.; 4 AT&SF; 5 US 56, K-51.

ROSE HILL, Butler (F-9) pop. 324; 1 KGE; 2 GSC; 4 AT&SF; Rose Hill State Bank $2,400,000.

ROSSVILLE, Shawnee (C-11) pop. 811; 1 KPL; 2 KPL; 3 Mun.; 4 UP; 5 US 24; Peoples State Bank $2,100,000; newspaper — Shawnee County Reporter.

ROZEL, Pawnee (E-5) pop. 244; 1 KPL; 4 AT&SF; 5 US 183, US 156.

RUSH CENTER, Rush (D-5) pop. 260; 1 Central Kansas Elec. Co-op. Assn.; 4 AT&SF; 5 US 183, K-96.

°RUSSELL, Russell (C-6) pop. 6,254; 1 Mun.; 2 KPL; 3 Mun.; 4 UP; 5 US 281, US 40; The Home State Bank, Russell State Bank $25,000,000; newspapers — Russell Daily News, Russell Record. Plaque and monument, 16½ miles northwest of Russell, mark the site of Carrie Oswald No. 1, discovery well of the Fairport pool and one of Kansas' most famous oil wells. Two miles northwest of Russell is Kit Fork's Canyon, from which a band of Indians rushed to attack a party of railroad section workers in 1869. Wilson Dam has recreation areas available.

Russell County — Earnings per cap. $1,974; sales tax collections $438,281; employed in industry 1,798; number of farms 798; crop value $5,349,840; livestock value $3,682,510; mineral production $24,831,832. County ranked third in petroleum production and third in total mineral value. Crude petroleum output nearly 8.5 million barrels. Natural gas production up 12 per cent to 439 million cubic feet. Paving sand and gravel produced. Completion of Wilson Dam and Reservoir came late in 1965.

RUSSELL SPRINGS, Logan (C-2) pop. 98; 1 CKP; 5 K-25.

SABETHA, Nemaha (A-11) pop. 2,440; 1 Mun.; 2 GSC; 3 Mun.; 4 CRIP, UP; 5 US 75; Farmers State Bank $5,700,000; newspaper — Sabetha Herald. Sabetha is home of Wenger Manufacturing, world-wide manufacturers and distributors of feed pellet making mills and the nation's leading manufacturers of pre-cooked dog food machines. During July, Sabetha has an annual 3-day rodeo and in August annual 1-day speed boat racing at the city lake. Sabetha has two large resorts within seven miles of town: Sycamore and Sun Springs.

°ST. FRANCIS, Cheyenne (A-1) pop. 1,675; 1 Mun.; 2 K-NG; 3 Mun.; 4 CB&Q; 5 US 36, K-27; Cheyenne County State Bank, Citizens State Bank $7,000,000; newspaper — Herald.

Cheyenne County — Earnings per cap. $1,786; sales tax collections $143,961; employed in industry 280; number of farms 713; crop value $5,618,650; livestock value $4,543,980; mineral production $81,478. Sand and gravel produced for building, paving and fill. Output of crude petroleum 1,690 barrels.

ST. GEORGE, Pottawatomie (B-10) pop. 273; 1 KPL; 2 KPL; 4 UP.

°ST. JOHN, Stafford (E-6) pop. 1,750; 1 Mun.; 2 KPL; 3 Mun.; 4 AT&SF; 5 US 281; First National Bank, St. John National Bank $6,700,000; newspapers — St. John Capital, St. John News. The Great Salt Marsh area in Stafford-Rice-Reno counties, northeast of St. John, is being developed into a national wildlife refuge by the U. S. Fish and Wildlife Service. This includes approximately 20,000 acres on Rattlesnake Creek.

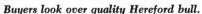
Buyers look over quality Hereford bull.   *Aerial view of St. Francis in extreme northwest Kansas.*

ST. FRANCIS: *trading, recreational center*

If your sizzling steak is particularly tender, juicy and full-flavored it could be from quality registered Hereford cattle fattened on the ranges near St. Francis and sold here.

Residents boast that St. Francis has more registered cattle within a 50-mile radius than any other community in the world. Each February, members of the Western Republican Valley Hereford Association sell their highest quality herd bulls, chosen long before sale date. Requests from buyers are sent in early making the advance price on these animals not less than $400 to $500 each. The event attracts buyers from several hundred miles.

St. Francis is located in good wheat growing area. Due to abundant underground water and increased irrigation, the agricultural outlook is bright. There are more than 200 wells in the county. Irrigation has greatly increased the demand for supplies, seed, fertilizer and irrigation equipment and will continue to do so. Wheat is always one of the best crops. Milo and other feed grains are grown extensively. Livestock feeding is increasing.

St. Francis, county seat of Cheyenne County, is the furthermost city north and west in Kansas. It is the hub of a trade territory that extends into Colorado and Nebraska. The community has a hospital, five rest homes, municipal airport with 3500-foot grass runway and cross runways, 10 churches, banks, a weekly newspaper, library, theater, and a county fair each August. Best of all, say the residents, it has ideal climate with cool nights even during midsummer (elevation: 3,355 feet).

The economy of the community is based almost entirely on agricultural production, chiefly wheat and cattle. A number of construction firms in town serve an area up to 70 miles away.

Educationwise, St. Francis is meeting the growing needs of its students — 233 in high school and 430 in the elementary grades. A $500,000 high school construction program will provide added classrooms and a gym. The elementary school $50,000 addition is underway.

For recreation, the city offers swimming instructions in a heated pool, nine-hole sand green golf course and clubhouse, bowling alley, baseball diamonds and parks. Still in the planning stage is a new recreation center to include a nine-hole grass green golf course, tennis courts, skeet range, shuffleboard, clubhouse, small fishing lake and camping area.

During hunting season St. Francis plays host to large crowds of sportsmen hunting pheasants and water fowl. In fact, pheasant hunters must make reservations well in advance. The deer population is increasing continually, with 1965 the first open limit deer season.

Closest metropolitan center is 170 miles away at Denver where the better restaurants feature tender, mouth watering, quality cut steaks . . . quite possibly from St. Francis, Kansas!

Stafford County — Earnings per cap. $1,730; sales tax collections $172,394; employed in industry 779; number of farms 879; crop value $6,769,800; livestock value $4,674,020; mineral production $15,804,410. Stafford County ranked seventh in crude petroleum production; output totaled 5.3 million barrels. Rychlec oil field and Emerson West gas field important discoveries. Natural gas production 3 billion cubic feet. Sand and gravel produced for building, paving and road maintenance.

ST. MARYS, Pottawatomie (B-11) pop. 1,482; 1 Mun.; 2 KPL; 3 Mun.; 4 UP; 5 US 24, K-63; The St. Marys State Bank $3,100,000; newspaper — St. Marys Star. St. Mary's College, now a Jesuit Seminary, was an outgrowth of St. Mary's Catholic Mission founded in 1848 for the Pottawatomie Indians. A boulder on the campus marks the site of the first Cathedral between the Missouri River and the Rocky Mountains. In the Church of the Immaculate Conception is a rare painting by an Italian Court painter of the 16th century, which was a gift of Pope Pius IX to the Pottawatomie in 1854.

ST. PAUL, Neosho (F-13) pop. 765; 1 KPL; 2 St. Paul Gas Co.; 3 Mun.; 4 MKT; 5 K-57; Exchange State Bank $1,400,000; newspaper — St. Paul Journal. Neosho County state lake is 6 miles south.

°SALINA, Saline (C-8) pop. 41,293; 1 KPL; 2 KPL; 3 Mun.; 4 AT&SF, CRIP, MP, UP; 5 I-70, US 281, US 40; 6 CEN; 7 Kansas Wesleyan University, Marymount College; The First National Bank and Trust Co., First State Bank of Salina, National Bank of America, Planters State Bank $64,000,000; newspapers — Salina Globe Sun, Salina Journal, Inc. Four miles east of Salina is a prehistoric Burial Pit containing more than 140 skeletal remains of Indians six feet or more tall who antedate Coronado. It is covered by a permanent structure which also contains a collection of Indian artifacts. Salina is the nation's fifth largest flour milling center. The Roman Catholic Cathedral of the Sacred Heart resembles a wheat elevator in architectural design. Smoky Hill Historical Museum in Oakdale Park features departments on stone-age man, the American Indian, the pioneer and his life, natural history and oriental art. Schilling Air Force Base is two miles southwest of Salina. Located in Salina are Kansas Wesleyan University (Methodist); Marymount College for Girls (Catholic); St. John's Military School (Episcopal), noted for rehabilitation work with wayward youngsters.

Saline County — Earnings per cap. $2,015; sales tax collections $2,074,934; employed in industry 10,185; number of farms 980; crop value $7,478,030; livestock value $4,706,430. The county ranked third in value of sand and gravel production, used mainly for building and paving. Output of crude petroleum 745,000 barrels. Pihl oil field important discovery.

SATANTA, Haskell (F-2) pop. 1,144; 1 WLT; 2 NNG; 3 Mun.; 4 AT&SF; 5 US 56, K-190; State Bank of Satanta $1,900,000. A teepee to house Indian artifacts and historical information is along US 56 underneath water tower.

SAVONBURG, Allen (F-13) pop. 123; 1 Mun.; 2 UGS; 3 Mun.; 4 MKT; 5 K-212.

SAWYER, Pratt (F-6) pop. 181; 1 WLT; 3 Mun.; 4 AT&SF; 5 US 281, K-42; newspaper — Sawyer News.

SCAMMON, Cherokee (G-13) pop. 476; 1 EDE; 2 AG; 3 Mun.; 4 SLSF, NEO; 5 K-102, K-7.

SCANDIA, Republic (A-8) pop. 607; 1 WLT; 2 KPL; 3 Mun.; 4 CRIP, MP; 5 US 36; Scandia State Bank $1,500,000; newspaper — Scandia Journal.

SCHOENCHEN, Ellis (E-5) pop. 197; 1 WLT; 5 US 183.

°SCOTT CITY, Scott (D-3) pop. 4,006; 1 Wheatland Elec. Co-op., Inc.; 2 K-NG; 3 Plains Utility Water; 4 AT&SF, MP; 5 US 83, K-96; First National Bank, Security Bank $8,000,000; newspaper — News Chronicle Printing Co., Inc. The 1,280-acre Scott County State Park, one of the state's most attractive areas, is 12 miles north of here. Monument marks El Quartelejo ruins, an important archeological site. The ruins were excavated in 1898, revealing a pueblo built by Picurie Indians and occupied by them from 1650-1720. Pueblo shows traces of an irrigation system. Today the ruins are mostly buried by drifting soil. Monument Rocks are 32 miles northeast of Scott City. The Kiva Indian Museum is located one-half mile west of city.

Scott County — Earnings per cap. $1,937; sales tax collections $248,818; employed in industry 747; number of farms 408; crop value $7,644,720; livestock value $4,831,750; mineral production $153,325. Crude petroleum production 53,000 barrels. Petroleum refinery operated at Shallow

Water. Natural gas output 23 million cubic feet.

SCOTTSVILLE, Mitchell (B-8) pop. 71; 1 WLT; 4 MP.

SCRANTON, Osage (C-11) pop. 542; 1 Mun.; 4 AT&SF; 5 US 56.

°SEDAN, Chautauqua (G-11) pop. 1,736; 1 Caney Valley Elec. Co-op. Assn., Inc.; 2 UGS; 3 Mun.; 4 MP; 5 US 166, K-99; First National Bank, Sedan State Bank $6,300,000; Newspaper — Sedan Times-Star.

Chautauqua County — Earnings per cap. $1,744; sales tax collections $133,736; employed in industry 542; number of farms 647; crop value $1,785,740; livestock value $4,257,360; mineral production $2,384,258. Yield of crude petroleum up 3 per cent; secondary recovery operations supplying a large part of the output. Natural gas recovery 280 million cubic feet, a 101 per cent increase.

SEDGWICK, Harvey (E-9) pop. 1,090; 1 KGE; 2 Mun. and GSC; 3 Mun.; 4 AT&SF; Sedgwick State Bank $1,200,000; newspaper — Sedgwick Pantagraph.

SELDEN, Sheridan (B-3) pop. 358; 1 CKP; 3 Mun.; 4 CRIP; 5 US 36, K-83; Farmers State Bank $851,000; newspaper — Selden Advocate.

°SENECA, Nemaha (A-11) pop. 2,259; 1 Mun.; 2 KPL; 3 Mun.; 4 UP; 5 US 36, K-63; Citizens State Bank $6,600,000; newspaper — Courier-Tribune. The 356-acre Nemaha County State Lake is 4 miles south of Seneca. There is a recreational area on the west edge of the city. "Fort Markley," a recreation-type facility located in a replica of a frontier fort, features the "oldest, authentic cowboy jail," gravity house, ceramics of prehistoric life, covered wagons, teepees, buggies, riding horses, bow and arrow range and a kart track, fishing lake and lake for ice skating; open all year.

Nemaha County — Earnings per cap. $1,460; sales tax collections $309,210; employed in industry 791; number of farms 1,577; crop value $8,581,870; livestock value $11,635,340; mineral production $80,916.

SEVERANCE, Doniphan (A-12) pop. 202; 1 Mun.; 4 UP; 5 K-120.

SEVERY, Greenwood (F-11) pop. 531; 1 KPL; 2 Stryker Gas Co.; 3 Mun.; 4 AT&SF, SLSF; 5 K-99, K-96; Severy State Bank $840,000; newspaper — Severyite.

SEWARD, Stafford (E-6) pop. 84; 1 Mun.; 4 MP; 5 K-219.

SHARON, Barber (G-7) pop. 291; 1 WLT; 3 Mun.; 4 AT&SF; 5 US 160; Sharon Valley State Bank $740,000.

°SHARON SPRINGS, Wallace (C-1) pop. 1,062; 1 Mun.; 3 Mun.; 4 UP; 5 US 40, K-27; Peoples State Bank $2,800,000; newspaper — Western Times. Five miles northwest of the city is the Old Maid's Pool, a geological sink filled with water to a depth of 200 feet. The pool, which has never gone dry, was used as a watering place for the early settlers and transient caravans.

Wallace County — Earnings per cap. $1,597; sales tax collections $71,048; employed in industry 108; number of farms 299; crop value $3,165,200; livestock value $2,102,500; mineral production includes diatomaceous marl with principal uses as paint filler and whiting material. Gravel produced for paving and road maintenance.

SHAWNEE, Johnson (C-13) pop. 13,730; 1 KCPL; 2 GSC; 3 K. C. Suburban Water Co.; 5 K-10; Shawnee State Savings Bank $11,000,000; newspaper — Johnson County Herald, Inc.

SILVER LAKE, Shawnee (C-11) pop. 408; 1 KPL; 2 KPL; 3 Mun.; 4 UP; 5 US 24; Silver Lake State Bank $1,800,000.

SIMPSON, Cloud and Mitchell (B-8) pop. 136; 1 WLT; 3 Mun.; 4 UP; 5 K-194; Simpson State Bank $300,000.

°SMITH CENTER, Smith (A-6) pop. 2,707; 1 WLT; 2 GSC; 3 Mun.; 4 CRIP; 5 US 281, US 36, K-204; First National Bank, Smith County State Bank $11,000,000; newspaper — Smith County Pioneer. On the banks of Beaver Creek about 17 miles northwest of Smith Center is a one-room cabin, home of Dr. Brewster M. Higley, pioneer Kansas doctor who wrote the words to the famous song, "Home on the Range," in the early 1870's. It was later adopted as the Official State Song. The tune was written by Daniel Kelley, a carpenter-musician who lived in nearby Gaylord. The cabin was dedicated as a historic memorial to Higley in 1954. It is open daily. A quaint octagonal Dutch windmill, five stories high, stands in the city park.

Century Refining Company, subsidiary of Panhandle Eastern Pipeline.

Floyd Fairleigh Feed Yards.

SCOTT CITY: *"confidence in the future"*

Confidence in future prosperity of this city of more than 4,000 is reflected in current new construction of business and government facilities. Completed in 1965 were a new telephone exchange with dial system, motel, restaurant, new high school field house and stadium, and Scott County Library. Underway are a new bank building, rest home and post office.

Scott City is the seat of Scott County. The city is located 100 miles from the Oklahoma state line, 100 miles from Nebraska and 60 miles from Colorado. Elevation is 2,971 feet above sea level. Average annual rainfall is over 19 inches. This second-class city is governed by a mayor and council.

For recreation there are the city park and playground, bowling alley, golf course and two riding clubs. One of Kansas' most attractive recreation facilities is Scott County State Park. Covering 1,280 acres, the lake and park are 12 miles north of here.

The Scott City Chamber of Commerce is directing its major effort toward development of new businesses to process the county's major agricultural products — grain and livestock. Irrigation assures year-round cattle feeding operations. The county has an abundance of natural resources and utilities. Water supply is from an underground reservoir of more than 600 square miles. Electricity is produced here by Wheatland Electric Co-op. Kansas-Nebraska Natural Gas Company provides gas from the Hugoton Field in southwest Kansas. A $1,250,000 expansion program at the compressor station site is underway with a new unit to be in operation by mid-winter. The new plant will cover about 10 acres and will be fully automatic, processing two million cubic feet of gas a day. The extracted gas is used by refineries.

Century Refining Co., located here, is a wholly-owned subsidiary of Panhandle Eastern Pipeline Co. The refinery has 140 employes, half of which live here. In 1964, the refinery processed 1,250,000 barrels of crude oil.

Scott City's population has doubled since 1945. This is due to several factors. Frontier Hybrids Seed Company, Kansas-Nebraska Natural Gas Co., Wheatland Electric Co-op, and Century Refining Co. have all expanded in the last few years, bringing in many new families. Many farmers also are moving to town so their children may attend city schools.

"A source of great pride" to Scott City is its schools. "Our elementary, junior high, high and parochial schools are modern and are operated by high-calibre staffs." The junior high school was built in 1958. A gymnasium, auditorium and classrooms were added to the high school in 1961. St. Joseph's parochial school was completed the same year.

Rolling hills spotted with timber.   *Pleasant view around every bend.*

SEDAN: *friendly town in scenic wilderness area*

Seat of Chautauqua County in southeast Kansas, Sedan is the marketing center of a prosperous community engaged in ranching, farming and oil production. Most recently it has become a center of tourist attraction.

Six years ago, Sedan and Cedar Vale, 18 miles to the west, sponsored a Redbud tour in the spring when redbud trees are in full bloom. It became an annual event sponsored by the Chamber of Commerce. Maps are provided. Redbud seedlings are given to visitors in some 2,000 cars which tour the area.

Early in 1965, the Chamber of Commerce sponsored the marking of a wilderness trail so that tourists might enjoy scenic drives the year around. An annual autumn color tour was added to the tourist schedule. Along the trails, tourists may find signs calling attention to historical landmarks. The Blackdog Trail Indian Museum at Chautauqua and the historical museum at Elgin are stopping points.

Sedan Chamber of Commerce and several business firms underwrote the cost of marking two drives. One goes north and east and returns to Sedan. The other goes south to Chautauqua through Elgin and ends at Cedar Vale.

Sedan is located near the southern end of the Flint Hills, adjacent to the Osage Cuestas. A cuesta is a gently sloping hill with an abrupt face. Osage Cuestas begin in northeastern Oklahoma and extend well into Kansas.

Sedan is the center of four watershed districts created to correct a history of frequent flash floods. Constructed or underway are 80 dams in the community. These will create water storage lakes five to 350 acres in size. These are privately owned. Landowners are urged to develop recreational facilities at the lakes. Dams are designed to protect 90 per cent of the county from floods.

Sedan recently completed a new city lake. It more than doubles the city's water supply. The shoreline will be developed for recreation and summer homes.

Sedan was founded in 1873. It was named after Sedan, France.

The Kansas town quickly became an agricultural trading center. About the turn of the century, development of oil production brought a boom to its economy. At present, ranchers graze about 45,000 cattle. The county has 4,500 producing oil wells.

Among industrial firms in town are Sedan Floral, largest bedding plant wholesaler east of California; Economy Manufacturing, maker of truck beds, feeders, cattle chutes; McCunningham's, manufacturer of tanks, hydraulic oil field pumps, trash racks; and Sedan Plastics, maker of plastic boxes for shipping bedding plants.

Smith County — Earnings per cap. $1,485; sales tax collections $186,685; employed in industry 418; number of farms 1,141; crop value $7,375,790; livestock value $6,985,230; mineral production $320,732.

SMOLAN, Saline (C-8) pop. 209; 1 KPL; 2 KPL; 3 Mun.; 4 MP.

SOLDIER, Jackson (B-11) pop. 183; 1 KPL; 5 K-62.

SOLOMON, Dickinson (C-9) pop. 1,137; 1 DS&O Rural Elec. Co-op. Assn., Inc.; 2 KPL; 3 Mun.; 4 AT&SF, UP; 5 K-221; Solomon National Bank $2,200,000; newspaper — Solomon Valley Tribune.

SOUTH HAVEN, Sumner (G-9) pop. 459; 1 WLT; 2 WLT; 3 Mun.; 4 AT&SF; 5 US 177, US 166, US 81; newspaper — South Haven New Era.

SOUTH HUTCHINSON, Reno (E-8) pop. 1,967; 1 KPL; 3 Mun.; 5 K-61, K-17; Farmers & Merchants State Bank $3,000,000.

SPEARVILLE, Ford (E-5) pop. 661; 1 WLT; 3 Mun.; 4 AT&SF; 5 US 56, US 50; First National Bank, Ford County State Bank $3,000,000; newspaper — Spearville News.

SPEED, Phillips (A-5) pop. 75; 1 WLT; 2 K-NG; 3 Mun.; 4 MP; 5 K-9.

SPIVEY, Kingman (F-7) pop. 108; 1 WLT; 4 AT&SF; 5 K-42.

SPRING HILL, Johnson (C-13) pop. 1,036; 1 KPL; 2 UGS; 3 Mun.; 4 SLSF; 5 US 169, K-7; State Bank of Spring Hill $1,900,000.

STAFFORD, Stafford (E-7) pop. 1,946; 1 Mun.; 2 KPL; 3 Mun.; 4 AT&SF, MP; 5 US 50; Farmers National Bank $4,100,000; newspaper — Stafford Courier, Inc.

STARK, Neosho (F-13) pop. 104; 1 KGE; 4 MKT; 5 K-201; Stark State Bank $1,007,000.

STERLING, Rice (E-7) pop. 2,024; 1 Mun.; 2 Ark.-La. Gas Co.; 3 Mun.; 4 AT&SF, MP; 5 K-96, K-14; 7 Sterling College; The Farmers State Bank in Sterling, First National Bank $4,400,000; newspaper — Sterling Bulletin.

°STOCKTON, Rooks (B-5) pop. 2,032; 1 Mun.; 2 K-NG; 3 Mun.; 4 MP; 5 US 183, US 24; Stockton National Bank $3,600,000; newspaper — Rooks County Record. Twelve miles southeast are Twin Mounds standing 200 feet above the prairie and used as a landmark and signal point by the Indians. Also near Stockton is Sugar Loaf Mound, over 300 feet high, which was an Indian lookout. A replica of the original log hotel in Stockton, near west city limits, is maintained as a museum. Webster Dam and Reservoir are southwest of Stockton.

Rooks County — Earnings per cap. $1,596; sales tax collections $282,350; employed in industry 980; number of farms 835; crop value $4,458,390; livestock value $4,325,750; mineral production $16,088,113. Rooks County ranked fifth in production of crude petroleum, nearly 5.6 million barrels. Building sand recovered from deposits near Alton.

STRONG CITY, Chase (D-10) pop. 603; 1 KPL; 2 Strong City Gas Co.; 3 Mun.; 4 AT&SF; 5 US 50, K-57, K-13; Strong City State Bank $860,000; newspaper — Chase County Leader-News.

°SUBLETTE, Haskell (F-3) pop. 1,252; 1 WLT; 2 NNG; 3 Mun.; 4 AT&SF; 5 US 56, K-145; Haskell County State Bank $4,700,000; newspaper — Haskell County Monitor-Chief.

Haskell County — Earnings per cap. $1,863; sales tax collections $99,874; employed in industry 423; number of farms 289; crop value $6,083,510; livestock value $2,889,540; mineral production $9,751,081. Crude petroleum output slightly less than 1.5 million barrels. Nearly 44 billion cubic feet of natural gas produced. Sand obtained for paving and road maintenance.

SUMMERFIELD, Marshall (A-10) pop. 259; 1 Mun.; 3 Mun.; 5 K-99; First National Bank $614,000; newspaper — Summerfield Sun.

SUN CITY, Barber (G-6) pop. 145; 1 WLT; 4 AT&SF.

SUSANK, Barton (D-6) pop. 73; 1 WLT; 3 Mun.; 4 AT&SF.

SYLVAN GROVE, Lincoln (C-7) pop. 543; 1 WLT; 2 GSC; 3 Mun.; 4 UP; 5 K-181; Sylvan State Bank $2,400,000; newspaper — Sylvan Grove News.

SYLVIA, Reno (E-7) pop. 397; 1 KPL; 2 Mun.; 3 Mun.; 4 AT&SF; 5 US 50; Sylvia State Bank $840,000; newspaper — Sylvia Press.

°SYRACUSE, Hamilton (E-1) pop. 1,989; 1 Wheatland Elec. Co-op., Inc.; 2 PNG; 3 Mun.; 4 AT&SF; 5 US 270, US 50, K-27; First National Bank, Valley State Bank $7,200,000; newspaper — Syracuse

Journal. Great Plains Historical Museum has complete collection of Colt shoulder arms, starting with Colt-Patterson revolving rifles made in 1836-42; Indian relics; cowboy equipment and tools and mementoes of the Old West. Perkins Park Zoo is in Syracuse. Hamilton County State Lake is 5 miles northwest.

Hamilton County — Earnings per cap. $2,208; sales tax collections $97,230; employed in industry 264; number of farms 377; crop value $2,492,430; livestock value $1,920,670; mineral production $330,740. Natural gas production up 92 per cent to 2.3 billion cubic feet. Crude petroleum production 11,000 barrels, up 17 per cent. Sand produced for building, paving and road maintenance.

TAMPA, Marion (D-9) pop. 168; 1 KPL; 2 Greeley Gas Co.; 4 CRIP; Tampa State Bank $970,000.

TESCOTT, Ottawa (C-8) pop. 464; 1 KPL; 2 KPL; 3 Mun.; 4 UP; 5 K-18; Bank of Tescott $4,000,000.

THAYER, Neosho (F-12) pop. 394; 1 KPL; 2 UGSv; 4 AT&SF; 5 US 169; First State Bank $2,500,000.

TIMKEN, Rush (D-6) pop. 146; 1 WLT; 2 KPL; 3 Mun.; 4 AT&SF; 5 K-96; Timken State Bank $1,200,000.

TIPTON, Mitchell (B-7) pop. 283; 1 Mun.; 3 Mun.; 4 AT&SF; 5 K-181; Tipton State Bank $400,000.

TONGANOXIE, Leavenworth (C-13) pop. 1,543; 1 KPL; 2 GSC; 3 Mun.; 4 UP; 5 US 40, US 24, K-16; First State Bank $2,700,000; newspaper — Tonganoxie Mirror. Leavenworth County State Lake, 2 miles west on K-16, includes a park area of 506 acres and a 175-acre lake.

*TOPEKA, Shawnee (C-12) pop. 122,008; 1 KPL; 2 GSC; 3 Mun.; 4 AT&SF, CRIP, MP, UP; 5 KTA, I-470, I-70, US 75, US 40, US 24, K-4; 6 CEN; 7 Washburn University of Topeka; Commerce State Bank, Fidelity State Bank, First National Bank, Kaw Valley Citizens State Bank, Merchants National Bank, Southwest State Bank, State Savings Bank, Topeka State Bank $205,000,000; newspaper — Topeka Capital-Journal. The state capitol building is located in a 20-acre square near the center of Topeka. East of the statehouse is the Kansas Memorial Building, headquarters of the Kansas State Historical Society with scores of displays and exhibits. The Society's newspaper collection is the largest in the country excepting that of the Library of Congress. East of the statehouse is the large general office building of the Santa Fe Railroad, the rail line which laid its first tracks from Topeka in 1868 headed for the trade area of the southwest. West of the statehouse is the new State Office Building, completed in 1957.

Topeka is the home of Alfred M. Landon, Republican candidate for President in 1936, and Harry H. Woodring, Secretary of War 1936-40. Charles Curtis, part Kaw Indian and U. S. vice president 1929-33, lived at Topeka and is buried here. The late Dr. Charles M. Sheldon, author of "In His Steps," was for many years pastor of the Central Congregational Church.

The Menninger Foundation near west city limits is world-famous psychiatric clinic, hospital and training center. Topeka VA Hospital is one of the principal psychiatric hospitals of the Veterans Administration. Also here are Topeka State Hospital (mental), the State Industrial School for Boys, and Stauffer Publications, Inc., founded by the late Sen. Arthur Capper. Important industries are the Santa Fe shops; the Goodyear Tire and Rubber Company, and DuPont cellophane plant. South of Topeka is Forbes Air Force Base. On the campus of Washburn University of Topeka is the Mulvane Art Museum with valuable permanent collections of paintings and sculpture. Reinisch Rose and Rock Garden in Gage Park is one of the most beautiful in the nation. One of the Midwest's larger zoos and special "Storybook Zoo" are also in Gage Park. Mid-America fair grounds contain 80 acres.

Shawnee County — Earnings per cap. $2,250; sales tax collections $5,671,464; employed in industry 27,840; number of farms 1,376; crop value $5,826,730; livestock value $4,256,410; mineral production $615,365. Shawnee County ranked fourth in value of sand and gravel produced. Included are building, paving and fill sand and gravel, engine sand and other industrial sands. Limestone quarried and crushed for concrete aggregate and roadstone.

TORONTO, Woodson (F-11) pop. 461; 1 Mun.; 2 WLT; 3 Mun.; 4 MP; 5 K-105; First National Bank $1,100,000; newspaper — Toronto Republican. Woodson County state park and lake (Lake Fegan), 5 miles east of Toronto, is one of the most beautiful of the state lakes. A prehistoric cave

Aerial view of Topeka.

TOPEKA: *citizens have faith*

People of Topeka show great faith in the future of their city. They are investing money, time and talent to keep it a city in which they will want to live and raise families.

All of the city's progress is based on a planned approach to growth.

Today, Topeka is acquiring a new face. Business and residential construction is booming. The appearance of Kansas Avenue (Main Street) is being altered rapidly. New buildings are replacing old. Businessmen are undertaking extensive remodeling. Eighteen shopping centers for outlying areas are completed or under construction.

New schools and parks are being built to prepare for anticipated growth. Construction is progressing at triple the pace of 1952. Building permits the past 10 years were valued at more than $100 million. Of that total, more than $80 million paid for new homes. Over $20 million went for new business facilities. Fifteen new public schools were built. Private enterprise construction amounted to $16.5 million the past two years. Programming through 1967 will bring an additional $26 million in construction.

By far the most ambitious undertaking is an Urban Renewal project "Keyway," which had its inception in 1957. Keyway is designed to consolidate many small parcels of land to provide efficient larger tracts needed by modern business and industrial operations. It is Topeka's pilot urban renewal program.

The project encompasses 27 city blocks adjacent to the north and east side of downtown business district. It is converting mixed residential, industrial and commercial usage to a planned industrial-commercial section. Major streets, railroad facilities, Kansas River and the business core area are boundaries of the renewal project. A portion of the project area became right-of-way for the new Interstate-70 highway.

Both large and small industries provide an important way of life in the capital city of Kansas.

Employing nearly 4,500 is Atchison, Topeka and Santa Fe Railroad Company — one of the nation's leading railroads. Santa Fe offices, maintenance shops, and hospitals are located here.

Goodyear Tire and Rubber Company employs 3,000 in its Topeka plant. The company has

45 acres under roof. Nearly 800 types and sizes of tires are manufactured for vehicles ranging from automobiles to huge earthmovers.

Stauffer Publications employs 800. It publishes the Topeka Daily Capital, Topeka State Journal and is one of the nation's largest publishers of farm magazines and newspapers. Stauffer publishes Capper's Weekly Farm Magazine and nine other newspapers.

E. I. du Pont de Nemours and Company, Inc., employs 600. The plant operates three shifts to produce 50 million pounds of cellophane annually.

Topeka is the home of The Fleming Company, one of the nation's leading voluntary group food distribution systems. Many smaller industrial plants employ from 20 to 300.

Topeka's stable, expanding economy is due to diversification of industrial and agricultural income. Located in the middle of the Great American Wheat Belt, Topeka plays a major role in agriculture. Because of development of irrigation systems and water conservation, it has become a leader in the Midwest among communities actively interested in prosperity of the farmer.

Topeka is situated in the heart of the fertile Kaw (Kansas River) Valley. It is an ideal location for food processing. Among its important industries are milling and storage of grain. Elevator capacity is more than 73.5 million bushels.

Retail sales, commercial construction, industrial payrolls, bank deposits, savings and other business barometers indicate an increasing business growth at a rate far more rapid than the national average. Per capita and family income also is substantially higher than average. In Kansas, average individual income is $2,041. In Topeka, it is $2,344. Average Kansas family income is $6,605. Here it is $7,365.

Effective buying power of Topeka's 23-county trade area was $961 million in 1964, according to Sales Management's survey of buying power. Topeka has primary retail trade in 11 counties and secondary trade in 12 counties.

Because of its size and location, Topeka plays a major role in many business, industrial and cultural activities of Kansas. Retail firms maintain credit accounts for people living two and three hundred miles away.

Four major railroads provide transportation to and from the city. They are Santa Fe, Missouri Pacific, Rock Island and Union Pacific lines.

Thirty-one trucklines serve the city, and 20 maintain agencies here. Central Airlines serves the city with 12 daily flights. Topeka is a popular convention center, hosting over 100,000 delegates each year.

Because of varied transportation facilities and its proximity to the geographic center of the

Veterans Administration Hospital.

Beautiful Lake Shawnee.

212

Large Mammal Building,
Topeka Zoological Park.

Atchison, Topeka and Santa Fe Railway shops.

United States, Topeka often is referred to as "the crossroads of the nation."

Topeka plays a part in the more serious business of national defense. Located seven miles south of the city is Forbes Air Force Base. Operated by Tactical Air Command, Forbes is a base for RB-47 and C-130 aircraft. The base has 6,000 personnel. Flights are made from here to all parts of the world. Salaries for Forbes' military personnel total $25.8 million a year. Civilians employed at the base receive an additional $2.5 million.

In addition to being the state capital, Topeka has the distinction of being "Psychiatric Capital of the World." Contributing to this title are Menninger Foundation, Topeka Veterans Administration Hospital and Topeka State Hospital. Menninger's is recognized world-wide as a leading psychiatric center. Last year, over 200 patients were admitted to Menninger Memorial Hospital. They were from 34 states and four foreign countries. Nearly 100 more were admitted to the day hospital, 150 to children's hospital and over 350 were treated as outpatients. Foundation neurologists and neurosurgeons interviewed 1,825 persons.

Veterans Hospital is housed in a new $21 million facility with 1,011 beds. VA Hospital has 1,057 employees and $6.75 million annual payroll. Topeka State Hospital has 1,044 beds and employs 840. Annual payroll is $4.7 million. Kansas Neurological Institute employs 521. Payroll is $1.6 million annually.

Other facilities are Kansas Treatment Center for Children, Kansas Boys Industrial School, Topeka Institute for Psychoanalysis, VA Mental Hygiene Clinic and Shawnee Guidance Center.

For cultural stimulus, productions are presented by Topeka Civic Theatre group. The Topeka Community Concert group offers outstanding musical events. Topeka Civic Symphony Orchestra and Mulvane Art Theatre League each presents an annual series.

Topeka Library, rebuilt in 1953, has approximately 182,000 volumes. The library includes a fine arts division, recording section, film library and bookmobiles. Topeka also has the State Library with 325,000 volumes. These include law and medical sections, in addition to public, business, political science and industrial publications. Kansas State Historical Society here has a newspaper collection second only in the nation to the Library of Congress.

Topeka High School ranks among the top secondary schools in the nation for academic and general development programs. Two of its faculty members achieved national acclaim. The late Mrs. Marjorie French won national teacher-of-the-year award for 1961. Mrs. Dorothy Greer was elected journalism teacher of the year the same year. Mrs. French was presented her award at the White House by the late President John F. Kennedy.

Continuously top-ranked in national educational surveys, Topeka High is equipped to teach 2,200 pupils annually. There are five other public high schools, 2 Catholic high schools, 11 junior high and 35 elementary schools. Also there are 8 Catholic and one Lutheran elementary schools.

Upon completion of high school, Topekans can attend municipally supported Washburn University. With enrollment over 4,400, Washburn has a reputation as one of the outstanding law schools. It also offers liberal arts and science programs. Topeka is 25 miles west of University of Kansas at Lawrence and 55 miles east of Kansas State University at Manhattan.

Recreation is abundant. Known as "the beautiful city of trees," Topeka has 46 parks with a total area of 1,043 acres. Most popular among outdoor recreational centers is Lake Shawnee, just southeast of the city. A 411-acre lake is encircled by 1,165 acres of wooded park. People throng there for boating, swimming, picnicking, fishing and other recreation.

Three country clubs and two municipal parks have 18-hole golf courses, in addition to three private 9- and 18-hole courses. Washburn University teams compete in all major sports. The football stadium seats 8,000. Big Eight Conference games are played at both Kansas State University and University of Kansas. Major league baseball and pro football are an hour away at Kansas City.

Mid-America Fair draws nearly 450,000 visitors annually. It begins the Friday after Labor Day and runs six days. More than $5 million is invested in permanent fair buildings to house amusements, exhibits and homemaking and agricultural events.

Topeka Zoological Park is Kansas' most progressive zoo. It covers 20 acres in Gage Park. The zoo exhibits over 225 specimens of about 100 species of mammals, birds, reptiles, amphibians, fish and invertebrates from six continents of the world. The zoo exercises a major influence in conservation of the world's diminishing wildlife. Attendance is 395,000 per year. Within a five-month period, the zoo had visitors from all 50 of the United States and Canada, Mexico, Japan, Germany, East Africa and Russia. Among visitors are youngsters from Capper Foundation for Crippled Children, staff and patients from Kansas Neurological Institute, Topeka State Hospital, Veterans Administration Hospital, Menninger Foundation, personnel and families from Forbes Air Force Base and students from Haskell Indian Institute at Lawrence.

A cooperative program with Topeka public school system includes educational tours of the zoo and lecture-demonstration programs in classrooms by members of the zoo staff. Sixty species of trees and shrubs are on the zoo grounds. A children's zoo is located west of the main zoo facility. It features domestic animals in a barnyard setting, sculptured concrete animals designed for the climbing antics of children, and performing animals. First major phase of a future master zoo development plan was completed in late 1965. It was a facility for elephants, giraffes, hippopotamuses and other large primates.

The community's history dates back four centuries when Vasques de Coronado, a Spaniard, was first to explore this territory. Two centuries later, French trappers established a headquarters near here and explored the area. Settlement of Topeka was stimulated in 1854 when a group of New England pioneers moved west to seek a new home. Their leader, Cyrus K. Holliday, later founded the Santa Fe Railroad. The city's original 684 acres was purchased from a Wyandotte Indian for $1,200. Incorporation occurred in 1857. Topeka became the state capital four years later. Population was 700 in 1865.

Goodyear Tire and Rubber Co.

Science Hall at Washburn University.

Municipal Auditorium and City Building.

Pioneer Woman sculpture.

Population is projected to grow from a current 130,000 to 180,000 in the next decade. To prepare for this rapid expansion, the city is acquiring a new "face." All but three buildings between Crane and Fifth streets on the east side of Kansas Avenue have been razed as part of Keyway Urban Renewal project. Southwestern Bell Telephone Company purchased three sites for future office building requirements between Fourth and Fifth on the west side of

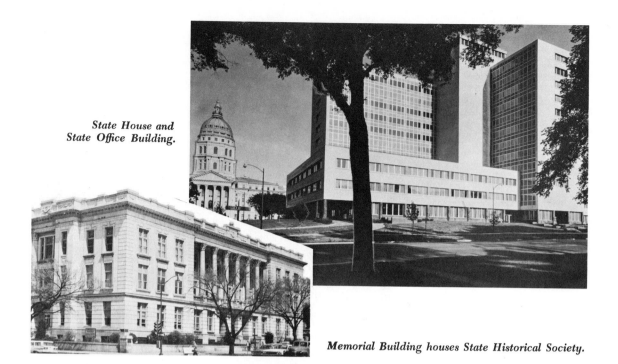

State House and State Office Building.

Memorial Building houses State Historical Society.

Kansas. Capitol Federal Savings purchased three sites and constructed a 7-story building at Seventh and Kansas. Macy's, Inc., department store bought three sites at Eighth and Kansas plus Eighth Street frontage from Quincy to Kansas Avenue for a new store and parking garage. A private developer bought two sites and built an 11-story building for Kansas Power and Light Company at 818 Kansas.

In the planning phase in 1965 is Keyway Center, a 2¼-square block addition to the urban renewal area. If this second phase of Keyway is approved, buildings between Fifth and Sixth streets and Monroe and Kansas Avenue will be razed for future development.

In the past five years, 15 store fronts along Kansas Avenue from Fifth to 10th streets have been remodeled. In the same period, two new high schools, four elementary schools and one junior high have been completed.

The 27-block Keyway area contained mostly sub-standard housing and business buildings. Major new construction in that area are Ramada Inn Motel, Duffen's Optical Company, Topeka Tent and Awning Company, McEntire Brothers, Inc. Mattress Company, a fire station, fire department academy, and Hallmark Cards' new 250,000-square foot plant. Only four blocks of the original 27 remained unsold to developers in October, 1965.

As an agricultural marketing center, Topeka has three flour mills, four dairy product processing plants, meat packing firms and fertilizer and alfalfa dehydrating plants.

Due to availability of almost an unlimited supply of water at shallow depths in the Kaw Valley, many farms near here have put down irrigation wells. Irrigation water supplements rainfall to produce maximum crop yields. A number of rural water districts have been organized, securing their water supply either from wells or from large lakes constructed for that purpose.

Construction of several large reservoirs on tributaries of the Kansas River has resulted in water conservation, flood control and development of park facilities. Through efforts of the Soil Conservation Service and Agricultural Stabilization and Conservation Service, a number of watershed districts were organized in this area.

216

New office facility in Topeka ready for 1966 occupancy.

SECURITY BENEFIT LIFE:

a story of growth

Nearly three-quarters of a century ago in a corner drugstore in Topeka, a small group of men conceived the idea of organizing a life insurance society. In 1892, those 11 men with $11 formed the company known today as Security Benefit Life.

The home office is still in Topeka not far from the corner drugstore where it was founded. Topeka has grown from a small midwestern city almost in the center of the United States to a bustling metropolis of almost 140,000 people; a rail and agricultural center; the site of manufacturing plants and a worldwide center for psychiatric treatment.

While Topeka and the nation were growing, so was Security Benefit Life. The resources of the company have multiplied many times over the original $11. Today, the lives of thousands of people in 49 states, the District of Columbia and Puerto Rico are affected by its business operations. The company provides life, health and disability insurance for 250,000 people through a network of agency offices. It offers both individual and group policies. Plans offered by the company include juvenile, savings, family, term, education, wife insurance, retirement and mortgage cancellation insurance.

Construction of a new home office is well underway, with occupancy scheduled for late 1966. The company reached a milestone in December, 1964, when it surpassed a billion dollars of insurance in force. At the same time, company records showed it had paid $167,000,000 to policyowners and their beneficiaries. Security Benefit Life is a mutual life insurance company.

It has no stockholders and its first responsibility is to its policyholders. The company has received recognition for its research which led to the offering of life insurance protection to persons who had previously been termed other than standard insurance risks.

There are 300 fulltime career field life underwriters. The company uses 275 people to process over a billion dollars of insurance — a total far below national average for insurance companies. The firm attributes this efficiency to careful control of all operations and use of electronic data processing equipment.

containing mysterious Indian writings is 13 miles north of Toronto. South of town is Toronto Dam and Reservoir with 2,800 acres of water and 51 miles of shoreline.

TOWANDA, Butler (F-9) pop. 1,141; 1 KGE; 2 GSC; 3 Mun.; 4 MP; 5 K-245; Towanda State Bank $800,000; newspaper — Western Butler County Times.

TREECE, Cherokee (G-13) pop. 286; 1 EDE; 2 Baxter Springs Gas Co.; 3 Mun.; 4 SLSF, NEO; 5 US 69, K-7.

°TRIBUNE, Greeley (D-1) pop. 1,144; 1 Wheatland Elec. Co-op., Inc.; 2 K-NG; 3 Mun.; 4 MP; 5 K-96, K-27; First National Bank $3,100,000; newspaper — Greeley County Republican.

Greeley County — Earnings per cap. $1,870; sales tax collections $59,084; employed in industry 150; number of farms 273; crop value $2,254,810; livestock value $1,769,420; mineral production $3,836.

°TROY, Doniphan (A-12) pop. 1,149; 1 Mun.; 2 GSC; 3 Mun.; 4 CRIP, UP; 5 US 36, K-7; First National Bank, Troy State Bank $3,000,000; newspaper — Kansas Chief.

Doniphan County — Earnings per cap. $1,477; sales tax collections $148,405; employed in industry 295; number of farms 1,065; crop value $8,138,760; livestock value $5,374,920; mineral production $457,386. Limestone quarried and crushed for concrete aggregate, roadstone and riprap. Gravel produced for paving and road maintenance.

TURON, Reno (F-7) pop. 511; 1 KPL; 2 GSC; 3 Mun.; 4 CRIP, MP; 5 K-61; The Turon State Bank $1,700,000.

TYRO, Montgomery (G-11) pop. 255; 1 CED; 2 UGS; 4 MP; 5 US 166.

UDALL, Cowley (F-9) pop. 615; 1 Mun.; 2 GSC; 3 Mun.; 4 AT&SF; 5 K-55, K-15; Bank of Commerce $900,000.

°ULYSSES, Grant (F-2) pop. 3,610; 1 Pioneer Co-op. Assn., Inc.; 2 PNG; 3 Mun.; 4 AT&SF; 5 US 270, US 160, K-25; Grant County State Bank $6,800,000; newspaper — Ulysses News. Large carbon black plants are located in the Ulysses region, one east of Hickok and another near Ryus. A natural gas capital, Ulysses is also an irrigated farming region famous for its onions, honeydew melons and cantaloupes. A National Historic Landmark is south of Ulysses on US 270 — Wagon Bed Springs, a popular but perilous watering spot on the Santa Fe Trail. Close by is a memorial to the noted Western explorer and fur trader, Jedediah S. Smith.

UNIONTOWN, Bourbon (E-13) pop. 266; 1 KGE; 3 Mun.; 4 MP; 5 K-3; Union State Bank $1,500,000.

UTICA, Ness (D-4) pop. 336; 1 WLT; 3 Mun.; 4 MP; 5 K-4; Citizens State Bank $1,200,000.

VALLEY CENTER, Sedgwick (E-9) pop. 2,440; 1 KGE; 2 GSC; 3 Mun.; 4 AT&SF, SLSF; Arkansas Valley State Bank $3,700,000; newspaper — Valley Center Index.

VALLEY FALLS, Jefferson (B-12) pop. 1,080; 1 KPL; 2 GSC; 3 Mun.; 4 AT&SF; 5 K-16, K-4; Citizens State Bank, Kendall State Bank $4,300,000; newspaper — Valley Falls Indicator.

VERMILLION, Marshall (A-11) pop. 238; 1 Mun.; 3 Mun.; 4 MP; 5 K-88; Vermillion State Bank $600,000.

VICTORIA, Ellis (C-6) pop. 1,258; 1 CKP; 2 KPL; 3 Mun.; 4 UP; 5 US 40; Farmers National Bank $3,300,000. St. Fidelis Church at Victoria, known as "The Cathedral of the Plains," took three years to build. Each parishioner was assessed $45 and six loads of stone. This Romanesque structure is of natural limestone and has two towers. The Christmas crib on display in the church yard consists of eight life-sized wood carved statues fashioned in Oberammergau, Germany. Also in the city is a Union Pacific railroad memorial and cemetery for laborers killed by Cheyennes in 1867.

VINING, Washington and Clay (B-9) pop. 122; 1 WLT; 2 KPL; 4 CRIP; 5 K-9.

VIOLA, Sedgwick (F-8) pop. 200; 1 WLT; 2 Mun.; 4 AT&SF; 5 K-49, K-42; Citizens State Bank $487,000.

VIRGIL, Greenwood (E-11) pop. 239; 1 KPL; 2 Quincy Pipeline Co.; 3 Mun.; 4 AT&SF.

°WAKEENEY, Trego (C-4) pop. 2,663; 1 CKP; 2 CKP; 3 Mun.; 4 UP; 5 I-70, US 283, US 283 spur, US 40; First National Bank, Trego-WaKeeney State Bank $6,700,000; newspaper — Western Kansas World. West of WaKeeney are fossil-rich chalk beds of the Smoky Hill River Valley.

Giant shovel gouges coal from the earth in Southeast Kansas mining area.

Eighteen miles southeast of town is Cedar Bluff Dam and Reservoir. The dam is 12,560 feet long and rises 134 feet above the stream bed. The lake covers 6,600 acres with 154 miles of shoreline. The reservoir stocked with channel cat, bass, crappie and walleyes. Cedar Bluff State Park is located on the north.

Trego County — Earnings per cap. $1,604; sales tax collections $155,648; employed in industry 362; number of farms 690; crop value $3,928,610; livestock value $3,919,990; mineral production $4,645,882. Crude petroleum output 1.6 million barrels. Muhlheim oil field important discovery. Building, paving and fill sand produced. Gravel obtained for paving and road maintenance. Limestone quarried and crushed for concrete aggregate.

WAKEFIELD, Clay (B-9) pop. 581; 1 KPL; 2 KPL; 3 Mun.; 4 UP; 5 K-82; Farmers & Merchants State Bank $900,000.

WALDO, Russell (C-6) pop. 165; 1 WLT; 3 Mun.; 4 UP; 5 US 281, K-18.

WALDRON, Harper (G-7) pop. 30; 1 Alfalfa Elec. Co-op., Inc.

WALLACE, Wallace (C-1) pop. 118; 1 Great Plains Co-op.; 3 Mun.; 4 UP; 5 US 40. Here is the Fort Wallace Memorial Museum, stage station and roadside park on US 40. At old Fort Wallace Cemetery 2 miles southeast of Wallace, the monument erected by Custer's 7th Cavalry to many of their men is still standing.

WALNUT, Crawford (F-13) pop. 395; 1 Walnut Gas & Elec.; 2 Walnut Gas & Elec.; 3 Mun.; 4 AT&SF, MKT; 5 K-146; Farmers State Bank $1,300,000.

WALTON, Harvey (E-9) pop. 225; 1 KGE; 3 Mun.; 4 AT&SF; 5 US 50; Walton State Bank $840,000.

WAMEGO, Pottawatomie (B-10) pop. 2,458; 1 Mun.; 2 KPL; 3 Mun.; 4 UP; 5 US 24, K-99; First National Bank, Kaw Valley State Bank $6,300,000; newspaper — Wamego Times. An old Dutch mill (1875) in the city park was transported stone by stone from a farm 12 miles north of town. Pottawatomie State Lake No. 1 is 17 miles north. Wamego is located in the Tuttle Creek Dam area.

°WASHINGTON, Washington (A-9) pop. 1,812; 1 Mun.; 2 KPL; 3 Mun.; 4 CB&Q, MP; 5 US 36, K-15W; First National Bank $5,200,000; newspaper — Washington County News.

Washington County — Earnings per cap. $1,369; sales tax collections $203,846; employed in industry 564; number of farms 1,754; crop value $9,522,380; livestock value $10,932,050.

Federal Fish Hatchery has 23 ponds on 382 acres.

"The Christmas City of
the High Plains."

WAKEENEY: *highway brings new business*

Exactly halfway between Kansas City and Denver is WaKeeney. The location is the *only* thing halfway about this community! It desires to "go all the way" in seizing opportunities to build a successful town.

WaKeeney's strategic location at the junction of two highways is the basis for a growing industry. Business men have begun to sell WaKeeney as a tourist and truck stop now and trucking center in the future. Improvement of U.S. 283 is in preliminary stages. Interstate-70 has six new service stations and truck stopping is "really taking hold." The town has four motels, one hotel and a 26-unit motel, now nearly completed. Town leaders who worked to get the new state trucking laws also have made contacts with firms to promote WaKeeney as a trucking terminal.

A year ago the WaKeeney Jaycees conducted a survey to see what the residents thought about their town. It showed that major assets were the friendly citizens, the attractive town with wide streets, excellent utilities services, above average school staffs and facilities, variety of churches, attractive downtown and residential Christmas decorations. WaKeeney Development, Inc., was formed to seek out industrial prospects. A one-mill industrial levy was approved with funds available in 1967. Also, Galloway Airport, a grass strip, was developed four miles north of town. It has a lighted sod landing strip and telephone service.

The following industries are located in WaKeeney: Trego Manufacturing; Malson Terracing, with new location southeast; Cline Manufacturing, and Northwest Manufacturing.

WaKeeney Grade School has had three additions since 1950. A science lab was added in 1963. This past year a gym was added to the 14-year-old Trego Community High School building. A vocational agriculture building was completed in the early '60's.

WaKeeney is the seat of Trego County. Basically, it is an agricultural community drawing trade from a 1,000-square-mile area. With 690 farms in the county, mostly cash grain and livestock, much business revolves around the farmer selling his products and buying his supplies. The county produces some of the highest protein wheat in the world — yields of 61.2 to 61.9 pounds per bushel, protein content 12.0 to 12.4.

Eighteen miles to the southeast is Cedar Bluff Dam and Reservoir with 154 miles of shoreline. This state park is easy to reach on highway 147 or other good access roads and there is a landing strip for aircraft. Here also is Cedar Bluff National Fish Hatchery. Using water from the reservoir, the hatchery provides fish for stocking western Kansas lakes and portions of Colorado, New Mexico, Oklahoma and Texas.

WaKeeney is often called "The Christmas City of the High Plains." The beautiful handmade Christmas decorations draw thousands of visitors. A downtown display features three miles of electrical wiring and 6,800 bulbs. Homes also deck out in holiday attire. As one resident explains it, "This season seems to have a special meaning to our area. It's a time when we all work together on a community project." And, being WaKeeney, they "go all the way!"

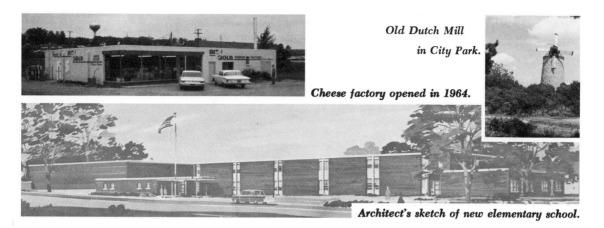

Old Dutch Mill
in City Park.

Cheese factory opened in 1964.

Architect's sketch of new elementary school.

WAMEGO: *small city on the move*

During the winter of 1965, 33 new snow plows cleared mountain passes in Yugoslavia. They were manufactured here by Balderson, Inc., producer of earthmoving equipment for Caterpillar. The company also has many other overseas and domestic markets for its tractor blades.

Harmony Gardens, producer of floral plants, is the largest grower of tropical plants in Kansas. Harmony supplies wholesalers over a 300-mile radius. The Sackrider Floral Co., also in Wamego, supplies vegetable and flowering plants to dealers over much of Kansas.

Bit-O-Gold Cheese, Inc., which opened in June, 1964, manufactures cheese for wholesale and retail trade. R and W Milling Company distributes alfalfa pellets throughout the Midwest. Two feed mills and elevators have added new facilities and constructions. A new Butler building completed this year houses the new Easy Wash of 24 washers and 12 dryers.

Local investors have formed Colonial Laboratories, Inc., to develop and manufacture crystals and other component parts for radio and other signal apparatus.

Located in the Kansas River basin, Wamego never has been flooded. There is ample room for industrial expansion. This city in southeast Pottawatomie County has more than 2,500 population. It is the birthplace of Walter P. Chrysler, founder of Chrysler Motors Corporation.

Wamego is headquarters for P. R. and W. Electric Cooperative, which provides power to Pottawatomie, Riley, Wabaunsee, Geary and Jackson counties. The municipally-owned light and water plant supplies the electrical and water needs of the city.

New construction in the city includes an electrically heated and air-conditioned elementary school and high school addition, independently-owned dial telephone company building with its new plant serving 2,200 customers and three exchanges, convent for Catholic nuns, educational unit for First Methodist Church and 500,000-gallon water tower. A $483,000 bond issue was approved late in 1962 for the school.

Several city parks provide recreation. The main park covers 20 acres. One of the city's main community events of the year, Fourth of July celebration, is held there. The local golf course attracts memberships from miles around Wamego. Also in City Park is a famed landmark — Old Dutch Mill. The 90-year-old mill was hauled, stone by stone, from a farm 12 miles north of the city and rebuilt here.

There are four new housing additions in the city. Wamego has several nursing homes and a 20-bed hospital. Another city hospital is being planned. Wamego has city manager form of government. Several industrial sites are available east and west of the city. Sites are adjacent to the UP Railroad or highways U.S. 24 and K-99.

WATERVILLE, Marshall (A-10) pop. 770; 1 Mun.; 2 KPL; 3 Mun.; 4 MP; 5 US 77, K-9; Citizens State Bank $2,600,000; newspaper — Waterville Telegraph.

WATHENA, Doniphan (A-13) pop. 1,027; 1 Mun.; 2 GSC; 3 Mun.; 4 CRIP, UP; 5 US 36; Farmers State Bank $2,900,000; newspaper — Wathena Times.

WAVERLY, Coffey (D-12) pop. 527; 1 KPL; 2 AG; 3 Mun.; 4 AT&SF; 5 K-31; First National Bank $1,300,000; newspaper — Waverly Gazette.

WEBBER, Jewell (A-8) pop. 62; 1 Mun.; 4 AT&SF.

WEIR, Cherokee (G-13) pop. 712; 1 EDE; 2 GSC; 3 EDE; 4 SLSF; 5 K-103; Citizens Bank $1,200,000; newspaper — Weir Spectator.

°WELLINGTON, Sumner (G-9) pop. 8,350; 1 Mun.; 2 Wellington Gas Co.; 3 Mun.; 4 AT&SF, CRIP; 5 US 160, US 81; First National Bank, National Bank of Commerce, Security State Bank $13,700,000; newspapers — Daily News, Monitor-Press. Woods' Park in Wellington is 183-acre spot with 5,000 trees and sports facilities. Harbaugh museum includes a collection of 1,000 canes, many unusual clocks, large collection of guns, vehicles, farm items, arrowheads and other mementoes.

Sumner County — Earnings per cap. $1,859; sales tax collections $635,297; employed in industry 2,105; number of farms 1,971; crop value $17,848,000; livestock value $7,049,870; mineral production $8,788,328. Crude petroleum production 3 million barrels. Natural gas output 527 million cubic feet, up 64 per cent. Sand and gravel produced for building, paving and road maintenance.

WELLSFORD, Kiowa (F-6) pop. 24; 1 WLT; 4 CRIP; 5 US 54.

WELLSVILLE, Franklin (C-13) pop. 1,189; 1 KCPL; 2 GSC; 3 Mun.; 4 AT&SF; 5 K-33; Wellsville Bank $2,800,000; newspaper — Wellsville Globe.

°WESTMORELAND, Pottawatomie (B-10) pop. 487; 1 KPL; 2 KPL; 3 Mun.; 5 K-99; Farmers State Bank $1,900,000; newspaper — Recorder. Town was one of the camping places on the Oregon Trail. Pottawatomie County State Lake No. 1 is on K-99 about 4 miles north.

Pottawatomie County — Earnings per cap. $1,540; sales tax collections $271,761; employed in industry 630; number of farms 1,197; crop value $5,701,440; livestock value $8,694,980; mineral production $217,922. Dimension limestone prepared. Limestone quarried and crushed for concrete aggregate, roadstone and agstone. Sand and gravel produced mainly for building and paving.

WESTPHALIA, Anderson (E-12) pop. 236; 1 KGE; 4 MP; State Bank of Westphalia $1,100,000.

WESTWOOD, Johnson (C-13) pop. 2,548; 1 KCPL; 2 GSC; 3 Water Dist. No. 1, Johnson Co.; 5 US 69, US 56, US 50.

WESTWOOD HILLS, Johnson (C-13) pop. 498; 1 KCPL; 2 GSC; 3 J. C. Nichols Co.; 5 U S 69, US 56, US 50.

WETMORE, Nemaha (A-11) pop. 399; 1 KPL; 3 Mun.; 4 MP; 5 K-9; First National Bank $1,300,000.

WHEATON, Pottawatomie (B-10) pop. 141; 1 KPL; 2 KPL; 5 K-16.

WHITE CITY, Morris (C-10) pop. 484; 1 KPL; 2 Greeley Gas Co.; 3 Mun.; 4 CRIP; 5 K-4; First National Bank $1,400,000; newspaper — White City Register.

WHITE CLOUD, Doniphan (A-12) pop. 242; 1 Doniphan Elec. Co-op. Assn.; 5 K-7; First State Bank $950,000.

WHITEWATER, Butler (E-9) pop. 543; 1 KGE; 2 GSC; 4 CRIP, MP; 5 K-196; Bank of Whitewater $1,700,000; newspaper — Independent.

WHITING, Jackson (B-12) pop. 252; 1 KPL; 2 GSC; 4 CRIP, MP; 5 K-9; State Bank of Whiting $1,100,000.

°WICHITA, Sedgwick (F-9) pop. 265,366; 1 KGE; 2 GSC and Ark.-La. Gas Co.; 3 Mun.; 4 AT&SF, CRIP, SLSF, MV, MP; 5 KTA, I-235, I-35, US 81, US 54, K-254, K-96, K-42, K-15; 6 CEN, BNF, TWA, CAL; 7 Wichita State University, Friends University (Society of Friends), Sacred Heart College (Catholic); Boulevard State Bank, Central State Bank, East Side National Bank, Federal Intermediate Credit Bank, Federal Land Bank, First National Bank, The Fourth National Bank & Trust Co., Kansas State Bank, National Bank, Parklane National Bank, Seneca National

Downtown Wichita from the air.

WICHITA: *All-America City*

From her cowtown days to the present, the largest city in Kansas has been a magnet attracting people, industries and tourists.

What is the promise of Wichita? How is it being fulfilled? These two big questions, and others, must be answered satisfactorily if the progressive trend in business, industry, education and the arts is to continue. Is there profitable work here? What are the living costs? Business operating costs? What is there to see and do in Wichita?

Each year the answers must come anew as changing population becomes an influencing factor. Fifty per cent increases in population were recorded in each of the past two decades. The 1965 figure showed 280,000 persons living in Wichita and 384,000 in the metropolitan area which sprawls over 182 square miles.

This aerial view shows a modern downtown Wichita with the Arkansas River winding through. Mostly, the photo shows Wichita's stores, where retail sales in 1965 rose to $550 million; office buildings, such as 14 banks with deposits close to a half billion dollars each year; hotels, with a total of 2,500 rooms; and manufacturing enterprises, 620 of them, employing 45,000 persons. Shown west (left) of the river is Lawrence Stadium, home of the semipro National Baseball Congress. Stretching out in all directions from downtown are 124 public and parochial schools, three colleges, seven hospitals with more than 2,000 rooms, 45 parks covering 1,139 acres; 424 churches and 107,722 homes.

This is the face of Wichita, governmental seat of Sedgwick County and 1962 National Municipal League choice as All-America City!

Wichita's first boom era started in 1872 when the rail line reached here and 350,000 longhorn cattle were driven over the Chisholm Trail and sold for $2 million. Two years later, the first flour mill was built. Second boom came when oil was discovered in neighboring Butler County in 1914 and the first airplane built in 1917. In that decade, Wichita's future as a center of aviation, trade, transportation, oil and industry was assured. Today, Wichitans are building aircraft, small and large, for the nation's commerce and defense. They are producing vast quantities of meat, flour and household goods for homes all over the country.

Utilities, Transportation, Government

Wichita's water comes from the Equus Beds, Cheney Reservoir and local wells. The Equus Beds are water-saturated gravel deposits underlying 800 square miles of central Kansas. Cheney Reservoir on the Ninnescah River was completed in 1965 at a cost of $18.2 million. The water supply and distribution facilities are owned and operated by the city.

Two companies supply Wichita's natural gas. It is brought into the city through independent mains, fed from gasfields in Kansas, Oklahoma and Texas. A 26-inch pipeline from the Hugoton Field was constructed in 1964 to provide gas capacity for large increases in industrial needs for the next several years. Coal and oil are also available.

Aircraft industry is a major one for Wichita.

Wichita is served by Kansas Gas and Electric Company and its inter-connections with other electric utility systems. Power costs are comparable to, or lower than, other areas in the nation. KG&E invested $11 million in new facilities in 1965, costliest item being addition of a 380,000-kilowatt generating unit.

Four airlines, five railroads, 58 common carrier truck lines, a cross-country bus system and two smaller bus lines connect Wichita with the rest of the nation. At Municipal Airport, landings and takeoffs top 200,000 annually. Wichita's central location helps assure good service to all parts of the country for passengers, cargo and mail. Within the city, the Rapid Transit Lines, Inc., serves local routes with air-conditioned buses. In recent years, the city has subsidized the bus company.

City and county governments cooperate in six areas of service to the metropolitan area — flood control maintenance, planning, health, mental health, civil defense and refuse disposal. Wichita, with a commission-manager form of government, has local property tax consistently among the lowest for first class cities in Kansas. Economics have been effected and the city operates with 40 per cent fewer employes than the national average. Biggest building boom since 1940 added $26 million assessed valuation to provide a broader base over which to spread costs.

Organized crime, particularly in the form of vice operations, has been kept out of the city by the alert work of the police department which operates with a smaller corps of employes than average for cities its size. The department maintains a clearance in Class 1 crimes which rates 10-15 per cent above national average for comparable cities. Combined efforts of the fire and water departments give Wichitans low Class 3 rates on fire protection insurance.

Agricultural Resources

Sedgwick County and Wichita are in the center of an extensive, fertile agricultural area. To the west are vast wheat acreages. To the east are the blue stem pastures. North and south the rich Arkansas Valley. Hence, agriculture is important and diversified. Wichita is the main agricultural market in Kansas. With its Board of Trade, wheat and flour milling facilities, it is the largest market for wheat in a state which, on the average, grows more than one-fifth of all the wheat in the United States. The city has over 89 million bushels of grain storage facilities — ranking third in the nation. More than 7 million hundredweights of flour were milled here in 1964. For years the largest broom corn market in the world, the city has approximately 30,000 tons marketed through local firms.

Wichita is among the 15 leading livestock terminal markets and meat packing centers. Union Stock Yards receives 1,141,000 head of livestock annually, valued at over $100 million. Capacity at the yards is 21,000 cattle, 15,000 hogs and 5,000 sheep. Major packing companies here process over 817,000 head of livestock each year.

This is the leading market for dairy production in Kansas. Seven Grade A dairy processing plants serving Wichita have milk sales of over $8.5 million annually; dairy products over $7 million.

Fruit production is a growing and prosperous agricultural business in Sedgwick County. Nearly 40,000 peach trees located in the Haysville area produce over 60,000 bushels of peaches. Seven orchards have formed the Sedgwick County Peach Growers Cooperative Association, invested in packing equipment, and now sell Golden Valley peaches wholesale to grocers as well as retail at the orchards.

"Air Capitol of the World"

The Wichita facility of The Boeing Company's Military Airplane Division is located on 579 acres with more than 132 under cover. Employing 15,000, it ranks as Kansas' largest industrial employer. During the 1957 peak, employment eclipsed 35,000. Since 1962, Boeing-Wichita

Serpentine wall and trees add interest to Douglas Avenue.

Architect's sketch of Auditorium complex.

efforts have turned to modification and maintenance of the 244-ton B-52 Stratofortresses, major manned deterrent power for the U. S. Air Force. Boeing workers, serving as tool fabricators and producers of components, are concerned with producing the first stage booster for the Saturn V moon rocket. Also, they assist in producing parts and assemblies for the company's commercial airliners and helicopters.

Wichita is international corporate headquarters for three companies engaged in making private and business aircraft. Beech Aircraft Corp., with 8,200 employes, makes nine models of business airplanes. Diversified operations include projects involving rockets, missiles and spacecraft for NASA's Apollo and Gemini programs. More than 22,000 Beechcraft airplanes have been delivered in the company's 33-year history.

Cessna Aircraft Company made delivery of its 60,000th airplane during 1965. It is the world's largest producer of business and private aircraft. A gain of 1,500 employes in Wichita and

Hutchinson plants is forecast for 1966. The company is conducting its own training schools to supplement those being operated by the community. Underway is construction of a new assembly building for twin-engine aircraft production. Both Beech and Cessna set new private and executive plane output records during 1965 and the Lear Jet Corporation moved into high gear in building of jet executive craft. Lear's plant opened in 1963. Two years later 50 jets had been delivered. Lear Jet has become a publicly-owned corporation with some 3,400 stockholders owning two million shares. Employment is about 2,000. The company seeks a third revenue bond issue to expand its facilities here. All four aircraft companies were expanding personnel as 1966 began.

As a fitting air memorial for the city, Wichita asked for and received a Boeing-built six-jet B-47 bomber being phased out of service. According to William Tarrant, Wichita's mayor in 1965-66, the memorial "will not be considered a tribute to that which has passed, but a challenge for the future."

Oil and Other Industries

As oil refining is Kansas' largest industrial enterprise, so petroleum production and all related activities are important to Wichita. Besides hundreds of firms listed as oil operators, producers and well drilling contractors, there are marketers, refiners, testers, oilfield supply companies, geologists and scores of others in "oil business." Large employers here are Derby Refining Company and Cardwell Company, oil field equipment maker. A Wichita firm, Rains & Williamson Oil Company, was the state's 1965 wildcat drilling champion. Two other Wichita companies tied for second and two more shared third place with a Texas firm.

The outing products division of The Coleman Company was named "Brand Name Manufacturer of 1964" by over 800 retailers in the department store markets. Coleman, long well known for its heating and air conditioning equipment, is expanding its outdoor division. In 1965, it acquired canvas products companies in western states in two separate million-dollar transactions.

Frontier Chemical Co., a division of Vulcan Materials Co., produces various grades of liquid and flake caustic. Expansion at the anhydrous ammonia plant will provide a 50 per cent increase of production, bringing capacity to about 65 tons per day; storage space to 10,000 tons. Also in Wichita is Davis Mfg. Inc., maker of industrial equipment such as trenchers, backhoes and bulldozers.

Racon Inc., new Wichita firm, chose a 15-acre site adjoining Frontier for its $3.7 million fluoro-carbon refrigerant gas plant. The city had 14 new industries started in 1965.

Financing programs for new and existing industries are available through industrial revenue bonds and Wichita Area Development, Inc., a non-profit community development corporation.

Educational Scope Widens

Wichita schools at all levels have shown enrollment gains. Wichita State University jumped above 10,000 and plans to double the size of its Campus Activities Center by 1967 at a cost of $1.8 million. Friends University reached 715 and dedicated its $600,000 art center. Sacred Heart College, now co-educational, showed an increase while readying a new science building and new dormitory. Industries here depend upon the adult industrial training program operated by the Department of Vocational Education. Many communities have adopted the system pioneered in Wichita.

New programs for Wichita schools include a library demonstration center at Buckner Elementary to serve the entire state; an adult literacy program with centers in schools and neighborhood centers, workshops to prepare teachers to deal with children from culturally deprived homes and programs for these children. New Catholic schools slated for use in fall 1966 will be a $1 million high school for girls and an elementary school.

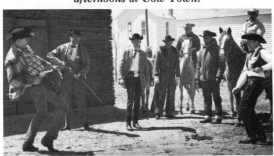

Quick draw artists entertain on Sunday afternoons at Cow Town.

National youth groups serve all ages of youth in Wichita. Camp Fire Girls, working in City Greenhouse, transfer seedlings to pots before planting outdoors.

This city is known internationally for the Institute of Logopedics, largest residential speech and hearing center in the world. Wichita State offers a course of studies leading to the Doctor of Philosophy in logopedics. In 1965, a new Starkey School for Retarded Children replaced one ruined by a storm. The Catholic Diocese opened the Holy Family Center for retarded youngsters of all denominations.

Cultural Excitement

A new Civic Cultural Center — by far the most ambitious municipal project in Wichita's history — is taking shape. It will be paid for with a $15 million bond issue. Federal participation is expected to reach $4.5 million, so the total value of the municipal construction will come close to $20 million by the time it is completed. It will be composed of an auditorium complex, new public library, park areas and parking for nearly 1,000 vehicles. The library will be ready by November, 1966. The auditorium complex, slated for completion two years later, will contain an exhibition hall with 50,000 square feet, auditorium to seat 5,700 and fully equipped stage, music hall with 2,200 seats, "Little Theater" with 670 seats, and meeting rooms for groups from 10 to 300 people.

Attendance at the Wichita Art Museum increases 25 per cent each year. More than 1,000 visit the museum each Sunday. The Wichita Art Association has erected an $800,000 center in eastern Wichita. It houses galleries, workshops, classrooms and a 500-seat theater.

During the first half of the 1960's, the modern image cast by the city's action in developing cultural facilities has resulted in a surge of new office and business structures in a variety of architectural designs and apartment buildings in every section of the city. Wichitans are eagerly looking ahead to more leisure-time and cultural enjoyments of urban living.

In addition to the Civic Center, urban renewal projects either completed, approved or on the drawing boards include: property abutting the Center to be developed by private enterprise; Glenn Village cleared and now site of the largest elementary school in Kansas; Park Plaza project in central Riverside being cleared for construction of high-rise and garden type apartments, a new marina on the banks of the Arkansas River, park areas and a shopping center; Skyline project downtown cleared and awaiting redevelopment; and the Northend Industrial project to be redeveloped as an industrial park.

This city benefits from conventions which bring $7-8 million here annually. The Wichita Chamber of Commerce has organized a conventions and visitors bureau which expects to double convention volume within a reasonable time after completion of the Civic Center.·

Priority projects listed by the Wichita Chamber are: downtown redevelopment, development of a giant convention center, metropolitan area planning, development of regional medical complex, creation of new industries and businesses, educating youth and re-educating adults, further development of aviation complex, insuring of future water resources and improving transportation networks.

ADVANCE PRODUCTS CO.:

from furnaces to audio-visual school furniture

There was a time when the Advance Furnace Company of Wichita manufactured only furnaces.

Then the firm decided to try something different and the Advance Products Company, Inc., was born. Educators then were beginning to stress the value of audio-visual aids in the schoolroom. Audio-visual dealers pointed out products the firm could manufacture which would be useful to schools. So Advance introduced a welded steel table for projectors.

From then on, the demand for audio-visual equipment expanded in many directions. New models of tables were introduced by Advance for almost every type of school equipment. Storage facilities for materials, as well as basic equipment, were added. Bookcases and booktrucks were designed and sold.

Then came the language laboratory. The Wichita Board of Education put Advance Products into the language laboratory furniture business by ordering a great quantity of lab furniture for 13 intermediate and high schools. These sophisticated electronics learning systems permit much more rapid and deeper learning.

Newest addition is study booths for library or classroom use, either with or without electronics equipment.

In most parts of the country, the words "It's A Cozy" have been almost a household phrase, referring to the Cozy brand of furnaces by Advance. Now, Pixmobile brand school equipment is familiar to educators. It is used in every state and every major city in the United States and Canada and its usage has spread to six continents.

The Advance Furnace Company and Advance Products Company, Inc., are located at 2300 East Douglas Avenue, Wichita, Kansas.

W. D. DeVore, general manager

Steel fabricating jobs come in all shapes.
Here, a huge custom-built cylinder takes form.

WATKINS INC.: *steel fabricator,*
industrial supplier

Equipment for installations on five continents and the Philippine Islands has been built from steel fabricated at Watkins Inc. in Wichita. Everything produced is built to the customers' basic designs; nothing under the Watkins name. The fabricating division is engaged in structural steel and plate fabrication. This 55-year-old company also operates a warehouse division involving steel service center distribution, wholesale heavy hardware and industrial supply distribution.

In its steel fabrication work, Watkins serves the chemical, carbon black and the petroleum refining industries. In addition, equipment and structures are fabricated such as waterworks, sewage disposal plants and natural gas transmission stations. Here in Kansas, jobs produced by Watkins Inc. include the Wichita State University Fieldhouse, Dodge City Auditorium and the Big Arkansas Turnpike Crossing Bridge. However, 85 per cent of Watkins' fabrication work is for jobs *outside* of Kansas.

Watkins' warehouse division distributes steel items such as cold rolled and hot rolled round steel, hot rolled bars and sheets, pipe and pipe fittings, structural shapes and plates, wire and nail products. Supplies include bolts, nuts and cap screws, welding electrodes, plow shares, sweeps, hand tools, machine tools, precision tools, twist drills, files, taps and dies. Equipment handled are well-known brands of electric tools, band saws, air tools and pipe tools, welding and metal working equipment, iron blenders, lathes, hoists and trolleys. The firm serves as industrial distributor in most of Kansas, northern one-third of Oklahoma, Texas Panhandle and eastern Colorado. Salesmen are based in Chanute, Dodge City, Garden City, Hutchinson, Lawrence, Liberal, Salina, Wichita and Winfield, Kansas, and Enid, Oklahoma.

Recognition in several national distributors' newsmagazines has been given to Watkins Inc. for its successful record of staging industrial shows. For the past 20 years, the shows have attracted approximately 80 manufacturers' exhibits and an average of 2,500 guests per show.

The firm has changed its name twice and has changed locations, too, during its growth years. About 1910, the firm started as a grey iron foundry, adding some light steel fabrication 10 years later. A small heavy hardware department flourished during the 1930's. The company became Watkins Inc. in 1940 and the present property was acquired the following year. The fabricating shop was built in 1942; warehouse in 1946, and present office building in 1953. At one time the general offices, engineering department, industrial supply warehouse and sales counter were housed in a 40'x80' two-story building later sold to Coleman Company. Physical facilities for Watkins Inc. now cover nine acres with 90,000 square feet under roof. Employment is currently around 160. During World War II, the firm was awarded the Maritime "M" for building boiler-casings for Type C3 cargo ships, weighing 30 tons each. Five stars were added at six-month intervals.

Bank, Southwest National Bank, Stockyards National Bank, Union National Bank, Wichita State Bank $479,600,000; newspapers — Wichita Eagle and Beacon, The Democrat.

Wichita, largest city in Kansas, is first in the world in production of personal airplanes and an important military airplane manufacturing center. The Beech, Boeing and Cessna plants are here, and smaller plants make airplane parts. The old municipal airport has become McConnell Air Force Base. New municipal airport, 6 miles southwest, is also headquarters of the National Flying Farmers Assn. Wichita is a major flour milling, meat packing, oil producing and refining center. It is the largest broomcorn market in the world, and home of Coleman lighting and heating equipment. Here also is Veterans Administration Center Hospital and the Institute of Logopedics, one of the world's outstanding speech correction centers.

On the banks of the Arkansas River the Cow Town of 1872 has been reconstructed by Historic Wichita, Inc. Many of the first buildings in town and others in keeping with that period have been moved there.

In the city are Wichita State University, Friends University, and Sacred Heart College. On Friends campus is a museum containing Indian and pioneer relics, an authentic covered wagon and numerous mounted African animals. On Wichita State University campus is Walter H. Beech Memorial Wind Tunnel which can create an artificial hurricane of 200-mph velocity to test airplane models. Both Wichita Art Museum and Wichita Art Association galleries have ever-changing exhibitions of fine and applied arts. The national Semipro Baseball Tournament is held annually in Lawrence Stadium. Wichita maintains Lake Afton 23 miles WSW of Wichita off US 54. Cheney Dam, a federal project 25 miles west of Wichita, was completed in 1965 and reservoir is attracting water enthusiasts.

Sedgwick County — Earnings per cap. $2,283; sales tax collections $13,595,626; employed in industry 89,137; number of farms 1,984; crop value $15,962,970; livestock value $7,500,360; mineral production $11,753,521. Sedgwick County ranked second in salt and sand and gravel production and fourth in recovery of natural gas liquids. Fifteen commercial sand and gravel producers and one Government-and-contractor producer reported production. Building, paving, fill and blast sand, and building, paving, and fill gravel were produced. One firm pumped brine from wells to manufacture chlorine and caustic soda and began operating its ammonia plant. Crude petroleum output 2.5 million barrels. Petroleum refinery operated at Wichita. Natural gas production 65 million cubic feet. Firm exfoliated vermiculite, using crude vermiculite purchased in Montana.

WILLARD, Shawnee (C-11) pop. 103; 1 KPL; 4 CRIP.

WILLIAMSBURG, Franklin (D-12) pop. 279; 1 KCPL; 2 AG; 3 Mun.; 4 AT&SF; 5 US 50. Three miles west, whitewashed limestone buildings mark the site of Old Silkville, a silk-growing colony of the 1870's.

WILLIS, Brown (A-12) pop. 125; 1 Mun.; 2 GSC; 4 MP.

WILLOWBROOK, Reno (E-8) pop. 79; 1 KPL; 2 Island Park Homes Co.

WILMORE, Comanche (G-5) pop. 121; 1 WLT; 4 AT&SF; Wilmore State Bank $605,000.

WILSEY, Morris (D-10) pop. 246; 1 KPL; 2 Greeley Gas; 4 MP.

WILSON, Ellsworth (C-7) pop. 1,150; 1 Mun.; 2 Wilson Gas Co.; 3 Mun.; 4 UP; 5 US 40, K-232; Wilson State Bank $2,400,000; newspaper — Wilson World.

WINCHESTER, Jefferson (B-12) pop. 496; 1 KPL; 3 Mun.; 5 K-192; newspaper — Winchester Star.

WINDOM, McPherson (D-8) pop. 191; 1 KPL; 2 Mun.; 3 Mun.; 4 AT&SF.

°WINFIELD, Cowley (G-9) pop. 10,286; 1 Mun.; 2 Mun.; 3 Mun.; 4 AT&SF, SLSF, MP; 5 US 160, US 77, K-15; 7 Southwestern College (Methodist), St. John's College (Lutheran); First National Bank, The State Bank $19,500,000; newspaper — Daily Courier. Located here are Winfield State Hospital and Training Center. Island Park surrounded by a lagoon attracts thousands of visitors annually. A huge mural, 62½ feet long and 13 feet high, on a wall of the First National Bank, depicts the history of Winfield since 1872.

Cowley County — Earnings per cap. $1,983; sales tax collections $1,079,445; number of farms 1,644; crop value $8,569,850; livestock value $9,437,880; mineral production $12,291,775. County

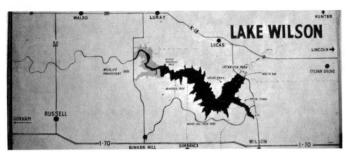

Kansas Scenic Waterland.

Stone fence posts still in use.

WILSON: *highways and reservoir encourage growth*

Early landmarks have been bulldozed down to make way for Interstate 70 highway and the Wilson Reservoir.

Reaping the benefits of the progress is the town of Wilson, located three miles north of the Smoky Hill River and 10 miles south of Saline.

Here the alert people are proving that life is far from dead in the "dead center" of Kansas. Their town of 1,150 residents is providing all the necessities of a small trading center. It is developing an outstanding school system, good churches with expanding emphasis on youth, city summer recreation programs, and new municipal buildings. But, futurewise, it is eyeing new industries and doing its best to attract them.

The men till the same rich soil their great grandparents tilled, yet sit down with neighbors and talk modern language of "efficient city management, industrial expansion and recreational development."

The town began in 1871. Czech settlements in 1874 brought to the area strong, ambitious people with the will and patience to develop a prosperous agricultural community. An early industry was rock quarrying which supplied native stone for posts and buildings. Many are still in use. Old Country customs still exist. Old World flavor which lives yet at the dinner table is delicious Czech cooking. Authentic oldtime recipes have been treasured from one generation to another. Many favorites are still served and still delight the modern appetite — the bierocks or hot bread with ground beef, cabbage and onion stuffing; the houska, braided holiday fruit bread; and, of course, the ever popular kolaches (filled fruit roll).

Wilson, today, with a mayor-council form of government, has a newly constructed fire station and jail and new post office. Church buildings were completed within the past year. The town has two grain elevators with approximately 1,500,000-bushel capacity, a bank, hotel, weekly newspaper and city library. Organizations are the Chamber of Commerce, Lions Club, and the American Legion and Auxiliary. A new industry is now being developed which will market an outdoor camper.

Most noteworthy development in recent years in the area has been the construction of the multiple-purpose Wilson Dam and Reservoir 10 miles north of the town on the Saline River. Construction started in 1960 and completion came late in 1965. Estimated cost was $21,200,000. The reservoir will provide a high degree of protection to 60,000 acres and several towns in the Saline River flood plain. A pleasant by-product of the flood control and irrigation project is the creation of recreational activity.

The drive from Wilson to the reservoir on the newly constructed highway 232 is considered one of the most scenic in Kansas. Perhaps it is safe to predict that Wilson soon will have itself another industry — tourists!

To build St. Fidelis Church, Victoria, each parishioner was assigned 45 dollars and six loads of stone.

ranked 10th in petroleum production; output nearly 3.8 million barrels. Exploratory drilling resulted in discovery of Cooley oil field. Refinery operated at Arkansas City. Natural gas recovery more than 3.7 billion cubic feet, up 35 per cent. Dimension limestone quarried; crushed limestone produced for concrete aggregate, roadstone and agstone. Sand and gravel for building, paving, fill and engine sand produced.

WINONA, Logan (C-2) pop. 393; 1 CKP; 3 Mun.; 4 UP; 5 US 40; Farmers State Bank $2,000,000; newspaper — Winona Leader.

WOODBINE, Dickinson (C-9) pop. 189; 1 KPL; 4 CRIP; 5 K-209; Citizens State Bank $602,000.

WOODSTON, Rooks (B-6) pop. 295; 1 WLT; 3 Mun.; 4 MP; 5 US 24; Rooks County State Bank $940,000.

°YATES CENTER, Woodson (E-12) pop. 2,009; 1 KGE; 2 UGS; 3 Mun.; 4 MP; 5 US 75, US 54; State Exchange Bank $4,000,000; newspaper — Yates Center News. The city is an important hay shipping point in a large hay producing section. Woodson County state park (Lake Fegan) is located 8 miles southwest of Yates Center.

Woodson County — Earnings per cap. $1,467; sales tax collections $119,101; employed in industry 261; number of farms 740; crop value $2,580,790; livestock value $3,895,380. Output of crude petroleum 824,000 barrels; waterflooding supplying a large part of output. Natural gas production 1.2 million cubic feet.

ZENDA, Kingman (F-7) pop. 173; 1 WLT; 4 AT&SF; 5 K-42.

ZURICH, Rooks (B-5) pop. 231; 1 WLT; 2 K-NG; 4 UP; 5 K-18.

KANSAS AUTHORS

by Zula Bennington Greene

In these 112 years since Kansas became a territory, hundreds of its people have taken pen in hand to set down their thoughts and feelings, from the fire-breathing abolitionists to gentle lady poets. This state, unlike any other, was created in a fire of conflict, and hardly had men arrived on its soil until they began to write. The newspaper often preceded the town.

When one undertakes to define a Kansas book, the line jiggles. The library at the Kansas State Historical Society has shelf after shelf of Kansas books, under a wide category that includes any book by or about a Kansan, or about this area of the Midwest.

The ideal Kansas author would be one who was born here, lived here his whole life and wrote here. There is another group that was born in the state, but left early and developed a literary career elsewhere. A third group includes authors who came here to live during a significant period of their lives and absorbed a breath of Kansas flavor.

In the early 1930's, self-conscious literati were lamenting that Kansas had no writers. Of course there were Ed Howe and William Allen White, stalwarts of a good many years, and there was Dr. Charles M. Sheldon, whose book "In His Steps," while hardly a literary work, had held national attention and had sold, it was claimed, more copies than any other book except the Bible.

But even as they lamented, Kansans were writing, and the year 1938 was a notable one. Four books published that year by Kansans stayed high on best-seller lists: White's biography of Calvin Coolidge, "A Puritan in Babylon"; his son, William L. White's novel, "What People Said" — what they said was that it was based on the Finney bond scandal; Dr. Karl A. Menninger's book about the conflicts warring within each person, "Man Against Himself"; and Dr. A. E. Hertzler's "The Horse and Buggy Doctor," which was a Book-of-the-Month club selection. A few years before this, Dr. Menninger's "The Human Mind" had been a Literary Guild selection.

And due to blossom in the next two decades were several young Kansas novelists — Paul Wellman, Joseph Stanley Pennell, Kenneth Davis — and dramatist William Inge. Pulitzer prizes and awards were to be won by them.

In the pre-Civil War years newspapers from the East and from England sent correspondents to Kansas to report the critical struggle going on for control of the state. An early list of Kansas books includes several of these, such as Edward Everett Hale's "Kanza and Nebraska," 1854, which has been called the first Kansas book. Soon afterwards Henry Harvey, missionary, wrote a history of the Shawnee Indians. Evander C. Kennedy, of Leavenworth, was the author of one of the first books written in the Territory.

At any rate, books were written before furrows were turned. It was estimated that between 1854 and 1899 there were 264 Kansas books. Another account said that between 1888 and 1892 there were 67 books published and by 1903 the total in the state had reached 750. Since that date, hundreds more have been published.

Ed Howe   Mrs. Sara T. D. Robinson   Edward Everett Hale

Mrs. Sara T. D. Robinson, whose husband became the first governor of Kansas, came to Lawrence in 1854 and three years later published her "Kansas — Its Interior and Exterior Life," which has not been surpassed for state fervor. An ardent abolitionist, in the same breath she praised the view from Mt. Oread and denounced man's inhumanity to man. In one sentence she said, "Our food is mush, bacon and molasses plentifully sprinkled with dirt a more beautiful country I never saw." Hardships were brushed aside — if the roof leaked, the few pieces of furniture were moved to the other side of the room. The book went into at least 10 editions. Governor Robinson in later years wrote a book, "The Kansas Conflict."

The fight against slavery dominated the writing until after the Civil War. Then with the westward movement, the theme was the frontier, the cattle range, pioneer life. Histories, novels, diaries, poetry, essays, editorials poured from the people testifying to their faith in the new country and in themselves.

The 1880's were marked with a flowering of literature — 1885 brought several notable publications: Howe's "Story of a Country Town," Eugene Ware's "Rhymes of Ironquill," another edition of Mrs. Robinson's book. It was the year with which Daniel Wilder ended his second volume of "Annals of Kansas," a chronological history of the state from Coronado through 1885. Wilder, a Harvard graduate, edited a number of papers and was one of the founders of the Historical Society. He wrote a life of Shakespeare and was one of the compilers of Bartlett's "Familiar Quotations."

In 1886, Frye Giles published his "Thirty Years in Topeka," which turned out to be a valuable record of those years. In 1960, Stauffer Publications issued a reprint for the state's Centennial, with the addition of photographs and maps.

After Howe's "Country Town" had been rejected by several publishers, he ran off 1,000 copies on the press of his Atchison Globe and sent them to these editors and others. It was an instant success. Men who had turned it down now begged to publish it. The book was soon being read all over the country.

Howe was a couple of generations ahead of his times — a realist in an age of romanticism and sentimentality. He wrote sparsely, sometimes bluntly, in short sentences minus embroidery, which allowed them to shine in their own simplicity. He was the author of a number of other books and in 1928 he wrote an autobiography, "Plain People."

"I come from a long line of plain people," he said. "I do not recall a distinguished man or woman related to me. In visiting homes I frequently see old pictures, silver or furniture coming down from ancestors. I have nothing of this kind. The only relic I have of my father is an old spectacle case. I have no picture of my mother nor anything touched by her hands. I do not believe she ever had a picture taken."

Howe's father was a stern abolitionist, a Methodist, harsh in his religion. When young Ed had a toothache, his father knocked the tooth out with a hammer and chisel and whipped the boy because he cried.

"I was brought up in my own father's family like a bound boy," he wrote, "for if he ever had any affection for me I never knew it." Yet in his later years he had understanding for his father, a man who had himself been nurtured on harshness.

He was honored at a dinner in New York in 1927, a glittering gathering of literary lights presided over by Irvin Cobb, and in 1934 by a similar dinner in Topeka with William Allen White as toastmaster.

His daughter, Mateel Howe Farnham, wrote half a dozen novels, of which "Rebellion," in 1927, received a $10,000 prize.

Ware, called the Dean of Kansas Poets, was a man of rich gifts. A Civil War veteran, he came to Ft. Scott in 1867, started a harness shop and acquired a farm. He studied law and edited the Ft. Scott Monitor, in which he printed poems signed "Ironquill," a name derived from two other anonymous writers, "Goosequill" and "Iron Pen."

His poetry ranged from deep feeling, as "The Washerwoman's Song" to gay trivia, as a verse he wrote of a law case, one in which he was not involved:

> "The defendant while at large
> Was arrested on a charge
> Of burglarious intent.
> And direct to jail he went."

He moved to Topeka in 1893, and left a library with books and real estate to Ft. Scott valued at $10,000. He and his wife traveled in Europe, where he found and translated an account of Coronado's travels in Kansas, which was published in a literary magazine here, the first time it had been published in English.

Besides several editions of his poems in this country, he had three London editions. He died in 1912 and in 1939 a 15th edition of his poetry was published with a foreword by White.

It was said that Ware was the person who gave White the idea for his famous "What's the Matter with Kansas" editorial that landed him in national prominence. White was visiting in Ware's office in the summer of 1896, listening to the lawyer's blast against the Populists. He went home and put it into his own prose.

In Kansas at least the personality of White overshadows his writing. Those who knew him — bright, gay, impudent, curious, unpretentious, inquisitive, warm-hearted — do not think of him in relation to what he wrote, but for himself.

He fits the ideal tradition of a Kansas writer. Born in Emporia of a father who came from colonial Massachusetts stock and a school teacher mother who was the daughter of Irish immigrants — the date was Feb. 10, 1868 — he remained in the state to distinguish it and the town of his birth. He attended the College of Emporia and Kansas University but did not graduate, learned the printing trade in El Dorado and was a reporter in Kansas City before he married Sallie Lindsay in 1893.

Two years later he bought the Emporia Gazette for $3,000, a paper with a circulation of 400, and turned it into a property worth a quarter of a million. He began writing short stories, selling them to magazines, then publishing them as a collection. The first book was "The Real Issue," published in 1896. The money he made from these stories made it easy to pay for the Gazette and put it on a profitable basis.

Daniel W. Wilder · *Charles Sheldon* · *William Allen White*

As his popularity grew, attractive offers came from the big cities in the East. He refused them all, as he had turned away from the siren song of politics when he had been offered a choice of profitable offices under McKinley. He became a close friend of Theodore Roosevelt, whose influence changed White from conservative leanings to a progressive. He was a behind-the-scenes power in Kansas politics, a role that he enjoyed for most of his life, though he never held a public office.

His first novel, "A Certain Rich Man," was published in 1909 and the first of his biographies in 1924. It was "Woodrow Wilson, the Man, the Times, and His Task." He wrote nearly a score of books and was one of the original five judges, in 1926, who chose the book-of-the-month for the club of that name.

He said, "I have never been bored an hour in my life. I get up every morning wondering what new strange glamorous thing is going to happen and it always happens at fairly regular intervals. Lady Luck has been good to me and I fancy she has been good to every one. Only some people are dour, and when she gives them the come hither with her eyes, they look down or turn away and lift an eyebrow. But me, I give her the wink and away we go."

White's fiction emphasized moral values without being preachy. The worth of honesty, uprightness and sobriety were implied in the lives of his characters, some of whom came to ruin for the lack of these virtues.

At a big dinner in Emporia on his 70th birthday, Feb. 10, 1938, he made it clear that he would do the talking — no tiresome tributes were wanted, just "no speeches and plenty of gravy." He died Jan. 29, 1944.

His autobiography was published two years later. In a foreword he said that despite all the pains he had put into its writing, the book was probably fiction. "So in all candor I wish to warn the reader not to confuse this story with reality, for God only knows the truth. I am hereby trying in my finite way to set down some facts which seem real and true to me. At best this is only a tale that is told."

He said that he had started out as Willie White, became Will, then W. A. and finally William Allen. "But under any name," as Jennie Small Owen said, "nobody was ever like him." Miss Owen, who began writing for the Gazette when she was a student at Emporia State Teachers College, was one of the many new writers in whom he took an interest and helped guide to a career of writing. "No matter who he was with," she said, "he was always at ease and always the same."

Among the Kansas books about the frontier one that stands out because of its imagination and charm is Col. Henry Inman's "The Old Santa Fe Trail," published in 1897. Men of dash and daring come to life once more along that famous road which felt the soft moccasins of the Indians and the heavy foot of the Spaniards as well as the tramp of oxen and horses and cattle and men.

Rising up are the ghosts of Kit Carson, who rode with Inman along the Trail, of El Solitario, the hermit who was said to have lived in a cave under bluffs at Council Grove, the great wagon trains and the bullwhackers who drove them. The book is inscribed to Hon. William F. Cody, "as a slight tribute to a generous nature and noble manhood." Cody (Buffalo Bill) wrote a foreword, saying equally nice things about Inman. He also said that between 1868 and 1881, $2,500,000 was paid for buffalo bones gathered on Kansas prairies, mostly destined for carbon works in St. Louis. By calculation he arrived at the fact that this meant the killing of 31 million buffalo.

Inman watched from a nearby hilltop: "A caravan of white covered wagons, the last that would ever travel the old trail, was slowly crawling toward the setting sun, loaded with supplies for some remote military post. It was the beginning of the end, for on Feb. 9, 1880 the first A. T. and S. F. train arrived in Santa Fe, New Mexico and the old trail as a route of commerce was closed forever."

A noted cowboy book was Andy Adams' "Log of a Cowboy," published in 1903. Mrs. Custer, widow of the General, took up writing and penned, "My Life on the Plains." Stanley Vestal, who was Dr. Walter Stanley Campbell, a professor at the University of Oklahoma, wrote a number of books, including biographies of pioneers and Indians. Frank Root, C. C. Post and Hal G. Evarts are others who contributed notably to preserving the history of the frontier. George S. Ogden wrote fiction with a background of the Old West.

F. B. Sanborn, a Harvard graduate, friend and confidante of John Brown, wrote a Brown biography which included his letters. He also wrote biographies of Emerson and Thoreau, famous residents of Sanborn's old home at Concord, Mass.

Novels were being written all over as new settlers felt the urge to write down their experiences, or more likely the experiences of their parents. Pioneer living was a way of life they knew was passing. These books had backgrounds of the rough frontier or the little towns springing up everywhere. They spoke of the hardships, and the courage with which they were met, the faith of the people and their work to build homes. There were sorrow and loss and disappointment and treachery and weakness in the books, but all were illuminated with a love story sweet as a morning meadowlark.

J. E. Williamson, principal of Topeka High School, gave an address before the Academy of Language and Literature on Dec. 31, 1885, in which he acknowledged his surprise at the numbers of works of romance he had turned up in his preparation for the talk.

"In fact," he said, "the multiplicity of our authors has lowered us in the estimation of the literary world." The multiplicity of his long words and involved sentences does something of the same thing for him.

He said the great trouble was that the authors "have all been poor in the world's goods and what they wrote was written at odd times snatched from a regular job."

"Our authors," he said, "have been farmers toiling six days a week, editors cudgeling their brains to fill their morning columns or fearfully worried to find pleasant expressions to describe the last wedding, physicians stealing spare time that should be spent studying their profession, and lastly the tired mothers who should have been napping the weariness from their limbs and the ashes from their brains while the noisy children are away at school instead of laboring to tickle the ears of strangers or pave the road to fame."

What, he asks, may we expect from such as these? Then answers his question — A lot of carelessly composed books.

He said of Howe, whose "Country Town" had been published that year, "If he took more time and pains he might write something that would have a permanent place." Howe had, of course, snatched time from his work on the Globe to write his famous book, in lean prose unburdened with the foliage of the school principal's talk.

The epitaph for these early novelists might be carved in a paragraph about one of them in a local history that ran in the Garden City News in 1937, written by Hamer Morris. He said, "Cy Cole engaged in the shoe business in Garden City, but he was a dreamer and romancer more than a salesman and he wrote a novel here that created more than local interest, which entitles him to a place with our other novelists. It is doubtful if a single copy of his novel could be found, so fleeting is fame."

Perhaps the most fleeting fame came to John Preston Campbell, whose book of poetry was printed by Crane and Co. in Topeka, but before it was distributed the printing house burned along with all the copies. Only the few that had been distributed early were saved. A dozen volumes of verse were printed in the 1880's and 90's.

In 1872, Capt. Henry King started the Kansas Magazine, aiming at a literary publication. It folded in the second year, for lack of material, it was stated, with a reported debt of $10,000, the amount for which the venture was set up, in shares of $50.

Among the contributors to the first issue was Cora M. Downes, who later became the first woman on the board of regents. In making the appointment, Gov. St. John said he would no doubt be criticized by some, yet he thought it right to have a woman on the board of institutions "where females are educated." Mrs. Downes' granddaughter, Dr. Cora M. Downes, was a professor of bacteriology at Kansas University.

Mrs. Downes said in the magazine that we "might be spared many a tiresome epic . . . if authors would only believe that great libraries are the graves of men's souls." She said that footprints for coming generations turned to fossils, and she generally lamented "the underdone efforts, the drizzling poetry of the raw period of life." The lady had a way with words.

Another contributor, Hattie McCoy North, was a militant feminist. "Everywhere within the pale of civilization," she declared, "woman is higher and purer and nobler than man." She said that whatever tends to weaken the body, weakens the mind — that "since chignons have come into vogue, cerebral diseases have increased 71 per cent."

James W. Steele, a Santa Fe official, wrote a number of books about Mexico, Cuba, and the Southwest, as well as short stories. He was considered a brilliant writer, but this quotation from an article in the magazine makes him hardly a compassionate human being: "In any event the Indian is doomed. The inscrutable purpose for which he was created is almost accomplished. On general grounds it is much better that he should go . . . He lacks the instinct of self-preservation. He would rather be aggressive and die than be peaceful and live."

"Agora" was another attempt at a literary magazine which lasted five issues. Another was started in Wichita in 1905 and survived a few years. In 1933, there was a revival of the Kansas Magazine at Kansas State University with Prof. Charles E. Rogers as editor. It has been published continuously since that time.

John J. Ingalls was one of the most brilliant men the state has produced and was looked on as a man destined to make his mark on literature, until he got elected to the Senate, where he served Kansas for 18 years, 1873-1891. His spoken words were as eloquent as his written, and he left his mark on the U. S. Senate. In 1905, his statue was placed in the Hall of Fame in the national Capitol.

He had the gift of the poetic phrase, shined and polished, erudite and scholarly, a gift that was sparked with a warmth of feeling. Much quoted is his words on grass, a classic: "Grass is the forgiveness of nature . . . It yields no fruit in earth or air and yet should its harvest fail for a single year, famine would depopulate the world." He graduated from Williams College in Massachusetts, in 1855.

His poem "Opportunity" also became a classic, along with "Each in His Own Tongue" by William Herbert Carruth, German language professor at Kansas University, and a few others.

Ingalls, who came to Kansas in 1858, was secretary of the Kansas Senate when the "vexed question" of a design for a state seal was considered. Among the suggestions for the motto were "We will" and its opposite "We Won't," and Ingalls is credited with supplying the one adopted on May 25, 1861, "Ad Astra per Aspera."

In the first decades of this century novels began to be written with character development as the chief theme, but the majority continued to be aware of the newness of the state. Margaret Lynn was the author of several historical novels. Elmer T. Peterson and Anna Carlson each wrote novels about Swedish settlers in Kansas. Vance Randolph wrote a novel about Russian settlers, but he is best known for his work in recording and preserving the native folk music of the Ozarks, and of writing about the people in that part of the country.

Novels during this period were published by May Griffee Robinson, Fletcher M. Sisson, Reynolds Knight, L. Addison Bone, George Alfred Brown, Tacy Stokes Paxton, Effie Graham, Dana Gatlin, Louisa Cooke Don-Carlos and, a little later, Frances Kaltenborn. Some of these novels were propaganda, which never creates lasting fiction.

The most popular and successful of the Kansas novelists of this period was Margaret Hill McCarter, who wrote 20 novels with backgrounds of the Great West, the frontier or pioneer life. She was an intelligent, vigorous woman, active in women's clubs — she organized the Sorosis club in Topeka and served as president of the State Federation of Clubs — civic betterment and politics. She said once that she was the first woman to be sent outside the state by the Republican party to campaign in a national election. She came to Kansas in 1888 and lived in Topeka, where she died in 1938.

An unusual literary venture was the publication of Little Blue Books by Emanuel Haldeman-Julius, who was way out front in the business of paper backs. They were small books three and a half by five inches and sold for a dime — some for a nickel. He claims to have sold 300 million of the 881 titles which ran the scale of literary subjects — the classics, essays, a few poems, philosophy, science, and discussion tending toward what was then thought radical. His publishing business was at Girard, where he lived a stormy life and died in 1951. He and his wife wrote a novel, "Dust," about an unhappy marriage.

Kansas was the birthplace of several noted writers who did not remain. Dorothy Canfield Fisher was born in Lawrence, where her father was a professor at Kansas University. Edgar Lee Masters came from Garnett and may have modeled some of his "Spoon River Anthology" characters on people he knew there. Damon Runyon, born in Manhattan, was a distinguished journalist who made Broadway his beat, a street where he knew the "Guys and Dolls." After his death from cancer a fund was established in his name. He was cremated and his ashes scattered over Times Square by his friend, Eddie Rickenbacker.

Rex Stout, a former Topekan, writes mystery stories around his well-known character of Detective Nero Wolfe. Brock Pemberton left Emporia for Broadway and became a playwright — "Miss Lulu Bett," "Strictly Dishonorable," "Personal Appearance."

William Inge, one of the foremost young dramatists, was born in Independence. His "Come Back Little Sheba" was runnerup for the Critics Circle Award. It was followed by "Picnic," which won a Pultizer Prize, and by "Bus Stop" and "The Dark at the Top of the Stairs." All were Broadway successes, road shows and were sold for motion pictures.

Carleton Beals left Medicine Lodge and became a journalist. He is the author of a biography of his fellow townswoman, Carry A. Nation, "Cyclone Carry." Carry herself laid down her hatchet and took up her pen to write the story of her life.

Charles B. Driscoll, born near Wichita, became a columnist and author of books for children. Alice Nichols moved from Liberal, but spent 10 years writing a book about her native state, "Bleeding Kansas." Margaret Whittemore, who illustrated her books about Kansas, now lives in Florida.

Noted authors, or some who later became noted authors, wandered into Kansas, graced it for a time, then left. One of the first was Frank Harris, who lived in the Flint Hills as a ranch hand in the middle seventies, and studied law at Kansas University. Brilliant, arrogant and boastful, he angered both men and women in his disloyalties and stirred bitter controversies. He later wrote biographies of Shakespeare, Wilde and Shaw, wrote for magazines in New York, and repeated his pattern of making himself disliked. His genius never quite came to flower.

Harry Kemp blew into Lawrence in 1906. The townspeople and University students might have used the word "unkempt," for he came without a hat, which in that year was pretty far out. He also had no money, but he entered the University and was "discovered" by William Allen White, at whose home he met Ida Tarbell, who helped him on his way to becoming a poet.

In 1909, he was told he could have a free ticket to the football game between the Jayhawks and Ichabods if he could get himself to Topeka, where the game was to be played. He left Lawrence on foot at 11:15 p.m. the Friday before the game, and arrived in Topeka 8:15 the next morning. He also walked back to Lawrence. He was smiled at by most of the students as a fool and a crank, but, at least in the matter of hatlessness, he was 50 years ahead of his time.

Vachel Lindsay, already an established poet, tramped through Kansas in the second decade of the century, living off the land, distributing his rhymes and preaching the gospel of beauty.

William Gibson lived in Topeka in the 1940's and wrote his play, "A Cry of Players," which won a national award offered by the Topeka Civic Theatre. He moved to Stockbridge, Mass., and wrote two Broadway successes — "Two for the Seesaw" and "The Miracle Worker." Both have also been made into motion pictures, as was his novel, "The Cobweb," laid in a mental hospital. Topekans tried to fit the setting and characters to hospitals here — Gibson's wife, Dr. Margaret Brenman, was on the staff of the Menninger Foundation.

A valuable addition to the state's literature are books that Kansans have written about their profession. Leading these are Dr. Karl A. Menninger and Dr. William C. Menninger. In writing about mental illness in a way that is understandable to the general reader, they have laid stout planks across the gap that in earlier years set the sufferer of emotional illness apart from society. Many writers have come to Topeka to obtain stories about the Menninger Foundation, which was started by these two doctors and their father, Dr. C. F. Menninger, in a farmhouse.

Their mother, Flo V. Menninger, wrote a warm-hearted story of her early life, her marriage and family — "Days of My Life."

Dr. Gardner Murphy, who directed research at the Foundation, is one of the nation's most renowned psychologists and has contributed significantly to man's efforts to understand himself and his fellowman. His "Human Potentialities," 1958, blazed new pathways into the tangle of human relations. He and his wife, Dr. Lois Murphy, known for her work with children, travel and write of people in other parts of the world.

Dr. Harry Levinson, of the Foundation staff, is the author of a book dealing with the relations of employers and employes, in ways that could lessen frustrations and contribute to the satisfactions, and, as a result, to the efficiency of men who work in large groups.

Dr. Hertzler, as plain-spoken as Ed Howe, grew up in central Kansas and established a hospital and clinic in Halstead. Fired with the success of "Horse and Buggy Doctor," he followed it with several others.

Dr. Samuel Crumbine's "Frontier Doctor," 1948, tells the engaging story of his efforts to promote public health in Kansas — the banishment of the roller towel and common drinking cup, the bricks he had a Topeka brickmaker imprint with "Don't Spit on the Sidewalk," and the fly swatters, which were first made at Weir City, Kansas. Dr. Crumbine thought of the name when he was at a ball game and heard fans yelling for a fly and for the batter to swat the ball. To him a fly meant a pesky insect that spread disease, not a ball making a parabola in the air. Walt Mason wrote in the Emporia Gazette:

> "Whose policies are good and wise?
> Who taught us how to swat the flies
> Between their doggoned blooming eyes?
> Doc Crumbine."

Martin and Osa Johnson of Chanute wrote books about big game hunting and the adventures on their trips to far countries.

Waldo R. Wedel, of the Smithsonian Institute staff, did some exploring in Kansas that led to a valuable book, "An Introduction to Kansas Archeology."

Lewis Dyche, for whom the Dyche Museum at Kansas University is named, wrote accounts of his polar trips with both Cook and Peary. N. S. Goss, whose collection of stuffed birds is in the Historical Society, wrote interestingly about them.

Clementine Paddleford is a Kansas woman who has become a top writer about foods. Nell Nichols, formerly of Topeka, was also a foods expert on eastern magazines.

Robert A. Taft, who was chemistry professor at Kansas University, wrote a book about his outside interest rather than his profession. His "Photography and the American Scene" is a valuable book, profusely illustrated, that deals with the technical and social revolution of picture making.

Another Kansas University professor, James C. Malin, has done important historical research, particularly for his book, "John Brown and the Legend of Fifty-Six," published in 1942.

John Ise, a stormy economics professor at Kansas University, now retired, is an acid critic of the popular scene. But he wrote a book in another vein, "Sod and Stubble," a story lived by his parents.

William Frank Zornow, who taught at both Washburn and Kansas State University, is the author of one of the newest of Kansas histories. Bliss Isely and W. M. Richards wrote a well-known history, "Four Centuries in Kansas." Isely wrote other books, as did his wife, who wrote under the name of Kunigunde Duncan.

Snowden D. Flora, a long time Kansas meteorologist, wrote interesting and valuable books about climate and weather.

Dr. Everett Rich, professor of Emporia State Teachers College, wrote a biography — "William Allen White: The Man From Emporia" and a book "Heritage of Kansas."

Two young college teachers collaborated on a charming book that is a bit off beat from the scholarly tradition. William Koch, English teacher at Kansas State University, and Sam J. Sackett, English teacher at Hays State Teachers College, published "Kansas Folklore," for which they went up and down the state, interviewing and observing. It is a book as valuable

John J. Ingalls   *Margaret Hill McCarter*   *William Inge*

as it is engaging, for it was derived from a source that will soon be gone. A Kansas-born woman, Mrs. Eva O. Jessye, wrote a book about spirituals.

Nelson Antrim Crawford was a scholarly man who made no compromises with taste and quality. When he edited the Household Magazine he turned it into a literary publication any author was proud to be in. He wrote a novel, "Unhappy Wind," and many articles. His book about cats, 1947, has become a classic for cat lovers everywhere. In his later years — he died in 1963 — he worked as an editor for writers at the Menninger Foundation and co-authored a book with Dr. Karl Menninger.

Kate Stephens, a Greek teacher at Kansas University, wrote about her beloved "Laurel Town" and another or two books on controversial subjects. She published the love letters of Byron Caldwell Smith, a young professor to whom she was engaged, after he died of tuberculosis. The book was written "because she grudged him to oblivion."

Mrs. L. M. Alexander of Baldwin won a $10,000 Dodd-Mead prize in 1932 for a first novel, "Candy," a story of her native South Carolina. She said she was 20 years writing it, sitting in a rocking chair by a window, a portable typewriter on her lap. A desk seemed too cold for writing fiction.

Dr. Charles H. Lerrigo, who wrote a few books in his earlier life, authored in his later years "The Better Half of Your Life," which undertakes to tell "how to live in health and happiness from forty to ninety." His daughter, Marion Lerrigo McWilliams, who now lives in Larchmont, N. Y., is the author of a number of health books. The latest, published 1965, was in collaboration with Dr. Benjamin Spock.

Kansas lays claim to Laura Ingalls Wilder, author of the famous "Little House" books, stories of various places in which her parents had taken their children in their movings — "Pa" was a great one for pushing on to a new place. Eileen Charbo, cataloguer at the Historical Society, has located the family in the 1870 census in Montgomery County, the place where "Baby Caroline" was born.

Thomas Craven was a Salina artist who wrote books that drew national interest. He published "Paint" in 1923 and "Men of Art" in 1931.

In a list of those who wrote about their work, Emmett Dalton should not be overlooked. He was a member of the Dalton Gang of southeast Kansas which achieved some fame in activities outside the law. In 1931, he published "When the Daltons Rode."

Kansas received popular attention in a children's book that became famous, both as a publication and as a motion picture — "The Wizard of Oz" by Frank Baum, about a girl named Dorothy who lived in Kansas and was carried away in a cyclone to the land of Oz.

Among writers of children's books is Edna Becker, Topeka, who has written stories — "Hugh and Dennis" is one — with a background of the middle ages. But her most popular book is her delightful "900 Buckets of Paint" which has sold more than 70,000 copies and is still selling.

Alice Huggins, who taught in a missionary school in China, is the author of some half dozen books around the people and country of China. Among them are "The Red Chair Waits" and her newest, "Spend Your Heart."

Holly Wilson, a prolific writer of books for girls, lived a number of years in Topeka. Most of her books have an added attraction of a historical background. Jean Bailey's "Cherokee Bill," the story of a horse, won the 1955 William Allen White award for a children's book.

Eula Mark Phillips won the $3,000 Follett award in 1957 with her "Chucko." Bernice Anderson, Partridge, is an author of children's books. Her best-known is "Indian Sleep-Man Tales." Mary Frances Shura is a Kansas-born writer of children's books. Others are Elizabeth Searle Lamb, Jessie Wright Whitcomb, and Dr. Thomas Clark Hinkle.

Kansas has a writer of confession stories, but not under her own name, Marie Wilsman, formerly of Burr Oak, Kansas, now of Franklin, Nebraska. She has confessed to a multitude of sins, but she knows the rules of her trade — the heroine must have some appeal to win the reader's sympathy, but she must suffer. For instance, instead of getting the nice clean-cut young man she has to be satisfied with a second-hand widower.

The 1930's and 1940's brought several promising young novelists. Paul Wellman had published several stories prior to his "Jubal Troop," which was made into a motion picture starring Gary Cooper. "The Bowl of Brass" also became a movie, as did "The Iron Mistress," a story about the career of James Bowie. "The Chain" was a Literary Guild selection of 1949. Cimarron is thought to be the "Jerico" of some of his books. Wellman's brother, Manly, is also a novelist. Frederic Wakeman, who was born in Scranton, began writing when he was in military service. A book about the advertising world, "The Hucksters" was chosen as book-of-the-month in June 1946, and was made into a movie. Both book and picture attracted much attention and comment. Other books were "The Wastrel," "Mandrake Root" and "The Fabulous Train." The last was a book about a small town, a drab picture of both people and town. Heads naturally turned toward Scranton.

Joseph Stanley Pennell, of Junction City, son of a noted photographer, papered his room at Kansas University with rejection slips before he won success with "The History of Rome Hanks and Kindred Matters" in 1944. One reviewer said it was a novel of the Civil War, "a roaring, brutal novel, the finest talent of the year." In it the author goes searching into the past and in doing so, mixes past with present. A second novel was "The History of Nora Beckham," 1949. Pennell died in 1963.

Kenneth Davis of Manhattan published "In the Forests of the Night," 1942, which might be described as a character study of a man going to pieces. It was followed by a biography of Eisenhower. In 1942, a good year for fiction in Kansas, Michael Amrine published "All Sons Must Say Goodby," which deals with the conflict between father and son and the old and the new generation. It was followed by "The Great Decision," a story of the atomic bomb. In 1963, Russell Laman, Kansas State University instructor, published a novel about the Populist movement, "Manifest Destiny."

Vivien Bretherton, Lawrence, also wrote a novel in 1942, "The Rock and the Wind," which created the popular character, Andy Hardy. Elinor Pryor, Wichita, is another novelist who had a story out in 1942, "And Never Yield." Her "The Big Play," 1951, was a story about oil that was sold for a picture starring Jane Russell.

Among young writers of today are Warren Kliewer, who writes both poetry and prose. He lived in Topeka during the war, later taught English at Bethany College in Lindsborg and is now teaching in Earlham College, Richmond, Ind. — assistant professor of English. In 1964, he published "The Violators," a story of life in a Canadian village.

"The Velvet Bubble," published in 1965 by Alice Winter, a young woman in Kansas City, Kansas, won the Morrow Honor award. It is a first novel of great promise.

Writing about the poets is difficult, for they are, comparatively, like the stars in the sky in numbers. Scores of poets are turning out verse, each in their separate stars, and mostly for the joy of working, though many poets sell their work and have published a volume or two. The Kansas Authors Club, organized in 1904, has an active membership.

The feminine gender seems to predominate in the poets of today, but such was not the case in earlier years. Along in the 80's and 90's and early in the century, the Kansas editors at their annual meeting elected a poet for the coming year, just as they elected a president. It was an honor bestowed on Ingalls, King, Steele, White, Ewing Herbert, Charles Harger, J. M. Cavaness, and others. It was the duty of the poet to compose and deliver a poem for the next year's meeting. Most of the editors wrote poetry and were proud of their output.

Richard Realf is called the first Kansas poet. He came to Lawrence in the 1850's and became one of John Brown's men. Said to have been a protege of Lady Byron, he was moody and introspective, and passionately idealistic. He killed himself in Oakland in 1878. A volume of his poetry, "Free State Lyrics," was edited by Richard Hinton and published in 1890.

A number of Anthologies of Kansas verse have been published. Perhaps the first was compiled by Hattie Horner in 1891. It has three poems by Will A. White in a folksy dialect that would have done credit to James Whitcomb Riley. They are "Sence Idy's Gone," "A Twelfth Month Idyl" and "The Ol' Wood Pump," which begins:

> "They's differ'nt things about a farm 'at takes a feller's eye;
>   Some think that pigs is pickchuresk, though durned if I see why."

White was a young man 23 years old, a reporter in Kansas City. Just as he went from Willie to Will to William Allen, he went from folksy rhymes to short stories to top quality discussion and biography.

In 1914, an anthology, "Sunflowers," was edited by Willard Wattles, a young poet who was a professor at Kansas University, and in 1927 one by Helen Rhoda Hoopes, also a KU professor and a gifted poet. An anthology was edited by Henry Harrison in 1935.

May Williams Ward is acknowledged as the present dean of Kansas poets. Bright, gay, witty, also thoughtful and durable, she graduated from KU in mathematics, a Phi Beta Kappa. She edited The Harp, a poetry magazine that was formerly published in the state, now lives in Wellington with her husband Merle. Between 1921 and 1926 she had 300 poems published in 35 magazines. She has published five books of verse and has had poems in some 75 publications. Her fifth book, "Wheatlands," 1954, is a beautifully printed volume illustrated with her own woodcuts. Besides her poetry, Mrs. Ward writes book reviews for a Wellington newspaper, the Daily News.

As in a line from one of her poems saying that poets "praise beauty in a thousand ways," she praises it in many moods and manners, from whimsy to drama. The closing line of "The Tornado" illustrates the latter —

> "And the monstrous horn of the unicorn
>   Gored the world."

Mrs. Ward and Whitelaw Saunders, a Wamego poet, were the first Kansans to be elected to the Poetry Society of America.

Esther Clark Hill

Charles Harger

Three members of the English faculty at Kansas State University are writing superior poetry — W. R. Moses, who has a new book just out, "Identities," Dr. Earle Davis and Fred Higginson. Bruce Cutler of Wichita University, is one of the promising young poets. He is author of "A West Wind Rises." Kenneth Porter's "The High Plains" won the Golden Rose award in 1938 of the New England Poetry Club and he has been a steady contributor to the Kansas Magazine, as has Paul Newman.

A distinguished Negro poet who was born in Topeka is Gwendolyn Brooks, whose "Annie Allen" won the Pulitzer prize for poetry in 1949. An earlier volume, "A Street in Bronzeville," established her talent as a poet.

Langston Hughes lived a number of years in Topeka and Lawrence. Besides several volumes of poetry he has written a novel and an autobiography, "I Wonder As I Wander," 1956.

Edna Becker writes poetry as well as children's stories, poetry for both children and adults that sparkles with imagination and whimsy. Irma Wassall, of Wichita, is a gifted poet who has a volume of distinctive verse, "Loonshadow." The lofty spirit of Myra Perrings, Topeka, soared in several volumes of verse written under severe physical handicap. Clara Aiken Speer, Kansas City, Kansas; Velma West Sykes, Garnett; Nora B. Cunningham, Chanute; and Billy Cooper, Neodesha, are active poets who are being published.

Eunice Wallace Shore wrote delicate poems that had a mystical quality, and was the last editor of The Harp. Her father, Leslie Wallace, a newspaper editor in Larned, wrote articles and some verse for magazines. Madeleine Aaron, Wichita, published a book of poetry in 1939, "Prairie Galleons." Edna Worthly Underwood, who read 15 languages, wrote verse as well as prose, most of it with a flavor of other countries. Elizabeth Barr Arthur, a poet and editor, was born in a dugout in Lincoln County and retained an individualistic outlook in all her work.

Albert Bigelow Paine, an itinerant photographer, came to Ft. Scott and remained. In 1893, he and White collaborated in a volume of verse, "Rhymes of Two Friends," with a foreword by Ewing Herbert. Paine later wrote 40 books, some of which were biographies. He refused to write Coolidge's — no sense of humor.

A popular early poet was Ellen Palmer Allerton, whose "Walls of Corn" was often quoted. Vingie Roe caused trouble in the Wichita Eagle office around 1912. Victor Murdock, who wrote a novel himself, liked her poetry and wanted it on the front page, but Dave Leahy, the managing editor, defied the boss and said he would "be torn asunder by wild sawhorses" before he'd print it anywhere but on the want-ad page. Later Vingie sold a novel to Dodd-Mead that became a best seller

When Esther Clark Hill was homesick in California she wrote a poem that has become a state classic, "The Call of Kansas," which was printed in the Lawrence Journal-World in 1907. In her later years — she died in 1932 — she worked at the Historical Society.

During her last illness when a blood transfusion was needed, Kirke Mechem, then secretary of the Society, and Nyle Miller, a member of the staff, volunteered to donate blood. She knew Mechem but had not become acquainted with Miller, and asked to meet him before the transfusion took place. Her doctor said it would not be necessary, that the blood was the right type and everything was ready.

But she insisted and when Miller came into the room she raised her head and fixing him with her bright eyes, asked, "Young man, were you born in Kansas?" Fortunately he was, and the transfusion went ahead.

Many others are writing or have written poetry that deserves to be mentioned — Harriett Lull Alden, who was born in Emporia; Violet Leighty, a farm woman near Logan; Lois Paulsen of Concordia, and Lynn Martin of Brookville, who sometimes wrote under the name of George Martin. His poems are sensitive, musical and have a depth of feeling.

The repository of all this Kansas writing is the Historical Society, which was organized in 1875 by men who foresaw the value of preserving publications and other writing — books, diaries, letters, programs — a foresight that has made this the most complete collection of historical material in any of the states.

In addition to being a repository, it is a fountain that feeds itself by supplying authors with material, not only authors in this state, but in others and many foreign countries.

William E. Connelley, an early secretary of the Society, was the author of a good many books of Kansas history and biography. Mechem is also an author, of poetry, plays and prose of a high literary quality. His play, "John Brown," 1939, received the Maxwell Anderson award. In 1936, he wrote a mystery novel, "A Frame for Murder."

Miller, the present Secretary, and Joseph W. Snell are the authors of a fascinating book, "Why the West was Wild," which could serve as a handbook for producers of westerns and other users of material about the wild and wicked cow towns of Kansas. The book was researched from newspapers and material in the Society.

It sponsored the publication of several books for the Centennial — a book of Kansas newspapers, a pictorial history of the state and a book of maps.

It published two more volumes of Kansas Annals, with Mechem as editor and Miss Owen as annalist, bringing the chronological history through the year 1925. Miss Owen is author of a book, "Fodder," a compilation of her columns in the El Dorado Times. It is a sprightly and nostalgic little book about pioneer life, written with insight and humor. Though now out of print, it is still asked for.

From the beginning, most Kansas authors have been editors. Both Howe and White earned their living from their newspapers and other editors have, in addition to good writing in their own papers, produced articles, novels, histories and poetry.

Charles Harger, of Abilene, wrote articles and poetry and his successor on the Chronicle, Henry Jameson, published a book about early days, "Heroes by the Dozen." Mack Cretcher, Newton, wrote a novel, "The Kansan," and Noble Prentis was an early editor with a literary bent. Cora G. Lewis of Kinsley wrote verse and articles.

Writers that came from Capper Publications are Marco Morrow, Tom McNeal, Jay House, who went to the Philadelphia Public Ledger, and the Jarrells — Frank and Myra and their children, Arch, Sanford, Jack and Barbara; good writing fairly oozed out of the Jarrells, who all wrote other things while doing newspaper work.

Paul Jones, Lyons editor, made a contribution to Kansas history with his "Coronado and Quivira," 1937, for which he did a great deal of research. W. G. Clugston, who was a fiery reporter on the old Kansas City Journal-Post and on the Topeka State Journal, is author of a number of books, of which "Rascals in Democracy," 1941, is best known.

Ben Hibbs is a Kansas editor who became editor of the Saturday Evening Post and is now doing some writing for Reader's Digest. William L. White wrote books that are "in depth" reporting, in which instance Truman Capote's new book, "In Cold Blood," about the Clutter murders at Garden City, should be included as a Kansas book.

Frank Clough, an Emporia Gazette reporter, wrote a biography of his boss. Alfred Hill is a Kansas newspaperman who has moved on to other writing, as did Ralph Wallace.

Kansas editors are still keeping up the tradition of good writing. Some that might serve as examples are Jack Harris, Hutchinson; Rolla Clymer, El Dorado; Marion Ellet, Concordia; Rolland Jacquart, Sublette; Angelo Scott of Iola, as did his father, Charles F. Scott. Going back again into the past, there was Jay Iden, poet and romancer from the hills. He is the one who coined the phrase, "Give till it hurts."

It is often said that present editors are kept so busy getting ads, keeping up civic duties and attending meetings that they are not giving the attention to writing that early editors did. The pioneer stalwarts had nothing to lose or worry about — an old press and a few handfuls of type — so they could afford to snort fire.

Talk about the Great American Novel is going the way that talk did about the Great American Desert, meaning the Midwest. Novels will be written, great novels, one hopes, but hardly "The" great novel. The nation is too large, too varied, its people and interest too diverse, for one novel to encompass the whole. A bright light turned on one small place can result in a great novel.

The state has turned out a good quota of authors, compared with other states. Driscoll, scanning the literary horizon, said, "Kansans have produced more printable work and more lookable pictures than they are entitled to."

And this article has not even mentioned Kansas' most distinguished and successful author, Dwight David Eisenhower, who modestly declared, "I'm just a hack and I know it." There isn't a hack in the state who wouldn't love to have the royalties rolling in as they are to this author of three popular and valuable books.

KANSAS PROGRESS BELIES TAG

by Jim Petterson

Long, long ago, when the word had a much less odious meaning, Kansas was mislabeled as a conservative state. This erroneous tag, hung on her by writers and speakers with only cursory knowledge of her heritage, has plagued Kansas more or less through each of her 105 years of statehood.

And still, today, despite a glowing, historic record to the contrary, the Sunflower State struggles to free herself from these ill-deserved and foreign-forged fetters.

Kansas, described by many as the buckle on the Bible belt, has a strong and stern religious background. This is understandable. Only men of great faith would willingly have braved the rigors, the dangers and uncertainties facing them as they carved and formed the untamed territory into the 34th state in the Union.

The state's birth as an anti-slavery force symbolized for all time its citizens' love of freedom, their stubborn insistence on independent thinking and their high regard for the rights of all mankind.

These attributes do not deserve the conservative label.

The pioneers who first settled the rolling prairies and fertile valleys of Kansas, risked their futures, yes, and their lives, daily as they waited for rain, dreaded disease or serious injury, feared Indian attacks, fought lawlessness and clung tenaciously to their right to worship in the churches they chose and built.

These efforts do not deserve the conservative label.

Born in strife and turmoil, "Bleeding Kansas" sought better things. Tired of bloodshed and danger, weary of war, Kansans sought to improve their state. During its relatively tender years, there were tendencies to experiment through legal channels. Lotteries were, and are, forbidden by the original constitution of the state.

Later, alcoholic beverages and all forms of gambling were outlawed. And long before they were tagged with the threat of lung cancer, cigarettes were banned by statute to protect the state's youth from poisonous "furfural."

All of these acts were the echoes of the strong moral voice that sounded across the broad expanses of the state. In time, and belatedly, the laws were changed in part. The nobility of the experiments had been overestimated and the effect of unpopular restraints was recognized. The laws against alcoholic beverages and sale of cigarettes were liberalized.

Experimentation, even with public morals, cannot be labeled conservative.

Kansas has never really resisted change. It only seeks thorough examination and assurance before it moves. Jayhawkers were born in determination and have lived in stability. Their reluctance to embark on pointless voyages was the abundant harvest of disappointment. It is evident yet in legislative halls.

Suffragettes go after the vote in 1912, riding in Gov. W. R. Stubbs automobile.

Governor Capper signing the "Bone Dry" law passed by 1917 Legislature.

A willingness to change, even when it means admission of error, certainly cannot be labeled conservative.

An example is the amendment to the Kansas Constitution, adopted by the voters in 1912, giving women the right to vote in all elections. A similar amendment had been defeated in 1867.

When the Kansas Constitution was drawn up in July, 1859, the vote was reserved for white males. Influenced by the days of reconstruction, the Kansas Legislature enacted a Civil Rights Act in 1874. It was the third state in the Union to do so.

While this first venture into the now explosive field was not accompanied by an enforceable law, it did rocket the state to the front as one that legally recognized the rights of every citizen.

In 1953, Kansas became the 12th state to enact an anti-discrimination law. The law, referred to by its author, Rep. Miles Stevens of Kansas City, Kans., as a "toothless tiger," was revised in 1961 and again in 1963. It was broadened into the Kansas Act against Discrimination in 1965.

In the final act, the Legislature wrote:

"It is declared to be the policy of the State of Kansas to assure equal opportunities and encouragement to every citizen regardless of race, religion, color, national origin or ancestry, in securing and holding without discrimination, employment in any field of work or labor for which he is properly qualified, and to assure equal opportunities to all persons within this state to full and equal public accommodations without distinction on account of race, religion, color, national origin or ancestry."

Certainly, this firm step forward is not to be labeled as conservatism.

While Kansas moved rapidly in the field of civil rights, perhaps it was because the citizenry recognized this bid for freedom and fairness was of paramount importance. This action probably was related more to personal morality than some of the state's more widely publicized endeavors.

When alcoholic liquors were banned by constitutional amendment in 1880, and enforced by a 1918 statute of far-reaching extent; and when cigarettes were illegal to sell after a law enacted in 1911, the state suffered intense agonies. Bootleggers bubbled to the surface in all areas. Liquor was available always for a price and cigarettes were sold freely under the counter. The laws and the constitution were flouted constantly. It took time, but both were repealed by the people and their legislators.

This slow, but orderly, retreat from limiting behavioral legislation is not conservatism.

Governor Huxman signing bill in 1937 which gave women equal vote with
men in political party organization.

Alf M. Landon

Gov. William H. Avery, elected in 1964, described his home state in these words:

"We have in Kansas a good example of the blending of New England pragmatism, Southern traditionalism and frontier realism. Not all of Kansas during the early years of the state's development was made by gun-toting cowboys, regardless of what the movie-makers and television writers say. A strong back was sometimes more important than a fast draw."

The accent ever on the worker, Kansas was a leader in securing the right of workers to join or not join a labor union. Sponsored by business and responsible citizens, the so-called right-to-work movement was begun. It ended in adoption of a constitutional amendment in 1958 which guaranteed that right.

Organized labor unions fought the effort tooth and toe-nail, but the amendment was adopted by a plurality of about 80,000 votes. Union leaders denounced the amendment as an employer's tool, but that did not explain away the tremendous favorable vote. The big "yes" vote, to reach that size, necessarily included many union members.

After losing similar battles in 17 other states, organized labor concentrated on a congressional act to void state right-to-work laws or constitutional amendments in the several states. This met strong opposition in a supposedly friendly Congress in 1965 and was delayed.

But the right-to-work amendment was not the first attempt by Kansans to solve the problems that have plagued labor-management relations through the years. During the administration of Gov. Henry J. Allen of Wichita, the Kansas Legislature enacted the Industrial Court Act. It created a Court of Industrial Relations where management and labor could confront each other, solve their differences and avoid wasteful strikes that are equally costly to both parties. The court was empowered to hear both sides of a labor controversy and adjudicate it.

Strangely, it was not labor, but business, who brought the court to a legal end. The court, established by an act of the 1920 special legislative session, was abolished in 1925.

The Wolf Packing Company of Topeka, disputing the right of the court to settle a strike in its plant, appealed through the lower courts to the U. S. Supreme Court where the legislation was declared unconstitutional.

It wasn't until the early days of the New Deal administration of President Franklin D. Roosevelt that the nation accepted similar laws.

Out of the Great Depression that followed the 1929 crash of the New York stock market, the National Labor Relations Act was sired. It included many of the features of the defunct Kansas law.

Could anyone call that Kansas act conservatism?

251

This federal backing and filling convinced Kansas legislators of the futility of adopting progressive legislation without a firm foundation. In casting about for an answer, Kansas lawmakers took two forward steps that were to pattern legislation in nearly every other state in the Union.

One was the Cash Basis and Budget Law and the other was the act creating the Kansas Legislative Council. Both were voted by the 1933 legislative session.

The Cash Basis Law, which forbade governmental agencies from spending beyond their budgets, was a product of the administration of Gov. Alf M. Landon. It drew so much attention nationally, it skyrocketed him to the Republican presidential nomination in 1936.

The Cash Basis Law was simply a public expression of Kansas philosophy: No one should live beyond his income, and each should pay his just debts.

Before the Depression, the state, counties, cities, towns and school districts could, and did, spend money in anticipation of tax collections. But property values dropped, jobs disappeared and Kansans had no money to pay taxes. Along with their residents, counties, cities, towns and school districts were short of funds. At least one Kansas town was bankrupted.

The Cash Basis Law was the first state step back to solvency. No tax money now can be spent unless it has first been budgeted and taxes already collected. All speculation was removed from government financing. It was progressive and sound. There was no more guess work. Because of that one law, Kansas emerged from the Depression with her bills paid.

Completing this double step forward in 1933 was the creation of the Legislative Council. This new division of government proved so popular 38 states now have similar agencies. Accomplishments of the Legislative Council are reflected in laws enacted by the Legislatures since its inception.

Members of the Kansas House and Senate never need look to paid lobbyists for information or advice on proposed bills. This information is supplied by the council. Still, the lobbyist was not banned, nor was this an intended by-product.

Measures recommended by the council have been studied and researched for a minimum of two years. Only facts — facts on both sides of any controversial subject — are placed before the legislators.

Since its creation, 60 per cent of the measures it researched and recommended have been accepted by the Legislature. Obviously, the Legislature has learned that "the blending of New England pragmatism, Southern traditionalism and frontier realism," has resulted in progress on controversial and touchy questions.

If this is conservatism in government, the nation needs more of it.

The importance of advice offered by the Legislative Council is evident in the work-load of the Kansas Legislature. In the 1965 session alone, more than 1,000 bills were introduced in both houses. About half were enacted into law.

Looking back over the years at the record of "conservative" Kansas, progressive legislation appears as thick as quills on a porcupine. None was on untested ground. Lawmaking reached the jet-age before the voters had named it.

During the administration of Gov. Payne H. Ratner some giant strides were stepped off. The state civil service system, guarantee-tenure to state employees, was not the least. Nor was the retirement act for school teachers a step backward.

The civil service system for Kansas was approved in 1940 as an amendment to the constitution. Implementing legislation was enacted in the 1941 Legislature.

Governor Ratner acknowledged the need even then for Kansas to doff a part of its time-honored, but limiting mantle of agriculturalism. The Kansas Industrial Development Commis-

Henry Allen   *Frank Carlson*   *Payne Ratner*   *William Avery*

sion was created. It subsequently was renamed the Kansas Economic Development Commission, and adequate funds appropriated. These forward steps were taken in the period from 1939 to 1943.

During the administration of Gov. Walter A. Huxman, just prior to that of Governor Ratner, the state's first sales tax was imposed. There are those who believe it cost him re-election to a second term, but it still is with us and has been increased to 3 cents on the dollar. The sales tax was voted originally for welfare, education and tax reduction. The first two items now command most of its monetary attention.

Conservatism was not a factor in consideration of these proposals.

When Frank Carlson, previously a Kansas congressman and later a United States senator, was governor, Kansas kicked aside one of its nationally recognized shackles. Voters were permitted to decide whether alcoholic liquor should be sold in the state. They voted in favor of its sale by a margin of 65,000 votes.

Governor Carlson also initiated the state's first long-range highway program. It was designed to project the state's needs for 20 years. He appointed a statewide commission to study the highway program begun under the administration of Gov. Clyde M. Reed. He was governor in 1929 and 1930.

More important than all else was Governor Carlson's drive to improve the state program for the care and treatment of the mentally ill. Under his direction and guidance, Kansas, with the considerable help of the Menninger Foundation, rose rapidly toward the top in the nation in the field of mental health. Mental hospitals at Topeka, Larned and Osawatomie gained in stature and efficiency. Kansas still maintains much of this mental health prestige. Its treatment program has been expanded to include area health facilities for the mentally ill.

Those looking for conservatism in Kansas still are searching.

Gov. Edward F. Arn, who succeeded Governor Carlson, kept the wheels of government progress rolling forward. The Kansas Turnpike Authority was created and the Turnpike from Kansas City through Lawrence, Topeka, Emporia and Wichita to the Oklahoma-Kansas border, was constructed. The State Office Building, long needed, was begun. Also, the state's finances were placed under the control of a new Department of Administration.

None of these accomplishments could be labeled conservative.

State support of elementary schools was begun in the administration of Governor Ratner. It was increased during the Carlson tenure and high school aid was added during the administration of Gov. Fred Hall. While the state increased the amount of money it returned to school districts, districts were being reduced in number through reorganization.

Following a rip-roaring political campaign in 1964, which was won by Governor Avery, a former congressman, the School Foundation Finance program was enacted. It greatly increased the state's contribution to school districts and was designed to reduce property taxes for school purposes. The act was effective in most areas — but not all.

In the same 1965 session, the Legislature established a junior college system. It outlined procedures for starting junior colleges and provided state aid for their financial support. Since adjournment of the Legislature, activity in that area has heightened measurably. Supervision of the system rests with the state superintendent of public instruction.

Through all the years, Kansas legislators, speaking for their constituents, have supported education at all levels. Never have state colleges and universities been neglected. Each has been adequately financed and each has shown great growth. A special tax levy insures continued building construction programs at the state schools.

Find something conservative in that!

In Kansas, welfare programs have been supported by sufficient federal, state and county funds. This includes participation in early enactments by Congress as well as later ones such as the Kerr-Mills Bill and Medicare. The state legally concerns itself with many special education problems of both retarded and brilliant children.

This is hardly conservatism.

Although Kansas has clung stoutly to the tenets of the Republican party, it refuses to be taken for granted. When Republicans fail to satisfy the electorate, it rebels. Consider the take-over by the Populists in 1893 after a near tax revolt. Of course, there was the Bull Moose revolt in 1912 when Kansas Republicans strayed from Taft to the ebullient Teddy Roosevelt. Taft won, but Kansans went down swinging. The voters also swatted the Ku Klux Klan in the early 1920's. So ringing was its failure at the polls, its strength declined steadily. Today, the Klan is virtually non-existent in Kansas.

A hotbed of John Birch Society members in Wichita has produced more heat than light in the wake of the massive defeat of Sen. Barry Goldwater for the presidency. Kansans were so against the conservative type his campaign appeared to be, they favored the election of President Lyndon B. Johnson. That they were selective in their choice is shown by election of a solid slate of Republican state officials and congressmen.

No true conservative would call that conservatism.

Still, Kansas and Kansans worry. The conservative tag has clung over the years despite evidence to the contrary. It stems from a false premise at the start.

The Sunflower State began its existence as an agricultural entity. Eli Thayer founded the Emigrant Aid Company in Massachusetts in 1854 to promote free-state migration to the Kansas Territory.

With the free-staters, a religious and industrious people, came the state's first lawmakers. It was not unnatural then that booze and gambling should be considered sinful and something to be banned by statute.

The subsequent years of publicity, mostly during the "Roaring 20's," gave the state an unjust reputation of ultra-conservatism. The period of transition gave the state's critics food for thought. They complained bitterly — and effectively. But Kansas grew despite them.

The truth is, Kansans did what they pleased, adopted those programs they considered good and rejected those that had been tried and found wanting. They also dared to blaze their own legislative trails. History supports this.

Where, oh where, did the conservative label originate?

THE KANSAS HISTORICAL
SOCIETY: *preserver of the state's heritage*

Kansans have been making history for more than a century, and for almost as long have been systematically preserving it through the medium of the Kansas State Historical Society in Topeka.

The Society as it exists today was organized and incorporated in 1875, the result of a resolution adopted that year at the annual meeting of the Kansas Editors' and Publishers' Association. The resolution noted that earlier efforts to establish a historical society had failed and declared that such an organization was "imperatively demanded" if the records of 21 years of eventful history were to be preserved. A five-member committee was appointed to organize a society and to ask the legislature for an appropriation of "not less than $1,000, annually."

This resolution was introduced by Daniel Webster Wilder, a Harvard graduate, lawyer, newspaper editor, the compiler of Wilder's *Annals of Kansas,* and at the time auditor of state. The five members of the committee were Floyd P. Baker, Daniel R. Anthony, John A. Martin, Sol Miller and George A. Crawford, all prominent Kansas newspapermen. The first president of the Society, after its incorporation, was Samuel A. Kingman, chief justice of the state supreme court.

Franklin G. Adams became the first permanent secretary in January, 1876. Adams was a newspaperman, too, and a man who loved Kansas and its history. He devoted the rest of his life to the Society, serving as secretary until his death in 1899. In the early years his only assistant was his daughter, Zu, and since the only income was from membership fees, two dollars annually or $20 for life, the two-member staff was at first unsalaried except for a small remuneration paid from this source. The Society's first headquarters was in the statehouse, in a corner of the auditor's office, where Mr. Wilder also made available a bookcase to house the embryonic collections. These consisted chiefly of books from the library of Chief Justice Kingman but soon were increased by newspaper files donated by most of the state's publishers. This practice has continued ever since, and is the source of the Society's great collection of Kansas newspapers.

About six months after Mr. Adams took office he was given his own quarters, a newly constructed room under the stairway to the senate gallery. The first state appropriation, $3,000, was made in 1877. Two years later the legislature designated the Society the official trustee of the state, prescribed its duties, and granted an appropriation of $2,500 with the provision that half be used for salaries. Mr. Adams and Zu thus became official state employees.

Until 1914 the Society was housed in various rooms, corridors and vaults of the state capitol. In that year the Memorial Building was completed, at Tenth and Jackson streets, as a home for the Society and a memorial to the Grand Army of the Republic, which also was to have its headquarters in the building. Construction was authorized by the 1909 legislature and payment was made largely with funds appropriated by Congress to reimburse the state for Civil War claims. Records in the Society's collections were the basis of proof of these claims, and as a later secretary remarked: "The state could at least furnish the Society with as much room as it needed in order to care for these same records."

In 1914, at the time of the removal across the street to the Memorial Building, the Society's collections had grown to about 43,000 books, 44,500 volumes of newspapers and magazines, 150,000 pamphlets, 150,000 archival records (items ranging in size from single pieces of paper to large bound volumes), 44,600 manuscripts, 9,100 pictures and photographs, and 7,600 maps, atlases and charts. There was a staff of eight and the operating budget for the fiscal year ending June 30, 1915, was just under $12,000.

In the half century that has followed, the Society has grown and developed, not spectacularly but solidly. Its general purposes and responsibilities, as defined in the act of 1879, have been enlarged, but the basic emphasis remains on the collecting, arranging, cataloging and making available for public use the materials illustrating the history of the Kansas area. Today the collections include approximately 111,000 volumes of books, clippings and periodicals; 74,000 bound volumes of newspapers; 160,000 pamphlets; 6,100 atlases and maps; 5,700 cubic feet of archival and manuscript materials; 13,500 reels of microfilm; and 46,000 photographs. Inconsistencies between these figures and those of 1914 are the result of combinations, discarding, and new methods of measurement.

To perform its duties and render the services necessary, the Society is organized in several major divisions. The library is a reference and research department specializing in Kansas, Western and Indian history, and in genealogy. In these fields it is one of the finest libraries in the Middle West. The newspaper section cares for the vast collection of newspapers, including some 12,000 bound volumes of out-of-state papers dating from the late 1700's to

Historical society archeological field party at work.

Official state archives are housed in state historical society building.

256

the present. Almost every Kansas publisher sends in his current issues and these are bound and preserved. The archives and manuscript division is in charge of all non-printed records, public and private, including personal letters, diaries, and church and business records that relate to Kansas history. This division also includes the maps, atlases and photographs. The museum's function is self-evident. Archeology is a separate department which works principally in the field of prehistory. The Society also has a staff photographer and a complete photographic laboratory for processing and printing, and a microfilm camera on which not only newspapers but library and archival materials are filmed.

The staff has increased to 50 full-time and a varying number of part-time and seasonal employees, while the annual budget is approximately half a million dollars — a substantial figure but still small (about one-tenth of one per cent) in comparison to the total state budget. The Society administers 11 historic sites in addition to its headquarters operation in Topeka, publishes *The Kansas Historical Quarterly* and a bimonthly news bulletin which are sent to all members, and is increasingly involved with local historical societies, museums and other local groups as the services of its staff are requested.

In 1965 nearly 15,000 people made personal use of the Society's research facilities, plus additional thousands whose inquiries were served by mail and telephone. The most popular department, of course, is the museum in the Memorial Building, whose modern, well-organized exhibit areas were visited by nearly 80,000 people. If recent trends continue, these figures will grow by eight to 10 per cent a year, though lack of adequate parking facilities are a handicap.

Since 1905 the Society has been the official archival agency of Kansas. State agencies and departments have periodically turned over those records of historical or legal importance after they were no longer needed for current business. Kansas also has a records disposal law administered by a state records board. The secretary of the Society is a member of the board and the state archivist, who is a member of the Society's staff, is its secretary. In this way the interests of history are safeguarded adequately and with a minimum of red tape.

An important archival series held by the Society is the federal and state census records. These are original manuscript volumes of the federal census taken in 1855, 1860 and 1870 and the state census taken in 1865 and every 10 years thereafter through 1925. For the past 20 years these records have been in constant daily use, since certified copies from them are valid documentary proof of age for people needing delayed birth certificates, or to qualify for Social Security and other retirement plans. Copies have also been in great demand by genealogists. A few years ago the Society was providing about 18,000 such certified copies annually, without cost, a service possibly unique in this country. When it became necessary to charge a one dollar fee, however, the number of applications dropped off sharply, though the rush to qualify for Medicare, in late 1965 and early 1966, sent requests soaring again.

About six years ago the Society moved to fill a major gap in its areas of activity. Archeology had been a neglected field, untilled for half a century except by amateurs and out-of-state investigators. With the aid of National Park Service contracts for work in federal reservoir areas, an archeological program was begun. Each year since it has expanded until the staff now includes two professional archeologists, with a third on temporary duty, with all the tools and equipment necessary for their work. An archeological publications series is underway and appraisal reports and full-scale technical studies are issued at intervals.

In its capacity as trustee for the state, the Society administers 11 state-owned historic sites. These are the Shawnee Methodist Mission, in Fairway, a suburb of Kansas City; Kaw Methodist Mission at Council Grove; the Iowa, Sac and Fox Presbyterian Mission near Highland; First Territorial Capitol on the Fort Riley military reservation; the Funston Memorial Home north of Iola; Frontier Historical Park at Hays; Marais des Cygnes Massacre Park in Linn

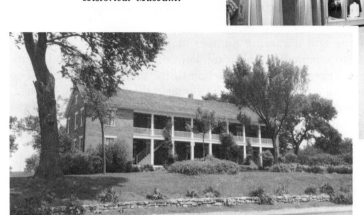

Military gallery in Kansas State Historical Museum.

North Building of Shawnee Methodist Mission in Johnson County. Built in the 1840's, it is operated as a museum by the state historical museum.

County; Hollenberg Pony Express Station near Hanover; the John Brown Museum at Osawatomie; the Pawnee Indian Village site in Republic County; and Pawnee Rock Park at Pawnee Rock. Museums, open to the public without charge, are located at all except the last two, and plans are being developed for a complete archeological museum at the Pawnee village site dealing with Indians.

As time and funds permit, the Society publishes books on various aspects of Kansas history. In 1954 and 1956 a two-volume *Annals of Kansas, 1886-1925*, was published. This was a continuation of Wilder's famous *Annals*. Compilation and editing took about eight years. In 1961, as part of the state's centennial observance, three staff members prepared *Kansas, A Pictorial History*, a book of more than 300 pages and 800 illustrations. Other volumes have included *Kansas Post Offices, Kansas in Maps*, and *Kansas in Newspapers*, which were published with financial assistance from Robert Baughman and the Baughman Foundation; and *Why the West Was Wild*, published in 1963. Copies of all except the last named are still available from the Society.

For 25 years the Society has been a partner in a historical marking program, co-operating with the State Highway Commission to bring "history in a nutshell" to the motoring public. The Society determines the historical authenticity of the subject and prepares the marker text; the Commission obtains the sign and erects and maintains it in a roadside park or other suitable area adjacent to the highway. About 90 state historical markers are now in place, and this number will gradually increase for some time to come. Kansas is rich in history, and these capsule stories make some of it available to the thousands of motorists who travel Kansas highways.

The Historical Society exists to serve the public. Its collections are available to everyone, though much of the material must be used in the Memorial Building since it could not be replaced if lost or damaged. The Society welcomes the support of all who are interested in Kansas history and invites them to become members. Dues are nominal: $5 annually or $50 for life membership, in return for which members receive *The Kansas Historical Quarterly* and the bimonthly news bulletin, *The Mirror*, plus the satisfaction of knowing that they are helping to preserve Kansas history.

View of Beech Aircraft Corp. Plant 1 in Wichita.

KANSAS INDUSTRY IN REVIEW

by Jack Lacy

For more than three decades a monumental struggle has been taking place within the borders of Kansas.

The outcome of the struggle will shape the destiny of a state and mould a pattern for the future of a new generation of Kansans. The antagonists of this battle are the people of Kansas. Their enemy is an unseen force that can best be described as the opposite of prosperous existence.

The battle was joined after the turmoil of depression and drought of the 1930's. The silent challenge of economic decay, apathy and poverty was staring Kansas in the face.

The challenge was answered and is still being answered. During 1965, there were 148 new industries located in Kansas, 20 more than in the previous year. Names like Ford Motors, Westinghouse Electric Corporation, Certainteed and scores of other large corporations are taking advantage of the Kansas market and central location as a distribution center to the midwest.

The future of industry in Kansas has taken a new turn during the last three decades with noticeable changes occurring during the past three years. The Kansas people have indicated their willingness to take on a program of development and have asked their legislators to provide the tools. Kansas is competitive with any state in the union in attracting industry at the present time, and more work is being done everyday to keep this movement underway.

Perhaps the development movement started when the bit of enterprise was committed on Kansas soil, but the organized movement in Kansas today was started about 1934 in a meeting of Kansas State Chamber of Commerce secretaries. Howard VanAuken, then secretary of the Wichita Chamber of Commerce developed a panel discussion on "What can we do in an organized way to promote industrial development in Kansas."

Prior to this, several prominent Kansans had given serious thought to an organized effort along these lines in view of the changing times. Even at this early date, a noticeable change was taking place on the predominately rural scene in the state. Farms were getting larger, technology and modern farm machinery were eliminating numerous farm jobs and former rural citizens were moving out of state to more urbanized industrial areas where work was available.

The problems were two-fold. Small towns, dependent on the farm trade, found their customers going to the city. Empty homes and stores left a heavier tax burden on those who remained. Meanwhile, the metropolitan areas were gaining an unprecedented population increase causing housing, service and employment problems.

Actually, these problems were not as acute as the drought and depression in the 30's, but noticeable trends were set and the more aware citizens of the state could see a bleak future for the state if immediate steps were not taken.

After VanAuken's panel discussion in 1934, the State Chamber of Commerce named a special industrial committee composed of Kansas Chamber of Commerce secretaries. The chairman was George B. Weeks, secretary of the Pittsburg Chamber of Commerce. As the program developed, scores of Kansas leaders representing every phase of community life and activity were consulted. Investigations were made into every conceivable economic and social condition resulting in volumes of material.

These early, far-sighted leaders, after digesting reams of information came to the conclusion that Kansas industry needed a shot in the arm to boost the number of job opportunities. They also decided that the state had the resources to do the job if there was a way to develop and popularize them.

The general opinion of these leaders was that new thinking was needed to change the retail-agriculture duet into a trio of retail-agriculture and manufacturing.

The State Chamber Committee set about forming an educational program that featured a speakers bureau, publicity and demonstrations, and included two tours of eastern industrial communities in 1937 and 1938 which included stops at St. Louis, Indianapolis, Cincinnati, Akron, Dayton, Wheeling, Pittsburgh, Wilmington, Washington, Charleston, Buffalo, Cleve-

Kansas City Power & Light Co.,
Paola.

W. W. Manufacturing Co., Inc.,
Dodge City.

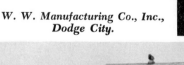

land, Detroit, Battle Creek, Kalamazoo and Chicago, by 125 businessmen.

The program was so successful that in 1938, later elected governor Payne Ratner, called a state-wide conference at Parsons for the drafting of a legislative program to officially put Kansas into the industrial development business.

The program was later adopted by the Kansas legislature with an almost unanimous vote. Actually, the law setting up the Kansas Industrial Development Commission was a rather revolutionary piece of legislation and considering the fact that it was the first time any such legislation was introduced, it could be said that the State Chamber of Commerce program was quite successful.

The idea of state supported industrial development was comparatively new even in older, more industrialized states and no state in the mid-western area had ever undertaken such a program. It was the first of many progressive moves the Kansas legislature would make toward the economic development of the state.

The original appropriation was for $125,000. The 1941 legislature increased the yearly appropriation of $60,000 to $70,000, and the 1943 legislature added $90,000 a year for scientific research.

Rolla Clymer, veteran El Dorado publisher, who was appointed as the first director of the new commission, recalls the first purchase he made upon arrival in his new cubbyhole office in the State Capitol Building in Topeka was a fly-swatter.

The first job of the new commission is contained in the following resolution:

> "That the Commission staff proceed to assemble and to index properly for convenient use the known information gathered by various research bureaus of this state as to its raw material resources and the possible uses that can be made of them."

This information proved invaluable in the wartime production that followed almost immediately, the formation and organization of the new commission. During the Second World War, the world got a glimpse of the potential of Kansas when the state convinced federal authorities that Kansas was more than a mere food producer. During the war, Kansas supplied: a full quota of men and women to the armed forces; an unprecedented amount of food; and suddenly became one of the nation's more important war production centers. The record shows that Kansas produced $2,599,597,000 of aircraft; $174,020,000 of ordnance; $36,543,000 of ships and $128,333,000 of miscellaneous items for the war effort.

While the state was producing the more than three and a third billion dollars worth of war materials, Kansas farms produced two and a half billion dollars worth of farm products.

History has proven that the early efforts of aware citizens who recognized an industrial lag in Kansas were correct in their summaries of Kansas potential. It was also probably due to these efforts that Kansas was able to shift into a new entity as an industrial state in such a short time. The change from predominately rural-agricultural life to complete industrialization was nothing short of amazing.

The demand for war ships, military aircraft and guns ended abruptly in 1945, but much thought had already been given to post-war industrial changes.

The Industrial Mill Levy legislation, which enabled communities in Kansas to provide tax money for industrial promotion was a reality and several communities were already using it when the war ended.

After the post-war slump, employment immediately started rising and has continued at a steady pace since that time. Much credit should be given the aircraft industry greats such as Walter Beech, Clyde Cessna and Lloyd Stearman for Kansas' ability to produce during the war years. Beech Aircraft, Cessna Aircraft and Boeing Aircraft, founded by Stearman, were going concerns when the war started. Mostly through their efforts, Kansas was able to produce an eighth of all military aircraft for the United States during the war.

Production at Beech and Cessna was again turned toward the production of private business aircraft after the war with a minimum of defense work, while Boeing continued as a source of new military aircraft production and maintenance to the present day. Wichita has become the center of the world's private aircraft production due to Beech Aircraft and Cessna and the latest addition of Lear Jet.

The war effort also provided the impetus in technology that was to rock the world after 1945 and the end of the war. The trend toward more modern farming speeded up. Agriculture gained in production, but the number of people employed on farms steadily decreased.

The importance of the industrial payroll was more and more apparent. Figures from the U. S. Department of Commerce show a rise in industrial income in Kansas from $71,000,000 in 1940, to $668,000,000 in 1957. By 1959, Kansas had 270 of the major industrial categories found in the United States, and 69 of the 500 largest industrial plants in the United States had one or more plants in Kansas.

In the meantime, more communities began using the tools provided by the legislature. The following is a list of cities using the Industrial Mill Levy in 1965.

	City First Class	Mill Levy		City	Mill Levy		City	Mill Levy
1	Coffeyville	.855	16	Council Grove	.473	32	Marysville	.87
2	Fort Scott	.500	17	Ellis	.40	33	McPherson	.96
3	Junction City	1.00	18	Emporia	.483	34	Neodesha	.943
4	Parsons	.947	19	Eureka	.50	35	Norton	.50
5	Pittsburg	.505	20	Florence	.47	36	Osawatomie	.95
	Second Class		21	Galena	.96	37	Osborne	.93
6	Abilene	.75	22	Girard	.455	38	Oswego	1.00
7	Anthony	.83	23	Great Bend	.477	39	Paola	.80
8	Baxter Springs	.94	24	Harper	1.00	40	Sabetha	.76
9	Burlington	.98	25	Hiawatha	1.00		**Third Class**	
10	Chanute	.96	26	Hillsboro	1.00	41	Baldwin City	.835
11	Cherryvale	.93	27	Independence	.94	42	Blue Rapids	.37
12	Chetopa	.475	28	Iola	.47	43	Downs	.50
13	Clay Center	.50	29	Larned	1.00	44	Moran	1.00
14	Columbus	.47	30	Lyons	.48	45	Smith Center	.41
15	Concordia	.369	31	Marion	.52	46	WaKeeney	.50

In 1961, the state legislature gave the people of Kansas another tool for industrial development — the industrial revenue bond. Senate Bill 298 was later validated by the State Supreme Court, and in 1963, Senate Bill 42 was passed specifying that property acquired and constructed by the issuance of these bonds were free from ad valorem taxation for 10 years.

The revenue bond act provides that any city shall have the authority to issue bonds to purchase, construct, reconstruct, equip, maintain or repair facilities; to acquire sites; to enlarge and remodel such facilities and to equip them for agricultural, commercial, industrial, natural resources and recreational development and to lease the facilities to firms or corporations.

Also, any city may issue the bonds without regard to the amount. Retirement of the bonds comes only from rents and revenues from the facility.

Since the conception of revenue bonds in Kansas, 34 cities have issued 54 bonds for industrial expansion capital expenditures of $34,738,000. Cities using revenue bonds include Lenexa, Belleville, Downs, Topeka, Chetopa, Emporia, McPherson, Fort Scott, Oxford, Oswego, Olathe, Elwood, Kansas City, Haysville, Clearwater, Council Grove, Newton, Pleasanton, Halstead, Hesston, Hutchinson, Independence, Wichita, Osborne, Coffeyville, Great Bend, Lyndon, Paola, Pittsburg, Girard, Leavenworth, Osage City, Parsons and Shawnee. Revenue bonds have been used to finance everything from the manufacture of jet planes to a nursing home. While revenue bonds and other means of financing have provided a wealth of capital for Kansas expansion, a noticeable slack was felt in certain areas of financing industry in Kansas. To fill this need, a movement started in 1964 to fill this gap.

The solution, in the form of a new organization in Kansas called the Kansas Development Credit Corporation, was chartered in June of 1965 and became operative in September 1965. Don C. Steffes, former McPherson Chamber of Commerce manager, assumed the position of executive vice-president of the corporation in December of 1965.

Purpose of the new corporation is to assist in meeting the long-term financial needs of industry as a means of creating needed new jobs for Kansans. The corporation will supplement existing sources of credit and add to the efforts of community and area groups in promoting more business and industrial activity toward an expanding Kansas community. The initial goal of the corporation is the sale of $500,000 in common stock at par value $5.00 per share, which will be the basis of a loan pool in a 10 to 1 ration from the banks of Kansas through their membership pledges of 3 per cent of capital and surplus for a loan pool of about $5 million. It is hoped that the Development Credit Corporation will complete the supply of necessary financial tools for development in Kansas. The workers to use the tools, in addition to the Kansas Department of Economic Development, are found in dozens of different Kansas communities in local Chamber of Commerce offices and in special organizations designed to represent the community in the acquisition and encouragement of new industry.

The following is a list of local industrial development corporations in Kansas:

Abilene Industrial Corporation	Abilene	Iola Ind., Inc.	Iola
Arkansas City Industries, Inc.	Arkansas City	Independence Industries, Inc.	Independence
Anthony Ind. Dev. Corporation	Anthony	Junction City Ind. Dev., Inc.	Junction City
Atchison Industry, Inc.	Atchison	Kingman Ind. Dev. Corp.	Kingman
Augusta Industries, Inc.	Augusta	Kismet Dev. Corp.	Kismet
Baxter Springs Ind. Dev.	Baxter Springs	Larned Community Dev. Corp.	Larned
Belleville Ind. Dev., Inc.	Belleville	Lawrence Ind. Dev. Corp., Inc.	Lawrence
Beloit Ind. Dev. Corp., Inc.	Beloit	Leavenworth New Industries, Inc.	Leavenworth
Blue Rapids Dev. Corp.	Blue Rapids	Liberal Zomto, Inc.	Liberal
Caney Industries, Inc.	Caney	Rice County Dev. Corp.	Lyons
Canton Ind. Dev. Corp.	Canton	Manfax, Inc.	Manhattan
Chanute Dev. Corp.	Chanute	Marysville Ind. Dev. Corp.	Marysville
Cherryvale Industries, Inc.	Cherryvale	McPherson Ind. Dev. Corp., Inc.	McPherson
Clay Center Ind. Dev. Corp., Inc.	Clay Center	Medicine Lodge Stockade, Inc.	Medicine Lodge
Coffeyville Industries, Inc.	Coffeyville	Industrial Dev. Corp.	Minneapolis
Colby Dev., Inc.	Colby	Morganville Dev. Corp.	Morganville
Columbus Ind. Dev. Corp.	Columbus	Moundridge Ind. Dev.	Moundridge
Concordia Dev. Corp.	Concordia	Neodesha Industries, Inc.	Neodesha
Greater Morris County Dev. Corp.	Council Grove	Newton Ind. Foundation, Inc.	Newton
Dodge City Ind. Dev. Corp.	Dodge City	Norton Dev. Corp., Inc.	Norton
Downs Enterprises, Inc.	Downs	Onaga Dev. Corp., Inc.	Onaga
El Dorado Dev. Corp., Inc.	El Dorado	Osage Industries, Inc.	Osage City
Emporia Enterprises, Inc.	Emporia	Osawatomie Dev., Inc.	Osawatomie
Enterprise Dev. Corp., Inc.	Enterprise	Oswego Industries, Inc.	Oswego
Eureka Ind. Dev. Corp.	Eureka	Ottawa Ind. Dev., Inc.	Ottawa
Fort Scott Industries	Fort Scott	Paola Industries, Inc.	Paola
Fredonia Development Corp., Inc.	Fredonia	Parsons Industries, Inc.	Parsons
Galena Ind. Dev. Corp.	Galena	Phillipsburg Dev., Inc.	Phillipsburg
Development, Inc.	Garden City	Pittsburg Ind. Dev. Corp.	Pittsburg
Garnett Ind. Dev. Corp., Inc.	Garnett	Plainville Dev. Corp.	Plainville
Goodland Development Corp.	Goodland	Pratt Ind. Dev., Inc.	Pratt
Great Bend Ind. Dev., Inc.	Great Bend	Russell Ind., Inc.	Russell
Halstead Ind. Foundation, Inc.	Halstead	Sabetha Ind. Dev. Corp.	Sabetha
Hanover Ind. Dev. Corp.	Hanover	Salina, Inc.	Salina
Hays Industries	Hays	Satanta Dev. Corp.	Satanta
Herington Ind. Corp.	Herington	Seneca Ind. Dev. Corp.	Seneca
Hiawatha Industries	Hiawatha	Tonganoxie Dev., Inc.	Tonganoxie
Doniphan County Ind. Corp.	Highland	Industrial Foundation, Inc.	Topeka
Hoisington Developments, Inc.	Hoisington	Wamego Ind. Dev. Corp.	Wamego
Holton Dev. Corp.	Holton	Wellington Ind. Dev. Corp.	Wellington
Hope Community Dev. Corp.	Hope	Wichita Area Dev. Corp.	Wichita
Hugoton Dev. Corp.	Hugoton	North Wichita Ind. Ass'n.	Wichita
Hutchinson Ind. Dev. Corp., Inc.	Hutchinson	Winfield Dev., Inc.	Winfield

One of Cessna Aircraft Company's newer buildings. This structure, built in 1963, is located at the company's large Wallace Plant complex in west Wichita.

MODERN KANSAS

The events leading up to the change in perspective in Kansas during the 1930's and the developments since then were the prelude to recognition of Kansas as a major factor in the economics of the United States.

Sweeping changes were made in 1963 when the legislature revamped the development program in Kansas with the emerging Kansas Department of Economic Development under the leadership of Commission Chairmen, William Muchnic, Robert Harkins and the present chairman, Mark Robeson, and the directorship of Jack Lacy, the scope of operations on the state level have broadened.

Probably the most important factor of the new department is the added emphasis on planning. On February 11, 1965, the Kansas Economic Development Commission approved a prospectus for state development and planning and programming for Kansas calling for a 38-month effort, broken into three phases. The prospectus recommends the preparation of a long range, integrated economic development plan for the state and the regions of the state.

A total budget of $723,000 for the project was suggested, with one-third of the required funds to come from staff contributions from various planning and development agencies of the state, and two-thirds of the funds to be provided by the Housing and Home Finance Agency of the Federal Government with a cash grant under the provision of Section 701 of the Federal Housing Act.

Work is being done by the staff of the Kansas Water Resources Board, the State's Forestry, Fish and Game Commission, the State Board of Health, the State Park and Resources Authority, the Kansas Geological Survey, the Kansas State Highway Commission, Board of Agriculture and several other departments and agencies. Personnel at the State's universities will also be involved.

The program includes Water Policy Studies, an Outdoor Recreation Plan, Economic and Population studies and studies of urban development in the state. Needs for an integrated education policy for the state, the social resources of the state, (employment-labor-welfare relationships) and long run agricultural policy, and opportunities and problems will also be delineated and studied.

Regional economic development programs will be prepared, with an initial pilot project to concentrate in a six-county area reaching from Topeka to Salina.

The planning program will also provide information on a community level that has never before been available and will also provide a means to keep this information up to date. Past experience has taught state leaders that changes in technology can change the whole pattern of state development. History is filled with examples of this type of change. The beauty of the new state planning program is that the continuing sources of information being fed into the plan allow for possible changes in the plan itself to meet the changing patterns of economic life.

The plan provides for action in the present to prevent chaos in the future. Added to the action program provided by the state wide planning is the work still being done toward the acquisition and encouragement of industry within the state.

Constant contact is maintained with dozens of large corporations located in other parts of the United States who might be planning an expansion into the Midwest. Regular advertisements are placed in numerous national magazines and direct mail contacts are made at regular intervals. When the industrial division of the department obtains a lead, a stepped up mail program is initiated. If the contact shows further interest, a personal contact is made by a representative of the department.

If enough interest in shown, the prospect is invited to tour areas of the state in which he has expressed interest.

Meanwhile, an in-state program of business appreciation is carried on at all times. Such programs as the annual Inventors Congress, held for the first time in 1965, are organized to provide an outlet for new thought and productive minds. Inventors are invited to show their wares to manufacturers and businessmen who might be interested in producing some of the new ideas.

The Kansas Department of Economic Development acts as coordinator for these programs along with coordination of advertising, publishing of literature about the state, such as the KANSAS! Magazine and the KDED Monthly Report, brochures, movies and slide presentations on all phases of the Kansas economy. The department's Commerce Division also acts as a clearing house for industrial and economic data collected through dozens of various sources. Probably one of the most important aspects of the department as a whole is the responsibility for keeping the development spark alive and moving within the state.

The results of these programs and the years of work are beginning to tell. In 1958, there were 114 new industries started in Kansas and 38 expansions. In 1964 there were 128 new industries and 106 plant expansions.

The record shows 148 new industries and 90 expansions during 1965 with a total new employment of 1,900; capital expenditure of $18,226,100 for the expansions and $27,692,200 for the new industry.

Of the 1965 new plants, 118 were started by Kansans. These plants accounted for 881 of the

Fiberglas plant in Kansas City, Kansas.

new employees. These new plants include four with more than 100 employees and 16 with employment between 25 and 99.

The really big story and the result of the concentrated push begin to show in the projections for 1966. Twenty-eight new plants announced plans for building completion for 1966, including a giant plant for Westinghouse at Salina which will employ 500.

The estimated capital expenditure for 1966 plants is already $43,040,000. The estimated employment from these new plants is 3,714 with a payroll of about $22,694,000. A new warehousing operation of the Ford Motor Company under construction at Lenexa will provide employment for 100 more people.

Beech Aircraft and Cessna Aircraft, together producing 50 per cent of the nation's business and light commercial aircraft, both reported record years in fiscal 1964 and again in the first half of 1965. Transportation equipment exports have placed Kansas high on the list of midwestern export states along with food products. The opening of the trade zone in Kansas City, Kansas, is expected to add to the export totals in Kansas in the very near future.

Kansas leaders are striking out in several directions in a concentrated effort to up the export totals from Kansas. Almost 100 business leaders accompanied Kansas Governor William H. Avery to Mexico City on a trade mission during the fall of 1965. Further trade missions are expected to follow during the next few years.

The attitude of progress has taken a foothold in Kansas. Other innovations for the state in recent years are the office of Economic Analysis and the Kansas Research Foundation, headed by Dr. Christopher Barthel. New concepts in technical training are being applied in a new system of Vocational Training Schools located all over the state, to provide the skilled labor for the manufacturing industry.

Most important of all, is the fact that most of the state's two million population is aware of the need of a concentrated effort for development. Old ideas are being carefully examined and new concepts are being considered. The immense changes that started three decades ago are becoming a part of the daily life. Projects such as the sprawling reservoir system in Kansas are needed and accepted to protect against serious growing pains.

The full potential of Kansas as an economic entity within the United States is probably not even close to being reached. Constant technological breakthrough in agriculture and manufacturing step up the production of the state constantly, and unemployment has generally been at a minimum.

This is the modern Kansas — still a peaceful place to live, but becoming steadily a more prosperous place to build a home.

MR. KANSAS

Harry Darby

To present a composite description of a typical Kansas businessman would be dull. To pick one who typifies businessmen of Kansas would be difficult. So many would qualify.

A poll in this regard would bring a great number of votes for Harry Darby, Kansas City, Kans., industrialist who still lives and works in the city of his birth. His industrial, farming and financial interests stretch from Kansas City to Coffeyville. No worthwhile community effort escapes his support.

Darby, at age 31, was president of the Kansas City Chamber of Commerce. He borrowed from local banks funds to buy from his father's estate a business in which he had grown up. He weathered depressions and competition, absorbed less fortunate firms into his own, expanded them and made them succeed. He served in government and politics by appointment, but always returned to his first love — making things out of steel, such as bombs and boats during the war, mammoth pressure vessels, towers and railway cars.

He was named Kansan of the Year in 1962 at the annual banquet of Native Sons and Daughters of Kansas. He was honored as Kansan of the Year in 1965 by the Kansas Society of Washington, D. C.

With Missouri Boiler Works Company, he rose from helper to mechanic, boilermaker and structural iron worker at 16 years of age. He was gang foreman until 1915, shop superintendent two years and vice president until 1919. Early in the 1920's, he purchased the company. Later, he purchased the Kaw Steel Construction Company and organized The Darby Corporation, of which he was president until 1945 when he became chairman of the board. He also is chairman of the board and founder of Leavenworth Steel, Inc., Leavenworth, and The Darby Railway Cars, Inc., of Kansas City, Kans.

He is a director of the Chicago, Rock Island and Pacific Railroad Company, Commercial National Bank, Gas Service Company, Kansas City Stockyards Company, Preferred Fire Insurance Company of Topeka, Mississippi Valley Association of St. Louis, University of Kansas Research Foundation, Wyandotte Hotel, Inc., Kansas Heart Association, Inc., and Starlight Theatre Association of Kansas City, Inc.

He was United States Senator from Kansas in 1949-50, was a delegate to the Republican National Conventions from 1940 through 1960.

From 1933 to 1937, he was chairman of the Kansas State Highway Commission. He was vice president 15 years, president 12 years and currently is chairman of the Board of Governors of the American Royal Live Stock and Horse Show. He is a trustee of the National Cowboy Hall of Fame, member of the executive committee of the Agricultural Hall of Fame and served as co-chairman of the Governor's National Committee for the Eisenhower Presidential Library at Abilene. He is chairman of the Eisenhower Presidential Library Commission and vice president and trustee of The Eisenhower Foundation at Abilene. He was chairman of the national fund-raising drive for the Eisenhower Presidential Library. The campaign for $2.5 million was successfully completed and the library was constructed at Abilene. All of these and many, many more are his contributions to Kansas and these United States.

1940's and early 1950's placed unprecedented burdens on the elementary and secondary schools of the state. New buildings had to be constructed. Instructional methods and curricular content had to be brought into line with the advances of modern education.

In addition to the specific problems of the various local institutions, the role of the different levels of government in supporting elementary and secondary education needed re-examination. Given the cost of a modern educational system, it became apparent that less and less reliance could be placed on the traditional mainstay of school finance, that is, the property tax. Furthermore, the varied distribution of the ability to support education throughout the state had to be examined. The accident of birthplace could not be used to justify unequal educational opportunities.

With these problems in mind, I recommended to the 1965 Kansas Legislature a comprehensive School Foundation Program. With the enactment of this program, and its formula for participation by the state in financing Kansas' schools, we have seen a reduction in the reliance on the property tax. The program also is based on an aid formula which encourages improved standards of instruction and equalization of educational opportunities throughout the state. By passing the Foundation Act and setting up, in effect, a progressive system of state support for elementary and secondary education, Kansas has been able, at this level, to meet the challenge posed by the post-war birth rate. This, in turn, has led to a shift in our attention to areas of higher education.

At the peak of the educational hierarchy, in a sense, stand the six degree granting state colleges and universities. Kansas has not been able to ride out the pressures for increased higher educational effort as have some eastern states. Although there are many private colleges of which Kansas can be proud, we have no long standing structure of private higher education comparable to that of many Atlantic seaboard states. But neither has Kansas been able to use the presence of several private higher educational institutions as an excuse for shirking its own obligation in this area.

Clearly the challenge for the future in Kansas rests in the area of higher education. At the time of this writing, the six state degree granting institutions were growing at a rate of over twelve per cent a year, and these six schools represent only part of the picture.

Kansas has also guaranteed itself a place in the forefront of community higher education. State assistance to community junior colleges throughout Kansas has been expanding commensurate with the enrollment in these schools. New vocational-technical schools are being established regularly to serve the high school and post-high school needs of those not desiring or needing to attend a degree granting college or university.

In summary, education continues to be the major obligation of state and local government in Kansas. This is an economic necessity in modern America.

But in Kansas, education is for "living," not just for "making a living." Given the thrust of contemporary society, education must be designed to serve the entire spectrum of one's life experiences, not merely as a tool for acquiring a paycheck. This, then, raises the second area in which Kansas has responded to the challenge of modern America.

Development of Human Resources

Although the phrase "human resources" is somewhat vague, it does capture the impact of this particular segment of state governmental activities. I am including here some aspects of education, recreation, and cultural arts; certain facets of conservation, and care for the disadvantaged. Many of these items are discussed at great length with considerable historical perspective elsewhere in this volume. Therefore, I shall concentrate more on specific state activities in the mid-1960's.

One area in which Kansas has long held a position of leadership is in her care for the mentally ill. By means of cooperation with the staff of the world famous Menninger Clinic, located in Topeka, and a high degree of sensitivity of governmental officials, Kansas has been able to benefit from the latest knowledge of psychiatric and rehabilitative techniques.

An example of this progressive approach has been the move toward creation of comprehensive local mental health clinics. A further example is a recent act requiring tests for PKT (phenylketomuria), a disease which has been found to be a major cause of retardation.

The psychological problems of a modern society, however, should not be met solely in a specific or remedial manner, or only in the extreme cases warranting actual medical care. Kansas is recognizing and planning ahead to alleviate some of the sources of individual problems that characterize much of the country today.

The chronic claustrophobia, for example, that often goes undetected in urban areas must be guarded against. As a larger and larger proportion of our citizens are compressed in relatively smaller areas, opportunities for diversion and relaxation must be afforded. For most people, this means a chance to get out of doors, away from cars and concrete, people and pressure.

To the person not familiar with the patterns of population movement in Kansas, this concern for breathing space may seem a bit premature. After all, is not Kansas the gateway to the Great Plains? Is it not blessed with vast acres of open land? Indeed it is! Yet these facts have not blinded policy makers to the changes taking place within the state. Between 1950 and 1960, the proportion of the Kansas population residing in urban areas increased from 52.1 to 61.0 per cent. Add to this the absolute growth in population, the mobility of the citizenry, the rising standard of living, and the increase in leisure time. The need for a significant investment in recreational facilities is clear.

In recognition of this trend, Kansas has been attentive to the needs for areas in the out of doors where her citizens can obtain a welcome and refreshing change from the pattern of daily activity. The state expenditure for outdoor recreation between 1951 and 1960 was $15.9 million. When added to cooperative programs between the state and the federal government, the outlay for outdoor recreation in that period comes up to $26.5 million.

A variety of agencies have cooperated to advance outdoor recreation in Kansas — the State Forestry, Fish and Game Commission; the State Park and Resources Authority; the State Historical Society; and the Kansas State Highway Commission. The total private and public recreational resources of the state are more than 700,000 acres. Of these, 18,000 acres are in 15 state parks.

And, by way of planning intelligently for future needs, in 1965 the Kansas Joint Council on Recreation was formed. This group has drawn up a comprehensive outdoor recreation plan. The plan will be maintained to keep up with anticipated needs and to form the basis for further state and federal cooperation in this area.

Closely associated with the continued and growing state encouragement of education at all levels have been other efforts to bring opportunities for intellectual enrichment to all the people throughout the state. Two recent actions in this regard are worthy of mention. In 1965 a new system of regional libraries went into effect. This program is designed to take full advantage of today's communications efficiency and to get broader use of available library facilities. It also aims at expanding the holdings of the various libraries of the state and seeks to improve the services available in every community.

The second step taken in 1965 for the overall enrichment of intellectual opportunities was the creation of the Kansas Cultural Arts Commission. Composed of twelve eminent leaders in a number of fields, this Commission is designated as the official agency of the state for

continued on page 271

BIG MEN FROM SMALL TOWNS RUN KANSAS

by John R. Peach

Kansas is one of the larger of the United States, with 105 counties and approximately 300 incorporated cities, ranging in population from 100 to nearly 300,000. Most of our representatives and 40 senators in the Legislature come from cities under 10,000.

Believers in the one-man, one-vote theory, of course, say this is bad because the big population centers do not have proper representation, as each county is given by our State Constitution one member of the House of Representatives and 20 others are divided among counties with larger cities.

There are many arguments presented for both sides. Some have to do with the quality of the members. Some uninformed people consider rural area legislators "hicks from the sticks." They say these do not conform to modern thinking, are too conservative, don't know what's going on in the world, pass legislation to benefit rural areas to the detriment of cities. In other words they are not as well qualified to run the state as their city brothers.

Our governors, historically, are from smaller towns. Some have been farmers, most were lawyers, with a sprinkling of bankers, newspaper men and business men to round out the list.

Topeka has had only one, Governor Capper, who went there from Garnett and entered the newspaper and farm publication fields. Henry Allen, another newspaper man, came from Wichita but originally was a western Kansas farm boy. Ed Arn was a big-city Governor. He was raised in Kansas City, moved to Topeka where he became active in politics. He was elected attorney general and later appointed to the Supreme Court. Then he was elected Governor and claimed Wichita, where he now lives, as his home.

But it is the Legislators who make the laws and represent the people. Governors have a program, but it is Legislators — living in their communities the year around — who know what the people are talking about and pretty much know what the people want.

Legislators from big cities usually represent a geographic area of the city, predominate with minorities or special interest. At the same time rural area Legislators represent not only farmers, but people from cities in their counties — white, Negro, rich, poor, bankers, businessmen. In fact, they represent larger interests of the state rather than groups or minorities.

They usually are pretty big frogs in a little pond. City members more likely are little frogs in a big pond. Seldom will a large city banker or big business man run for public office. Some lawyers do, as a stepping stone to something bigger. But they don't stay in office long.

Officers and leaders of the House and Senate in most every case are from small towns. They wear better, not only with their home folks, but also with other Legislators. Paul Wunsch of Kinsley was called the ruler of the Senate for many years. But, he had ability to bring factions together into compromise. Much of the progressive legislation the past 20 years was under his leadership. None seriously challenged him. No Governor overrode his leadership on legislative matters. Wunsch worked with Governors and fellow Legislators. They respected and trusted him. Other strong men have provided leadership in both houses. But, in every case, they have been from small towns.

Why have small towns developed such leaders? They have more leadership opportunities because there are fewer in their communities to take over responsibilities. They start out in leadership in school affairs, business and civic clubs, farm organizations, directorships in banks and business. If they tend to the business at hand, do their homework in studying problems, soon they become responsible in the community and are looked up to for even more responsible leadership. They are encouraged to seek election.

Not only do we find these small-town men holding high government offices, but the same also applies to the Kansas Bankers Association, State Chamber of Commerce, education groups and other statewide organizations. They travel more than city folks, not only over the United States, but also abroad. They are great readers of current events in the best newspapers and magazines, both general and trade. In my experience, the average citizen from a small town is much better informed than the average citizen from a big city, clear to New York. A small-town citizen must be right more often because his actions are more critically evaluated.

Most Kansas people believe in the big-men-from-small-towns theory, for this leadership continues and is rewarded.

KANSAS STATE GOVERNMENT
continued from page 269

the development and coordination of the cultural arts. It is given authority to support and aid in the development of various programs of significance. It also coordinates programs between different governmental units and private organizations for the advancement of the cultural arts throughout Kansas.

Conclusion

Many of the things I have discussed in this brief essay are still in their beginning stages. Others are continuing, changing programs. But it should be borne in mind that the title of the essay is "Kansas State Government in Modern America." The implication of this is that Kansas is prepared to move in a position of leadership and strength with the rest of the nation. This calls for foresight. What I have presented here is not so much history as it is prediction of things to come.

I should also emphasize that I have not attempted to construct a complete documentation of all I feel reflects Kansas state government's concern for the future. Rather I have chosen a few typical examples. When viewed in conjunction with the total array of state activities and plans, the result is a solid note of optimism mixed with a large element of pride.

To ignore a problem is to compound that problem. But to ignore achievement is to dilute good judgment. Optimism and realism are synonymous in Kansas today.

MAJESTY OF THE HILLS

by R. A. Clymer

The Flint Hills stand off there along the horizon, in serried ranks stretching from the Kaw to Oklahoma fastnesses, brooding over what mysteries no man knows. They guard their secrets jealously. But every year, in their quiet way, they turn out a vast product to sate the world's hunger.

The Flint Hills comprise a factory of sorts — yet one eternally fascinating and unique. They operate no machines, the workadays' whistle's blast never sounds over their far-flung reaches, no smoke clouds befog their serene skies. Yet their output is tremendous and of supreme utility. The Hills represent an unexampled institution in Kansas cosmos — and their story never grows old.

Once a visitor arrives in the Flint Hills, he passes into substantially a different world from the one he left with its hurly-burly and carking cares. In the bluestem pastures, there is always abiding peace and calm and compelling beauty at every season of the year. June, with its gorgeous greens, brings out the peak points of their charm — while their lure is ever present and their soothing benediction ever ready for those who are spiritually attuned to accept it.

Even in February or March, when the prairie grass is sere and brown and no stir of life appears as far as the eye can see over shimmering expanses, a dip into deep canyons between the chains of hills will reveal unsuspected activity. For in these hidden valleys hundreds of docile beasts are winter feeding, springs are busily creating rippling rills, and birds and small furry creatures are going soberly about their manifold business. On stilly nights the shrill, quavering voice of the coyote — individualist supreme — sounds over snow-covered wastes.

At that season, comes the period of quiet before the earth bursts into a renewal of its age-old functions. Within brief days the sweet-scented bluestem — best pasturage for beef cattle to be found upon the continent — will be peering through the soil along with myriad prairie flowers of brightly twinkling hues. And then, in the midst of the Month of Many Rains, the Big Beef Steer — monarch and ruler of all he surveys — will dominate the scene until summer runs it course.

The Big Beef Steer is one overlord who clings steadfastly to his kingdom. The domains of royalty have been well shattered by the explosive events of recent years. Kings have fled from their empires or sit with shaky and anxious seats upon their tinselled thrones. But the Big Beef Steer persists in his sovereignty. His rule is wise and benevolent and attended only by the trappings of peace.

He comes from the southland when spring smiles in welcome; he moves with vast dignity and intent during the lush pasture glory of May and June and July. His realm is a surpassingly lovely creation of emerald-coated ranges, fading off into mystic, purplish haze shrouding the far distances. All therein is touched with stillness and tranquility. The World of wars and its "alarums," of human strife for place and prestige, seems far away. It is far away — as far almost as the stars — for in the dominion of the bluestem only one mighty objective rules — and that is the making of beef by which a waiting world may be nourished. This magic and silent process calls for no struggle, no outburst of violent effort — and the majestic quiet that hovers over the scene is broken only by the trill of the meadowlark or his various winged cousins.

The Flint Hills are changeless and unchanging — and have so stood since their limestone ridges first broke from beneath the surface of prehistoric seas. All modern development, the growing complexity of civilization's advance have surrounded and hemmed them in but have failed to alter their essential character. They vie not in grandeur with the mighty Rockies, nor do they aspire to eminence among the nation's fondly cherished landmarks. Yet they possess unique glory and appeal, which stems from their gentle and healing moods. For those who would flee "far from the madding crowd," they provide a sure retreat and sanctuary. For ones bowed by worldly discouragement and disillusion, they offer spiritual enchantment through eyes opened to their beauty and constancy.

Endlessly plying their wonder-working formula through the centuries, the Flint Hills serve as silent monitors of the credo that the race of men would be supremely blessed by gearing its manifold activities to their simplicity and unswerving purpose.

KANSAS' FAVORABLE BALANCE OF TRADE
by John R. Peach

Our federal government has been concerned for years with the international balance of trade, which finds gold leaving our country to make up our trade deficit.

The opposite is true in Kansas. Financial leaders of this state like to point out Kansas' favorable balance of trade, which each year finds total bank deposits, savings and loan associations and insurance company assets growing with surplus trade dollars. In 1965, these totals were 12 times as much as in 1940.

This has not always been so. Statistics show very slow economic growth prior to 1940. But the evolution of Kansas' economy since that year has been most interesting. And the factors responsible for this change have been many. Prior to 1940, the state depended mostly on agriculture. The farmer was not much better off than the share cropper who owed the company store about as much as he produced. Farmers harvested from July to October and took a depressed price because the year's production had to be absorbed by the market during the short harvest period.

Kansas banks strove to help the farmer hold back the flood of produce but bank reserves were too limited. The main thing that helped the farmer was federal legislation that stabilized market prices beyond the harvest period.

The first substantial crops after the "dirty thirties" came in 1941. Land prices, bank deposits and business in general climbed. Kansas industry began supplying more of the needs of farms, mills, mines and the expanding oil-gas industry. Some consumer goods were manufactured here.

The war clouds of Europe started a new boom for Kansas industry. American entry into the war set off unprecedented industrial growth. Aircraft production in Wichita by Beech, Cessna and Stearman corporations (Stearman later was purchased by Boeing) increased from hundreds to thousands of aircraft a year.

As prime contractors and subcontractors, Kansas factories, such as Coleman Company at Wichita, and many machine shops over the state began manufacturing thousands of items never produced before here. A dozen new chemical plants used raw material from the earth and air to produce such tongue twisters as perchloroethylene and tripolyphosphate, as well as helium, hydrogen and ammonia. Hundreds were employed and millions of dollars came to Kansas.

Great gas fields at Hugoton, Otis and McPherson soon were piping billions of cubic feet of gas to markets as far off as Michigan. Compressor stations and processing plants in Kansas extracted petro-chemicals from gas to supply other Kansas industries.

Milling companies began shipping scientifically-prepared feeds for fowls and livestock from coast-to-coast.

Cattlemen formerly raised and pastured cattle to be sent to other states for fattening and finishing. Today, great feedlots dot every corner of the state. Kansas packing plants process

Farm machinery from Hesston Manufacturing Company in Hesston moves on its way eventually to be transported to foreign markets.

cattle and hogs and ship the carcasses all over the nation. Other Kansas plants process all forms of table and prepared meats. Livestock formerly was shipped to big packing centers at Kansas City, Chicago and Omaha for processing.

Kansas' industrial "know how" and markets have brought into the state such industries as General Motors, DuPont, Westinghouse, General Electric, Owens-Corning and Goodyear, with the largest exclusive tire factory in the world turning out 30,000 tires a day.

Then there are Kansas names such as Coleman, McNally, Stein, Cross, Didde-Glaser, Balderson, Guston-Bacon, Darby, Reuter, Davis and Henry, shipping products to the four corners of the world. They bring back additional millions of dollars to Kansas. These firms are not found only in Wichita, Topeka and Kansas City. Towns like Cawker City and Lewis have their own home-grown industries whose products are in demand nationwide.

Numerous newspaper headlines tell of new plants, new ideas, new progress being made to give Kansas a better share of her own markets. One of the compelling reasons for industrial growth is that Kansas has 63,000 boys and girls in its 24 four-year colleges. Nearly 60 per cent of our high school graduates go on to college.

Also, junior colleges with vocational schools give special training and introduction into college close to home. If students want to continue, they can go on to our great universities and continue through graduate schools that give degrees in medicine, law, engineering, arts, humanities and sciences.

All of this means that Kansas is a balanced state. It is about as self-sufficient as a state can be. It could feed the world if all its acres and talents were put to full production. It can supply much in every field of manufacture from automobiles and airplanes to camp equipment and batteries.

It means that Kansans want a better place for their children to live and work. In 25 years, Kansas has grown from a "good state to be from" to a great state with power and glory and beauty in its hills, lakes and rivers, symphony orchestras and art galleries. It has beautiful girls like Deborah Bryant, Miss America 1965. It has rugged boys like Jim Ryun, the great young mile runner, learning the qualities of leadership and challenge that make them champions.

Kansas has a most favorable balance of trade. It has so much here that other people want. It has the abundance and talents to produce it. Its unemployed are not a problem, just a

A Speed-Klect collator is loaded for delivery in London, England, after being manufactured in Emporia, Kansas, at the Didde-Glaser plant.

President Lyndon Johnson presents special "E" award for excellence in exporting to Dwane L. Wallace, president of Cessna Aircraft Company of Wichita.

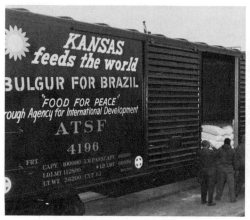

Carload of Kansas-produced bulgur presented to Brazil.

Coleman Company products are known throughout the world.

challenge. Its weaknesses are its strength. They make Kansans work harder to correct them. Their faith is in their heritage. Their motto is "to the stars through difficulties."

"The important thing to keep in mind is the new role Kansas is assuming.

"We're no longer just Midway America. We're now Midway World," said Jack Lacy, director of Kansas Department of Economic Development.

Kansas' new identity is the result of its extensive network of highway, railway, air and other transportation systems. This enables manufacturers to ship products easily to seaports and on to foreign markets. Kansas is going after the world market in an ambitious manner.

Kansas exported $117 million worth of manufactured goods and about $200 million in agricultural products in 1963. Kansas exported $61.3 million worth of food to lead the seven-state West North Central Region. Wheat and beef were the major food exports. Transportation equipment, mostly airplanes, totaled 68 per cent of Kansas' exports.

1965-1966 State Chamber President C. Y. (Kit) Thomas.

T. J. (Tom) Griffith, Chairman of the Board.

STATE CHAMBER

"The greatest single accomplishment of the State Chamber of Commerce is that it does speak up for Kansas business and industry at the state and national levels every time it is important and necessary for the 'Voice of Kansas Business' to be heard."

This statement was made by T. J. (Tom) Griffith of Manhattan as he completed his term as president of the Kansas Chamber during the 1964-65 fiscal year and became Chairman of the Board of Directors for 1965-66.

How, specifically, was this "speaking up" accomplished?

One method was in providing witnesses to present the business point of view at Kansas Legislature committee hearings. During the 1965 legislative session, State Chamber witnesses appeared at 22 hearings: four on the Assessment Ratio Study (HB 521), three on Workmen's Compensation (HB 581, 582 and SB 251), two on In-State Bidders' Preference (HB 831, 832), two on Unemployment Compensation (HB 1061), and others on Sunday Sales Legislation (SB 16), Right-to-Work Implementation (SB 30), Warehoused Goods Property Tax Exemption (HB 589), Kansas Citizens Council (HB 713), School Foundation Finance (SB 281), Air Conservation Bill (HB 734), Permissive County Manager Government (HB 718), State Division of Aeronautics (HB 699, 700), Toll Road Feasibility Study (SB 104), Financial Institutions Tax (SB 128), and Administrative Allowance for Collecting Sales Tax (SB 289).

In connection with the legislative sessions, 20 area "Decisions/65" Pre-Legislative conferences

Each "Eggs and Issues" breakfast meeting conducted in 1965 was well attended.

Typical view of conferences between potential buyers and sellers.

Over-flow crowd at conference listens intently to remarks by Fred Rausch, Topeka, State Workmen's Compensation Director.

were conducted by the State Chamber and co-sponsored by the local Chambers of Commerce in the 20 host cities. Main objectives were: (1) to explain some of the major state legislative issues expected to confront the 1965 Legislature; (2) to obtain, through pro and con discussion, local views on legislative issues; and (3) to stimulate greater interest and participation in governmental affairs by business people. The 1,873 Kansas citizens from 153 different communities (including 105 Kansas Legislators) who attended the 20 conferences represented a cross-section of the agricultural, business, industrial, professional, civic and governmental leadership in the state.

Also, relative to the Session, four lively "Eggs and Issues" Breakfast meetings were held in Topeka in early 1965. The purpose of these State Chamber-sponsored meetings was to present the pros and cons of important, selected issues being considered by the Legislature and then have an open-forum discussion with the speakers. Through this "Town Hall" method, a free exchange of viewpoints gave better understanding of the major topic under consideration.

Issues discussed were:

"Should the method of Selecting District Court Judges Be Changed?"
"Should the Sunday Sales Bill (SB 16) Be Enacted?"

"Should the Minimum Age for Obtaining Drivers' Licenses Be Increased as Proposed in Senate Bill 26?"

"Should the Legislature Submit for Popular Vote a Constitutional Amendment That Would Permit Liquor By the Drink?"

These breakfast meetings were well attended by legislators, business people, lobbyists, and the general public. Average number of legislators in attendance was more than 100.

What have been the big projects by the State Chamber recently?

One notable accomplishment was the formation of a Kansas Development Credit Corporation. It attempts to aid the statewide effort toward accelerating economic growth and providing more jobs for Kansans. The project was carried out as a joint venture by the State Chamber and the Kansas Bankers Association. The corporation is a privately financed organization. It pools loan funds for making long-term and capital loans to deserving businesses in "gray area" situations where regular bank credit is not available. Upon achieving the initial goal of the issuance of $500,000 in common stock, the corporation will provide a loan pool near $5 million. These loan funds will be available through the banks of Kansas that become members of the corporation by pledging 3 per cent of the capital and surplus on call. (See article on Kansas Banking)

The State Chamber also co-sponsored the Kansas Business Opportunities Unlimited Conference in Topeka. More than 200 representatives of Kansas manufacturers, suppliers and service industries attended. They had the opportunity to develop first-hand knowledge on how to obtain profitable government contract business. Representatives of many prime contractors and government agencies having major procurement functions were present to tell, in detail, how to secure government work. They conducted across-the-table discussions regarding individual firm capabilities and government needs.

A comprehensive statewide Workmen's Compensation Conference was co-sponsored by the State Chamber, the Wichita Chamber and seven statewide associations. Held in Wichita, it brought together more than 400 top management men, attorneys, governmental officials, industrial physicians, industrial relations and personnel executives, insurance men, and safety engineers, representing over 50 cities from all areas of Kansas. It sought to (1) give broader employer understanding of the objectives, employer liabilities, and costs of the Kansas workmen's compensation program; (2) highlight current problems in the program; and (3) mobilize support for needed improvements.

The State Chamber continued its KABIE tours for Kansas teachers. A tour (Kansas Agriculture-Business-Industry-Education Tour) is a 2,000-mile statewide study trip for which the participants may receive college credit. To date more than 700 Kansas teachers have taken part in this event. Many have said that, as a result of these study tours, their classes are receiving more accurate and detailed information about the Kansas economy and the state's potential.

Also, the State Chamber co-sponsored the annual Master Farmer-Master Farm Homemaker Recognition Banquet; awarded a scholarship for the winner of a writing contest for high school students conducted by the Kansas Governor's Committee on Employment of the Physically Handicapped; honored members of the Kansas Congressional Delegation at a reception and dinner in Washington, D.C.; and hosted more than 400 business, industrial and professional leaders from all parts of the state at the Chamber's annual convention. A legislative roundup and economic development forum were popular sessions at the convention.

Why a State Chamber of Commerce, anyway?

To make Kansas a better place in which to live, learn, work, earn, play and do business.

GENERAL OFFICERS 1965-66

President

C. Y. (Kit) Thomas
Mission Hills

Chairman of the Board

T. J. (Tom) Griffith
Manhattan

Senior Vice President

Wesley Sowers
Wichita

Vice President, Finance

Carl K. Suderman
Newton

Treasurer

Harrison F. Johnson
Independence

PAST PRESIDENTS

Roy F. Bailey
Salina

Ross Beach
Hays

Maurice L. Breidenthal, Sr.
Kansas City

Ellis K. Cave
Dodge City

Robert A. Finney
Humboldt

John N. Landreth
Los Angeles

Frank L. Lombard
Enterprise

E. C. Mingenback
McPherson

J. Hardin Smith
St. Louis, Mo.

Fred W. Stein
Atchison

280

Carl K. Suderman
Newton

Cliff Titus
Wichita

M. W. Watson
Topeka

DISTRICT OFFICERS

District One

Ralph E. Bates
Kansas City

District Two

Thad M. Sandstrom
Topeka

District Three

H. Gordon Angwin
Pittsburg

District Four

John M. Peck
Concordia

District Five

Paul Kitch
Wichita

District Six

John F. Hayes
Hutchinson

District Eight

Kenneth J. Powell
Liberal

District Seven

Willis E. Stout
Goodland

DIRECTORS COMPLETING TERM IN 1965

Ray A. Acker
Topeka

H. Gordon Angwin
Pittsburg

Ralph E. Bates
Kansas City

W. I. Boone
Eureka

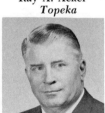

Earl C. Brookover
Garden City

Ray E. Dillon, Jr.
Hutchinson

Ned Fleming
Topeka

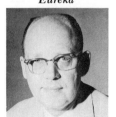

Henry B. Jameson
Abilene

281

Paul Kitch
Wichita

M. W. Kraemer
Hays

Leslie Matthews
Newton

Thomas P. Murphy
Kansas City

John M. Peck
Concordia

Harlan Potter
Kansas City

Kenneth J. Powell
Liberal

Fred Rice
Salina

Neill Richards
Wichita

Thad M. Sandstrom
Topeka

Willis E. Stout
Goodland

Bill Tucker
Elkhart

John W. Warren, Jr.,
M.D., *Wichita*

Walter H. Wulf
Humboldt

HOLD-OVER DIRECTORS

J. H. Abrahams
Topeka

Frank A. Boettger
Wichita

M. L. Breidenthal, Jr.
Kansas City

C. C. Brewer
Manhattan

282

William Bruckner
Emporia

A. Dwight Button
Wichita

William A. Dearth
Parsons

John F. Hayes
Hutchinson

Paul Hill
Lyons

Bill House
Cedar Vale

W. W. Keith
Winfield

G. H. Lavely
Topeka

W. E. Lehmberg
McPherson

G. W. Marble
Fort Scott

H. W. Reece
Scandia

Carl V. Rice
Kansas City

Robert E. Schmidt
Hays

Henry Schulteis, Jr.
Topeka

Albert J. Schwartz
Salina

O. B. States
Dodge City

C. H. Thomas
Leawood

Dan J. Dreiling
Seneca

Jack Elliott
Leavenworth

Don A. Farmer
Pratt

283

R. B. Harkins
Liberal

Milton A. Nitsch
Oberlin

Robert D. Payne
Lawrence

Robert L. Price
Coffeyville

Paul Radke
Liberal

Nestor R. Weigand
Wichita

Dr. W. Clarke Wescoe
Lawrence

Roger Williams
Russell

Walter G. Wilson
Newton

Lyle E. Yost
Hesston

Although early Chambers in the United States were designed almost exclusively as trade bodies and functioned in that respect for nearly 100 years, they now have broadened their scope to work for general community development along commercial, industrial and civic lines. Here in Kansas, the State Chamber serves as coordinator of the Chamber team at the state level. The 230 Local Chambers in Kansas form the team base to mobilize forces to help put unity in each individual Kansas community.

How is the State Chamber organized for action?

Through 14 councils (large committees) and a number of supporting departments. The task of each council is to carry on a study program and to initiate, formulate and recommend to the Board of Directors policies on which to base a program of action. Each council concentrates on issues relating to its own particular field of interest. Each consists of from about 40 to more than 100 active, participating members from all parts of the state — with a total representation of well over 1,000 Kansans. Final authority in determining policies for the State Chamber rests with the Board of Directors. It is composed of 85 members who come from every section of the state and represent every important segment of the state's business economy.

What has each council done recently?

AGRICULTURAL RELATIONS COUNCIL — Recognizing the need for good working relationships between farm and urban enterprise, this 93-member council: sought ways to cement the bond between farmers and other businessmen in efforts to maintain free enterprise and a strong economy; continued to support the Master Farmer-Master Farm Homemaker program;

cooperated in efforts to develop broader agricultural research programs, to find new uses and markets for Kansas' agricultural products, and to improve soil and water conservation practices.

CHAMBER EXECUTIVES ADVISORY COUNCIL — Continuing in an advisory capacity to the Board of Directors on ways and means of better coordinating and strengthening Chamber programs, this 67-member council: cooperated in Pre-Legislative conferences; urged business people to take more active interest in political affairs; encouraged local Chambers to disseminate important information of legislative issues; stimulated grass-roots legislative action in support of proposals to improve state's business climate.

EDUCATION COUNCIL — Recognizing the mutual interests of business and education, this 90-member council: worked with other groups in developing a sound school foundation finance proposal for submission to the Legislature and supported enactment of the finance plan; supported continuation of school district unification in Kansas; continued to encourage more and better economic education at all levels; gave support to the state's new vocational-technical training program; provided a forum for discussion of problems in diverse areas such as the teaching of English in Kansas schools and providing facilities for dental education.

TRANSPORTATION AND COMMUNICATION COUNCIL — Working to unite diverse interests in the transportation and communication fields, this 37-member council: brought leaders of various segments of the transportation industry together to seek solutions to current problems; successfully sought designation of the Kansas Department of Economic Development as the official state aviation agency for promotional, educational, and advisory purposes; studied problem of freight rates as applied to current problems of the milling industry and other industries; and sought solutions to problems caused by freight rate differentials.

HIGHWAY DEVELOPMENT COUNCIL — Recognizing that better roads mean better business, this 121-member council: worked to bring highways, roads and streets up to satisfactory standards for safety and use; worked for adequate financing system of taxes and fees paid by highway users; strongly supported continuing programs of highway safety.

INDUSTRIAL AND DEVELOPMENT RESEARCH COUNCIL — Emphasizing need for maximum use of Kansas' total resources in creating new jobs, new markets and increased production, this 156-member council: promoted the organization of the privately financed Kansas Development Credit Corporation; continued to promote industrial research facilities and projects to stimulate expansion of present industries and attraction of new ones; urged Kansas communities to analyze their own industrial potential and make necessary adjustments, and encouraged top-level state officials to participate actively in economic development efforts.

ECONOMIC SECURITY COUNCIL — Voicing the views of Kansas business on social benefit programs affecting employer costs and individual economic security, this 67-member council: conducted and published survey on how various states handle certain troublesome case problems in workmen's compensation; co-sponsored conference on workmen's compensation; prepared and vigorously supported state legislation to clarify employer liabilities and eliminate abuses under the present workmen's compensation system, together with amendments to tighten benefit payments and to stabilize the fund for payment of unemployment compensation; cooperated with groups dealing with social security issues at the federal level.

KANSAS RETAIL COUNCIL — This 117-member council: served as a vehicle through which Kansas retailers and retail trade associations worked together; served as spokesman for Kansas retailers on state and national issues affecting retailers; issued informational and action bulletins; supported legislation which was enacted to strengthen Kansas Trading Stamp Act; supported proposed legislation which, if enacted, would have authorized an "administrative allowance" to retailers for collecting sales tax for the State of Kansas, and restricted Sunday sale of merchandise which does not need to be purchased on Sunday; joined forces with other groups in efforts to improve free enterprise system and the state's economic climate.

GENERAL ADMINISTRATION

C. C. (Bud) Kilker
*Executive Vice President and
General Manager*

Carl C. Nordstrom
*Assistant General Manager
Research Director, Corp. Secretary*

Clinton C. Acheson

Clara Miller

Charles R. Roter

Ken Dodderidge

Dorothy Rake

Noble W. Drake

Raymond Riley

Norlan Foster

George Weeks

Roy H. Johnson

James Winn

Thomas E. Slattery

LABOR-MANAGEMENT RELATIONS COUNCIL — Striving for a labor-management relations climate that will stimulate economic growth, the 56-member council: published an 18-page booklet, "What To Do When Labor Problems Confront You," as ready reference for employers in labor-relations matters; supported retention and implementation of right-to-work provision of the Kansas Constitution; studied and testified on various labor-management issues pending before Kansas Legislature and U. S. Congress; prepared and disseminated reports to businessmen on major labor relations issues and developments.

POLITICAL PARTICIPATION COUNCIL — Recognizing critical need for making the "Voice of Kansas Business" more articulate in the political arena, this 91-member, bi-partisan council: stressed need for vigorous political participation by individual business people through the political party of their choice; sought more effective means of encouraging all business people to express their views directly to their elected public officials on crucial issues at all levels of government; expanded efforts to influence more able, business-oriented people to run for public office; issued periodic bulletins to disseminate important bi-partisan political information to the business community.

TAXATION AND FINANCE COUNCIL — FEDERAL — This 41-member council: continued to follow developments at federal level and express the viewpoint of Kansas business; stressed need for a balanced federal budget and an end to deficit financing; emphasized importance of a tax system more conducive to individual incentive and economic growth.

TAXATION AND FINANCE COUNCIL — STATE — This 90-member council: supported programs for achieving greater equality in the assessment of property for taxation; helped develop proposals for improving annual real estate assessment ratio study; worked for a new foundation finance plan for schools, including a control to insure property tax relief; stressed need for a vehicle for continuing study of state and local fiscal policy and governmental organization and operations toward boosting efficiency and cutting costs.

TOURIST AND RECREATION PROMOTION COUNCIL — Maintaining active support of programs to stimulate greater tourist travel and recreation in Kansas, this 93-member council: cooperated in launching and promoting "Play-A-Day Midway U.S.A." tourist and travel promotion program; helped to get Fort Larned established as a national historical site; encouraged programs to develop more state pride among Kansans; worked to achieve better coordination of tourist and travel promotion efforts of various groups; encouraged development of more recreational areas and facilities and other tourist attractions.

WATER RESOURCES COUNCIL — This 71-member council: supported proposed state water plan for long-range development and control of Kansas' water resources, as initiated by the Kansas Water Resources Board; formulated recommendations with respect to Kansas projects and studies submitted to Congress; held a special conference, with Resources Board, in attempt to reconcile differences of position with regard to selected water projects.

Here is the list of members of the Board of Directors for 1965-66, their home towns and business affiliations. Heading up the Board are the general officers: president, C. Y. (Kit) Thomas, Mission Hills, The Pittsburg and Midway Coal Mining Co.; chairman of the board, T. J. (Tom) Griffith, Manhattan, Griffith Lumber Co., Inc.; senior vice president, Wesley Sowers, Wichita, Racon Inc.; vice president of finance, Carl K. Suderman, Newton, Suderman Co., Inc.; treasurer, Harrison F. Johnson, Independence, Union Gas System, Inc.

Board members serving as district vice presidents are: District One, Dan J. Dreiling, Seneca, Citizens State Bank; District Two, J. H. Abrahams, Topeka, Security Benefit Life Insurance Co.; District Three, G. W. Marble, Fort Scott, The Fort Scott Tribune; District Four, H. W. Reece, Scandia, Reece Construction Co., Inc.; District Five, Walter G. Wilson, Newton, Wilson Drug Store; District Six, Paul Hill, Lyons, Lyons Savings & Loan Assoc.; District Seven, Robert E. Schmidt, Hays, KAYS, Inc.; District Eight, Paul Radke, Liberal, Radke, L. Light Lumber Co.

The general officers and district officers form the Executive Committee of the Board.

Past presidents are active members of the Board of Directors and ex-officio members of the Executive

Committee. They are: Roy F. Bailey, Salina, Bailey-Krehbiel Newspaper Agency; Ross Beach, Hays, Kansas Natural Gas, Inc.; Ellis K. Cave, Dodge City, The Dodge City Terminal Elevator Co.; Robert A. Finney, Wichita, Farm & Ranch Life Insurance Co.; John N. Landreth, Los Angeles, Calif., Coast Lines, Atchison, Topeka and Santa Fe Railway Co.; Frank L. Lombard, Enterprise; E. C. Mingenback, McPherson, The Farmers Alliance Mutual Casualty Co.; J. Hardin Smith, St. Louis, Mo., Southwestern Bell Telephone Co.; Fred W. Stein, Atchison, Stein Laboratories; Cliff Titus, Wichita, Beech Aircraft Corp.; M. W. Watson, Topeka, M. W. Watson, Inc.

Other board members: Ray A. Acker, Topeka, Southwestern Bell Telephone Co.; Frank A. Boettger, Wichita, Cessna Aircraft Co.; M. L. Breidenthal, Jr., Kansas City, Security National Bank; C. C. Brewer, Manhattan, Brewer Motor Co.; William Bruckner, Emporia, Bruckner's; A. Dwight Button, Wichita, The Fourth National Bank & Trust Co.; F. B. Conrad, Topeka, Goodyear Tire & Rubber Co.; Cloud L. Cray, Sr., Atchison, Midwest Solvents Co., Inc.; William A. Dearth, Parsons, Bill Dearth Insurance, Inc.; Leslie F. Eaton, M.D., Salina, Mowery Clinic; Jack Elliott, Leavenworth, Bell Laundry, Inc.; Gordon W. Evans, Wichita, Kansas Gas & Electric Co.; Don A. Farmer, Pratt, Jetts Department Store; R. J. Fegan, Junction City, Junction City Telephone Co.; John F. Hayes, Hutchinson, Gilliland, Hayes, Miller & Goering; Carl Hemstreet, Emporia, Kansas Chamber of Commerce Executives; A. T. Heywood, Kingman, C. R. Calvert Co.; Fred C. Hiller, Humboldt, Monarch Cement Co.; Prof. Leland Hobson, Manhattan, Kansas State University; Bill House, Cedar Vale, House Hereford Ranch; J. E. Isaacs, Wichita, Beech Aircraft Corp.; W. W. Keith, Winfield, Winfield Daily Courier; J. Lyle Kimsey, Manhattan, Kimsey's Shoes; Jack Lacy, Topeka, Kansas Department of Economic Development; G. H. Lavely, Topeka, E. I. du Pont de Nemours & Co., Inc.; W. E. Lehmberg, McPherson, The McPherson & Citizens State Bank: Robert S. Lemon, Kansas City, attorney; Marion P. Mathews, Winfield, Christenson, Mathews & Mathews; Leslie A. Matthews, Salina, Salina Chamber of Commerce; G. W. McCarty, Wichita, The Boeing Company; Dwight McCreight, Chanute, The Chanute Tribune; J. A. Mermis, Jr., Great Bend, Security State Bank; C. M. Miller, Colby, Farmers & Merchants State Bank; John D. Montgomery, Junction City, Junction City Daily Union;

Russell Mosser, Lawrence, Centron Corp., Inc., Iron Mueller, Bird City, Rancher; Thomas P. Murphy, Kansas City, General Motors Corp.; George E. Nettels, Jr., Girard, John J. Stark Contractor; Jack R. Nicholson, Ellis, Ellis State Bank; Milton A. Nitsch, Oberlin, Nitsch & Nitsch, Inc.; C. C. Otto, Fort Scott, The Western Insurance Companies; Robert D. Payne, Lawrence, Hallmark Cards, Inc.; Robert L. Price, Coffeyville, Oklahoma Tire & Supply Associate Store; Carl V. Rice, Kansas City, The Rodar Co., Inc.; Emil Salyer, Garden City, Wheat Lands Motel & Restaurant; R. G. Sanborn, Abilene, The A. L. Duckwall Stores Co.; Thad M. Sandstrom, Topeka, WIBW AM-FM-TV; Henry Schulteis, Jr., Topeka, The Atchison, Topeka & Santa Fe Railway Co.; Deryl Schuster, Wichita, Kansas Jaycees, Southwest National Bank; Albert J. Schwartz, Salina, The Lee Hardware Co.; O. B. States, Dodge City, Palace Drug Store, Inc.; Stanley H. Stauffer, Topeka, Topeka Capital-Journal; Clifford W. Stone, El Dorado, Walnut Valley State Bank; C. H. Thomas, Leawood, Standard Oil Division of American Oil Co.; Nestor R. Weigand, Wichita, J. P. Weigand & Sons; Dr. W. Clarke Wescoe, Lawrence, University of Kansas; Robert L. Williams, Wichita, Imperial Oil Co.; Roger Williams, Russell, R. C. Williams, Inc.; W. L. Worford, Wichita, Cessna Aircraft Co.; Lyle E. Yost, Hesston, Hesston Manufacturing Co., Inc.

INDEX TO MANUFACTURERS

Southern Kansas Produce Co., Inc., Box 323, Anthony: Poultry, eggs.
Stafford Poultry & Egg Co., 112 W. Stafford, Stafford: Poultry, eggs.
Swift & Co., 10 Berger, Kansas City: Poultry and eggs.
Swift & Co., 2000 Crawford, Parsons: Poultry.
Swift & Co., Fifth and Elm, Salina: Dressed poultry, turkeys, and shell eggs.
Thompson's Dressed Poultry, 1105 E. Lincoln, Iola: Dressed poultry.
Tindell's Hatchery, Burlingame: Eggs.
Tip Top Dairy Co., Hillsboro: Eggs.
Triplett Leghorn Hatchery, 1827 E. 21st, Topeka: Eggs.
Washington County Co-op. Creamery, Linn: Poultry, eggs.
Wheat Belt Buyers, Route 1, Garden City: Processing of jack rabbits for mink food.

Dairy Products

Creamery Butter

Ark Valley Co-op Dairy Assn., 911-923 S. M in, Hutchinson: Butter.
Arkansas City Co-op. Milk Assn., Inc., 615 W. Chestnut, Arkansas City: Butter.
Beatrice Foods Co., Box 622, Salina: Butter.
Beloit Dairy Products, 122 W. Second, Beloit: Butter.
Bennett Creamery Co., N. Walnut, Ottawa: Butter.
Chappell Creamery, 118 N. Fourth, Manhattan: Butter.
DeCoursey Cream Co., 1901 E. Douglas, Wichita: Butter.
Fairmont Foods Co., Norton: Butter.
Jo-Mar Dairies Co., 1300 E. Iron, Salina: Butter.
Meadow Gold Dairy Products, Great Bend: Butter.
Milk Producers Marketing Co., 3250 Fairfax Rd., Kansas City: Butter.
Nemaha Co-op. Creamery Assn., Seventh and Oregon, Sabetha: Butter.
Neosho Valley Co-op. Creamery, 403 S. Main, Erie: Butter.
Shawnee Creamery & Dairy, 1200 N. Kansas, Topeka: Butter.
Strahan Creamery Co., 108 N. Fifth, Salina: Butter.
Sunflower Co-op. Creamery Assn., Inc., Valley Falls: Butter.
Swift & Co., 10 Berger, Kansas City: Butter.
Swift & Co., Fifth and Elm, Salina: Butter.
Tip Top Dairy Co., Hillsboro: Butter.
Washington County Co-op. Creamery, Linn: Butter.

Natural Cheese

Anco Cheese Co., Inc., 59 and 31 Highway Jct., Garnett: Cheddar cheese.
Burlington Creamery, 509 Neosho, Burlington: Cheddar cheese.
Central Kansas Cheese Milk Co., Inc., 816 N. Pine, Hoisington: Barrel cheese.
DeCoursey Cream Co., Moline: Cheddar cheese.
Dwight-Alma Dairy Products, Inc. (Alma Div.), Alma: Cheese.
Dwight-Alma Dairy Products, Inc. (Dwight Div.), Dwight: Cheese.
Fairlane Cheese Co., 534 Holliday, Osage City: Cheddar cheese.
Gardiner Dairy & Ice Cream Co., 305 N. Eighth, Garden City: Cheese.
Kraft Foods Co., 907 Illinois, Oswego: Cheddar cheese.
Meadow Gold Dairy Products, Great Bend: Cheese.
Nemaha Co-op. Creamery Assn., Seventh and Oregon, Sabetha: Cheese.
Paola Butter Co., 24 E. Wea, Paola: Cheese.
The Southwest Milk Producers Assn., 722 S. Main, Pratt: American cheese.
Swift & Co., 10 Berger, Kansas City: Cheese.
Swift & Co., 2000 Crawford, Parsons: Cheese.
Tescott Cheese Co., Tescott: American, cheddar cheese.
United Dairies Products, Case St., Norton: Cheese.
Whiting Cheese Factory, Horton: Longhorn cheddar cheese.

Condensed and Evaporated Milk

Anco Cheese Co., Inc., 59 and 31 Highway Jct., Garnett: Dried whey.
Arkansas City Co-op. Milk Assn., Inc., 615 W. Chestnut, Arkansas City: Condensed milk, sterile canned milk, dry milk solids, ice cream mixes.
Beatrice Foods Co., 2012 Belmont, Parsons: Ice cream mix.
Bennett Creamery Co., N. Walnut, Ottawa: Condensed milk, ice cream mix, spray milk powder.
Bircher Dairy, Inc., Box 184, Ellsworth: Ice cream mix.
Carnation Co., 221 S. Ozark, Girard: Evaporated milk.
Central Processing Co., 609 W. Kansas, McPherson: Ice cream mix.
Fellers Dairy Co., 810 Fourth, Clay Center: Mixes.
Milk Producers Marketing Co., 3250 Fairfax Rd., Kansas City: Condensed and powdered milk.
Nemaha Co-op. Creamery Assn., Seventh and Oregon, Sabetha: Condensed and powdered milk.
Neosho Valley Co-op. Creamery, 403 S. Main, Erie: Condensed milk, dry milk solids.
The Page Milk Co., Coffeyville: Evaporated milk.
Pet Milk Co., Iola: Evaporated milk and ice cream mix.
Shawnee Creamery & Dairy, 1200 N. Kansas, Topeka: Ice cream mix.
Sunflower Co-op. Creamery Assn., Inc., Valley Falls: Powdered and condensed milk.
Tip Top Dairy Co., Hillsboro: Condensed milk and milk powder.

Canning and Preserving Fruits, Vegetables and Sea Foods

Canned Fruits, Vegetables, Preserves, Jams and Jellies

Heinemann Coffee & Supply, Inc., 1341 Sierra Dr., Wichita: Jellies.
Pioneer Foods, 2331 W. Maple, Wichita: James, preserves and jellies.
Stokely-Van Camp, Inc., Tenth and Maryland, Lawrence: Pork and beans, hominy and other dry pack items, fruit juice.
Western Food Products, 126 E. Second, Hutchinson: Jams, jellies, preserves, apple butter, tomato juice, green beans, wax beans.

Pickled Fruits and Vegetables; Vegetable Sauces and Seasonings; Salad Dressings

Heinemann Coffee & Supply, Inc., 1341 Sierra Dr., Wichita: Barbecue sauce.
Hickory Foods Co., 1716 Main, Winfield: Hickory sauce.
Lady Baltimore Foods, Inc., 35 Southwest Blvd., Kansas City: French dressing, barbecue sauce.
Phipps Products Co., 555 Industrial Blvd., Kansas City: Spaghetti and barbecue sauces.
Pickle King Food Products Co., 4220 W. 21st, Topeka: Pickles, salads, kraut.
Poulson's Copper Kettle Chili Co., 511½ S. Estelle, Wichita: Barbecue sauce, chili.
Taco Grande, Inc., 1057 N. Mosley, Wichita: Sauces.
Western Food Products, 126 E. Second, Hutchinson: Pickles, salad dressing, mustard, barbecue sauce, catsup.
Byron Willcuts Food Products, Inc., 608 N. Kansas (Box 478), Topeka: Horseradish products, relish-dip.

Frozen Fruits, Fruit Juices, Vegetables, and Specialties

Agricultural Building, Inc., 5620 Wolcott Dr., Bethel: Vegetable packing.
Gerald Blood Co., 6346 S. Broadway, Wichita: Frozen applesauce.
Boogaart Meat Products, Inc., Concordia: Frozen foods.
Everest Locker Plant, Everest: Frozen food.
Tom Foley, Wholesale Meats, 508 E. 21st, Wichita: Frozen foods (fruits, vegetables, juices, sea foods).
Jack's Locker Service, 124 S. Chisholm, Caldwell: Frozen foods.
Midwest Cold Storage & Ice Corp., 1101 S. Fifth, Kansas City: Refrigerated and frozen products.
Mini Max Provisions, Inc., Smith Center: Frozen foods.
Parsons Ice & Cold Storage, Parsons: Blast freezing of foods.

Southwest Bean & Elevator Co., 110 Railroad, Ulysses: Pinto bean, dried bean and white corn packaging.
Valley Growers Packing Co., Inc., Turner (Mailing add.: Box 267, Edwardsville): Vegetable packing.

Grain Mill Products

Flour and Other Grain Mill Products

Abilene Flour Mills, 211 N. E. Third, Abilene: Flour.
Barton County Flour Mills Co., 1812 16th, Great Bend: Flour.
Bay State Milling Co., 316 S. Fifth, Leavenworth: Flour.
Buhler Mills, Inc., Buhler: Flour, bran and shorts.
Claassen Flour Mills, 124 E. Sixth, Newton: Flour, bran and shorts.
Claflin Flour Mill, Claflin: Flour.
Consolidated Flour Mills Co., Box 605, Winfield: Flour.
Dixie Portland Flour Mills, Inc., Box 698, Arkansas City: Flour.
Flour Mills of America (Rosedale Mill), 914 Division, Rosedale Station, Kansas City: Flour.
General Mills, Inc., 430 E. 18th, Wichita: Flour.
Grain Products, Inc., E. Chestnut, Dodge City: Milo grits, germ, bran.
Hunter Milling Co., 801 South F, Wellington: Flour.
International Milling Co., 301 Main, Newton: Flour.
International Milling Co., 511 N. Santa Fe, Salina: Flour.
Ismert-Hincke Milling Co., 126 N. Jefferson, Topeka: Flour.
Kansas Milling Co., 715 E. 13th, Wichita: Flour, malted wheat and barley flour.
William Kelly Milling Co., 414 S. Main, Hutchinson: Flour.
Light Grain & Milling Co., Inc., 140 S. Kansas (Box 919), Liberal: Flour.
Moore-Lowrey Flour Mills, Inc., 1310 Maple, Coffeyville: Flour.
Moundridge Mill & Elevator Co., Moundridge: Flour.
New Era Milling Co., 309 W. Madison, Arkansas City: Flour.
Oxford Milling Co., Oxford: Flour.
The Pillsbury Co., 1149 Main, Atchison: Flour.
Rodney Milling Co., McPherson: Flour.
Rodney Milling Co., Norris and N. Quincy, Topeka: Flour.
Ross Industries, Inc., 300 E. Broadway, Newton: Flour and ground grains.
J. L. Saunders Milling Co., Main and Sixth, Council Grove: Flour and corn meal.
Seaboard Allied Milling Corp., Kingman (Mailing add.: 1550 W. 29th, K. C., Mo.): Flour.
Security Milling Co., Inc., 309 S. Elm, Abilene: Flour.
Stafford County Flour Mills Co., Hudson: Flour.
Wall-Rogalsky Milling Co., 400 Main, McPherson: Flour.
Wamego Milling Co., Wamego: Flour.
Weber Flour Mills Co., 348 N. Seventh (Box 58), Salina: Flour.
The Western Star Mill Co., 215 E. Iron, Salina: Flour.
Whitewater Flour Mills Co., Whitewater: Flour.
Wichita Flour Mills Co., 17th and Santa Fe, Wichita: Flour.
Willis Norton Co., 524 N. Kansas, Topeka: Flour.
Willis Norton Co., 701 E. 17th, Wichita: Flour.

Cereal Preparations

Farmers Co-op. Commission Co. (Bulgar Plant), 715 Wiley Bldg., Hutchinson: Bulgur.
Jones Milling & Mfg. Co., Ninth and Santa Fe, Wichita: Breakfast cereals.
Light Grain & Milling Co., Inc., 140 S. Kansas (Box 919), Liberal: Breakfast cereals.
Jack Stevens Grain Co., 231 S. Lorraine, Hutchinson: Debranned wheat.
Wall-Rogalsky Milling Co., 400 Main, McPherson: Breakfast cereals.

Blended and Prepared Flour

Blair Milling & Elevator Co., Inc., 1000 Main, Atchison: Pancake mixes.
Hol'n One Donut Co. of Ks., 1552 Pattie, Wichita (11): Doughnut mix.
Light Grain & Milling Co., Inc., 140 S. Kansas (Box 919), Liberal: Pancake, waffle, cornbread and muffin mixes.

Confectionery and Related Products

Baden's, 109½ W. Main, Independence: Cinnamon flavored toothpicks.
Bogdon's Candies, 6330 Goddard, Shawnee: Candies.
Cero's Provincial Candy Shoppe, 329 S. Minneapolis, Wichita: Homemade candy.
Dayton Candy Co., 3610 Rainbow, Kansas City: Kid-bits, licorice, stick candy.
Fife and Drum, 5231 E. Central, Wichita: Candy.
Henry & Son Candy Co., Box 294, Dexter: Candy and hand-dipped chocolates.
Hi Plains Bakery, 1118 Main, Goodland: Candy.
Larson Bros. Co., Inc., 226-228 N. James, Kansas City: Popped corn, plain, cheese, and caramel.
Lester's Sweet Shop, 210 W. Sixth, Concordia: Home-made candy.
Nifty Nut House, 603 Kansas, Topeka: Candy and nuts.
Nifty Nut House, 312 E. Murdock, Wichita: Salted nuts, peanuts in shells.
Victor Peck Candies, Emporia: Candy of all types.
Reklites Candy Kitchen, 1417 W. Sixth, Topeka: Candies and nuts.
Steve's Candy Shop, 5231 E. Central, Wichita: Chocolates.
Sunshine Biscuits, Inc., Seventh and Sunshine Rd., Kansas City: Candy.
Welton Candy Co., 5871 Merriam Dr., Merriam: Raw sugar candy.

Beverage Industries

Wines, Brandy, and Brandy Spirits

D. A. Winters Co., 207 Kansas, Topeka: Wines.

Distilled, Rectified, and Blended Liquors

Midwest Solvents Co., Inc., 1300 Main, Atchison: Grain alcohol, gin, vodka.

Flavoring Extracts and Flavoring Syrups, Not Elsewhere Classified

Heinemann Coffee & Supply, Inc., 1341 Sierra Dr., Wichita: Syrups (waffle and fountain).
Ideal Syrups, Inc., 608 Burton, Wichita: Flavored syrups for fountains, etc.
Melbert Citrus Products Co., 1401 Fairfax Trafficway, Kansas City: Beverage syrups and drink concentrates.
Nifty Nut House, 312 E. Murdock, Wichita: Syrup.
Pioneer Foods, 2331 W. Maple, Wichita: Syrup.
Richardson Corp., Bonner Springs: Soft drink syrups and ice cream toppings.

Miscellaneous Food Preparations and Kindred Products

Soybean Oil Mills

Archer-Daniels-Midland Co., Box 191, Fredonia: Soybean oil and meal.
Cargill, Inc., 1501 N. Mosley, Wichita: Soybean oil, meal and pellets.
Kansas Soya Products Co., Inc., Emporia: Crude soybean oil and soybean oil meal.
Producers Co-op. Assn., Buffalo St., Girard: Crude soybean oil and soybean oil meal.

Grease and Tallow

A. C. Hide, Iron & Metal Co., Route 1, Arkansas City: Tankage.
Acme Rendering Co., 18 Central, Kansas City: Inedible fats, tankage.
Arkansas City Rendering Co., Route 1, Arkansas City: Animal fats.

Ellis Rendering Co., Inc., Ellis: Meat scraps, animal fat.
Excel Packing Co., Inc., 900 E. 21st, Wichita: Meat scrap and tallow.
Hill Packing Co., 401 Harrison, Topeka: Grease.
Hull & Dillon Packing Co., W. Fourth, Pittsburg: Grease.
Kaw Valley Rendering Co., 28 N. Second, Kansas City: Tallow.
Midwest Rendering Co., 74 Ewing, Kansas City: Tallow.
Mid-West Rendering, Inc., Box 444, Belleville: Grease.
National By-Products, Inc., 2050 N. Mosley, Wichita: Tallow, grease, meat scraps.
Standard Rendering Co. (Div. Darling-Delaware Co., Inc.), 685 Adams, Kansas City: Grease, tallow and meat scraps.
Swift & Co., 10 Berger, Kansas City: Tallow and grease.

Animal and Marine Fats and Oils, Except Grease and Tallow

Swift & Co., 10 Berger, Kansas City: Industrial oil.

Shortening, Table Oils, Margarine and Other Edible Fats and Oils, Not Elsewhere Classified

Ark Valley Co-op. Dairy Assn., 911-923 S. Main, Hutchinson: Margarine.
Swift & Co., 10 Berger, Kansas City: Oleomargarine.

Macaroni, Spaghetti, Vermicelli, and Noodles

American Beauty Macaroni Co., 501 Funston Rd., Kansas City: Macaroni, spaghetti, egg noodles.
Topeka Pizza Co., 520 Branner, Topeka: Fresh frozen egg noodles.

Food Preparations, Not Elsewhere Classified

Arnholz Coffee & Supply Co., 920 E. First, Wichita: Coffee processing.
Aunt Anna's, Inc., 813 W. Douglas, Wichita: Natural food products (flour, cereals, breads, pastry and special foods).
Barkman Honey Co., Inc., Highway U. S. 56 E., Hillsboro: Honey.
Dick Brooks Honey, Route 4, Paola: Honey.
Cain's Coffee Co., 330 Commerce, Wichita: Coffee, instant coffee, tea, spices.
Cardel Tortilla Factory, 2112 E. Fourth, Hutchinson: Tortillas.
E. C. Conroy Coffee Co., 1529 Lake, Kansas City: Coffee and tea.
Davis Coffee House, 102 S. Main (Box 127), Lindsborg: Coffee.
Dixie Creme Donut Shop, 4220 W. 21st, Topeka: Potato salad, jello salads, pickles, kraut.
Emporia Wholesale Coffee Co., 302-08 Commercial, Emporia: Coffee roasting.
Frito-Lay, Inc., 713 E. Eighth (Box 857), Topeka: Potato chips, cheetos.
Gilk's Potato Chip Co., 213 W. Fifth, Holton: Potato chips (bar-b-que, onion-garlic flavored, and ripple chips).
Guy's Foods, Inc., 430 N. Mosley, Wichita: Potato chips and cheese stix.
Hales Potato Chip Co., 521 N. 13th, Salina: Potato chips.
Hawley Honey Co., 220 N. Elm, Iola: Honey.
Heinemann Coffee & Supply, Inc., 1341 Sierra Dr., Wichita: Coffee.
Henson Sorghum Mill, Chetopa: Sorghum molasses.
Hickory House, 1625 E. Central, Wichita: Potato salad, slaw, kraut, relishes, gelatin salads, crispy fry.
Hillsboro Refrigerated Lockers, 415 S. Ash, Hillsboro: Cracklins.
Jamestown Honey, Extracting Plant, Jamestown: Honey.
Kitty Clover Potato Chip Co., 2034 Northern, Wichita: Potato chips.
Klaasen Honey Farms, Whitewater: Honey.
Krispy Krunch Potato Chips, 1623 N. Smelter, Pittsburg: Potato chips.
Larson Bros. Co., Inc., 226-228 N. James, Kansas City: Fried bacon rind.
Lehman Orchard, E. 15th, Horton: Apple cider.
Midland Food Lab., Inc., 18th and Kansas, Kansas City: Bakery and ice cream supplies (ingredients), stabilizers and emulsifiers.
Midwest Popcorn Co., 25th and Parallel, Kansas City: Popcorn.
Mitchell's Honey, Altoona: Honey.
Safeway Stores, Inc. (Milk Dept.), 1243 Argentine (Box 461), Kansas City: Delicatessen products.

Salina Coffee House, Inc., 113-15 N. Seventh, Salina: Coffee.
Seibel Sausage House, Highway 50 and Walnut, Peabody: Cracklins.
Southwest Bean & Elevator Co., 110 Railroad, Ulysses: Packaged popcorn.
Sta-Krisp Potato Chip Co., 307 S. Hydraulic, Wichita: Potato chips.
Stewart In-Fra-Red Commissary of Wichita, Inc., 2812 E. English, Wichita: Sandwiches.
Superior Wholesale Meat Co., 2150 E. Douglas, Wichita: Chili.
Taco Grande, Inc., 1057 N. Mosley, Wichita: Taco shells.
Topeka Spice Mills, Inc., 2514 Kansas, Topeka: Coffee.
Vette Co., Inc., Box 304, Leavenworth: Chili, mush, prepared salads.
Weigand Tea & Coffee Co., 160 N. Emporia (Box 455), Wichita: Coffee.
W. S. Welshimer Co., 325 S. Market, Wichita: Coffee.
Western Food Products, 126 E. Second, Hutchinson: Vinegar.
White Coffee Co., 1202 S. Summit Dr., Arkansas City: Coffee roasting.
Wichita Vinegar & Cider Works, 3200 W. Central, Wichita: Vinegar.

TEXTILE MILL PRODUCTS

Knitting Mills

Cholly Knit Co., 1108 N. Washington, Wellington: Men's golf and argyle socks.

Floor Covering Mills

Kansas Foundation for the Blind, 223 W. Third, Wichita: Door mats.
Kansas Industries for the Blind, 925 Sunshine Rd., Kansas City (15): Throw rugs.
Kansas Industries for the Blind, 425 Mac Vicar, Topeka: Yarn and rag rugs.

Miscellaneous Textile Goods

Paddings and Upholstery Filling

American Felt Mfg. Co., 14-16-18 Ewing, Kansas City: Cotton batting and pads.

Artificial Leather, Oilcloth, and Other Impregnated Coated Fabrics Except Rubberized

Champion Textile Finishing Co., La Cygne: Water, mildew, and flame resistant finished materials.
Hallmark Cards, Inc., Box 99, Lawrence: Gift wrap ribbon.

Textile Goods, Not Elsewhere Classified

Bemis Bros. Bag Co., 1000 E. 13th, Wichita: Bags (burlap and cotton).
Hutchinson Bag Corp., 2155 Poplar (Box 868), Hutchinson: Bags (cotton, burlap, mailing, parts, etc.).
Taylor Bag Co., 1206 Elm, Coffeyville: New and used burlap and cotton bags.
Taylor Bag Co., 410 E. 21st, Wichita: Process used bags.

APPAREL, AND OTHER FINISHED PRODUCTS MADE FROM
FABRICS AND SIMILAR MATERIALS

Men's, Youths', and Boys' Suits, Coats, and Overcoats

Fruhauf Southwest Garment Co., Inc., 312 E. English, Wichita: Uniforms for high school and college bands, military uniforms.
Land Mfg. Co., 1709 E. Lincoln, Wichita: Flying suits, jackets and tailored goods.
Parker Brothers, Winfield: Tailor-made clothes.
Fred Ronald Mfg. Co., Commercial Dr., Parsons: Boys' clothing.
Stevie Togs, Inc., 89th and Rosehill Rd., Lenexa: Boys' clothing.
Stevie Togs, Inc., N. Eighth, Neodesha: Boys' clothing.

Rock City is the name given to the strange rock formations near Minneapolis, Kansas.

Men's, Youths', and Boys' Furnishings, Work Clothing, and Allied Garments

Men's, Youths', and Boys' Shirts (Except Work Shirts), Collars, and Nightwear

Albert Land, Shirtmaker, 2 Orpheum Bldg., Topeka: Custom made shirts, pajamas, lightweight sport jackets.
Lerner Brothers Mfg. Co., Inc., 130 E. 12th, Baxter Springs: Sports shirts.
Nat Nast, Inc., Box 415, Bonner Springs: Bowling shirts, campus sportswear.
Wichita Shirt Co., 1101 S. Santa Fe, Wichita: Custom-made shirts and dental smocks.

Men's, Youths', and Boys' Underwear

Albert Land, Shirtmaker, 2 Orpheum Bldg., Topeka: Custom-made shorts.

Men's, Youths', and Boys' Neckwear

Ti-Not Tie Co., 438 N. Roosevelt, Wichita: Neckties.
Wisby Art Studio, Box 323, Turon: Silk screen processed advertising ties (livestock a specialty).

Men's, Youths', and Boys' Separate Trousers

Allee-Berry, Inc., Columbus: Boys' trousers.
Cherryvale Mfg. Co., 200 Galveston, Cherryvale: Casual slacks.

Work Clothing

Arotex Uniform Co., Inc., 201 N. Waco, Wichita: Washable uniforms.
Glenn Berry Mfrs., Inc., 307 Illinois, Oswego: Boys' dungarees.
Bruce Co., Inc., 120 E. 15th (Box 19), Ottawa: Whipcord jackets, blanket lined jackets (whipcord and denim).
Burlington Mfg. Co., Chanute: Work clothing.
Chetopa Mfg. Co., Chetopa: Work clothes.
Key Work Clothes, Inc., 523 E. Wall, Fort Scott: Overalls, coveralls, work pants, work shirts, jeans, lined and unlined jackets.

Men's, Youths', and Boys' Clothing, Not Elsewhere Classified

Dick Jones, Tailor, 239 W. Seventh, Junction City: Riding breeches.

Women's, Misses' and Juniors' Outerwear

Blouses, Waists, and Shirts

Lucy Frock, Inc., Herington: Blouses.
Mode O'Day Corp., 607 W. Main, Osawatomie: Ladies' blouses.
Osage Mfg. Co., Osage City: Blouses.
Raynell Fashions, 605 Washington, La Crosse: Girls' blouses.

Dresses

Horton Garment Co., 112 S. Second, Atchison: Women's, misses' and junior dresses.
Horton Garment Co., 138-40 E. Eighth, Horton: Junior dresses.
Doris Johnson, 841 Fairland, Wichita: Women's dresses (originals).
Lucy Frock, Inc., Herington: Girls' dresses.
H. L. Miller and Son, Inc., 405-415 W. Madison, Iola: Cotton dresses.
Mode O'Day Corp., 403½ S. Main, Ottawa: Women's dresses.
Slimaker Dress Co., Holton: Women's half size dresses.
Smith & Co., 102 W. Kaskaskia, Paola: Ladies' dresses.

Suits, Skirts, and Coats, Except Fur Coats and Raincoats

Annshire Garment Co., Inc., 101½ E. Kansas, Pittsburg: Ladies' suits and coats.
Braemoor Garment Co., Pleasanton: Ladies' coats and suits.
Cliff Mfg. Co., Inc., 609 Massachusetts, Lawrence: Women's sportswear (jackets, blouses, skirts, etc.).
Jan Mfg. Co., State Bank Bldg., Olathe: Women's sportswear.
Onaga Sportswear Mfg. Co., Onaga: Women's outerwear.
Osage Mfg. Co., Osage City: Jackets, slacks, skirts, two-piece suits.
Smith & Co., 102 W. Kaskaskia, Paola: Sportswear.

Women's, Misses', and Juniors' Outerwear, Not Elsewhere Classified

Tom Broderick Co., 2400 Broadway, Parsons: Girls' gym togs.
Champion Textile Finishing Co., La Cygne: Aprons.
Kansas Industries for the Blind, 425 Mac Vicar, Topeka: Aprons.
Don Lutton & Son, La Cygne: Novelty aprons and caps.
Sunbonnet Mfg. Co., Atwood: Ladies' sunbonnets.
Trump Apron Co., Frankfort: Ladies' fancy aprons, cobblers, tunics and bibs.

Hats, Caps

Hats and Caps, Except Millinery

Champion Textile Finishing Co., La Cygne: Cloth caps.

Girls', Children's, and Infants' Outerwear

Dresses, Blouses, Waists, and Shirts

Glenn Berry Mfrs., Inc., 307 Illinois, Oswego: Toddlers' dungarees.
Modern American Co., Inc., 101 S. Main, Hillsboro: Children's clothing.
Warner Mfg. Co., 412-14 Cedar, Garnett: Children's clothing.
Winett, Inc., 3059 N. 27th, Kansas City: Infants' and children's clothing.

Miscellaneous Apparel and Accessories

Robes and Dressing Gowns

Smith & Co., 102 W. Kaskaskia, Paola: Robes.

Leather and Sheep Lined Clothing

Hurd Leather Shop, Ashland: Zipper chaps (leather).
Roberts Rodeo Equipment Mfg. Co., Strong City: Naugahyde and leather chaps, children's chaps.

Apparel Belts

Hillmer Leather Shop, 115 E. Sixth, Topeka: Leather belts.
Kansas Industries for the Blind, 425 Mac Vicar, Topeka: Leather belts.
The Sewing Nook, 1517 W. Sixth, Topeka: Belts.
Singer Sewing Machine Co., 722 Kansas, Topeka: Dress belts.
Wichita Pleating & Button Co., 300 E. Douglas, Wichita: Cloth covered belts.

Miscellaneous Fabricated Textile Products

Curtains and Draperies

T. L. Collins Upholstering, 736 N. Ninth, Salina: Draperies.
Bill Davis Shop, 855 Minnesota, Kansas City: Draperies.
The Drapery Den, 416 W. Sixth, Emporia: Custom made draperies.
Forsell, Inc., 1421-23 Lane, Topeka: Draperies.

Hinshaw's Slip Covers & Draperies, 2040 Woodland, Wichita: Draperies.
Home Decorating Service, Caney: Draperies.
Hunton's Carpets & Draperies, 250 S. Santa Fe, Salina: Draperies.
Don Lutton & Son, La Cygne: Custom made school and stage curtains.
Mastercraft Interiors, Beloit: Draperies.
The Nickel Shop, 607 W. Eighth, Hutchinson: Custom made draperies.
Dwight Putnam Interiors, 415 E. Iron, Salina: Draperies.
Rohr's Venetian Blind Factory, 727 E. 12th, Hays: Draperies.
Skau Shop, 2417 N. 55th, Kansas City (4): Draperies.
Stiefel's, 119 N. Santa Fe, Salina: Draperies.
Textile Drapery Shop, 1427 Burns, Wichita (3): Draperies and cornices.
Young Drapery Shop, 521 W. 18th, Hutchinson: Draperies.

Housefurnishings, Except Curtains and Draperies

Arotex Uniform Co., Inc., 201 N. Waco, Wichita: Towels, napkins, linens, sheets, etc.
B & J Mattress Co., 132 W. Fifth, Newton: Bedding.
Bill Davis Shop, 855 Minnesota, Kansas City: Slip covers, bed spreads.
The Drapery Den, 416 W. Sixth, Emporia: Slip covers.
Hinshaw's Slip Covers & Draperies, 2040 Woodland, Wichita: Slip covers.
Home Decorating Service, Caney: Slip covers.
Interstate Mattress Co., 2100 N. 13th, Kansas City: Pillows and cushions.
Kansas City Feather Co., Inc., 1619 N. Third, Kansas City: Pillows and cushions (feather, down and dacron and polyurethane).
Kansas Foundation for the Blind, 223 W. Third, Wichita: Wet mops, dust cloths, ironing board covers and pads, basket liners, clothespin bags, dish cloths, wash cloths, baby bibs, dampening bag, shamicloth, terry tea towels, kitchen mitts, silver polishing cloth, window polish cloth, shoe polishing cloth.
Kansas Industries for the Blind, 925 Sunshine Rd., Kansas City (15): Dacron pillows.
Kansas Industries for the Blind, 425 Mac Vicar, Topeka: Ironing board covers and pads, pillowcases, clothespin bags, mops, etc.
McEntire Brothers, Inc., 227 Quincy, Topeka: Pillows.
Myers Brush-Broom & Mop Co., 300 S. Tenth, Kansas City (2): Mops.
The Nickel Shop, 607 W. Eighth, Hutchinson: Custom made slip covers, bedspreads.
Saunders Mfg. Co., 11th and Main, Atchison: Mops.
Lester Sircoulomb Co., Caney: Mops, window washers.
Skau Shop, 2417 N. 55th, Kansas City (4): Slip covers, bedspreads, cornices.
E. W. Starne Mfg. Co., Attica: Ironing board covers.
Sunny Seal Specialty Mfg. Co., 415 W. 20th, Wichita: Clothespin bags.
Textile Drapery Shop, 1427 Burns, Wichita (3): Slip covers, bedspreads.
Western Kushion Co., Oberlin: Cushions (attached handles).
Wichita Brush & Chemical Co., Inc., 234 N. Main, Wichita: Mops.
Winfield Mattress Co., 1019 Main, Winfield: Pillows.
Young Drapery Shop, 521 W. 18th, Hutchinson: Bedspreads, pillows.
Zelinkoff Co., 345-57 N. Main, Wichita: Mops, dusters, wash mitt, cellulose sponge products.

Canvas Products

Aircraft Specialties Co., 3425 W. Central, Wichita: Custom manufacturing (canvas), aircraft seat covers.
Airway American Mfg., Inc., 325 N. St. Francis, Wichita (2): Custom textile and synthetic production fabricators (coated, laminated and dyed finishes).
Anderson Canvas Works, Great Bend: Harvester aprons, oil field windbreaks and tarpaulins.
Anderson Leather Shop, 118 N. Santa Fe, Salina: Canvas products.
Atchison Leather Products Co., 316 Commercial, Atchison: Canvas specialty items.
Atherton Awning Co., 1012 Fruitland, Independence: Awnings, fitted covers, tarps, truck seats (re-built), boat covers, canopies.
Bigelow Awning Co., 521 E. Kansas, Arkansas City: Canvas goods.
E. A. Brown Mfg. Co., 418 Walnut, Dodge City: Canvas goods (awnings, tents, truck covers, sporting goods).
Buckley Awning & Mattress Co., 105 N. 11th, Atchison: Awnings.
Burk Awning & Mfg. Co., 706 Massachusetts, Lawrence: Awnings and canvas goods.
Champion Textile Finishing Co., La Cygne: Awnings, tractor umbrellas.
Colby Supply & Mfg. Co., 285 E. Third, Colby: Canvas products (tarpaulins, harvester canvas, drapers for swathers, binders, and windrowers).
Coles Ornamental Iron Co., 204 W. Fifth, Wichita: Awnings and canvas goods.
Crawford Mfg. Co., 12th and Graham, Emporia: Canvas goods (awnings, seat covers, hassocks, and cushions).
Emporia Tent & Awning Co., 612 Merchant, Emporia: Canvas products (tents, awnings, etc.).
Henry Enz & Son, 127 E. Sixth, Newton: Car and house awnings, convertible tops, boat covers and tops, tarpaulins, industrial, agricultural and furniture canvas.
Evans Rug & Upholstery, 215 S. Gordy, El Dorado: Canvas products, awnings.
Fort Scott Home Furnishings, 105-107 Scott, Fort Scott: Awnings, tarpaulins.
Gray's Canvas Shop, 1422 W. Oklahoma, Arkansas City: Canvas goods.
Hutchinson Tent & Awning Co., 627 S. Main, Hutchinson: Awnings, tarps, tents, etc.
Krause Auto Trim, 421 S. Poplar, Wichita (11): Convertible tops.
Land Mfg. Co., 1709 E. Lincoln, Wichita: Canvas goods.
Langdon Mfg. Co., 222 N. Hydraulic, Wichita: Missile and aircraft protective covers, portable shelters and windbreaks for drilling rigs.
Newacheck Supply Co., 512 Main, Larned: Combine and binder canvases, irrigation dams, tarpaulins, and other canvas products.
Rub-R-Slat Draper Co., 225 E. Tenth, Halstead: Combine canvases, windrower canvases.
Salina Tent & Awning Co., 515 E. Walnut, Salina: Canvas awnings, store marquees, and tarpaulins.
Taylor Mfg. Co., Inc., 300 E. Pacific, Salina: Tool bags, canvas connectors, baseball bases, campers.
Textile Fabricators, 604 S. Main, Hutchinson: Oil field canvas, tarpaulins, truck covers, canvas specialties.
Topeka Auto Fabric Co., Inc., 225 E. Fifth, Topeka: Boat tops, boat covers.
Topeka Tent & Awning Co., 130-34 Kansas, Topeka: Tents, awnings, tarps, etc.
Turner Auto Fabric Co., 1521 Minnesota, Kansas City: Convertible tops.
Wichita Ponca Canvas Products Co., 611 E. Central, Wichita: Awnings, tents, truck covers, canvas products for aircraft, builders canvases, boat covers, miscellaneous fabricated canvas items.
Wyandotte Awning & Storage, Inc., 1315 Central, Kansas City: Awnings and canvas goods.

Pleating, Decorative and Novelty Stitching, and Tucking for the Trade

Price's Stencils, 1207 W. Trail, Dodge City: Painted textiles.
Wichita Pleating & Button Co., 300 E. Douglas, Wichita: Pleating, monograms, uniform and athletic letters, etc.
Williams Bros. Mfg. Co., 1405 W. 15th, Topeka: Silk screened T-shirts, pennants, etc.

Apparel Findings and Related Products

Wichita Pleating & Button Co., 300 E. Douglas, Wichita: Fancy settings and dress trimmings.

Fabricated Textile Products, Not Elsewhere Classified

Coad Saddlery, Cawker City: Blankets for horses and cattle.
Don's Upholstery Clinic, 106 E. Main, Marion: Auto seat covers.
Henry Enz & Son, 127 E. Sixth, Newton: Seat covers.
Goodson Auto Trim, 207 Poyntz, Manhattan: Automobile upholstery.
Hiawatha Seat Cover Co., 106 N. Eighth, Hiawatha: Auto seat covers.
Johnson Auto Fabric, 407 N. Sixth, Kansas City: Auto tops, seat covers, upholstery carpets.

Kansas Foundation for the Blind, 223 W. Third, Wichita: Auto seat belts.
Krause Auto Trim, 421 S. Poplar, Wichita (11): Seat covers, automobile upholstery, truck seats.
Lapstrap, Inc., 443 N. St. Francis, Wichita: Seat belts.
Morgan-Bulleigh Mfg. Co., 346 N. Washington, Wichita: Automobile seat covers, carpets, trunk mats.
Q-Lifesaver Co., Inc., Box 102, Tampa: Auto safety belts (nylon webbing).
Rayco Mfg. Co., 1516 E. Central, Wichita: Auto seat covers.
Richardson Upholstery Co., 145 N. Hydraulic, Wichita: Seat covers (auto, aircraft, boat).
Salina Upholstering Co., 127 S. Fourth, Salina: Auto seat covers.
Smith Chenille & Embroidery Co., 123 S. Third, Atchison: Emblems, pennants, chenille award letters, bowling shirt lettering.
Spooner Auto Trim, 1916 Grand, Parsons: Seat covers.
Standard Precision, Inc., 4105 W. Pawnee (Box 1297), Wichita: Automotive seat belts.
Topeka Auto Fabric Co., Inc., 225 E. Fifth, Topeka: Seat covers.
Turner Auto Fabric Co., 1521 Minnesota, Kansas City: Seat covers.

LUMBER AND WOOD PRODUCTS (Except Furniture)

Sawmills and Planing Mills

Sawmills and Planing Mills, General

American Walnut Co., 1021 S. 18th, Kansas City: Walnut lumber.
Barton's Saw Mill, Route 4, Independence: Rough lumber.
E. F. Bedford, 733 Shute, Fort Scott: Walnut, maple, and hackberry lumber.
Eichman's Saw Mill, Route 2, Westphalia: Sawmill.
Roy Johnson, 813 Carnahan, Topeka: Native lumber.
La Rue Sawmill, Erie: Sawmill.
Meyer Saw Mill, Hanover: Lumber.
C. Nauman Lumber, Inc., 1626 S. Main, Ottawa: Walnut and maple lumber.
Frank Purcell Walnut Lumber Co., Inc., 13th and Kaw River, Kansas City: Walnut lumber.
Sitka Spruce Lumber & Mfg. Co., 50 Kansas, Kansas City: Aircraft spruce lumber.
Earl Welch Saw Mill, Perry: Walnut lumber and squares.

Hardwood Dimension and Flooring Mills

American Walnut Co., 1021 S. 18th, Kansas City: Walnut gunstock blanks.
E. F. Bedford, 733 Shute, Fort Scott: Gunstocks.
Gunstocks, Inc., Perry: Custom made walnut gunstocks.
Earl Welch Saw Mill, Perry: Walnut gunstock blanks.
Wilson Bros. Walnut Lumber Co., 2718 Dirr, Parsons: Hardwoods for furniture factories.

Special Product Sawmills, Not Elsewhere Classified.

Independent Stave Co., Holton: Rough barrel headings.

Millwork, Veneer, Plywood, and Prefabricated Structural Wood Products

Millwork Plants

Adamson Machine Shop, Highway 196, Potwin: Woodworking.
Allen Millworks, 1025 N. Hoover, Wichita: Millwork.
Beisecker Sash & Door Co., 127 N. Van Buren, Topeka: Millwork (windows, doors, storm sash).
Berthot Planing Mill, 106 N. Ashby, Chanute: Millwork.
John A. Briggs, 113 S. Pennsylvania, Independence: Wooden cabinets and built-ins.
Brown's Cabinet Shop, E. Highway 24, Colby: Millwork cabinets.
Century Mfg. Co., Inc., E. Ninth (Box 121), Hays: Wood prime windows.
Component Builders, Inc., 410 N. Franklin, Colby: Prehung doors.
Danielson & Schnug Mill & Lumber Co., 218 W. Lewis, Wichita: Sashes, doors, frames, cabinets.
Erickson Building Supply, Third and Lincoln, Clay Center: Doors, windows.
Frantz Wood Products, 101 Commercial, Atchison: Architectural custom woodwork.
Good Wood Shop, 12317 E. Central, Wichita (8): Shutters, flower fence, arbors, trellises.
Goodjohn Sash & Door Co., Third and Santa Fe, Leavenworth: Stock sash, doors, frames, screens.
Hays Planing Mill, 1013 Elm, Hays: Millwork.
Hessler Planing Mill, 218-20 W. Sixth, Newton: Millwork.
Highland Millshop, 2112-2116 Pennsylvania, Topeka: Millwork.
Hill Woodcraft Shop, 423 Sherman, Wichita: Millwork.
Ed Holtzen Woodwork, Inc., 317 N. Osage, Wichita (3): Millwork.
Ingroum Planing Mill, 207 N. State, Iola: Doors, windows, etc.
Iola Planing Mill, 404 North St., Iola: Sash and door.
Justice Mfg. Co., 800 S. First, Hiawatha: Shutters.
Kaaz Woodwork Co., Inc., 201-211 Delaware, Leavenworth: Millwork.
King Bros. Cabinet Co., Inc., 2329-31 Metropolitan, Kansas City: Mantels and special millwork.
J. A. Knight & Son, 123 Stout, Pratt: Millwork.

Padbloc Co., Inc., 110 N. Lorraine, Wichita: Dunnage for packing specification packages for military items.
Par-Kan Mfg. Co., 722 S. 22nd, Parsons: Boxes.
Larson Lumber Co., 208-226 S. Fourth, Salina: Window units.
McGee Woodworking Shop, 523 S. Kansas, Liberal: Woodwork.
A. Messenger Lumber & Millwork Construction Co., 822 E. Fourth, Pittsburg: Millwork.
Meyer Lumber Co., 10815 W. 63rd, Shawnee: Millwork (sash and doors).
Michaelis Millwork Co., Inc., Jefferson and Oak, Osborne: Millwork.
Miller's Mill and Cabinet Shop, 2124 N. Buchanan, Topeka: Cabinets, millwork.
Munson Millworks, Inc., 417 E. Elm, Salina: General planing mill work, windows, doors, cabinets.
Ostermann Cabinet Shop, Sylvan Grove: Window frames and woodwork.
Ottawa Millwork Co., N. Locust, Ottawa: Millwork.
Rock Island Millwork Co., 1340 N. Mosley, Wichita: Millwork.
Roddis Lumber & Veneer Co., Inc., 1016 Southwest Blvd., Kansas City: Doors, moldings.
Rounds & Porter Co., 1004 W. Trail, Dodge City: Millwork.
Rounds & Porter Co., 430 N. Waco, Wichita: Millwork.
Salina Planing Mill, Inc., 1100 W. Crawford, Salina: Millwork.
Shawnee Planing Mill, Inc., 401 S. Adams (Box 924), Hutchinson: Architectural millwork.
Southard Home Improvement, 1005 Williams (Box 219), Great Bend: Doors and windows.
Specialty Millworks, Inc., 1423 S. Ridge Rd., Wichita: Crates, cabinets, furniture, specialty millwork.
W. P. Stark Lumber Co., Inc., Fairfax Rd. and Quindaro, Kansas City: Lumber products.
The Sun Lumber Co., 1945 N. Broadway, Wichita: Millwork.
Topeka Cabinet & Fixture Co., 800 N. Kansas, Topeka: Millwork, office equipment (custom made).
Topeka Mill Co., 410 E. Second, Topeka: Millwork.
Topeka Millwork Co., 414 E. Second, Topeka: Cabinets, doors, fixtures, millwork.
United Sash & Door Co., 13602 E. Central, Wichita: Millwork.
Walling Sash & Door Co., Inc., 911 E. Indianapolis, Wichita: Millwork.
Whelan's, Inc., 715 E. Fourth, Topeka: Architectural millwork.
Wichita Millwork Co., Inc., 141-147 N. Washington, Wichita: Millwork.
Wood Products Co., 1201 Sharps Dr., (Box 313), Newton: Screen and combination doors, louver doors, sash.
Woodwork Mfg. & Supply Co., 14-16 W. Fourth, Hutchinson: Millwork.

Veneer and Plywood Plants

Aero Supply & Equipment, 139th and Antioch Rd., Olathe (Mailing add.: Box 373, K. C. [41], Mo.): Aircraft and marine plywood.
J. B. Anthony Co., 724 N. Lee, Belle Plaine: Plywood.
Roddis Lumber & Veneer Co., Inc., 1016 Southwest Blvd., Kansas City: Plywood.
Sitka Spruce Lumber & Mfg. Co., 50 Kansas, Kansas City: Plywoods.

Prefabricated Wooden Buildings and Structural Members

Baldwin Display Products Co., Route 2, Derby: Custom homes.
Barber Ready Built Homes, W. Highway 50, Garden City: Ready made buildings.
Blaker Lumber & Grain Co., La Cygne: Prefabricated buildings.
Century Homes Co., Inc., 102nd St. and Kaw Dr. (Box 307), Edwardsville: Pre-cut wood homes and buildings, roof trusses.
Century Mfg. Co., Inc., E. Ninth (Box 121), Hays: Roof trusses and wall components.
Component Builders, Inc., 410 N. Franklin, Colby: Wooden truss rafters with gissmo gusset.
Component Builders, Inc., 1000 Franklin, Salina: Wooden truss rafters with gissmo gusset.
Custom Houses & Components, Inc., 411 W. Lincoln (Box 1402), Salina: Wall sections, trusses, gable ends, built up interiors.
Eichman's Saw Mill, Route 2, Westphalia: Portable buildings.
H & W Service, 115 S. Foster, Stockton: Portable cattle sheds.
Handy Man Service (Prefab Homes Div.), 201 Scott, Fort Scott: Prefab homes and buildings.
Hunt Movable Homes, Haysville (Mailing add.: 7464 S. Broadway, Wichita): Sectionalized homes.
Mid-West Lumber Co., Smith Center: Roof trusses.
Norton Lumber Co., 202 N. State, Norton: Roof trusses.
Perfection Truss Co., 3000 Old S. Lawrence, Wichita (17): Wooden roof trusses.
Ready Made Buildings, Inc., DeSoto (Mailing add.: 706 Massachusetts, Lawrence): Prefab homes and buildings.
Standard Homes Co. (Div. R. L. Sweet Lumber Co.), 4400 Roe Blvd., Kansas City: Precut homes.

Wooden Containers

Nailed and Lock Corner Wooden Boxes and Shook

B-T Box Co., 201 S. Baltimore, Derby: Wooden boxes and crates.
Burgess Mfg. Co., 320 E. 21st, Wichita: Wooden boxes, crates.
Dirks Wood Mfg. Co., Buhler: Shipping boxes and blocks.
Heaton Mfg., 102 E. Railroad, Erie: Wood boxes (casket), crating.
Love Mfg., Inc., 700 E. 37th, Wichita: Wood boxes, wood cleated crates.

Specialty Millworks, Inc., 1423 S. Ridge Rd., Wichita: Walk in cold storage boxes and deep freeze boxes.
Topeka Cabinet & Fixture Co., 800 N. Kansas, Topeka: Boxes.
United Mfg. Co., Shawnee, Kansas City: Wooden boxes and crates.
Wichita Box Co., Inc., 4202 K42 W., Wichita: Wood boxes, crates, containers.

Wirebound Boxes and Crates

Cramer & Son Sheet Metal Shop, 721-29 S. Oak, Garnett: Dog shipping crates.
Industrial Lumber Co., 655 Industrial Blvd., Kansas City: Pallets, crates and industrial woods.
Roy Johnson, 813 Carnahan, Topeka: Shipping boxes and crates.
Topeka Cabinet & Fixture Co., 800 N. Kansas, Topeka: Crates.

Cooperage

Black, Sivalls & Bryson, Inc., Box 166, Ellinwood: Wood tanks for oil field use.
Greif Bros. Cooperage Corp., 17th and Osage, Kansas City: Wooden barrels.
O'Neill Tank Co., Fifth and C Sts., Westport Addition, Route 1, Great Bend: Redwood storage tanks.
Sauder Tank Co., Inc., Madison: Wood oil field tanks.

Miscellaneous Wood Products

Allen's Sawmill, 114 W. Jefferson, Pittsburg: Hickory chips for barbecue-grills.
American Crossarm & Conduit Co., 2838 N. 27th, Kansas City: Wooden crossarms, braces and allied products for electric power and telephone industry.
Aurel Products, 1147 Jewell, Topeka: Wooden clothing hangers and book ends (children's).
B-T Box Co., 201 S. Baltimore, Derby: Pallets.
Beckner Cabinet Shop, 120 E. Fifth, Garnett: Wood frames for aluminum door and window displays, hardware displays.
Buller Mfg. Co., Hillsboro: Folding truck ladders.
Burgess Mfg. Co., 320 E. 21st, Wichita: Wood pallets.
D & B Truck Bed Co., Pawnee Rock: Stepladders.
Eichman's Saw Mill, Route 2, Westphalia: Truck stokes, truck flooring, pipe line skids, building materials, hog slot flooring, chicken house slot flooring.
Elbe's Woodwork Shop, 111 E. Eighth, Harper: Wood products.
G & S Mfg. Co., Route 2 (Box 56), McPherson: Wood novelties.
Good Wood Shop, 12317 E. Central, Wichita (8): Porch boxes, bird houses and feeders.
Haul-Mor Co., Inc., Valley Falls: Wood pallets and crates, forage boxes.
Harold L. Heaton Mfg. Co., 102 E. Railroad, Erie: Surveyors' stakes, pallets.
Home Novelty Shoppe, 323 N. Elizabeth, Wichita: Wood souvenirs and novelties.
Kansas Industries for the Blind, 925 Sunshine Rd., Kansas City (15): Chair cane.
Kechi Corner Lumber Co., 6149 N. Broadway, Wichita: Redwood fences, trellis, picnic tables.
Marlow Woodcuts, Inc., Americus: Wood gifts.
Novel Woodcraft, Hanover: Gift items (wooden).
Par-Kan Mfg. Co., 722 S. 22nd, Parsons: Ladders, wooden specialties.
Anton Pearson Studio, 505 S. Main, Lindsborg: Original sculptured wood objects.
Rarewoods Mfg. Co., 2449 N. Broadway, Wichita: Redwood fences.
Red Barn Studio, Lindsborg: Wood carvings.
Ross Hickory Chip Co., Osawatomie: Hickory chips.
Rylko Fence Co., 5704 Highland Dr. (Box 1081), Hutchinson: Wooden fences.
John Shively, Osawatomie: Trophies (all types).
Sinclair Mfg. Co., 1816 Wabash, Wichita (14): Wood products.
Thyfault's Wood & Window Shop, 316 Main, Stockton: Lumber and wood products.
Wallace Mfg. Co. (Div. Cook Paint & Varnish Co.), Industrial Park Area, Pittsburg: Pre-finished plywood products.
Wichita Box Co., Inc., 4202 K42 W., Wichita: Pallets, skids.

FURNITURE AND FIXTURES

Household Furniture

Wood Household Furniture, Except Upholstered

A & H Woodwork, 1600 Nickerson, Hutchinson: Cabinet work.
Amco, Inc., 112 E. Second, Halstead: Wood products and custom furniture.
American Wood Works, Great Bend: Cabinets.
Armstrong Cabinet Co., 6481 Holliday Rd., Kansas City: Custom made kitchen cabinets.
Beckner Cabinet Shop, 120 E. Fifth, Garnett: Custom cabinets and furniture.
Bix Stripping Service Co., 2017 Tenth, Great Bend: Furniture stripping and refinishing.
Bradshaw & Son Construction Co., Melvern: Custom built furniture (cabinets, picture frames, lamps, tables, chairs, etc.).
Bratton Construction Co., 1410 Ninth, Dodge City: Custom built furniture.
Central Cabinet & Fixture Co., 732 N. Ninth, Salina: Cabinets and cupboards, formica tops.
Century Wood Products, Inc., Park and Church, Olathe: Cabinet work.
Chastain Lumber Co., 121 Pattie, Wichita: Wood furniture and cabinets.
Colby Mattress Co., E. Fourth, Colby: Small furniture.
Cooper's Custom Products, 216 N. Washington, Wichita: Custom built furniture.
Julian Costillo, 318 Pierre, Manhattan: Cabinets, antique reproductions.
Cowboy's Furniture Corral, 104 Second, Dodge City: Cabinets, furniture.
D & B Truck Bed Co., Pawnee Rock: Lawn chairs.
Deese Cabinet Shop, Inc., 803 Quindaro, Kansas City: Custom built cabinets, formica cabinet tops.
Dor-Nic Mfg. Co., 1625 Military, Baxter Springs: Patio table and bench combination.
C. Downing Casting & Cabinet Shop, Route 2, Sedan: Custom built furniture and cabinet work.
Emporia Woodworking Shop, 113 S. Commercial, Emporia: Cabinet work.
Erickson Building Supply, Third and Lincoln, Clay Center: Special and stock millwork cabinets.
Frantz Wood Products, 101 Commercial, Atchison: Wood household furniture.
Garrett Cabinet & Supply, Gridley: Sink and counter tops.
Gaskill Custom Furniture Mfg., 1109 E. Harry, Wichita: Custom furniture.
Fred V. Gentsch, Inc., Box 345, Newton: Furniture for mobile homes.
Good Wood Shop, 12317 E. Central, Wichita (8): Shelves, etc.
Gragg's Cabinets & Fixtures, 217-219 W. Main, Cherryvale: Custom kitchen cabinets.
Gunnerson Cabinet Shop, 1424 Madison, Topeka: Cabinets.
Gunstocks, Inc., Perry: Walnut table legs, walnut coffee tables, walnut table lamps.
Haul-Mor Co., Inc., Valley Falls: Display furniture.
Highland Millshop, 2112-2116 Pennsylvania, Topeka: Custom kitchens.
Hill Woodcraft Shop, 423 Sherman, Wichita: Cabinets.
Ed Holtzen Woodwork, Inc., 317 N. Osage, Wichita (3): Cabinets.
Ingroum Planing Mill, 207 N. State, Iola: Cabinets.
Iola Planing Mill, 404 North St., Iola: Kitchen cabinets.
Jay's Woodwork Shop, 202 N. Second, Norton: Cabinets, unfinished furniture.
Jim's Cabinet Shop, Winchester: Built-in cabinets, custom furniture.
Kaaz Woodwork Co., Inc., 201-211 Delaware, Leavenworth: Plastic covered counters and cabinets, architectural woodwork and cabinets, wardrobes.
King Bros. Cabinet Co., Inc., 2329-31 Metropolitan, Kansas City: Kitchen cabinets.
Kufeld Cabinet Shop, Great Bend: Cabinets.
Larson Lumber Co., 208-226 S. Fourth, Salina: Cabinets.
Love Mfg., Inc., 700 E. 37th, Wichita: Tri-wall containers.
Mastercraft Interiors, Beloit: Furniture (custom built).
Meader's Wood Shop, 705 Dearborn, Augusta: Custom furniture, junior recliners, novelties.
A. Messenger Lumber & Millwork Construction Co., 822 E. Fourth, Pittsburg: Cabinets.
Miller Cabinet Shop, 159 S. Green, Hoisington: Cabinets.
Moddrell Cabinet Shop, 207 N. E. Tenth, Abilene: Kitchen cabinets.
Modern Millwork, 620 Kansas City Rd., Olathe: Cabinets.
Monty's Fixture Mfg. Co., 2121 S. Poplar, Wichita: Wooden cabinets, desks, wood products.
Al Mouthuy's Furniture Factory, 206 N. Rouse, Pittsburg: Custom furniture and antique refinishing.
Nedrow Wood Products, 3400 Rowland, Kansas City: Custom built cabinets and fixtures (residential, commercial, and industrial).
North End Mattress Co., 721 N. Main, Wichita: Hollywood beds.
Novel Woodcraft, Hanover: Cabinets, furniture.
Ostermann Cabinet Shop, Sylvan Grove: Furniture and kitchen cabinets.
Ottawa Millwork Co., N. Locust, Ottawa: Cabinets.
Paul W. Otto Furniture Co., 1238 Lane, Topeka: Wood furniture and cabinet work.
Overland Cabinet Co., 5948 Merriam Dr., Shawnee Mission: Kitchen cabinets.
Princes Furniture, 128 N. Main, Lindsborg: Banquet tables, end tables, cocktail tables, ping pong tables, custom furniture.
Dwight Putman Interiors, 415 E. Iron, Salina: Custom furniture.
Rankin's Cabinet Shop, Box 196, Gardner: Kitchen cabinets, woodwork.
Sam Ross, Cabinet Maker, Weir: Cabinets.
Schallo Awning & Mfg. Co., Inc., 1203 N. Broadway, Pittsburg: Cabinets.
Scott City Builders, Inc., Scott City: Formica fabrication.
Seneca Planing Mill & TV Shop, Seneca: Cabinet work.
Shawnee Cabinet, Inc., 11114 W. 60th, Shawnee: Custom wood work.
Songer Woodworking & Upholstering, 328½ S. Kansas, Olathe: Household built-ins, small furniture.
Standard Cabinet Shop, 1302 W. Trail, Dodge City: Cabinets.
Stewart's Builders & Supply, 1213 E. 13th, Hutchinson: Woodwork, cabinets.
Sturm Fixture Co., 1910-1912 Brown, Coffeyville: Household cabinets.
Topeka Cabinet & Fixture Co., 800 N. Kansas, Topeka: Cabinets, doors, fixtures, furniture, lawn furniture.
W. H. Traylor & Son, W. Chestnut, Dodge City: Cabinets, furniture and woodworking.
Turon Hardware & Lumber Co., Turon: Kitchen built-ins.
R. E. Ward & Sons Mfg. Co., 535 N. Hydraulic, Wichita (14): Plastic laminated cabinet tops.
Alvin Weaver Co., 1647 S. 47th, Kansas City: Custom furniture.
Whelan's, Inc., 715 E. Fourth, Topeka: Residential cabinetry.
Wichita Cabinet Co., Inc., 1313 E. Harry, Wichita (11): Custom built cabinets.
Wichita Millwork Co., Inc., 141-147 N. Washington, Wichita: Cabinets.
Willard Mfg. Co., Vermillion: Furniture.
Chet Willey Fixture Co., Route 2, Caldwell: Kitchen cabinets.
L. W. Wilson Cabinet Shop, Route 5, Manhattan: Cabinets.

Wood Household Furniture, Upholstered

Artistic Furniture Co. of K. C., Inc., 1800 N. Seventh, Kansas City (1): Upholstered living room furniture.
Bailey's Upholstery Shop, 1505 N. Lorraine, Hutchinson: Upholstered furniture.
Carters Upholstery & Repair, 517 Watson, Topeka: Upholstering.
College Hill Upholstery, 1413 W. 15th, Topeka: Upholstery.
Don's Upholstery Clinic, 106 E. Main, Marion: Furniture upholstery.
Duo-Bed Corp., 1812 W. Second, Wichita: Furnishings for hotels, motels and institutions.
Hays Furniture Upholstery, 716 Galaxy Dr., Manhattan: Custom built upholstered furniture.
Home Decorating Service, Caney: Upholstering.
Lyon Custom Upholstery, 904 S. Main, Hutchinson: Upholstering.
Meader's Wood Shop, 705 Dearborn, Augusta: Upholstery.
Monarch Furniture Mfg. Co., 719 S. St. Francis, Wichita: Upholstered furniture.
Princeton Chair Co., 419½ Main, Galena: Chairs.
Rak Furniture Repair & Refinishing, 323 Polk, Topeka: Custom furniture.
Rok-A-Chair Mfg. Co., 125 E. Eighth, Coffeyville: Chairs and trailer furniture, boat seats.
Simmons Co., Fairfax and Eagle Rds., Kansas City: Sofas.
Songer Woodworking & Upholstering, 328½ S. Kansas, Olathe: Upholstered furniture.
Textile Drapery Shop, 1427 Burns, Wichita (3): Upholstering.
Wertzberger Upholstery, 3400 W. Sixth, Topeka: Upholstered furniture.
Wilson Upholstering Co., 2015 W. Sixth, Topeka: Upholstered furniture.

Metal Household Furniture

Becker Mfg. Co., Downs: Picnic tables.
Brockhoff Mfg. Co., 15 Oregon (Box 267), Sabetha: Picnic tables.
Gilmore-Tatge Mfg. Co., Box 133, Clay Center: Picnic tables.
Hanover Mfg. Co., Inc., Hanover: Picnic tables.

Mattresses and Bedsprings

Arkansas City Mattress Factory, 1102-04 S. Summit, Arkansas City: Mattresses.
Barnett Mattress Co., 604½ N. Fifth, Independence: Mattresses.
Behee Mattress Co., East Trail, Dodge City: Mattresses.
Buckley Awning & Mattress Co., 105 N. 11th, Atchison: Mattresses.
Colby Mattress Co., E. Fourth, Colby: Mattresses, box springs.
Edna Mattress Factory, Box 36, Edna: Mattresses and box springs.
Eldredge Mattress Factory, 411 N. Main, Hutchinson: Mattresses and box springs.
Fort Scott Home Furnishings, 105-107 Scott, Fort Scott: Mattresses.
Fred V. Gentsch, Inc., Box 345, Newton: Bedding for mobile homes.
Interstate Mattress Co., 2100 N. 13th, Kansas City: Mattresses, box springs.
Kansas Industries for the Blind, 925 Sunshine Rd., Kansas City (15): Mattresses (cotton felted and innerspring), box springs.
Kansas Industries for the Blind, 425 Mac Vicar, Topeka: Mattresses and box springs.
Kansas Mattress Co., Inc., 830 S. St. Francis, Wichita: Mattresses.
McEntire Brothers, Inc., 227 Quincy, Topeka: Mattresses, bedsprings.
Manhattan Mattress Co., 414 S. Fourth, Manhattan: Mattresses.
Monarch Mattress Mfg. Co., 719 S. St. Francis, Wichita: Mattresses and box springs.
North End Mattress Co., 721 N. Main, Wichita: Mattresses.
Salina Upholstering Co., 127 S. Fourth, Salina: Mattresses and box springs.
Sanitary Bedding Co., 118 Ruby, Topeka: Mattresses.
Seneca Furniture Co., 423 Main, Seneca: Mattresses.
Simmons Co., Fairfax and Eagle Rds., Kansas City: Mattresses, box springs, hide-a-beds.
Stevens Spring Co., Inc., Box 292, Newton: Innerspring, box and sofa springs.
United Mattress Co., 834 S. Kansas, Liberal: Mattresses.
Vickery Mattress Co., Hiawatha: Mattresses.
West Side Mattress Co., 605 W. Douglas, Wichita: Bedding, cotton felt, station wagon mattresses.
Wichita Mattress Co., Box 644, Wichita: Mattresses, box springs.
Winfield Mattress Co., 1019 Main, Winfield: Mattresses, box springs, cot and glider pads.
Wyandotte Mattress Co., 1520 Central, Kansas City: Mattresses.

Office Furniture

Wood Office Furniture

Custom Craft, Highway 81, Concordia: Office furniture.
Gragg's Cabinets & Fixtures, 217-219 W. Main, Cherryvale: Office desks.

Metal Office Furniture

Cramer Posture Chair Co., Inc., 625 Adams, Kansas City (5): Secretarial and executive posture chairs, side chairs, office machine stands.
Hoch Publishing Co., Inc., Marion: Office furniture.
Steel Fixture Mfg. Co., Seventh and Adams, Topeka: Steel filing equipment.

Public Building and Related Furniture

Advance Products Co., 2300 E. Douglas, Wichita: Language laboratory furniture.
Cramer Posture Chair Co., Inc., 625 Adams, Kansas City (5): School furniture.
Custom Craft, Highway 81, Concordia: Church and store furniture.
Dorton Mfg. Co., Bonner Springs: Chairs and seats (homes, hospitals, theaters, buses, etc.).
Erickson Building Supply, Third and Lincoln, Clay Center: Church furniture, school cabinets.
Garnett Church Furniture & Mfg. Co., Ninth and Oak, Garnett: Church furniture.
Hays Planing Mill, 1013 Elm, Hays: Church furniture.
McEntire Brothers, Inc., 227 Quincy, Topeka: Seating equipment for railroads.
Mid-Am Mfg. Co., Calhoun Bldg., McCune: Wooden school furniture and allied products.
T-K Specialty Co., Commercial Natl. Bank Bldg., Kansas City: Club room furniture.
Topeka Bench Co., 399 Cecil Rd., Topeka: Bus benches.
Whelan's, Inc., 715 E. Fourth, Topeka: School furniture (wood).

Partitions, Shelving, Lockers, and Office and Store Fixtures

Wood Partitions, Shelving, Lockers, and Office and Store Fixtures

American Wood Works, Great Bend: Store fixtures.
Baldwin Display Products Co., Route 2, Derby: Store fixtures, kitchen, etc.
Central Cabinet & Fixture Co., 732 N. Ninth, Salina: Fixtures.
Chastain Lumber Co., 121 Pattie, Wichita: Wood fixtures.
Danielson & Schnug Mill & Lumber Co., 218 W. Lewis, Wichita: Store fixtures.
Erickson Building Supply, Third and Lincoln, Clay Center: Fixtures.
Frantz Wood Products, 101 Commercial, Atchison: Wood store fixtures.
Gragg's Cabinets & Fixtures, 217-219 W. Main, Cherryvale: Store fixtures.
Hays Planing Mill, 1013 Elm, Hays: Wood fixtures.
Harold L. Heaton Mfg. Co., 102 E. Railroad, Erie: Shelving units.
Highland Millshop, 2112-2116 Pennsylvania, Topeka: Store fixtures and special displays.
Hunt's Store Modernization Service, Burns (Mailing add.: 1167 Woodhull, Topeka): Fixtures and office equipment for stores.
Jay's Woodwork Shop, 202 N. Second, Norton: Store fixtures.
King Bros. Cabinet Co., Inc., 2329-31 Metropolitan, Kansas City: Store fixtures.
Larson Lumber Co., 208-226 S. Fourth, Salina: Fixtures, shelving.
Moddrell Cabinet Shop, 207 N. E. Tenth, Abilene: Fixtures.
Monty's Fixture Mfg. Co., 2121 S. Poplar, Wichita: Store fixtures, displays.
Pechin Store & Cafe Fixture Co., 1005 E. Douglas, Wichita: Bar fixtures (wood).
Schallo Awning & Mfg. Co., Inc., 1203 N. Broadway, Pittsburg: Store fixtures.
Sitka Spruce Lumber & Mfg. Co., 50 Kansas, Kansas City: Store and display fixtures.
Stewart Multi-Roll Wallpaper Display Co., Wamego: Wallpaper display fixtures.
Sturm Fixture Co., 1910-1912 Brown, Coffeyville: Store fixtures.
R. E. Ward & Sons Mfg. Co., 535 N. Hydraulic, Wichita (14): Fixtures.
Chet Willey Fixture Co., Route 2, Caldwell: Hardwood store fixtures.
Woodwork Mfg. & Supply, Inc., 14-16 W. Fourth, Hutchinson: Store fixtures.

Metal Partitions, Shelving, Lockers, and Office and Store Fixtures

Charles Products Co., 415 N. Poplar, S. Hutchinson: Oil can display racks, barrel stands.
Industrial Shelving & Storage Equipment, 1100 S. McComas, Wichita: Steel shelving, parts bins and related products.
Midland Metalcraft, Inc., 1100 S. McComas, Wichita: Industrial steel shelving and parts bins, display shelving for variety stores.
Steel Fixture Mfg. Co., Seventh and Adams, Topeka: Steel fixtures (custom-built).

Miscellaneous Furniture and Fixtures

Venetian Blinds and Shades

A-B Window Shade Shoppe, 2405 Main, Parsons: Window shades, Venetian blinds, awnings.
All Weather Products Co., 816 N. Main, Wichita: Aluminum awnings.
Allied Blind & Linoleum Co., 724 N. Main, Wichita: Venetian blinds (wooden and metal).
Aluminum Home Products Co., Phillipsburg: Aluminum awnings.
Aluminum Products Co., 302 W. Second, Washington: Aluminum awnings.
Aluminum Screen & Window Co., Inc., 535 W. Douglas, Wichita: Aluminum awnings.
Armstrong Venetian Blind Mfg. Co., 720 N. Main, Wichita: Aluminum, steel and wooden Venetian blinds.
Boatwright Supply, Inc., 33 Provence, Olathe: Awnings.
Boyd Shade & Drapery Co., 1623 Central, Kansas City: Window shades, Venetian blinds.
L. J. Bromert Co., 319 W. Fifth, Hutchinson: Window shades, venetian blinds, vertical blinds.
Cooks Aluma-Fab Mfg. Co., 1221 E. River, Eureka: Prefab awnings.
Cool-Temp Awning Co., Inc., 229-235 S. Wichita, Wichita: Aluminum and redwood awnings.
Bill Davis Shop, 855 Minnesota, Kansas City: Window shades, Venetian blinds, traverse rods.
Emporia Tent & Awning Co., 612 Merchant, Emporia: Venetian blinds, aluminum awnings.
Evans Venetian Blind Mfg. Co., 613 W. Douglas, Wichita: Venetian blinds (aluminum and steel), draw draperies (metal), window shades (cloth).
Exterior Art Co., 3550 Southeast Blvd., Wichita (16): Aluminum and fiberglass awnings.
Forsell, Inc., 1421-23 Lane, Topeka: Venetian blinds, aluminum awnings, window shades.
Hawley Brothers, 403 W. Wyatt Earp, Dodge City: Venetian blinds and aluminum awnings.
Humphrey Products, Inc., 719 E. Zimmerly, Wichita (11): Aluminum awnings.
Jaxon Mfg. Co., 215 W. Fifth, Topeka: Venetian blinds, aluminum awnings.
Johnson's Wood Shop, 406 N. E. 14th, Abilene: Aluminum awnings.
Lasting Mfg. Co., Inc., 119 W. Central, El Dorado: Aluminum Venetian blinds.
The Laurie Co., 2331 S. Mead (Box 3911), Wichita: Metal Venetian blinds, vertical draw drapes, roller shades.
Mid-West Weatherstrip & Venetian Blind Mfg. Co., 1647 S. Ida, Wichita: Metal Venetian blinds.
Peerless Products, Inc., 21st and Adlie, Fort Scott (Mailing add.: 3105 Euclid, K. C. [9], Mo.): Aluminum and fiberglass awnings.
Joe W. Pittman Co., 831 N. Kansas, Topeka: Aluminum awnings.
Rohr's Venetian Blind Factory, 727 E. 12th, Hays: Custom made blinds.
Salina Tent & Awning Co., 515 E. Walnut, Salina: Aluminum awnings.
Salina Venetian Blind Factory, Route 2, Salina: Venetian blinds.
Schallo Awning & Mfg. Co., Inc., 1203 N. Broadway, Pittsburg: Awnings (wood and aluminum).
Schammerhorn Blind Co., Inc., 124 S. Seneca, Wichita: Venetian blinds, window shades, shutters, vertical blinds, bamboo blinds.
Schultz Home Modernizing Co., 510 W. First, Larned: Awnings and awning shutters, patio covers.
Sears Home Improvement Co., Arkansas City: Aluminum awnings.
Shadelite Marquee Co., 1724 N. Main, Newton: Aluminum marquees and canopies.
Spangler Insulation & Mfg. Co., 1327 17th, Belleville: Marquees, awnings.
Van's Incinerator Co., Route 4, Wellington: Aluminum awnings.
Wilson All Weather Window Co., 1010-12 S. Main, Hutchinson: Aluminum awnings and canopies.
Zephyr Mfg., Inc., 400 E. Second, Hutchinson: Aluminum awnings.
Zephyr Ventilated Awning Co., Inc., 2109 Metropolitan, Kansas City: Ventilated redwood and aluminum awnings, patio covers, screen rooms, marquees.

Furniture and Fixtures, Not Elsewhere Classified

A & A Cabinet Shop, 1637 Laura, Wichita: Restaurant fixtures.
Ablah Hotel Supply Co., Inc., 800 E. 11th, Wichita: Restaurant fixtures and equipment.
Pechin Store & Cafe Fixtures Co., 1005 E. Douglas, Wichita: Restaurant fixtures (wood).
Pyramid Mfg., Inc., 1301 E. Funston, Wichita: Restaurant fixtures.
Salina Coffee House, Inc., 113-15 N. Seventh, Salina: Restaurant and bar fixtures.
Skilman & Steele Mfg. Co., 301 N. Cedar, Abilene: Restaurant equipment.
Valentine Mfg., Inc., 1020 S. McComas, Wichita: Restaurant fixtures.
White Coffee Co., 1202 S. Summit Dr., Arkansas City: Restaurant equipment, fixture manufacturing.

PAPER AND ALLIED PRODUCTS

Converted Paper and Paperboard Products, Except Containers and Boxes

Paperboard Mills

Packaging Corp. of America, Box 1033, Hutchinson: Paperboard.

Paper Coating and Glazing

Arundel Book & Printing Co., 526 Arundel (Box 206), Emporia: Gummed litho labels.

Envelopes

Service Envelope Co., 541 Central, Kansas City: Envelopes.

Bags, Except Textile Bags

Bemis Bros. Bag Co., 1000 E. 13th, Wichita: Paper bags.
Central Bag & Sack Co., 707 S. Main, Hutchinson: Bags.
Dura-Lee Corp., 1102 S. Mill, Kansas City: Cellophane, polyethylene, saran wraps and bags.

Die Cut Paper and Paperboard; and Cardboard

Mid-Continent Tab Card Co., Seventh and Sunshine Rd., Kansas City: Data processing machine cards.
Western Bindery Products Co., 323 W. Fifth, Topeka: File folders.

Converted Paper and Paperboard Products, Not Elsewhere Classified

Insul-Seal Insulation Co., Inc., 1867 S. Glendale, Wichita: Insulation (cellulose wood fiber).
Osage Products Co., Box 17, Osage City: Paper products for home use.
Wallace Mfg. Co. (Div. Cook Paint & Varnish Co.), Industrial Park Area, Pittsburg: Pre-finished wallboard.
Western Bindery Products Co., 323 W. Fifth, Topeka: Blank paper, scratch pads, mailing wrappers.

Paperboard Containers and Boxes

Folding Paperboard Boxes

Hazelwood Paper Box Co., 121 S. Main, Lindsborg (Mailing add.: 254 N. Santa Fe, Salina): Folding paper boxes.
Hazelwood Paper Box Co., 254 N. Santa Fe, Salina: Folding paper boxes.
Neosho Paper Products, 113 W. Main, Chanute: Gift boxes, garment boxes.
Wichita Box Co., Inc., 4202 K42 W., Wichita: Folding paper boxes.

Set-Up Paperboard Boxes

Hazelwood Paper Box Co., 121 S. Main, Lindsborg (Mailing add.: 254 N. Santa Fe, Salina): Set-up paper boxes.
Hazelwood Paper Box Co., 254 N. Santa Fe, Salina: Set-up paper boxes.
Ward Paper Box Co., 3150 Chrysler Rd., Kansas City (15): Set-up paper boxes.
Wichita Box Co., Inc., 4202 K42 W., Wichita: Set-up paper boxes.

Corrugated and Solid Fiber Boxes

C. F. Downey Box Div. (Central Fibre Prod. Co.), Funston and Fiberglas Rd., Kansas City: Corrugated shipping containers.
Hinde & Dauch (Div. W. Virginia Pulp & Paper Co.), 530 Sunshine Rd., Kansas City: Corrugated shipping boxes.
International Paper Co. (Container Div.), 2101 Kansas, Kansas City: Corrugated shipping containers.
Lawrence Paper Co., Lawrence: Corrugated shipping containers.
Love Box Co., Inc., 700 E. 37th, N. Wichita: Corrugated cartons.
Olin Mathieson Chemical Corp., 464 E. Donovan Rd., Kansas City: Corrugated containers.
Packaging Corp. of America, Box 1033, Hutchinson: Corrugating medium, egg packaging products.
Packaging Corp. of America, 3111 Fiberglas Rd., Kansas City: Corrugated shipping containers and packaging materials.

Sanitary Food Containers

Sealright Co., Inc., 2925 Fairfax Rd., Kansas City: Plastic coated paper food containers, aluminum and plastic composite containers, sanitary paper food packages, milk bottle caps and closures, milk bottles.

Fiber Cans, Tubes, Drums, and Similar Products

Greif Bros. Cooperage Corp., 17th and Osage, Kansas City: Fibre drums.
R. C. Can Co., 5500 Kansas, Kansas City: Fibre cans and tubes.

Building Paper and Building Board Mills

Insul-Wool Insulation Corp., 121 N. Dodge, Wichita: Vinylboard siding.
Lawrence Paper Co., Lawrence: Weatherproof asphalt impregnated concrete construction grade beams and tubes.
Packaging Corp. of America, Box 1033, Hutchinson: Wallboard.

PRINTING, PUBLISHING, AND ALLIED INDUSTRIES

Periodicals: Publishing, Publishing and Printing

Ag Press, Box 1009, Manhattan: Area farm paper.
Allen Press, 1041 New Hampshire, Lawrence: Scientific magazines.
Bucklin Banner, Bucklin: Trade publication.
Capper's Weekly, 616 Jefferson, Topeka: Farm paper.
Central States Construction Magazine, 4125 Gage Center Dr., Topeka: Construction magazine.
Continental Color Press, Inc., 550 Industrial Blvd., Kansas City (15): Publications.
Defender's, Inc., 2502 E. Douglas, Wichita (Mailing add.: Box 601, Oklahoma City (1), Oklahoma): Magazine.
Dormois Type Shop, 751 Minnesota, Kansas City: Magazine.
The Downtowner, 831 Minnesota, Kansas City: Publication.
Exchange Publishing Co., 201 S. Ninth, Marysville: Real estate exchange publication.
Goodnight Printing Co., 508 N. Tenth, Kansas City: Publications.
Gossip Printery, Inc., 116-118 E. Fifth, Holton: Magazines.
Herald & Banner Press, 7415 Metcalf, Overland Park: Religious publication.
Herald Publishing Co., Box 318, Newton: Religious publishing.
Kansas Color Press, Inc., 2201 Haskell, Lawrence: Magazines.
Kansas Masonic Digest, KMD Bldg., 429 W. Third (Box 707), Wichita: Magazine.
Kansas-Oklahoma Oil Reporter, Box 5525, Wichita: Periodical.
Kansas Press Association, 701 Jackson, Topeka: Magazine.
Lawrence Daily Journal-World, Lawrence: Magazines.
M. B. Publishing House, 135-137 N. Main, Hillsboro: Religious periodicals.
Midwest Industry Magazine, 4125 Gage Center Dr., Topeka: Industrial publication.

Mid-West Publishing Co., Inc., 120 N. Main, Yates Center: Magazine.
Mission Press, 8715 Johnson Dr., Merriam: Publications.
Pittcraft, Inc., 104-118 S. Locust, Pittsburg: Periodicals.
Prairie Printers, Inc., 155 N. Franklin, Colby: Historical journal.
Printing Press, 113 E. Third, Pratt: Magazines.
Stauffer Publications, Inc., 616 Jefferson, Topeka: Periodicals.
Wake Publications, 1307 W. 30th (Box 797), Topeka: Magazines.
Weekly Publishers, 2723 E. Kellogg, Wichita: Publications.
Wichita Eagle Press, 317-19 S. Market, Wichita: Publications.
World Co., Sixth and New Hampshire, Lawrence: Magazines, professional journals, fraternal publications.
Henry Wurst, Inc., 550 Industrial Blvd., Kansas City: Publications.

Books

Books: Publishing, Publishing and Printing

Central Press-Pictorial, Inc., 525 N. Kansas, Topeka: Publishing.
Hutch-Line, Inc., 408-410 N. Main, Hutchinson: Books.
Kansas Labor Weekly, 1005-07 W. Sixth, Topeka: Publishing.
Little-Blue-Book Co., Box 31, Girard: Book publishing.
McCormick-Mathers Publishing Co., 1440 E. English, Wichita: Schoolbooks, etc.
Parker & Sons Printing Co., 1952 S. Washington, Wichita: Books and pamphlets.
Tilma Printers & Publishers, 323 N. Main, Wichita: Publishing.

Book Printing

Allen Press, 1041 New Hampshire, Lawrence: Book printing.
American Yearbook Co. (Myers Div.), 501-503 Gage, Topeka: Yearbooks (high schools and colleges).
Continental Color Press, 550 Industrial Blvd., Kansas City (15): Catalogs.
Hall Lithographing Co., Inc., 1947 N. Topeka, Topeka: Book production.
Kansas Color Press, Inc., 2201 Haskell, Lawrence: Catalogs.
Moundridge Journal, 135 S. Main, Moundridge: Catalogs.
Pittcraft, Inc., 104-118 S. Locust, Pittsburg: Book printing.
World Co., Sixth and New Hampshire, Lawrence: Book and pamphlet printing.

Miscellaneous Publishing

Miscellaneous Publishing

The Allen Publishing Co., 111 E. Seventh, Newton: Telephone directories.
American Coin Publishing Co., 323 Jackson, Topeka: Coin books and supplies for collectors.
Artec, Inc., 117 S. Hydraulic, Wichita (11): Technical publications and advertising art.
Artmaster Yearbooks, 4700 W. 52nd, Mission: Publishing.
Campgrounds Unlimited, Blue Rapids: Campground guides.
City Publishing Co., 118 S. Eighth, Independence: Cross reference directories.
Dietzgen of Kansas, Inc., 131-135 S. Laura, Wichita: Oil maps and oil industry forms.
Fort Scott Printing & Advertising Co., Inc., 5 Market, Fort Scott: Calendars.
L. F. Garlinghouse Co., Inc., 820 Quincy, Topeka: Residence plans and plans books.
Goodwin Publishing Co., 1600 W. 51 St., N., Wichita: Newspapers, tabloids, handbills, price sheets, cards, etc.
R. A. Hoffman, Inc., 1421 Coolidge, Wichita (3): Church and school music.
Kansas Law Publishing Co., 1216 W. Eighth, Topeka: Law briefs and abstracts.
Perkins-Bowman, Box 3747, Wichita: Publishing.
R. L. Polk and Co., Lorraine and Santa Fe R. R., Hutchinson: City directories.
R. L. Polk and Co., 216 N. Third (Box 636), Manhattan: City directories.
Printcraft Co., 2500 Buchanan, Topeka: Publishing.
Printing, Inc., 344 N. St. Francis, Wichita: Directories, price lists.
Seaton Publishing Co., Inc., Box 787, Manhattan: Newspaper publishing.
Standard Printing Co., Inc., 702 Harrison, Topeka: Publishing.
Wilkinson-Akers, Inc., 725 Kansas, Kansas City: Calendars.

Commercial Printing, Lithographic

Acme Lithographer-Printers, 513 S. St. Francis, Wichita: Lithographing, offset printing.
American Yearbook Co. (Myers Div.), 501-503 Gage, Topeka: General litho-printing.
Anderson Printing Co., 406 N. Seneca, Wichita: Lithographing.

Arundel Book & Printing Co., 526 Arundel (Box 206), Emporia: Offset printing, letterpress printing.
Bayouth Printing Co., 811 E. Douglas, Wichita: Lithographing.
Glenn E. Bish, 513 S. St. Francis, Wichita: Lithographing.
Branch Printing Co., 101 W. Seventh, Junction City: Lithographing.
Brooks Printing & Litho, Inc., 321 N. Main, Wichita: Litho advertising and addressing.
Warren Burdick Co., 1815 N. Broadway, Wichita: Decals.
E. R. Callender Printing Co., Inc., 740 Nebraska, Kansas City: Lithographing.
Central Press, 14 S. Walnut, Hutchinson: Lithographing.
Consolidated Printing & Stationery Co., 113 N. Santa Fe, Salina: Lithographing.
Continental Color Press, Inc., 550 Industrial Blvd., Kansas City (15): Color printing.
Saml Dodsworth Printing & Stationery Co., 655 Sunshine Rd., Kansas City (15): Lithographing.
Donlevy Lithograph, Inc., 409-411 W. Douglas, Wichita: Lithographing.
Duke Printing, Inc., 1329 S. McLean, Wichita: Lithographing.
Elliott Printers, Inc., 206 N. Seventh (Box E), Garden City: Lithographing.
George Eschbaugh, Wilson: Decals, posters, emblems.
Paul F. Etrick & Associates, 1300 W. Wyatt Earp, Dodge City: Lithographing.
Paul F. Etrick & Associates, 404 E. Fulton, Garden City: Lithographing.
Herbert Etrick, Printers, 17 W. Third, Liberal: Lithographing.
Fine Arts Lithographing Co., Inc., 101 Greystone, Kansas City (3): Advertising and general commercial lithographing.
Fredonia Litho Plate Co., Box 247, Fredonia: Litho plates.
Fryer Printing & Stationery, Inc., 1209-11 Southwest Blvd., Kansas City: Lithographing.
Garman Printing & Lithographing, 8410 W. Highway 54, Wichita: Lithographing.
Hall Lithographing Co., Inc., 1947 N. Topeka, Topeka: Lithographing (color).
J. M. Hart & Co., Inc., 210 W. Sixth, Topeka: Lithographing.
Hutch-Line Inc., 408-410 N. Main, Hutchinson: Lithographing.
Inland Printing Co., 1111 E. Douglas, Wichita: Lithographing.
Kansas Color Press, Inc., 2201 Haskell, Lawrence: Broadsides.
Kansas Press, 108 S. Washington, Wichita: Lithographing.
Kennedy Printing Co., Fifth and Madison (Box 192), Fredonia: Lithographing.
Krusemark Printing Co., 115 N. Eighth, Atchison: Lithographing.
McCormick-Armstrong Co., 1501 E. Douglas, Wichita: Lithographing.
The M-J Printing Co., Box 68, Little River: Lithographing.
Midwestern Litho, Box 129, Fredonia: Lithographing and embossing.
Miller Printers, Great Bend: Lithographing.
Miracle Sign Co., 734 Washington, Wichita: Decals.
Mutual Press, Inc., 201 East B (Box 868), Hutchinson: Lithographing.
Myers Printing Co., 214 W. Commercial, Lyons: Lithographing.
Les Neel Litho, 833 W. Euclid, McPherson: Lithographing and related services.
New Era Printing Co., Gardner: Lithographing.
Parker & Sons Printing Co., 1952 S. Washington, Wichita: Lithographing.
Pittcraft, Inc., 104-118 S. Locust, Pittsburg: Lithographing.
Printcraft Co., 2500 Buchanan, Topeka: Lithographing.
Printcraft, Inc., 230 W. Ninth, Hays: Lithographing.
Quinius Multi-Letter Corp., 222 N. Market, Wichita: Lithographing.
Rea Feed Tag Service, 220 Main, Halstead: Formula feed tags.
Republic Printing Co., Box 328, Junction City: Offset printing.
The Shaeffer Printing Co., Inc., 125 N. Emporia, Wichita: Lithographing.
Tallman Printing Co., 602-604 N. Main, Ottawa: 4-color web offset printing.
Telescope Publishing Co., 1320 19th, Belleville: Lithographing.
Western Lithograph Co., First and Topeka, Wichita: Lithographing.
Western Star, Coldwater: Lithographing.
Woods-Beeton Decals, Inc., 1710 Laura, Wichita: Decals (custom order, screen printed).
Henry Wurst, Inc., 550 Industrial Blvd., Kansas City: Color printing, lithographing.

Engraving and Plate Printing

Bowman Horn Engraving, 245 N. Broadway, Wichita: Steel and copper, engraving and printing.
Capper Engraving Co., 616 Jefferson, Topeka: Engravings (zinc and copper half tones, zinc etchings, mats, electros).
Kingman Journal, Inc., Kingman: Commercial engraving.
Meade Globe-Press, Meade: Engraving.
Mid-Continent Engraving Co., 120 S. St. Francis, Wichita: Engravings and art.
Printcraft, Inc., 230 W. Ninth, Hays: Engraving.
Shadinger-Wilson Printers, Inc., 207 N. E. Third, Abilene: Engraving.

Construction of reservoirs and ponds will play major role in solution of Kansas water problems.

Stauffer Publications, Inc., 616 Jefferson, Topeka: Engravings.
Western Newspaper Union, 201 S. St. Francis, Wichita: Commercial stereotypes and advertising mats.
Wichita Eagle & Beacon Publishing Co., Inc., 825 E. Douglas, Wichita: Engravings.

Greeting Card Manufacturing

Hallmark Cards, Inc., Box 99, Lawrence: Greeting cards and related products.
Hallmark Cards, Inc., 1110 N. Second, Leavenworth: Greeting cards.
Hallmark Cards, Inc., 1029-1035 Kansas, Topeka: Greeting cards.
Reo Card Co., Inc., 269 N. Tenth, Kansas City: Contemporary cards.

Bookbinding and Related Industries

Blankbooks, Loose Leaf Binders and Devices

Adams Business Forms, Inc., 200 Jackson (Box 91), Topeka: Sales books, cafe checks, order books, one-time carbon forms, misc. business forms, NCR sets.
Armstrong Mfg. Co., 2732 Ohio, Topeka: Sales and catalog binders, post binders, ring books.
Beck-Nor Systems Co., Box 266, Salina: Simplified accounting systems.
Black and White Record Co., Box 129, Fredonia: Bookkeeping and record forms for service stations and hospitals.
Burns Publishing Co., 521 Kansas City Rd., Olathe: NCR business forms, carbon sets.
Central Check Co., 121 W. Third, Ottawa: Business records (dashboard delivery).
Childs Mfg. Co., 1100 S. Denver, El Dorado: Prescription blanks and records.
Commercial Publishers, Inc., 17th and Elliott (Box 206), Parsons: Business forms.
Consolidated Printing & Stationery Co., 113 N. Santa Fe, Salina: County records.
De Luxe Check Printers, Inc., 25 Funston Rd., Kansas City: Bank checks.
The Garden Press, 404 E. Fulton, Garden City: Business forms.
Groh Printing Co., 9 E. Fourth, Emporia: Hospital case records.
J. M. Hart & Co., Inc., 210 W. Sixth, Topeka: Accounting systems.
Hill City Times, Hill City: Office supplies.
Hoch Publishing Co., Inc., Marion: Office supplies.
Horner Co., 110 N. Emporia, Wichita: Printed business forms.
The Hospital Record Co., 125 N. Emporia, Wichita: Hospital and physicians record forms.
Hutch-Line, Inc., 408-410 N. Main, Hutchinson: Snap-out forms.
Lockwood Co., Inc., 125 N. Fifth, Atchison: County record loose-leaf binders and forms.
Mid-America Business Forms, Inc., 220 Scott, Fort Scott: One time carbon interleaved forms.
Salts Mfg. Co., 5021 Irving Dr., Wichita: Printed forms (tourist court).
Service Business Forms, Inc., 815 E. Second, Wichita: Snap-out business forms.
The Schaeffer Printing Co., Inc., 125 N. Emporia, Wichita: Business forms.
Superior School Supply, 213½ S. Central, Parsons: School supplies.
Traf-O-Teria System, Inc., 124 S. Gordy, El Dorado: Envelope type parking violation and traffic tickets.
Va-Co-Hy Business Forms, Inc., Cherokee and Magnolia, Girard: One-time carbon forms.

Bookbinding, and Miscellaneous Related Work

Acme Bindery Co., 1912 Sandusky, Kansas City: Bookbinding.
American Bindery, 914 Jefferson, Topeka: Bookbinding.
Armstrong Mfg. Co., 2732 Ohio, Topeka: Gold stamping, silk screening.
Capitol City Bindery Co., 2018 E. 28th, Topeka: Bookbinding (hard, flexible, plastic and stripping), Bible rebinding, loose leaf binders, record books, index cutting, gang punching, gold stamping and embossing.
Central Press, 14 S. Walnut, Hutchinson: Wire-o-binding.
Handy Bindery, 1204 Laramie, Marysville: Bookbinding.
Mid-West Bindery, Inc., 210 S. Emporia, Wichita (2): Bookbinding.
F. M. Steves & Sons, 1017 Kansas, Topeka: Binding.
Western Bindery Products Co., 323 W. Fifth, Topeka: Bookbinding, machine ruling, perforating, punching, loose leaf binding, plastic binding, folding, die cutting, etc.
Wichita Bindery, 415 S. St. Francis, Wichita: Bookbinding.
Wichita Eagle & Beacon Publishing Co., Inc., 825 E. Douglas, Wichita: Bookbinding.
World Co., Sixth and New Hampshire, Lawrence: Book binding.

Service Industries for the Printing Trade

Typesetting

Ted Andrews & Sons, 437 N. St. Francis, Wichita: Typography.
Dormois Type Shop, 751 Minnesota, Kansas City: Typesetting.
Missouri-Central Type Foundry, 703-711 E. Murdock, Wichita: Printer's type.
Topeka Typeshop, 511 Jackson, Topeka: Line composed type, reproproofing.

Photoengravings

Arrow Litho Camera, 100 W. Fifth, Topeka: Offset plates and negatives.
Beloit Daily Call, 122 E. Court, Beloit: Electronic engraving (plastic halftone plates).
Edwards Typographic Service, Inc., 340 Pattie, Wichita: Negatives and offset plates, industrial photography, complete art and composition.
Etchrite, Inc., 1337 Massachusetts (Box 228), Lawrence: Printing plates of all types.
Graphic Arts Engraving Co., Inc., 705 N. Eighth, Kansas City: Photoengravings.
Mainline Printing Co., 206 W. Fourth, Topeka: Offset printing, negatives, plates.
Marysville Publishing Co., 1000 Broadway, Marysville: Photoengraving.
Mid-Continent Engraving Co., 120 S. St. Francis, Wichita: Photoengravings, offset plates.
Midwestern Litho, Box 129, Fredonia: Die cutting.
Sun Engraving Co., Inc., 1818 Broadway, Parsons: Photoengravings, offset negatives and plates, 3 and 4 color process plates and commercial art, wraparound letter press plates.
Topeka Engraving Co., Inc., 110 W. Sixth, Topeka: Photoengravings, offset plates and negatives.
Tribune Publishing Co., 2014-16 Forest, Great Bend: Photoengravings.

CHEMICALS AND ALLIED PRODUCTS

Industrial Inorganic and Organic Chemicals

Alkalies and Chlorine

Frontier Chemical Co. (Div. of Vulcan Materials Co.), Municipal Airport Terminal (Box 545), Wichita (1): Chlorine, caustic soda (50% and 73%), caustic soda (flake and solid).
Thompson-Hayward Chemical Co., 5200 Speaker Rd., Kansas City (6): Alkalies and chlorine.

Industrial Gases

Air Reduction Sales Co., (Div. of Air Reduction Co., Inc.), 1100 S. Packard, Kansas City: Oxygen, acetylene, helium, argon, nitrogen.
Air Reduction Sales Co. (Div. of Air Reduction Co., Inc.), 602 E. 29th, Wichita: Oxygen, acetylene, helium, argon.
Cities Service Helex, Inc., Route 1, Satanta: Helium, crude liquid hydrocarbons.
FMC Corp. (Inorganic Chemicals Div.), Ninth and Maple, Lawrence: Dry ice.
Jayhawk Welding Supply Co., 317 Jackson, Topeka: Carbon dioxide gas.
Kansas Carbonic Co., 707 N. Main, Wichita: Carbonic gas, soda dispensers and allied accessories.
Kansas Oxygen, Inc., Box 551, Hutchinson: Oxygen and acetylene gases.
Linde Co. (Div. of Union Carbide Corp.), 550 E. 17th, Wichita: Oxygen, acetylene, nitrogen, hydrogen, argon.
National Cylinder Gas Products (Div. Chemetron Corp.), 1614 State, Kansas City: Oxygen, hydrogen, nitrogen, acetylene, argon.
National Helium Corp., Liberal: Helium.
Northern Helex Co., Bushton: Helium.
Pure Carbonic Air Reduction, 7th and Kindleberger, Kansas City: Carbon dioxide (solid and liquid).
Spencer Chemical Co., Pittsburg: Dry ice, liquid carbon dioxide.
U. S. Dept. of Interior, Bureau of Mines (Otis Helium Plant), Otis: Helium.

Dyes, Dye (Cyclic) Intermediates, and Organic Pigments (Lakes and Toners)

Frontier Chemical Co. (Div. of Vulcan Materials Co.), Municipal Airport Terminal (Box 545), Wichita (1): Benzene hexachloride (high and low gamma), pentachlorophenol, benzoic acid.
Skelly Oil Co., Box 1121, El Dorado: Phenol.

Inorganic Pigments

Eagle-Picher Co., Galena: Lead and zinc pigments.
The Sherwin Williams Co. (Ozark Smelting & Mining Div.), W. Fourth (Box 855), Coffeyville: Lithopone, leaded zinc oxide, zinc oxide, zinc sulphate, cadmium, barium carbonate, barium monohydrate.

Industrial Organic Chemicals, Not Elsewhere Classified

Abbott Laboratories (Wichita Chemical Div.), 6601 S. 71st, Wichita: Cyclohexylamine.
Callery Chemical Co., Box 199, Lawrence: Boron fuel and chemicals.
Frontier Chemical Co. (Div. of Vulcan Materials Co.), Municipal Airport Terminal (Box 545), Wichita (1): perchloroethylene, carbon tetrachloride, chloroform, methylene chloride, methyl bromide.
Reichhold Chemicals, Inc., Sunshine and Fiberglas Rds., Kansas City: Formaldehyde.
Spencer Chemical Co., Pittsburg: Methanol.

Industrial Inorganic Chemicals, Not Elsewhere Classified

Air Reduction Sales Co. (Div. of Air Reduction Co., Inc.), 1100 S. Packard, Kansas City: Carbide.
Air Reduction Sales Co. (Div. of Air Reduction Co., Inc.), 602 E. 29th, Wichita: Carbide.
Chemi-Sol Sales, 2412 E. Fourth, Hutchinson: Oil field chemicals.
Cooperative Farm Chemicals, Box 80, Lawrence: Ammonium nitrate, anhydrous ammonia, nitrogen solutions, urea-nitrate solutions.
Eagle-Picher Co., Galena: Sulfuric acid.
FMC Corp. (Inorganic Chemicals Div.), Ninth and Maple, Lawrence: Chemicals (tetrasodium pyrophosphate, sodium tripolyphosphate, phosphate, disodium phosphate, monosodium phosphate, sodium hexametaphosphate).
Frontier Chemical Co. (Div. of Vulcan Materials Co.), Municipal Airport Terminal (Box 545), Wichita (1): Muriatic acid (20° and 22° baume), anhydrous hydrogen chloride, anhydrous ammonia.
Homolka Grain & Supply, 910 W. 12th, Ellsworth: Stock salt.
Linde Co. (Div. of Union Carbide Corp.), 550 E. 17th, Wichita: Carbide.
O'Kan Chemical Co., 17 Kansas, S. Hutchinson: Oil well chemicals.
Philadelphia Quartz Co., 17th and Kansas, Kansas City: Silicates of soda.
Reichhold Chemicals, Inc., Sunshine and Fiberglas Rds., Kansas City: Liquid phenolic resins, polyvinyl acetate emulsions.
Spencer Chemical Co., Pittsburg: Anhydrous ammonia (tank cars), refrigeration grade ammonia (cylinders), ammonium nitrate (fertilizer grade and 83% solution), ammoniating solutions, nitric acid.
Thompson-Hayward Chemical Co., 5200 Speaker Rd., Kansas City (6): Industrial chemicals.
Thompson-Hayward Chemical Co., 727 E. Osie, Wichita (2): Industrial chemicals.
U. S. Industrial Chemicals, De Soto: Sulfuric acid.

Plastics Materials and Synthetic Resins, Synthetic Rubber, Synthetic and Other Man-Made Fibers, Except Glass

E. I. du Pont de Nemours & Co., Inc., Box 481, Topeka: Cellophane.
Mid-Con Plastics, Inc., 1556 Pattie, Wichita (11): Plastic materials and tooling resins, epoxy concrete binder and coatings.
Plastifloor, Inc., 1105 E. 30th, Hutchinson: Liquid plastic floor coating (for woods, asphalt, masonite and cement).
Sherwood and Co., Inc., 2100 E. 37th N. (Box 3647), Wichita: Plastic resins and specialized adhesives.
Thompson-Hayward Chemical Co., 5200 Speaker Rd., Kansas City (6): Plastic materials and synthetic resins.

Drugs

Biological Products

Bio Laboratories, Inc., 6320 Kansas, Kansas City: Veterinary biologicals.
Chemical Commodities, Inc., Olathe: Chemical products (veterinary).
Guilfoil Serum Co., 14-22 N. Second, Kansas City: Anti-hog-cholera serum and virus.
Hill Packing Co., 401 Harrison, Topeka: Glands for pharmaceutical usage.
Johnson Serum Co., 422 E. Crane, Topeka: Anti-hog-cholera serum.
National Laboratories Corp., 210 Central, Kansas City: Anti-hog-cholera serum and virus.
Southwestern Laboratories, Inc., 821 E. 21st (Box 1540), Wichita (1): Anti-hog-cholera serum, virus and vaccines.
Southwestern Vaccine Corp., Inc., Box 1540, Wichita: Hog cholera vaccine.
Vetline Laboratories, Inc., 12230 Santa Fe Dr., Lenexa: Veterinary biological products.
Vita-Vex, Inc., Sixth and Santa Fe, Coffeyville: Live yeast cultures.

Medicinal Chemicals and Botanical Products

Vita-Vex, Inc., Sixth and Santa Fe, Coffeyville: Vitamin concentrates.

Pharmaceutical Preparations

Airosol Co., Inc., 525 N. 11th (Box 240), Neodesha: Pharmaceuticals.
Archer-Taylor Drug Co., 335 W. Lewis, Wichita: Pharmaceuticals (medicinal elixirs, tablets, ointments, etc.).
Bear Mfg. Co., Inc., 606 Main, Winfield: Mentholated ointment.
Central Specialty Co., 10 N. Baltimore, Kansas City: Liniment.
Chemical Commodities, Inc., Olathe: Solvents.
Cramer Chemical Co., W. Warren, Gardner: Athletic trainers' supplies.
Curts Laboratories, Inc., 70 Central, Kansas City (18): Veterinary pharmaceuticals.
Dermal Products Co., 523 Mills Bldg., Topeka: Chigger-tox.
Excel Packing Co., Inc., 900 E. 21st, Wichita: Pharmaceuticals.
W. W. Gavitt Medical Co., 601-603 E. Fourth (Box 26), Topeka: Herb tablets.
Haver-Lockhart Laboratories, 12707 W. 63rd, Shawnee: Veterinary medicines.
Jensen-Salsbery Labs, Inc., 2000 S. 11th, Kansas City: Veterinary supplies.
Kinreco Products, 1408 W. 15th (Box 513), Topeka: Medicines.
Physicians & Surgeons Pharmacal Co. (E & J Laboratory), 710 N. Sixth, Kansas City: Pharmaceuticals.
Pruitt Laboratories, 901-1029 W. 29th, Wichita: Poultry remedies.
Sifer's, Inc., 118 W. Jackson, Iola: Aerosol medicines.
Unruh's Hatchery, Galva: Poultry remedies.

Soap, Detergents and Cleaning Preparations, Perfumes, Cosmetics, and Other Toilet Preparations

Soap and Other Detergents, Except Specialty Cleaners

Attica Chemical Co., Attica: Soap.
Central Chemical Co., Inc., 3130 Brinkerhoff Rd., Kansas City (15): Surgical and liquid hand soaps.
Colgate-Palmolive Co., 17th and Kansas, Kansas City: Soap, detergents and glycerin.
Manufacturer's Chemical & Soap, 823 S. Main, Hutchinson: Chemical soaps.

Procter & Gamble Mfg. Co., 19th and Kansas, Kansas City: Soap, detergents, and glycerine.
Puro-O-Zone Chemical Co., Inc., 708-718 Connecticut (Box 227), Lawrence: Soap.
Safeway Stores, Inc. (Brookside Div.), 219 N. Monroe, Hutchinson: Liquid detergents and cleaners.
Swift & Co., 10 Berger, Kansas City: Soap and glycerin.
Vibra-Clean Products, 1016 S. Coy, Kansas City: Industrial soap.
Whitaker & Co., 816 N. Glendale, Wichita: Soap compounds.

Specialty Cleaning, Polishing, and Sanitation Preparations, Except Soap and Detergents

Airosol Co., Inc., 525 N. 11th (Box 240), Neodesha: Glass cleaner, deodorizers, moth proofers, repellants, pet sprays, spray shoe polish, spray wax.
Attica Chemical Co., Attica: Cleaning preparations, radiator cleaner, exterminators, repellants, deodorant.
Carbro, Inc., 209-11-13 N. St. Francis (Box 487), Wichita: Window cleaner and insecticides, air fresheners.
Central Chemical Co., Inc., 3130 Brinkerhoff Rd., Kansas City (15): Disinfectants, polishes and waxes, liquid and powered cleansers, insecticides and deodorants.
Champion Packaged Products, Inc., La Cygne: Fabric treating compounds.
C. A. Fowler & Sons, 211 S. St. Francis, Wichita: Linoleum cleaners and waxes.
Hanlon Chemical Co., Inc., 1016 S. Coy, Kansas City: Skin cleanser, cleaning compounds, white wall tire cleaner.
Kaufman Laboratories, 734 Commercial, Atchison: Liquid soaps, waxes and polishes, disinfectants.
Keystone Chemical Co., 2808 Ohio (Box 2337), Wichita: Automotive cleaning compounds.
Kleen Sheen Products Inc., Wilson: Silver, brass and copper kleen.
Line-X Co., Inc., 1602 East St., Iola: Cleaners.
Mira-Kleer Products, 113 N. Main, Smith Center: All-purpose cleaner and polish.
Mitchell Janitor Supply Co., 1232 E. Douglas, Wichita: Liquid glass cleaner.
Mystic Mist Corp., 801 S. Main, Hutchinson: Liquid and powder cleaners for automotive, janitorial, household and industrial cleaning.
National Laboratories Div. (Sekan Chemicals, Inc.), 2001 Broadway, Parsons: Cleaning compounds.
Nova Products, Inc., Kansas at Railroad, Kansas City: Cleaning compounds.
Permatex Co., Inc., 3255 Harvester Rd., Kansas City: Cleaners and polishes, parts cleaners.
Pittsburg Chemical Co., Inc., 109 W. Jackson, Pittsburg: Dry cleaners supplies.
Private Brands, Inc., 300 S. Third, Kansas City: Household insecticides.
Process Solvent Co., Inc., 1040 Chelsea Trafficway, Kansas City: Radiator cleaner, hand soap, carburetor cleaner, block and radiator flusher, industrial concrete remover, brick cleaner, curing compounds, marine equipment cleaners, etc.
Pur-O-Zone Chemical Co., Inc., 708-718 Connecticut (Box 227), Lawrence: Liquid dishwashing detergent, dishwashing compound, boiler treatment, mop treatment, cleaners (floor, glass, upholstery).
Reid Supply Co., Inc., 2709 Seward, Topeka: Various cleaning compounds.
Rockwell Laboratories, Inc., 300 S. Third, Kansas City: Household insecticides.
Safeway Stores, Inc. (Brookside Div.), 219 N. Monroe, Hutchinson: Household waxes and floor cleaners.
Spanglers, Inc., 836 N. Madison, Topeka: Dance wax.
Sutherland-Becker Labs., Inc., Burlingame: Cleaners and anti-fogging compounds, automotive and optical).
Thompson-Hayward Chemical Co., 5200 Speaker Rd., Kansas City (6): Laundry and dry cleaning supplies.
Thompson-Hayward Chemical Co., 727 E. Osie, Wichita (2): Laundry-dry cleaning supplies.
Warwick Wax Div. (Western Petrochemical Corp.), Box 558, Chanute: High melting point microcrystalline and oxidized waxes.
Water Treat Chemicals, Inc., 920 Perry, Wichita: Radiator and boiler cleaner.
Waxene Products Co., 2023 N. Broadway, Wichita: Sweeping compounds, sawdust and oil absorbents.
Western Oh-Zo-Dry Co., Tonganoxie: Dry cleaner.
Whitaker & Co., 816 N. Glendale, Wichita: Disinfectants, household insecticides.
Wichita Brush & Chemical Co., Inc., 234 N. Main, Wichita: Cleaning chemicals.
Zelinkoff Co., 345-57 N. Main, Wichita: Polishes.

Perfumes, Cosmetics, and Other Toilet Preparations

Bear Mfg. Co., Inc., 606 Main, Winfield: After-shave lotion, brushless shave cream, shampoo, hand cream, hair dressing.
Carbro, Inc., 209-11-13 N. St. Francis (Box 487), Wichita: Hair spray and hand creme.
Central Specialty Co., 10 N. Baltimore, Kansas City: Cosmetics, barber supplies.
Colgate-Palmolive Co., 17th and Kansas, Kansas City: Toilet preparations.
Cressler Products Co., 223 E. Eighth, Newton: Tablet dentifrice.
Mr. Harolds, 6627 E. Kellogg, Wichita (7): Hair cosmetics and grooming aids.
Nellie Harrison Cosmetics, 2602 E. Douglas, Wichita: Face cream, face lotion, eye cream, scalp ointment.
Sifer's, Inc., 118 W. Jackson, Iola: Aerosol cosmetics.

Paints, Varnishes, Lacquers, Enamels, and Allied Products

Airosol Co., Inc., 525 N. 11th (Box 240), Neodesha: Spray paint.
Aluminum & Lead Paint Co., 200 N. Millwood, Wichita: Paints.
Harry Byers & Sons, Inc., 500 N. Plummer, Chanute: Masonry paint.
M. L. Campbell Co., 2909 Chrysler Rd., Kansas City: Industrial finishes, lacquers, synthetic enamels and primers, thinners and furniture repair specialties.
Chas. Dutcher Paint & Varnish Mfg. Co., 1330 E. 37th St. N., Wichita: Paint and varnish.
Enmar, Inc., 1424 E. 25th, Wichita: Lacquers, enamels, thinners.
Kansas Paint & Color Co., 132 N. Mosley, Wichita: Paints and protective coatings.
Osage Paint & Varnish Co., 720 Kansas, Kansas City: Paint and varnishes, roof coatings.
Pur-O-Zone Chemical Co., Inc., 708-718 Connecticut (Box 227), Lawrence: Penetrating floor seals and finishes.
Reliance Chemical Co., Pauline: Paint for traffic lines.
Salina Concrete Products, Inc., 1102 W. Ash, Salina: Paints.
Sifer's, Inc., 118 W. Jackson, Iola: Aerosol paints.
Western Oh-Zo-Dry Co., Tonganoxie: Paint.
Wilko Paint, Inc., 5613 N. Broadway, Wichita: Paint and allied products.

Gum and Wood Chemicals

Chetopa Charcoal Co., Inc., Chetopa: Raw charcoal.

Agricultural Chemicals

Airosol Co., Inc., 525 N. 11th (Box 240), Neodesha: Insecticides.
Anthony Chemical Co., Box 27, Anthony: Poisonous insecticide.
Attica Chemical Co., Attica: Insecticides.
Chemi-Sol Sales, 2412 E. Fourth, Hutchinson: Agricultural chemicals.
Frontier Chemical Co. (Div. of Vulcan Materials Co.), Municipal Airport Terminal (Box 545), Wichita (1): Grain fumigants.
W. T. Muncy Co., 300 S. Third, Kansas City: Agricultural chemicals.
National Laboratories Div. (Sekan Chemicals, Inc.), 2001 Broadway, Parsons: Insecticides and herbicides, disinfectants and rodenticides.
Nova Products, Inc., Kansas at Railroad, Kansas City: Insecticides.
Odor Aire, Inc., 1019 E. Second (Box 1892), Wichita: Insecticides, moth blocks.
Patterson Packaging Div. (Patterson Chemical Co.), 625 James, Kansas City (Mailing add.: 1400 Union, K. C., Mo.): Insecticides, fungicides, rodenticides.
Phinney's, 317 Broadway, Larned: Pesticides.
Private Brands, Inc., 300 S. Third, Kansas City: Agricultural chemicals (insecticides, weed killers, etc.).
Pruitt Laboratories, 901-1029 W. 29th, Wichita: Insecticides.
Sifer's, Inc., 118 W. Jackson, Iola: Aerosol insecticides.
Spencer Chemical Co., Pittsburg: Herbicides.
Thompson-Hayward Chemical Co., 5200 Speaker Rd., Kansas City (6): Agricultural chemicals, feed chemicals.
Thompson-Hayward Chemical Co., 727 E. Osie, Wichita (2): Agricultural chemicals.
Robert S. Wise Co., Inc., 502 E. 33rd St. N. (Box 2381), Wichita: Herbicides, insecticides and rodenticides.

Miscellaneous Chemical Products

Glue and Gelatin

H. B. Fuller Co. of Mo., 200 Funston Rd., Kansas City: Industrial adhesives.
Gifford's Lapidary, Box 416, Haysville: Adhesive liquid to cement gems.
Leech Products, Inc., Fourth and Hendricks, Hutchinson: Glues, liquid cement (all purpose adhesive).
Swift & Co., 10 Berger, Kansas City: Gelatin and adhesives, glue, casings.

Carbon Black

Columbian Carbon Co., Route 1 (Box 114), Ulysses: Carbon black.

Chemicals and Chemical Preparations, Not Elsewhere Classified

Airosol Co., Inc., 525 N. 11th (Box 240), Neodesha: Charcoal lighter.
American Salt Corp., Lyons: Salt and compressed salt pellets for water softening plants.
Barton Salt Co., Box 989, Hutchinson: Salt.
Beal, Inc., 4001 Kaw Dr., Kansas City: Custom compounding and packaging of chemicals.
Carey Salt Co., 1800 Carey, Hutchinson: Salt.
Cleveland Lithichrome, Inc., 1024 E. Wall, Fort Scott: Coloring for stone and glass, stone adhesive and waterproofer.
Clorox Co., (Procter & Gamble), 1815 Bayard, Kansas City: Household bleaches.
Deady Chemical Co., 1401 Fairfax Trafficway, Kansas City (15): Water treating chemicals.
Frontier Chemical Co. (Div. of Vulcan Materials Co.), Municipal Airport Terminal (Box 545), Wichita (1): Salt.
Global Brands, Inc., 141 N. Elizabeth, Wichita: Permanent antifreeze.
Independent Salt Co., Kanopolis: Rock salt.
Keystone Chemical Co., 2808 Ohio (Box 2337), Wichita: Industrial cleaning compounds, de-greasers, packing house, dairy, food processing cleaners, bleach solution.
Line-X Co., Inc., 1602 East St., Iola: Bleach, water treating chemicals, chemical specialties.
Lubri-Gel Products Mfg. Co., WaKeeney: Drilling mud.
McPherson Custom Products, 500 W. Hayes, McPherson (Mailing add.: 504 W. Kansas): Drilling starch.
McPherson Mud Seal Co., 504 W. Kansas, McPherson: Mud seal for drilling well.
Mid-West Oil Co., 50-60 S. James, Kansas City: Antifreeze.
Morton Salt Co., Box 753, Hutchinson: Salt.
Nova Products, Inc., Kansas at Railroad, Kansas City: Chemical specialties.
Odor Aire, Inc., 330 N. Mosley, Wichita: Bathroom deodorants.
Pawnee Salt Co. (Div. Davis Mud & Chemical, Inc.), Pawnee Rock (Mailing add.: Box 523, Great Bend): Granulated salt, water softening salt pellets, chemicals.
The Penn-Central Co., Inc., Roe at Merriam Blvd., Kansas City: Chemicals.
Permatex Co., Inc., 3255 Harvester Rd., Kansas City: Sealing compounds, surface coatings, lubricating oils, hydraulic fluids.
Physicians & Surgeons Pharmacal Co. (E & J Laboratory), 710 N. Sixth, Kansas City: Cleaning and boiler compound.
Private Brands, Inc., 300 S. Third, Kansas City: Antifreeze compounds.
Process Solvent Co., Inc., 1040 Chelsea Trafficway, Kansas City: Water pump lubricant, form oil.
Pur-O-Zone Chemical Co., Inc., 708-718 Connecticut (Box 227), Lawrence: Neutral rubber dressing, disinfectants and deodorants.
Quaker Oats Co., Hiawatha: Chemicals.
Reid Supply Co., Inc., 2709 Seward, Topeka: Boiler compounds, battery acid, swim pool chemicals.
Reid Supply Co., Inc., 306 W. Second, Wichita: Chemicals, laundry and dry cleaning, dairy and bottles supplies, boiler compounds, battery acid, swim pool chemicals.
Safeway Stores, Inc. (Brookside Div.), 219 N. Monroe, Hutchinson: Household bleaches, liquid starch.
Security Oil Co., 920 E. 19th, Wichita: Antifreeze.
Sutherland-Becker Labs, Inc., Burlingame: Chemical specialties, synthetic lubricant.
Universal Motor Oil Co., Inc., Box 3145, Wichita: Antifreeze.
Vonolite Corp, Iola: Fireproof insulating compound.
Western Oh-Zo-Dry Co., Tonganoxie: Waterproofing materials.

PETROLEUM REFINING AND RELATED INDUSTRIES

Petroleum Refining

American Oil Co., 1101 Illinois, Neodesha: Petroleum products.
American Petrofina, Box 551, El Dorado: Petroleum products.
Apco Oil Corp., Arkansas City: Petroleum products.
Century Refining Co., Shallow Water (Mailing add.: Box 127, Scott City): Petroleum products, LPG and natural gasoline.
Chanute Refining Co., Box 431, Chanute: Petroleum products.
Cities Service Oil Co., Route 1, Hutchinson: Liquid petroleum products.
Cities Service Oil Co., (Wichita Gasoline Plant), 901 W. MacArthur Rd., Wichita: LPG and natural gasoline, oil.
Columbian Carbon Co., Route 1 (Box 114), Ulysses: LPG and natural gasoline.
Co-op. Refinery Assn., Coffeyville: Petroleum products.
Co-op. Refinery Assn., Box D, Phillipsburg: Petroleum products.
Derby Refining Co., (Div. of Colorado Oil & Gas Corp.), 202 W. First, Wichita: Petroleum products.
Dunn-Mar Oil & Gas Co., Albert: LPG and natural gasoline, crude oil.
Hugoton Production Co., Garden City: LPG and natural gasoline.
Kansas Hydrocarbons Co., Burrton (Mailing add.: 3424 East G, Hutchinson): Butane, propane and natural gasoline.
Kansas Hydrocarbons Co., Cheney (Mailing add.: 3424 East G, Hutchinson): Butane, propane and natural gasoline.
Kansas-Nebraska Natural Gas Co., Deerfield: LPG and natural gasoline.
Kewanee Oil Co., Box 2093, Wichita (1): Crude oil.
Mid-America Refining Co., Inc., Box 31, Chanute: Petroleum products.
Mobil Oil Co. (Div. Socony Mobil Oil Co., Inc.), Box 546, Augusta: Petroleum products.
Mobil Oil Co. (Div. Socony Mobil Oil Co., Inc.), Ulysses: LPG and natural gasoline.
National Co-op. Refinery Assn., Box 770, McPherson: Petroleum products.
Northern Gas Products Co., Bushton: Propane, butane, isobutane, natural gasoline.
Northern Natural Gas Co., Sublette: Natural gasoline.
Phillips Petroleum Co., 2029 Fairfax Trafficway, Kansas City: Petroleum products.
Rounds & Stewart Natural Gas Co., Inc., Marion (Mailing add.: 820 Union Center Bldg., Wichita): Gasoline, propane and butane.
Skelly Oil Co., Box 1121, El Dorado: Petroleum products, natural gasoline.
Skelly Oil Co., Medicine Lodge, Petroleum products.
Skelly Oil Co., Minneola: Propane and natural gasoline.
Spivey Gasoline Plant, Mobil Oil Co. (Div. of Socony Mobil Oil Co., Inc.), Box 129, Attica: LPG and natural gasoline.
Texaco, Inc., Burden (Mailing add.: Box 504, Winfield): LPG and natural gasoline.

Ulysses Plant of Pan American, Route 3 (Box 21A), Ulysses: Propane, isobutane, normal butane, natural gasoline.
Vickers Refining Co., Box 2240, Wichita: Petroleum products, petroleum chemicals.

Paving and Roofing Materials

Paving Mixtures and Blocks

Asphalt Sales Co., 1440 Kansas, Kansas City: Paving material.
Aubel Asphalt Co., E. Highway 40 (Box 261), Hays: Hot mix asphalt.
Hankamer Asphalt Co., Inc., 2150 Kansas, Topeka: Asphalt.
Holland Construction Co., Inc., Box 396, Lenexa: Asphalt paving mixtures.
Inland Asphalt Co., 107 Osage, Kansas City: Hot and cold mixed asphalt concrete.
Irontite of Kansas, Inc., Marion (Mailing add.: Scott City): Foamed asphalt concrete, crack filler and sealer.
Kansas Asphalt Co., Coffeyville: Asphalt.
Kansas Emulsions, Inc., 800 E. Tenth (Box 1264), El Dorado: Emulsified asphalts.
Peerless Quarries, Inc., 6300 Inland Dr., Kansas City: Hot mix asphalt.
Ritchie Bros. Construction Co., 1820 N. Mosley, Wichita (4): Asphalt paving mixtures.

Asphalt Felts and Coatings

Royal Brand Roofing, Inc., Phillipsburg: Packaged asphalt, composition, roll roofing and shingles.

Miscellaneous Products of Petroleum and Coal

Lubricating Oils and Greases

Beal, Inc., 4001 Kaw Dr., Kansas City: Custom compounding and packaging of petroleum.
Global Brands, Inc., 141 N. Elizabeth, Wichita: Motor oils, upper cylinder oil, lubricating oils and greases (custom packaging).
Home Oil Co., Inc., 125 N. Elizabeth, Wichita: Lubricating oils and greases (custom packaging).
Inter-State Oil Co., Inc., 87 Shawnee, Kansas City: Lubricating oils and greases.
K-T Oil Corp., 1028 E. 21st, Wichita: Blended oils.
Lehunt Oil & Gas Co., Inc., Box 338, Cherryvale: Lubricating oils and greases.
McDonald Oil Co., 1603 S. Walnut, Coffeyville: Rerefined oil.
Mid-West Oil Co., 50-60 S. James, Kansas City: Lubricating oils and greases.
Mobil Oil Co. (Div. of Socony Mobil Oil Co., Inc.), 966 Sunshine Rd., Kansas City: Lubricants.
The Penn-Central Co., Inc., Roe at Merriam Blvd., Kansas City: Lubricating oils.
Radium Petroleum Co., Box 61, Shawnee Mission: Refined motor oils.
Security Oil Co., 920 E. 19th, Wichita: Lubricating oils, motor fuels.
Southwest Grease & Oil Co., Inc., 220 W. Waterman, Wichita: Petroleum lubricating greases, petroleum specialties.
Super Refined Oil Co., 915 E. 21st, Wichita (14): Oil Reclaiming.
Universal Motor Oil Co., Inc., Box 3145, Wichita: Lubricating oils and greases.

Products of Petroleum and Coal, Not Elsewhere Classified

Jayhawk Charcoal Co., Inc., 406 Maple, Chetopa: Charcoal briquettes.
Mackie Clemens Fuel Co., Pittsburg: Washed coal.
Pittsburg & Midway Coal Mining Co., Mine No. 19, Hallowell: Coal processing and washing.

RUBBER AND MISCELLANEOUS PLASTIC PRODUCTS

Tires and Inner Tubes

The Goodyear Tire and Rubber Co., (Topeka Plant), Box 1069, Topeka: Tires.
Hudson & Odom Tire Co., Inc., 3349 Harvester Rd., Kansas City (15): Tire retreading for truck and earth mover equipment.
Press Wheels, Unlimited, (Div. Stewart Investments, Inc.), Airport Rd. and Santa Fe R. R., Hutchinson: Tires for grain drill press wheels, lister and planters.

Fabricated Rubber Products, Not Elsewhere Classified

Jackord Co., 111 N. Jefferson, Plainville: Rubber door knob lever.
Kansas Foundation for the Blind, 223 W. Third, Wichita: Industrial tire link floor mats.
Kansas Industries for the Blind, 925 Sunshine Rd., Kansas City (15): Tire strip mats.
Kansas Industries for the Blind, 425 MacVicar, Topeka: Tire link and rubber floor mats.
Moore Rubber & Plastic Co., Municipal Airport (Box 852), Great Bend: Sheet rubber tank coverings and linings, hazardous liquid handling hose (continuous lengths), rubber and plastic lined pipe, spouting, valves and fittings.
O'Neill Tank Co., Fifth and C Sts., Westport Addition, Route 1, Great Bend: Rubber lined products for corrosive and abrasive services.
H. K. Porter Co., Inc., (Thermoid Div., Chanute Works), 201 N. Allen, Chanute: Flexible rubber hose.
Rubber Supply, Inc., 719 E. Third, Wichita (2): Die cut rubber products.
Superior Foam Co., Inc., 1400 N. Fifth, Kansas City: Bonded shredded foam rubber, and bonded shredded polyurethane.
Topeka Rubber Supply, Inc., 408 W. First, Topeka: Fabricated rubber products.

Miscellaneous Plastic Products

Ames Industries, Inc., 528 W. Douglas (Box 3426), Wichita (13): Plastic apron bands.
Bergman Sign Co., (Plastic Div.), 116 E. Eighth, Coffeyville: Plastic signs.
Brown Neon Sign Co., 1305 N. 38th, Kansas City: Plastic signs.
Burnham Products, Inc., 4203 W. Harry, Wichita: Molders and fabricators of fiberglass laminates and plastic tooling, fibre-lok tool panels, fish transporting bottles.
Cantrall Sign Co., Inc., 940 Osage, Kansas City: Plastic signs.
Carbro, Inc., 209-11-13 N. St. Francis (Box 487), Wichita: Decorative plastic containers, plastic laminates, plastic products.
Century Plastics, 111 W. Locust (Box 789), El Dorado; Luminiscent reel handle knobs and light scopes for checking gun barrels, custom injection molding of thermo-plastics.
Childs Mfg. Co., 1100 S. Denver, El Dorado: Signs (engraved plastic).
Cleveland Lithichrome, Inc., 1024 E. Wall, Fort Scott: Epoxy coatings and adhesives.
Consolidated Plastics, Inc., 500 W. First, McPherson: Plastic extrusions from vinyl and polyethylene, plastic pipe (PVC sizes ⅜ inch 6 inch).
Durapane Corp., 112 Osage, Kansas City: Plastic panels (fiberglass reinforced) flat or corrugated, fiberglass reinforced polyester tanks or cylinders, panels, cardboard or aluminum honeycomb cores, skins as specified.
Electronic Motors, Inc., Fifth and Richmond, Kansas City: Plastic products (motor components for medical and electronic industries) specialty plastics molding.
The Fortune Co., 1100 W. 37 N., Wichita (4): Plastic pipe fittings and parts, plastic tank linings.
Gott Mfg. Co., Inc., 1608 Wheat Rd., Winfield: Plastic containers.
Green Contracting & Engineering Co., Inc., 1135 N. Washington, Wichita: Plastic pipe fittings and parts, plastic tanks, tank linings and pit liners.
Hedges Neon Sales, Inc., 616 Reynolds, Salina: Signs (plastic).
Hiline Plastics, Inc., 600 E. Main, Gardner: Custom plastic extrusions, injection molding.
A. G. Holwick Co., 1604 Railroad, Phillipsburg: Kleerview plastic windshield covers.
IXL Mfg. Corp., 1709-11 W. Second, Wichita (3): Small household items (plastic).
Kansas Plastic Pipe Co., 1632 Terminal, Garden City: Plastic pipe, industrial tubing, custom extrusions.
Lofland Sail-Craft, Inc., 4123 N. Broadway, Wichita (19): Misc. fiberglass products.
Lucille's, Lindsborg: Plastic comfy tabs (for brush rollers).
Mason Plastics Co., Inc., 911 Osage, Kansas City: Plastic processing of bowling pins.
Midwest Plastics Corp., 7015 Pueblo, Wichita: Nameplates, dies, plastic forming.
Monarch Molding, Inc., 120 Liberty, Council Grove: Injection molding articles.
Moore Rubber & Plastic Co., Municipal Airport (Box 852), Great Bend: Fiberglass reinforced plastic pipe (continuous lengths).
Multi-Plastics, Inc., 2148 S. Hoover, Wichita: Barricades (fiberglass products).
Plastic Fabricating Co., Inc., 722 E. Ninth, Wichita: Fiberglass reinforced plastics, compression molding, plastic sheet forming.
Plasti-Craft, Inc., 616 Pennsylvania, Wichita: Plasti-foam, plasti-pak packing materials, flora foam, flotation plasti-panels, walls and partitions.
Precision Plastics Molding Co., Inc., Fort Scott: Plastic injection moldings.
Rock Island Oil & Refining Co., Inc. (Fiberglass Pipe Div.), 2501 S. West, Wichita (Mailing add.: 321 W. Douglas): Fiberglass reinforced epoxy pipe.
Walter Schwarz, 707 N. 11th, Marysville: Plastic fraternal novelties.
Scientech Co., 812 Hill (Box 511), Independence: Plastics (castings, coatings, adhesives, laminations), models, patterns and prototypes.
Serv-A-Car Products, 2530 Morgan, Parsons: Plastic manufacturing, vinyl and plastisol coatings (dishwashing machine racks, display racks, chemical tanks, etc.), vacuum forming, drive-in restaurant equipment, plastic magneto covers for industrial engines and specialties, plastic blister packaging.
Sfeld Co., 1125-281 By-Pass, Great Bend: Plastic items.
Sta Nu Plastic Co., 607 N. Madison, Hutchinson: Plastic covers (photos, passports, etc.).
Stewart-Shattuck, Inc., 1225 E. Pawnee, Wichita (11): Prefabing, laminated plastic on plywood or wood products.
Styro Products, Inc., 1401 Fairfax Trafficway, Kansas City: Expanded plastics.
Sun Enclosure, Inc., 448 N. Mosley, Wichita: Aluminum and fiberglass pool cover, green house, etc.
Thomas-Warren, Inc., Cottonwood Falls: Crating ends, pill boxes for vets, seed boxes for nurseries (foamed plastics).
Western Control Corp., 2533 S. West St. (Box 1202), Wichita: Blow-molded plastic containers, plastic parts.
Wilco Name Plates, 1303 E. 37th N., Wichita: Engraved plates, signs, plaques, plastic laminates.
Wimp Plastic and Engineering Co., 103 S. Vine, Wichita: Plastic fittings.
Winfield Reinforced Plastics Co., Strother Field, Winfield: Fiberglass products.

LEATHER AND LEATHER PRODUCTS

Leather Tanning and Finishing

Clyde D. White, 868 Gilman, Wichita (3): Custom tanning and leather goods.

Footwear, Except Rubber

G. C. Blucher Boot Co., 214 N. Cherry, Olathe: Cowboy boots.
Gooch Shoe Shop, 105 Second, Dodge City: Hand made custom boots.
C. H. Hyer and Sons, 130 N. Chestnut, Olathe: Cowboy boots and shoes.
Carl McDowell Boot Shop, 603 E. 21st, Wichita: Cowboy boots, orthopedic shoes.
Shaffer Mfg. Co., 308 E. Lincoln, Wichita (11): Shoes.

Luggage

Hillmer Leather Shop, 115 E. Sixth, Topeka: Custom luggage, luggage covers, brief cases, salesmen cases.
Quinn Luggage Co., 122½ N. Santa Fe, Salina: Brief cases and Gladstone bags.
United Products of Kansas, Box 23, Gardner: Luggage and hat boxes.

Handbags and Other Personal Leather Goods

Hillmer Leather Shop, 115 E. Sixth, Topeka: Billfolds.
Leachman Friesen Co., 510 W. Third, Oakley: Cosmetic, jewelry, men's toiletry, and silverware cases.
Quinn Luggage Co., 122½ N. Santa Fe, Salina: Key cases.

Leather Goods, Not Elsewhere Classified

Anderson Leather Shop, 118 N. Santa Fe, Salina: Hand-tooled leather bags, gun holsters, brief cases, dog supplies, sample cases, grain probe cases, tool cases, truckers' wallets.
Atchison Leather Products Co., 316 Commercial, Atchison: Auto and aircraft safety belts, shoulder harnesses, pistol holsters, leather strap work, specialty items.
Coad Saddlery, Cawker City: Stock saddles, show halters, Shetland pony harness.
English Leather Shop, 150 W. Eighth, Horton: Gun belts, holsters, saddles and other riding equipment.
Handy Bindery, 1204 Laramie, Marysville: Leather tooling.
Henson Dairy Supply, 415 N. Main, Hutchinson: Halters.
Hillmer Leather Shop, 115 E. Sixth, Topeka: Horse goods, dog goods.
Litson Leathers, Box 27, Gove: Soft leather garments, purses, hand carved leather, show trophies.
L. J. Pracht Mfg. Co., Box 1857, Wichita: Leather watch bands.
Roberts Rodeo Equipment Mfg. Co., Strong City: Bull ropes, bronc reins, bridles, saddle pads.
Shaffer Mfg. Co., 308 E. Lincoln, Wichita (11): Custom eyeletting, custom die cutting.
Harry Shepler Saddle Co., 6501 W. Kellogg, Wichita (9): Telephone and electric tool kits, steel workers safety belts and pouches, special cases, saddles and harness.
Standard Precision, Inc., 4105 W. Pawnee (Box 1297), Wichita: Aircraft seat belts.
Tavella and Depaoli, 209 N. Broadway, Pittsburg: Harness and saddlery equipment.

STONE, CLAY, AND GLASS PRODUCTS

Glass and Glassware, Pressed or Blown

Kansas Glass, Inc., Caney: Pressed and blown glassware.

Cement, Hydraulic

Ash Grove Lime & Portland Cement Co., N. Santa Fe, Chanute: Cement.
Fort Scott Hydraulic Cement Co., Box 267, Fort Scott: Cement (natural and masonry).
General Portland Cement Co., Box 479, Fredonia: Cement (portland, masonry, high early strength, air entraining).
General Portland Cement Co., Route 3, Olathe: Cement.
Lehigh Portland Cement Co., Box 309, Iola (Plant at Bassett): Cements (portland and masonry).
Lone Star Cement Corp., Bonner Springs: Cement (portland, type I & II), masonry, high early strength, oil well.
Monarch Cement Co., Humboldt: Cements (portland and masonry).
Universal Atlas Cement, Box 428, Independence: Portland cement.

Structural Clay Products

Brick and Structural Clay Tile

Acme Brick Co., Buffalo: Brick and tile.
Acme Brick Co., Coffeyville: Face brick, building tile.
Acme Brick Co., Box 98, Kanopolis: Face bricks in buffs, pinks, reds, white, grays (mingled or straight shades), hollow building tile, and paving blocks.
Acme Brick Co., Weir: Brick and tile.
Cloud Ceramics, First Natl. Bank Bldg., Concordia: Face brick.
Excelsior Brick Co., Box 32, Fredonia: Common and face brick, hollow building tile.
Humboldt Brick & Tile Co., 910 New York, Humboldt: Common and face brick, building tile.
Kansas Brick and Tile, Inc., Hoisington: Bricks.

Ceramic Wall and Floor Tile

Acme Brick Co., Box 98, Kanopolis: Floor tile, clay tile, glazed tile.
Pomona Tile Mfg. Co., Box 918, Arkansas City: Glazed ceramic floor and wall tile.

Clay Refractories

Acme Brick Co., Box 98, Kanopolis: Fire brick.

Structural Clay Products, Not Elsewhere Classified

Acme Brick Co., Coffeyville: Flue lining, drain tile.
Acme Brick Co., Box 98, Kanopolis: Flue liners and drain tile.
W. S. Dickey Clay Mfg. Co., 900 E. Second, Pittsburg: Flue lining, drain tile, sewer pipe, wall coping.
Excelsior Brick Co., Box 32, Fredonia: Drain tile.
Humboldt Brick & Tile Co., 910 New York, Humboldt: Drain tile.

Pottery and Related Products

Acme Brick Co., Box 98, Kanopolis: Acid proof brick, and acid rings.
Brown's Ceramic, 138 W. Main, Solomon: Ceramics.
Cyclo Pottery House, 302 W. 25th, Hutchinson: Ceramic pieces, fired stain for ceramics.
Fincham's Gifts & Ceramics, Route 1, Blue Rapids: Ceramic items.
Frontier Gift & Ceramic, 411 W. Wyatt Earp, Dodge City: Ceramic giftware.
Heart of America Ceramics, 758 Central, Kansas City: Ceramics.
Mrs. Alma Jackson, 229 Broadway, Augusta: Ceramic artware.
Ju Rene Ceramic Molds, Franklin: Ceramic molds.
Albert Meyers, Hanover: Ceramics.
Pittsburg Pottery Co., Inc., Box 5, Pittsburg: Stoneware, artware, flower pots.
Red Barn Studio, Lindsborg: Ceramics.
Ross Mold Co., Kingman: Ceramic molds.
Santner Ceramics Supply Co., 1727 E. Central, Wichita: Ceramic products.
Shadow Box Ceramics Studio, 308 W. Cloud, Salina: Ceramics.
Sunflower Mfg. Co., 116 E. Harry (Box 3882), Wichita: Ceramic ash trays.
Theresa's Gifts, 302 S. Rothsay, Minneapolis: Ceramic gift items and advertising novelties.
Van Riper Art Studio, 1501 N. Halstead, Hutchinson: Greenware, ceramics.
Ye Ole Contemporary Pott Shoppe, 365 W. Lindsborg (Box 485), Lindsborg: Ceramics and pottery (earthenware, stoneware, cast items).
Zella Ceramic Mfg., 7315 State, Kansas City: Ceramics.

Concrete, Gypsum, and Plaster Products

Lime

Fort Scott Hydraulic Cement Co., Box 267, Fort Scott: Hydraulic hydrated lime.
Midwest Lime Co., Inc., Box 107, Bonner Springs: Pebble quick lime.

Gypsum Products

Bestwall Gypsum Co., Blue Rapids: Industrial plasters, wall plasters, wallboard.
National Gypsum Co., Medicine Lodge: Gypsum products (wallboard, wall plaster, lath, Keene's cement).
L. R. Parsons Co., Inc., 281 By-pass and Broadway (Box 987), Great Bend: Gypsum deck.

Cut Stone and Stone Products

Bandera Stone Quarry, Redfield: Stone.
Bayer Stone, Inc., 508 Riley, Manhattan: Building stone.
Becker Memorials, 1410 Beverly Dr., Salina: Granite memorials.
Bell Memorials, Beloit: Monuments.
Bruce Marble & Granite Works, Inc., 315 N. National, Fort Scott: Granite monuments and mausoleums.
Byrd Memorial Co., 215-219 Commercial, Atchison: Granite memorials, polish granite for construction, fireplaces.
Cremers Monument Co., Inc., 617 S. Broadway, Pittsburg: Monuments.
W. H. Dawson Monument Co., 1309-17 Main (Box 912), Winfield: Monuments, burial vaults.
Day Monument Co., 907 S. Summit, Arkansas City: Monuments and burial vaults.
Fairchild Memorials, 314 W. Ninth, Coffeyville: Monuments and mausoleums, building marble and soft stone.

Fairfax Granite, Inc., Chrysler and Industrial Blvd., Fairfax District, Kansas City: Building granite, monumental granite.
Fort Scott Hydraulic Cement Co., Box 267, Fort Scott: Limestone.
Guild Monument House, 135 E. 29th, Topeka: Memorials.
Hutton Monument Works, 201 Topeka, Topeka: Monuments, markers and mausoleums.
Individual Mausoleum Co., 909 Commercial, Atchison: Monuments, individual mausoleums.
Junction City Stone Co., Box 127, Junction City: Veneering stone, sawed slabs, quarry blocks.
Kansas Brick and Tile, Inc., Hoisington: Stone.
Kansas Natural Stone Co., Hays: Cut stone, veneer and architectural carvings.
Kerford Quarry Co., 415 Utah, Atchison: Limestone products.
J. T. Lardner Cut Stone Contractor, 128 N. Van Buren, Topeka: Cut stone.
Leavenworth Quarries, Route 1, Leavenworth: Limestone.
Loring Quarries, Bonner Springs: Stone.
Marion Marble & Granite, 159 Main, Marion: Monuments and markers.
Memorial Art Co., 507 S. Second, Dodge City: Marble and granite memorials.
Memorial Art Co., 1508 Nickerson, Hutchinson: Monuments.
Memorial Crafts, Inc., 3608 State, Kansas City: Monuments.
Mid-West Victorian Marble, Inc., 159th and 69 Highway, Stanley: Marble products (table tops, vanity tops, etc.).
Norton Memorials, Inc., 126 W. Sixth, Newton: Monuments.
R. W. Parks & Sons, Inc., 1707 E. Douglas, Wichita: Monuments, markers, mausoleums, burial vaults, interior marble.
Peerless Quarries, Inc., 6300 Inland Dr., Kansas City: Stone.
Pittsburg Mosaic Stone Co., 103 W. 20th, Pittsburg: Mosaic stones.
Pratt Monument Co., 1305 E. First, Pratt: Memorials.
Quiring Monument Co., Inc., 925 N. Hillside and Frisco Tracks, Wichita: Monuments, marble facings and hearths, marble table tops, etc.
Reeble Monuments, 1 S. Commercial, Emporia: Monuments and markers.
Riddle Quarries, Inc., Box 1268, Salina: Commercial rock.
Rock-Hill Stone & Gravel Co., Inc., Sterling: Aggregates, plaster, concrete, mortar, engine sand.
Russell Building Stone, Inc., 731½ Main, Russell: Building and veneer stone.
Salina Memorial Art. Co., 1608 S. Ninth, Salina: Monuments and markers.
Silverdale Cut Stone Co., Silverdale: Natural building stone.
Silverdale Limestone Co., Route 3 (Box 165), Arkansas City: Silverdale limestone.
Stewart Memorials, 118 W. 15th, Ottawa: Monuments.
Stone Facing & Wholesale Co., 926 W. Second, Wichita: Building and veneer stone.
Trusswall Stone Co., 1136 Southwest Blvd., Kansas City: Cast stone joists, roof and floor slabs.
Wallmax Cut Stone Co., Glen Elder: Veneer cut stone.
Wolf's Exclusive Memorials Co., 205 W. Ninth, Ellis: Granite and marble memorials, cornerstones for buildings, table tops and furnishings for home or business.

Abrasives, Asbestos, and Miscellaneous Nonmetallic Mineral Products

Abrasive Products

K. C. Abrasives, 3140 Dodge Rd., Kansas City (15): Abrasives (industrial, optical, electronic).

Asbestos Products

Corrosion Proof Fitting Co., Inc., 607 Holland, Great Bend: Threaded transite, (asbestos cement), fittings and specialties.

Steam and Other Packing, and Pipe and Boiler Covering

Gasket Products, Inc., 319 S. Wichita, Wichita (2): Gasket materials, gaskets.
Tru-Line Die Cutting Co., 705 E. Third, Wichita (2): Gaskets.

Mineral Wool

Buckley Construction Industries, 1600 E. Murdock (Box 574), Wichita: Insulation.
Dodson Mfg. Co., Inc., 1463 Barwise, Wichita: Insulation.
Gustin-Bacon Mfg. Co., 3000 Fairfax Rd. and 3031 Fiberglas Rd., Kansas City: Glass fiber insulation and organic fiber mats (thermal and acoustical).
Insulation Products Co., Jct. U. S. Highway 24 and K14, Beloit: Insulation material.
Insul-Wool Insulation Corp., 121 N. Dodge, Wichita: Insulation.
Modern Insulating Co., 504 W. Kansas, McPherson: Thermal wool insulation.

Restful summer day at a Kansas state lake.

Owens-Corning Fiberglas Corp., Sunshine and Fiberglas Rds., Kansas City: Thermal insulation, mat products, and acoustical products.
Spangler Insulation & Mfg. Co., 1327 17th, Belleville: Insulation.

Nonmetallic Mineral Products, Not Elsewhere Classified

Cartercraft, 212 W. Third, Concordia: Decorative wall plaques.
Ceramic Sales, Inc., 315 W. Fifth, Concordia: Plaster wall plaques, figures, and bisque ware.

PRIMARY METAL INDUSTRIES

Blast Furnaces, Steel Works, and Rolling and Finishing Mills

Blast Furnaces (Including Coke Ovens), Steel Works, and Rolling Mills

Prolerized Steel Corp., 1115 S. 12th, Kansas City: Conversion of scrap to steel particles.

Steel Pipes and Tubes

Applequist-Lagerberg Mfg., Inc., 921 Bishop, Salina: Lock seam tubing.
Brown-Strauss Corp., 14th and Osage, Kansas City: Fabricators of pipe and steel.
Buzbee-Thompson Steel, Inc., 5726 Merriam Dr., Merriam: Steel pipe.
Doerr Metal Products, 320 E. Sixth, Larned: Irrigation and industrial well casing and screen, arc welded steel pipe.
Hutchinson Foundry & Steel Co., D and Washington, Hutchinson: Well casing (cast iron and bronze).
R & R Tank Co., Inc., Box 231, Pratt: Large piping for industrial plants.
Sonken-Galamba Corp., Second and Riverview, Kansas City: Steel pipe.

Iron and Steel Foundries

Gray-Iron Foundries

Acme Foundry & Machine Co., 1502 Spruce, Coffeyville: Castings (gray-iron and semisteel).
Atchison Specialty Mfg. Co., 1620 Pacific, Atchison: Cast iron plumbing and drainage material, iron castings.
P. J. Bays Foundry, Fort Dodge Rd., Dodge City: Gray-iron castings.
Beard Foundry & Machine Works, 723 S. First, Arkansas City: Gray-iron castings (surface and sewer drainage, industrial, municipal and construction).
Crescent Foundry, 824 S. Heylman (Box 176), Fort Scott: Gray-iron castings.
J. B. Ehrsam & Sons Mfg. Co., Enterprise: Gray-iron castings.
Ehrsam Wichita Foundry (Plant No. 1), Box 2837, S. Wichita Station, Wichita: Gray-iron castings.
M. W. Hartmann Mfg. Co., Inc., 120-122 N. Adams, Hutchinson: Gray-iron castings.
Hutchinson Foundry & Steel Co., D and Washington, Hutchinson: Gray-iron castings.
Jensen Bros. Mfg. Co., Inc., 14th and Pacific, Coffeyville: Castings (gray-iron, semisteel and nodular iron).
Kramer Machine & Engineering Products Co., 320 S. Second, Leavenworth: Gray-iron castings.
McNally Pittsburg Mfg. Corp., Drawer D, Pittsburg: Specification cast iron, stress relieving.
McNally Pittsburg Mfg. Corp. (Foundries Div.), Drawer D, Pittsburg: Process and alloy iron castings.
The Mid-West Specialty Mfg. Co., 1230 Commercial, Atchison: Cast iron plumbing and drainage material.
Salina Foundry, Inc., 1024 W. Elm (Box 111), Salina: Gray-iron castings.
Service Iron Foundry, 340 N. Rock Island, Wichita: Gray-iron and semisteel castings.
Sooby Foundry, 1205 N. Main, Garden City: Tractor wheel weights, small castings.
Topeka Foundry & Iron Works Co., 326 Jackson, Topeka: Gray-iron castings.
Walton Foundry, Inc., East and Kentucky, Iola: Gray-iron castings.
Western Iron & Foundry Co., Inc., 702 E. Second, Wichita (2): Gray-iron and semisteel castings, sewer manhole and street castings.
Winfield Foundry, Route 3, Winfield: Gray-iron castings.
Wyatt Mfg. Co., Inc., 500 N. Fifth, Salina: Gray-iron castings.

Malleable Iron Foundries

J. B. Ehrsam & Sons Mfg. Co., Enterprise: Ductile castings.
Ehrsam Wichita Foundry, Inc. (Plant No. 2), Box 2837, S. Wichita Station, Wichita: Ductile iron castings.
M. W. Hartmann Mfg. Co., Inc., 120-122 N. Adams, Hutchinson: Ductile iron castings.
Midwest Foundry, Inc., 805 E. Boston, Wichita (11): Irosteel, ductile iron, NI resist ductile, and kronalloy castings.
Service Iron Foundry, 340 N. Rock Island, Wichita: Ductile castings.

Steel Foundries

The LFM Mfg. Co., Inc. (Subs. of Rockwell Mfg. Co.), Third and Park, Atchison: Steel castings.

Primary Smelting and Refining of Nonferrous Metals

Cherryvale Zinc Co., Inc., Martin and School (Box 240), Cherryvale: Non-ferrous metals.

Rolling, Drawing and Extruding of Nonferrous Metals

Rolling, Drawing, and Extruding of Aluminum

Brown Supply Co., 1504 Terminal (Box 323), Garden City: Aluminum pipe.
Extrusions, Inc., 2401 S. Main, Fort Scott: Aluminum extrusions.
Kansas Mfg. Co., 623 Vermont, Lawrence: Drawing (small aluminum).
Roll Formed Products, Inc., Moundridge: Roller dies, custom roll forming.
Sonken-Galamba Corp., Riverview at Second, Kansas City: Aluminum billets, coils and sheets.
Sterling Mfg. Co., Inc., 1134 N. Fairview (Box 1789), Wichita: Roll forming.

Rolling, Drawing, and Extruding of Nonferrous Metals, Except Copper and Aluminum

Extrusion Products Co., Box 1093, El Dorado: Lead wire, solder, special lead alloy wire, bullet metal, pistol bullets.
Sioux Chief Mfg. Co., Inc., 41 Shawnee, Kansas City (5): Flexible magnesium rods for domestic hot water heaters.

Drawing and Insulating of Nonferrous Wire

Dor-Et Mfg. Co., 1021 Walnut, Coffeyville: Battery cables.

Nonferrous Foundries

Aluminum Castings

A & I Engineering Works, 408 E. Third, Pittsburg: Aluminum die castings.
Ace Pattern & Foundry Co., Inc., 1001 Sunshine Rd., Kansas City: Aluminum castings.
Basham Foundry Co., 2487 N. Hillside, Wichita: Aluminum castings.
Berners Novelty & Machine Works, 821 S. First, Arkansas City: Aluminum castings (flamingoes, donkeys and carts), yard furniture and decorations.
C & L Aluminum Foundry & Mfg. Co., 509 N. Locust, Pittsburg: Aluminum alloy castings.
Cable Spinning Equipment Co., Inc., 3100 Topeka, Topeka: Custom aluminum casting.
Cordray Pattern Works, 308 N. Olive, Pittsburg: Aluminum castings and manufacturing.
Degginger's Foundry, Crane and Topeka, Topeka: Building plaques and letters, street and memorial markers.
C. Downing Casting & Cabinet Shop, Route 2, Sedan: Aluminum castings.

J. B. Ehrsam & Sons Mfg. Co., Enterprise: Aluminum and aluminum alloys castings.
Eschraft Foundry, 520 E. Fourth, Cherryvale: Aluminum castings.
M. W. Hartmann Mfg. Co., Inc., 120-122 N. Adams, Hutchinson: Aluminum castings.
Manhattan Aluminum Casting, 1219 Claflin Rd., Manhattan: Permanent mold aluminum castings (trivets, planters, bells, etc.).
Midland Foundry Co., 608 N. Washington, Wichita: Aluminum castings.
Midwest Machine Co., 111 N. Fourth, Atchison: Aluminum castings.
The Mid-West Specialty Mfg. Co., 1230 Commercial, Atchison: Aluminum castings.
Monarch Brass & Aluminum Works, 2008 S. Holbrook, Fort Scott: Nonferrous castings.
Ivan Morrow Pattern Shop & Foundry, Inc., 1115 W. 12th, Coffeyville: Aluminum castings.
Pittsburg Industries, Rose and Elm, Pittsburg: Aluminum castings.
Pressure Cast Products, 1217 Elm, Coffeyville: Precision castings (aluminum).
R. D. Foundry, Atchison: Permanent mold aluminum castings.
Reed Home Improvement Co., 116 E. Harvey, Wellington: Aluminum products.
Scientech Co., 812 Hill (Box 511), Independence: Precision centrifugal metal castings.
Service Brass & Aluminum Foundry, Inc., 911 E. Third, Wichita: Aluminum castings.
Sonken-Galamba Corp., Second and Riverview, Kansas City: Aluminum ingots.
Wichita Brass & Aluminum Foundry, 412 E. 29th, Wichita: Aluminum castings, Kirksite dies.
Winfield Foundry, Route 3, Winfield: Aluminum castings.

Brass, Bronze, Copper, Copper Base Alloy Castings

Basham Foundry Co., 2487 N. Hillside, Wichita: Brass and bronze castings.
Cable Spinning Equipment Co., Inc., 3100 Topeka, Topeka: Custom brass casting.
M. W. Hartmann Mfg. Co., Inc., 120-122 N. Adams, Hutchinson: Brass and bronze castings.
Midland Foundry Co., 608 N. Washington, Wichita: Brass and bronze castings.
The Mid-West Specialty Mfg. Co., 1230 Commercial, Atchison: Brass castings, plumbing and drainage material.
Ivan Morrow Pattern Shop & Foundry, Inc., 1115 W. 12th, Coffeyville: Bronze and brass castings.
Service Brass & Aluminum Foundry, Inc., 911 E. Third, Wichita: Brass castings, bronze grave markers.
Sonken-Galamba Corp., Second and Riverview, Kansas City: Brass ingots.
Sooby Foundry, 1205 N. Main, Garden City: Bronze castings.
Wichita Brass & Aluminum Foundry, 412 E. 29th, Wichita: Brass castings.

Nonferrous Castings, Not Elsewhere Classified

Ace Pattern & Foundry Co., Inc., 1001 Sunshine Rd., Kansas City: Magnesium castings.
Chrome Fixture Mfg. Co., Inc., Redel Rail Siding, Stanley: Diecasting.
The LFM Mfg. Co., Inc. (Subs. of Rockwell Mfg. Co.), Third and Park, Atchison: Crushing equipment castings, earth moving equipment castings.
Midland Foundry Co., 608 N. Washington, Wichita: Magnesium castings.
Wichita Brass & Aluminum Foundry, 412 E. 29th, Wichita: Magnesium castings.

Miscellaneous Primary Metal Industries

Iron and Steel Forgings

Santa Fe Rail Mill, W. First, Newton: Crossing frogs, switch points and rods, guard rails, gauge plates.
Wilde Tool Co., Inc., 13th and Pottawatomie, Hiawatha: Drop forgings.

Primary Metal Industries, Not Elsewhere Classified

Ace Pattern & Foundry Co., Inc., 1001 Sunshine Rd., Kansas City: Aluminum heat treating.
Oxwell, Inc., 600 E. 15th, Wellington: Heat treating, age hardening.
Ransdell Heat Treaters, 1551 Barwise, Wichita: Heat treating.
Walcher Metal Treat, Inc., 1019 S. McLean, Wichita: Heat treating.

FABRICATED METAL PRODUCTS
(Except Ordnance, Machinery, and Transportation Equipment)

Metal Cans

Downing Sheet Metal, Route 1, Arkansas City: Ice water cans.
Egan Mfg. Co., 306-308 S. Main, El Dorado: Water cans and coolers.
Gott Mfg. Co., Inc., 1608 Wheat Rd., Winfield: Metal containers.

Cutlery, Hand Tools, and General Hardware

Hand and Edge Tools, Except Machine Tools and Hand Saws

Garwin, Inc., 1326 Walnut, Wichita: Special tools.
Goodrich Co., Box 247, Lenora: Portable propane heating torch.
Haivala Concrete Tools, Inc., 1017 Walker, Wichita: Concrete contractors' tools.
Harmon Machine Co., Inc., 225 W. Lewis, Wichita: Carpenter levels, cement finishing tools, carpenter squares, trowels, hawks and darbies, diamond wheels and tools.
Holloway Mfg. Co., 306 W. Holloway, Yates Center: Bale hooks.
Kansas Jack, Inc., McPherson: Body and fender repair tools.
Lind Fabricating Co., Lebo: Adjustable spanner wrenches.
McCulley Cook, Inc., 307 Commercial, Oswego: Coach lifts.
McCunningham Mfg. Co., Box 197, Sedan: Floor leveling jacks.
Ottawa-Warner Corp., 634 King, Ottawa: Posthole digger.
Perine Bros. Iron Works, 809 Quincy, Topeka: Cement finishers' tools.
Saturn Mfg. Corp., Inc., Barclay (Mailing add.: Box 592, Topeka): Carpenters' squares.
Wilde Tool Co., Inc., 13th and Pottawatomie, Hiawatha: Hand tools.

Hardware, Not Elsewhere Classified

Advanced Metal Sales Corp., 213 N. Summit, Arkansas City: Drapery hardware, extrusions for mobile homes.
Crescent Foundry, 824 S. Heylman (Box 176), Fort Scott: Sash weights.
Flanders Mfg. Co., 315 S. High, Pratt: Portable pulley assembly.
Gilmore-Tatge Mfg. Co., Box 133, Clay Center: Vacuum bottle holders.
Kansas Mfg. Co., 623 Vermont, Lawrence: Seals (aluminum railroad car, truck).
Midwest Machine Co., 111 N. Fourth, Atchison: Steel handles.
Paco Mfg. Co., 601 E. Murdock (Box 1898), Wichita: Concrete accessories, building hardware.
Saturn Mfg. Corp., Inc., Barclay (Mailing add.: Box 592, Topeka): Multi-purpose brackets.
Snyder Stamp & Key Co., 1021 Kansas, Topeka: Keys.
Woodwork Mfg. & Supply, Inc., 14-16 W. Fourth, Hutchinson: Building hardware and materials.

Heating Apparatus (Except Electric) and Plumbing Fixtures

Plumbing Fixture Fittings and Trim (Brass Goods)

Advanced Metal Sales Corp., 213 N. Summit, Arkansas City: Plumbing supplies for mobile homes.
Baker Mfg. Co., 216 W. Second, Hutchinson: Plumbing supplies.
Cantrell Supply Co., Inc., 910 E. Second, Wichita: Lead drum traps for bathtubs.
M. W. Hartmann Mfg. Co., Inc., 120-122 N. Adams, Hutchinson: Lawn sprinklers.
Punco Specialty Sales & Service (Div. Push-Tite Mfg. Co.), 215 S. Parker, Olathe: Valve stems and faucet washer replacement units.
Sonner Burner Co., 412-420 E. Sixth (Box 903), Winfield: Nonfreeze valves.
Taylor Forge & Pipeworks of Kansas, Inc., Box 231, Paola: Extruded nozzle header.

Heating Equipment, Except Electric

Advance Products Co., 2300 E. Douglas, Wichita: Gas floor furnaces and wall heaters.

Air Conditioning Equipment Co., Waco and Douglas, Wichita: Furnaces (custom-built).
Bowlby Air Devices Co., 300 W. Indianapolis, Wichita: Conversion burners for furnaces, overhead heaters.
Bruest, Inc., 20th and Sycamore, Independence: Flameless gas heaters.
Brumme Mfg. Co., 1521 Seward, Topeka (Mailing add.: 609 Freeman): Draft inductors, warm air boosters.
The Coleman Co., Inc., 250 N. St. Francis, Wichita: Heating systems (gas and oil, LPG), floor furnaces (electric, gas, oil, LPG), forced air furnaces (gas and oil), wall heaters (gas, LPG), space heaters (gas, oil, LPG).
Gordon & Piatt, Inc., Box 914, Winfield: Commercial and industrial gas and oil burners.
Jet Burner, Inc., Box 709, Hutchinson: Portable space heaters, conversion burners, burner heads, asphalt kettle burners.
Kansas Air Conditioning, Inc., 314-22 E. 15th, Topeka: Furnaces (commercial and industrial).
Shaw Burner Co., Pine and Indiana, Columbus: Commercial and industrial burners, heater for house trailers and pick-up coaches (butane).
Sonner Burner Co., 412-420 E. Sixth (Box 903), Winfield: Conversion gas burners.
Van's Incinerator Co., 114 S. Washington, Wellington: Incinerators.
Western Supply Co. (Mfg. Div.), 315 W. Third, Hutchinson: Heat pumps, oil and gas furnaces.
Western Supply Co. (Western-Aire Products Div.), Nickerson (Mailing add.: 315 W. Third, Hutchinson): Gas and oil furnaces, heat pumps.

Fabricated Structural Metal Products

Fabricated Structural Steel

A & A Iron Works, 1632 N. Mosley, Wichita: Structural and plate steel, steel warehousing.
Armco Steel Corp. (Metal Products Div.), Box 1009, Topeka: Steel buildings, steel water pipe.
Blue Rapids Blacksmith & Welding Shop, Blue Rapids: Metal fabrication.
Boge Iron & Metal Co., Inc., 800 S. St. Francis (Box 3182), Wichita: Structural steel fabrication.
Brockhoff Mfg. Co., 15 Oregon (Box 267), Sabetha: Steel bar joists and steel rafters for buildings.
Buzbee-Thompson Steel, Inc., 5726 Merriam Dr., Merriam: Structural steel and miscellaneous fabrication.
Capital Iron Works Co., Seventh and Adams, Topeka: Structural steel fabrication.
Firman L. Carswell Mfg. Co., 501 S. Valley, Kansas City: Steel fabrication.
Casebeer Supply, Inc., 1007 W. North (Box 862), Salina: Structural steel fabrication, contract manufacturing.
Ceco Steel Products Corp., Kindelberger and Harvester Rds., Kansas City: Reinforcing steel and steel joists.
Geo. C. Christopher & Son, Inc., 1220 Blaine, Wichita: Fabricated steel.
Cofer Sales & Mfg., Ransom: Television towers.
Conaway Welding & Repair, Box 132, Kensington: Self supporting antenna poles.
Consumers Co-op. Assn. (Big Chief Div.), Box 473, Hutchinson: Steel buildings (farm, industrial, etc.).
Cotton Welding Service, Larned: All steel car canopies.
Darby Corp., First and Walker, Kansas City: Towers, steel and stainless steel fabrication, structural steel fabrication, aluminum fabrication.
Field Tool, Inc., 605 Spring, Coffeyville: Steel fabrication.
Paul Gorzik Steel Co., 332 Brotherhood Bldg., Kansas City: Structural steel and steel products.
Haller Sales & Mfg. Co., Blue Rapids: Television antennas.
Harding Glass of Kansas, Inc., 724-30 Jackson, Topeka: Metal fabrication.
The Herrmann Co., Inc., 539 S. Tenth, Kansas City: Metal buildings.
Humphrey Roll Forming, Inc., 719 E. Zimmerly, Wichita (11): Cold roll forming (tubular and structural shapes and angles).
Hutchinson Foundry & Steel Co., D and Washington, Hutchinson: Fabricated structural steel and reinforcing steel.
Joe's Welding Shop, Ninth and Oak, Garnett: Steel trusses for buildings.
Johnson Steel Co., Inc., Route 4, Olathe: Structural steel fabrication.
Kansas City Structural Steel Co., 21st and Metropolitan, Kansas City: Steel buildings, bridges and platework, structural warehouse steel.
Kaw Valley Steel Co., 1103 S. Mill, Kansas City: Miscellaneous steel, light structural steel.
Kechi Corner Lumber Co., 6149 N. Broadway, Wichita: Steelcoat pole buildings.
Kellner Jetties Co., 415 E. Gordon, Topeka: River bank and bridge protection systems.
Kenco Mfg. Co., 617 Ottawa (Box 337), Baxter Springs: Steel fabrication.
Kent Mfg. Co., Tipton: Television towers, steel buildings.
Lasley Co., Inc., 109 Kansas, Kansas City: Steel fabrication.
Leavenworth Steel, Inc., Main and Cherokee, Leavenworth: Structural steel.
Lind Fabricating Co., Lebo: TV towers.
W. L. Luedke Mfg. Co., Box 184, Colony: Radiation and storm shelters (family type unit).
McCulley-Cook, Inc., 307 Commercial, Oswego: Steel buildings.
McNally Pittsburg Mfg. Corp., Drawer D, Pittsburg: Structural fabrication.
Machinery Tank & Supply Co., Inc., 1600 W. Douglas, Wichita: Fabricated steel products.
Missouri Valley Steel, Inc., Box 89, Leavenworth: Fabricated structural steel (buildings, bridges, sewage plants, etc.).
Ornico, Inc., 6002 Merriam Dr., Merriam: Steel fabricators.
Palmer Welding & Tank Co., Garden City: Television aerials.
Peltier Foundry, 105 W. Fifth, Concordia: Structural steel products.
Petrowsky Motor Co., Bucklin: Television towers.
Progressive Mfg. Co., 969 Kansas, Kansas City: Metal fabrication.
Pyramid Mfg., Inc., 1301 E. Funston, Wichita: Portable steel buildings.
Rehfeld Steel Jetty Co., 2116 Elm Lane, Manhattan: Jetties.
Russell Steel Products Co., 2205 Metropolitan, Kansas City: Steel fabrication.
Ryan Welding Co., 228 Humboldt, Manhattan: Metal fabrication.
Salina Mfg. Co., 606 N. Front (Box 26), Salina: Structural steel.
Schmidt Sheet Metal Works, 117 W. Maple, Independence: Metal fabrication.
Schroeder Steel Engineering Co., 7528 Juniper Dr., Prairie Village: Steel buildings.
Simlo, Inc., Seventh and McBratney, Clay Center: Galvanized and stainless steel products.
Smith-Moon Steel Co., Strother Field, Winfield: Fabricated steel, structural steel, stainless steel plate work.
Sonken-Galamba Corp., Second and Riverview, Kansas City: Structural, plate and sheet steel.
Southwest Ornamental Iron Co., Box 275, Bonner Springs: Misc. and structural steel fabrication.
Spencer-Safford Loadcraft Co., Inc., Augusta: Steel underground fallout shelters.
Topeka Foundry & Iron Works Co., 326 Jackson, Topeka: Structural steel.
Uni-Temp Products, Inc., 1032-38 W. Kansas, McPherson: Custom rollforming.
W. W. Mfg. Co., Box 728, Dodge City: Large metal buildings, television towers.
Watkins, Inc., 711 W. Second (Box 117), Wichita: Steel fabrication.
Western Foundry & Machine Works, 1801 Madison (Box 439), Topeka: Steel, stainless steel and aluminum fabrication.
Western Iron & Foundry Co., Inc., 702 E. Second, Wichita (2): Structural steel fabrication, steel warehouse.
Wichita Steel Fabricators, Inc., 3400 N. Broadway, Wichita: Carbon and stainless steel fabrication.
Wichita Structural Steel Co., 1319 S. Mosley, Wichita: Structural steel.
R. G. Wise Machine Works, 527 S. St. Francis, Wichita: Steel fabrication.

Metal Doors, Sash, Frames, Molding, and Trim

All Weather Products Co., 816 N. Main, Wichita: Aluminum storm doors and windows.
Aluminum Home Products Co., Phillipsburg: Aluminum storm doors and screens.
Aluminum Products Co., 302 W. 2nd, Washington: Aluminum combination storm doors and windows.
Aluminum Screen & Window Co., Inc., 535 W. Douglas, Wichita: Aluminum storm windows.
American Glass Co., 1402 N. Seventh, Kansas City (1): Aluminum store fronts, windows and doors.
Beisecker Sash & Door Co., 127 N. Van Buren, Topeka: Screens.
Boatwright Supply, Inc., 33 Provence, Olathe: Aluminum combination storm windows, doors, screens.
Ceco Steel Products Corp., Kindelberger and Harvester Rds., Kansas City: Steel and aluminum window sash, metal frame screens.
Century Mfg. Co., Inc., E. Ninth (Box 121), Hays: Aluminum combination windows.
Columbia Metal Products Co., Inc., Riverview Park, Iola (Mailing add.: 1824 McGee, K. C., Mo.): Aluminum storm doors and windows.
Cooks Aluma-Fab Mfg. Co., 1221 E. River, Eureka: Prefab storm windows and doors.
Danielson & Schnug Mill & Lumber Co., 218 W. Lewis, Wichita: Screens.
Drake Refrigerator Works, 253 N. Market, Wichita: Refrigerator doors.
Exterior Art Co., 3550 Southeast Blvd., Wichita (16): Aluminum storm windows and doors.
Forsell, Inc., 1421-23 Lane, Topeka: Storm windows.
Hawley Brothers, 403 W. Wyatt Earp, Dodge City: Combination storm windows and screens, aluminum prime windows.
Hehr Midwest, Box 278, Newton: Windows and accessories for mobile homes, travel trailers and pickup coaches.
Homestead Mfg. Co., Fifth and Richmond, Kansas City: Aluminum storm doors and windows.
Humphrey Products, Inc., 719 E. Zimmerly, Wichita (11): Aluminum windows (combination storm and screen), storm doors primary windows, screen.
Hurlburt Construction & Mfg. Co., 1414 W. Pine, El Dorado: Aluminum combination storm windows and doors.
ILC Products of Ks., Inc., Chanute: Windows and doors for mobile homes.
Insul-Wool Insulation Corp., 121 N. Dodge, Wichita: Storm windows and doors.
Jaxon Mfg. Co., 215 W. Fifth, Topeka: Aluminum storm windows and doors.
Johnson's Wood Shop, 406 N. E. 14th, Abilene: Aluminum storm windows, screens.
Larsons Electric, 134 N. Main, Lindsborg: Aluminum storm windows.
Lincoln Aluminum Door Co., 717 N. Fourth, Lincoln: Aluminum storm doors, screen doors, windows.
The M. S. W. Co., Inc., D/B/A Solar, 201 W. Dennis, Olathe: Steel primary replacement windows, steel and aluminum storm windows and doors, porch enclosures.
Mid-West Weatherstrip & Venetian Blind Mfg. Co., 1647 S. Ida, Wichita: Metal weatherstrip.
Modern Products, Inc., 1032-38 W. Kansas, McPherson: Aluminum screen doors, storm doors, mobile home doors.
Modern Vent Co., 1622 W. Harry, Wichita: Basement windows.
Peerless Products, Inc., 21st and Adlie, Ft. Scott (Mailing add.: 3105 Euclid, K. C. (9), Mo.): Aluminum combination storm windows and doors.
Philips Industries of Kansas, Inc., Box 203, Newton: Aluminum windows, storm sash, doors and screens for mobile homes.
Joe W. Pittman Co., 831 N. Kansas, Topeka: Aluminum combination storm windows and doors.
Quality Aluminum Products, W. Highway 40 (Box 364), Ellis: Aluminum storm doors and windows.
Reed Home Improvement Co., 116 E. Harvey, Wellington: Combination storm windows, metal door and window screens.
Todd Roberts Insulation Co., 510 W. 29th, N. (Box 2366), Wichita (14): Aluminum screens and storm windows.
Russell Steel Products Co., 2205 Metropolitan, Kansas City: Metal sash.
Salina Tent & Awning Co., 515 E. Walnut, Salina: Aluminum storm windows and doors.
Schallo Awning & Mfg. Co., Inc., 1203 N. Broadway, Pittsburg: Aluminum storm windows.
Schultz Home Modernizing Co., 510 W. First, Larned: Aluminum doors, prime and storm windows of all types.
Scott City Builders, Inc., Scott City: Aluminum storm doors and windows (residential and commercial buildings).
Sears Home Improvement Co., Arkansas City: Aluminum self-storing storm windows and doors.
Smith-Rouse & Co., Inc., Box 8, Oskaloosa: Aluminum storm doors and windows.
Spangler Insulation & Mfg. Co., 1327 17th, Belleville: Storm windows.
Sutton Mfg. & Sales Co., 506 E. Martin, Stafford: Aluminum storm windows and doors.
Tailormade Industries, Inc., 515 Madison (Box 475), Fredonia: Aluminum windows for mobile homes.
Uni-Temp Products, Inc., 1032-38 W. Kansas, McPherson: Metal sash components.
Wilson All Weather Window Co., 1010-12 S. Main, Hutchinson: Aluminum combination storm doors and windows.
Zephyr Mfg., Inc., 400 E. Second, Hutchinson: Storm windows and doors.

Fabricated Plate Work (Boiler Shops)

Barnett Welding Shop, Sixth and Prairie, Emporia: Steel storage tanks.
Bates & Sons, 256 S. Green, Hoisington: Tanks, metal fabrication.
Beeker Mfg., Inc., 11125 Johnson Dr., Shawnee: Steel products.
Darby Corp., First and Walker, Kansas City: Smokestacks, breeching, elevated water tanks, storage tanks, pressure vessels, bins and hoppers.
Doerr Metal Products, 320 E. Sixth, Larned: Stock tanks, sheep watering tanks, water storage tanks, pneumatic tanks, water hauling tanks, fuel storage tanks, septic tanks, grain bins.
Eaton Metal Products Corp., 110 N. Pershing, Hutchinson: Storage tanks.
Elmer's Welding & Tank Co., Wellsville: Oil field storage tanks.
Hutchinson Foundry & Steel Co., D and Washington, Hutchinson: Steel tanks.
Joe's Welding Shop, Ninth and Oak, Garnett: Storage tanks and bins.
Leavenworth Steel, Inc., Main and Cherokee, Leavenworth: Steel plate products.
Luthy Bros., Inc., 956 Scott, Kansas City: Steel fabrication, boilers.
Luxra Co., 1018 Commercial, Atchison: Glass lined tanks.
McDonald Tank & Equipment Co., Box 73, Great Bend: Oil field tanks.
M-E-C Co. (Div. Altamil Corp.), 1402 Main, Neodesha: Welded steel storage tanks.
Machinery Tank & Supply Co., Inc., 1600 W. Douglas, Wichita: Steel tanks and boilers.
Marley Co., 3001 Fairfax Rd., Kansas City: Industrial and air conditioning water cooling towers, air cooled refrigerant condensers, evaporative condensers.
Merker Machine & Boiler Works, 2000 S. Main, Fort Scott: Boiler work.
O'Neill Tank Co., 5th and C Sts., Westport Addition, Route 1, Great Bend: Welded steel storage tanks.
R & R Tank Co., Inc., Box 231, Pratt: Steel tanks (farm, bulk and service stations).
Sauder Tank Co., Inc., 220 Weaver, Emporia: Redwood and steel oil field tanks and emulsion treaters.
Superior Boiler Works, 3400 E. Fourth, Hutchinson: High and low pressure boilers and equipment.
Taylor Forge & Pipe Works of Kansas, Inc., Box 231, Paola: Pressure vessel fabrication.
Thompson Machine Works, Fourth and Parallel, Conway Springs: Steel tanks.
Topeka Supply & Boiler Co., Inc., Second and Jefferson (Box 207), Topeka: Smokestacks, breechings, water and oil storage tanks.
We-Mac Mfg. & Supply, Route 3, U. S. Highway 59, Atchison: Steel and aluminum storage tanks.
Wichita Steel Fabricators, Inc., 3400 N. Broadway, Wichita: Steel tanks (storage and truck), smokestacks, pipe line paint kettles, boiler breechings.

Architectural and Miscellaneous Metal Work

A & A Iron Works, 1632 N. Mosley, Wichita: Ornamental iron.
Aluminum Home Products Co., Phillipsburg: Porch railing and posts.
Angle's Ornamental Castings, 1510 E. Waterman, Wichita: Ornamental castings.
Architectural Art Mfg. Co., 3239 N. Hillside, Wichita: Ornamental iron, bronze and aluminum, expansion joint covers, aluminum railings.
Bob's Ornamental Iron Studio, 1144 Southwest Blvd., Kansas City (3): Ornamental iron.
L. J. Bromert Co., 319 W. Fifth, Hutchinson: Ornamental iron.
Capital Iron Works Co., Seventh and Adams, Topeka: Steel stairs and fire escapes.
Century Iron Works, 2121 Metropolitan, Kansas City: Ornamental iron, grills, grates, etc.
Cofer Sales & Mfg., Ransom: Steel steps.
Cramer Posture Chair Co., Inc., 625 Adams, Kansas City (5): Safety step ladders.
Dalton-Brecheisen Mfg. Co., Garnett: Custom wrought iron work.
Don Dye Co., Kingman: Tank battery walkway and stair treads.
Exterior Art Co., 3550 Southeast Blvd., Wichita (16): Ornamental iron.
Flye Repair & Welding Service, 5551 W. 21st, Topeka: Ornamental railings, house columns.
Gilmore-Tatge Mfg. Co., Box 133, Clay Center: Metal farm gates.
Gott Mfg. Co., Inc., 1608 Wheat Rd., Winfield: Misc. metal products.

Grain Spouting & Elevators of Kansas, Inc., Box 371, Hutchinson: Portable metal buildings.
Hawley Brothers, 403 W. Wyatt Earp, Dodge City: Ornamental iron railing.
Hutchinson Foundry & Steel Co., D and Washington, Hutchinson: Fire escapes, steel stairs, building specialties.
Kaw Valley Steel Co., 1103 S. Mill, Kansas City: Steel railings, fire escapes, window guards and steel stairs.
Landwehr Mfg. Co., 416 S. McComas, Wichita: Ornamental iron.
Load-King Mfg. Co., Kingman: Farm gates.
Luthy Bros., Inc., 956 Scott, Kansas City: Fire escapes.
McCulley-Cook, Inc., 307 Commercial, Oswego: Combination steel step and bumper.
McCunningham Mfg. Co., Box 477, Sedan: Walks and stairs.
M-F Welding Co., 211 Colorado, Manhattan: Fire escapes, etc.
Metal Arts Co., 5819 Slater, Merriam: Ornamental iron.
Ornamental Iron Works, 711 Old Main, Newton: Ornamental iron railings, fire escapes.
Perine Bros. Iron Works, 809 Quincy, Topeka: Fire escapes, gratings and ornamental railings, window bars, flag poles, wrought iron yard furniture, porch columns.
Rylko Fence Co., 5704 Highland Dr. (Box 1081), Hutchinson: Metal fences.
Schallo Awning & Mfg. Co., Inc., 1203 N. Broadway, Pittsburg: Ornamental iron.
Schultz Home Modernizing Co., 510 W. First, Larned: Decorative iron.
The Sloyd, 104 W. Saline, Lindsborg: Wrought iron railings.
Valentine Mfg., Inc., 1020 S. McComas, Wichita: Movable steel restaurants, diners, carry-outs, service stations and other similar type buildings.
We-Mac Mfg. & Supply, Route 3, U. S. Highway 59, Atchison: Collapsible ladders for tank trucks.
Wilson All Weather Window Co., 1010-12 S. Main, Hutchinson: Ornamental iron.
Young Sales & Erection Co., 701 W. Second, Hutchinson: Metal buildings.
Zenoniani Ornamental Iron Works, 918 E. Sixth, Hutchinson: Ornamental iron work (columns, railings, fire screen, weathervanes, room dividers).

Screw Machine Products, and Bolts, Nuts, Screws, Rivets and Washers

Alexander Mfg. Co., 2025-31 Grand, Parsons: Precision screw machine parts.
Baker Machine Co., 5827 S. Hydraulic, Wichita: Screw machine products.
Consolidated Equipment Co., Inc., 4202 Highway 42 W. (Box 2216), Wichita: Toggle clamps.
D-K Mfg. Co., 823 Main, Neodesha: Screw machine products.
Gehlbach Machine Co., 1115 W. Sycamore, Independence: Screw machine products.
Johnson Screw Products, 1215 Argentine, Kansas City: Automatic screw machine products.
Nibarger Tool Service, 1765 N. Emporia, Wichita: Special tools for screw machines, B and S cams.

Metal Stampings

A & I Engineering Works, 408 E. Third, Pittsburg: Kitchen utensils.
Capitol Stamp & Seal Co., 422 E. Tenth, Topeka: Name plates, dog tags.
Chrome Fixture Mfg. Co., Inc., Redel Rail Siding, Stanley: Punch press and small steel products.
J. C. Darling Stamp & Seal Co., 734 Kansas, Topeka: Name plates, dog tags.
Davies Implement Co., Pratt: Popcorn poppers and picnic accessories.
Don Dye Co., Kingman: Wrought iron washers, special washers and stampings.
Globe Engineering Co., 1539 S. St. Paul, Wichita: Metal spinning.
Harper Trucks, Inc., 901 Oak, Harper: Heavy duty tool boxes.
Hayes Tool & Die Co., 597 Rodgers Rd., Olathe: Metal stamping.
Kirkhart's, 1120 S. Santa Fe, Wichita: Metal stamping.
Machine Specialties Co., Route 4, (Box 888), Topeka: Metal spinning.
Machinery Tank & Supply Co., Inc., 1600 W. Douglas, Wichita: Stampings.
Midwest Machine Co., 111 N. Fourth, Atchison: Stampings.
National Sign Co., Inc., 1204 N. Main, Ottawa: Promotional auto tags.
Neosho Small Parts, Box 102, Erie: Metal stampings.
Pauls Mfg. Co., Glen Elder: Tractor tool boxes.
Quincraft Products, Quincy: Aluminumware, corn poppers, metal spinning.
Snyder Stamp & Key Co., 1021 Kansas, Topeka: Dog tags, name plates.
Sterling Mfg. Co., Inc., 1134 N. Fairview (Box 1789), Wichita: Metal stamping.
V. M. Mfg., Airport Rd. and Santa Fe R. R., Hutchinson: Steel stampings.
Vita Craft Corp., Sixth and Johnson, Shawnee: Aluminum and stainless steel cooking utensils.
Western Control Corp., 2533 S. West St. (Box 1202), Wichita: Metal stampings.
Wilco Name Plates, 1303 E. 37th N., Wichita: Brass, aluminum and steel nameplates, plaques, etc.

Coating, Engraving, and Allied Services

Electroplating, Plating, Polishing and Anodizing and Coloring

American Plating, Inc., 400 N. Emporia, Wichita: Plating of metals, chrome, nickel, cadmium, copper, brass, gold and silver.
Anderson Antiques, 4409 W. 17th, Topeka: Silver plating.
Bauersfield Service, 15 E. Fourth, Liberal: Shaft grinding and metallizing.
Bush Plating Co., 1129 Southwest Blvd., Kansas City: Electroplating.
Cable Spinning Equipment Co., Inc., 3100 Topeka, Topeka: Cadmium plating.
Chrome Fixture Mfg. Co., Inc., Redel Rail Siding, Stanley: Plating.
Chromium, Inc., Kansas and Railroad St., Kansas City (5): Electroplating, hard chromium plating, cylindrical grinding.
Dawson Brothers, 3720 W. Pawnee, Wichita: Electroplating.
Fairchild Memorials, 314 W. Ninth, Coffeyville: Sand blasting.
Fairchild Memorials, 108 E. Chestnut, Independence: Sand blasting.
Grandpre Shop, Concordia: Plating.
Industrial Chrome, Inc., 834 N. Madison, Topeka: Hard chrome, nickel chrome, nickel, cadmium and copper plating.
Industrial Engineering, Inc., 901 W. Euclid, McPherson: Hard chrome plating.
Kansas Plating, Inc., 1110 N. Mosley, Wichita: Electroplating service.
Ladd Machine Shop, 323 S. Main, Garden City: Metalizing.
Machine Tool Products Co., 1518 Walnut, Coffeyville: Electroplating.
Marquart Plating Plant & Music Shop, 4103 Gage Center Dr., Topeka: Electroplating.
Metal Finishers, Inc., 3125 Brinkerhoff Rd., Kansas City: Chrome plating of diesel cylinder liners.
Metal Finishing Co., 1423 S. McLean, Wichita: Electroplating and anodizing.
Nance Machine & Paint Co., 2943 Wellington Pl., Wichita: Cadmium plating.
National Allied Chemical Co., 122 S. Main, Ottawa: Chrome plating kit.
Oxwell, Inc., 600 E. 15th, Wellington: Anodizing, chromodizing.
R. W. Parks & Sons, Inc., 1707 E. Douglas, Wichita: Commercial sandblasting.
Ed Peters Chrome Plating, 345 Convesse, Colby: Hard chrome plating on farm machinery parts (discs, sweeps, knives, combine cylinder parts, sickle sections, etc.).
Salina Sand Blasting Co., Inc., 108 E. Iron, Salina: Sandblasting.
Thompson Plating Co., 1025 E. Harry, Wichita: Chrome, nickel, cadmium plating, dow treating, spray painting, electroplating.
Topeka Supply & Boiler Co., Inc., Second and Jefferson (Box 207), Topeka: General plate metal work.
Walcher Metal Treat, Inc., 1019 S. McLean, Wichita: Sandblasting.
Wichita Brass & Aluminum Foundry, 412 E. 29th, Wichita: Sandblasting.

Coating, Engraving, and Allied Services, Not Elsewhere Classified

Cota-Matic, Inc., 512 E. 21st, Wichita: Coating of aluminum and steel.
Field Tool, Inc., 605 Spring, Coffeyville: Spray metallizing (hardsurfacing all alloys and ceramics).
McCunningham Mfg. Co., Box 477, Sedan: Plastic coating.
Metal Processing Co., 728 W. Douglas, Wichita: Aircraft parts painting, phosphate coatings, electro-film (solid film lubricant, commercial paintings) gas fired oven, vapor hone.
Multi-Plastics, Inc., 2148 S. Hoover, Wichita: Fiberglass spraying (coatings).
Standard Precision, Inc., 4105 W. Pawnee (Box 1297), Wichita: Engraving and etching, precision silk screen work.
Tapco, Inc., E. Highway 40 (Box 588), Russell: Protective coatings for tanks, pipe and other tubular goods.

Miscellaneous Fabricated Wire Products

Ankortite Products, Inc., 1900 Wilson, Parsons: Wire work, wire bar supports and basket assemblies (for reinforced concrete), snap ties and bar ties.
Atlas Wire Products Co., Inc., 6615 Inland Dr., Kansas City (6): Wire merchandise displays.
Beeker Mfg., Inc., 11125 Johnson Dr., Shawnee: Wire novelties and gifts, welded wire products.
Brinkman Mfg. & Fence Co., Huntoon and Auburn Rd., Topeka: Portable runs and pens (pets, live-stock, kennel, veterinarian hospitals, research), overload springs.
Ceco Steel Products Corp., Kindelberger and Harvester Rds., Kansas City: Reinforcing steel (wire mesh).
Central Spring Co., 1901 N. Tenth, Kansas City: Furniture springs (box, sofabed, mattress, pillow, divan, chair).
Dalton-Brecheisen Mfg. Co., Garnett: Wire products (crates, grills, hangers, baskets, display racks).
Farris-Burns Corp., 1032 S. 26th, Kansas City: Wire products (clips, handles, hooks, etc.).
G & S Machine Shop, 1020 E. Sixth, Emporia: Bar ties.
Hopkins Mfg. Corp., 428 Peyton (Box 230), Emporia: Oil display rack, tire display rack.
The Lane Myers Co., Protection: Concertina barbed wire, wire products.
Ratzlaff Mfg. Co., Goessel: Wire products.
Sinclair Mfg. Co., 1816 Wabash, Wichita (14): Wire products.
Western Control Corp., 2533 S. West St. (Box 1202), Wichita: Wire shapes and forms, springs.
Wichita Wire Products, 624 E. Harry, Wichita: All types of springs, wire forms, display racks, wire grills and baskets, window guards and partitions.

Miscellaneous Fabricated Metal Products

Metal Shipping Barrels, Drums, Kegs, and Pails

Drumco, Inc., 116-130 N. Sycamore, Wichita (Mailing add.: 630 Pennsylvania [14]): Reconditioning of steel drums.
Greif Bros. Cooperage Corp., 17th and Osage, Kansas City: Steel drums.
Greif Bros. Cooperage Corp., Strother Field, Winfield: Steel drums.
Jones-Laughlin Steel Corp. (Container Div.), Funston and Chrysler Rd., Kansas City: Steel shipping containers.
Sims Barrel Co., Inc., 6 Greystone, Kansas City: Steel shipping barrels and drums.

Valves and Pipe Fittings, Except Plumbers' Brass Goods

Ball Valve Co., 6212 Carter, Shawnee Mission: Valves for air, natural gas and ammonia compressors.
The LFM Mfg. Co., Inc. (Subs. of Rockwell Mfg. Co.), Third and Park, Atchison: Valves.
Liberal Industries, Inc., Syracuse (Mailing add.: Box 93, Liberal): Water inlet valve for toilet tanks.
McNally Pittsburg Mfg. Corp., Drawer D, Pittsburg: Valves.

Fabricated Pipe and Fabricated Pipe Fittings

Darby Corp., First and Walker, Kansas City: Piping fabrication.
K & E Industries, Inc., 1009 S. West St., Wichita: Union type steel coupling for thin wall pipe.
Metal-Fab, Inc., 430 S. Commerce, Wichita: Gas vent pipe and fittings.
Piping & Engineering Co., Box 1065, Wichita: Pipe and fittings.
Taylor Forge & Pipe Works of Kansas, Inc., Box 231, Paola: Pulsation dampeners.
Topeka Supply & Boiler Co., Inc., Second and Jefferson (Box 207), Topeka: Pipe fabricators.

Fabricated Metal Products, Not Elsewhere Classified

A-1 Barrel Co., 1412 N. Grove, Wichita: Clothesline poles, trash containers and burners.
Advanced Metal Sales Corp., 213 N. Summit, Arkansas City: Sink and bar tops for mobile homes.
Ankortite Products, Inc., 1900 Wilson, Parsons: Metal building specialties, metal products for masonry construction.
Barrel Rite, Inc., 1109 Fifth, Dodge City: Trash barrel holders.
Beeker Mfg., Inc., 11125 Johnson Dr., Shawnee: Welded magnesium products, animal cages.
Berners Novelty & Machine Works, 821 S. First, Arkansas City: Novelties.
Besco, Inc., 408 E. 21st, Wichita: Metal products.
Bolin Furniture & Mfg. Co., Route 3, Fort Scott: Combination launderette basket and cart.
Calvert Metal Products Co., 440 N. Meridian, Wichita: Wall ties, flashing, form spreader ties, metal edging and building specialties.
The Carlson Co., Inc., 6045 N. Broadway, Wichita: Metal fabrication.
Childs Mfg. Co., 1100 S. Denver, El Dorado: Prescription files.
The Coleman Co., Inc., 250 N. St. Francis, Wichita: Portable coolers, picnic jugs, portable camp stoves (gasoline, LPG).
Dalton-Brecheisen Mfg. Co., Garnett: Trailer ice boxes, auto refrigerators.
C. Downing Casting & Cabinet Shop, Route 2, Sedan: Novelty items (metal).
Downing Sheet Metal, Route 1, Arkansas City: Cistern filters.
E-Z Tripod Co., Ludell: Tripods.
Empire Mfg. Co., Inc., 3939 Maple, Wichita: Light metal products (foot scrapers, etc.).
Farris-Burns Corp., 1032 S. 26th, Kansas City: Metal products(clips, handles, hooks, etc.).
Flye Repair & Welding Service, 5551 W. 21st, Topeka: Grinding service, steel lintels, guards (sash and door).
Gus Hobby Shop, Beloit: Pop case repair item.
Hanover Mfg. Co., Inc., Hanover: Park benches.
Jackson & Usher, 910 E. Fifth, Newton: Clothesline tighteners.
Kamen Iron & Metal Co., 616 E. Murdock, Wichita: Clothesline posts and other steel fabrication.
Luce Coal & Material Co., 2110 W. Second, Wichita: Metal fabrication.
Meyer Welding Co., 114 S. Pennsylvania, Independence: Metal parts.
Midwest Vending, Inc., Neodesha: Portable soft drink fountains.
Modern Vent Co., 1622 W. Harry, Wichita: Form ties, brick wall ties, anchor bolts.
Oliva Machine Works, 129 E. Third, Newton: Wire stretcher.
Oliver Mfg. Co., 1436 Payne, Wichita: Portable drafting equipment case, auto-desk.
Palmer Welding & Tank Co., Garden City: Metal fabrication.
Ralph Peatman, Mound City: Lighted growing bins for house plants.
Perma-Weld Co., Inc., 1947 N. Topeka, Topeka: Portable aluminum trash barrels.
Pewther Mfg. Co., 1519 S. Dodge, Wichita: Gopher and mole traps.
Phillips Mfg. Co., Inc., 201 N. Waco, Wichita: Portable metal clothes driers.
Quality Mfrs., Inc., 3158 S. Hoover Rd., Wichita (15): Fabricated metal products.
Red Barn Studio, Lindsborg: Metal works.
Reliance Mfg. & Sales Co., 1131 Kansas, Kansas City: Metal products.
S-W Supply Co., Girard: Temporary grave markers and nursery and plant markers.
Schultz Home Modernizing Co., 510 W. First, Larned: Ambulance shade screens.
Sinclair Mfg. Co., 1816 Wabash, Wichita (14): Metal goods.
Sterling Mfg. Co., Inc., 1134 N. Fairview (Box 1789), Wichita: Custom metal work.
Thyfault's Wood & Window Shop, 316 Main, Stockton: Fabricated metal products.
Traf-O-Teria System, Inc., 124 S. Gordy, El Dorado: Parking fine collection boxes.
United Mfg. & Engineering Corp., 1947 N. Topeka, Topeka: Aluminum and steel fabrication.
Van's Incinerator Co., Route 4, Wellington: Incinerators.
W. B. Mfg. Co., 157 N. Waco, Wichita: Hose and tire rack.
We-Mac Mfg. & Supply, Route 3, U. S. Highway 59, Atchison: Gas tank stands, strainers for farm storage tanks.
Western Mfg. Co., Inc., Arkansas City: Contract manufacturing.
Wilson Tool & Die, Inc., 104 S. Tenth, Kansas City: Metal specialties.

MACHINERY (Except Electrical)

Engines and Turbines

Thomas Engineering, 2203 S. Millwood, Wichita: Outboard motors.

Farm Machinery and Equipment

Aeroglide Corp., Aeroglide St. and South Ave., Emporia: Grain drying machinery (commercial and grain bank types).
Agricultural Business Co., Inc., Box 36, Lawrence: Fertilizer application equipment.
Agricultural Business Co., Inc., 203 N. Main, Scott City: Fertilizer application equipment.
Airosprayer Co., Neodesha: Trombone-type brass sprayer, jar sprayer, power airosprayer.
Allen Mfg. Co., 517 Reynolds, Salina: Combine electric lift.
Al's Garage, Lehigh: Farm implements.
American Products, Inc., Box 95, Spearville: Wire rollers, crustbreaker, implement trailers.
Amy Mfg. Co., Inc., Box 808, Dighton: Portable disc roller.
Ankenman Machine Shop, Norton: Adapto-hitches.
Ansel Mfg. Co., S. Missouri, Ulysses: Combine and tractor cabs, irrigation gates, metal reel batts.
Applequist-Lagerberg Mfg., Inc., 921 Bishop, Salina: Grain augers.
Ark Valley, Inc., 721 Sunnyside, Dodge City: One-way plows, tandem discs, replacement parts for farm machinery, implement hitches.
Ausherman Mfg. Co., 3500 N. Topeka, Wichita (19): Reversible rasp cylinder bars for combines.
B & D Mfg. Co., Phillipsburg: Spoutliners (forage cutters and field choppers).
B & J Mfg. Co., Mullinville: Stock racks, racks, gates, feed mixers, feeder wagons, automatic hitches.
B-M Mower Co., Main St., Blue Mound: Power lawn mowers (rotary).
B-M-B Co., Inc., Holton: Farm machinery (rotary mowers, shredders, tractor chains).
B & W Trailer Co., Route 2, Salina: Livestock tables.
Baldwin Metal Products, Route 2, Ottawa: Grain augers, tractor conversion power shift wheels.
Bar-Six Feed Dispenser Co., Protection (Mailing add.: Box 621, Pratt): Cake feed dispenser (livestock).
P. J. Bays Foundry, Fort Dodge Rd., Dodge City: Wheel weights.
Becker Mfg. Co., Downs: Farrowing crates, pig holders, pig feeders, waterers.
Bennett & Son Machine Works, Holyrood: Baled hay elevators.
Bergen General Repairing and Blacksmithing, Goessel: Hog feeders.
Bircher Machine Shop, Box 62, Kanopolis: Stock racks, loading chutes, fence panels, bale loaders.
Bloomstrom Welding Shop, Nortonville: Metal bases for liquid cattle feeders.
Boettcher Supply, 118 W. Court, Beloit: Anhydrous ammonia knives.
Borell Mfg. Co., 410 E. Lincoln, Lindsborg: Lifthitch.
Bowers Mfg. Co., Bird City: Propane weed burner.
Brockhoff Mfg. Co., 15 Oregon (Box 267), Sabetha: Sickle grinders, hydraulic harrow carriers, hydraulic manure loaders, sled curler cultivator, bale loaders.
Buller Mfg. Co., Hillsboro: Elevator ladders, tractor hitches, cattle and hog oilers, feed bunks, drawbar rollers, LP gas brackets.
C & S Applicator Co., Route 3, Iola: Cattle oilers.
Central Machine Shop, Russell: Wide front axle for farm tractors.
Chain Machine Co., Box 202, Haven: Nursery thresher.
Chrome Fixture Mfg. Co., Inc., Redel Rail Siding, Stanley: Lawn mower parts.
Cofer Sales & Mfg., Ransom: Silo unloaders, self-propelled wheel barrows, lawn mowers.
Coontz Implement & Mfg. Co., 131 N. Sixth, Kiowa: Bulldozer attachment for farm wheel tractors.
Cotton Welding Service, Larned: Drill hitches, cattle stocks and feeders.
Dalton-Brecheisen Mfg. Co., Garnett: Grain saver guards.
H. C. Davis Sons Mfg. Co., Inc., Box 395, Bonner Springs: Farm and ranch feed rolling and mixing equipment.
Dawkins Machine Shop, Bucklin: Hay loading tool.
Dirks Wood Mfg. Co., Buhler: Reel batts and reel arms.
Dodson Mfg. Co., Inc., 1463 Barwise, Wichita: Silo and bunk unloaders.
Doerr Metal Products, 320 E. Sixth, Larned: Hog and cattle feeders, hog troughs, bulk feed units, feed mill hoppers and cones.
Doonan Implement Co., Great Bend: Grain loaders and unloaders, grain blowers.
Durite Corp., Inc., 29 Davis, Iola: Rotary tillers, power lawn mowers.
East Side Garage, 410 E. Ave. A, Syracuse: Drill hitches and one way transports, tractor hitches.
Economy Trailer Co., 248 E. Main, Sedan: Branding and dehorning chutes, grain beds, cattle feeders, calf creep feeders.
Edson Co., Box 367, Baxter Springs: Fertilizer equipment.
Elson Farm Tools, Inc., 16th and Halstead (Mailing add.: Landmark Hotel), Hutchinson: Farm tools, loaders, tractor blades, draw bar rollers, hoists, springtooth harrows, tool bars, grain augers.
Excel Industries, Inc., Hesston: Cabs (combine, tractor, cotton picker).
Farm Equipment Parts & Sales Co., Inc., 835 Highland, Salina: Combine attachments.
Farrar Machine Shop, Norwich: Variable speed V-belt traction drives for agricultural machines, sprockets, pressed steel V-pulleys and improvement parts for farm machinery.
Ferguson Service, Belleville: Stalk cutter, plows, farm implements.
Field Queen, Inc., Box 37, Maize: Self-propelled alfalfa and forage grass cutter and self-unloading trailer.
Filson Mfg. Co., Main St., Protection: Branding chutes and calf cradles.
Flop-Over Trailer Mfg. Co., Caldwell: Implement trailers, tractor hitch, drill hitch and measuring wheel.
Florence Implement Co., Florence: Agricultural chemical sprayers.
Forgy Plow Co., Vermillion: Plow bases, steel sled curlers, cultivators.
W. S. Fred & Son, Macksville: Scooter lawn mowers.
Full Vision, Inc., 523 W. First (Box 321), Newton: Cabs for combines, tractors, industrial machinery.
General Distributing Co., Inc., Box 205, Newton: Cardboard chick feeders.
Gilmore-Tatge Mfg. Co., Box 133, Clay Center: Milo guards, feed bunks, fence line bunks, crop driers, mineral feeders, power feeders.
Gravely Tractors (Div. Studebaker Corp.), 2423 S. Main (Box 191), Fort Scott: Rotary power lawn mowers.
Great Bend Mfg. Co., Inc., 1912 11th (Box 1057), Great Bend: Tractor attached equipment.
H & W Service, 115 S. Foster, Stockton: Loading chutes.
Hainke Mfg. Co., Kensington: Power lawn mowers.
Hansen Machine Shop, Strong City: Dehorning chutes.
Harvester Co., Inc., Pratt Municipal Airport, Pratt: Wheel-mounted disc harrows, one-way plows, power weeders.
Heckendorn Mfg. Co., Inc., Cedar Point: Industrial mowers.
Henson Dairy Supply, 415 N. Main, Hutchinson: Calf weaners, bull staffs.
Hesston Mfg. Co., Inc., Hesston: Agricultural equipment (combine accessories, straw choppers, self-propelled grain and hay windrowers, hay conditioners, corn and cotton harvesting equipment, turf mowers, beet topper/windrower, row crop saver).
Hey Machinery Co., Inc., Baldwin: Implement wheel conversions for airplane tires.
Hiebert Mfg. Co., 512 W. Grand, Hillsboro: Cattle oilers.
H. P. Holman, Route 2, Arkansas City: Pressure wing weights.
Holmstrom Machine Works, Holcomb: Stock tank heaters, land levelers.
Horton Digger Co., 118 E. Ninth, Horton: Power augers.
Hull Mfg. Co., 1020 W. 53rd, Wichita: Garden tractor.
Hume-Fry Co., Inc., E. Highway 50 (Box 757), Garden City: Portable grain driers, bearings for one-way plows, planter attachments, pick-up reels.
Hutchinson Foundry & Steel Co., D and Washington, Hutchinson: Agricultural equipment (soil packer wheel weights).
Hutchinson Mfg. Co., Inc., W. Crawford (Box 33), Clay Center: Grain augers and grain roller mills.
Independent Mfg. Co., Inc., 301 N. 11th, Neodesha: Plows, landscrapers, disc harrows (lift type and wheel mounted), rear grader blades.
Jackson Mfg. Co., Simpson: Baled hay elevator, mechanical cattle oilers.
Jet Burner, Inc., Box 709, Hutchinson: Weed burners, flame cultivators, stock tank heaters.
Jet Flow Mfg. Co., La Cygne: Supplemental natural air drying fans and heaters, special augering equipment (agriculture), sequence batch hopper scales (automatic, electronic), poultry, hog and cattle feeding systems.
Johnson Equipment Co., 529 N. Mead, Wichita: Broomcorn harvesting machinery.
Jones Alfalfa Milling Co., 622 Van Buren, Topeka: Live bottom trailers, metal tanks, collectors, coolers and shakers.
Jones Electric Matchinery Co., 622 Van Buren, Topeka: Attachments for green forage harvesters.
Jones Milling & Mfg. Co., Ninth and Santa Fe, Wichita: Power lawn mowers.
Kenison, Inc., 603 N. Eighth, Salina: Grain saving guards.
Kent Mfg. Co., Tipton: Grain driers, fertilizer spreaders.
Kingman Mfg. Co., Inc., Cunningham: Metal feed troughs, cattle oilers, creep feeders, hay feeders, mineral feeders, self-feeders.
Kramer Machine & Engineering Products Co., 320 S. Second, Leavenworth: Farm machinery.
Krause Corp., 305 S. Monroe, Hutchinson: Farm implements.
Lasley Co., Inc., 109 Kansas, Kansas City: Grain bins, grain handling equipment.
Leavenworth Steel, Inc., Main and Cherokee, Leavenworth: Farm implements.
Load-King Mfg. Co., Kingman: Rubber-tired press wheels, sweeprakes.
Luttig Trailer Co., Emmett: Cattle feeders.
McBratney Implement & Mfg., Centralia: Hay-loading, silage and other farm equipment.
McCracken Tri-Bar, McCracken: Undercutting blades.
A. E. Mapes Co., Norcatur: Grain driers.
Martin Tire & Supply Co., 154 N. Emporia, Wichita: Agricultural implement tire wheel assemblies.
Mayrath Machinery Co., Inc., E. Trail, Dodge City: Corn and hay elevators, standard and truck augers, junior augers, center drive augers, crop sprayers, bale movers.
Meade Mfg., Inc., Highways 54 and 160 W., Meade: Individual seeding hoppers for grain drills, tractor combine cabs, tractor cabs, riding type power lawn mowers.
Michael Mfg. Co., Winona: Farm equipment carrier, stock tank heater.
Mid-States Truck Hitch Co., Bucklin: Truck hitch.
Midwest Machine Co., 111 N. Fourth, Atchison: Rotary lawn mowers.
J. V. Mitchell Mfg. Co., N. Locust, Ottawa: Poultry and turkey crops, feeding batteries.
Monarch Brass & Aluminum Works, 2008 S. Holbrook, Fort Scott: Power lawn mowers.
Moridge Mfg. Co., Moundridge: Grain driers and augers, automatic tube cattle feeders, springtooth harrows.
Harold Mulville, Dighton: Deep furrow attachment.
Newacheck Supply Co., 512 Main, Larned: Rubber feed conveyors and replacement parts for combines, hydraulic lift for one-way plows.
Newton Mfg. Co., 110 E. 17th, Newton: Farm implements.
Ed Norden, Kensington: Wide front adjustable axle for tractors.
Nu Way Mfg. Co., Box 97, Barnard: Bale stacker.
Oakley Reel Mfg. & Fix-It, 801 Clinton, Beloit: Steel rods for combines, wooden blades for reels.
Oswalt Industries, Inc., Garden City: Ensilage loader, power feed box.
Ottawa-Warner Corp., 634 King, Ottawa: Land levelers, fertilizer spreaders, metal combine and tractor cabs.
P & N Equipment Co., 1000 N. Chemical, Hutchinson: Portable livestock corrals, stock racks and assorted livestock handling equipment.
Palmer Welding & Tank Co., Garden City: Steel cattle feeder.
Pauls Mfg. Co., Glen Elder: Rear mounted tractor blades.
Perma-Weld Co., Inc., 1947 N. Topeka, Topeka: Hydraulic tractor attachments.
Pratt Mfg. Co., Box 232, Pratt: Rod weeder attachment, hydraulic lift attachment.
Press Wheels, Unlimited (Div. Stewart Investments, Inc.), Airport Rd. and Santa Fe R. R., Hutchinson: Press wheel attachment assemblies.
Pyramid Welding & Mfg. Co., E. 13th, Hays: Cabs for tractors, combines and other heavy equipment.
Rawdon Bros. Aircraft, Inc., Box 1119, Wichita (1): Aircraft spray equipment, aircraft seeding and dusting equipment.
Raye's Welding & Machine, Harper: Dirt scrapers and springtooth carriers.
Reed Mfg. Co., Colby: Tractor wheel weights.
Regier Mfg. Co., Route 2, Moundridge: Riding lawn mowers.
Reschke Machine Works, 908 N. Washington, Wichita: Agricultural equipment.
Rich Implement Store, 105 E. Fourth, St. John: Governor attachment for tractors.
Richardson Mfg. Co., Inc., Cawker City: Pick-up reel attachments, combine straw walker covers, milo guard, bale loader, mulch treader, trench silo unloader, stubble mulch plow, wire winder, dual hitch.
Roberts Machine Shop, 520 S. Lincoln, Liberal: Power lawn mowers.
Root Mfg. Co., Inc., 127 E. 11th, Baxter Springs: Riding, self-propelled type rotary lawn mowers, power tillers.
Rylko Home Supply Co., 1314 E. Fourth, Hutchinson: Grease hose attachment.
Schafer Plow Co., Inc., 208 W. Simpson, Pratt: One-way plows, tandem discs, chisel plows.
Schermuly Mfg. Co., 812 N. Wichita, Wichita: Ridge busters, one-way plow and disc harrow bearings, twin press wheels.
Security Stock Table Co., Municipal Airport, Hutchinson: Livestock treating table.
Seibel Welding Shop, Leoti: Farm machinery.
Shaw Mfg. Co., Inc. (Div. of Bush Hog, Inc.), Galesburg: Power farm mowers, garden and small farm tractors, riding, power lawn mowers.
Simpson-Oliver, Inc., 401 N. Poplar, S. Hutchinson: Farm equipment.
Speck Sales & Mfg. Co., 206 Main, Galena: Adjustable front axles for row crop tractors, grain savers.
Speed King Mfg. Co., Inc., Ft. Dodge Rd., (Box 1039), Dodge City: Auger type grain loaders and attachments, hand portable posthole diggers, belt conveyers.
Stroberg Equipment Co., 4901 N. Monroe, Hutchinson: Porta loading chutes, porta corrals, catch pens, farm gates, pickup stock racks, feed lot equipment.
Sunflower Mfg. Co., 312 S. Pine, Beloit: Soil packers, seeder attachments, plow bearings, grain augers, rotary hoes, milo misers, bin levelers, wide sweep stubble mulch blades, flexible stubble mulch plow.
The Sun-Mastr Corp., 501-9 S. Kansas, Olathe: Tractor saw (weed and brush cutter), mowers, silage loader, hammermill type mowers, shredders, rotary mowers, gang lawn mowers.
Tedford Mfg., Inc., 130 E. Birch, Liberal: Subsoil mulcher, plows, plow sweep attachment, flexible coulters, rolling.
Ternes Silo Unloader Co., Conway Springs: Silo unloader.
Thielen Brothers, Dorrance: Grain blowers.
Thompson Machine Works, Fourth and Parallel, Conway Springs: Farm load haulers, bulk unloaders, double drill hitches, hardfacing farm tools.
Topeka Hiway Mower Co., Box 301, Ottawa: Mowing machines, chemical sprayers, loaders, angledozers.
Trego Mfg. Co., 212 S. First, WaKeeney: Stacker, hydraulic load, cable hoist, self-unloader, bale trailer, combine building.
Turon Hardware & Lumber Co., Turon: Feed bunks, grain bins, brooder houses.
Twin-Feed Blower Co., 111 Main (Box 185), Larned: Greaser systems for agricultural machinery, combine-tractor hydraulic systems, hydraulic steering for tractors and combines, front end tractor loaders.
United Mfg. & Engineering Corp., 1947 N. Topeka, Topeka: Automatic cattle feeder.
Unruh Industry Co., Durham: Combine cabs.
Victory Hopper Co., Lewis Addition, Dodge City: Grain hoppers.
Viking Mfg. Co., 1600 Yuma (Box 68), Manhattan: Farm feed grinders, farm elevators, roller blade for leveling, grading, seeding and fertilizing.
W-W Grinder Corp., 2957 N. Market, Wichita: Permanent magnetic separators.
W. W. Mfg. Co., Box 728, Dodge City: Cattle chutes, calf cradles, stock racks, portable corrals, feed bunks.
Walker Bros. Mfg., Macksville: Wheel track planter.
Charles Wampler, Glasco: Hydraulic truck hoist.
Webb Mfg. Co., 1115 N. G St. (Box 47), Arkansas City: Power lawn mower and lawn mower blades.
Welch Mfg., Inc., S. Fifth, Herington: Animal insecticide applicator, bale loader.
Wenger Mfg., Inc., Box 150, Sabetha: Front end hydraulic loader, combine clutch.

Wheat Belt Supply Co., Box 1015, Dodge City: Grain driers.
White Star Enterprises, Inc., Box 1052, Wichita (1): Road grader, maintainer or agricultural leveler tractor attachment.
Wilbeck Machine & Mfg. Co., 418 N. Poplar, S. Hutchinson: Bale elevators, three point plows, tandem disc and chisels.
Robert S. Wise Co., Inc., 502 E. 33rd St. N. (Box 2381), Wichita: Spraying equipment.
Wonder Tool Co., Johnson: Windlass attachment for pickup truck wheel.
Wyatt Mfg. Co., Inc., 500 N. Fifth, Salina: Farm-industrial augers, auger elevators and conveyors, subsoilers, V-plows, ditchers, farm-type feed mill, corn stalk lifters, automatic hog feeding systems.

Construction, Mining, and Materials Handling Machinery and Equipment

Construction Machinery and Equipment

Balderson, Inc., Wamego: Bulldozers, loaders.
Balzer Machine Shop, Moundridge: Steel scrapers and land levelers.
Ceco Steel Products Corp., Kindelberger and Harvester Rds., Kansas City: Concrete forms.
Geo. C. Christopher & Son, Inc., 1220 Blaine, Wichita: Cement mixers.
Conmaco, Inc., 820 Kansas, Kansas City: Pile driving equipment and accessories.
Davis Mfg., Inc., 1500 McLean Blvd., Wichita: Trenching and earth moving equipment.
Henry Industries, Inc., 525 N. Ninth, Salina: Parts and sub-assemblies.
Henry Mfg. Co., Inc., 1700 N. Clay (Box 521), Topeka: Hydraulic earthmoving and materials handling equipment (backhoes, loaders, fork lifts, drop hammers and hydraulic jackhammers).
Hydra-Bumber Co., Box 775, McPherson: Hydraulic bumper and scraper.
The LFM Mfg. Co., Inc. (Subs. of Rockwell Mfg. Co.), Third and Park, Atchison: Heavy machinery.
Luttig Trailer Co., Emmett: Trailers.
McNally Pittsburg Mfg. Corp., Drawer D, Pittsburg: Coal preparation equipment (bins, loaders, chutes, breakers, cleaners, crushers, dryers, feeders, gates, hoppers, screens).
Monatco Mfg. Corp., 2214 Front, Kansas City: Asphalt road planers.
Perine Bros. Iron Works, 809 Quincy, Topeka: Curb and gutter mules.
Sherman Brothers Machine Works, Box 305, Great Bend: Terracers.
Topeka Arc Welding, 1928 N. Topeka, Topeka: Front end loaders.
Tucker's, Inc., 102½ N. Cedar, Marion: Dirt elevator attachment, terracer.
Tumaco Equipment, 1206 E. Main, Marion: Multi-grader terracers.
Universal Pulleys Co., Inc., 330 N. Mosley, Wichita: Cement mixers.
Viking Mfg. Co., 1600 Yuma (Box 68), Manhattan: Rolling straightedge for highway and airport construction.
Wichita Steel Fabricators, Inc., 3400 N. Broadway, Wichita: Rollers (sheepfoot, flat, pneumatic tired and self-propelled).
Young Spring & Wire Corp. (Ottawa Steel Div.), Box 49, Ottawa: Hydraulic front end loaders, hydraulic concrete breakers, backfill tampers, heavy duty backhoes, piggy back rail trailer loaders, mobile chemical weed control distributors with highway sign water attachment.

Oil Field Machinery and Equipment

Augusta Welding & Machine Shop, W. Seventh, Augusta: Oil field equipment.
Boydston Machine & Tool Co., 1100 S. Denver, El Dorado: Oil field equipment (valve spacer, sucker rod wrenches).
Brandberry Machine Shop, Russell: Oil field supplies.
Byers Portabase, Inc., 500 N. Plummer, Chanute: Oil well pump jack base.
C & W Machine Works, Inc., Box 12, Great Bend: Oil field tools and equipment (toolhouses, tanks, rathole diggers).
C & W Machine Works, Inc., Box 670, Liberal: Oil field supplies.
Cardwell Mfg. Co., 801 S. Wichita, Wichita: Oil well drilling and servicing equipment, oil well mud pumps.
Central Enterprises, 707 N. Grand, Lyons: Gas generators.
Central Machine Shop, Russell: Oil field supplies.
Central Machine Works, Inc., Box 276, Plainville: Oil field tools and equipment (toolhouses, tanks, etc.).
Chase Welding Co., Box 302, Chase: Oil field equipment.
Churchill, Inc., 316 W. Cherry, Chanute: Core barrels for oil field use, pump jack.
Construction Service Co., 1722 E. Third, Great Bend: Sectionalized engine houses for oil fields.
Corrision Proof Fitting Co., Inc., 607 Holland, Great Bend: Cast-ite products.
Easter Welding Service, Russell: Oil field supplies.
Eaton Metal Products Corp., 110 N. Pershing, Hutchinson: Oil equipment.
Farley Machine Works Co., Great Bend: Oil field supplies.
Federal Supply & Machine Co., 200-220 E. 5th, Winfield: Rotary drill collars, subs, oil field specialties.

Flexweight Drill Pipe Co., Inc., 1314 Park (Box 507), Great Bend: Special weighted rotary drill pipe.
Gehlbach Machine Co., 1115 W. Sycamore, Independence: Oil well pumping equipment.
Giffin Mfg. Co., Box 27, Kechi: Oil field specialty tools.
J & M Machine Co., Canton: Oil field machinery and equipment.
Jensen Bros. Mfg. Co., Inc., 14th and Pacific, Coffeyville: Oil well pumping jacks, geartorks and speed reducers, jet, submersible and beam counter-balanced pumps, water systems.
The LFM Mfg. Co., Inc. (Subs. of Rockwell Mfg. Co.), Third and Park, Atchison: Oil field machinery and castings.
Lind Fabricating Co., Lebo: Oil field equipment.
Herman Long, Edna: Oil and gas field supplies.
Loomer Machine & Welding Co., 510 W. Cottonwood, Independence: Oil field accessories.
McCartney Mfg. Co., 635 W. 12th, Baxter Springs: Oil field and refinery valves.
McCunningham Mfg. Co., Box 477, Sedan: Storage tanks, tanks for trucks, skid mounted tanks, engine starters, stop locks, vent valves.
Manufacturing Enterprises, Inc., 200½ N. Millwood (Box 878), Wichita: Oil well pumping equipment.
Mountain Iron Co., W. Seventh, Augusta: Oil field supplies.
National Tank Co., Great Bend: Oil field equipment.
Norm Engineering Co., Russell: Oil field and various metal supplies.
O'Neill Tank Co., Fifth and C Sts., Westport Addition, Route 1, Great Bend: Oil and gas processing equipment.
Parkersburg (Div. of Textron, Inc.), 12th and Oak (Box 573), Coffeyville: Oil well pumping units, hydromatic brakes and hydrotarders.
Petroleum Specialty Co., Russell: Oil well paraffin scrapers.
R & R Tank Co., Inc., Box 231, Pratt: Oil field tanks and equipment.
Radaco Engine Houses, Chase: Oil field engine houses.
Robinson Packer Co., 14th and Spruce, Coffeyville: Oil and gas field equipment.
Russell Tool Co., Russell: Oil field supplies.
Salco Co., Inc., Hill City: Impervious lining for sealed brine ponds.
Star Drilling Supply Co., 202 W. Fourth, Chanute: Cable tool and rotary well drilling machinery, tools.
Charles Wheatley Co., Caney: Check valves, etc.

Elevators and Moving Stairways

Alexander Mfg. Co., 2025-31 Grand, Parsons: Freight elevators.
J. B. Ehrsam & Sons Mfg. Co., Enterprise: Passenger and freight elevators (commercial and industrial).
Jackson Mfg. Co., Simpson: Basement elevators.
Olathe Lifts, 125 N. Water, Olathe: Automatic residential lifts (dumb waiter).
Western Mfg. Co., Inc., Arkansas City: Passenger elevator car enclosures, elevator hatchway doors and frames.

Conveyors and Conveying Equipment

J. B. Ehrsam & Sons Mfg. Co., Enterprise: Elevating and conveying machinery.
Hutchinson Mfg. Co., Inc., W. Crawford (Box 33), Clay Center: Screw conveyors.
McNally Pittsburg Mfg. Corp., Drawer D, Pittsburg: Conveyors, conveyor chain, elevator chain, elevators and elevator buckets, belt and belt carriers.
Mid-West Conveyor Co., Inc., 450 E. Donovan Rd., Kansas City: Conveyors.
Peerless Conveyor & Mfg. Co., Inc., 3341 Harvester Rd., Kansas City: Conveying machinery for handling sand, crushed rock, gravel, etc.
Vacu-Blast Co., (Abilene Div.), 600 N. Washington, Abilene: Air conveying equipment.

Hoists, Industrial Cranes, and Monorail Systems

Baldwin-Ward Mfg. Co., Inc., 1630-44 S. Main, Ottawa: Aerial crane.

Industrial Trucks, Tractors, Trailers, and Stackers

Alexander Mfg. Co., 2025-31 Grand, Parsons: Truck winches (electric).
Consolidated Equipment Co., Inc., 4202 Highway 42 W. (Box 2216), Wichita: Handling equipment (dollies).
Curtis Machine Co., 715 S. Second, Dodge City: Small winches.
J. B. Ehrsam & Sons Mfg. Co., Enterprise: Engineered materials handling systems.
Hanover Mfg. Co., Inc., Hanover: Truck hoists, trailer box hoist.
Harper Trucks, Inc., 901 Oak, Harper: Industrial material handling carts.
Kenison, Inc., 603 N. Eighth, Salina: Two-wheel hand trucks, four-wheel platform trucks, beverage trucks.

Mid-West Conveyor Co., Inc., 450 E. Donovan Rd., Kansas City: Material handling equipment.
P. D. G. Mfg., Inc., Box 98, Rose Hill: Vehicles, transporters, trailers.
W. C. Rickel & Son Mfg. Co., Basehor: Tricycle hydraulic dump tractor (for stockyards).
S/M Hydraulics, Clearwater: Truck lifts.
Western Foundry & Machine Works, 1801 Madison (Box 439), Topeka: Material handling equipment.

Metalworking Machinery and Equipment

Machine Tools, Metal Cutting Types

Clark Motor Co., 204 E. Eighth, Liberal: Metal lathe work.
Lawco, Inc., 217 W. Second, Hutchinson: Portable power pipe threader.
Salts Mfg. Co., 5021 Irving Dr., Wichita: Hobbyists' lathe, lathe kits, grinding and polishing heads.

Machine Tools, Metal Forming Types

Air Reduction Sales Co. (Div. of Air Reduction Co., Inc.), 1100 S. Packard, Kansas City: Cutting equipment and supplies.
Air Reduction Sales Co. (Div. of Air Reduction Co., Inc.), 602 E. 29th, Wichita: Cutting equipment and supplies.
Geo. C. Christopher & Son, Inc., 1220 Blaine, Wichita: Combination punch and shear bar cutters.
Henry Industries, Inc., 525 N. Ninth, Salina: Hydraulic hammers.
Murrell Tool Service, 1938 N. Mead, Wichita: Cutting tools, gauges and grinding (internal and cylindrical).
Oxwell, Inc., 600 E. 15th, Wellington: Drop hammers.

Special Dies and Tools, Die Sets, Jigs and Fixtures

Ammann Mfg. Co., Inc., 3915 Maple, Wichita: Tools and dies.
Applequist-Lagerberg Mfg., Inc., 921 Bishop, Salina: Tools and dies.
Beardsley & Couchman, Inc., 231 N. St. Francis, Wichita: Tools and dies.
Blue Rapids Supply Co., Blue Rapids: Rubber molds.
Bruest, Inc., 20th and Sycamore, Independence: Tools and dies.
C-B-S Machine Works, 219 W. Fourth, Chanute: Tool design.
Center Line Machine Shop, 2020 Main, Parsons: Tools, dies, jigs and fixtures.
Consolidated Equipment Co., Inc., 4202 Highway 42 W. (Box 2216), Wichita: Plate dies, aircraft tools and dies.
Cox Machine Shop, 5920 W. 21st, Wichita: Aircraft and tooling.
Crole Machine Shop, 331 N. Seneca, Wichita: Tools, dies, jigs and fixtures.
Flint Hills Machine Works, 1217 Industrial, Emporia: Tools and dies, production machinery.
Gasket Products, Inc., 319 S. Wichita, Wichita (2): Steel rule dies.
General Tool Co., Inc., 912 E. Zimmerly, Wichita: Tools and dies.
Gramling Tool & Die, Inc., 4719 Merriam Lane, Merriam: Tools and dies, stampings.
Hayes Tool & Die Co., 597 Rodgers Rd., Olathe: Tool dies, plastic molds, fixtures.
Kirkhart's, 1120 S. Santa Fe, Wichita: Tools and dies.
Loomer Machine & Welding Co., 510 W. Cottonwood, Independence: Tools and dies.
Wayne McCarrier Mfg. Co., 2801 N. Athenian, Wichita (24): Tools.
Magic Circle Mfg. Co., Inc., 1209 Buckeye (Box 657), Coffeyville: Tools and dies.
Mal Mfg., Inc., 1120 S. Santa Fe, Wichita: Custom tools and dies.
Martin Tool Co., 435 N. Water, Wichita: Tools, dies, special machines, contract manufacturing.
Mead Mfg. Co., 1430 S. Washington, Wichita: Aircraft jigs and dies.
Midwest, Inc., Box 6, Wellington: Tools and dies.
Midwest Machine Co., 111 N. Fourth, Atchison: Tools, dies and machine parts.
Milling Precision Tool, Inc., 116 N. Martinson, Wichita (12): Tools and dies.
Neosho Small Parts, Box 102, Erie: Tools and dies.
Nickelson Tool & Die Co., 1105-1107 S. West St., Wichita: Blank and pierce dies, jigs and fixtures.
Don Osborne Machine Plant, 2-17 Crestview, Hutchinson: Tools, dies and fixtures.
Page Airways Machine Tool, 522 Woodlawn, Atchison: Machine tools.
Product Engineering & Mfg. Co., Inc., 434 W. First, Wichita: Tools and dies.
Ransdell Heat Treaters, 1551 Barwise, Wichita: Tools and dies.
Roll Formed Products, Inc., Moundridge: Tools and press dies.
Ross Engineering & Equipment Co., 631 N. Bluff, Wichita: Tools, dies, jigs and fixtures.
Southwest Machine Shop, Elkhart: Jigs and fixtures.
Superior Industrial Machine Co., 521-23 E. Murdock, Wichita: Tools and dies.
Tru-Line Die Cutting Co., 705 E. Third, Wichita (2): Steel rule dies, die-cutting.
Union Machine & Tool Works, Box 2308, Kansas City: Aircraft tools.
V. M. Mfg., Airport Rd. and Santa Fe R. R., Hutchinson: Tools and dies.
Weaver Engineering & Mfg. Co., 1005 E. 17th, Wichita (14): Tools and dies.
Wilson Tool & Die, Inc., 104 S. Tenth, Kansas City: Tools and dies.

Machine Tool Accessories and Measuring Devices

Center Line Machine Shop, 2020 Main, Parsons: Portable boring equipment.
Roy E. Davis, 416½ S. Kansas, Liberal: Shear sharpener.
Erhardt's, Inc., 7 Kansas, S. Hutchinson: Disc sharpening tools, measuring devices.
Harlow Tool Service, Inc., 922 N. Santa Fe, Wichita: Special tools, carbide tipped countersink cutters, H. S. countersink cutters, micro rivet shaver cutters and production parts.
Lungstrom Machine & Mfg. Co., 415 E. Union, Lindsborg: Porcelain tube cutters.
Master Mfg. Co., Inc., 1300 Ave. A, E., Hutchinson: Milling, boring, drilling heads, feed tables, machine tool attachments, portable machine tools, erector type machine components.
Mid-Western Tool, Inc., 909 S. Main, Hutchinson: Portable power tools.
Mower-Mate Tool Co., Box 100, Riverton: Drill attachment for sharpening rotary lawn mowers.
Nibarger Tool Service, 1765 N. Emporia, Wichita: Cutting tools.
Ross Engineering & Equipment Co., 631 N. Bluff, Wichita: Machine-tool accessories.
Vernon's Supply Co., Inc., 123 N. Santa Fe, Salina: Spiral balance weight adjusting wrench, plane grounding plugs, inspection mirrors.

Metalworking Machinery, Except Machine Tools

Air Reduction Sales Co. (Div. of Air Reduction Co., Inc.), 1100 S. Packard, Kansas City: Welding equipment.
Air Reduction Sales Co. (Div. of Air Reduction Co.), 602 E. 29th, Wichita: Welding equipment.
Harper Trucks, Inc., 901 Oak, Harper: Welding equipment carts.
Linde Co. (Div. of Union Carbide Corp.), 550 E. 17th, Wichita: Welding equipment.
Topeka Arc Welding, 1928 N. Topeka, Topeka: Shears, metal cutting.

Special-Industry Machinery, Except Metalworking Machinery

Food Products Machinery

Aeration & Dust Control, Inc., 707 S. Main, Hutchinson: Aeration and dust control equipment for commercial elevators.
Allison Mfg. Co., Inc., Route 3 (Box 264), Olathe: Feed mill equipment.
Beeker Mfg., Inc., 11125 Johnson Dr., Shawnee: Tubing products.
Chillicothe Industries, Inc., Leavenworth (Mailing add.: 2519 Madison, K. C., Mo.): Feed mixers, grain rollers, food processing machinery.
Cofer Sales & Mfg., Ransom: Egg washing machines, poultry house supplies.
Creason Corrugating & Machinery, Inc., 5836 N. Broadway, Wichita: Regrinding and corrugating of flour and feed mill rolls.
H. C. Davis Sons Mfg. Co., Inc., Box 395, Bonner Springs: Feed mill and elevator equipment.
J. B. Ehrsam & Sons Mfg. Co., Enterprise: Grain elevator and feed processing machinery.
G-R Mfg. Co., Hunter Island (Route 2), Manhattan: Meat testers.
Grain Belt Supply Co., U. S. Highway 81 N. (Box 629), Salina: Grain elevator, flour and feed mill equipment, aeration equipment.
Grain Spouting & Elevators of Kansas, Inc., Box 371, Hutchinson: Grain spouting, bucket elevators, hoppers, and grain conveying equipment.
Great Western Mfg. Co., 208-220 Choctaw, Leavenworth: Flour mill sifters, grain elevators, feeders, separators (for hammermills).
Jayhawk Mfg. Co., Inc., 120 N. Adams, Hutchinson: Colloid mills for food and grease.
Kenco Mfg. Co., 617 Ottawa (Box 337), Baxter Springs: Grain aeration equipment.
Kice Metal Products Co., 2040 S. Mead, Wichita (11): Air systems (pneumatic conveying, grain cleaning, dust control).
M-E-C Co. (Div. Altamil Corp.), 1402 Main, Neodesha: Grinding, mixing, conveying and drying equipment for agricultural and industrial processing.
Mid-States Mill Equipment Co., Inc., 1547 N. Mosley, Wichita: Flour and feed mill equipment, dust control systems.
Millcraft, Inc., 1127 Merriam, Kansas City (3): Laboratory equipment for flour milling industry.
Nelson Co., Inc., W. Main, Oxford: Feed packing equipment.
Nor-Vell, Inc., Box 671, Fort Scott: Flour mill machinery, supplies and repair parts, sifters, sieve frames, bleaching machines, etc.
Perma-Weld Co., Inc., 1947 N. Topeka, Topeka: Replacement rolls for pellet mill machines.
Pierpoint Mfg. Co., Yates Center: Semi-false floors for grain bins.
Ranney-Davis, Fifth Ave. at First, Arkansas City: Coffee roasters.
Reschke Machine Works, 908 N. Washington, Wichita: Grain handling, drying and milling equipment, dehydrating equipment.
Salina Mfg. Co., 606 N. Front (Box 26), Salina: Mill and elevator equipment, pneumatic conveying.
Seymour Foods, Inc., 101 N. Kansas, Topeka: Automatic egg-handling machinery.
Simlo, Inc., Seventh and McBratney, Clay Center: Mill and elevator machinery, grain handling equipment, dust systems and areation equipment.
Stapleton's Atom Feed Products, 907 Ayers, Coffeyville: Ice cream machine items.
Stickelber & Sons, Inc., 1150 Southwest Blvd., Kansas City: Bakery machinery and equipment.
United Mfg. & Engineering Corp., 1947 N. Topeka, Topeka: Perma-weld rolls and dies for pellet mills.
W-W Grinder Corp., 2957 N. Market, Wichita: Agricultural and industrial hammermills and roller mills.
Wenger Mfg., Inc., Box 150, Sabetha: Feed mixers.

Woodworking Machinery

Buller Mfg. Co., Hillsboro: Saw frames and sets.
Root Mfg. Co., Inc., 127 E. 11th, Baxter Springs: Power saws and chain saws.
V. M. Mfg., Airport Rd. and Santa Fe R. R., Hutchinson: Tree saw wheels and guards.
Valley Saw, Mound Valley: Tractor power saw.

Printing Trades Machinery and Equipment

Brackett Stripping Machine Co., 505 Jackson, Topeka: Stripping machine, paper jogging machine, machine for bookbinders and printers.
Didde-Glaser, Inc., Highway 50 and W. 12th, Emporia: Gathering and gluing collator, sheet and signature collator, offset printing presses.
Missouri-Central Type Foundry, 703-711 E. Murdock, Wichita: Paper cutters, stereotype casters and supplies, lead and slug cutters-miterers, metal feeders, melting pots, job and cylinder chases.
Don Osborne Machine Plant, 2-17 Crestview, Hutchinson: Printing trades machinery.
V-M Tipper Co., Spearville: Tipping and collating machines.

Special Industry Machinery, Not Elsewhere Classified

Alexander Mfg. Co., 2025-31 Grand, Parsons: Shell loading ordnance equipment.
Bircher Machine Shop, Box 62, Kanopolis: Automatic brick unloader.
Bowers Mfg. Co., Bird City: Tire truing machine, tractor tire removing tool.
Center Line Mfg. Co., 4741 St. Louis, Wichita: Tire repair equipment (passenger, truck, tractor).
Darby Corp., First and Walker, Kansas City: Refinery and chemical plant equipment.
Elliott, Inc., 926 Oxford Dr., Emporia: Roof nailing machine.
Great Western Mfg. Co., 208-220 Choctaw, Leavenworth: Sifting and screening machines.
Insul-Wool Insulation Corp., 121 N. Dodge, Wichita: Home insulating machine.
Jayhawk Mfg. Co., Inc., 120 N. Adams, Hutchinson: Colloid mills for paint.
Johnson Equipment Co., 529 N. Mead, Wichita: Broom equipment.
Koch Engineering Co., Inc., 321 W. Douglas, Wichita: Refinery equipment (designer and fabricator of modern trays).
Lungstrom Machine & Mfg. Co., 415 E. Union, Lindsborg: Pipe wrapper.
McCartney Mfg. Co., 635 W. 12th, Baxter Springs: Petro-chemical equipment.
McNally Pittsburg Mfg. Corp., Drawer D, Pittsburg: Complete lightweight aggregate plants, rotary kilns, dryers, component equipment, barge loading systems, car handling system.
Merker Machine & Boiler Works, 2000 S. Main, Fort Scott: Stone splitters.
Research Engineering & Development Co., 10901 Mission Rd., Overland Park: Meat processing equipment.
Rogers Mfg. Co., Inc., 202 N. Mahaffee, Olathe: Litterlift for gathering litter.
Supreme Power Cleaner Mfg. Co., 111 S. Hydraulic (Box 4141), Wichita: Cleaning machine (for office machines, motor parts, parking meter clocks, cash registers, teletypes).
Thompson Dehydrating Co., Laurent and N. Taylor, Topeka: Alfalfa dehydrating equipment.

General Industrial Machinery and Equipment

Pumps, Air and Gas Compressors, and Pumping Equipment

Boettcher Supply, 118 W. Court, Beloit: Portable sprayers.
Cessna Aircraft Co. (Industrial Products Div.), Hutchinson: Hydraulic pumps.
Charles Products Co., 415 N. Poplar, S. Hutchinson: Barrel pumps.
Geo. Cox & Sons, Clifton: Irrigation systems.
Fairbanks Morse & Co., Turner Industrial Dist., Kansas City: Pumps.
M. W. Hartmann Mfg. Co., Inc., 120-122 N. Adams, Hutchinson: Irrigation and home water pumps and accessories, jet pumps.
Hoffman Engine Co., 813 Elk, Seneca: Portable air compressors.
McCunningham Mfg. Co., Box 197, Sedan: Pumping units, air balanced, hydraulic actuated.
McNally Pittsburg Mfg. Corp., Drawer D, Pittsburg: Centrifugal pumps.
Sioux Chief Mfg. Co., Inc., 41 Shawnee, Kansas City (5): Utility pumps.
Speck Sales & Mfg. Co., 206 Main, Galena: Diaphragm pumps.
Wichita Machine Tool Co., 2957 N. Market, Wichita: Industrial paint spraying equipment.
Wilmit Mfg. Co., Inc., 117 E. Pine, Independence: Inflator for tires and other inflatable objects.
Ed Winter, Marion: Air compressors.

Ball and Roller Bearings

Don Dye Co., Kingman: Unground ball bearings.
Federal-Mogul Service Div. (Federal-Mogul-Bower Bearings, Inc.), 330 W. First, Wichita (1): Roller and ball bearings.
McNally Pittsburg Mfg. Corp., Drawer D, Pittsburg: Roller bearings.
Roberts Mfg., Inc., Salina: Precision and commercial grade ball bearing pillow blocks, flange units, and special ball bearing assemblies.
Twin Feed Blower Co., 111 Main, Larned: Ball bearing conversion units.

Blowers, Exhaust and Ventilating Fans

Tony's Radiator & Tin Works, Box 1161, Dodge City: Dust collecting systems.
Western Supply Co. (Mfg. Div.), 315 W. Third, Hutchinson: Attic fans and blowers.

Industrial Patterns

Atchison Pattern Works, 1531 Main, Atchison: Wood, metal and plastic patterns.
C & L Aluminum Foundry & Mfg. Co., 509 N. Locust, Pittsburg: Wood and metal patterns.

Clark Pattern Works, 315 N. Mead, Wichita: Wood, metal, plaster and plastic patterns.
Coffeyville Matchplate, Inc., 1115 W. 12th, Coffeyville: Metal patterns, pressure cast matchplates.
Cordray Pattern Works, 308 N. Olive, Pittsburg: Wood and metal patterns and matchplates for use in foundries.
Bob Esch Pattern Shop, 602¼ E. Eighth, Coffeyville: Iron shell core boxes and patterns, wood and metal patterns for foundry use.
Eshcraft Foundry, 520 E. Fourth, Cherryvale: Patterns (wood and aluminum).
Lee Pattern Works, 1103 S. Santa Fe, Wichita (11): Wood and metal patterns.
Ivan Morrow Pattern Shop & Foundry, Inc., 1115 W. 12th, Coffeyville: Patterns (wood and metal), pressure cast matchplates.
Precision Pattern Co., 1339 N. Santa Fe, Wichita: Close tolerance wood and metal patterns.
Pressure Cast Products, 1217 Elm, Coffeyville: Aluminum production pattern equipment.
Service Brass & Aluminum Foundry, Inc., 911 E. Third, Wichita: Pattern shop.

Mechanical Power Transmission Equipment, Except Ball and Roller Bearings

Applequist-Lagerberg Mfg., Inc., 921 Bishop, Salina: V-belt sheaves.
Barney's Bearing Mfg. Co., 329 Pattie, Wichita: Bearings.
Curtis Machine Co., 715 S. Second, Dodge City: Power transmission equipment, gear boxes.
J. B. Ehrsam & Sons Mfg. Co., Enterprise: Power transmission equipment.
Federal-Mogul Service Div. (Federal-Mogul-Bower Bearings, Inc.), 330 W. First, Wichita (1): Sleeve bearings, bushings, needle rollers, oil and grease seals, O-rings.
Funk Mfg. Co., 1211 W. 12th, Coffeyville: Power transmission devices.
McNally Pittsburg Mfg. Corp., Drawer D, Pittsburg: Gears, pulleys, shafts, sprockets, bearings, roller-drive chain, couplings, shaft drives.
Mid-States Industrial Clutch Co., 6045 N. Broadway (Box 848), Wichita: Industrial clutches and brakes.
Murdock Electric & Supply, 800 E. Central, Wichita: V-belt sheaves.
Simlo, Inc., Seventh and McBratney, Clay Center: Industrial transmission drives.
Speed Flow, Inc., 911 E. Third, Wichita: Variable speed hydraulic drive.
Vun Ruhe Vee Clutch, Route 2, Great Bend: Clutch device for small engines.
Western Iron & Foundry Co., Inc., 702 E. Second, Wichita (2): Pulleys, V-belt sheaves.

General Industrial Machinery and Equipment, Not Elsewhere Classified

Baker Engineering Co., 700-702 W. Douglas, Wichita: Hydraulic power units.
Brackett Stripping Machine Co., 505 Jackson, Topeka: Gypsum wallboard sawing and taping machines, lath bundlers.
Cessna Aircraft Co. (Industrial Products Div.), Hutchinson: Hydraulic filters.
Double J Mfg. Co., Inc., 1141 S. 12th, Kansas City: Electrical jacks.
Field Tool, Inc., 605 Spring, Coffeyville: Oil field valve, water meter, high pressure pump reconditioning.
Heckendorn Mfg. Co., Inc., Cedar Point: Earth boring equipment.
Kramer Machine & Engineering Products Co., 320 S. Second, Leavenworth: Production machining, tank and automotive.
Lind Fabricating Co., Lebo: Hydraulic equipment, hydraulic pump piston reloading sleeve, rotary tumbling tables.
Luxra Co., 1018 Commercial, Atchison: Compressor guards.
Midwest Machine Works, Inc., 1615 N. Topeka, Topeka: Industrial machinery parts.
Monatco Mfg. Corp., 2214 Front St., Kansas City: Mobile foam generators.
Olin-Dixon, Inc., McGugin Air Field, Coffeyville: Ordnance ground support items, industrial equipment.
P. D. G. Mfg., Inc., Box 98, Rose Hill: Jacks, links, locking devices.
Research Engineering & Development Co., 10901 Mission Rd., Overland Park: Hydraulic lifting jacks.
Santa Fe Wheel Co., Inc., 130 N. Water, Olathe: Industrial wheels (cast aluminum and pressed steel).
Taylor Forge & Pipe Works of Kansas, Inc., Box 231, Paola: Gas cleaners-air washers, mufflers for large gas diesel engines.
Topeka Supply & Boiler Co., Inc., Second and Jefferson (Box 207), Topeka: Dehydrator drums, dust collectors.
Universal Pulleys Co., Inc., 330 N. Mosley, Wichita: Cast iron V-belt sheaves.
Viking Fire Protection Co., 501 Sunshine Rd., Kansas City: Automatic sprinkler system.
W-W Grinder Corp., 2957 N. Market, Wichita: Compost grinders and shredders.

Office, Computing, and Accounting Machines

Scales and Balances, Except Laboratory

Nelson Co., Inc., W. Main, Oxford: Automatic scales.

Service-Industry Machines

Automatic Merchandising Machines

Harmon Machine Co., Inc., 225 W. Lewis, Wichita: Vending machines.
Kenfern Industries, Route 2 (Box 105), Galena: Vending machines.
E. J. Shurtz Mfg. Co., Inc., 240 W. Tenth, Wichita (3): Ice vending machines.

Commercial Laundry, Dry Cleaning, and Pressing Machines

Bader Mfg. Co., 118 E. Kansas, McPherson: Dry cleaning equipment (garment finishers, pants stretchers, etc.).
Saturn Mfg. Corp., Inc., Barclay (Mailing add.: Box 592, Topeka): Laundry and dry cleaners conveyors.
Wichita Precision Tool Co., Inc., 450 N. Seneca, Wichita: Pillow renovating machine, pants topper, and garment finisher.

Refrigerators and Refrigeration Machinery, Except Household; and Complete Air Conditioning Units

Addison Mfg. Co., Cimarron: Ice making machine.
Air Conditioning Equipment Co., Waco and Douglas, Wichita: Air conditioners (custom-built).
B & W Trailer Co., Route 2, Salina: Cold storage walk-in units.
The Coleman Co., Inc., 250 N. St. Francis, Wichita: Air-conditioning systems.
Dawson Metal Products, Inc., 1529 Barwise, Wichita: Air conditioning parts.
M. W. Hartmann Mfg. Co., Inc., 120-122 N. Adams, Hutchinson: Air conditioning pumps.
Kansas Air Conditioning, Inc., 314-22 E. 15th, Topeka: Air conditioning (commercial and industrial).
Koch Refrigerators, Inc., 401 Funston Rd., Kansas City (15): Commercial refrigerators.
Permatex Co., Inc., 3255 Harvester Rd., Kansas City: Cooling system products.
Planco Mfg. Co., Inc., Box 643, Wichita: Refrigeration equipment.
Stevens, Inc., 225 S. Main, Hutchinson: Air conditioner.
Western Supply Co. (Mfg. Div.), 315 W. Third, Hutchinson: Air conditioning units and parts.
Western Supply Co. (Western-aire Products Div.), Nickerson (Mailing add.: 315 W. Third, Hutchinson): Air conditioning equipment.

Measuring and Dispensing Pumps

Allen Mfg. Co., 517 Reynolds, Salina: Portable six and twelve volt high pressure grease guns.
Sheldon Tractor Filler Co., Cunningham: Gasoline pumps.

Service Industry Machines, Not Elsewhere Classified

Ablah Hotel Supply Co., Inc., 800 E. 11th, Wichita: Ranges, fry stations, steam tables.
Independence Clean Dish Service, Inc., Route 3, Independence: Commercial dishwashers.
Leahearn Mfg. Co., 215 Commercial, Emporia: Cleaning tank for engines and automotive parts.
Midwest Machine Works, Inc., 1615 N. Topeka, Topeka: Liquid mixers (paint, etc.).
Pallister Co., Inc., 530 W. Douglas, Wichita: Water softeners.
Phillips Mfg. Co., 808 W. Carthage (Box 624), Meade: Water treatment filter.
Smith and Loveless (Div. Union Tank Car Co.), 96th and Old Highway 50, Lenexa: Sewage lift stations and sewage treatment equipment.
United Industries, Inc., 618 W. Douglas, Wichita: Misc. municipal supplies, swimming pool supplies.

Miscellaneous Machinery, Except Electrical

Allison Mfg. Co., Inc., Route 3 (Box 264), Olathe: Custom manufacturing.
Ammann Mfg. Co., Inc., 3915 Maple, Wichita: Contract manufacturing.
Applequist-Lagerberg Mfg., Inc., 921 Bishop, Salina: Contract manufacturing.
Beardsley & Couchman, 231 N. St. Francis, Wichita: Special machines.
Berners Novelty Machine Works, 821 S. First, Arkansas City: Small machine items.
Bigbee Blacksmith & Welding, Route 2, Manhattan: Contract manufacturing.
Cessna Aircraft Co. (Industrial Products Div.), Hutchinson: Hydraulic valves and cylinders.
Chance Mfg. Co., Inc., 4219 Irving, Wichita (9): Amusement park rides.
Chrome Fixture Mfg. Co., Inc., Redel Rail Siding, Stanley: Tube fabrication and bending.
Clayton Carburetor Works, 1512 W. Laurel, Independence: Carburetors for natural gas, butane, propane.
Cross Mfg. Co., Lewis: Hydraulic cylinders.
Darby Corp., First and Walker, Kansas City: Contract manufacturing.
General Tool Co., Inc., 912 E. Zimmerly, Wichita: General manufacturing.
H & H Parts Co., Inc., 1234 Wellington Pl., Wichita: Custom manufacturing.
Hanover Mfg. Co., Inc., Hanover: Merry-go-rounds, teeter-totters, tug-of-wars, rock-aways.
Hydra Hose, Inc., 2208 S. Mead, Wichita: Hydraulic and industrial hose assemblies and fittings.
Hydro-Flex Corp., 1318 N. Taylor (Box 1165), Topeka: Flexible metal hose assemblies.
Inland Industrial Equipment Co., 632 N. Washington, Wichita: General manufacturing.
Joe's Machine Shop, Blue Rapids: Machinery parts.
Ken's Sales & Repair Service, 110 N. Ash, McPherson: Small parts, tools, and precision sharpening.
Kirkhart's, 1120 S. Santa Fe, Wichita: Contract manufacturing.
Leavenworth Steel, Inc., Main and Cherokee, Leavenworth: Contract manufacturing.
Loomer Machine & Welding Co., 510 W. Cottonwood, Independence: Special machines.
McPherson Machine & Tool Co., Galva: Foundry and machine shop.
Machine Tool Products Co., 1518 Walnut, Coffeyville: Contract machine work, tooling and metal fabrication.
Mal Mfg., Inc., 1120 S. Santa Fe, Wichita: Machine work.
Milne Machine & Tool Co., Inc., 1011 W. Second, Wichita: Machine and tool shop.
P. D. G. Mfg., Inc., Box 98, Rose Hill: General mechanical equipment fabrication.
Planco Mfg. Co., Inc., Box 643, Wichita: Contract manufacturing.
Precision Engineering Co., Box 120, N. Topeka: Recondition locomotive diesel crankshafts and diesel engine parts.
Frank Reese Welding Service, Lindsborg: Contract manufacturing.
Roy Reeves Service, 116 N. Osage, Wichita: Gas forge.
Sunnyside Machine Works, 3813 W. Harry, Wichita: Machine production work.
Swick-Guth, Inc., 400-410 N. Chestnut, McPherson: Diesel cylinder head rebuilding.
Theel Mfg. Co., Lawrence and Spruce Sts., Leavenworth: Merry-go-rounds and amusement park rides.
Vacu-Blast Co. (Abilene Div.), 600 N. Washington, Abilene: Air blasting and cleaning equipment.
Viking Mfg. Co., 1600 Yuma (Box 68), Manhattan: Contract manufacturing.
Wheat Belt Supply Co., Box 1015, Dodge City: Flexible metal tube.

ELECTRICAL MACHINERY, EQUIPMENT, AND SUPPLIES

Electric Transmission and Distribution Equipment

Electric Measuring Instruments and Test Equipment

Hopkins Mfg. Corp., 428 Peyton (Box 230), Emporia: Headlight intensity meter.

Power, Distribution, and Specialty Transformers

Atkinson Armature Works Co., 116 E. First, Pittsburg: Special transformers.

Switchgear and Switchboard Apparatus

Atkinson Armature Works Co., 116 E. 1st, Pittsburg: Portable switchgear, control units and assemblies.
Custom Control Mfrs., Inc., 5601 Merriam Dr., Merriam: Electric, electronic and/or pneumatic control panels and programmers.
Elec-Tron, Inc., 2050 Northern, Wichita: Electrical switches.
Kooken Electric, Inc., 201 Belle Springs (Box 17), Abilene: Various electrical distribution and control panels.

Electrical Industrial Apparatus

Motors, Generators, Etc.

Atkinson Armature Works Co., 116 E. First, Pittsburg: Portable substations.
Mayfield Electric, 238 W. Sixth, Concordia: Motor rewinding.
Mears Electric Co., 625 N. Washington, Wichita: Electric motor rebuilding, electric power equipment.
Mesh Mfg. Co., 1101 E. Third, Hutchinson: Electric generators and generator sets.
Tarrant Electric Machinery Co., 447 S. Washington (Box 853), Wichita (1): Distribution transformers, heavy electric machinery rebuilding and transformers rewound.
Zimmerman Electric Machine Co., 3756 N. Broadway, Wichita: Electric motors, generators and transformers (rewound).

Welding Apparatus

DeLuxe Marine Specialties, 221 S. Walnut, Hutchinson: Seam welding equipment.
Harper Steel & Supply, Inc., 901 Oak, Harper: Welding equipment carts.
Holgerson's Service, Box 319, Canton: AC welders.
Tweco Products, Inc., 1450 S. Mosley, Wichita: Electrode holders, ground clamps and cable connections for electric welding.
Wessam Mfg. Co., Bazine: Power take-off portable electric welder.

Electrical Industrial Apparatus, Not Elsewhere Classified

Central Kansas Electric, Inc., 912 W. North, Salina: Electrical supplies and machinery.
Ingersoll Machine & Welding, Paola: Electric wincher.

Household Appliances

Household Laundry Equipment

General Mfg. Co., Inc., 518 N. Star, El Dorado: Electric clothes driers.

Electric Housewares and Fans

Monarch Brass & Aluminum Works, 2008 S. Holbrook, Fort Scott: Exhaust fans.
Perma-Health, 614 N. Grandview, Hutchinson: Vapor units (germ and insect killing).
Pur-O-Zone Chemical Co., Inc., 708-718 Connecticut (Box 227), Lawrence: Electric polishers and scrubbing machines.
Research Engineering & Development Co., 10901 Mission Rd., Overland Park: Floor scrubbing and polishing machines.

Household Appliances, Not Elsewhere Classified

The Coleman Co., Inc., 250 N. St. Francis, Wichita: Water heaters (gas, oil, LPG, electric).
Cris Lab, Inc., 616 N. Main, Pratt: Instantaneous flash type water heater, electric coil heated (no tank).
Luxra Co., 1018 Commercial, Atchison: Automatic water heaters.
Sunshine Mantle Co., Inc., 201 E. First, Chanute: Gas water heaters.

Electric Lighting and Wiring Equipment

Electric Lamps

Sfeld Co., 1125-281 By-Pass, Great Bend: Lamps and related items.
Sunflower Mfg. Co., 116 E. Harry (Box 3882), Wichita: Table lamps, early American lamps.
Esther E. Wulf, Argonia: Lamps.

Lighting Fixtures

Berry Irrigation Supply Co., Box 185, Rossville: Electrical fixtures.
Bruest, Inc., 20th and Sycamore, Independence: Lawn lites.
The Coleman Co., Inc., 250 N. St. Francis, Wichita: Portable gasoline lanterns, LPG lanterns.
Geeco, 405 N. Second, Lawrence: Fishing lights (bite lite, ice lite, bank lite).
H & M Mfg. Co., Inc., 109 N. Main, Ottawa: Safety flag lights, neon transistor flasher safety light.
Machine Specialties Co., Route 4 (Box 888), Topeka: Outdoor gas lights and posts, electric lighting fixtures, television lamps, brooder lamps.
Mal Mfg., Inc., 1120 S. Santa Fe, Wichita: Inspection light.
Phillips Mfg. Co., Inc., 201 N. Waco, Wichita: Porto safety flashers.
Sunshine Mantle Co., Inc., 201 E. First, Chanute: Outdoor gas post lanterns.

Current Carrying Wiring Devices

Atkinson Armature Works, 116 E. First, Pittsburg: Special wiring troughs.
O. D. Dye & Co., Kingman: Switch boxes.
Elec-Tron, Inc., 2050 Northern, Wichita: Wiring assemblies, terminal strips, electrical components.
Sunshine Mantle Co., Inc., 201 E. First, Chanute: Stove and range connectors.

Communication Equipment

Sound Equipment, Electrical

Drive-In-Theatre Mfg. Co., Fifth and High (Box 247), Edwardsville: In car speakers, junction boxes, directional lighting, patio speakers, general loud speakers, box office and projection room products.

Telephone and Telegraph Apparatus

Cable Spinning Equipment Co., Inc., 3100 Topeka, Topeka: Telephone supplies (tools for the erection and maintenance of aerial cables).

Radio and TV Transmitting, Signaling and Detection Equipment and Apparatus

Armstrong Templeman, Inc., Box 209, Abilene: Audio visual and sales promotional sound recording equipment.
Caswell & Co., Quenemo: Component parts for hi-fi and radio baffles and speakers.
Diversified Avionics, Inc., 2516 E. Douglas, Wichita: Electronic all-weather landing systems.
King Radio Corp., Box 106, Olathe: Aircraft radio and navigation equipment.
King Radio Corp., 1806 W. Second, Wichita: Aircraft instruments.
Olin-Dixon, Inc., McGugin Air Field, Coffeyville: Radar tracking antennae and antenna mounts.
Radio Industries, Inc., 1307 Central, Kansas City: Electronics, radio.
Wesco Mfg. Co., 17-19 Central, Kansas City: Sound equipment.

Electronic Components and Accessories

Cathode Ray Picture Tubes

E & P Electronic Tube Mfg. Co., 2402 E. Ninth, Wichita (14): Remanufactured television picture tubes.

Electronic Components and Accessories, Not Elsewhere Classified

Electra Mfg. Co., 20th and Sycamore, Independence: Solid tantalum capacitors, integrated circuits, micro-modular packaging, high reliability resistors.
Hisonic, Inc., 249 N. Troost, Olathe: Electronic components.
Midland Mfg. Co., Inc., 3155 Fiberglas Rd., Kansas City: Quartz crystals, filter crystals, crystal ovens, oscillators, filters, discriminators.
Precision Devices, Inc., 619 Vermont, Lawrence: Piezo electric quartz crystals, ovens for temperature control of electronic components, oscillators and other electronic components.

Miscellaneous Electrical Machinery, Equipment and Supplies

Storage Batteries

American Battery Mfg. Co., 1700-18 Kansas, Kansas City: Automobile batteries.
Delco-Remy Div. (General Motors Corp.), Olathe: Storage batteries.
Globe-Union, Inc., Emporia: Storage batteries.
Gould-National Batteries, Inc., 1901 S. Fourth, Leavenworth: Automotive truck, bus and diesel batteries.

Electrical Equipment for Internal Combustion Engines

Aviation Electronics, Inc., 1026 N. Mosley, Wichita: Electronic ignition systems (automotive).
Edmco, Inc., Box 111, Holton: Electronic motor starting devices.
Electra Mfg. Co., 20th and Sycamore, Independence: Automotive voltage regulators, deposited carbon resistors, metal film resistors.
General Armature & Mfg. Co., Kansas and Railroad, Kansas City: Automotive armatures, generators, and starting motors.
Simpson Industries, Tribune: Generators.
Standard Precision, Inc., 4105 W. Pawnee (Box 1297), Wichita: Motors, AC, DC, electronic equipment.
Ted Mfg. Corp., 11415 Johnson Dr., Shawnee: Aircraft electrical connectors.

Electrical Machinery, Equipment, and Supplies, Not Elsewhere Classified

Speck Sales & Mfg. Co., 206 Main, Galena: Electro magnets.

TRANSPORTATION EQUIPMENT

Motor Vehicles and Motor Vehicle Equipment

Motor Vehicles

Balderson, Inc., Wamego: Snow plows.
Deibler Trackless Trains, 914 Claflin, Manhattan: Trackless trains.
General Motors Corp., Fairfax and Kindelberger, Kansas City: Automobiles (Buick, Oldsmobile, Pontiac).
H & M Mfg. Co., Inc., 109 N. Main, Ottawa: Sidewalk snow removal plows.
Tripp Mfg. Co., Burlington: Assembly of fire engines.
Walker Mfg. Co., Fowler: Power trucks.
Wentz Equipment Co., 600 N. Van Buren, Topeka: Snow plows.

Truck and Bus Bodies

Adams Welding Machine Co., 1008 W. Main, Lyons: Truck beds.
B & W Trailer Co., Route 2, Salina: Truck bodies.
Baldwin Metal Products, Route 2, Ottawa: Truck bed hoists.
C-B Manufacturers, Box 263, Chanute: Implement cabs and jeep tops.
Clark Mfg., Inc., Box 485, Wellington: Aluminum truck tops.
D & B Truck Bed Co., Pawnee Rock: Truck beds.
Economy Trailer Co., 248 E. Main, Sedan: Enclosed aluminum bodies for pickups, truck beds and stock racks.
Flye Repair & Welding Service, 5551 W. 21st, Topeka: Truck bodies, glass racks (truck).
H & W Service, 115 S. Foster, Stockton: Pickup stock racks.
Hansen Machine Shop, Strong City: Truck beds.
Haul-Mor Co., Inc., Valley Falls: Truck beds.
Hiawatha Industries, Inc., Hiawatha: Truck bodies.
Joe's Welding Shop, Ninth and Oak, Garnett: Truck beds.
Kansas Missouri Trailer & Equipment, 549 S. Fifth, Kansas City: Truck and trailer equipment.
Landwehr Mfg. Co., 416 S. McComas, Wichita: Hydraulic truck hoists.
Laverne Truck Bed Co., 905 S. Kansas, Olathe: Truck beds.
Load King Mfg. Co., Kingman: Steel truck beds.
Leo L. McKenzie Body Works, 117 W. First, Wichita: Truck and trailer bodies of all types, custom fire trucks (industrial, etc.), sleeper cab annex to fit all standard type trucks, etc.
Meade Mfg., Inc., Highways 54 and 160 W., Meade: Stock racks for pickups.
Midwest Works, Inc., W. Seventh, Augusta: Special truck bodies and hoists.
Mobilefreeze Co., Inc., 44 S. Central (Box 691), Parsons: Refrigerated steel or plastic truck bodies and trailers.
Monatco Mfg. Corp., 2214 Front St., Kansas City: Hydraulic equipment, steel dumping bodies.
Moser Tank & Trailer, Inc., 2550 N. Market, Wichita: Petroleum products semitrailer transports.
Pauls Mfg. Co., Glen Elder: Steel stock racks for pickups.
Plett's Machine Shop, Inman: Truck beds.
Sun-Jay Mfg. Co., South St., Arma: Truck and trailer panels.
Tradewind Industries, Inc., Liberal Air Base, Liberal: Truck bodies, stock racks, steel grain bodies, wood floored grain bodies, wood platforms, steel platforms, grain sides with end gates.
Truck Parts & Equipment Inc., 820 E. Harry, Wichita: Oil field truck beds, tailboards and snatch blocks for trucks.
Turon Hardware & Lumber Co., Turon: Truck beds.
Western Equipment, Inc., 109 Kansas, Kansas City: Truck and special utility bodies.
Western Mfg. Co., Great Bend: Oil field truck beds and trailers.
Wichita Body & Equipment Co., Inc., 1926 N. Broadway, Wichita: Utility service, refrigerated bodies and custom built van bodies.
Wichita Steel Fabricators, Inc., 3400 N. Broadway, Wichita: Truck bodies.

Motor Vehicle Parts and Accessories

Allred Tire & Brake Service, 520 W. Ninth, Winfield: Pickup truck bumpers.
Bangs Auto Parts Rebuilders, Route 4, El Dorado: Rebuilt shock absorbers.
C. F. Bender Co., Inc., 14th and Scott (Box 814, Packers Station), Kansas City: Automobile transporting trailer parts, oil reservoirs.
Bowman Farm Implements & Truck Co., 236-40 E. Eighth, Junction City: Motors rebuilt.
Charles Products Co., 415 N. Poplar, S. Hutchinson: Fuel strainers.
Consolidated Rebuilders, 528 W. First, Hutchinson: Rebuilt automobile engines and parts, connecting rods, transmissions.
Dexter Axle Co., Inc., U. S. Highway 160 E. (Box 466), Winfield: Trailer axles.
The Easton Mfg. Co., Inc., 1023 S. Santa Fe (Box 889), Wichita: Automotive replacement parts (clutch collars, water outlet fittings).
Les Endres Service, Box 561, Independence: Reconditioning of internal combustion motors of truck, car, tractors, and aircraft engines.
Federal-Mogul Service Div. (Federal-Mogul-Bower Bearings, Inc.), 330 W. First, Wichita (1): Connecting rods.
Hewitt's, Inc., 104 E. Central, Medicine Lodge: Automotive tools, parts and equipment.
Holmstrom Machine Works, Holcomb: Bumper hitch.
Hopkins Mfg. Corp., 428 Peyton (Box 230), Emporia: Body-fender tool, head light focusing device, flexible trouble lamp, split image transit level, air filter tester, oil an-oil-izer.
Jones Milling & Mfg. Co., Ninth and Santa Fe, Wichita: Automobile compasses.
Kansas Cylinder Head Co., Inc., First and Baer, McPherson: Repair of cracked diesel cylinder heads and blocks.
Kansas Rebabbiting Co., Inc., 314-318 S. Wichita, Wichita: Connecting rods, main bearings.
Kool-Fin Industries, Garnett: Aluminum brake cooling fins for automobiles.
Martin Tire & Supply Co., 154 N. Emporia, Wichita: Wheel hubs, axles, etc.
Miro-Flex Co., Inc., 1824 E. Second, Wichita: Reflector flares, clearance marker lights, tail lamps, combination stop-tail lights, rear vision mirrors, directional signals.
Moody Mfg. Co., 328 N. Sixth, Arkansas City: Metering plugs for motor oil lines.
Perine Bros. Iron Works, 809 Quincy, Topeka: Automobile springs.
Power Steering Co., Pratt: Power steering units for tractors and combines, hydraulic systems.
Ransdell Heat Treaters, 1551 Barwise, Wichita: Automotive parts.
Service Mfg., Inc., 1120 S. Santa Fe, Wichita (11): Front end corrective parts for automobiles.
Tradewind Industries, Inc., Liberal Air Base, Liberal: Tire carriers, front and rear bumpers.
Western Mfg. Co., Great Bend: Pickup bumpers.
Wyatt Mfg. Co., 500 N. Fifth, Salina: Truck hoists.

Truck Trailers

Allred Tire & Brake Service, 520 N. Ninth, Winfield: Trailers and hitches.
B & W Trailer Co., Route 2, Salina: Trailers.
East Side Garage, 410 E. Ave. A, Syracuse: Alfalfa trailers.
Hey Machinery Co., Inc., Baldwin: Farm tractor trailers.
Jackson & Usher, 910 E. Fifth, Newton: Farm trailers.
Joe's Welding Shop, Ninth and Oak, Garnett: Trailers.
Langhover Trailer Works, 3039 N. Broadway, Wichita: Trailers.
Martin Tire & Supply Co., 154 N. Emporia, Wichita: Trailer wheel assemblies.
W. G. Olsson Repair Shop, Jamestown: Trailers.
Peterson Supply Co., Smith Center: Trailers.
Spencer-Safford Loadcraft Co., Inc., Augusta: Truck trailers, components and parts, loadcraft air ride for trucks and trailers.
Train Trailer Co., Inc., 436 N. Chicago, Salina: Commercial truck trailers.
Truck Parts & Equipment, 820 E. Harry, Wichita: Oil field and pole trailers.
Truck-Trailer Supply Co., Inc., Stafford: Oil field trailers and truck beds.
Wilbeck Machine & Mfg. Co., 418 N. Poplar, S. Hutchinson: Implement trailers.

Aircraft and Parts

Aircraft

Beech Aircraft Corp., Wichita: Aircraft (commercial and military), major assemblies and components, missile target aircraft.
The Boeing Co., Wichita: Aircraft.
Cessna Aircraft Co. (Commercial Aircraft Div.), 5800 E. Pawnee Rd., Wichita: Commercial aircraft.
Cessna Aircraft Co. (Military Aircraft Div.), K42 Highway W., Wichita: Aircraft (military and commercial), helicopters (military and commercial).

Lear Jet Corp., Municipal Airport (Box 1280), Wichita: Executive jet aircraft, avionics.
Mid-States Mfg. Div. (Helio Aircraft Corp.), Pittsburg: Helio airplanes.
Rawdon Bros. Aircraft, Inc., Box 1119, Wichita (1): Aircraft.
Rock Island Oil & Refining Co., Inc. (Aircraft Div.), Municipal Airport, Hutchinson: Structural redesign and modification of corporation aircraft.
Rotary Wing Aircraft, 506 N. Summit, Arkansas City: One place autogyro aircraft.
Spencer-Copters, Inc., 1241 E. 31st S., Wichita (16): Gyrocopter.

Aircraft Parts and Auxiliary Equipment, Not Elsewhere Classified

Aero Machine Co., 1957 N. Santa Fe, Wichita (14): Precision machined aircraft and missile parts, tools and assemblies.
Aero Supply & Equipment, 139th and Antioch Rd., Olathe (Mailing add.: Box 373, K. C. [41], Mo.): Lumber and aircraft supplies.
Aircraft Tool Co., 1409 E. Douglas, Wichita: Aircraft sheet metal parts.
Ammann Mfg. Co., Inc., 3915 Maple, Wichita: Aircraft parts.
Associated Co., Inc., 1441 S. McLean, Wichita: Aircraft and missile assemblies and components, engine design, R & D, ground supporting equipment.
Atchison Leather Products Co., 316 Commercial, Atchison: Runway overrun barriers (nylon webbing).
Attica Engineering, Inc., Attica: Airplane parts.
Beech Aircraft Corp., Liberal Air Field, Liberal: Aircraft parts and assemblies.
Beech Aircraft Corp., Wichita: Ground support equipment, jettisonable fuel tanks, high energy fuel containers.
Blanchat Machine Co., 3323 Maple, Wichita: Aircraft and missile machined parts.
The Boeing Co., Wichita: Aircraft components.
Brocar, Inc., Box 487, Wichita: Aircraft subcontracting.
Cessna Aircraft Co. (Commercial Aircraft Div.), 5800 E. Pawnee Rd., Wichita: Aircraft parts.
Cessna Aircraft Co. (Military Aircraft Div.), K42 Highway W., Wichita: Major subcontract assemblies, ordnance work, ground handling equipment.
Chastain Lumber Co., 121 Pattie, Wichita: Aircraft parts.
Clark Mfg., Inc., Box 485, Wellington: Aircraft parts.
Consolidated Equipment Co., Inc., 4202 Highway 42 W. (Box 2216), Wichita: Aircraft assemblies and parts.
D & H Machine Shop, 1408 S. Osage, Wichita (13): Airplane parts.
Eamco, Inc., 1922 N. Mead, Wichita: Aircraft parts and assemblies.
Fibercraft, Inc., 328 E. Ave. North, Lyons: Reinforced fiberglass components (primarily military aircraft).
General Electric Co., Strother Aircraft Service Shop, Box 797, Arkansas City: Aircraft equipment overhaul.

Globe Engineering Co., 1539 S. St. Paul, Wichita: Aircraft tubular work, heliarc welding.
H & H Parts Co., 1234 Wellington Pl., Wichita: Aircraft assemblies.
Javelin Aircraft Co., Inc., 9175 E. Douglas, Wichita (7): Automatic pilots, trim systems, auxiliary fuel systems for airplanes, industrial fluid drive torque convertors, gyro stabilizers.
Kramer Machine & Engineering Products Co., 320 S. Second, Leavenworth: Aircraft.
L & S Machine Co., Inc., 541 S. Tracy, Wichita: Aircraft and missile parts.
Line-O-Site, Box 539, Baxter Springs: Instrument practice hoods for aircraft.
Lyons Mfg. Co., Inc., 711 E. Main, Lyons: Precision machined component parts and assemblies.
Wayne McCarrier Mfg. Co., 2801 N. Athenian, Wichita (24): Aircraft parts and assemblies.
McCartney Mfg. Co., 635 W. 12th, Baxter Springs: Aircraft parts and assemblies.
Machinery Tank & Supply Co., Inc., 1600 W. Douglas, Wichita: Aircraft parts finishing (X-ray magnetic inspection), aircraft tools and jigs.
Maize Flying Service, Inc., Box 301, Maize: Tanks and dispersal equipment for agricultural aircraft, aircraft component parts, major overhaul of airframes and engines, overseas fuel tanks for aircraft, airplane painting.
Mid-States Mfg. Div. (Helio Aircraft Corp.), Pittsburg: Aircraft subassemblies and parts.
Midwest, Inc., Box 6, Wellington: Aircraft sheet metal shop.
Nance Machine & Paint Co., 2943 Wellington Pl., Wichita: Machine parts (aircraft and commercial).
Nelson Co., Inc., W. Main, Oxford: Aircraft machined parts, tool and die.
Olin-Dixon, Inc., McGugin Air Field, Coffeyville: Aircraft and missile components.
Ott Brothers Machine Co., 331 E. 37th S., Wichita: Aircraft hardware, special machine parts, both aircraft and commercial, small assemblies.
Oxwell, Inc., 600 E. 15th, Wellington: Aircraft parts, frame.
Paramount Products Corp., Peabody: Aircraft parts.
H. K. Porter Co., Inc. (Thermoid Div., Chanute Works), 201 N. Allen, Chanute: Impregnated fabric ducting (aircraft).
Precision Metalcraft, Inc., 2853 S. Hillside, Wichita: Aircraft and missile components, precision tool and die.
Precision Pattern Co., 1339 N. Santa Fe, Wichita: Design and fabrication of aircraft cabin tables, cabinets, etc.
Product Engineering & Mfg. Co., Inc., 434 W. First, Wichita: Aircraft parts and assemblies (sheet metal).
Quality Mfrs., Inc., 3158 S. Hoover Rd., Wichita (15): Aircraft sheet metal fabrication.
R & L Parts Co., La Crosse: Aircraft machine work.
Ransdell Heat Treaters, 1551 Barwise, Wichita: Aircraft parts.
Rawdon Bros. Aircraft Inc., Box 1119, Wichita (1): Aircraft accessories.
Art Roll Co., 3520 McCormick, Wichita: Production machine parts and assemblies.
Sinclair Mfg. Co., 1816 Wabash, Wichita (14): Heliarc welding on aircraft parts.
Southwest Mfg. Co., 1712 Mildred, Wichita (14): Aircraft tooling and machine work.

A windmill, turning briskly in the western Kansas wind, pulls up cool fresh water.

Spencer-Safford Loadcraft Co., Inc., Augusta: Container for storage and transportation of guided missiles and air craft tanks.
Standard Precision, Inc., 4105 W. Pawnee (Box 1297), Wichita: Electro mechanical actuators, aircraft instrument and accessories, relief tubes, special machine products.
Stearman Aircraft Products, 2495 N. Hillside, Wichita: Engineering, tool design and fabrication, precision machine parts.
Tammany Industries, 330 N. Mosley (Box 487), Wichita: Aircraft parts and assemblies.
Weaver Engineering & Mfg. Co., 1005 E. 17th, Wichita (14): Aircraft machined parts and assemblies.
John Weitzel, Inc., La Crosse: Precision aircraft parts, sheet metal assemblies.
John Weitzel, Inc., 3310 W. Central, Wichita: Precision aircraft and missile parts, sheet metal assemblies.
Welco, Inc., 1423 North A, Wellington: Aircraft machine parts.
Wellington Machine, Inc., 1510 North A, Wellington: Tool and die for plane parts.
Westholt Mfg. Co., Inc., 925 W. Harry, Wichita: Aircraft and missile subassemblies, components and accessories.
Wichita Precision Tool Co., Inc., 450 N. Seneca, Wichita: Airplane parts.
Wilson Machine Co., Inc., 217 W. Second, Hutchinson: Aircraft parts and tools.

Ship and Boat Building and Repairing

Bail-Master Co., Hillsboro: Boat bailing devices.
Blue Rapids Industries, Inc., Blue Rapids: Fiberglass boats.
Bow Guide Mfg. Co., 333 S. Kansas, Liberal: Boat loader.
Cherryvale Fiberglass Co., Route 1, Cherryvale: Fiberglass canoes.
DeLuxe Marine Specialties, 221 S. Walnut, Hutchinson: Marine accessories for outboard motor boats.
Flex-Prop Co., Inc., Marion: Variable pitch propeller for outboard motors.
Hopkins Mfg. Corp., 428 Peyton (Box 230), Emporia: Go-boat.
Iola Molded Plastics, Box 321, Iola: Fiberglass boats.
Jayhawk Marine, Inc., Box 243, Parsons: Fiberglass marine parts.
Lofland Sail-Craft, Inc., 4123 N. Broadway, Wichita (19): Sailboats.
Missouri Valley Steel, Inc., Box 89, Leavenworth: Boats and barges.
Starcraft Boat Co. of Kansas, Independence: Fiberglass pleasure boats.
Sun-Jay Mfg. Co., South St., Arma: Fiberglass boats.
Wendell Vail Co., Mound Valley: Pontoon floats.
Wes Craft, S. Washington, Great Bend: Fiberglass boats, fiberglass tooling, custom parts, boat repair.
Winfield Reinforced Plastics Co., Strother Field, Winfield: Fiberglass boats.

Railroad Equipment

A. T. & S. F. Railway Co., 1300 Hiram, Wichita: Freight car equipment.
A. T. & S. F. Railway Shops, Crane and Branner, Topeka: Freight cars, passenger cars, parts for locomotives and cars.
General American Transportation Corp., 41st and Argentine, Kansas City: Rebuild railroad tank cars.
Griffin Wheel Co., 7111 Griffin Rd. (Box 8), Muncie: Steel railroad car wheels.
The LFM Mfg. Co., Inc. (Subs. of Rockwell Mfg. Co.), Third and Park, Atchison: Railroad equipment and castings.
M-K-T Railroad, Box 737, Parsons: Railroad equipment.
North American Car Corp., 1620 Spruce, Coffeyville: Tank, hopper, refrigerator car rebuilding and repair.
North American Car Corp., Route 3, Country Club Rd., Pittsburg: Rebuild railway cars.
Salzberg Railway Parts, Inc., Box 188, Osawatomie: Rebuilding of freight equipment.
Union Pacific Railroad Shops, Ellis: Railroad equipment.

Motorcycles, Bicycles, and Parts

Auto-Craft Inc., 1301 E. Fourth, Hutchinson: Small motor driven cars (auto midget power driven).
Durite Corp., 29 Davis, Iola: Small racing carts, motor scooters.
Hickman Aviation Services, Municipal Airport, Stafford: Power driven competition go-karts.
Topeka Arc Welding, 1928 N. Topeka, Topeka: Small sports car.

Miscellaneous Transportation Equipment

Trailer Coaches (Mobile Dwellings)

Adventure Line Mfg. Co., Inc., 3339 Main, Parsons: Custom built coaches for pick-up trucks.
Allison Construction Co., 416 W. Kansas, Arkansas City: Camp trailers for pick-up trucks.
American Coach Co., Box 358, Newton: Mobile homes.
Blair Trailers, Route 2, Erie: Pick-up campers.
C-B Manufacturers, Box 263, Chanute: Pick-up coach trailer.
Comet Mobilhomes, Hill Airport (Box 857), Coffeyville: Mobile homes.
Coons Custom Coach Mfg. Co., Inc., U. S. Highway 59 and K96, Oswego: Custom built coaches for pick-up trucks.
Detroiter Mobile Homes Mfg., Inc., 400 S. Halstead, Hutchinson: Moblie homes.
Guerdon Industries, Inc., Box 338, Newton: Mobile homes.
Honorbuilt Trailer Mfg. Co., Inc., Minneapolis: Travel trailers, camping coaches for pick-up trucks.
The Huntsman, 815 W. Fifth, Oswego: Custom built coaches for pick-up trucks.
Kit Mfg. Co., Inc., McPherson: Mobile homes.
Marlette Coach Co., Municipal Air Base, Great Bend: Mobile homes.
Meade Mfg. Inc., Highways 54 and 160 W., Meade: Pick-up travel coach, camper-on-wheels.
Neosho Coach Div. (Gearhart Bldg. Materials), 701 Oregon, Oswego: Custom camper coaches for pick-ups, trucks or trailers.
Princess Homes, Inc., 901 N. 25th, Parsons: Mobile homes.
Richard & Clark Mfg. Co., Erie: Travel trailers.
Scotsman Industries, Inc., McGugin Field, Highway 169 N., Coffeyville: Travel trailers.
Skyline Homes, Inc., W. Madison, Arkansas City: Mobile homes.

Transportation Equipment, Not Elsewhere Classified

B & L of Kansas, Inc., 102 S. Forest, Douglass: Trailer roofs.
Beck Welding & Mfg. Co., 824 W. Madison, Arkansas City: Steel frames for mobile homes.
Blair Trailers, Route 2, Erie: Horse trailers.
East Side Garage, 410 E. Ave. A, Syracuse: Horse trailers.
Erhardt's, Inc., 7 Kansas, S. Hutchinson: Golf carts.
Flye Repair & Welding Service, 5551 W. 21st, Topeka: Trailers.
Fumetco, Inc., U. S. Highway 59 and K-96, Oswego: Aluminum fabrication (outside skins for mobile homes, special shapes and designs).
Hamilton's, 2106 E. Central, Wichita (2): Factory cycles, unicycles, special cycles for handicapped, ice cream vending cycles.
Hansen Machine Shop, Strong City: Wagon beds.
Haul-Mor Co., Inc., Valley Falls: Wagon beds.
Hiawatha Industries, Inc., Hiawatha: Wagon boxes.
Hoffman Engine Co., 813 Elk, Seneca: Motorized golf car.
Irwin's Trailers, 7330 N. Broadway, Wichita: Horse and stock trailers, vans, custom manufacturing.
Jato Mfg., Inc., 427 S. Broadway, Salina: Riding golf carts.
Load-King Mfg. Co., Kingman: Farm wagons.
Midwest Works, Inc., W. Seventh, Augusta: Farm wagons.
Morse Trailer Assembly Plant, 702 E. Tenth, Great Bend: Utility trailers.
Nu-Wa Camp Trailers, Inc., Route 1 (Box 136A), Chanute: Folding camp trailers.
Petrowsky Motor Co., Bucklin: Trailer.
Riblet Products of Kansas, Inc., Box 274, Newton: Mobile home chassis.
Art Roll Co., 3520 McCormick, Wichita: Boat trailers.
Simon All America Rentals, Inc., 1501 E. Kellogg, Wichita: Utility trailers.
Dale Smith, Marion: Trailers.
Westholdt Mfg. Co., Inc., 925 W. Harry, Wichita: All purpose camping trailer.
Whitney Mfg. Co., Lebo: Automotive service equipment.
Wilbeck Machine & Mfg. Co., 418 N. Poplar, S. Hutchinson: Farm wagons.

PROFESSIONAL, SCIENTIFIC, AND CONTROLLING INSTRUMENTS; PHOTOGRAPHIC AND OPTICAL GOODS; WATCHES AND CLOCKS

Engineering Laboratory, and Scientific and Research Instruments and Associated Equipment

Garwin, Inc., 1326 Walnut, Wichita: Aircraft instruments and accessories, test equipment.
Instruments & Flight Research, Inc., 2716 George Washington, Wichita (14): Instrument flight systems, aircraft instruments, aircraft accessories and industrial precision equipment.
Instruments, Inc., 205 E. Lewis, Wichita: Aircraft instruments and parts.
Midwest Instrument Co., 205-207 N. Front, Salina: Grain temperature measuring instruments.
Fred Stein Laboratories, Inc., 121 N. Fourth, Atchison: Electronic apparatus for testing moisture, oil and fats, electric seed germinator, electric laboratory mills (grinder-extractor).
Wheat Belt Supply Co., 306 S. Second, Dodge City: Grain moisture testers.

Instruments for Measuring, Controlling, and Indicating Physical Characteristics

Mechanical Measuring and Controlling Instruments, Except Automatic Temperature Controls

Carmac Co. (Erickson Specialties Div.), 10917 Johnson Dr., Shawnee: Barometric pressure switches.
Farebox Corp. of America, Inc., 1101 E. Central, Wichita: Fare register boxes.
G-R Mfg. Co., Hunter Island (Route 2), Manhattan: Bend testing device for steel.
GTE Co., 478 Pamela, Wichita (12): Oil field tank gauge.
McCartney Mfg. Co., 635 W. 12th, Baxter Springs: Extreme pressure equipment.
Phillips Mfg. Co., 808 W. Carthage (Box 624), Meade: Aircraft control devices.
Solid State Sonics & Electronics, Inc., Highway 4 and Silver Lake Rd., Topeka: Ultrasonic axle tester, ultrasonic equipment for ultrasonic detector cars, intruder control systems and various other electronic and sonic devices.
Standard Precision, Inc., 4105 W. Pawnee (Box 1297), Wichita: Aircraft and industrial dials.
Vernon Mfg. Co., Gypsum: Coin operated automatic water salesman.
Western Control Corp., 2533 S. West St. (Box 1202), Wichita: Controls for engines (flexible mechanical remote, lever type, push-pull, button-type).

Automatic Temperature Controls

Mo-Re, Inc., 201 Oak (Box 244), Bonner Springs: Miniature thermocouples.
Salina Metal Products (Div. of Salina Roofing Co.), Ninth and Bishop, Salina: Automatic draft control.

Surgical, Medical, and Dental Instruments and Supplies

Surgical and Medical Instruments and Apparatus

Howard Beuoy, Mfg., Cedar Vale: Caponizing and surgical instruments.

Orthopedic, Prosthetic, and Surgical Appliances and Supplies

American Optical Co., Mills Bldg., Topeka: Safety products, industrial goggles, clothing respirators, etc.
Bolin Furniture & Mfg. Co., Route 3, Fort Scott: Hospital walking chair.
A. H. Bosworth, 416 N. Water, Wichita (2): Surgical braces.
Cramer Chemical Co., W. Warren, Gardner: First-aid supplies.
Gambill Mfrs., Inc., La Harpe (Mailing add.: Box 4, Iola): Hospital bed unit.
Kansas City Brace & Splint Co., 906 N. 18th, Kansas City: Orthopedic supplies.
Mid-States Laboratories, Inc., 600 N. St. Francis (Box 1140), Wichita: Custom earmolds, plastic accessories and accouterments peculiar to the hearing aid industry.
Scott Specialties, Inc., Box 266, Belleville: Elastic rib belts, cotton webbing rib belts, abdominal binders and short leg cast supports.
Smith Truss Co., Inc., 1119 W. Tenth, Topeka: Trusses, orthopedic braces, surgical belts.
Steven Motor Chair Co., 1702 Rosedale Dr., Kansas City: Motorized wheelchair.
Tilson Co., Box 554, Ulysses: Safety rails for bathtubs, stools, etc.
The Winkley Co., Inc., 3128 E. Douglas, Wichita: Artificial limbs and orthopedic appliances.

Dental Equipment and Supplies

J. Chamberlain Dental Lab., 640 Minnesota, Kansas City: Denture plate work.
Cressler Products Co., 223 E. Eighth, Newton: Dental instruments.
E K Dental Laboratory, 138½ S. Santa Fe, Salina: Dental supplies.
Easthouse Dental Laboratory, 512 Natl. Reserve Bldg., 1000 Kansas, Topeka: All types of prosthetic dentistry.
Hansen's Labiodentals, Inc., 4301 Huntoon, Topeka: Dental appliances.
Heumann Dental Labs, 1007 Monroe, Topeka: Restorative dental appliances of all types.
Latta Dental Laboratory, Marysville: Dentures.
Myron Dental Laboratory, 1106 N. 13th, Kansas City: Dental plates.
Rooney Dental Laboratory, 1007 Vassar Dr., Salina: Dental prosthetics.
Salina Dental Laboratory, United Bldg., Salina: Dental prosthetics.
Vinson Dental Laboratory, Box 791, Dodge City: Dentures, full and partial plates.

Ophthalmic Goods

American Optical Co., 407 Hoke Bldg., Hutchinson: Optical goods.
American Optical Co., 419 United Bldg., Salina: Optical goods.
American Optical Co., Mills Bldg., Topeka: Optical goods.
American Optical Co., 150 S. Ida, Wichita: Optical goods.
Doolin-Shaw Optical Dispensers, 141 N. Main, Wichita: Optical goods.
Duffens Contact Lens Co., Inc., 110 W. Iron, Salina: Contact lens.
Duffens Optical Co., 112 E. Sherman, Hutchinson: Optical goods.
Duffens Optical Co., 831 Kansas, Topeka: Optical goods.
G & H Optical Service, Inc., 1819 Grandview, Kansas City: Optical goods.
Hawkins Optical Laboratory, 115 E. Seventh (Box 721), Topeka: Optical goods.
McBratney Optical Co., 1321 Minnesota, Kansas City: Optical goods.
Magic Circle Contact Lens Labs., Fourth and Halligan, Caney: Contact lenses.
Minuteman Nylon Products, Inc., 417 School, Augusta: Eyeglass frames.
Parmelee Products, Inc., 634 King, Ottawa: Optical frames and parts, industrial safety equipment.
Payton Optical Co., 10 W. Second, Hutchinson: Optical goods.
Pittsburg Optical Service, 105 W. Fifth, Pittsburg: Optical goods.
Singleton-Joyce Optical Service, 9 W. First, Hutchinson: Optical goods.

Photographic Equipment and Supplies

Advance Products Co., 2300 E. Douglas, Wichita: Projection and television tables, portable easels, rear projection audio visual systems.
Gordon Electric Retoucher, 904 Anderson, Garden City: Electric photo retouching machine.
Hand Co., 346 N. St. Francis, Wichita: Solid aluminum screen for daylight projection.
Kreonite, Inc., 715 E. Tenth (Box 2099), Wichita: Photographic fiberglass sinks and laboratory equipment.
Le Roy E. Pickard Co., 1127 Hillside Dr., Concordia: Solid aluminum screen for daylight projection.

MISCELLANEOUS MANUFACTURING INDUSTRIES

Musical Instruments and Parts

Evans Products, Inc., 201 First (Box 58), Dodge City: Plastic drum heads.
Charles W. McManis Co., Tenth and Garfield, Kansas City: Organs.
Oliver Mfg. Co., 1436 Payne, Wichita: Double-bass cart.
Reuter Organ Co., 614-620 New Hampshire, Lawrence: Pipe organs.
Milo Wright, 2200 N. Roosevelt, Wichita: Music teachers' supplies.

Toys, Amusement, Sporting and Athletic Goods

Games and Toys, Except Dolls and Children's Vehicles

Chance Mfg. Co., Inc., 4219 Irving, Wichita (9): Miniature trains and equipment.
Dow-Lee Co., 7442 Warren, Wichita (12): Indoor games.
Novel Woodcraft, Hanover: Toys.
Prue Mfg. Co., 1937 S. 14th, Kansas City: Skill game (metal and wood).
T-K Specialty Co., Commercial Natl. Bank Bldg., Kansas City: Dice, games, etc.

Dolls and Doll Clothing

Cholly Knit Co., 1108 N. Washington, Wellington: Apparel for dolls.

Sporting and Athletic Goods, Not Elsewhere Classified

Air Flo Target Works, Box 486, Hutchinson: Clay pigeons.
All-Weld Playground Equipment Co., 2000 W. 48th, Shawnee Mission: Heavy duty playground equipment.
F. F. Anderson, 1181 Meadowbrook Lane, Manhattan: Sinker molds.
Ashley Bait Co., 421 S. Sylvan, Emporia: Catfish baits.
Atchison Leather Products Co., 316 Commercial, Atchison: Sporting-athletic equipment (baseball bases, bat bags, football helmets, shoulder pads, blocking dummies, school equipment bags).
Bal-Brock Bait Co., Box 5, Kensington: Channel catfish bait.
Becker Mfg., Downs: Folding tent frames.
Bennett & Son Machine Works, Holyrood: Fish pole molders.
W. R. Blake Co., 122 W. Tenth (Box 126), Baxter Springs: Fiberglass water skiis.
Bob's Tackle Shop, 1338 N. Fourth, Arkansas City: Fishing lures.
Buckeye Bait Corp., 120 Liberty, Council Grove: Plastic fishing floats, lures and misc. terminal tackle.
Cholly Knit Co., 1108 N. Washington, Wellington: Golf club covers and accessories.
Deel, Inc., 202 S. Factory (Box 58), Enterprise: Bowling equipment, marine and water ski accessories.
Domestic Athletic Co., Inc., 109 Ellis, Wichita: Football pads.
Exer-Matic, Inc., 1020 Maple (Box 1212), Wichita: Exercise machine (electric).
F & M Mfg. Co., 1653 Northeast Parkway, Wichita: Storage rack for table tennis paddles and balls.
Fishing Equipment Mfg. Co., Inc., 5 N. Silver, Paola: Fishing rod tender, dock brackets and ground stakes.
Irl Fitzgerald, 1110 Coolidge, Wichita: Roque sets.
Francis Fly Co., 605 W. Euclid, Pittsburg: Fishing lures.
Geeco, 405 N. Second, Lawrence: Fishing pole holder, skinning holder for small fish.
Geiger Specialties, Horton: Carp and channel catfish baits.
Delmer F. Harris Co., Concordia: Playground equipment.
Home Oil Co., Marion: Shotgun shell reloaders.
Hook-O-Matic Mfg. Co., Route 2, Goodland: Automatic fishing equipment.
Hunter Mfg. Co., 124 E. Third (Box 376), Pratt: Hunters' hoist.
Jackson Mfg. Co., Simpson: Playground equipment.
Lectromatic Sports of Kansas, Jennings: Solid and hollow fiberglass fishing poles.
Lowe's Poultry & Sporting Goods, 143 S. Fourth, Salina: Sporting goods.
Rainbolt & Son Bait Center, Burlington: Fish bait.
Rohr Bait Service, 1131 N. Main, El Dorado: Fish bait.
Shaffer Mfg. Co., 308 E. Lincoln, Wichita (11): Golf accessories.
Kenneth Smith Golf Club Co., Lenexa: Golf clubs, golf club scales and supplies.
Ultra Modern, 9028 W. Kellogg, Wichita (9): Swimming pool equipment and accessories.
George Wylie Co., Inc., Box 55, Clay Center: Fishing calculator and bait.

Pens, Pencils, and Other Office and Artists' Materials

Pens, Pen Points, Fountain Pens, Ball Point Pens, Mechanical Pencils and Parts

Wilkinson-Akers, Inc., 725 Kansas, Kansas City: Ball point pens, mechanical pencils, wood pencils.

Lead Pencils, Crayons and Artists' Material

Binney & Smith, Inc., Winfield: School and artists crayons.

Marking Devices

Capitol Stamp & Seal Co., 422 E. Tenth, Topeka: Rubber stamps, notary and corporation seals, stencils.
Childs Mfg. Co., 1100 S. Denver, El Dorado: Rubber stamps, seals (notary and corporate).
J. C. Darling Stamp & Seal Co., 734 Kansas, Topeka: Rubber stamps, notary and corporate seals, stencils.
Elliott Printers, Inc., 206 N. Seventh (Box E), Garden City: Rubber stamps.
L. F. Garlinghouse Co., Inc., 820 Quincy, Topeka: Personalized rubber stamps.
Polly-Dell Stencils, Glasco: Textile painting stencils.
Price's Stencils, 1207 W. Trail, Dodge City: Textile painting stencils.
Chas. K. Schweizer Co., 1401 Fairfax Trafficway, Kansas City: Rubber printing plates.
Snyder Stamp & Key Co., 1021 Kansas, Topeka: Rubber stamps, notary and corporate seals.
Vera Waters Stencils, Fowler: Textile stencils.
West Rubber Stamp Co., Inc., 1001 E. Douglas (Box 575), Wichita: Rubber stamps, marking devices, stencils and shipping room supplies.
Wichita Stamp & Seal Co., 309 W. Douglas, Wichita: Notary and corporation seals, shipping stencils, rubber stamps.
Wilbur's Rubber Stamps, 405 Pine (Box 2), Peabody: Rubber stamps.

Costume Jewelry, Costume Novelties, Buttons, and Miscellaneous Notions, Except Precious Metal

Costume Jewelry and Costume Novelties, Except Precious Metal

Anna R. Hensley, Route 2, Eureka: Jewelry.
E. M. Lovell, 108 W. Ninth, Topeka: Jewelry.
Snyder Jewelry Repair & Mfg. Co., 729 Kansas, Topeka: Jewelry.

Feathers, Plumes, and Artificial Flowers

Beckner Cabinet Shop, 120 E. Fifth, Garnett: Memorial and Christmas decorations.

Gary Holiday Wreath Co., 127½ Oak, Bonner Springs: Memorial and Christmas wreaths and sprays.
Karjim, 112 W. Lincoln, Wellington: Wreaths and sprays (artificial).
Rindom's Wreaths, 132 S. Lawrence, Box 645, Emporia: Wreaths and decorative merchandise.
Roy's Wreaths, Mankato: Wreaths, crosses, Bibles, sprays for grave memorials, corsages, Christmas door knockers, centerpieces.

Miscellaneous Manufacturing Industries

Brooms and Brushes

Broce Mfg. Co., Inc., 110 Cherry (Box 390), Dodge City: Self propelled highway brooms (power).
Chanute Broom Co., 603 N. Evergreen, Chanute: Brooms (standard and warehouse).
Dungan Broom Co., Mulberry: Brooms, whisk brooms and toy brooms.
H & M Mfg. Co., Inc., 109 N. Main, Ottawa: Rotary sweeping brooms (metal).
Kansas Foundation for the Blind, 223 W. Third, Wichita: Cornbrooms, whisk brooms, toy brooms.
Kansas Industries for the Blind, 925 Sunshine Rd., Kansas City (15): Push brooms.
Kansas Industries for the Blind, 425 Mac Vicar, Topeka: Brooms, floor brushes.
Lindsay Broom Co., 5311 State, Kansas City: Brooms.
Lyndon Broom Co., Lyndon: Brooms and whisk brooms.
Myers Brush-Broom & Mop Co., 300 S. Tenth, Kansas City (2): Brooms and brushes.
Lester Sircoulomb Co., Caney: Brooms.
Standard Broom Co., 1515 S. Mosley, Wichita: Brooms.
United Broom Co., Inc., 936-38-40 Miami, Kansas City: Brooms.
Wichita Brush & Chemical Co., Inc., 234 N. Main, Wichita: Brushes.
Wyandotte Brush Mfg. Co., 1211 Orville, Kansas City: Industrial and packing house brushes.

Lamp Shades

Sunflower Mfg. Co., 116 E. Harry (Box 3882), Wichita: Lamp shades.
Textile Drapery Shop, 1427 Burns, Wichita (3): Lamp shades.

Morticians' Goods

Arkansas City Funeral Supplies, 1110 N. D, Arkansas City: Ladies' and men's burial garments, casket veils.
Artco Casket Co., 1621 N. 25th, Kansas City: Metal and wooden caskets.
Central Casket Shell Co., Second and Nebraska, Kansas City (1): Casket shells (redwood).
Rex-Art Casket Co., 1608 N. 13th, Kansas City: Caskets.
Superior Metallic Casket Co., 612-14 N. Sixth, Kansas City (1): Metal caskets (steel, copper and bronze).
Wichita Casket Co., 3737 W. Harry, Wichita: Burial caskets.
Wyandotte Casket Co., 16 N. James, Kansas City (18): Caskets.

Furs, Dressed and Dyed

Mid-West Rendering, Inc., Box 444, Belleville: Furs.

Manufacturing Industries, Not Elsewhere Classified

Ames Industries, Inc., 528 W. Douglas (Box 3426), Wichita (13): Wrist pincushion, pressing cushions, sleeve rolls, point-seam pressers, pounding boards.
Da Mar Mfg. Co., 436 N. St. Francis, Wichita (2): Models (three dimensions).
Envel-O-Pener, Inc., Citizens Bank Bldg., Independence: Envelope opener.
Hopkins Mfg. Corp., 428 Peyton (Box 230), Emporia: Car and window washers.
Horner Co., 110 N. Emporia, Wichita: Badges.
Kamen Wiping Materials, Inc., 441 N. Santa Fe, Wichita (2): Wiping cloths.
Lassen Pipe Shop, 127 E. First, Wichita (2): Custom made pipes (tobacco).
Mid-America Enterprises, Inc., 530 N. Main, Ottawa: Car washers and washing compound.
Minit Mitt Mfg. Co., 1006 N. Cedar, Ottawa: Car washing mitt with water supply means.
H. K. Porter Co., Inc. (Thermoid Div., Chanute Works), 201 N. Allen, Chanute: Impregnated fabric ducting (industrial).
Max Rollins & Don McElfresh, Lebanon: Miniature U. S. center markers.
Songer Woodworking & Upholstering, 328½ S. Kansas, Olathe: Novelties and gift wares.
E. W. Starne Mfg. Co., Attica: Safety fountain for rodent poison.
Water and Waste Co., 501 Sunshine Rd., Kansas City: Fabricators of material for fire prevention installations.
Wellborn, Inc., 1727 E. Second, Wichita: Cast plaster items.
Wichita Precision Tool Co., Inc., 450 N. Seneca, Wichita: Firearms cartridge reloading equipment.
Wilbeck Machine & Mfg. Co., 418 N. Poplar, S. Hutchinson: Wheel and rim conversions for flotation tires.

MISCELLANEOUS BUSINESS SERVICES

Duplicating, Addressing, Blueprinting, Photocopying, Mailing, Mailing List, and Stenographic Services

Capitol City Blue Print Co., 421 Kansas, Topeka: Films, blueprint papers.
City Blue Print, Inc., 1200 Waterman, Wichita: Blueprints, photostats and supplies.
Dietzgen of Kansas, Inc., 131-135 S. Laura, Wichita: Photographic copies and blow ups, blue prints, printing.
Keuffel & Esser Co., 139 N. Topeka, Wichita: Reproductions, optical metrology, audiovisual, photogrammetry.
Morris Mimeographing & Menu Service, 108 S. St. Francis, Wichita: Menus and letter shop, forms, cards, etc.
Topeka Blue Print Co., 608 Jackson, Topeka: Blueprints, photo-copy.
Wichita Mapping & Engineering Co., 248 N. Market, Wichita: Blueprints, oil field maps, etc.

MOTION PICTURES

Motion Picture Production and Distribution

Centron Corp., Inc., Avalon Rd. at W. Ninth, Lawrence: Sound motion pictures, sales meeting and sound filmstrip production.
Library Filmstrip Center, 140 N. Old Manor, Wichita (8): Educational filmstrips for libraries.
Morley Productions, 448 S. Westfield, Wichita (9): Documentary and educational films.
Sanderson Films, Inc., 3303 E. Harry, Wichita: Aviation films.
Steve Smith Pictures, 636 Kansas, Topeka: Motion pictures, slides.
South-West Films, 231 Ida, Wichita: Sound slidefilms, motion pictures, tape recordings.

From listings on page 144.

°GREAT BEND, Barton (D-6) pop. 18,233; 1 Mun.; 2 KPL; 3 WLT; 4 AT&SF, MP; 5 US 281, US 281 Alt., US 56, K-96, K-45; 6 CEN; 7 American State Bank, First National Bank in Great Bend, Security State Bank $32,520,000; newspapers — Great Bend Daily Tribune, Western Kansas Press. Great Bend, known as "Oil Capital in the Heart of the Wheat Belt," is located at the great bend of the Arkansas River. Its famous Tenth Street, site of scores of supply houses and allied oil businesses, is known as "the oil artery of Kansas." A historical marker, three miles east of Great Bend, marks the site of old Fort Zarah. Cheyenne Bottoms is located 6½ miles northeast of Great Bend.

Barton County — Earnings per cap. $1,977; sales tax collections $1,531,960; employed in industry 6,325; number of farms 1,373; crop value $7,631,490; livestock value $4,891,910; mineral production $25,540,779. The county ranked second in petroleum production and second in value of mineral production. Petroleum 8.6 million barrels. Chaffee oil field, with initial production of 229 barrels per day, was important discovery. Natural gas up 25 per cent. Evaporated salt produced from brine wells at Pawnee Rock. Fire clay used for building brick. Building and paving sand and gravel produced.

ABOUT THE PUBLISHER

John Peach of Kansas can't recall a time when he didn't think of his home state with affection. In his early teens, he spent two summers chauffeuring an insurance examiner over roads in every county in Kansas, getting his first comprehensive look at the entire state. Since then, his interest in Kansas has never lagged. He traveled over the United States, too, and found many false impressions of his beloved Sunflower State. Each time, he felt keen personal disappointment and wanted to do something to change those false impressions. Also, he wanted to give his fellow Kansans the latest concise information and photos of their state. And so began the compilation of data for Kansas, Its Power and Its Glory.

Peach is a building operator and investment developer who makes his home in Topeka. He has worked in politics and enjoyed flings at newspapering here in Kansas. His favorite occupation is his present one, investment developer in the exciting world of business. His indoor hobby is listening to symphonic music (usually while the telephones are ringing and he's talking real estate). His outdoor passion is cars. As a boy of 11, back in Emporia, he took a job in a garage to be near cars. He was either washing, cranking, or selling cars, teaching others to drive those models of his youth, or traveling hundreds of thousands of miles himself in cars of every description. Since 1955, he has been building racing cars and driving them in sports car races for the thrill of it.